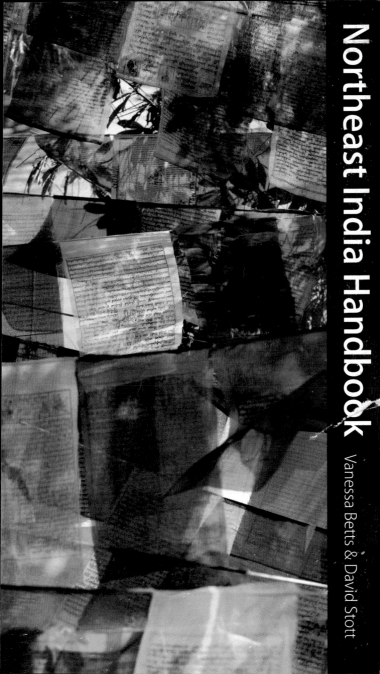

Northeast India Handbook

Vanessa Betts & David Stott

Veteran broadcaster Mark Tully perfectly summed up India's Northeast when he described the country as "a land where there are no full stops". Here, the India of old – steam trains lumbering through misty tea gardens, Bengal tigers stalking the mangrove forests, golden monasteries perched on mountain peaks – collides with the tensions that underlie the modernization of the New India.

As societies long starved of opportunity now race to grab their share of the consumer dream, and governments embrace a vision of progress involving forcible land grabs, the marginalized millions strike back for any number of issues – Maoism, separatism or national independence – that in themselves seem to keep the nation in its miraculous equilibrium.

A journey through the Northeast can take you from a coffee house political debate in intellectual Kolkata to ash-smeared Varanasi, gazing across the Ganga through plumes of smoke – another soul's blissful release into *moksha*; from Bodh Gaya, where pilgrims seek peace beneath the Buddha's Bodhi tree, to Puri, home to one of Hinduism's most riotous festivals; from tiny Sikkim, so ethnically Himalayan and so clean that you can forget you're in India altogether, to the Christianized hills on the frontier with Myanmar, where elders in hornbill-feather headgear oversee traditions that predate the 'universal' religions by millennia. More than any other region of India, in he Northeast you can escape the paths trodden by mass tourism and not see another foreign face for weeks.
The romantic rhythms, the chaos and madness are all here. This is a land of unrelenting change and colour – the India of your imagination.

Northeast India highlights

1 Kolkata, intellectual, cultural and sporting capital of India. ▶▶ page 61.

2 Historic Bengali ruins at Murshidabad on the banks of the Ganges. ▶▶ page 98.

3 Darjeeling tea estates and trekking in the shadow of the Himalaya. ▶▶ page 110.

4 Tiger-spotting at Sunderbans among the mangrove archipelago. ▶▶ page 129.

5 Khangchendzonga, monasteries, orchids and more in Sikkim. ▶▶ page 131.

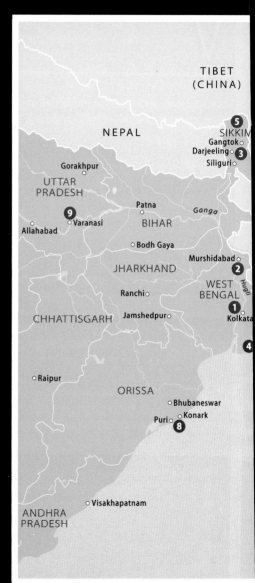

TIBET (CHINA)

NEPAL

5 SIKKIM
Gangtok
Darjeeling **3**
Siliguri

Gorakhpur

UTTAR PRADESH

Patna

Ganga

9 Varanasi

BIHAR

Allahabad

Bodh Gaya

JHARKHAND

Murshidabad **2**

WEST BENGAL

Ranchi

Hugli

CHHATTISGARH

Jamshedpur

1
Kolkata

4

Raipur

ORISSA

Bhubaneswar

Puri Konark
8

Visakhapatnam

ANDHRA PRADESH

ARUNCHAL PRADESH

BHUTAN

Brahmaputra

Guwahati

ASSAM **6**

NAGALAND

Shillong○

MEGHALAYA

MANIPUR

MYANMAR (BURMA)

TRIPURA

○ Agartala

MIZORAM

BANGLADESH

N

100 km
100 miles

The Government of India states that "the external boundaries of India are neither correct nor authenticated"

ay of Bengal

Andaman Islands

10

Nicobar Islands

6 One-horned rhinos in Kaziranga National Park before Assam tea on the veranda. ▶▶ page 165.

7 Buddhist isolation at Tawang Monastery in secretive Arunachal Pradesh ▶▶ page 192.

8 Exquisite temples, hectic festivals and sandy beaches at Puri and Konark. ▶▶ pages 233 and 236.

9 Varanasi, India in the raw. ▶▶ page 274.

10 Scuba, snorkel and scooter in the Andaman Islands, a pristine paradise. ▶▶ page 290.

Top Kolkata.
Mid-left Murshidabad.
Mid-right Darjeeling tea estate.
Above Sunderbans Tiger Reserve.
Right Sikkim.

Title page Buddhist prayer flags, Bodh Gaya.
Pages 2-3 View of Khangchendzonga
from Darjeeling.

6

Left Kaziranga National Park.
Below left Tawang Monastery.
Below right Konark.
Bottom Varanasi.
Next page Andaman Islands.

Contents

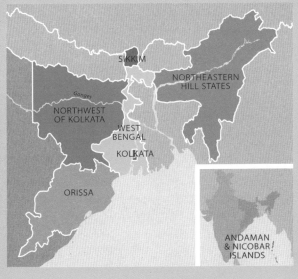

Contents

Footprint features

Essentials

Planning your trip

Where to go

Northeast India encompasses a vast land of diverse peoples, languages, adventures and geography. Although many of the key destinations are connected by an overnight train ride, and cheaper domestic flights are making the distances involved less daunting, if you have limited time it is best to stick to your main goals and not get over-ambitious. If, however, you have more than a couple of weeks at your disposal, the Northeast offers the chance to experience beach life, the Himalaya and tribal cultures, as well as some of the country's holiest places, all in one trip. Travel agencies, which can make the necessary arrangements for a relatively small fee, are listed throughout the text, but remember that air tickets can be difficult to get at short notice for some trips (such as to the Andamans during Indian holiday periods, and to Varanasi at any time). Regardless of budget, travel in India is invariably tiring so build in an opportunity for a rest: Puri on the east coast, the hill stations and Bodh Gaya are all relaxing places to spend a few days. Kolkata, where you are likely to start your trip, is both a good and a bad introduction to India. On one hand, expect poverty, over-crowding and choking pollution, yet because it is not as heavily touristed as other points of entry (such as Delhi or Mumbai) there is less risk of being scammed and locals are genuinely friendly. There are plenty of top- and mid-range hotels in Kolkata and Varanasi, and it is advisable to book your first night in advance if you're a first-time visitor.

Two weeks

Starting in Kolkata, give yourself a couple of days to acclimatize and view the wealth of colonial architecture and cultural offerings. If you are feeling overwhelmed by the city, leave this for the end of the trip when you are better adjusted. Fly or take an overnight train to Siliguri, then a jeep to Kalimpong or Darjeeling for a few days to soak up the Kangchendzonga views, before heading to Varanasi by train. Steep yourself in the holiest Hindu city, then strike east to catch the Buddhist vibe at Bodh Gaya. From here return to Kolkata and spend time in the city, or kick back on a launch among the islands of the Sunderbans.

An excellent trekking experience is manageable in Sikkim or the north of West Bengal in a fortnight. Head straight up to Darjeeling or Gangtok, where the majority of treks last three to eight days, and breathe the Himalayan air. After your trek, retreat and relax for a couple of nights in a quiet settlement such as Mirik (near Darjeeling) or Khecheopalri Lake (Sikkim) to just admire the snowy peaks. Back down in the plains, head east and get up close to the wildlife in Jaldapara Park before hopping slowly south to Kolkata via Malda's historic ruins and sleepy Murshidabad's charms.

For two weeks in paradise, take a flight to the Andamans and make for Havelock or (depending on boat schedules) one of the more pristine, isolated islands such as Little Andaman or Neil Island. For more accessible beach action, head south to Puri, where you might coincide with a Yatra festival if it's April or July. Take in the majestic Sun Temple at Konark, then perhaps head south down the coast, diverting inland to visit the tribal belt of southern Orissa. Do this trip in reverse if you prefer to unwind at the end of a holiday.

Packing for India

You can buy most essentials in larger cities and shops in five-star hotels. Items you might find useful include a loose-fitting, light cotton clothes including a sarong (women should dress modestly at all times; brief shorts and tight vest tops are best avoided, though on the beach modest swimwear is fine). It can be cold in the north from December to February and everywhere over 1500 m, where warmer clothing is essential. Comfortable shoes, sandals or trainers are essential. Take high-factor sun screen and a sun hat. Earplugs and an eyemask are also essential. Indian pharmacies can be very cheap but aren't always reliable, so take a supply of medicines from home, including inhalers and anti-malarial drugs (Proguanil is not available). For protection against mosquitoes, take repellent. See also Health, page 48.

Photocopies of documents, passport ID and visa pages, and spare photos are useful when applying for permits or in case of loss or theft.

For budget travellers: moquito nets aren't always provided in cheap hotels so take one with you. Take a good padlock to secure your budget room too, though these are cheaply bought in India. A cotton or silk sheet sleeping bag is useful when you can't be sure of clean linen.

For trekking equipment and clothing, see page 18.

Three weeks

Visit the Northeastern Hill States, flying from Kolkata to Guwahati and on to Tezpur, where you can branch off into Arunachal Pradesh for the four-day journey to the magical Tawang Monastery. Back in Tezpur, it's a short road trip to Kaziranga to spot one-horned rhinos. Next, if it's December, the Hornbill Festival in jungly Nagaland is worth a detour and while there absorb Kohima and its memories of the Second World War. Otherwise, carry straight on by road to Meghalaya to see the archery stakes and colourful bazars in Shillong, from where day trips allow you to visit Jaintia tribal villages or the wettest place on earth, Mawsynram. Cross over again to Guwahati to fly back to Kolkata or, if you have time to spare, fly to Bagdogra and travel by land to Sikkim, Darjeeling or Murshidabad.

Four weeks

In a month and at a brisk pace, it is possible to see all the main sights of Northeast India (excluding the Hill States) and really get an impression of the distinct regional cultures. Flying wherever possible, you could take on Kolkata, the Himalaya, Jaldapara, Varanasi, Bhubaneswar, and either Puri/Digha/Havelock. Alternatively, selecting two or three states, and seeing them at a more leisurely pace, meandering through less touristy towns (such as Kurseong, Bishnupur or Sasaram) could be more enriching and less stressful.

When to go

As in most of India, the best time to be in the Northeast is from the end of the monsoon in October to the end of March, after which the temperatures and humidity level in the lowlands begin to build up. Some of the country's great festivals, such as Dasara and Diwali across India and Durga Puja in West Bengal, are celebrated in the autumn and winter. From April to June the Himalayan hill stations bring much needed respite from the heat, while the monsoon months of June to September can bring serious disruption in the shape of flooding and landslides. On the other hand, the spectacular Rath Yatra festival in Puri is one compelling reason to visit during July, and devotees of wet weather might pick this time of year to visit Meghalaya – officially home of the wettest town on earth – if only to see nature at one of its extremes.

Trekking in the eastern Himalaya is best in October, with clear blue skies and relatively mild temperatures; the spring months are also good, though visibility may by hazy. Winter in the mountains can be extremely cold, and many guesthouses close.

What to do

There are many opportunities in adventure sports. Such thrills can be combined with more conventional sightseeing. Apart from the activities listed here, you can also try ballooning, heli-skiing, hang-gliding, mountain or rock climbing, and even motor rallying. ▸▸ For tour operators, see page 55.

Biking

For those keen on moving faster along the road, by travelling on the 2 wheels of a motorbike (preferably a 'Bullet'), see page 33.

Birdwatching

The country's diverse and rich natural habitats harbour over 1200 species of birds of which around 150 are endemic. Visitors can enjoy spotting Oriental species whether it is in towns, in the countryside or more abundantly in the national parks and sanctuaries. On the plains, the cooler months (Nov-Mar) are the most comfortable for a chance to see migratory birds from the hills, but the highlands themselves are ideal in May-Jun and again after the monsoons when visibility improves in Oct-Nov. Bodies of water of all sizes draw visiting water fowl from other continents during the winter.

It is quite easy to get to some parks from the important tourist centres. *A Birdwatcher's Guide to India* by Krys Kazmierczak and Raj Singh (Prion Ltd, Sandy, Bedfordshire, UK, 1998), is well researched and comprehensive with helpful practical information and maps. See also Background, page 364.

Contact

www.delhibird.net, www.kolkatabirds.com, www.orientalbirdclub.org, www.sacon.org.

Bird Link, biks@giasdl01.vsnl.net.in, is concerned with conservation of birds and their habitat.

Cricket

Cricket has an almost fanatical following across India. Reinforced by satellite TV and radio and a national side that enjoys high world rankings and much outstanding individual talent, cricket has become a national obsession. Stars have cult status, and you can see children trying to model themselves on their game on any and every open space.

Contact

India's cricket board (BCCI), www.bcci.cricket.deepthi.com, keeps up to date with all the latest in Indian cricket, and for other information and tickets.

Cycling

Cycling offers a peaceful and healthy alternative to cars, buses or trains. Touring on locally hired bicycles is possible along country roads – ideal if you want to see village life and the lesser known wildlife parks. Consult a good Indian agent for advice. Expert guides, bicycles and support vehicle, accommodation in simple rest houses or tents, are included in most tours. See also page 32.

Football

Football is played from professional level to kickabout in any open space. The season is Oct-Mar and details of matches are published in the local papers. Top class game tickets are Rs 25, but they are sold for much more on the black market. The crowds generate tremendous fervour for big matches, and standards are improving. African players are now featuring more frequently with Indian teams and monthly salaries have risen to over Rs 40,000 per month, an excellent wage by Indian standards.

Contact

www.indianfootball.com, for the latest news.

Trekking

See page 16. For tour operators, see page 55.

Water sports

Snorkelling, parasailing, windsurfing and waterskiing are among the attractions along the long stretches of unspoilt coastal India. There are scuba diving centres in the Andamans. Courses are well run and cost US$85 for an introductory dive, US$400 for 4 days, or US$600 for a 2-week Dive Master course.

Contact

PADI Europe, Oberwilerstrasse 3, CH-8442, Hettlingen, Switzerland, T52-304 1414, admin@padi.ch. **PADI International Head Office**, Unit 6, Unicorn Park, Whitby Rd, Bristol, BS4 4EX, T0117-971 1717, www.padi.co.uk.

Whitewater rafting

The snow-fed rivers that flow through regions such as Sikkim offer excellent whitewater rafting. The popular waters range from Grades II-III for amateurs to the greater challenges of Grades IV-VI for the experienced (eg Rangit and Teesta in Sikkim). In Arunachal, the Siang (Upper Brahmaputra) has Grade III-IV navigable rapids and trips run Nov-Dec each year. Trips range from a half day to several days and allow a chance to see scenery, places and people off the beaten track. The trips are organized and managed by professional teams who have trained abroad. The rivers are in flood during the rainy season, which, in the east of India, runs from Apr/May-Sep, often resulting in around 2 m of rainfall. They can be dangerous in Aug and Sep.

Yoga and meditation

There has been a growing Western interest in the ancient life disciplines in search of physical and spiritual wellbeing, as practised in ancient India. Yoga is supposed to regulate the nervous system and aims to attain the union of body, mind and spirit through the practice of *asanas* (body postures), breath control, discipline, cleansing, contemplation and awareness. It seeks to achieve moral purification through abstinence and restraint (dietary and sexual). Meditation which complements yoga to relieve stress, increase awareness and bring inner peace prescribes the practice of *dhyana* (purposeful concentration) by withdrawing oneself from external distractions and focusing ones attention to consciousness itself. This leads ultimately to *samadhi* (release from worldly bonds). Hatha yoga has captured the Western imagination as it promises good health through postural exercises, while the search for inner peace leads others to learn meditation techniques.

Centres across the country offer courses for beginners and practitioners. Some are at special resort hotels which offer all inclusive packages in idyllic locations, some advocate simple communal living in an ashram while others may require rigorous discipline in austere monastic surroundings. Whether you wish to embark on a serious study of yoga or sample an hour's introductory meditation session, India offers opportunities for all, though you may need to apply in advance for some popular courses. The **International Yoga Festival** is held in annually in Feb/Mar.

Himalayan Environment Trust Code of Practice

Deforestation Make no open fires and discourage others making one for you. Limit use of firewood and heated water and use only permitted dead wood. Choose accommodation where kerosene or fuel-efficient wood burning stoves are used.

Litter Remove it. Burn or bury paper and insist that guides and porters do the same, and carry away any non-degradable litter. If you find other people's litter, remove it too. Pack food in biodegradable containers.

Water Keep local water clean. Do not use detergents and pollutants in streams and springs. Where there are no toilets be sure you are at least 30 m away from water source and bury or cover. Do not allow cooks or porters to throw rubbish in nearby streams and rivers.

Plants Do not take cuttings, seeds and roots – it is illegal in all parts of the Himalaya.

Traditions and culture Respect people's privacy and ask permission before taking photographs; respect holy places, never touching or removing religious objects, and removing shoes before entering temples; dress modestly particularly when visiting temples and shrines and while walking through villages avoiding shorts, skimpy tops and tight-fitting outfits. Do not hold hands and kiss in public. Don't swim or bathe nude in rivers or hot springs. When trekking, don't give money, cigarettes, sweets, etc indiscriminately, but do give alms to pilgrims and holy men.

Best yoga retreats
Cochrane Place, Kurseong, West Bengal, www.imperialchai.com.
Bihar School of Yoga, Bihar, www.yogavision.net.

Glenburn Tea Estate, West Bengal, www.glenburnteaestate.com.
Yoga Adventure with Jane Craggs, West Bengal, www.janecraggs.co.uk.

Trekking

The Himalaya offers unlimited opportunities to view the natural beauty of mountains, rare flora and fauna, and the diverse groups of people who live in the ranges and valleys, many of whom have retained unique cultural identities because of their isolation. The treks described in this book are only for guidance. They try to give you a flavour of an area or a destination. Some trails fall within the 'Inner Line' for which special permits are required, see pages 19 and 161. For books on trekking, see page 369.

Independent trekking There are some outstandingly beautiful treks, though they are often not through the wilderness sometimes conjured up. However, trekking alone is not recommended as you will be in unfamiliar territory where you may not be able to communicate with the local people and if injured you may not have help at hand. Independent trekkers should get a specialist publication with detailed route descriptions and a good map. Remember, mountain topography is subject to constant change, and tracks and crossings can be affected very rapidly. Speak to those who know the area well and have been trekking to the places you intend visiting.

Backpacking camping Hundreds of people arrive each year with a pack and some personal equipment, buy some food and set off trekking, carrying their own gear and choosing their own campsites or places to stay. Serious trekkers will need a framed backpack. Supplies of fuel wood are scarce and flat ground suitable for camping rare. It is not always easy to find isolated and 'private' campsites.

Trekking without a tent Although common in Nepal, only a few trails in India offer the ease and comfort of this option. Exceptions are the Singalila Ridge trail in the Darjeeling area and the Sikkim Khangchendzonga trek. On these, it is often possible to stay in trekking huts or in simple village homes. You carry clothes and bedding, as with youth hostelling, and for not much money a night you get a space on the floor, a wooden pallet or a camp bed, or in the more luxurious inns, a room and shower. The food is simple, usually vegetable curry, rice and dhal which, although repetitive, is healthy and can be tasty. This approach brings you into more contact with the local population, the limiting factor being the routes where accommodation is available.

Locally organized treks Porters can usually be hired through an agent in the town or village at the start of a trek. Porters hired in the bazar can be cheaper than agency porters but may be unreliable. They will help carry your baggage, often cook for you, and communicate with the local people. A good porter will know the area and some can tell you about local customs and point out interesting details en route. Away from roads, the footpath is the principal line of communication between villages. Tracks tend to be very good, well graded and in good condition. In remoter areas away from all habitation, tracks may be indistinct and a local guide is recommended. Although some porters speak a little English, you may have communication problems. Remember, you may be expected to provide your porter's warm clothing and protective wear including shoes, gloves and goggles on high altitude treks.

Hiring a *sardar* and crew is more expensive but well worthwhile since he will speak some English, act as a guide, take care of engaging porters and cooks, arrange for provisions, and sort out all logistical problems. A *sardar* will cost more and although he may be prepared to carry a load, his principal function will be as a guide and overseer for the porters. Make sure your *sardar* is experienced in the area you will be travelling in and can show good references which are his own and not borrowed.

Using a trekking agent Trekking agents based in Delhi or Kolkata or at hill stations (eg Darjeeling or Gangtok) will organize treks for a fee and provide a *sardar*, porters, cooks, food and equipment, but it requires effort and careful thought on your part. This method can be excellent and is recommended for a group, preferably with some experience, that wants to follow a specific route. You have to follow a pre-arranged itinerary in some areas, as required by the government, and also as porters expect to arrive at certain points on schedule. You can make arrangements from abroad in advance; often a protracted business. Alternatively, wait until you get to India but allow at least a week to make arrangements.

Fully organized and escorted trek A company or individual with local knowledge and expertise organizes a trip and sells it. Some or all camp equipment, food, cooking, planning the stages, decision-making based on progress and weather conditions, liaison with porters, shopkeepers, etc are all taken care of. When operating abroad, the agency may take care of all travel arrangements, ticketing, visas and permits. Make sure that both you and the trekking company understand exactly who is to provide what equipment. This has the advantage of being a good, safe introduction to the country. You will be able to travel with limited knowledge of the region and its culture and get to places more easily, which as an individual you might not reach, without the expense of completely kitting yourself out. You should read and follow any advice in the preparatory material you are sent, as your enjoyment greatly depends on it.

An escorted trek involves going with a group; you will camp together but not necessarily all walk together. If you are willing to trade some of your independence for careful, efficient organization and make the effort to ensure the group works well together, the experience can be very rewarding. Ideally there should be no more than 20 trekkers (preferably around 12). Companies have reputations to maintain and try to comply with Western concepts of hygiene. Before booking, check the itinerary – is it too demanding, or not adventurous enough? Also find out whether the leader is qualified and is familiar with the route, and what equipment is provided.

Local agents

Tourist offices and government-approved trekking agents in Delhi and the hill stations will organize fairly inexpensive treks. Tour operators and travel agents are listed in each town. The following are recommended:

Adventure Quests, www.adventurequests.net. Run by ex-servicemen, with a range of adventurous trekking and rafting trips in Arunachal Pradesh.

Aquaterra Adventures, S-507, Ground Floor, Greater Kailash-II, New Delhi, T011-2921 2641, www.treknraft.com. Trekking, rafting, kayaking, etc in all Indian Himalayan states.

Ibex Expeditions, see page 57.

Mountain Adventures, A-51, SFS Mount Kailash, New Delhi, T011-2622 2202, www.mountainindia.com.

NEI (Nature Expedition India), B-966 Ansals Palam Vihar, Gurgaon, New Delhi Suburb, T0124-236 8601, www.himalaya-india.com.

Wanderlust, G-18, 2nd floor, Masjid Moth, Greater Kailash Part-II, New Delhi 110048 T011-3292 0231, www.wanderlustindia.com.

Foreign operators

Australia and New Zealand

Adventure World, see page 57.

Himalayan Travellers, Wellington, T04-863325.

Peregrine Adventures, see page 58.

UK

Exodus, see page 55.

Explore Worldwide, T0870-333 4001, www.explore.co.uk.

High Places, T0845-257 7500, www.highplaces.co.uk.

Himalayan Kingdoms, T0845-330 8579, www.himalayankingdoms.com.

KE Adventure, T01768-773966, www.keadventure.com.

Snow Lion Expeditions, T0800-525 8735, www.snowlion.com.

USA

Air Treks, T1877-247 8735, www.airtreks.com.

Mercury, T0800-223 1474.

Mountain Travel Sobek, T1510-594 6000, www.mtsobek.com.

Equipment and clothing If you have good equipment, it is worth taking it, especially your own boots. Mountaineering and trekking equipment can sometimes be hired from various hill stations. Ask the tourist offices there. Guard against cold, wet, sudden changes of temperature, strong sun and wind! Waterproof jacket with hood and over-trousers (windproof, waterproof and 'breather' type); warm sweater; fleece jacket; tracksuit; hiking trousers or shorts (knee length but not cycling); cotton T-shirts; cotton underwear; thermal underwear (vests, long johns); gloves; balaclava or ski toque; sun hat; swimwear. Try to carry lightweight, quick-drying fabrics that can be easily washed in cold-water streams. (After the trek, you might consider offering clothes you can part with to your porter.) Good lightweight walking boots with ankle support should be comfortable and well worn in, as blisters can ruin a trek; spare laces, good trainers (for resting the feet; also suitable for many low-level treks except in snow and off-the-trails); polypropylene undersocks, heavy walking socks. Sunglasses (with UV filter), snow glasses if you are planning to go above the snow line, high-factor sun block (SPF 30+), lip cream, a good sleeping bag (cheap ones from a local market are unsuitable above 4000 m) plus cotton liner, a Thermarest pad or a double thickness foam sleeping mat, 2-m-sq plastic sheet (sold locally), torch (flashlight) with replacement batteries or a Petzl headtorch, a compass, binoculars, insulated bag water-bottle (to also take to bed!), a day pack, a tent (in certain areas). Those expecting to climb high, cross glaciers, etc may need to hire crampons, ice axes, snow gaiters, ropes, etc as well as a silver survival blanket and a reinforced plastic 'bivouac bag'. A kerosene stove and strong fuel container suitable for high altitudes (kerosene is widely available); water filter and containers; nesting cooking pots (at least two); enamel mug and spoon and bags for provisions. Be sure to eat a balanced diet. Local foods will be available along the trail, and in fact the porters' meal of chapati or rice, vegetables, dhal and sweet milky tea is quite nutritious. Some shops stock limited amounts of dry goods for trekkers (noodles, chocolate bars, canned foods, fruit, nuts, porridge oats, etc). You might prefer to take some freeze-dried packs of favourites from home. Remember to thoroughly boil the fresh (unpasteurized) local milk.

Maps Survey of India has started producing trekking maps, Scale 1:250,000, but at present these cover only the Himachal and Uttarakhand areas; none are available for the Northeast. For information on Sikkim trekking maps, see page 154.

Trekking seasons These vary with the area you plan to visit and the elevation. Autumn is best in most parts of the Himalaya though March to May can be pleasant. The monsoons (mid-June to end-September) can obviously be very wet and localized thunderstorms can occur at any time, particularly in the spring and summer. Start your trek early in the morning as the monsoon approaches. It often continues to rain heavily up to mid-October in the eastern Himalaya. Be prepared for extremes in temperatures in all seasons so come prepared with light clothing as well as enough waterproof protection. Winters can be exceptionally cold; high passes can be closed and you need more equipment. Winter treks on all but a few low-altitude ones (up to 3200 m) are only recommended for the experienced trekker accompanied by a knowledgeable local guide.

Darjeeling area (pages 110-113): April and May has a chance of occasional showers but the rhododendrons and magnolias are in full bloom; October and November are usually dry with excellent visibility. Early December is possible but very cold.

Sikkim (pages 154-156): Mid-February to late May and again October to early December are possible; April, May, October and November are best.

Arunachal (pages 189-196): October to February is best for trekking in this remote wilderness, although nights are extremely cold.

Trekking permits Trekking is permitted in all areas other than those described as Restricted or Protected and within the 'Inner Line', so that you may not go close to the international boundary in many places. Often, destinations falling within these 'sensitive' zones which have recently been opened for trekking, require treks to be organized by a recognized Indian Travel Agent for groups of at least four, travelling on a specified route, accompanied by a representative/liaison officer. Sometimes there are restrictions on the maximum number of days, season and type of transport used. The 'Inner Line' runs parallel and 40 km inside the international boundary. Other areas now open to tourists include Tsangu Lake, Lachung and Yumthang (Sikkim) and Kameng Valley (Arunachal Pradesh).

On arrival in India, Government-approved trekking agencies can obtain permits relatively easily, usually within three or four days. It can be much slower applying for trekking permits from abroad and may also slow down your visa application.

Some restricted areas are still totally closed to foreigners. For other restricted areas, permits are issued at the **Foreigners' Regional Registration Offices (FRRO)** in Delhi, Mumbai, Kolkata and Chennai.(and sometimes at a local FRRO), from Immigration officers at some points of entry, and sometimes at the District Magistrate's. See box, page 161.

There are also entrance fees for the various national parks and conservation areas which can be as much as Rs 350.

> ☾ *Always carry your passport. Without one you can be turned back or, if in a restricted area, be deported at one of the regular trekking permit inspection points.*

Being prepared **Health**: You will probably experience mountain sickness in its mildest form if you go much over 3000 m (very occasionally at lower altitudes). It is best to move at a slow pace and take plenty of rest and fluids. See page 48 for details.

Security: Thefts and muggings are very rare but on the increase. Guard your money at the point of departure. Keep your valuables with you at all times, make sure the tent 'doors' are closed when you are going for meals, and lock your room door in lodges. Be particularly careful with rucksacks carried atop buses on long journeys – always keep a watch on them when other passengers are loading/unloading their belongings. Be particularly careful of pickpockets at the start of a trek. Thieves sometimes hang around groups of trekkers knowing that many will be carrying all their money for the trek in cash.

Mountaineering courses Information on mountaineering is available from **Himalyan Mountaineering Institute**, Darjeeling, T0354-225 4083, www.himalayanmountaineering institute.com, which runs one-month beginners' and advanced mountaineering courses. **Indian Mountaineering Federation**, New Delhi, T011-2411 1211, www.indmount.org, funds serious mountaineering, skiing, high-altitude trekking expeditions. Their permission is required for scaling any of India's peaks.

Taking a tour
You may choose to try an inclusive package holiday or let a specialist operator quote for a tailor-made tour. Out of season these can be worth exploring. The lowest prices quoted from the UK vary from about US$550 for a week (flights, hotel and breakfast) in the low season to over US$3000 for three weeks during the peak season. Most will chalk out individual itineraries and cover the major sights with small groups. A list of specialist tour operators, who arrange anything from general tours to wildlife safaris to ashram retreats, can be found on page 55.

Getting there

Air

India is accessible by air from virtually every continent. Most international flights arrive in Delhi or Mumbai, both of which have good internal connections to Kolkata and other airports in Northeast India. Some carriers permit 'open-jaw' travel, arriving in and departing from different cities.

Buying a ticket

Discounts The cheapest fares from Europe tend to be with Central European, Central Asian or Middle Eastern airlines. With these airlines it pays to confirm your return flight as early as possible. You can also get good discounts from Australasia, Southeast Asia and Japan. If you plan to visit two or more South Asian countries within three weeks, you may qualify for a 30% discount on your international tickets. Ask your national tourist office. International air tickets can be bought in India though payment must be made in foreign currency.

Ticket agents Companies dealing in volume and taking reduced commissions for ticket sales can offer better deals than the airlines themselves. The national press carry their advertisements. **Trailfinders**, T0845-058 5858, www.trailfinders.co.uk, has worldwide agencies; **STA**, T0870-160 0599, www.statravel.co.uk, with over 100 offices worldwide, offers special deals for under-26s; **Travelbag**, T0800-082 5000, www.travelbag.co.uk, quotes competitive fares and is part of ebookers. General Sales Agents (GSAs) for specific airlines can sometimes offer attractive deals: try **Jet Air**, 188 Hammersmith Road, London W6 7DJ, T020-8970 1555, for Gulf Air, Kuwait Airways; **Welcome Travels**, 58 Wells Street, London W1P 3RA, T020-7436 3011, for Air India.

Stopovers and Round-the-World (RTW) tickets You can arrange several stopovers in India on RTW and long-distance tickets. RTW tickets allow you to fly in to one and out from another international airport. You may be able to arrange some internal flights using international carriers, eg **Air India** sometimes allows stopovers within India for a small extra charge. **Emirates/Sri Lankan** offers some attractive return fares to Australia that allow stops in Dubai, India, Sri Lanka and either Thailand or Singapore.

From Europe

The best deals are from the UK (try www.cheapflights.com, which also has lots of useful information). In 2010 a return flight direct to Kolkata from London Heathrow cost around £500, but rose above £700 approaching the high season of Christmas, New Year and Easter. Alternatively, an off-season return flight to Delhi can cost as little as £300, and airlines such as **Jet Airways** offer good deals on internal flights when booked in conjunction with an international leg.

Direct services from London to Kolkata are offered only by **Air India**, with a flight taking about 10 hours. **Lufthansa** and **Emirates** offer good discounts but fly via their hub cities, adding to the journey time. Flight consolidators in the UK offering competitive fares include: **Flight bookers**, T0800-082 3000, www.ebookers.com; and **North South Travel**, T01245-608291, www.northsouthtravel.co.uk (profits to charity). **Air India** has a companion-free scheme for routes from India to the USA/Canada/

UK/Europe and also to other destinations in Asia and the Middle East (valid until 31 December 2010, one-way and return trips).

From Australasia

Qantas, **Singapore Airlines**, **Thai Airways**, **Malaysian Airlines**, **Cathay Pacific** and **Air India** are the principal airlines connecting the continents, although **Qantas** is the only one that flies direct. Coming from Asia, **Singapore Airlines**, **Thai Airways**, **Jet Airways** and **Kingfisher Airlines** have direct services to Kolkata. **STA** and **Flight Centre** offer discounted tickets from their branches in major cities in Australia and New Zealand. **Abercrombie & Kent**, **Adventure World**, **Peregrine** and **Travel Corporation of India** organize tours; see Ticket agents and Airlines, below.

From North America

From the east coast, it is best to fly direct to India from New York via London by **Air India** (18 hours). Discounted tickets on **British Airways**, **KLM**, **Lufthansa**, **Gulf Air** and **Kuwait Airways** are sold through agents although they will invariably fly via their country's capital cities. From the west coast, it is best to fly via Hong Kong, Singapore or Bangkok to Delhi or Kolkata using one of those countries' national carriers. **Air Canada** operates between Vancouver and Delhi. **Air Brokers International**, www.airbrokers.com, is competitive and reputable. **STA**, www.statravel.co.uk, has offices in many US cities, Toronto and Ontario. Student fares are also available from **Travel Cuts**, T0800-6672887, www.travelcuts.com, in Canada.

Departure tax

Rs 500 is payable for all international departures other than those to neighbouring SAARC countries, when the tax is Rs 250 (not reciprocated by Sri Lanka). This is normally included in your international ticket; check when buying. (To save time 'Security Check' your baggage before checking in at departure.)

Ticket agents

Abercrombie & Kent, www.abercrombie kent.com, www.abercrombiekent.com.au.
Adventure Company, T0870-794 1009, www.adventurecompany.co.uk. Quotes competitive fares.
Adventure World, www.adventureworld.com.au.
Ebookers, T020-7757 3000, www.ebookers.com.
Flight Centres, www.flightcentre.com.
North South Travel, T01245-492882, www.northsouthtravel.co.uk. Profits go to charity.
Peregrine, www.peregrine.net.au. Adventure tours for small groups.
STA, London, T0871-230 0040, www.sta travel.co.uk. Over 100 offices worldwide.
Trailfinders, London, T0845-058 5858, www.trailfinders.com. Worldwide agencies.

Travel Corporation of India, www.tcindia.com.
Travel Cuts, www.travelcuts.com. US and Canadian agent.
Welcome Travels, 58 Wells St, London W1P 3RA, T020-7436 3011, www.welcome travels.com. For Air India.

Useful websites

www.bargainholidays.com
www.expedia.co.uk
www.lastminute.com
www.travelocity.com

Airlines

Air India, www.airindia.com
British Airways, www.ba.com
Cathay Pacific, www.cathaypacific.com
Emirates, www.emirates.com
Gulf Air, www.gulfairco.com

Jet, www.jetairways.com
Kingfisher, www.flykingfisher.com
KLM, www.klm.com
Kuwait Airways, www.kuwait-airways.com
Lufthansa, www.lufthansa.com
Malaysia Airlines, www.malaysiaairlines.com

Qantas, www.qantas.com.au
Royal Jordanian, www.rja.com.jo
Singapore Airlines, www.singaporeair.com
Thai Airways, www.thaiair.com
Virgin Atlantic, www.virgin-atlantic.com

Road

Crossings between India and its neighbours are affected by the political relations between them. Get your Indian visa in advance, before arriving at the border. Several road border crossings are open periodically, but permission to cross cannot be guaranteed. Those listed below are the main crossings which are usually open all year to tourists.

From Bangladesh

To Kolkata from Dhaka and Jessore. The Bangaon-Benapol crossing is the most reliable. On the Bangladesh side rickshaws are available from Benapol, while buses and minibuses go to Bangaon railway station from the border. **To Tripura** from Dhaka is only four hours by road from the border crossing, just 2 km from the centre of Agartala, with flights to Kolkata. The border post is efficient when open but arrive there before 1500, as formalities often take time. Regulations are subject to change so find out in advance. In London, Bangladesh High Commission, T020-7584 0081.

From Bhutan

The nearest airport at **Bagdogra** is four or five hours' drive from Jaigaon, the rather untidy and unkempt Indian border town. The Indian Immigration checkpost is on the main street, about 1 km from the 'Bhutan Gate' at the border town of Phuntsholing where it is possible to spend a night. To enter Bhutan you need to go through an authorized travel agent and arrange the full visit in advance; the daily fee is currently US$250.

From Burma/Myanmar

The recently reopened Moreh/Tamu border crossing links Myanmar with the state of Manipur. However, foreigners have reported great difficulty in securing permission to either leave or enter Myanmar by land. Anyone intending to try will need a permit to visit Manipur from the Indian government (see page 59 for permit information).

From Nepal

Four crossings are in common use: To **Delhi via Banbassa** is the shortest direct route between Kathmandu and Delhi, via the Nepali town of Mahendranagar and Banbassa. To **Varanasi via Gorakhpur** you must go to the **Sonauli-Bhairawa** crossing, the shortest and fastest route to Varanasi; many continue to Delhi from there. From Kathmandu or Pokhara you can get to Bhairawa, 6 km inside the Nepal border, Sonauli on the border itself, and Nautanwa on the Indian side. From there, buses take 3½ hours to Gorakhpur, with train connections for Delhi, or 5½ hours by bus to Varanasi, see page 287. To **Patna via Raxaul-Birganj** several buses run daily from Raxaul to Patna (five to seven hours) but timings are unreliable and the buses are crowded and uncomfortable. Night buses from Patna reach the border in the early morning; morning buses from Patna connect with the night bus to Kathmandu. Either way you have to have at least one night bus journey unless you stay overnight at Birganj or Raxaul, which is not recommended. The bus journey between Kathmandu or Pokhara and the border takes about 11-12 hours. Even Express buses are slow and packed. Tourist minibuses are the only moderately comfortable option. **Kakarbhitta** (Kakarvita) is on the Nepalese side of a wide river which forms the border here between India and Nepal. A kilometre-long road bridge links it to the Indian town of Raniganj on the east bank. Cycle rickshaws run between the two. A small notice and an Indian flag are all that mark the Indian Immigration checkpost which is in a shady grove of trees by the road. The larger Indian town of Bagdogra is 15 km away. For details see under Siliguri, page 105.

Getting around

Air

India has a comprehensive network linking the major cities of the different states. Deregulation of the airline industry has had a transformative effect on travel within India, with a host of low-budget private carriers offering sometimes unbelievably cheap fares on an ever expanding network of routes in a bid to woo the train-travelling middle class. Promotional one-way fares as low as Rs 9 (US$0.20) have not been unknown, and on any given day, booking a week or two in advance, you can hope to fly between Delhi and Kolkata for around US$65-100.

Kolkata is the hub of northeast air travel, with direct flights to the capitals of most states in the region, as well as to Delhi, Mumbai, Varanasi and other major cities. Guwahati in Assam, and Bagdogra, the air hub for the Himalayan hill stations, also have good connections to Delhi. Some approximate one-way fares include: Delhi–Guwahati US$70-200; Delhi–Bagdogra US$100-200; Kolkata–Varanasi US$60-200; Kolkata–Guwahati US$40-80; and Kolkata–Agartala US$40-80.

Competition from the efficiently run private sector has, in general, improved the quality of services provided by the nationalized airlines. It also seems to herald the end of the two-tier pricing structure, meaning that ticket prices are now usually the same for foreign and Indian travellers. The airport authorities too have made efforts to improve handling on the ground.

For covering vast distances, or awkward links on a route, internal flights are worth considering, though delays and re-routing can be irritating, and there are environmental issues to consider. For short distances it makes more sense to travel by train.

The best way to get an idea of the current routes, carriers and fares is to use a third-party booking website such as www.cleartrip.com or www.yatra.com; the latter also deals with international flights. Booking with these is a different matter: some refuse foreign credit cards outright, while others have to be persuaded to give your card special clearance. Tickets booked on these sites are typically issued as an email ticket or an SMS text message – the simplest option if you have an Indian mobile phone, though it must be converted to a paper ticket at the relevant carrier's airport offices before you will be allowed into the terminal.

National airlines
The following airlines were well established at the time of writing, though the pace of change is rapid:

Air India, www.airindian.com, is the nationalized carrier with a wide network of domestic routes.

Indigo, T099-1038 3838, www.goindigo.in. Comparable to SpiceJet.
Jet Airways, T1800-225522, T011-3989 3333, www.jetairways.com. The longest-established of the private airlines, offering full-service domestic flights.

Jetlite, www.jetlite.com. Comprehensive coverage of the country.
Kingfisher, T0124-284 4700, www.flyking fisher.com. Similar service and prices to Jet.
SpiceJet, T1800-180 3333, www.spicejet.com. No-frills service between major cities.

Airport information

The formalities on arrival in India have been increasingly streamlined during the last few years and the facilities at the major international airports greatly improved. However, arrival can still be a slow process. Disembarkation cards, with an attached customs declaration, are handed out to passengers during the inward flight. The immigration form should be handed in at the immigration counter on arrival. The customs slip will be returned, for handing over to the customs on leaving the baggage collection hall. You may well find that there are delays of over an hour at Immigration in processing passengers passing through immigration who need help with filling in forms.

Pre-paid taxis to the city are available at all major airports. Insist on being taken to your chosen destination even if the driver claims the city is unsafe or the hotel has closed down. ▸▸ *For details on getting from Kolkata airport into the city centre, see page 64.*

Air tickets

All the major airlines are connected to the local travel agents who will book your tickets for a fee if you don't want to spend precious time searching online or waiting in a queue. Remember that tickets are in great demand in the peak season so it is essential to get them weeks or months ahead. If you are able to pre-plan your trip, it is even possible to book internal flights at home when you buy your international air ticket. This can done through an agent or direct with the airline (eg **Air India** or **Jet Airways**). Both Jet and Air India offer a variety of flight passes, valid on certain sections of their networks; these can be useful if you plan to travel extensively and quickly in areas beyond the reach of the budget airlines. You can also book internal flights on the internet, www.welcome travel.com, and collect and pay for them on your arrival in India. **Air India** and **Jet Airways** both offer coupon schemes which can save money on internal flights. Jet also has special seven-, 15- and 21-day unlimited travel deals (US$360-950). Check airline websites for these 'special offers' when making a booking.

Delays

Be prepared for delays, especially during the winter. Nearly all northern routes originate in Delhi where from early December to February smog has become a common morning hazard, sometimes delaying departures by several hours. The same problem is common in Kolkata.

Air travel tips

Security You may need to identify your bags after they have been checked in and just before they are loaded onto the plane. All baggage destined for the hold must be X-rayed by security before checking in, so do this first on arrival at the airport.
Telephone There is a free telephone service at major airports (occasionally through the tourist office counter) to contact any hotel of your choice.
Waiting lists If you don't have a confirmed booking and are 'wait-listed' it pays to arrive early at the airport and be persistent in enquiring about your position.

Trains can still be the cheapest and most comfortable means of travelling long distances saving you hotel expenses on overnight journeys. It gives access to booking station Retiring Rooms, which can be useful from time to time (see page 36). Above all, you have an ideal opportunity to meet local travellers and catch a glimpse of life on the ground. Remember the dark glass fitted on air-conditioned coaches does restrict vision. See also Internet services, page 28.

High-speed trains

There are several air-conditioned 'high-speed' **Shatabdi** (or 'Century') **Express** for day travel, and **Rajdhani Express** ('Capital City') for overnight journeys. These cover large sections of the network but due to high demand you need to book them well in advance (up to 90 days). Meals and drinks are usually included.

Steam

For rail enthusiasts, the steam-hauled narrow-gauge train between Kurseong and Darjeeling in North Bengal (a World Heritage Site) is an attraction. See the IRCTC and Indian Railways website, www.irctc.co.in. **SD Enterprises Ltd** (see page 27) is recommended for tailor-made trips.

Classes

A/c First Class, available only on main routes, is very comfortable (bedding provided). It will also be possible for tourists to reserve special coaches (some air-conditioned) which are normally allocated to senior railway officials only. **A/c Sleeper**, two- and three-tier configurations (known as 2AC and 3AC), are clean and comfortable and good value. **A/c Executive Class**, with wide reclining seats, are available on many *Shatabdi* trains at double the price of the ordinary **a/c Chair Car** which are equally comfortable. **1st Class (non-a/c)** is gradually being phased out (now rather run down but still pleasant if you like open windows). **Sleeper Class** provides basic upholstered seats and is a 'Reserved' class though tickets are sometimes 'subject to available accommodation'. **2nd Class** (non-a/c) two- and three-tier (commonly called Sleeper) provides exceptionally cheap and atmospheric travel but can be crowded and uncomfortable, and toilet facilities can be unpleasant; it is nearly always better to use the Indian-style squat loos rather than the Western-style ones as they are better maintained. At the bottom rung is **Unreserved Second Class**, with hard wooden benches. You can travel long distances for a trivial amount of money, but unreserved carriages are often ridiculously crowded, and getting off at your station may involve a battle of will and strength against the hordes trying to shove their way on.

Indrail passes

These allow travel across the network without having to pay extra reservation fees and sleeper charges but you have to spend a high proportion of your time on the train to make it worthwhile. However, the advantages of pre-arranged reservations and automatic access to 'Tourist Quotas' can tip the balance in favour of the pass for some travellers. Tourists (foreigners and Indians resident abroad) may buy these passes from the tourist sections of principal railway booking offices and pay in foreign currency or by major credit card. Fares range from US$57 to US$1060 for adults or around half that

Riding the rails

High-class, comfortable, and by Indian standards, quick new Express trains have brought many journeys within daytime reach. But while they offer an increasingly functional means of covering long distances in comfort, it is the overnight trips which still retain something of the early feel of Indian train travel. The bedding carefully prepared – and now available on air-conditioned second-class trains – the early morning light illuminating another stretch of hazy Indian landscape, spontaneous conversations with fellow travellers – these are still on offer, giving a value far beyond the still modest prices. Furthermore, India still has a complete guide to its rail timetables.

for children. Rail-cum-air tickets are also to be made available. Indrail passes can also conveniently be bought abroad from special agents. For people contemplating a single long journey soon after arriving in India, the half- or one-day Pass with a confirmed reservation is worth the peace of mind; two- or four-day passes are also sold. The UK agent is **SD Enterprises Ltd**, 103 Wembley Park Drive, Wembley, Middlesex, HA9 8HG, UK, T020-8200 9549, www.indiarail.co.uk. They make all necessary reservations and offer excellent advice. They can also book Air India and Jet Airways internal flights.

Cost

A/c first class costs about double the rate for two-tier, and non a/c second class about half. Children (five-12) travel at half the adult fare. The young (12-30 years) and senior citizens (65 years and over) are allowed a 30% discount on journeys over 500 km (just show your passport). Fares for individual journeys are based on distance covered and reflect both the class and the type of train. Higher rates apply on the Mail and Express trains and the air-conditioned *Shatabdi* and *Rajdhani Expresses*.

Rail travel tips

Bedding It can get cold in air-conditioned coaches when travelling at night. Bedding is provided on second-class air-conditioned sleepers. On others it can be hired for Rs 30 from the Station Baggage Office for second class.

Berths It is worth asking for upper berths, especially in second-class three-tier sleepers, as they can also be used during the day when the lower berths are used as seats. Once the middle berth is lowered for sleeping the lower berth becomes too cramped to sit on.

Credit cards Some main stations now have separate credit card booking queues – even shorter than women's queues!

Delays Always allow plenty of time for booking and for making connections. Delays are common on all types of transport. The special **Shatabdi** and **Rajdhani Express** are generally quite reliable. Ordinary Express and Mail trains have priority over local services and occasionally surprise by being punctual, but generally the longer the journey time, the greater the delay. Delays on the rail network are cumulative, so arrivals and departures from mid-stations are often several hours behind schedule. Allow at least two hours for connections, more if the first part of the journey is long distance.

Food and drink It is best to carry some though tea, bottled water and snacks are sold on the platforms (through the windows). Carry plenty of small notes and coins on long journeys. Rs 50 and Rs 100 notes can be difficult to change when purchasing small food items. On long-distance trains, the restaurant car is often near the upper class carriages (bogies).

Getting a seat It is usually impossible to make seat reservations at small 'intermediate' stations as they don't have an allocation. You can sometimes use a porter to get you a seat in a second-class carriage. For about Rs 20 he will take the luggage and ensure that you get a seat!

Internet services Much information is now available online via the websites **www.railtourismindia.com**, **www.indianrail.gov.in** and **www.trainenquiry.com**, where you can check timetables (which change frequently), numbers, seat availability and even the running status of your train. Another very useful website for checking availability and planning itineraries is **www.erail.in**. Internet tickets can theoretically be bought at **www.irctc.co.in**, though a credit card is required; foreign cards are accepted, but persistence is needed with the website when registering. An alternative is to seek out a local agent who can sell e-tickets, which can cost as little as Rs 5-10 (plus Rs 20 reservation fee), and can save hours of hassle; simply present the printout to the ticket collector.

Left luggage Bags can be left for up to 30 days in station cloakrooms. These are especially useful when there is time to go sightseeing before an evening train. The bags must be lockable and you are advised not to leave any food in them (rats!).

Ladies' compartments A woman travelling alone, overnight, on an unreserved second class train can ask if there is one of these. Lone female travellers may feel more comfortable in air-conditioned sleeper coaches, which require reservations and are used extensively by Indian families.

Ladies' and seniors' queues Separate (much shorter) ticket queues may be available for women and senior citizens. Travellers over 60 can ask for a 30% discount on the ticket price.

Overbooking Passengers with valid tickets but no berth reservations are sometimes permitted to travel overnight, causing great discomfort to travellers occupying lower berths. Wait-listed passengers should confirm the status of their ticket in advance by calling enquiries at the nearest computerized reservation office. At the station, check the reservation charts (usually on the relevant platform) and contact the Station Manager or Ticket Collector.

Porters These can carry prodigious amounts of luggage. Rates vary from station to station (sometimes listed on a board on the platform) but are usually around Rs 10-25 per item of luggage.

Pre-paid taxis Many main stations have a pre-paid taxi (or auto-rickshaw) service which offers a reliable service at a fair price. Search these out on arrival, they can save you from nasty disagreements.

Quotas A large number of seats are technically reserved as quotas for various groups of travellers (civil servants, military personnel, foreign tourists, etc). Tourist quota is available at main stations. As a tourist you are not obliged to use it, but it can get you on an otherwise 'full' train; you will need your passport, and either pay in US dollars or pounds sterling or in rupees with a currency encashment certificate/ATM receipt. In addition, many stations have their own quota for particular trains so that a train may be 'fully booked' when there are still some tickets available from the special quota of other stations. These are only sold on the day of departure so wait-listed passengers are often able to travel at the last minute. Ask the superintendent on duty to try the 'Special' or 'VIP Quota'. The 'Tatkal' system releases a small percentage of seats at 0800 on the day before a train departs; you pay an extra Rs 75-200 (depending on class and season) to get on an otherwise heavily booked train.

Train touts

Many railway stations – and some bus stations – are heavily populated with touts. Self-styled 'agents' will board trains before they enter the station and seek out tourists, often picking up their luggage and setting off with words such as "Madam!/Sir! Come with me! You need top-class hotel …". They will even select porters to take your luggage.

For a first-time visitor such touts can be more than a nuisance. You need to keep calm and firm. Decide in advance where you want to stay. If you need a porter on trains, select one yourself and agree a price before the porter sets off with your baggage. If travelling with a companion one can stay guarding the luggage while the other gets hold of a taxi and negotiates the price to the hotel. It sounds complicated and sometimes it feels it. The most important thing is to behave as if you know what you are doing!

Security Keep valuables close to you, securely locked, and away from windows. For security, carry a good lock and chain to attach your luggage.

Tickets and reservations Unreserved second-class tickets are available at any station by queueing at the window – a skill in itself – and represent the quickest way to get on a train that is about to depart. On most trains (not *Rajdhani* or *Shatabdi Expresses*) you can attempt to upgrade an unreserved ticket by seeking out the Station Manager's office, or the black-suited TTE (Travelling Ticket Examiner, pronounced 'tee-tee') if the train is at the platform, and asking if a seat is available; an upgrade fee is payable. This can save time waiting in the slower line for reservations.

It is possible to reserve tickets for virtually any train on the network from one of the 520 computerized reservation centres across India. It is always best to book as far in advance as possible (usually up to 60 days). To reserve a seat on a particular train, note down the train's name, number and departure time, and fill in a reservation form while you line up at the ticket window; you can use one form for up to four passengers. At busy stations the wait can take an hour or more; you can save a lot of time and effort by asking a travel agent to get yours for a small fee, usually of around Rs 50-100. If the class you want is full, ask at the ticket window if special 'quotas' are available (see above). If not, consider buying a 'wait list' ticket, as seats often become available close to the train's departure time; phone the station on the day of departure to check your ticket's status. If you don't have a reservation for a particular train but carry an Indrail Pass, you may get one by arriving about three hours early. Be wary of touts at the station offering tickets, hotels or money changing.

Timetables Regional timetables are available cheaply from station bookstalls; the monthly 'Indian Bradshaw' is sold in principal stations. The handy 'Trains at a Glance' (Rs 30) lists popular trains likely to be used by most foreign travellers and is available in the UK from **SD Enterprises Ltd** (see under Indrail passes, page 27).

Road

Road travel is often the only choice for reaching many of the places of outstanding interest in which India is so rich. For the uninitiated, travel by road can also be a worrying experience because of the apparent absence of conventional traffic regulations and also in the mountains, especially during the rainy season when landslides are possible.

Vehicles drive on the left – in theory. Routes around the major cities are usually crowded with lorry traffic, especially at night, and the main roads are often poor and slow. There are a few motorway-style expressways, but most main roads are single track. Some district roads are quiet, and although they are not fast they can be a good way of seeing the country and village life if you have the time.

Bus

Buses now reach virtually every part of India, offering a cheap, if often uncomfortable, means of visiting places off the rail network. Very few villages are now more than 2-3 km from a bus stop. Services are run by the State Corporation from the State Bus Stand (and private companies which often have offices nearby). The latter allow advance reservation and though tickets prices are a little higher, they have fewer stops and are a bit more comfortable.

Bus categories Though comfortable for sightseeing trips, apart from the very best 'sleeper coaches' even **air-conditioned luxury coaches** can be very uncomfortable for really long journeys. Often the air conditioning is very cold so wrap up. Journeys over 10 hours can be extremely tiring so it is better to go by train if there is a choice. **Express buses** run over long distances (frequently overnight), these are often called 'video coaches' and can be an appalling experience unless you appreciate loud film music blasting through the night. Ear plugs and eye masks may ease the pain. They rarely average more than 45 km per hour. **Local buses** are often very crowded, quite bumpy, slow and usually poorly maintained. However, over short distances, they can be a very cheap, friendly and easy way of getting about. Even where signboards are not in English someone will usually give you directions. Many larger towns have **minibus** services which charge a little more than the buses and pick up and drop passengers on request. Again very crowded, and with restricted headroom, they are the fastest way of getting about many of the larger towns.

Bus travel tips Some towns have different bus stations for different destinations. Booking on major long-distance routes is now computerized. Book in advance where possible and avoid the back of the bus where it can be very bumpy. If your destination is only served by a local bus you may do better to take the Express bus and 'persuade' the driver, with a tip in advance, to stop where you want to get off. You will have to pay the full fare to the first stop beyond your destination but you will get there faster and more comfortably. When an unreserved bus pulls into a bus station, there is usually an unholy scramble for seats, while those arriving have to struggle to get off! In many areas there is an unwritten 'rule of reservation' using handkerchiefs or bags thrust through the windows to reserve seats. Some visitors may feel a more justified right to a seat having fought their way through the crowd, but it is generally best to do as local people do and be prepared with a handkerchief or 'sarong'. As soon as it touches the seat, it is yours! Leave it on your seat when getting off to use the toilet at bus stations.

Car

A car provides a chance to travel off the beaten track, and gives unrivalled opportunities for seeing something of India's great variety of villages and small towns. Until recently, the most widely used hire car was the Hindustan Ambassador. However, except for the newest model, they are often very unreliable, and although they still have their devotees, many find them uncomfortable for long journeys. For a similar price, Maruti cars and vans (Omni) are much more reliable and are now the preferred choice in many areas. Gypsy

4WDs and Jeeps are also available, especially in the hills, where larger Sumos have made an appearance. Maruti Esteems and Toyota Qualis are comfortable and have optional reliable air conditioning. A specialist operator can be very helpful in arranging itineraries and car hire in advance.

Car hire With a driver, car hire is cheaper than in the West. A car shared by three or four can be very good value. Be sure to check carefully the mileage at the beginning and end of the trip. Two- or three-day trips from main towns can also give excellent opportunities for sightseeing off the beaten track in reasonable comfort. Local drivers often know their way much better than drivers from other states, so where possible it is a good idea to get a local driver who speaks the state language, in addition to being able to communicate with you. In the mountains, it is better to use a driver who knows the roads. Drivers may sleep in the car overnight though hotels sometimes provide a bed for them. They are responsible for their expenses, including meals. Car (and auto) drivers increase their earnings by taking you to hotels and shops where they get a handsome commission (which you will pay for). If you feel inclined, a tip at the end of the tour of Rs 100 per day in addition to their daily allowance is perfectly acceptable. Check beforehand if fuel and inter-state taxes are included in the hire charge.

Cars can be hired through private companies. International companies such as **Hertz**, **Europcar** and **Budget** operate in some major cities and offer reliable cars; their rates are generally higher than those of local firms (eg **Sai Service**, **Wheels**). The price of an imported car can be three times that of the Ambassador.

Car with driver	Economy Maruti 800 Ambassador	Regular a/c Maruti 800 Contessa	Premium a/c Maruti 1000 Opel	Luxury a/c Esteem Qualis
8 hrs/80 km	Rs 800	Rs 1000	Rs 1400	Rs 1800+
Extra km	Rs 4-7	Rs 9	Rs 13	Rs 18
Extra hour	Rs 40	Rs 50	Rs 70	Rs 100
Out of town				
Per km	Rs 7	Rs 9	Rs 13	Rs 18
Night halt	Rs 100	Rs 200	Rs 250	Rs 250

Car travel tips When booking emphasize the importance of good tyres and general roadworthiness. On main roads across India **petrol stations** are reasonably frequent, but some areas are poorly served. Some service stations only have diesel pumps though they may have small reserves of petrol. Always carry a spare can. Diesel is widely available and normally much cheaper than petrol. Petrol is rarely above 92 octane. Drivers must have third party **insurance**. This may have to be with an Indian insurer, or with a foreign insurer who has a national guarantor. You must also be in possession of an International Driving Permit, issued by a recognized driving authority in your home country (eg the AA in the UK, apply at least six weeks before leaving). **Asking the way** can be very frustrating as you are likely to get widely conflicting advice each time you stop to ask. On the main roads, 'mile' posts periodically appear in English and can help. Elsewhere, it is best to ask directions often and follow the average direction! **Accidents** often produce large and angry crowds very quickly. It is best to leave the scene of the accident and report it to the police as quickly as possible thereafter. Ensure that you have adequate provisions, plenty of food and drink, and a basic tool set in the car.

Taxi

Yellow-top taxis in cities and large towns are metered, although tariffs change frequently. These changes are shown on a fare chart which should be read in conjunction with the meter reading. Increased night-time rates apply in some cities, including Kolkata, but there should not be any extra charge for luggage. Insist on the taxi meter being flagged in your presence. If the driver refuses, the official advice is to contact the police. This may not work, but it is worth trying. When a taxi doesn't have a meter, you will need to fix the fare before starting the journey. Ask at your hotel desk for a guide price.

At stations and airports it is often possible to share taxis to a central point. It is worth looking for fellow passengers who may be travelling in your direction and get a pre-paid taxi. At night, always have a clear idea of where you want to go and insist on being taken there. Taxi drivers may try to convince you that the hotel you have chosen 'closed three years ago' or is 'completely full'. Say that you have a reservation.

Rickshaw

Auto-rickshaws (autos) are almost universally available in towns across India and are the cheapest and most convenient way of getting about. It is best to walk a short distance away from a hotel gate before picking up an auto to avoid paying an inflated rate. In addition to using them for short journeys it is often possible to hire them by the hour, or for a half or full day's sightseeing. In some areas younger drivers who speak some English and know their local area well may want to show you around. However, rickshaw drivers are often paid a commission by hotels, restaurants and gift shops so advice is not always impartial. Drivers generally refuse to use a meter, often quote a ridiculous price or may sometimes stop short of your destination. If you have real problems it can help to note down the vehicle license number and threaten to go to the police. Beware of some rickshaw drivers who show the fare chart for taxis.

Cycle-rickshaws and **horse-drawn tongas** are more common in the more rustic setting of a small town or the outskirts of a large one. You will need to fix a price by bargaining. The animal attached to a tonga usually looks too undernourished to have the strength to pull the driver, let alone passengers.

Kolkata holds the dubious honour of being the only city in the world where **hand-pulled rickshaws** remain an essential means of transport; in the monsoon, they are often the only vehicles that can get through the flooded streets. The government periodically tries to ban them, but until another form of employment can be found for 18,000 men, they are likely to remain. Always agree a price before getting on board and expect a very bumpy ride.

Cycling

Cycling is an excellent way of seeing the quiet byways of India. It is easy to hire bikes in most small towns for about Rs 20-30 per day. Indian bikes are heavy and without gears, but on the flat they offer a good way of exploring comparatively short distances outside towns. In the more prosperous tourist resorts, mountain bikes are now becoming available, but at a higher charge. It is also quite possible to tour more extensively and you may then want to buy a cycle.

There are shops in every town and the local Hero brand is considered the best, with Atlas and BSA good alternatives; expect to pay around Rs 1200-1500 for a second-hand Indian bike but remember to bargain. At the end of your trip you could sell it easily at half price. Imported bikes have lighter weight and gears, but are more difficult to get repaired and carry the much greater risk of being stolen or damaged. If you wish to take your own, it is quite easy if you dismantle it and pack it in its original shipping carton; be sure to take all essential spares including a pump. It is possible to get Indian spares for 26" wheel cycles. All cyclists should take bungy cords (to strap down a backpack) and good lights from home, although cycling at night is not recommended; take care not to leave your bike parked anywhere with your belongings. Bike repair shops are universal and charges are nominal.

It is possible to cover 50-80 km a day quite comfortably. One cyclist reported that the national highways are manic but country roads, especially along the coast, can be idyllic, if rather dusty and bumpy. You can even put your bike on a boat for a backwater trip or on top of a bus. If you want to take your bike on the train, allow plenty of time for booking it in on the brake van at the Parcels office and for filling in forms.

It is best to start a journey early in the morning, stopping at midday and then resuming your journey in the late afternoon. Night riding, though cooler, can be hazardous because of lack of lighting and poor road surfaces. Try to avoid major highways as far as possible. Fortunately foreign cyclists are usually greeted with cheers, waves and smiles and truck drivers are sometimes happy to give lifts to cyclists (and their bikes). This is a good way of taking some of the hardship out of cycling round India. For expert advice contact the **Cyclists' Touring Club**, T0870- 873 0060, www.ctc.org.uk.

Motorcycling

This is a particularly attractive way of getting around. It is easy to buy new Indian-made motorbikes including the 350cc Enfield Bullet and several 100cc Japanese models, including Suzukis and Hondas made in collaboration with Indian firms; Indian Rajdoots are less expensive but have a poor reputation for reliability. Buying new at a fixed price ensures greater ease and reliability. Buying second hand in rupees takes more time but is quite possible (expect to get a 30-40% discount) and repairs are usually easy to arrange and quite cheap. You can get a broker to help with the paperwork involved (certificate of ownership, insurance etc) for a fee (see also Insurance, page 50). They charge about Rs 5000 for a No Objection Certificate (NOC), essential for reselling; it's easier to have the bike in your name. Bring your own helmet and an International Driving Permit. Vespa, Kinetic Honda and other makes of scooters in India are slower than motorbikes but comfortable for short hauls of less than 100 km and have the advantage of a 'dicky' (small, lockable box) for spares, and a spare tyre.

Hitchhiking

Hitchhiking is uncommon, partly because public transport is so cheap. If you try, you are likely to spend a very long time on the roadside. However, getting a lift on scooters and on trucks in areas with little public transport can be worthwhile, while those riding motorbikes or scooters in tourist areas can be expected to pick up the occasional hitchhiking policeman! It is not recommended for women on their own.

Maps

For anyone interested in the geography of India, or even simply getting around, trying to buy good maps is a depressing experience. For security reasons it is illegal to sell large-scale maps of areas within 80 km of the coast or national borders, and it is illegal to export any large scale maps.

The **Bartholomew** 1:4 m map sheet of India is the most authoritative, detailed and easy to use map available. It can be bought worldwide. **GeoCenter World Map** 1:2 m covers

India in three regional sections and are clearly printed. **Nelles'** regional maps of India at the scale of 1:1.5 m offer generally clear route maps, though neither the road classifications nor alignments are wholly reliable. The same criticism applies to the attractively produced and easy-to-read **Lonely Planet Travel Atlas of India and Bangladesh** (2001).

State and town plans are published by the **TTK Company**. These are often the best available though they are not wholly reliable. For the larger cities they provide the most compact yet clear map sheets (generally 50 mm by 75 mm format).

The Survey of India publishes large scale 1:10,000 town plans of approximately 70 cities. These detailed plans are the only surveyed town maps in India, and some are over 20 years old. The Survey also has topographic maps at the scale of 1:25,000 and 1:50,000 in addition to its 1:250,000 scale coverage, some of which are as recent as the late 1980s. However, maps are regarded as highly sensitive and it is only possible to buy these from main agents of the Survey of India.

Stanfords, 12-14 Long Acre, London, WC2, T020-7836 1321, www.stanfords.co.uk, offers a mail order service.addition to its 1:250,000 scale coverage, some of which are as recent as the late 1980s. However, maps are regarded as highly sensitive and it is only possible to buy these from main agents of the Survey of India.

Sleeping

India has an enormously wide range of accommodation. You can stay safely and very cheaply by Western standards right across the country. In all the major cities there are also high-quality hotels, offering a full range of facilities. In small centres even the best hotels are far more variable. The heritage hotels so widespread in Rajasthan are virtually unheard of in the Northeast. Hotels in hill stations, because of their location and special appeal, often deviate from the description of our different categories. In the peak season (October to April for most of India) bookings can be extremely heavy in popular destinations. It is sometimes possible to book in advance by phone, fax or email, but double check your reservation, and always try to arrive as early as possible in the day.

Hotels → *See box, page 35, for Sleeping price codes.*
Price categories The category codes used in this book are based on prices of double rooms excluding taxes. They are **not** star ratings and individual facilities vary considerably. The most expensive hotels charge in US dollars only. Modest hotels may not have their own restaurant but will often offer 'room service', bringing in food from outside. Many hotels operate a 24-hour checkout system. Make sure that this means that you can stay 24 hours from the time of check-in. Expect to pay more in Delhi and, to a lesser extent, Kolkata, for all categories. Prices away from large cities tend to be lower.

Off-season rates Large reductions are made by hotels in all categories out-of-season in many resorts. Always ask if any are available. You may also request the 10-15% agent's commission to be deducted from your bill if you book direct. Clarify whether the agreed figure includes all taxes.

Taxes In general most hotel rooms rated at Rs 1200 or above are subject to a tax of 10%. Many states levy an additional luxury tax of 10-25%, and some hotels add a service

Sleeping and eating price codes

LL over US$200	**B** US$46-65	**E** US$12-20
L US$151-200	**C** US$31-45	**F** US$7-11
AL US$101-150	**D** US$21-30	**G** under US$7
A US$66-100		

Price of a double room in high season, excluding taxes.

¶¶¶ over US$12   **¶¶** US$6-12   **¶** under US$6

Price of a two-course meal for one person, excluding drinks and taxes.

charge of 10% on top of this. Taxes are not necessarily payable on meals, so it is worth settling your meals bill separately. Most hotels in the **C** category and above accept payment by credit card. Check your final bill carefully. Visitors have complained of incorrect bills, even in the most expensive hotels. The problem particularly afflicts groups, when last-minute extras appear mysteriously on some guests' bills. Check the evening before departure, and keep all receipts.

Hotel facilities You have to be prepared for difficulties which are uncommon in the West. It is best to inspect the room and check that all equipment (air conditioning, TV, water heater, flush) works before checking in at a modest hotel.

In some states **power cuts** are common, or hot water may be restricted to certain times of day. The largest hotels have their own generators but it is best to carry a good torch. Usually, only category **C** and above have **central air conditioning**. Elsewhere air-conditioned rooms are cooled by individual units and occasionally by large 'air-coolers' which can be noisy and unreliable. When they fail to operate tell the management as it is often possible to get a rapid repair done, or to transfer to a room where the unit is working. During power cuts generators may not be able to cope with providing air conditioning. Fans are provided in all but the cheapest hotels.

Apart from those in the **A** category and above, 'attached bath' does not necessarily refer to a bathroom with a bathtub. Most will provide a **bathroom** with a toilet, basin and a shower. In the lower priced hotels and outside large towns, a bucket and tap may replace the shower, and an Indian squat toilet instead of a Western WC (squat toilets are very often cleaner). Even mid-price hotels, which are clean and pleasant, don't always provide towels, soap and toilet paper.

In some regions **water supply** is rationed periodically. Keep a bucket filled to use for flushing the toilet during water cuts. Occasionally, tap water may be discoloured due to rusty tanks. During the cold weather and in hill stations, hot water will be available at certain times of the day, sometimes in buckets, but is usually very restricted in quantity. Electric water heaters may provide enough for a shower but not enough to fill a bath tub! For details on drinking water, see page 38.

At some times of the year and in some places **mosquitoes** can be a real problem, and not all hotels have mosquito-proof rooms or mosquito nets. If you have any doubts check before confirming your room booking. In cheap hotels you need to be prepared for the presence of flies, cockroaches, spiders, ants and geckos (harmless house lizards).

Poisonous insects and scorpions are extremely rare in towns. Hotel managements are nearly always prepared with insecticide sprays. Few small hotels in mosquito-prone areas supply nets so it is best for budget travellers to take one from home. An impregnated, wedge-shaped one (for single-point fixing) is preferable, available in all good camping/outdoor shops. Remember to shut windows and doors at dusk. Electrical mats and pellets are now widely available, as are mosquito coils that burn slowly. One traveller recommends Dettol soap to discourage mosquitoes. Dusk and early evening are the worst times for mosquitoes so trousers and long-sleeved shirts are advisable, especially outdoors. At night, fans can be very effective in keeping mosquitoes off; remember to tuck the net under the mattress all round. As well as insects, expect to find spiders larger and hairier than those you see at home; they are mostly harmless and more frightened of you than you are of them!

Hotels close to temples can be very **noisy**, especially during festivals. Music blares from loudspeakers late at night and from very early in the morning, often making sleep impossible. Mosques call the faithful to prayers at dawn. Earplugs are invaluable.

Hotels in hill stations often supply **wood fires** in rooms. Usually there is plenty of ventilation, but ensure that there is always good air circulation, especially when charcoal fires are provided in a basket.

Where staff training is lacking, the person who brings up your cases may proceed to show you light switches, room facilities, TV tuning, and hang around waiting for a **tip**. Room boys may enter your room without knocking or without waiting for a response to a knock. Both for security and privacy, it is a good idea to lock your door when you are in the room. At the higher end, you should expect to tip bellboys a little for every favour.

Tourist 'bungalows'

The different state tourism development corporations run their own hotels and hostels which are often in places of special interest. These are very reasonably priced, though they may be rather dated, restaurant menus may be limited and service is often slow.

Railway and airport retiring rooms

Railway stations often have 'Retiring Rooms' or 'Rest Rooms' which may be hired for periods of between one and 24 hours by anyone holding an onward train ticket. They are cheap and simple though often heavily booked. Some major airports (eg Mumbai) have similar facilities.

Government rest houses

Rest houses may be available for overnight stays, especially in remote areas. They are usually very basic, with a caretaker who can sometimes provide a simple meal, with notice. Check the room rate in advance as foreigners can be overcharged. Government officials always take precedence, even over guests who have booked.

Indian-style hotels

These, catering for Indian businessmen, are springing up fast in or on the outskirts of many small- and medium-sized towns. Most have some air-conditioned rooms and attached showers. They are variable in quality but it is increasingly possible to find excellent value accommodation even in remote areas.

Hostels

The Department of Tourism runs 16 youth hostels, each with about 50 beds, usually organized into dormitory accommodation. The YHA also have sites in Kolkata, Darjeeling and Gangtok. Travellers may also stay in religious hostels (*dharamshalas*) for up to three days. These are primarily intended for pilgrims and are sometimes free, though voluntary offerings are welcome. Usually only vegetarian food is permitted; smoking and alcohol are not.

Camping

Mid-price hotels with large grounds are sometimes willing to allow camping. Regional tourist offices have details of new developments. For information on YMCA camping facilities contact: **YMCA**, The National General Secretary, National Council of YMCAs of India, PB No 14, Massey Hall, Jai Singh Rd, New Delhi 1.

Eating and drinking

Food → *For a glossary of food and drink, see page 372.*

You find just as much variety in dishes and presentation crossing India as you would on an equivalent journey across Europe. Combinations of spices give each region its distinctive flavour.

The larger hotels, open to non-residents, often offer **buffet** lunches with Indian, Western and sometimes Chinese dishes. These can be good value (Rs 250-300; but Rs 450 in the top grades) and can provide a welcome, comfortable break in the cool. The health risks, however, of food kept warm for long periods in metal containers are considerable, especially if turnover at the buffet is slow. We have received several complaints of stomach trouble following a buffet meal, even in five-star hotels.

It is essential to be very careful since food hygiene may be poor, flies abound and refrigeration in the hot weather may be inadequate and intermittent because of power cuts. It is best to eat only freshly prepared food by ordering from the menu (especially meat and fish dishes). Avoid salads and cut fruit.

If you are unused to spicy food, go slow! Stick to Western or mild Chinese meals in good restaurants and try the odd Indian dish to test your reaction. Popular local restaurants are obvious from the number of people eating in them. Try a traditional *thali*, which is a complete meal served on a large stainless steel plate (or very occasionally on a banana leaf). Several preparations, placed in small bowls, surround the central serving of wholewheat chapati and rice. A vegetarian *thali* would include *dhal* (lentils), two or three curries (which can be quite hot) and crisp poppadums, although there are regional variations. A variety of pickles are offered – mango and lime are two of the most popular. These can be exceptionally hot, and are designed to be taken in minute quantities alongside the main dishes. Plain *dahi* (yoghurt) in the south, or *raita* in the north, usually acts as a bland 'cooler'. Simple *dhabas* (rustic roadside eateries) are an alternative experience for sampling authentic local dishes.

Many city restaurants offer a choice of so-called **European options** such as toasted sandwiches, pancakes, apple pies, fruit crumbles and cheesecakes. Italian favourites (pizzas, pastas) can be very different from what you are used to. Western confectionery, in general, is disappointing. **Ice creams**, on the other hand, can be exceptionally good; there are excellent Indian ones as well as some international brands.

India has many delicious tropical **fruits**. Some are seasonal (eg mangoes, pineapples and lychees), while others (eg bananas, grapes and oranges) are available throughout the year. It is safe to eat the ones you can wash and peel.

Drink

Drinking water used to be regarded as one of India's biggest hazards. It is still true that water from the tap or a well should never be considered safe to drink since public water supplies are often polluted. Bottled water is now widely available although not all bottled water is mineral water; most is simply purified water from an urban supply. Buy from a shop or stall, check the seal carefully (some companies now add a second clear plastic seal around the bottle top) and avoid street hawkers; when disposing bottles puncture the neck which prevents misuse but allows recycling for storage. There is growing concern over the mountains of plastic bottles that are collecting and the waste of resources needed to produce them, so travellers are encouraged to use alternative methods of getting safe drinking water. Many hotels will have a water filter from which to fill your bottle, and in the more advanced towns and cities, even simple restaurants provide glasses of filltered water, which is generally quite safe to drink (see box, page 43). You may wish to purify water yourself, see box, page 49. A portable water filter is a good idea, carrying the drinking water in a plastic bottle in an insulated carrier. Always carry enough drinking water with you when travelling. It is important to use pure water for cleaning teeth.

Tea and **coffee** are safe and widely available. Both are normally served sweet, and with milk. If you wish, say 'no sugar' (*chini nahin*), 'no milk' (*dudh nahin*) when ordering. Alternatively, ask for a pot of tea and milk and sugar to be brought separately. Freshly brewed coffee is a common drink in South India, but in the North, ordinary city restaurants will usually serve the instant variety. Even in aspiring smart cafés, espresso or cappuccino may not turn out quite as you'd expect in the West.

Bottled **soft drinks** such as Coke, Pepsi, Limca and Thums Up are universally available but always check the seal when you buy from a street stall. There are also several brands of fruit juice sold in cartons, including mango, pineapple and apple. Don't add ice cubes as the water source may be contaminated. Take care with fresh fruit juices or *lassis* as ice is often added.

Indians rarely drink **alcohol** with a meal, water being on hand. In the past wines and spirits were generally either imported and extremely expensive, or local and of poor quality. Now, the best Indian whisky, rum and brandy (IMFL or 'Indian Made Foreign Liquor') are widely accepted, as are good Champagnoise and other wines from Maharashtra. If you hanker after a bottle of imported wine, you will only find it in the top restaurants and have to pay at least Rs 800-1000.

For the urban elite, refreshing Indian beers are popular when eating out and so are widely available. 'Pubs' have sprung up in the major cities. Elsewhere, seedy, all-male drinking dens in the larger cities are best avoided for women travellers, but can make quite an experience otherwise – you will sometimes be locked into cubicles for clandestine drinking. If that sounds unsavoury then head for the better hotel bars instead; prices aren't that steep. In rural India, local rice, palm, cashew or date juice *toddy* and *arak* is deceptively potent. However, the Sikkimese *chhang* makes a pleasant change drunk out of a wooden tankard through a bamboo straw!

Most states have alcohol-free dry days or enforce degrees of Prohibition. Some upmarket restaurants may serve beer even if it's not listed, so it's worth asking. For dry states and Liquor Permits, see page 47.

Entertainment

Despite the rapid growth of a young business class, Northeast India's 'nightlife' remains meagre and is mainly focused on discos in the largest hotels. Kolkata has a few such clubs to choose from, although new and more ambient bars/lounges are beginning to appear. For more basic drinking, there are options ranging from English-style pubs within hotels to men-only, cabaret-feel bars. More traditional, popular entertainment is widespread across the villages in the form of folk drama, dance and music, each region having its own styles, with open-air village performances. The hugely popular local film industry comes largely out of this tradition, and *Bhojpuri* films are now flourishing as a reaction against recent slick Bollywood and Tollywood offerings. It's always easy to find a cinema, even in small towns, but prepare for a long sitting with standard storylines and characters plus lots of action, singing and dancing. In big cities, multiplexes are becoming commonplace and usually show English-language movies as well as the latest Indian hits, while the Nandan complex in Kolkata has art-house and foreign film screenings. As the intellectual and cultural hub of India, Kolkata offers a wealth of opportunities and venues to see theatre, concerts and exhibitions in both Bengali and English. See also pages 14 and 15 for cricket and football, which are both popular forms of entertainment.

Festivals and events

Northeast India has an extraordinary wealth of festivals, many specific to a particular state or community or even a particular temple. The biggest festival of all, and the largest gathering of humanity on the planet, is the **Kumbh Mela**, which draws millions of pilgrims to four holy sites in India in a rotation system. One of these sites is Allahabad, 125 km to the west of Varanasi, where the next Maha (great) Kumbh Mela will be held from 27 January to 25 February in 2013. Festivals tend to fall on different dates each year depending on the Hindu lunar calendar, so check with the tourist office. Some major festivals are given below; details of these and others appear under the particular state or town.

A few count as national holidays: **Republic Day** (26 January); **Independence Day** (15 August); **Mahatma Gandhi's Birthday** (2 October); and **Christmas Day** (25 December). 1 January (when following the Gregorian calendar) is accepted officially as **New Year's Day**, but there are regional variations that fall on different dates, often coinciding with spring/harvest time, such as **Naba Barsha** in Bengal (14 April) and **Rongali Bihu** in Assam (mid-April). **Makar Sankranti** always falls on 14 January and is highly auspicious in Bengal, when the huge **Gangasagar Mela** sees the gathering of pilgrims at the mouth of the Ganga to mark the end of winter. During the spring festival of **Vasant Panchami** (January/February) people wear bright yellow clothes to herald the advent of the season with singing, dancing and feasting. In Bengal this festival is commonly called **Saraswati Puja**, as the goddess of learning is worshipped, and it is a state holiday. **Maha Sivaratri** (February/March) marks the night when Siva danced his celestial dance of destruction; it is celebrated with feasting and fairs at Siva temples, but preceded by a night of devotional readings and hymn singing. Varanasi sees Siva devotees collect en masse, when the ghats become a camping ground for sadhus, naga babas and their followers.

Holi, the festival of colours, occurs at the end of February or the start of March and is particularly vibrant in North India. On the first night, bonfires are lit symbolizing the end of winter (and conquering of evil). People have fun throwing coloured powder and water at each other and in the evening some gamble with friends. If you don't mind getting covered in colours, you can risk going out but celebrations can sometimes get very rowdy (and unpleasant, especially for lone women) in urban areas, even though alcohol is not for sale during festival. There is also a **Bengali Holi** (Dol Jatra) the day before, which means celebrations stretch over three days in many places in this region.

Purnima (full moon)

Many religious festivals depend on the phases of the moon. Full moon days are particularly significant and can mean extra crowding and merrymaking in temple towns throughout India, and are sometimes public holidays.

Buddha Jayanti, the first full moon night in April/May, marks the birth of the Buddha and Bodh Gaya collects pilgrims from all over the world to celebrate in its temples. Puri in Orissa witnesses the spectacle of Rath Yatra in June/July, when crowds gather to help tow Lord Jagannath and his brother and sister through the streets in extraordinary decorated chariots. **Raksha Bandhan** (or Rakhi Purnima) in July/August symbolizes the love between brother and sister. A sister says special prayers for her brother and ties artful coloured threads around his wrist to remind him of the special bond. He in turn gives a gift and promises to protect and care for her. August/September sees **Janmashtami**, when the birth of Krishna is celebrated at midnight at Krishna (ISKCON) temples. The September/October festival of **Dasara** has many local variations. In North India, celebrations for the nine nights (navaratri) are marked with **Ramlila**, various episodes of the Ramayana story (see page 332) being enacted with particular reference to the battle between the forces of good and evil. In Bengal, the focus is on Durga's victory over the demon Mahishasura and **Durga puja** is celebrated in a massive way, with huge pandals erected in public spaces, often themed to reflect current events or mimic world monuments, containing images of the Goddess, her consorts and her enemies.

In Bengal, **Lakshmi puja** follows soon after Durga puja, and offers worship to the Goddess of Wealth. However, the rest of India worships Lakshmi with **Diwali/Deepavali**, the festival of lights, which falls on the dark chaturdasi (14th) night (the one preceding the new moon) in October/November, when rows of lamps or candles are lit in remembrance and rangolis are painted on the floor as a sign of welcome. Fireworks have become an integral part of the celebrations, often set off days before Diwali. In Bengal, **Kali Puja** is celebrated the day before Diwali but is a distinct festival. The **Konark Dance Festival** (early December), held in Orissa, runs for five days and showcases classical Indian dance against a backdrop of the Sun Temple. **Christmas Day** sees Indian Christians celebrate the birth of Christ in much the same way as in the West, many churches hold midnight masses and decorations go up.

Muslim holy days

These are fixed according to the lunar calendar, see box, above. According to the Gregorian calendar, they tend to fall 11 days earlier each year, depending on the sighting of the new moon. **Ramadan** (12 August-10 September 2010, 1-30 August 2011, 20 July-19 August 2012) is the start of the month of fasting when all Muslims (except young children, the very elderly, the sick, pregnant women and travellers) must abstain from food and drink, from sunrise to sunset. **Id ul Fitr**, with much gift-giving, is the three-day festival that marks the end of Ramadan. **Id-ul-Zuha/Bakr-Id** (17 November 2010, 6 November 2011, 26 October 2012) is when Muslims commemorate Ibrahim's sacrifice of his son according to God's commandment; this is the main time of pilgrimage to Mecca (the Hajj). It is marked by the sacrifice of a goat, feasting and alms giving. **Muharram** is when the killing of the Prophet's grandson, Hussain, is commemorated by Shi'a Muslims. Decorated *tazias* (replicas of the martyr's tomb) are carried in procession by devout wailing followers who beat their chests to express their grief. **Murshidabad** (16 December, 5 December, 24 November) in West Bengal celebrates Murharram with much festivity, and the Muslim areas of Kolkata are highly atmospheric at this time.

Shopping

India excels in producing fine crafts at affordable prices through the passing down of ancestral skills. You can get handicrafts from the different states at the government emporia in the major cities, which guarantee quality at fixed prices, although many goods are poorly displayed. Upmarket shops and top hotel arcades offer better quality, choice and service but at a price. Vibrant and colourful local bazars are often a great experience but you must be prepared to bargain.

Bargaining can be fun and quite satisfying but it is important to get an idea of prices by asking at several different stalls before taking the plunge. Some shopkeepers will happily quote twice the actual price (or more) to a foreigner showing interest, so you might well start by halving the asking price. On the other hand, it would be inappropriate to do the same in an established shop with price tags, though a plea for the 'best price' or a 'special discount' might reap results even here. Remain good humoured throughout. Walking away slowly can test whether your custom is sought, if you are then called back. Taxi/rickshaw drivers and guides get a commission when they deliver tourists to certain shops, but prices are invariably inflated. Small shops can't always be trusted to pack and post your purchases: unless you have a specific recommendation from a person you know, only make such arrangements in government emporia or a large store. Never enter into any arrangement to help 'export' marble items, jewellery, etc, no matter how lucrative your 'cut' of the profits may sound. Make sure, too, that credit cards are run off just once when making a purchase. Export of certain items is controlled or banned (see page 46).

The superb hand-knotted **carpets** of Kashmir, using old Persian designs woven in wool or silk or both, are hard to beat for their beauty and quality, and Kashmiri traders can be found wherever there are foreign tourists. Tibetan refugees in Darjeeling and Gangtok also produce excellent carpets, which are less expensive. They will make carpets to order and parcel post them safely. You'll find **jewellery** catching your eye at wayside stalls and from sparkling shops, whether it's chunky tribal necklaces from the Himalaya, fine Orissan filigree, or glass bangles from Varanasi. It's best to buy from reputable shops as street stalls often pass off fake silver, gems and stones as real; and beware of being hustled in Kolkata's New Market. **Silver** and **gold** are sold by weight – check the price in newspapers. The choice of metal work is vast, from brass, copper and white-metal ware with ornate patterns, tribal lost-wax *dhokra* toys from Orissa and Bengal, to Tibetan 'singing' bowls which are available from refugee communities. Stone temple carvings are produced for sale in Orissa (Puri, Konark) while Santiniketan is renowned for colourful embossed **leatherwork**. Exquisite **textiles** are plentiful: handlooms produce skilful *ikat* from Orissa, brocades from Varanasi, golden *muga* from Assam, and printed silks and batiks from Bengal. Sober handspun *khadi*, tribal weaving from remote Himalayan villages and hand block-printed saris from Serampur are easier on the pocket. The pashmina shawl from Kashmir is available in dozens of colours, widths and qualities (often mixed with silk) in every city. All trade in *tush* (toosh) wool is banned. Cane and bamboo work is a speciality of the Northeastern Hill States, offering a variety of furniture or intricately **woven baskets** in unusual shapes and designs.

Responsible tourism

Local customs

Most travellers experience great warmth and hospitality. With it comes an open curiosity about personal matters. You should not be surprised if total strangers ask for details of your job, income and family circumstances or discuss politics and religion.

Conduct
Respect for the foreign visitor should be reciprocated by a sensitivity towards local customs and culture. How you dress is how people will judge you; cleanliness, modest clothes and a smile go a long way. Scanty, tight clothing draws unwanted attention. Displays of intimacy are totally inappropriate in public places. You may at times be frustrated by delays, bureaucracy and inefficiency, but displays of anger and rudeness will not achieve anything positive, and often make things worse. People's concept of time and punctuality is also often rather vague so be prepared to be kept waiting.

Courtesy
It takes little effort to learn common gestures of courtesy and they are greatly appreciated. The greeting when meeting or parting, used universally among the Hindus across India, is the palms joined together as in prayer, sometimes accompanied with the word *namaste* (North and West) or *namoshkar* (East). Muslims use the greeting *assalām aleikum*, with the response *waleikum assalām*, meaning 'peace be with you'; 'please' is *mehrbani-se*; 'thank you' is often expressed by a smile, or with the somewhat formal *dhannyabad* or *shukriya* (Urdu). For useful Hindi phrases, see page 372.

Hands and eating
Traditionally, Indians use the right hand for giving, receiving, shaking hands and eating, as the left is considered to be unclean since it is associated with washing after using the toilet. In much of rural India cutlery is alien at the table except for serving spoons, and at most humble restaurants you will be offered only small spoons to eat with. If you visit an ashram or are lucky enough to be invited to a temple feast day, you will almost certainly be expected to eat with your hands. Watch and copy others until the technique becomes familiar.

Women → *See also page 60.*
Indian women in urban and rural areas differ in their social interactions with men. To the Westerner, Indian women may seem to remain in the background and appear shy when

How big is your footprint?

As well as respecting local cultural sensitivities, travellers can take a number of simple steps to reduce, or even improve, their impact on the local environment. Environmental concern is relatively new in India, but don't be afraid to pressurize businesses by asking about their policies.

Litter Many travellers think that there is little point in disposing of rubbish properly when the tossing of water bottles, plastic cups and other non-biodegradable items out of train windows is already so widespread. You can immediately reduce your impact by refusing plastic bags and other excess packaging – use a small backpack or cloth bag instead – and if you do collect a few, keep them with you to store other rubbish until you get to a litter bin.

Filtered water versus bottled water Plastic mineral water bottles, an inevitable corollary to poor water hygiene standards, are a major contributor to India's litter mountain. However, many hotels, including nearly all of the upmarket ones, most restaurants and bus and train stations, provide drinking water purified using a combination of ceramic and carbon filters, chlorine and sometimes UV irradiation. Ask for 'filter paani'; if the water tastes at all like a swimming pool it is probably quite safe to drink, though it's worth introducing your body gradually to the new water. See box, page 49, for water purification.

Bucket baths versus showers The biggest issue relating to responsible and sustainable tourism is water. Much of Northwest India is afflicted by severe water restrictions, with certain cities in Rajasthan and Gujarat having water supply for as little as 20 minutes a day. The traditional Indian 'bucket bath', in which you wet, soap then rinse off using a small hand-held plastic jug dipped into a large bucket, uses on average around 15 litres of water, as compared to 30-45 for a shower. These are commonly offered except in four- and five-star hotels.

Support responsible tourism Spending your money carefully can have a positive impact. Sleeping, eating and shopping at small, locally owned businesses directly supports communities, while specific community tourism concerns provide an economic motivation for people to stay in remote communities, protect natural areas and revive traditional cultures, rather than exploit the environment or move to the cities for work.

Transport Choose walking, cycling or public transport over fuel-guzzling cars and motorbikes.

approached. Yet you will see them working in public, often in jobs traditionally associated with men in the West, in the fields or on construction sites. It is not considered polite for men to photograph women without their consent, so ask before you start snapping.

Women do not usually shake hands with men as physical contact between the sexes is not acceptable. A Westernized city woman, however, may feel free to shake hands with a foreign visitor. In certain, very traditional rural circles, it is still the custom for men to be offered food first, separately, so don't be surprised if you, as foreign guest (man or woman), are awarded this special status when invited to an Indian home.

Visiting religious sites

Visitors to all religious places should be dressed in clean, modest clothes; shorts and vests are inappropriate. Always remove shoes before entering (and all leather items in Jain temples). Take thick socks for protection when walking on sun-baked stone floors.

Menstruating women are considered 'unclean' and should not enter places of worship. It is discourteous to sit with one's back to a temple or shrine. You will be expected to sit cross-legged on the floor – avoid pointing your feet at others when attending prayers at a temple. Walk clockwise around a shrine (keeping it to your right).

Non-Hindus are sometimes excluded from the inner sanctum of **Hindu** temples and occasionally even from the temple itself. Look for signs or ask. In certain temples and on special occasions you may enter only if you wear unstitched clothing such as a *dhoti*.

In **Buddhist** shrines, turn prayer wheels in a clockwise direction. In **Sikh** *gurdwaras*, everyone should cover their head, even if it is with a handkerchief. Tobacco and cigarettes should not be taken in. In **Muslim** mosques, visitors should only have their face, hands and feet exposed; women should also cover their heads. Mosques may be closed to non-Muslims shortly before formal prayers.

Some temples have a register or a receipt book for **donations** which works like an obligatory entry fee. The money is normally used for the upkeep and services of the temple or monastery. In some pilgrimage centres, priests can become unpleasantly persistent. If you wish to leave a donation, put money in the donation box; priests and Buddhist monks often do not handle money. It is also not customary to shake hands with a priest or monk. *Sanyasis* (holy men) and some pilgrims depend on donations.

Guide fees
Guides vary considerably in their knowledge and ability. Government licensed guides are covered by specified fees. Local temple and site guides should charge less. Charges for four people for half a day are about Rs 280, for a full day Rs 400; for five to 15 people for half a day Rs 400, for a full day Rs 530. Rs 125 for a language other than English.

Begging
Beggars are found in busy street corners in large Indian cities, as well as at bus and train stations where they often target foreigners. Visitors can find this distressing, especially the sight of severely undernourished children or those displaying physical deformity. You may be particularly affected when some persist in making physical contact. In the larger cities, beggars are often exploited by syndicates which cream off most of their takings. Yet those seeking alms near religious sites are another matter, and you may see Indian worshippers giving freely to those less fortunate than themselves, since this is tied up with gaining 'merit'. How you deal with begging is a personal choice but it is perhaps better to give to a recognized charity than to make largely ineffectual handouts to individuals. Young children sometimes offer to do 'jobs' such as call a taxi, carry shopping or pose for a photo. You may want to give a coin in exchange. While travelling, some visitors prefer to hand out fruit to the many open-palmed children they encounter.

Charitable giving
A pledge to donate a part of one's holiday budget to a local charity could be an effective formula for 'giving'. Some visitors like to support self-help cooperatives, orphanages, refugee centres, disabled or disadvantaged groups, or international charities such as Oxfam, Save the Children or Christian Aid which work with local partners, by either making a donation or by buying their products. Also see information about charities and organizations that welcome volunteers on pages 60 and 89.

Concern India Foundation, 6K Dubash Marg, Mumbai, T022-2202 9708, www.concernindia.org. An umbrella organization working with local charities.
Oxfam, Sushil Bhawan, 210 Shahpur Jat, New Delhi 110049, T011-2649 1774; 274 Banbury Rd, Oxford OX2 7D2, UK, www.oxfam.org (400 grassroots projects).
SOS Children's Villages, A-7 Nizamuddin West, New Delhi 110013, T011-2435 9450, www.soscvindia.org. Over 30 children's projects in India, eg opposite Pital Factory, Jhotwara Rd, Jaipur 302016, T0141-228 0787.
Save the Children India, 4C Swapnalok, 47 LJ Mard, Mumbai 400036, www.savethechildrenindia.org.
Trek-Aid, 2 Somerset Cottages, Stoke Villages, Plymouth, Devon, PL3 4AZ, www.a38.com/trekaid. Health, education, etc, through self-help schemes for displaced Tibetan refugees.

Photography

Many monuments and national parks charge a camera fee ranging from Rs 20-100 for still cameras, and as much as Rs 500 for video cameras (more for professionals). Special permits are needed from the Archaeological Survey of India, New Delhi, for using tripods and artificial lights. When photographing people, it is polite to first ask – they will usually respond warmly with smiles. Visitors often promise to send copies of the photos – don't unless you really mean to do so. Photography of airports, military installations, bridges, and in tribal and 'sensitive border areas' is not permitted.

Essentials A-Z

Accident and emergency

Contact the relevant emergency service (police T100, fire T101, ambulance T102) and your embassy (see page 92). Make sure you obtain police/medical reports for insurance claims.

Children

Children of all ages are widely welcomed. However, care should be taken when travelling to remote areas where health services are primitive. Diarrhoea and vomiting are the most common problems, so take the usual precautions. In the big cities you can get safe baby foods and formula milk (although breastfeeding is best and most convenient for babies). Wet wipes and disposable nappies are difficult to find. The biggest hotels provide babysitting. See also Health, page 48.

Customs and duty free

Duty free

Tourists are allowed to bring in all personal effects 'which may reasonably be required', without charge. The official allowance includes 200 cigarettes, 0.95 litres of alcohol, a camera with 5 rolls of film and a pair of binoculars. Valuable personal effects and professional equipment including jewellery, camera equipment and laptop computers must be declared on a Tourist Baggage Re-Export Form (TBRE) in order for them to be taken back out of the country. These forms require the equipment's serial numbers. Details of imported equipment may be entered into your passport. Save time by completing the formalities while waiting for your baggage. Keep these forms to show to the customs when leaving India, otherwise considerable delays are very likely.

Prohibited items

The import of live plants, gold coins, gold and silver bullion and silver coins not in current use is subject to strict regulation. Enquire at consular offices abroad for details.

Export restrictions

Export of gold jewellery purchased in India is allowed up to a value of Rs 2000 and other jewellery (including precious stones) up to a value of Rs 10,000. Export of antiquities and art objects over 100 years old is restricted. Ivory, musk, skins of all animals and articles made from them are banned, unless you get permission for export. For further information, contact the Indian High Commission or consulate, or access the Central Board of Excise and Customs website, www.cbec.gov.in/travellers.htm.

Disabled travellers

India is not specially geared up for less able-bodied travellers. Access to buildings, toilets (sometimes squat type), pavements and public transport can prove frustrating, but it is easy to find people to give a hand to help with lifting and carrying. Provided you are prepared to pay for at least mid-price accommodation, car hire and taxis, travel in India should be fairly accessible.

Some travel companies specialize in exciting holidays, tailor-made for individuals depending on their level of disability. Global Access, Disabled Travel Network, www.globalaccessnews.com, provides travel information for 'disabled adventurers' and includes a number of reviews and tips. *Nothing Ventured*, edited by Alison Walsh (HarperCollins), gives personal accounts of worldwide journeys by disabled travellers, plus advice and listings. Accessible Journeys Inc, 35 West Sellers Av, Ridley Park, PA 19078, T610-521 0339, www.disability

travel.com, runs some packages to India. **Responsible Travel.com**, 3rd floor, Pavillion House, 6 Old Steine, Brighton, BN1 1EJ, UK, T01273-600030, www.responsible travel.com, specializes in eco-holidays and has some tailored to the needs of disabled travellers. See **www.asparkholidays.com**, based in New Delhi, for high-end tours designed for less able-bodied people.

Drugs

Certain areas, such as Puri (Orissa), have become associated with foreigners who take drugs. These are likely to attract local and foreign drug dealers but be aware that the government takes the misuse of drugs very seriously. Anyone charged with the illegal possession of drugs risks facing a fine of Rs 100,000 and a minimum 10 years' imprisonment. Several foreigners have been imprisoned for drugs-related offences in the last decade.

Electricity

India supply is 220-240 volts AC. There may be pronounced variations in the voltage, and power cuts are common. Power back-up by generator or inverter is becoming more widespread, though it may not cover a/c. Socket sizes vary so take a universal adaptor; low-quality versions are available locally. Many hotels, even in the higher categories, don't have electric razor sockets.

Embassies and consulates

For information on visas and immigration, see page 58. For a complete list of embassies and consulates, see http://meaindia.nic.in/onmouse/mission.htm.

Indian embassies abroad

Australia 3-5 Moonah Pl, Yarralumla, Canberra, T02-6273 3999, www.hcindia-au.org; Level 2, 210 Pitt St, Sydney, T02-9223 9500; 15 Munro St, Coburg, Melbourne, T03-9384 0141.

Canada 10 Springfield Rd, Ottawa, K1M 1C9, T613-744 3751, www.hciottawa.ca. Toronto, T416-960 0751, Vancouver, T604-662 8811.

France 15 Rue Alfred Dehodencq, Paris, T01-4050 7070, www.amb-inde.fr.

Germany Tiergartenstrasse 17, 10785 Berlin, T030-257950. Consulates: Bonn T0228-540132; Frankfurt T069-153 0050, Hamburg T040-338036, Munich T089-210 2390, Stuttgart T0711-153 0050.

Ireland 6 Leeson Park, Dublin 6, T01-497 0843, www.indianembassy.ie.

Nepal 336 Kapurdhara Marg, Kathmandu, T+9771-441 0900, www.south-asia.com/embassy-india.

Netherlands Buitenrustweg-2, 2517 KD, The Hague, T070-346 9771, www.indianembassy.nl.

New Zealand 180 Molesworth St, Wellington, T+64-4473 6390, www.hicomind.org.nz.

South Africa 852 Schoeman St, Arcadia, Pretoria 0083, T012-342 5392, www.india.org.za.

Switzerland 9 Rue de Valais, CH-1202, Geneva, T022-906 8686.

UK India House, Aldwych, London, WC2B 4NA, T020-7836 8484 (visas 0800-1200), www.hcilondon.net. Consulates: 20 Augusta St, Jewellery Quarter, Hockley, Birmingham, B18 6JL, T0121-212 2782, www.cgibirming ham.org; 17 Rutland Sq, Edinburgh, EH1 2BB, T0131-229 2144, www.cgiedinburgh.org.

USA 2107 Massachusetts Av, Washington DC 20008, T202-939 7000. Consulates: New York, T212-774 8600, San Francisco, T415-668 0662, Chicago, T312-595 0405.

Gay and lesbian travellers

Indian law forbids homosexual acts for men (but not women) and carries a maximum sentence of life imprisonment. Although it is common to see young males holding hands in public, this very rarely indicates a gay relationship and is usually an expression of friendship. Overt displays of affection between homosexuals (and heterosexuals) can offend and should be avoided. Nevertheless, in 2007 Kolkata held its inaugural **Gay and Lesbian Film Festival**, a sign that in the cities, at least, attitudes may be starting to shift. Likewise, the **Siddhartha Gautam Film Festival**, held in Siliguri and Kolkata in Mar 2010, aimed to de-stigmatize HIV and same-sex relationships.

Health

See your GP or travel clinic at least 6 weeks before departure for general advice on travel risks and vaccinations. Try phoning a specialist travel clinic if your own doctor is unfamiliar with health conditions in India. Make sure you have sufficient medical travel insurance, get a dental check, know your own blood group and if you suffer a long-term condition such as diabetes or epilepsy, obtain a Medic Alert bracelet/necklace (www.medicalert.co.uk). If you wear glasses, take a copy of your prescription.

Vaccinations
Confirm your primary courses and boosters are up to date. It is advisable to vaccinate against diphtheria, tetanus, poliomyelitis, hepatitis A and typhoid. Yellow fever is not required in India but you may be asked to show a certificate if you are entering from an area with risk of yellow fever transmission.

Vaccination against rabies is advised for those going to risk areas that will be remote from a reliable source of vaccine. Even when pre-exposure vaccines have been received urgent medical advice should be sought after any animal bite.

Malaria is a danger in India and, although it has some seasonality, it is too unpredictable to not take prophylaxis. Specialist advice should be taken on the best anti-malarials to use.

Health risks
Altitude sickness can creep up on you as just a mild headache with nausea or lethargy during your visit to the Himalaya. The more serious disease is caused by fluid collecting in the brain in the enclosed space of the skull and can lead to coma and death. The best cure is to descend as soon as possible. It is essential to get acclimatized before undertaking long treks or arduous activities.

The standard advice for **diarrhoea** prevention is to be careful with water and ice for drinking. If you have any doubts about where the water came from then boil it or filter and treat it. Bottled water is readily available and cheap. Food can also transmit disease. Be wary of salads, re-heated foods or food that has been left out in the sun. There is a simple adage that says wash it, peel it, boil it or forget it. Also be wary of unpasteurized dairy products as these can transmit a range of diseases. Diarrhoea may be also caused by viruses, bacteria (such as E-coli), protozoal (such as giardia), salmonella and cholera. It may be accompanied by vomiting or by severe abdominal pain. The key treatment with all diarrhoea is rehydration. Try to keep hydrated by taking the right mixture of salt and water. This is available as Oral Rehydration Salts (ORS) in ready-made sachets or can be made up by adding a teaspoon of sugar and a half teaspoon of salt to a litre of clean water. You can also use flat carbonated drinks. If the symptoms persist, consult a doctor.

Mosquitoes are more of a nuisance than a serious hazard but some, of course, are carriers of serious diseases, such as malaria, so it is sensible to avoid being bitten as much as possible. Sleep off the ground and use a mosquito net and some kind of

Water purification

There are various ways of purifying water in order to make it safe to drink. Dirty water should be strained through a filter bag, and then boiled or treated.

Bringing water to a rolling boil at sea level will make water safe for drinking, but at higher altitudes you have to boil the water for longer to ensure that all the microbes are killed.

Various sterilizing methods can be used, with preparations containing chlorine or iodine compounds. Chlorine compounds generally do not kill protozoa (eg giardia).

There are a number of water filters now on the market, available both in personal and expedition size. Mechanical filters are usually a combination of carbon, ceramic and paper. The disadvantage of mechanical filters is that they do not always remove viruses or protozoa. Chemical filters use a combination of an iodine resin filter and a mechanical filter. The advantage is that according to the manufacturers' claims, everything in the water will be killed. The disadvantage is that the filters need replacing, adding a third to the price.

insecticide. Mosquito coils release insecticide as they burn and are available in many shops, as are tablets of insecticide, which are placed on a heated mat plugged into a wall socket.

Rabies is endemic throughout certain parts of India, so avoid dogs that are behaving strangely and cover your toes at night from the vampire bats, which also carry the disease. If you are bitten by a domestic or wild animal, do not leave things to chance: scrub the wound with soap and water and/or disinfectant, try to at least determine the animal's ownership, where possible and seek medical assistance at once. The course of treatment depends on whether you have already been vaccinated against rabies.

The range of visible and invisible **sexually transmitted diseases** is awesome. Unprotected sex can spread HIV, hepatitis B and C, gonorrhea (green discharge), chlamydia (nothing to see but may cause painful urination and later female infertility), painful recurrent herpes, syphilis and warts, just to name a few. You can cut down the risk by using condoms, a femidom or avoiding sex altogether.

Make sure you protect yourself from the **sun** with high-factor sun screen and don't forget to wear a hat.

If you get sick

Contact your embassy or consulate for a list of doctors and dentists who speak your language, or at least some English. Doctors and health facilities in major cities are also listed in the Directory sections of this book. Make sure you have adequate insurance (see below).

Useful websites

www.btha.org British Travel Health Association.

www.cdc.gov US government site that gives excellent advice on travel health and details of disease outbreaks.

www.fco.gov.uk British Foreign and Commonwealth Office travel site has useful information on each country, people, climate and a list of UK embassies/consulates.

www.fitfortravel.scot.nhs.uk A-Z of vaccine/health advice for each country.

www.numberonehealth.co.uk Travel screening services, vaccine and travel health advice, email/SMS text vaccine reminders and screens returned travellers for tropical diseases.

Insurance

Buying insurance with your air ticket is the most costly way of doing things. For advice, see www.dh.gov.uk/policyandguidance/healthadvicefortravellers.

If you are carrying expensive equipment you may need to get separate cover for those items (claims for individual items are often limited to £250) unless they are covered by existing home contents insurance.

Check exactly what your medical cover includes, eg ambulance, helicopter rescue or emergency flights back home, and check for exclusions: you may find that activities such as mountain biking are not covered. Also check the payment protocol. You may have to pay first before the insurance company reimburses you.

Always carry with you the telephone number of your insurer's 24-hr emergency helpline and your insurance policy number.

Internet

India is at the forefront of the technology revolution and is the third largest internet user in the world. You're never far from an internet café or PCO (public call office), which also offers the service. Note that internet cafés now require you to produce ID.

In small towns there is less internet access and it is recommended to take precautions: write lengthy emails in Word, save frequently, then paste them into your web-based email server rather than risking the loss of missives home when the power fails or the connection goes down. Browsing costs vary dramatically depending on the location: these can be anything from Rs 20-100, with most charging somewhere in between. As a rule, avoid emailing from upmarket hotels as their prices can be exorbitant unless you are a guest, in which case it's often free. If you intend to stay in India for a while, sign up for membership with the internet chain I-way.

Language

The most widely spoken Indo-Aryan languages in Northeast India are Bengali (spoken by 8.3% of the Indian population) and Oriya (3.7%), spoken alongside Hindi in Orissa. Nepali and Sikkimese are the dominant languages in Sikkim. For food and drink and a glossary of terms, see page 372.

Media

International **newspapers** (mainly English language) are sold in the bookshops of top hotels in major cities and occasionally by booksellers elsewhere. India has a large and lively English-language press.

The best known are the traditionalist *The Hindu*, www.hinduonline.com/today. *The Hindustan Times*, www.hindustan times.com, the slightly more tabloid-establishment *Times of India*, www.timesof india.com and *The Statesman*, www.the statesman.org. *The Economic Times* is good for world coverage. *The Telegraph*, www.telegraphindia.com, has good foreign coverage. *The Indian Express*, www.express india.com, stands out as being consistently critical of the Congress Party and the government. *The Asian Age* is now published in the UK and India simultaneously and gives good coverage of Indian and international affairs. Some of the most widely read weeklies are current affairs *India Today*, *Frontline* and *The Week*, which are journals in the *Time* or *Newsweek* mould. *Business Today* is of course economy-based, while *Outlook* has a broader remit and has good general interest features.

India's national **radio** and **television** network, *Doordarshan*, broadcasts in national and regional languages but things have moved on. The advent of satellite TV has hit even remote rural areas and is now available even in modest hotels in the smallest of towns.

Money

Exchange rates (June 2010)
UK£ 1=Rs 68; €1=Rs 56; US$1=Rs 47;
AUS$1=Rs 38; NZ$1=Rs 31.
Indian currency is the Indian rupee (Re/Rs).
It is **not** possible to purchase these before
you arrive. If you want cash on arrival it is
best to get it at the airport bank. Rupee
notes are printed in denominations of
Rs 1000, 500, 100, 50, 20, 10. The rupee is
divided into 100 paise. Coins are minted
in denominations of Rs 5, Rs 2, Rs 1 and
50 paise. **Note** Carry money in a money
belt worn under clothing. Have a small
amount in an accessible place.

Credit cards

Major credit cards are accepted in the main
centres, but rarely in smaller cities and towns.
Payment by credit card can sometimes be
more expensive than payment by cash and
some credit card companies charge a
premium on cash withdrawals. **Visa** and
MasterCard have a growing number of ATMs
in major cities and several banks offer
withdrawal facilities for **Cirrus** and **Maestro**.
It is easy to obtain a cash advance against a
credit card. Some railway reservation centres
are now taking payment for train tickets by
Visa, which can be very quick as the queue
is short, but they cannot be used for Tourist
Quota tickets.

Another option is to use a pre-paid
currency card (such as **Caxton Card**,
www.caxtonfxcard.com), which is
equivalent to but more practical than
traditional traveller's cheques.

ATMs

By far the most convenient method of
accessing money, ATMs are appearing all
over India, usually attended by security
guards. Banks with ATMs for Cirrus, Maestro,
Visa and MasterCard include: **Bank of Baroda**,
**Citibank, HDFC, HSBC, ICICI, IDBI, Punjab
National Bank, State Bank of India** (SBI),
Standard Chartered and **UTI**. A withdrawal

fee is usually charged by the issuing bank
on top of the various conversion charges
applied by your own bank. Fraud prevention
measures may result in travellers having their
cards blocked by the bank when unexpected
overseas transactions occur; advise your bank
of your travel plans before leaving.

Changing money

The **State Bank of India** and several others
in major towns are authorized to deal in
foreign exchange. Some give cash against
Visa/MasterCard (eg **ANZ, Bank of Baroda**
who print a list of their participating
branches, **Andhra Bank**). The larger cities
have licensed money changers with offices
usually in the commercial sector. Changing
money through unauthorized dealers is
illegal. Premiums on the currency black
market are very small and highly risky.
Large hotels change money 24 hrs a day for
guests, but banks often give a much better
rate of exchange. It is best to exchange
money on arrival at the airport bank or the
Thomas Cook counter. You should be given
a foreign currency encashment certificate
when you change money through a bank
or authorized dealer; ask for one if it is not
automatically given. It allows you to change
Indian rupees back to your own currency on
departure. It also enables you to use rupees
to pay hotel bills or buy air tickets. The
certificates are only valid for 3 months.

Transferring money to India

HSBC, Barclays and **ANZGrindlays** and
others can make 'instant' transfers to their
offices in India but charge a high fee
(about US$30). **Standard Chartered Bank**
issues US$ TCs. Sending a bank draft (up
to US$1000) by post (4-7 days by
Speedpost) is the cheapest option.

Cost of travelling

Most food, accommodation and public
transport are exceptionally cheap. Budget
travellers sharing a room, using public
transport and eating nothing but rice

and dhal can get away with a budget of Rs 350-400 (about £5 or US$8) a day. This sum leaps up if you drink booze (about £1, US$2, Rs 80 for a pint), smoke or want to have your own wheels. Those planning to stay in fairly comfortable hotels and use taxis should budget at US$30 a day. Then again, you could always check into the **Park Hotel** in Kolkata and notch up a US$300 credit card bill on your room alone.

Opening hours

Banks Mon-Fri 1030-1430, Sat 1030-1230. Top hotels sometimes have a 24-hr money changing service. **Post offices** Mon-Fri 1000-1700 and Sat mornings. **Government offices** Mon-Fri 0930-1700, Sat 0930- 1300 (some on alternate Sat only). **Shops** Mon-Sat 0930-1800. **Bazars** keep longer hours.

Post

The post is frequently unreliable, and delays are common. It is best to use a post office where you can hand over mail for franking across the counter, or a top hotel post box. Valuable items should only be sent by registered mail. Government emporia or shops in the larger hotels will send purchases home if the items are difficult to carry.

Airmail services to Europe, Africa and Australia take at least a week and a little longer for the Americas. **Speed post** (which takes about 4 days to the UK) is available from major towns. Speed post to the UK from Tamil Nadu costs Rs 675 for the first 250g sent and an extra Rs 75 for each 250g thereafter. **Specialist shippers** deal with larger items, normally around US$150 per cubic metre. Courier services (eg **DHL**) are available in the larger towns. At some main post offices you can send small packages under 2 kg as **letter post** (rather than parcel post), which is much cheaper at Rs 220. Check that the post office holds necessary customs declaration forms (2-3 copies needed). Write 'No commercial value' if returning used clothes, books, etc. Sea Mail is being phased out to be replaced by **SAL** (Surface Air Lifted). The prices are fractionally lower than airmail, Rs 500-600 for the first kg and Rs 150-250 per extra kg. Delivery can take up to 2 months.

Poste restante facilities are widely available in even quite small towns at the GPO where mail is held for 1 month. Ask for mail to be addressed to you with your surname in capitals and underlined. When asking for mail at Poste Restante check under first name as well as surname.

Safety

Personal security

In general the threats to personal security for travellers in India are remarkably small. However, incidents of petty theft and violence directed specifically at tourists have been on the increase so care is necessary in some places, and basic common sense needs to be used with respect to looking after valuables. Follow the same precautions you would when at home. Avoid wandering alone outdoors late at night in these places. During daylight hours be careful in remote places, especially when alone. If you are under threat, scream loudly. Never accept food or drink from casual acquaintants, it may be drugged.

Following a major explosion on the Delhi to Lahore (Pakistan) train in Feb 2007 and the Mumbai attacks in Nov 2008, increased security has been implemented on many trains and stations. Similar measures at airports may cause delays for passengers so factor this into your timing. Also check your airline's website for up-to-date information on luggage restrictions.

Travel advice

Seek advice from your consulate before you travel. Also contact: **British Foreign &**

Commonwealth Office Travel Advice Unit, T0845-850 2829, www.fco.gov.uk. US State Department's Bureau of Consular Affairs, Overseas Citizens Services, Room 4800, Department of State, Washington, DC 20520-4818, USA, T202-647 1488, http://travel.state.gov. Australian Department of Foreign Affairs Canberra, Australia, T02-62613305, www.smartraveller.gov.au. Canadian official advice is on www.voyage.gc.ca.

Theft

Theft is not uncommon. Keep passports and valuables with you at all times. Don't regard hotel rooms as being automatically safe; even hotel safes don't guarantee secure storage. Avoid leaving valuables near open windows even when you are in the room. Use your own padlock in a budget hotel when you go out. Pickpockets and other thieves operate in the big cities. Crowded areas are particularly high risk. Take special care of your belongings when getting on or off public transport.

If you have items stolen, they should be reported to the police as soon as possible. Keep a separate record of vital documents, including passport details. Larger hotels will be able to assist in contacting and dealing with the police. Dealings with the police can be very difficult, the paperwork involved in reporting losses can be time consuming and irritating and your own documentation (eg passport and visas) may be demanded. In some states the police themselves sometimes demand bribes, though you should not assume that if procedures move slowly you are being expected to offer a bribe.

Confidence tricksters are particularly common around railway stations or places where budget tourists gather.

Travel safety

The traffic police are tightening up on traffic offences in some places. They have the right to make on-the-spot fines for speeding and illegal parking. If you face a demand for a fine,

insist on a receipt. If you have to go to a police station, try to take someone with you.

If you face really serious problems, for example in connection with a driving accident, you should contact your consular office as quickly as possible. Always ensure you have your international driving licence and vehicle documentation with you.

Motorcycles don't come fitted with helmets and accidents are commonplace so exercise caution, the horn and the brake.

Thefts on **trains**, particularly between Kolkata, Varanasi and Delhi, are on the rise. First-class compartments are self-contained and normally completely secure, although nothing of value should be left close to open train windows. Most thefts occur in non-a/c sleeper class carriages. Luggage should be chained to a seat for security overnight. Locks and chains are available at main stations and bazars. If you put your bags on the upper berth during the day, beware of fellow passengers climbing up for a 'sleep'. Be guarded with new friends on trains who show particular interest in the contents of your bag and be extra wary of accepting food or drink from casual acquaintances; travellers have reported being drugged and then robbed.

Senior travellers

Travellers over the age of 60 can take advantage of several discounts on travel, including 30% on train fares and up to 50% on some air tickets. Ask when booking, as these will not be offered automatically.

Smoking

Several state governments have passed a law banning smoking in all public buildings and transport but exempting open spaces. To avoid fines, check for notices.

Student travellers

Full-time students qualify for an ISIC (International Student Identity Card) which is issued by student travel and specialist agencies at home. The card allows certain travel benefits such as reduced prices and concessions into certain sites. For details see www.isic.org or contact STIC in Imperial Hotel, Janpath, New Delhi, T011-2334 3302. Those intending to study in India may get a year's student visa, see page 58. For insurance, see page 50.

Telephone

The international code for India is +91. The IDD prefix for dialling out of India is 00. International Direct Dialling is widely available in privately run call booths, usually labelled on yellow boards with the letters 'PCO-STD-ISD'. You dial the call yourself, and the time and cost are displayed on a screen. Cheap rate is 2100-0600, but expect queues. Calls from hotels are usually much more expensive, though some will allow local calls free of charge. Internet phone booths are the cheapest way of calling overseas.

A double ring repeated means it is ringing. Equal tones with equal pauses means engaged, similar to in the UK.

Due to the tremendous pace of the telecommunications revolution, millions of telephone numbers go out of date every year. Current telephone directories are often out of date and some of the numbers given in this book will have been changed even as we go to press. **The best advice is to put an additional 2 on the front of existing numbers**. Directory enquiries, T197, can be helpful but works only for the local area code.

Mobile phones are for sale everywhere, as are local SIM cards that allow you to make calls within India and overseas at much lower rates than using a 'roaming' service – sometimes for as little as Rs 0.5 per min. Private companies such as **Airtel, Hutch, Reliance** and **Tata Indicom** are easier to sign up with, but the deals they offer can be befuddling and are frequently changed. To connect you'll need to complete a form, have a local address (a hotel receipt with your name on should do), and present photocopies of your passport and visa plus 2 passport photos. Most phone dealers will be able to help, and can also sell top-up vouchers. India is divided into a number of 'calling circles' or regions, and if you travel outside the region where your connection is based (eg from West Bengal into Uttar Pradesh), you will pay higher charges for calls. In the northeast states, sim cards from other states do not work at all. Here, every state has its own network for security reasons and you have to get a new sim card in each – a real pain.

Time

GMT +5½ hrs. India doesn't change its clocks, so from the last Sun in Oct to the last Sun in Mar it is UK time +5½ hrs, and the rest of the year it's +4½ hrs (USA, EST +10½ and +9½ hrs; Australia, EST -5½ and -4½ hrs).

Tipping

A tip of Rs 10 to a luggage porter in a modest hotel (Rs 20 in a higher category) would be appropriate. In upmarket restaurants, a 10% tip is acceptable when service is not already included; in cheaper places round off the bill with small change. Indians don't normally tip taxi drivers but a small extra amount over the fare is welcomed. Porters at airports and railway stations often have a fixed rate displayed but will usually press for more. Ask fellow passengers what a fair rate is.

Tourist information

There are Government of India tourist offices in the state capitals, as well as state tourist offices (sometimes Tourism Development Corporations) in the major cities and a few important sites. They produce their own tourist literature and some also have lists of city hotels and guesthouses. The quality of material is improving though maps are often poor. Many offer tours of the city and sights, and overnight and regional packages. Some run modest hotels and midway motels with restaurants and may also arrange car hire and guides. The staff in the regional and local offices are usually helpful.

Tourist offices overseas

Australia Level 5, Glasshouse,135 King St, Sydney, NSW 2000, T02-9221 9555, info@indiatourism.com.au.

Canada 60 Bloor St West, Suite No 1003, Toronto, Ontario, T416-962 3787, indiatourism@bellnet.ca.

France 11-13 Bis Boulevard Hausmann, 75009, Paris T01-4523 3045.

Germany Baserler St 48, 60329, Frankfurt AM-Main 1, T069-242 9490, www.india-tourism.de.

Italy Via Albricci 9, Milan 20122, T02-805 3506, info@indiatourismmilan.com.

Japan B9F Chiyoda Building, 6-5-12 Ginza, Chuo-Ku, Tokyo 104-0061, T03-3571 5062, indiatourt@smile.ocn.ne.jp.

The Netherlands Rokin 9-15, 1012 KK Amsterdam, T020-620 8991, info@indiatourismamsterdam.com.

South Africa PO Box 412452, Craig Hall 2024, 2000 Johannesburg, T011-325 0880, goito@global.co.za.

UK 7 Cork St, London WIS 3LH, T020-7437 3677, T08700-102183, info@indiatouristoffice.org.

USA 3550 Wilshire Boulevard, Room 204, Los Angeles, California 90010, T213-380 8855, goitola@aol.com; Suite 1808, 1270 Av of Americas, New York, NY 10020-1700, T212-5864901, ny@itony.com.

Tour operators

UK

Ace, T01223-835055, www.acestudytours.co.uk. Expert-led cultural study tours.

The Adventure Company, Cross and Pillory House, Cross and Pillory Lane, Alton, GU34 1HL, T0845-450 5316, www.adventurecompany.co.uk. Adventure tours, small groups.

Colours Of India, Marlborough House, 298 Regent's Park Rd, London, N3 2TJ, T020-8343 3446, www.partnershiptravel.co.uk. Tailor-made cultural, adventure, spa and cooking tours.

Cox & Kings (Taj Group), T020-7873 5000, www.coxandkings.co.uk.

Discovery Initiatives, The Travel House, 51 Castle St, Cirencester, GL7 1QD, T01285-643333, www.discoveryinitiatives.com. Wildlife safaris, tiger study tours and cultural tours with strong conservation ethic.

Dragoman, T01728-861133, www.dragoman.com. Overland, adventure, camping.

Exodus, T0208-675 5550, www.exodus.co.uk. Small group overland and trekking tours.

Greaves Tours, 53 Welbeck St, London, T020-7487 9111, www.greavesindia.com. Luxury, tailor-made tours using only scheduled flights. Traditional travel such as road and rail preferred to flights between major cities.

Indian Explorations, Afex House, Holwell, Burford, Oxfordshire, OX18 4JS, T01993-822443, www.indianexplorations.com. Bespoke holidays, including to the Andaman Islands and Rajasthan.

Kerala Connections, School House Lane, Horsmonden, Kent, TN12 8BP, T01892-722 440, www.keralaconnections.co.uk. Excellent tailor-made tours throughout India, including Lakshadweep and Andaman Islands, with great homestays. Also trades under the name **Select Connections**, www.selectconnections.co.uk.

Kuoni, Kuoni House, Dorking, Surrey, RH5 4AZ, T01306-747002, www.kuoni.co.uk, and subsidiary upmarket brand **Voyage Jules Vernes**, www.vjv.co.uk. Run week-long culture and relaxation tours.

MAHout, The Manor, Manor Rd, Banbury, T01295-758 150, www.mahoutuk.com. Boutique hotels representation specialist.
Master Travel, T020-7501 6742, www.mastertravel.co.uk. History, Ayurveda and cultural study tours.
On the Go Tours, 68 North End Rd, London, W14 9EP, T020-7371 1113, www.onthego tours.com. Legendary tours and tailor-made itineraries at amazing prices.
Palanquin Travels, T020-7436 9343, www.palanquin.co.uk. Culture, wildlife.
Pettitts, T01892-515966, www.pettitts.co.uk. Unusual locations.
Red Dot Tours, Orchard House, Folly Lane, Bramham, Leeds, LS23 6RZ, T0113-815 1864, www.reddottours.com. Tailor-made specialist in Kerala and Rajasthan. Also organizes flights and cricket tours.
STA Travel, T0871-230 0040, www.statravel. co.uk. Student and young persons' travel agent.
Steppes Travel, 51 Castle St, Cirencester, Gloucestershire, GL7 1QD, T01285-880980, www.steppestravel.co.uk.
Trans Himalaya, 16 Skye Crescent, Crieff, PH7 3FB, T01764-650604, www.trans-himalaya.com. Under the direction of Gyurme Dorje, a Tibetologist and Tibet travel writer, they organize travel throughout the Tibetan plateau, as well as in Mongolia, China and the Himalaya (Bhutan, Sikkim, Nepal and Ladakh).

Trans Indus, 75 St Mary's Rd and the Old Fire Station, Ealing, London, W5 5RH, T020-8566 3739, www.transindus.com. Upmarket India travel specialists offering tailor-made and group tours and holidays. Unusual locations.
Tropical Locations, Welby House, 96 Wilton Rd, London, SW1V 1DW, T0845-277 3310, www.tropical-locations.com. Specialist tour company covering India and the Indian Ocean.

India
Aquaterra Adventures, S-507, Ground Floor, Greater Kailash-II, New Delhi, T011-29212641, www.treknraft.com. Trekking, rafting, kayaking, etc in all Indian Himalayan states.
Banyan Tours and Travels, www.banyan tours.com. Pan-Indian operator specializing in bespoke, upmarket travel, with strength in culture, heritage, adventure and wildlife.
The Blue Yonder, 23-24 Sri Guru Nivas, No 6 Amar Jyoti Layout, Nagashetty Halli, Sanjay Nagar, Bengaluru (Bangalore), T080-4115 2218, www.theblueyonder.com. Highly regarded and award-winning sustainable and community tourism operators, active in Kerala, Sikkim, Orissa and Rajasthan.
Getoff ur ass, www.getoffurass.com. Tailored trips to the Andamans.
Help Tourism, Kolkata/Siliguri/Guwahati, T033-2455 0917, www.helptourism.com. Eco-tours in Assam, Arunachal and North Bengal, involving local communities.

Trans Himalaya

Customised cultural tours, treks and botanical expeditions in India's northeast- Sikkim, West Bengal (Darjeeling and Kalimpong), Assam and Meghalaya, and Arunachal Pradesh (Tawang and Pemako), as well as in the adjacent mountain kingdom of Bhutan and throughout the Tibetan plateau.

For details and booking contact:
Trans Himalaya, 16 Skye Crescent, Crieff, Perth & Kinross PH7 3FB.
Tel: 0044-1764-650604, Fax: 0044-1764-650991
Email: info@trans-himalaya.com *Website*: www.trans-himalaya.com

Ibex Expeditions, 30 Community Centre, East of Kailash, New Delhi 110 065, T011-2646 0244, T011-2646 0246, www.ibex expeditions.com. Award-winning eco-aware tour operator specializing in tailor-made adventure and luxury holidays.

Indebo India, 116-117 Aurobindo Pl, Hauz Khas, New Delhi 110016, T011-4716 5500, www.indebo.com. Customized tours and travel-related services throughout India.

Paradise Holidays, 312 Ansals Classique Tower, Rajouri Garden, New Delhi 110027, T011-4552 0735/6/7/8, www.paradise holidays.com. Wide range of tailor-made tours, from cultural to wildlife.

Purvi Discovery, Jalannagarh, Dibrugarh, Assam, T0373-230 1120, www.purviweb.com, www.assamteatourism.com. Experienced in tours to Arunachal, Assam and other northeast destinations, a quality outfit with quality accommodation.

Royal Expeditions Pvt Ltd, 26 Community Center (11th floor), East of Kailash, New Delhi 110065, T011-2623 8545 (UK T020-8150 6158; USA T1-609-945 2912), www.royal expeditions.com. Tailor-made tours in culture, wildlife and photography. Specializes in easy options for senior travellers.

Terralaya Travels, Gangtok, Sikkim, T03592 252516, www.terralaya.com. Specialists in the Northeast states, with interesting sleeping options (including homestays): biking, trekking, spiritual, nature, etc journeys offered.

North America

Absolute Asia, 180 Varick St, 16th floor, New York, T1-800-736-8187, www.absolute asia.com. Luxury custom-designed tours: culinary, pilgrimage of the south, honeymoon, 'Jewish India' tour plus Tamil tour combining Tamil Nadu with Sri Lanka.

Adventures Abroad, T1-800-665 3998, www.adventures-abroad.com.

Greaves Tours, 121 W Wacker Dr, Chicago, T1-800-318 7801. See under UK entry, above.

High Asia, 33 Thornton St, Hamden, Connecticut, T609-269-5332. Adventurous and exploratory tours in Assam and Arunachal Pradesh, including elephant trekking, tribal culture tours and trips linking India to China via the Burma Road.

Myths and Mountains, T1-800-670 6984, www.mythsandmountains.com. Culture, crafts and religion.

Spirit of India, T1-888-3676147, www.spirit-of-india.com. General and spirituality-focused tours, local experts.

Australia and New Zealand

Adventure World, 73 Walkers St, North Sydney, T02-89130755, www.adventure world.com.au. Independent tour operator with packages from 7 nights in Kerala. Also 101 Great South Rd, Remuera, Auckland, T64-9524 5118, www.adventureworld.co.nz.

Classic Oriental Tours, 35 Grafton St, Woollahara, T02-9657 2020, www.classic oriental. com.au. Travel for groups and independent travellers, all standards from budget to de luxe.

India Unbound, 40 Leithead St, Brunswick, Victoria, T1300-889513, www.indiaunbound. com.au. Intriguing range of small-group trips and bespoke private tours.

Intrepid Travel, 11-13 Spring St, Fitzroy, Victoria 3065, T1300-364 512, www.intrepid travel.com. Cookery courses to village stays. Adventure, treks and aiming to be carbon neutral by end of 2010.

Peregrine Adventures, Australia, T613-8601 4444, www.peregrineadventures.com. Small group overland and trekking tours.

Continental Europe

Academische Reizen, World Travel Holland, Academische Reizen BV, Prinsengracht 783-785, 1017 JZ Amsterdam, T020-589 2940, www.academischereizen.nl. All-India group culture tours.

Chola Voyages, 190, rue du Faubourg St Denis, 75010 Paris, T01-4034 5564, delamanche@hotmail.com.

La Maison Des Indes, 7 Place St Sulpice, 75006 Paris, T01-5681 3838, www.maisondes indes.com. Bespoke or group cultural tours.

The Shoestring Company, Meidoornweg 2, 1031 GG Amsterdam, T020-685 0203, info@shoestring.nl. Group leisure and adventure tours.

Visas and immigration

For embassies and consulates, see page 47. Virtually all foreign nationals, including children, require a visa to enter India. The rules regarding visas change frequently and arrangements for application and collection also vary from town to town so it is essential to check details and costs with the relevant embassy or consulate. These remain closed on Indian national holidays. Now many consulates and embassies are outsourcing the visa process, it's best to find out in advance how long it will take. For example, in London where you used to be able to get a visa in person in a morning if you were prepared to queue, it now takes 2-3 working days and involves 2 trips to the office.

At other offices, it can be much easier to apply in advance by post, to avoid queues and frustratingly low visa quotas. Postal applications can take 15 working days to process.

Visitors from countries with no Indian representation may apply to the resident British representative, or enquire at the **Air India** office. An application on the prescribed form should be accompanied by 2 passport photographs and your passport which should be valid 6 months beyond the period of your visit. Note that visas are valid from the date granted, not from the date of entry. For up-to-date information on visa requirements visit www.india-visa.com.

Currently the following visa rules apply:
Transit For passengers en route to another country (no more than 72 hrs in India).
Tourist 3-6 month visa from the date of issue with multiple entry.
Business 3-6 months or up to 2 years with multiple entry. A letter from the company giving the nature of business is required.
5 year For those of Indian origin only, who have held Indian passports.
Student Valid up to 1 year from the date of issue. Attach a letter of acceptance from Indian institution and an AIDS test certificate. Allow up to 3 months for approval.
Visa extensions Applications should be made to the Foreigners' Regional Registration Offices at New Delhi, Mumbai, Kolkata or Chennai, or an office of the Superintendent of Police in the District Headquarters. After 6 months, you must leave India and apply for a new visa – the Nepal office is known to be difficult. Anyone staying in India for a period of more than 180 days must register at a convenient Foreigners' Registration Office.

Permits and restricted and protected areas

Some areas are politically sensitive and special permits may be needed to visit them, though the government is relaxing its regulations. The border regions, tribal areas and Himalayan zones are subject to restrictions and special permits may be needed to visit them.

Currently the following require special permits: **Arunachal Pradesh**, **Manipur** (for 5 days), **Mizoram** and **Nagaland**. Apply to the Under Secretary, Ministry of Home Affairs, Foreigners Division, Lok Nayak Bhavan, Khan Market, New Delhi 110003, at least 4 weeks in advance. Special permission is no longer needed to visit Assam, Meghalaya and Tripura. For **Sikkim**, permits for 15 days are issued by a large number of government offices; see box, page 135.

Work permits

Foreigners should apply to the Indian representative in their country of origin for the latest information about work permits.

Liquor permits

Periodically some Indian states have tried to enforce prohibition. To some degree it is in force in Mizoram and Manipur. When applying for your visa you can ask for an All India Liquor Permit. Foreigners can also get the permit from any Government of India Tourist Office in Delhi or the state capitals. Instant permits are issued by some hotels.

Weights and measures

Metric system has come into universal use in the cities. In remote areas local measures are sometimes used. One lakh is 100,000 and 1 crore is 10 million.

Women travellers

Independent travel is still largely unheard of for Indian women. Although it is relatively safe for women to travel around India, most people find it an advantage to travel with a companion. Even then, privacy is rarely respected and there can be a lot of hassle, pressure and intrusion on your personal space. Backpackers often meet like-minded travelling companions at budget hotels. Cautious solo women travellers recommend dying blonde hair black and wearing wedding rings, but the most important measure is to dress appropriately, in loose-fitting, non-see-through clothes, covering shoulders, arms and legs. Take advantage of the gender segregation on public transport, both to avoid hassle and talk with local women. In mosques women should be covered from head to ankle. **Independent Traveller**, T0870-760 5001, www.independenttraveller.com, runs women-only tours to India.

Unaccompanied women are most vulnerable in major cities, crowded bazars, beach resorts and tourist centres where men may follow them and touch them; festival nights are particularly bad for this. Women have reported that they have been molested while being measured for clothing in tailors' shops. If you are harassed, it can be effective to make a scene. Be firm and clear if you don't wish to speak to someone. The best response to staring, whether lascivious or curious, is to avert your eyes down and away. This is not the submissive gesture it might seem, but an effective tool to communicate that you have no interest in any further interaction. Aggressively staring back or verbally confronting the starer can be construed as a come-on. It is best to be accompanied at night, especially when travelling by rickshaw or taxi in towns. Be prepared to raise an alarm if anything unpleasant threatens.

Most railway booking offices have separate women's ticket queues or ask women to go to the head of the general queue. Some buses have seats reserved for women. See also page 42.

Working in India

See also Visas and immigration, page 58. It is best to arrange voluntary work well in advance with organizations in India (addresses are given in some towns, eg Darjeeling, Kolkata); alternatively, contact an organization abroad.

Students may spend part of their year off helping in a school or teaching English.

Voluntary work
UK
i to i, Woodside House, 261 Low Lane, Leeds, LS18 5NY, T0800-011 1156, www.i-to-i.com.
International Voluntary Service, IVS GB, Thorn House, 5 Rose St, Edinburgh, EH2 2PR, T0131-243 2745.
VSO, 317 Putney Bridge Rd, London, SW15 2PN, www.vso.org.uk.
Volunteer Work Information Service, Old School House, Pendomer, Yeovil, BA22 9PH, T01935-864458, www.workingabroad.com.

USA
Amerispan, 1334 Walnut St, 6th floor, Philadelphia, PA 19107, T1-800-879 6640, www.amerispan.com. Volunteer placements in Delhi and Jaipur.
Council for International Programs, 1700 East 13th St, Suite 4ME, Cleveland, Ohio, T216-566-108, www.cipusa.org.

Australia
www.ampersand.org.au has links to volunteer organizations, of which the biggest is:
Australian Volunteers International, 71 Argyle St, Fitzroy, VIC 3065, T03-9279 1788, www.australianvolunteers.com.

Contents

Footprint features

Kolkata (Calcutta)

At a glance

⊖ **Getting around** An efficient metro runs north-south, ferries cross the Hughly, taxis are cheap and buses cheaper, trams criss-cross the eastern city (very slowly) and of course there are hand-pulled rickshaws.

◉ **Time required** 3-4 days to get to grips with Kolkata.

☼ **Weather** Best during Oct-Feb, about the only time that isn't muggy.

✖ **When not to go** Extremely humid from Apr until the monsoon arrives in early Jun.

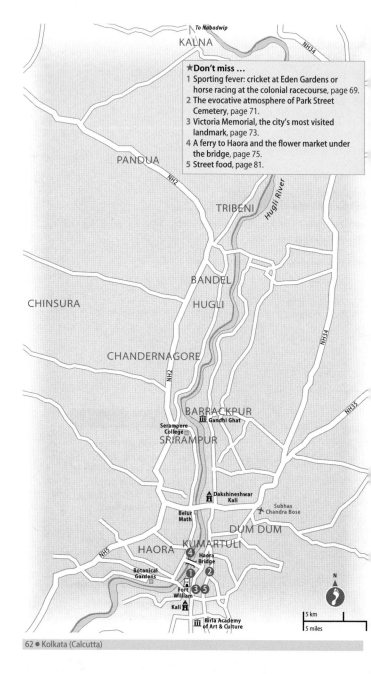

★Don't miss ...
1 Sporting fever: cricket at Eden Gardens or horse racing at the colonial racecourse, page 69.
2 The evocative atmosphere of Park Street Cemetery, page 71.
3 Victoria Memorial, the city's most visited landmark, page 73.
4 A ferry to Haora and the flower market under the bridge, page 75.
5 Street food, page 81.

To Nabadwip
KALNA
NH34
PANDUA
NH2
TRIBENI
Hugli River
BANDEL
CHINSURA
HUGLI
CHANDERNAGORE
NH2
NH34
BARRACKPUR
Gandhi Ghat
NH35
Serampore College
SRIRAMPUR
Dakshineshwar Kali
Subhas Chandra Bose
Belur Math
DUM DUM
HAORA
KUMARTULI
NH5
4 Haora Bridge
Botanical Gardens
2
Fort William
3 5
Kali
Birla Academy of Art & Culture

N

5 km
5 miles

Kolkata is considered by many to be the country's cultural and intellectual hub. The vibrant daily theatre and concert performances, sprawling annual book fair and art-house film festivals are rooted in the legacy of the great Tagore and evoke the iconic films of Satajit Ray. From being at the centre of the Indian Independence movement, politics and reform continue to be discussed amidst the fan-swirled smoke in the Indian Coffee House, and by the businessmen gathered for *adda* (chatting) in one of the historic clubhouses.

Many visitors have a preconceived idea of this oft-maligned city, and for a long time the 'black hole' tag and the work of Mother Teresa conjured up images of a disintegrating, filthy conurbation engulfed in desperate poverty. But a little time spent here is enough for those ideas to be rapidly dispelled, and to gain a fascinating glimpse of how 14 million people live together. From rich to poor and educated to illiterate, Kolkatans melt together in a way that isn't seen in other cities. Although the *bustees* (slums) continue to swell and street living is more visible here than anywhere, the warmth and humanity of the population is palpable. The city's many volunteers find that this is the memory that stays with them, as intensely as the smell of kathi-rolls cooking, the jingle of rickshaw bells and the ever-vocal horns of the city's yellow Ambassadors.

Since 2000, Kolkata has been rejuvenating itself economically and, more recently, visually: the impressive relics of colonialism are being given a facelift and Hoara Bridge is lit up at night. Kolkatans are immensely proud of their heritage and they love their city – and visitors to this fascinating and surprising metropolis generally discover that they do too.

Ins and outs → *For listings, see pages 78-92. Colour map 2, C2. Phone code: 033.*
Population: 13.22 million.

Getting there Subhas Chandra Bose airport at Dum Dum serves international and domestic flights. Taxis to the city centre take 30-60 minutes and there is a pre-paid taxi booth before exiting the airport. Haora (Howrah) station, on the west bank of the Hugli, can be daunting and the taxi rank outside is often chaotic; the prepaid taxi booth is to the right as you exit. Trains to the north use the slightly less chaotic Sealdah terminal east of the centre, which also has prepaid taxis. Long-distance buses arrive at Esplanade, 15-20 minutes' walk from most budget hotels. ►► *See Transport, page 89.*

Getting around You can cover much of Central Kolkata on foot. For the rest you need transport. You may not fancy using hand-pulled rickshaws, but they become indispensable when the streets are flooded. Buses and minibuses are often jam packed, but routes comprehensively cover the city – conductors and bystanders will help find the correct bus. The electric trams can be slightly better outside peak periods. The Metro, though on a limited route, is one of the easiest ways of getting around the city. Taxis are relatively cheap but allow plenty of time to get through very congested traffic. Despite the footpath, it is not permitted to walk across the Vidyasagar Bridge. Taxi drivers expect passengers to pay the Rs 10 toll.

Tourist information **India Tourism** ⓘ *4 Shakespeare Sarani, T033-2282 5813, Mon-Fri 0900-1800, Sat 0900-1300.* **West Bengal Tourism Development Corporation (WBTDC)** ⓘ *BBD Bagh, T033-2248 8271, Mon-Fri 1030-1600, Sat 1030-1300; also a counter at the station in Howrah, T033-2660 2518.*

Climate Kolkata can be very hot and humid outside mid-March-October. Asthma sufferers find the traffic pollution very trying.

Background

Calcutta, as it came to be named, was founded by the remarkable English merchant trader **Job Charnock** in 1690. He was in charge of the East India Company factory (ie warehouse) in Hugli, then the centre of British trade from eastern India. Attacks from the local Muslim ruler forced him to flee – first down river to Sutanuti and then 1500 km south to Chennai. However, in 1690 he selected three villages – Kalikata, Sutanuti and Govindpur – where Armenian and Portuguese traders had already settled, leased them from Emperor Aurangzeb and returned to what became the capital of British India.

The first fort here, named after King William III! (completed 1707), was on the site of the present BBD Bagh. A deep defensive moat was dug in 1742 to strengthen the fort – the Maratha ditch. The Maratha threat never materialized but the city was captured easily by the 20-year-old **Siraj-ud-Daula**, the new Nawab of Bengal, in 1756. The 146 British residents who failed to escape by the fort's river gate were imprisoned for a night in a small guard room about 6 m by 5 m with only one window – the infamous **'Black Hole of Calcutta'**. Some records suggest 64 people were imprisoned and only 23 survived.

The following year **Robert Clive** re-took the city. The new Fort William was built and in 1772 Calcutta became the capital of British administration in India with Warren Hastings as the first Governor of Bengal, see page 323. Some of Calcutta's most impressive colonial buildings were built in the years that followed, when it became the first city of British India. It was also a time of Hindu and Muslim resurgence.

Colonial Calcutta grew as new traders, soldiers and administrators arrived, establishing their exclusive social and sports clubs. Trade in cloth, silk, lac, indigo, rice,

Kolkata's place in the cosmic dance

Kolkata's site was particularly holy to Hindus. According to one myth, King Daksa was enraged when his daughter Sati married Siva. He organized a *yajna* (grand sacrifice) to which he invited everyone in the kingdom – except his son-in-law. Distraught, Kali (Sati) threw herself on the sacrificial flames. Siva in turn arrived on the scene to find his wife's body already burnt. Tearing it from the flames, he started his dance of cosmic destruction. All the other gods,

witnessing the devastation that Siva was causing in his anguish, pleaded with Vishnu to step in and end the chaos. Vishnu intercepted him with his *chakra* (discus-like weapon) and, in order to dislodge Kali's body from Siva's shoulder, chopped it into 51 pieces, which were flung far and wide. The place where each one fell became a *pithasthana* (place of pilgrimage). Kali's little toe fell at Kali Ghat. The place, Kalikshetra or Kalikata, gave the city its name.

areca nut and tobacco had originally attracted the Portuguese and British to Bengal. Later Calcutta's hinterland producing jute, iron ore, tea and coal led to large British firms setting up headquarters in the city. Calcutta prospered as the commercial and political capital of British India up to 1911, when the capital was transferred to Delhi.

Kolkata had to absorb huge numbers of migrants immediately after Partition in 1947. When Pakistan ceased trading with India in 1949, Kolkata's economy suffered a massive blow as it lost its supplies of raw jute and its failure to attract new investment created critical economic problems. In the late 1960s the election of the Communist Party of India Marxist, the CPI(M), led to a period of stability. The CPI(M) has become committed to a mixed economy and has sought foreign private investment.

Sights

To Bengalis Kolkata is the proud intellectual capital of India, with an outstanding contribution to the arts, services, medicine and social reform in its past, and a rich contemporary cultural life. As the former imperial capital, Kolkata retains some of the country's most striking colonial buildings, yet at the same time it is truly an Indian city. Unique in India in retaining trams, and the only place in the world to still have hand-pulled rickshaws, you take your life in your hands each time you cross Kolkata's streets. Hugely crowded, Kolkata's Maidan, the parkland, gives lungs to a city packed with some of the most densely populated slums, or bustees, anywhere in the world.

Central Kolkata

BBD Bagh (Dalhousie Square) and around

Many historic Raj buildings surround the square, which is quietest before 0900. Renamed Benoy Badal Dinesh (BBD) Bagh after three Bengali martyrs, the square has an artificial lake fed by natural springs. On Strand Road North is the dilapidated **Silver Mint** (1824-1831). The **Writers' Building** (1780), designed by Thomas Lyon as the trading headquarters of the East India Company, was refaced in 1880. It is now the state Government Secretariat. The classical block with 57 sets of identical windows was built like barracks inside. The **Great Eastern Hotel** (1841) was in Mark Twain's day "the best

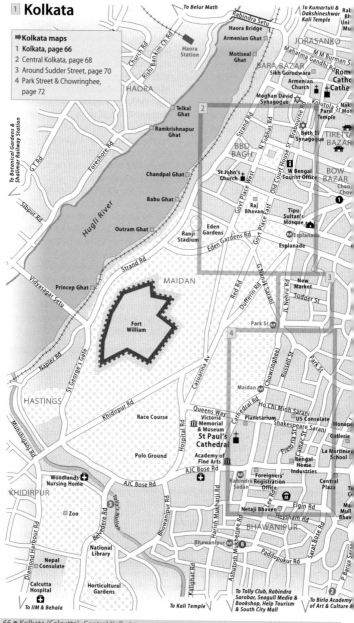

1 Kolkata

➡ **Kolkata maps**
1 Kolkata, page 66
2 Central Kolkata, page 68
3 Around Sudder Street, page 70
4 Park Street & Chowringhee, page 72

To Belur Math

To Kumartuli &
Dakshineshwar
Kali Temple

Rabindra Setu

Haora Bridge

Armenian Ghat

JORASANKO

Haora
Station

Motiseal
Ghat

Mahatma Gandhi Rd

M M Burman Rd

Rom
Cath
Cath

BARA BAZAR

Sikh Gurudwara

Armenian
Church

Kolutola St

Nak
Mos

Parsi
Temple

TIRETT
BAZAR

Telkal Ghat

Moghan David
Synagogue

Strand Rd

N Subhas Rd

Brabourne Rd

Beth El
Synagogue

Ramkrishnapur
Ghat

BBD
BAGH

Old Court House St

ℹ W Bengal
Tourist Office

BOW
BAZAR

Chan
Chov

Chandpal Ghat

St John's
Church

Govt Place West

Govt Place East

Raj
Bhavan

Tipu
Sultan's
Mosque

Babu Ghat

Eden
Gardens

Ⓜ Esplanade

Hugli River

Outram Ghat

Ranji
Stadium

Eden Gardens Rd

Govt Place East

G Nehru Sarani

Esplanade

Strand Rd

MAIDAN

Red Rd

Dufferin Rd

JL Nehru Rd

New
Market

Sudder St

Princep Ghat

Fort
William

Park St Ⓜ

HAORA

Church Rd

Right Bank Kim Ch Rd

Foreshore Rd

G L Rd

To Botanical Gardens &
Shalimar Railway Station

Sibpur Rd

Vidyasagar Setu

HASTINGS

KHIDIRPUR

66 ● Kolkata (Calcutta) Central Kolkata

Sleeping 🛏
Chrome **4**
New Haven Guest House **2**
Taj Bengal & Chinoiserie Restaurant **3**
Vedic Village **5**

Eating 🍴
Anand **1**
Banana Leaf **2**
Coffee House **3**
Mainland China **5**
Rehmania & Shiraz **7**
Mezze & Soho Bar **2**

Bars & clubs 🍷
Tripti's **8**

hotel East of the Suez", but from the 1970s it steadily declined and has been undergoing major restoration (no date set for re-opening). **Mission Row** (now RN Mukharji Road) is Kolkata's oldest street, and contains the **Old Mission Church** (consecrated 1770), built by the Swedish missionary Johann Kiernander.

South of BBD Bagh is the imposing **Raj Bhavan** (1799-1802), the residence of the Governor of West Bengal, formerly Government House. It was modelled on Kedleston Hall in Derbyshire, England (later Lord Curzon's home), and designed by Charles Wyatt, one of many Bengal engineers who based their designs on famous British buildings. The **Town Hall** (1813) has been converted into a **museum** ⓘ *1100-1800, foreigners Rs 10, no bags allowed*, telling the story of the independence movement in Bengal through a panoramic, cinematic display, starring an animatronic Rabindranath Tagore. The **High Court** (1872) was modelled on the medieval cloth merchants' hall at Ypres in Flanders.

Ochterlony Monument (1828), renamed Shahid Minar (Martyrs' Memorial) in 1969, was built as a memorial to Sir David Ochterlony, who led East India Company troops against the Nepalese in 1814-1816. The 46-m tall Greek Doric column has an Egyptian base and is topped by a Turkish cupola.

St John's Church (1787) ⓘ *0900-1200, 1700-1800*, like the later St Andrew's Kirk (1818), was modelled partially on St Martin-in-the-Fields, London. The soft subsoil did not allow it to have a tall spire and architecturally it was thought to be 'full of blunders'. Verandas were added to the north and south in 1811 to reduce the glare of the sun. Inside the vestry are Warren Hastings's desk and chair, plus paintings, prints and assorted dusty memorabilia of the Raj. *The Last Supper* by Johann Zoffany in the south aisle shows the city's residents dressed as the Apostles. Job Charnock is buried in the old cemetery. His octagonal mausoleum, the oldest piece of masonry in the city, is of Pallavaram granite (from Madras Presidency), which is named charnockite after him. The monument to the **Black Hole of Calcutta** was brought here from Dalhousie Square (BBD Bagh) in 1940.

② Central Kolkata

→Kolkata maps
1 Kolkata, page 66
2 **Central Kolkata, page 68**
3 Around Sudder Street, page 70
4 Park Street & Chowringhee, page 72

200 metres
200 yards

N

Sleeping 🛌
Broadway & Bar 1
Majestic 3
Oberoi Grand &
   Baan Thai Restaurant 2

Eating 🍴
Aaheli at Peerless Inn 3
Amber 1
Anand 2
Song Hay 4

Bars & clubs 🍸
Embassy 5
Local bars 6

Worship of the clay goddess

Durga Puja, the 17th-century festival in honour of the clay goddess, precedes the full moon in late September/early October, when all offices and institutions close down and the Metro only operates from the late afternoon.

Images of the 10-armed, three-eyed goddess, a form of Shakti or Kali (see page 341) astride her 'vehicle' the lion, portray Durga slaying Mahisasura, the evil buffalo demon. Durga, shown with her four children Lakshmi, Sarasvati, Ganesh and Kartik, is worshipped in hundreds of brightly illuminated and beautifully decorated *pandals* (marquees) made of bamboo and coloured cloth. The priests perform prayers at appointed times in the morning and evening. On the fourth and last day of festivities, huge and often emotionally charged processions follow devotees who carry the clay figures to be immersed in the river at many points along the banks. The potters return to collect clay from the river bank once again for the following year.

You can see the image makers in Kumartuli (see page 73) a few days earlier and visit the *pandals* early in the evening, before they become crowded. Local communities are immensely proud of their *pandals* and no effort is spared to put on the most impressive display. The images are decorated with intricate silver, golden or *shola* (white pith) ornaments, there are moving electric light displays and huge structures are built (sometimes resembling a temple) in order to win competitions. WBTDC offers an all-night bus tour (Rs 50) as well as a two-hour launch trip on the Hugli to watch the immersion ceremony on the last night.

Eden Gardens ⓘ *usually open for matches only, a small tip at Gate 14 gains entry on other days*, which are situated in the northwest corner of the Maidan, were named after Lord Auckland's sisters Emily and Fanny Eden. There are pleasant walks, a lake and a small Burmese pagoda (typical of this type of Pyatthat). Laid out in 1834, part forms the Ranji Stadium where the first cricket match was played in 1864. Today, Test matches (November-February), international tennis championships and other sports fixtures attract crowds of 100,000.

Around Sudder Street

Conveniently close to Chowringhee and the vast shopping arcade, New Market, Sudder Street is the focus for Kolkata's backpackers and attracts touts and drug pushers. Beggars on Chowringhee and Park Street often belong to organized syndicates who have to pay a large percentage of their 'earnings' for the privilege of working that area.

Around the corner from Sudder Street is the **Indian Museum** ⓘ *27 JL Nehru Rd, T033-2286 1679, Mar-Nov Tue-Sun 1000-1700, Dec-Feb 1000-1630, foreigners Rs 150, Indians Rs 10, cameras Rs 50/100 with tripod*, possibly Asia's largest. The Jadu Ghar (House of Magic) was founded in 1814 and has a worthwhile collection. The colonnaded Italianate building facing the Maidan has 36 galleries (though large sections are often closed off). Parts are poorly lit and gathering dust so it is best to be selective. Highlights include the geological collection with Siwalik fossils, natural history and anthropology, outstanding exhibits from the Harappa and Moenjodaro periods, a prized collection of Buddhist art, miniature paintings, 'Art and Textile' with ivory, glass and silverware, Theme Gallery with rare paintings and 200-year-old hand-drawn maps, and many more. You need permission to see the exceptional collection of over 50,000 coins. Allow a couple of hours.

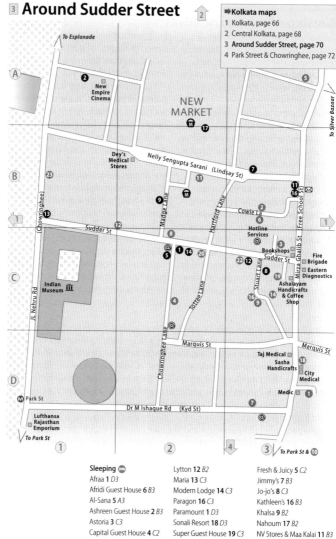

➡ **Kolkata maps**

1 Kolkata, page 66
2 Central Kolkata, page 68
3 **Around Sudder Street, page 70**
4 Park Street & Chowringhee, page 72

To Esplanade

New Empire Cinema

NEW MARKET

To Silver Bazaar

Dey's Medical Stores

Nelly Sengupta Sarani (Lindsay St)

Chowringhee

Madge Lane

Hartford Lane

Cowie La.

Free School St

Sudder St

Hotline Services

Bookshops

Fire Brigade

Eastern Diagnostics

Torree Lane

Stuart Lane

Mirza Ghalib St

Ashalayam Handicrafts & Coffee Shop

Indian Museum

JL Nehru Rd

Chowringhee Lane

Marquis St

Marquis St

Taj Medical

Sasha Handicrafts

City Medical

Medic

Park St

Dr M Ishaque Rd (Kyd St)

Lufthansa Rajasthan Emporium

To Park St

To Park St &

N

100 metres
100 yards

Sleeping
Afraa **1** D3
Afridi Guest House **6** B3
Al-Sana **5** A3
Ashreen Guest House **2** B3
Astoria **3** C3
Capital Guest House **4** C2
Crystal **7** D3
Emirates **7** D3
Fairlawn **8** C2
Galaxy **9** C3
Housez 43 **10** D3
Lindsay & Blue Beyond **11** B2

Lytton **12** B2
Maria **13** C3
Modern Lodge **14** C3
Paragon **16** C3
Paramount **1** D3
Sonali Resort **18** D3
Super Guest House **19** D3
Times Guest House **20** C2
Tourist Inn **22** C3
YMCA **23** B1

Eating
Blue Sky Café **1** C2
Brothers Snacks **2** A1

Fresh & Juicy **5** C2
Jimmy's **7** B3
Jo-jo's **8** C3
Kathleen's **16** B3
Khalsa **9** B2
Nahoum **17** B2
NV Stores & Maa Kalai **11** B3
Tirupati **12** C3
Zaranj & Jong's **13** B1
Zurich **14** C2

Park Street

Park Street Cemetery ① *daily 0800-1630, free, booklet Rs 100, security guard opens gate for foreigners and will expect you to sign the visitors' book*, was opened in 1767 to accommodate the large number of British who died 'serving' their country. The cemetery is a peaceful paradise on the south side of one of Kolkata's busiest streets, with a maze of soaring obelisks shaded by tropical trees. The heavily inscribed decaying headstones, rotundas, pyramids and urns have been restored, and gardeners are actively trying to beautify the grounds. Several of the inscriptions make interesting reading. Death, often untimely, came from tropical diseases or other hazards such as battles, childbirth and even melancholia. More uncommonly, it was an excess of alcohol, or as for Sir Thomas D'Oyly, through "an inordinate use of the hokkah". Rose Aylmer died after eating too many pineapples! Tombs include those of Col Kyd, founder of the Botanical Gardens, the great oriental scholar Sir William Jones, and the fanciful mausoleum of the Irish Major-General 'Hindoo' Stuart. Across AJC Bose Road, on Karaya Road, is the smaller and far more derelict **Scottish Cemetery** ① *daily 0700-1730, free, pamphlet by donation to the caretaker*. The Kolkata Scottish Heritage Trust begun work in 2008 to restore some of the 1600 tumbledown graves but the undergrowth is rampant and jungle prevails. Also known as the 'dissenters' graveyard', as this was where non-Anglicans were buried.

The **Asiatic Society** ① *1 Park St, T033-2229 0779, www.asiaticsocietycal.com, Mon-Fri 1000-1800, free*, the oldest institution of Oriental studies in the world, was founded in 1784 by the great Orientalist, Sir William Jones. It is a treasure house of 150,000 books and 60,000 ancient manuscripts in most Asian languages, although permission is required to see specific pieces. The museum includes an Ashokan edict, rare coins and paintings. The library is worth a visit for its dusty travelogues and titles on the history of Calcutta. Bring a passport as the signing-in process to visit the building itself is at least a triplicate process.

The Maidan

This area, 200 years ago, was covered in dense jungle. Often called the lungs of the city, it is a unique green, covering over 400 ha along Chowringhee (JL Nehru Road). Larger than New York's Central Park, it is perhaps the largest urban park in the world. In it stands Fort William and several clubhouses providing tennis, football, rugby, cricket and even crown green bowls. Thousands each day pursue a hundred different interests – from early-morning yogis, model plane enthusiasts, weekend cricketers and performers earning their living, to vast political gatherings.

The massive **Fort William** was built by the British after their defeat in 1756, on the site of the village of Govindapur. Designed to be impregnable, it was roughly octagonal and large enough to house all the Europeans in the city in case of an attack. Water from the Hugli was channelled to fill the wide moat and the surrounding jungle was cleared to give a clear field of fire; this later became the Maidan. The barracks, stables, arsenal, prison and St Peter's Church are still there, but the fort now forms the Eastern Region's Military Headquarters and entry is forbidden.

Chowringhee and around

You can still see some of the old imposing structures with pillared verandas (designed by Italian architects as residences of prominent Englishmen) though modern high-rise buildings have transformed the skyline of this ancient pilgrim route to Kalighat.

St Paul's Cathedral ① *0900-1200, 1500-1800, 5 services on Sun*, is the original metropolitan church of British India. Completed in 1847, its Gothic tower (dedicated in

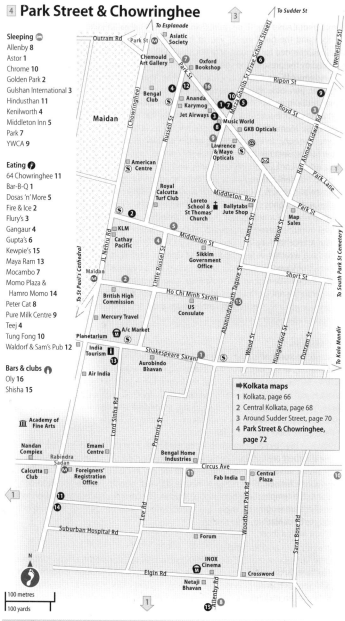

1938) was designed to replace the earlier steeples which were destroyed by earthquakes. The cathedral has a fine altar piece, three 'Gothic' stained-glass windows, two Florentine frescoes and the great West window by Burne-Jones. The original stained-glass East window, intended for St George's Windsor, was destroyed by a cyclone in 1964 and was replaced by the present one four years later.

Academy of Fine Arts ⓘ *Cathedral Rd, Tue-Sun 1200-1900, Rs 5*, was founded in 1933. The collection includes miniature paintings, textiles, works of Jamini Roy, Tagore and Desmond Doig and modern Indian sculpture in the gardens. Galleries exhibit works of local artists. Guide service and occasional films.

Victoria Memorial (1906-1921) ⓘ *Tue-Sun 1000-1630; museum 1000-1530 (very crowded on Sun), foreigners Rs 150, Indians Rs 10, cameras not permitted inside; son et lumière show, summer 1945, winter 1915, 45 mins, Rs 20 front seats, Rs 10 elsewhere*, was designed by Lord Curzon. The white marble monument to Queen Victoria and the Raj designed in Italian Renaissance-Mughal style stands in large, well-kept grounds with ornamental pools. A seated bronze Queen Victoria dominates the approach, while a marble statue stands in the main hall where visitors sometimes leave flowers at her feet. The building is illuminated in the evening; the musical fountain is a special draw. The statues over the entrance porches (including Motherhood, Prudence and Learning), and around the central dome (of Art, Architecture, Justice, Charity) came from Italy. The impressive weather vane, a 5-m-tall bronze winged figure of Victory weighing three tonnes, looks tiny from below. The principal gallery, covering the history of the city, includes a wealth of Raj memorabilia. There are fine miniatures, a rare collection of Persian manuscripts, and paintings by Zoffany, the two Daniells and Samuel Davis.

North Kolkata

Belur Math and the Dakshineshwar Kali Temple

Some 16 km north of the city is **Belur Math** ⓘ *0600-1200, 1600-1900*, the international headquarters of the **Ramakrishna Mission**, founded in 1899 by Swami Vivekananda, a disciple of the 19th-century Hindu saint Ramakrishna. He preached the unity of all religions and to symbolize this the *Math* ('monastery') synthesizes Hindu, Christian and Islamic architectural styles in a peaceful and meditative atmosphere.

On the opposite side of the river from Belur Math is the **Dakshineshwar Kali Temple** ⓘ *0600-1200, 1500-1800, 1830-2100, no photography allowed inside*. This huge Kali temple was built in 1847 by Rani Rashmoni. The 12 smaller temples in the courtyard are dedicated to Siva and there are also temples to Radha and Krishna. Because of the Rani's low caste, no priest would serve there until Ramakrishna's elder brother agreed and was succeeded by Ramakrishna himself. Here, Ramakrishna achieved his spiritual vision of the unity of all religions. The temple is crowded with colourfully clad devotees, particularly on Sundays when there are lengthy queues, and is open to all faiths. A boat (Rs 7) takes 20 minutes to/from to Belur Math across the Hooghly. Buses from BBD Bagh go to Dunlop Intersection, from where it's a short auto ride to the temple; trains run from Sealdah to Dakshineshwar.

Kumartuli

South of the Dakshineshwar temple is Kumartuli. Off Chitpur Road, the *kumars* or potters work all year, preparing clay images around cores of bamboo and straw. For generations they have been making life-size idols for the *pujas* or festivals, particularly of goddess Durga on a lion, slaying the demon. The images are usually unbaked since they are immersed in the holy river at the end of the festival. As the time of the *pujas* approaches, you will see thousands of images, often very brightly painted and gaudily dressed, awaiting the final finishing touch by the master painter. There are also *shola* artists who make decorations for festivals and weddings.

Just north of the Belgachia Metro station is a cluster of three Digambar Jain temples, one of the most tranquil spots in the city. The meticulously maintained and ornate **Paresnath Temple** ⓘ *0700-1200, 1500-2000, no leather*, is dedicated to the 10th Tirthankara. Consecrated around 1867, it is richly decorated with mirrors, Victorian tiles and Venetian glass mosaics.

College Street

This is the heart of intellectual Kolkata with the **university** and several academic institutions, including the old **Sanskrit College** and the elite **Presidency College**. Europeans and Indian benefactors established the Hindu College (1817) to provide a liberal education. In 1855, this became the Presidency College. A centre for 19th-century Bengali writers, artists and reformers, it spawned the early 20th-century Swadeshi Movement. The famous **Coffee House** (opened in 1944), cavernous haunt of the city's intelligentsia, still sells a good cup of coffee and has tonnes of atmosphere despite the recent lick of paint. Along the pavements are interesting second-hand book stalls. **Asutosh Museum** ⓘ *University Centenary Building, Mon-Fri 1030-1630, Sat 1030-1500, closed university holidays*, of eastern Indian art and antiquity, includes textiles, terracotta figures and Bengali folk art, but is poorly maintained with large sections frequently closed off.

Rabindra Bharati University Museum

ⓘ *6/4 Dwarakanath Tagore Lane (red walls visible down lane opposite 263 Rabindra Sarani), Mon-Fri 1000-1700, Sat 1000-1330, Sun and holidays 1100-1400*.
This museum, in a peaceful enclave away from the teeming chaos of Rabindra Sarani, occupies the family home of Rabindranath Tagore, who won the Nobel prize for Literature in 1913. It showcases Tagore's life and works, as well as the 19th-century Renaissance movement in Bengal.

Marble Palace

ⓘ *46 Muktaram Babu St, closed Mon and Thu, 1000-1600. Free pass from WBTDC (see page 64), 24 hrs ahead, or baksheesh (Rs 10 per person) to the security man at the gate, shoes must be removed, no photography allowed*.
Located in *Chor Bagan* ('Thieves' Garden'), the one-man collection of Raja Rajendra Mullick is in his ornate home (1835) with an Italianate courtyard, classical columns and Egyptian sphinxes. Family members still inhabit a portion of the house while servants' descendants live in the huts that encircle the grounds. Six sleeping marble lions and statuary grace the lawns and there is a veritable menagerie at the back. The galleries are crammed with statues, porcelain, clocks, mirrors, chandeliers and English (Reynolds), Dutch (Reubens) and Italian paintings, disorganized and gathering dust. The pink, grey and white Italian marble floors are remarkable, as is the solid rosewood statue of Queen Victoria. Allow one hour, or take a book and relax in the garden. The rambling museum on two floors has more than curiosity appeal – it is one of Kolkata's gems.

Haora Bridge area

North of the Marble Palace on Baghbazar Street is the **Girish Mancha**, the government theatre complex. The gorgeously well-kept **Armenian Church** of Holy Nazareth (1724) reminds us of the important trading role the small Armenian community who mostly came from Iran, played from the 17th century. Though the church is locked on weekdays you may ask to look around as the vestry is open during office hours. The 200 or so Armenians in the city still hold a service in Armenian in one of their two churches here every Sunday. Their college on Mirza Ghalib Street (also the birthplace of William Makepeace Thackery in 1811) only has about half-a-dozen pupils since it admits only those of Armenian descent. On its east side is the **Roman Catholic Cathedral** (1797) built by the Portuguese. The Jewish community, mostly Sephardic, of Baghdadi origin, was also once very prominent in commerce. Their two cavernous synagogues are well maintained and still used for services on alternate Saturdays. The grander of the two, **Moghan David Synagogue** in Canning Street, dates from 1884, and the smaller **Beth El Synagogue** is on Pollock Street nearby. There are only around 30 elderly Jews left in the city who continue to congregate at Nahoum's bakery in the New Market; the Jewish Girls School in Park Street has no pupils from the community. To view the interior of the synagogues, it is necessary to get a note of permission from Mr DE Nahoum, either at the bakery or from the office at 1 Hartford Lane.

Haora Bridge (pronounced How-ra), or Rabindra Setu, was opened in 1943. This single-span cantilever bridge, a prominent landmark, replaced the old pontoon bridge that joined the city with Haora and the railway station. To avoid affecting river currents and silting, the two 80-m-high piers rise from road level; the 450-m span expands by a metre on a hot day. It is the busiest bridge in the world in terms of foot passengers; go during rush hour to join the 100,000 commuters and men with improbable loads on their heads. Wrestlers can be seen underneath and there is a daily **flower market** beneath the eastern end, with piles of marigolds glowing against the mud. At night the bridge is illuminated, which makes a fine sight – if waiting for a night train at Howrah station go to first floor The pedestrian-free **Vidyasagar Setu**, further south, has eased the traffic burden slightly.

South Kolkata

Kali Temple

① *Off Ashok Mukherjee Rd, 0500-1500, 1700-2200.*

This is the temple to Kali (1809), the patron goddess of Kolkata, usually seen in her bloodthirsty form garlanded with skulls. There was an older temple here, where the goddess's little toe is said to have fallen when Siva carried her charred corpse in a frenzied dance of mourning, and she was cut into pieces by Vishnu's *chakra* (see box, page 65). Non-Hindus have limited access to this important Hindu pilgrimage centre. Where once human sacrifices were made, the lives of goats are offered daily on two wooden blocks to the south of the temple. When visiting the temple, priests will attempt to snare foreigners for the obligatory *puja*. A barrage may start as far away as 500 m from the temple. Don't be fooled in to handing over your shoes and succumbing to any priests until you are clearly inside the temple, despite being shown 'priest ID' cards. Once settled with a priest the experience can be well worth the initial hassle. An acceptable minimum donation is Rs 50-60. Books showing previous donations of Rs 1000 are probably faked. Having done the *puja*, you'll probably be left alone to soak up the atmosphere.

Mother Teresa's Homes

Mother Teresa, an Albanian by birth, came to India to teach as a Loreto nun in 1931. She started her Order of the Missionaries of Charity in Kalighat to serve the destitute and dying 19 years later. **Nirmal Hriday** ('Pure Heart'), near the Kali Temple, the first home for the dying, was opened in 1952. Mother Teresa died on 5 September 1997 but her work continues. You may see nuns in their white cotton saris with blue borders busy working in the many homes, clinics and orphanages in the city.

Birla Mandir and Birla Academy of Art and Culture

ⓘ *Birla Mandir, Gariahat Rd, 0600-1100 and 1630-2030; Birla Academy of Art and Culture, 108/109 Southern Av, T033-2466 2843, Tue- Sun 1600-2000.*

Housed in a modern high rise, the Birla Academy of Art and Culture concentrates on medieval and contemporary paintings and sculpture. It is worth visiting. Taking 22 years to complete, the shiny white edifice of Birla Mandir pulls in a lot of devotees and it is particularly impressive when lit up at night. Another gift of the Birla family, it is modelled on the Lingaraj Temple at Bhubaneshwar and is covered with carvings both inside and out. No photos are permitted inside.

Botanical Gardens

ⓘ *20 km south from BBD Bagh, 0700-1700, Rs 50, avoid Sun and public holidays when it is very crowded.*

Kolkata's Botanical Gardens, on the west bank of the Hugli, were founded in 1787 by the East India Company. The flourishing 250-year-old banyan tree, with a circumference of over 300 m, is perhaps the largest in the world. The original trunk was destroyed by lightning in 1919 but over 1500 offshoots form an impressive sight. The gardens are peaceful and deserted during the week and make a welcome change from the city. To reach the Botanical Gardens catch a bus from Esplanade; minibuses and CTC buses (No C-12) ply the route.

Around Kolkata

There are several interesting places for a day's outing north of Kolkata. It's best to take a train (buses are slow); avoid peak hours, and keep an eye on your possessions.

Barrackpur and Hugli District → *25 km away.*

The riverside **Gandhi Ghat** has a museum and there is a pleasant garden in memory of Jawaharlal Nehru. The bronze raj statues removed from their pedestals in Central Kolkata after Independence have found their way to the gardens of the bungalow of the former governor (now a hospital) in Barrackpur. The tower was part of the river signalling system.

Many European nations had outposts along the River Hugli. Hugli District has a rich history. When the Mughals lost power, several of the ancient seats of earlier rulers of Bengal became centres of foreign trade. The Portuguese and British settled at Hugli, the Dutch chose Chinsura, the French Chandernagore, the Danes Serampore, the Greeks had an outpost at Rishra, and the Germans and Austrians one at Bhadreswar!

Srirampur (Serampore) → *24 km north of Kolkata.*

Founded by the Danes in 1616 as Fredricnagore, Serampore, a garden city, became a Danish colony in 1755. From the early 19th century it was the centre of missionary activity, until sold to the East India Company in 1845. The Government House, two churches and a Danish cemetery remain. **College of Textile Technology** ⓘ *12 Carey Rd, 1000-1630 (Sat 1000-1300)*. The Baptist missionaries Carey, Marshman and Ward came to Serampore since they were not welcomed by the English administrators in Calcutta. They set up the Baptist Mission Press, which by 1805 was printing in seven Indian languages. **Serampore College** (1818) ⓘ *Mon-Fri 1000-1600, Sat 1000-1300, with permission from the principal*, India's first Christian Theological college, was allowed to award degrees by the Danish king in 1829. The library has rare Sanskrit, Pali and Tibetan manuscripts and the Bible in over 40 Asian languages.

Chandernagore

The former French colony, which dates back to 1673, was one of the tiny pockets of non-British India that did not gain Independence in 1947, but was handed over to India after a referendum in 1950. The churches, convents and cemeteries of the French are still there, although the old French street names have been replaced by Bengali. The former Quai de Dupleix, with its riverfront benches, still has a somewhat Gallic air. The Bhubaneswari and Nandadulal **temples** are worth visiting, especially during **Jagaddhatri Puja**. The **Institute Chandernagore** ⓘ *at the Residency, Mon-Sat except Thu 1600-1830, Sun 1100-1700*, has interesting documents and relics of the French in India. The orange-painted Italian missionary **church** (1726) also stands witness to Chandernagore's European past.

Chinsura and Hugli

The Dutch acquired Chinsura from the Nawab of Murshidabad in 1628 and built the **Fort Gustavus**, but it was exchanged with Sumatra (Indonesia) and became British in 1825. The octagonal **Dutch church** (1678) with its cemetery nearby, a 17th-century Armenian church and three East India Company barracks remain. The Dutch are still remembered at the **Shandesvar Siva Temple** on special occasions, when the lingam is bizarrely decked in Western clothes and a Dutch sword!

The Portuguese set up a factory in Hugli in 1537 but Emperor Shah Jahan took the important trading post in 1632. The East India Company built their factory in 1651, destroyed in skirmishes marking the following six years, but Clive regained Hugli for the Company in 1757.

The **Shi'a Imambara of Hazi Mohammed Mohasin** (1836-1876) has fine marble inlay decoration, a silver pulpit and elaborate lanterns. In **Chota Pandua** nearby, interesting Muslim buildings include the ruins of the 14th-century Bari Masjid that has elements of Buddhist sculpture. In Rajbalhat, the **Amulya Pratnasala Museum** ⓘ *closed 2nd and 4th Tue, Wed 1400-2100*, exhibits sculpture, coins, terracottas and manuscripts.

Bandel

Bandel (Portuguese *bandar* or wharf) is now a railway junction town. The Portuguese built **Bandel Church** to Our Lady of the Rosary around 1660, on the site of an older Augustinian monastery. The keystone of the original church (1599), perhaps the earliest in Bengal, is on the riverside gate. Destroyed in 1640 by Shah Jahan, the church was reinstated 20 years later. The seafaring Portuguese believed that the statue of Our Lady of Happy Voyages in the bell tower could work miracles. Lost in the river, while being carried to save it from Shah Jahan's soldiers, it miraculously reappeared two centuries later. The 18th-century stone and terracotta **Hanseswari Temple** is 4 km away.

Tribeni and Pandua

Originally *Saptagram* (seven villages), **Tribeni** (three rivers) is particularly holy, being at the confluence of the Ganga, Saraswati and Kunti. It has many Hindu temples and 11th- to 12th-century Vaishnavite and Buddhist structures. The remains of the **Mazar of Zafarkhan Ghazi** (1313), the earliest mausoleum in eastern India, shows how black basalt sculpture and columns of earlier Hindu temples and palaces were incorporated into Muslim buildings. **Pandua** (Hugli District) has several remains of the Pala and Sena periods. Shah Sufi-ud-din is thought to have built the 39-m **Victory Tower** after defeating the local Hindu ruler in 1340. Its circular base had a court house. Outside, a staircase spirals up the fluted surface, while inside there is enamelled decoration. Hoards of Kushana and Gupta Dynasty gold coins have been found in nearby **Mahanad**.

Kalna

The town north of Pandua, centred on the **Maharaja of Burdwan's palace**, has several fine 18th-century terracotta temples. Look for the *Ramayana* scenes on the large Lalji (1739), Krishna panels on the Krishnachandra (1752), assorted friezes on the Ananta Vasudeva (1754) and the later Pratapesvara (1849). Across the way is the unusual circular Siva temple (1809) with 108 small double-vaulted shrines. Kalna has trains from Kolkata and rickshaws at the station, 3 km from the temples.

Nabadwip

The birthplace of Sri Chaitanya (see page 100) is a pilgrimage centre for his followers and the river ghats are lined with temples where devotees worship by singing *keertans* and *bhajans*. **International Society for Krishna Consciousness** (**ISKCON**) has a **Chandrodaya Mandir** ⓘ *Mayapu, across the river, until 1300*, and a guesthouse (inexpensive four- to six-bed dorms, a/c rooms and cheap meals). Nabadwip has trains from Sealdah and Haora, and ferries across to Mayapur.

Kolkata listings

Hotel prices

LL over US$200	**L** US$151-200	**AL** US$101-150
A US$66-100	**B** US$46-65	**C** US$31-45
D US$21-30	**E** US$12-20	**F** US$7-11
G under US$7		

Restaurant prices

ᛘᛘᛘ over US$12	ᛘᛘ US$6-12	ᛘ under US$6

Sleeping

Watch out for 10% luxury tax, 10% service charge and 20% expenditure tax. Medium price and budget hotels attracting foreigners are concentrated in the **Sudder St** area. Mid-priced hotels often have a few a/c rooms but may not have a generator and so have power cuts, especially in summer. For telephone number changes T1952 (dial old number to get new). 'Ask Me', T033-2474 6363, advises on local affairs/ numbers/addresses, etc.

Kyd St, home to many of the budget hotels, has changed its name to Dr Md Ishaque Rd.

Central Kolkata *p65, maps p66, p68, p70 and p72*

LL Oberoi Grand, 15 JL Nehru, T033-2249 2323, www.oberoihotels.com. Atmospheric Victorian building opposite the Maidan, exquisitely restored, suites have giant 4-posters, tea lounge, excellent restaurants including Thai, lovely pool for guests.

LL Taj Bengal, 34B Belvedere Rd, Alipore, T033-2223 3939, www.tajhotels.com. Opulent and modern, restaurants are plush, imaginative, intimate, with good food (ground floor Indian cheaper than 5th floor), leisurely service, unusual Bengali breakfast, *Khazana* shop for excellent textiles, *Baluchari* saris, *kantha* embroidery, etc.

LL-L Park, 17 Park St, T033-2249 9000, www.theparkhotels.com. Trendy designer hotel, good restaurants, nightclubs, health club, 24-hr café, service can be disappointing, entrance themed on underground car park.

L Golden Park, 13 Ho Chi Minh Sarani, T033-2288 3939. Boutique hotel, 78 rooms with all facilities including pool and health club, restaurants. 30% discounts often available.

L-AL Astor, 15 Shakespeare Sarani, T033-2282 9957-9, www.astorkolkata.com. In a red-brick colonial building, comfortable a/c rooms with bath tubs, inferior annexe, have not retained original features, although public areas have fared better. The open-air restaurant and small bar are nice places to be, and become the sedate **Plush** lounge-bar at the weekends. Breakfast included, off-season discounts.

AL Lytton, 14 Sudder St, T033-2249 1872, www.lyttonhotelindia.com. Comfortable, tastefully furnished rooms, better in new block, good restaurants, bar, efficient, good value, breakfast included.

A Housez 43, 43 Mirza Ghalib St, T033-2227 6020, housez43@gmail.com. Newish 'value boutique' hotel making a slightly wide-of-the-mark attempt at trendy, nice public areas with beanbags, well-presented rooms, pleasant staff.

A Lindsay, 8-A Lindsay St, T033-2252 2237/8, hotellindsay@com. Recently refurbished hotel towering over Newmarket, mainly for business travellers, Wi-Fi in rooms, good breakfast. **Blue & Beyond** restaurant and the adjacent bar have panoramic city views.

B Fairlawn, 13A Sudder St, T033-2252 1510. 20 a/c old-fashioned rooms (including breakfast and afternoon tea), semi-formal meals at set times aren't the best. The hotel and management provide a throwback to the raj, bric-a-brac everywhere, quite a place and the terrace is great for a beer.

B Kenilworth, 7 Little Russell St, T033-2282 5325. The 'original' Kenilworth provides old-world comforts in enormous colonial rooms with antique furnishings. Bit faded but atmospheric, away from tourist scene, it's a unique and interesting place.

B-C Middleton Inn, 10 Middleton St, T033- 2216 0452, mchamber@vsnl.net. Pleasantly furnished a/c rooms with hot bath (fridge, TV), not particularly spacious though spotlessly clean, original art, quiet and convenient, breakfast included. Recommended.

C Gulshan International, 21B Royd St, T033-2229 0566. Efficient staff, 16 clean, comfortable rooms, complimentary breakfast.

C-D Astoria Hotel, 6 Sudder St, near fire station, T033-2252 2241. Offers 41 rooms of various standards. The top-floor room with a terrace has style.

D Majestic, 4C Madan St, T033-2212 6518/ 7701, majestichotelonline@rediffmail.com. A majestic old building with recently remodelled a/c rooms, veneer furniture, new tiled floors and TVs, but some oversights such as sheets and curtains being too short. A couple of rooms have balconies, try for these. 1st-floor bar can be noisy.

D Super Guest House, 30A Mirza Ghalib St, T033-2252 0995, super_guesthouse@ hotmail.com. This excellent guesthouse has the only truly spotless rooms in the area, a/c with hot bath, friendly management.

D YMCA, 25 Jl Nehru Rd, T033-2249 2192, www.calcuttaymca.org. 17 rooms, some a/c, with bath, in large, rambling colonial building, clean linen, recently renovated but check room first as some are nicer than others. Helpful staff, rates include breakfast.

E Ashreen Guest House, 2 Cowie Lane, T033-2252 0889, ashreen_guesthouse@ yahoo.com. Modern rooms of above-average standard with TV and hot water, a suitable place to break yourself into Kolkata gently, or to put up the parents, though prices are ever escalating. Pickup for late night flights, Rs 400.

E Crystal, 11/1 Dr Md Ishaque Rd (Kyd St), T033-2226 6400, hcrystal@vsnl.net. Decent, clean rooms (mostly a/c), phone and TV, those on top floor are light and airy (and cheaper). Bright tiled corridors lend a more upmarket air. Management willing to negotiate on price.

E-F Afridi Guest House, opposite Ashreen Guest House (see above), calcutta_guest house@yahoo.com. Recently remodelled (shared bathrooms) but many rooms are windowless. Book ahead.

E-F Al-Sana, Futnani Chamber (near Society Cinema), 6A SN Banerjee Rd, T033-2265 6210, hotel_alsana@yahoo.com. Go for one of the refurbished rooms with clean white paint, TV and new furniture, push for a window. It's close to the chaos of Newmarket and out of the backpacker scene. Some rooms have a/c.

E-F Broadway, 27A Ganesh Chandra Av, T033-2236 3930, http://business.vsnl.com/ broadway. Amazingly good-value hotel in a characterful building that hasn't changed much since it opened in 1937. Clean rooms are non-a/c but airy with antique furniture, some with common bath, plus 24-hr checkout. The bar is appealing.

E-F Emirates, 11/1 Dr Md Ishaque Rd (Kyd St), T033-2217 8487. Fresh, bright rooms in a building with character, some a/c, bathrooms are a bit jaded but there's a pleasant terrace.

E-F YWCA, 1 Middleton Row, T033-2229 2494. Old colonial building with good atmosphere, airy verandas and tennis courts. Some rooms with bath (Rs 555) but doubles with shared bath have windows (Rs 305), dorm, all spotless, very friendly staff. Rates include breakfast, alcohol forbidden, a pleasant oasis in the city. A recommended alternative to Sudder St for women travellers.

F Afraa, B/33/H/3 Mirza Ghalib St (Free School St), 3rd floor, T033-2217 7222, manager@hotelafraa.8k.com. Clean, small rooms in this warren are good value at Rs 350 for a double, TV, ask for one with a window. In the same building, the **Milan**, T033-3022 8621, is the same price but slightly better and often full. Brightest of all is the **Paramount**,

T033-2229 4295, which is marginally more expensive.

F Capital Guest House, 11B Chowringhee Lane, T033-2252 0598. Tucked away from the road in a freshly painted old building, Capital is relatively quiet and rooms have TVs, not a place to meet other travellers.

F Galaxy, 3 Stuart Lane, T033-2252 4565. 4 good tiled rooms with attached bath and TV, decent choice but often full of long-stayers. Try at around 1030 just after checkout.

F Sonali Resort, 21A Mirza Ghalib St (Free School St), T033-2252 4741. Set back from the main road, with 13 pokey but clean rooms with bath and TV, roof for drying washing.

F-G Paragon, 2 Stuart Lane, T033-2252 2445. Textbook backpacker haunt with 45 rooms and dorms (Rs 80/100 with shared/private bath), some tiny and prison-like but clean, rooftop rooms are better. Water heater to fill buckets. Open communal spaces, indifferent management.

G Maria, 5/1 Sudder St, T033-2252 0860. 24 clean, basic rooms (hard beds), some with bath, dorm (Rs 70), internet, shared TV, hot water, pleasant staff. Popular budget place with a good atmosphere.

G Modern Lodge, 1 Stuart Lane, T033-2252 4960. Very popular, almost always full with long-term volunteers, 14 rooms, attached or shared bath, breezy rooftop, sinister 'lounge', quirky staff, no reservations so try at 1000.

G Times Guest House, 3 Sudder St, T033-2252 1796. Get a room at the front with balcony to view the action on the street below. Has character, jolly staff.

G Tourist Inn, 4/1 Sudder St, T033-2252 9818. 9 small, clean rooms with common bath, rooftop catches the precious breeze.

South Kolkata *p75, map p66*

LL-L Chrome, 226 AJC Bose, T033-3096 3096, www.chromehotel.in. Space-age hotel opened Jan 2009, with, slick modern rooms, dense with gadgetry, 'adrenalin' showers and trendy colour schemes. 3 categories, The 'Edge' suites being the zennith, but all are supremely comfortable. Good city-scapes from the higher levels. Minimalist Khana Sutra restaurant is North Indian, with huge set lunch/dinner menus as well as à la carte, rooftop bar/club **Pulp** has a pure white Zen theme, and **Nosh** café in the lobby is good for speciality coffee. Swimming pool is planned. Discounts possible, especially for stays of a few days.

LL-L Hindusthan International, 235/1 AJC Bose Rd, T033-2283 0505, www.hindusthan. com. Comfortable quiet rooms on 8 floors are priced right, but staff are distracting with their demands for tips. The food is nothing special although there's an almost cool bar/coffee shop and **Underground** nightclub is popular, pool (non-residents Rs 340).

A Park Palace, Singhi Villa, 49/2 Gariahat Rd, T033-2461 9108-11, www.parkpalace hotel.com. The main draws are the peaceful residential area, **Mirsh Masala** restaurant/bar next door, and the roof terrace with excellent views. Rooms have fitted furniture and are large yet cosy, if twee. Staff delightful. Behind Pantaloons, to the right, off Gariahat Rd.

B Allenby Inn, 1/2 Allenby R, T033-2486 9984, allenbyinn.vsnl.net. Intimate and friendly hotel, rooms vary in size but all have quality (if gawdy) furnishings and large new bathrooms. No balconies, room service available.

C-D 66/2B The Guest House, 66/2B Purna Das Rd, T033-2464 6422/1. On a tree-lined street with some great restaurants a 2-min walk away, this guesthouse is smartly decorated and furnished, with small but decent baths, all rooms have a/c and flatscreen TV. A more relaxing area to stay in. Look for the sign for **Charcoal** restaurant.

D New Haven Guest House, 19B Ritchie Rd, T033 2475 4462. Simply furnished, cleanish rooms with bath, small front garden, only breakfast, residential area with good *dhaba* and Chinese restaurants within 10 mins' walk.

D-F Sharani Lodge, 71/K Hindustan Park, T033-2463 5717, gautam_sharani@ rediffmail.com. In a quiet area, yet close to hectic Rash Behari Av, this well-maintained and well-run lodge is very Indian in ambiance. The a/c rooms are not worth

the money, but non-a/c are a good deal (double Rs 500-600), ones with common bath also share balconies at the front, all have TV.

Other areas
LL-AL Vedic Village, T033-22802071, www.thevedicvillage.com. In Rajarhat, 20 mins from the airport on the eastern edge of the city, but a world away from the rest of Kolkata. The appeal is the clean air and rural surrounds as much as the luxurious rooms, fabulous pool and of course the spa. Top-end villas and suites are stunning while studio rooms are not unreasonable when compared to other Rs 5000 options in the city.

🍴 Eating

Thu is traditionally a 'meatless' day and in smaller places only chicken and fish are available. Licensed restaurants serve alcohol (some are no longer pleasant places to eat in since the emphasis is on drink). Be prepared for a large surcharge for live (or even recorded) music. This, plus taxes, can double the price on the menu. Many restaurants outside hotels do not accept credit cards. Special Bengali sweets are made fresh every afternoon at thousands of sweet shops (1600-1730): try *shingaras*, *kochuris* and *nimkis*.

Central Kolkata *p65, map p66*
🍴🍴 **Chinoiserie**, Taj Bengal (see Sleeping), T033-2223 3939. Good for a splurge on excellent Chinese.

BBD Bagh and around *p65, map p68*
🍴🍴 **Baan Thai**, Oberoi Grand (see Sleeping), T033-2249 2323. Excellent selection, imaginative decor, Thai-style seating on floor.
🍴 **Aaheli**, 12 JL Nehru Rd, T033-2228 0301. Excellent, unusual menu of Bengali specialities, carefully selected from around the state by the chef, comfortable a/c, fairly pricey.

¶¶ **Amber**, 11 Waterloo St, T033-2248 3477. Open 1100-2330, 2 floors of North Indian and continental gourmet delights (best for meat *tandoori*), generous helpings, fast service. **Essence** on 2nd floor fancies itself as a cocktail bar, but alcohol is served in both. There's also a functional bar on the ground floor (strictly no women).

¶¶-¶ **Song Hay**, 3 Waterloo St, T033-2248 0794. This small a/c restaurant is functional with formica tables and efficient staff. Hugely popular and with a huge menu, it attracts a varied clientele (cheap) alcohol served. Highly recommended. Women not permitted in the downstairs bar.

¶ **Anand**, 19 Chittaranjan Av. Closed Wed. Great South Indian. Mammoth *dosas*, all-vegetarian, family atmosphere and warmly decorated. Queues at busy times.

Around Sudder Street *p69, map p70*

¶¶¶ **Zaranj** and **Jong's**, 26 JL Nehru Rd. Adjacent restaurants, both tasteful, stylish, subdued decor, excellent food. Try *pudina paratha*, *murgh makhani*, *tandoori* fish in Zaranj, or delectable Burmese fare in Jong's.

¶¶-¶ **Gupta's**, 53C Mirza Ghalib St, T033-2229 6541. Open 1100-2300 for excellent Indian and Chinese. More intimate and softly lit upstairs, low ceilings (beware of the fans), try fish *tikka peshwari* and *bekti tikka*, alcohol reasonably priced.

¶¶-¶ **Jimmy's**, 14D Lindsay St. Chinese. Small, a/c, good *momos*, Szechuan dishes, ice cream. Alcohol served.

¶ **Blue Sky Café**, 3 Sudder St. Chiefly Western. Very popular travellers' meeting place, a/c, always full and cramped, opinions on the food vary.

¶ **Fresh and Juicy**, Chowringhee Lane, T033-2286 1638. Snug space for a sociable breakfast with some of the best coffee around, reasonably authentic Indian meals, attracts a loyal following. Phone ahead for parcel-order.

¶ **Jo-jo's**, Stuart Lane. Average Indian snacks and meals but superb juices, 1st floor a/c, good escape during summer.

¶ **Khalsa**, 4C Madge Lane, T033-2249 0075. Excellent *lassis*, Western breakfasts, Indian mains, all super-cheap, and beyond excellent service from utterly charming Sikh owners.

¶ **NV Stores**, T033-2252 9661, and Maa Kali, 12/2 Lindsay St. Closed Sun. Stand-up street eateries making surprisingly good sandwiches from any possible combination of ingredients; great *lassis* too.

¶ **Tirupati**, street stall next to **Hotel Maria**. A Sudder St institution; find a perch on the busy benches and enjoy enormous helpings of food from every continent.

¶ **Zurich**, 3 Sudder St. Attempts a café atmosphere, reliable snacks and breakfasts, often full, portions can be a bit niggardly.

Park Street *p71, map p72*

Visitors craving Western fast food will find plenty of familiar names in this area.

¶¶ **Bar-B-Q**, 43 Park St, T033-2229 9916. Always popular, always delicious. 3 sections serving Indian and Chinese food, bar.

¶¶ **Fire and Ice**, Kanak Building, Middleton St, T033-2288 4073, www.fireandicepizza.com. Open 1100-2330. Pizzas here are the real deal, service is excellent, and the ambience relaxing. Decor is very much what you would expect from a pizza-place at home. Definitely worth it.

¶¶ **Flury's**, 18 Park St. Classic Kolkata venue with hit-and-miss Western menu, but pastries and afternoon tea are winners and the bakery has brown bread.

¶¶ **Gangaur**, 2 Russell St. A wide menu of Indian delights, if you can resist the superb Rs 100 (plus tax) *thali* (1130-1530). Afterwards head next door for Bengali sweets.

¶¶ **Mocambo**, 25B Park St. International. A/c, pleasant lighting, highly descriptive menu. Long-standing reliable favourite.

¶¶ **Peter Cat**, 18A Park St (entrance on Middleton Row), T033-2229 8841. Chiefly Indian, with some international dishes. Good kebabs and sizzlers, hilarious menu of cheap cocktails, pleasant ambience but can rush you on busy weekend nights. No booking system, expect to queue outside.

¶¶ **Teej**, 2 Russell St, T033-2217 0730. Pure vegetarian Rajasthani delights washed down with cold beer, colourful *haveli*-esque setting.

¶¶ **Tung Fong**, Mirzah Ghalib St. Quality Chinese food for a reasonable price, the setting spacious and subtly Asian, white linens and Ming vases. Great Manchurian dishes, good fish and chilli garlic paneer, excellent deserts. Super-swift service.

¶¶ **Waldorf**, 13D Russell St, T033-6535 4952. Open 1200-2230. Excellent Chinese and Thai. Extensive menu, speciality fish and prawn dishes in a kitschy but cosy setting with white faux leather seats, fish tanks and other Chinese trinkets.

¶ **Dosas 'n' More**, 43 Park Mansion, Free School St, T(0)9831-425435. Free delivery and takeaways 0630-2230, upstairs restaurant opens at 0800. Sublime South Indian meals (Rs 65/85) have 4 flavours of rice, a wealth of *dosas* (try Mysore), all veg, in new a/c environs. Toilets could be better maintained.

¶ **Hamro Momo**, next to **Momo Plaza** (see below). Open 1300-2100. Cheap and good, in simple eat-and-run surroundings.

¶ **Maya Ram**, 1 Lord Sinha Rd, T033-6515 5837. Open 1100-2300. A good place to try 'snacks' such as *paw bhaji*.

¶ **Momo Plaza**, 2A Suburban Hospital Rd, T033-2287 8260. Open 1200-2200. With black half-tiling and sunflower and lime walls accentuated by kitsch ornaments, this little place could be intentionally bohemian. Highly recommended for plentiful and delicious meals. Try the chilli chicken, fried *momos* and *thukpa*. Staff are silently efficient.

South Kolkata *p75, map p66*

¶¶¶ **Mainland China**, 3A Gurusaday Rd, T033-2283 7964; also at South City Mall, 3rd floor. Sublime Chinese. Unusual offerings, especially fish and seafood, tastefully decorated with burnished ceiling and evocative wall mural, pleasant ambience, courteous. Book ahead.

¶¶¶ **Kewpie's**, 2 Elgin Lane (between Elgin Rd and Heysham Rds), T033-2475 9880. Tue-Sun 1200-1500, 1730-2245. Authentic Bengali,

home cooking at its best, add on special dishes to basic *thali* (Rs 200), unusual fish and vegetarian. Few tables in rooms in a residence, a/c, sells recipe book. Highly recommended, reserve in advance.

¶¶ **Mezze**, Ideal Plaza, 11/1 Sarat Bose Rd, T033-2289 6059. Daily 1200-1530 and 1930-2330. Mainly Mediterranean cuisine, good wine list, Sun brunch buffet (Rs 350) with North Indian and mezze choices, **Soho** bar and club next door.

¶¶-¶ **64 Chowringhee**, Alexandra Court, 64 Chowringhee, T033-2290 1206. Daily 1100-2300. A pleasant multi-cuisine a/c eatery, not too fussy, with especially good fish as well as other non-veg and veg dishes. Recommended.

¶¶-¶ **Tero Parbon**, 49C Purna Das Rd, T033-2463 2016. Daily 1200-2230, but best to go in the evening when a wider choice is available. Experiment with Bengali food in attractive Asian-colonial surrounds, reed blinds, dark wood ceiling fans and bamboo – no doubt inspired by the pricier **Oh Calcutta**. The emphasis is on fish, veg dishes are seasonal.

¶ **Banana Leaf**, 73-75 Rash Behari Av. Vegetarian South Indian, top-notch *dosas* and *thalis* plus superb *mini-iddli* and decent southern-style coffee.

¶ **Bhojohori Manna**, 13 PC Sorcar Sarani (aka Ekdalia Rd); also at JD Park and Salt Lake. Budget prices and a perfect little place to sample pure Bengali cuisine. Ticks on the wall menu indicate availability, try *echor dalna* (jackfruit curry) and *bhekti paturi* (mustard-drenched fish steamed in banana leaves). 2 people can order 4-5 different dishes to share. Decent toilet.

¶ **Bliss**, 53 Hindustan Park, T033-2463 5962. For eating Chinese in a fast-food environment, Bliss is ideal. Portions are generous, the soups delicious, it's tiny but there's seating.

¶ **The Dhaba**, P23 Ashutosh Choudary Av, Ballygunge Phari, T033-2461 5227. Daily 1100-2315. Functional and efficient as the name suggests, Indian and Chinese dishes (veg and non-veg, including liver) are delicious and authentic, many have the option of half-plates so you can sample a few, plus great rolls (including low-fat ones) and the *firni* and *lassis* are particularly fine.

South India Club, off Rash Behari Av. Mon-Sat 0700-1100, 1400-2130, Sun 0700-1200, 1500-2130. An authentic taste of the South in a canteen environment, full meals for Rs 35, and a good place to experiment with less commonly seen dishes such as *pongal* or *upma*. Highly recommended.

Other areas

Connoisseurs of Chinese cuisine go to South Tangra Rd off EM bypass, east of the city centre. The approach is none too picturesque, past tanneries and open drains, but among the maze of lanes (in places lit by lanterns) many eateries are quite swanky.

Beijing, 77/1A Christopher Rd, T033-2328 1001. Try garlic chicken, sweet and sour fish, chop suey, steamed fish, generous portions.

Golden Joy, **Kafulok** and **Sin Fa**, to name but a few, offer excellent soups, jumbo prawns and honey chicken, best to go early (1200 for lunch, 2000 for dinner).

Coffee shops, sweets and snacks

Ashalayam, 44 Mirza Ghalib St. Peaceful oasis run by NGO, sells handicrafts made by street children.

Coffee House, College St (see page 74).

Dolly's Tea Shop, Dakshinapan market, (just after Dhakuria Bridge). The quaintest place in the city for a variety of teas, refreshing iced-teas (try watermelon) and excellent toasties. Tea-chest tables, low basket chairs, indoor and outdoor seating, even the walls are lined with old tea-crates. Anglo-Indian Dolly is a fascinating lady.

Indthalia, 12a Hindustan Park (off Rash Behari Ave), Gariahat, T033-4008 6657. Daily 1000- 2300. Low-key unpretentious coffee shop for proper (cheap) latte and tasty multi-cuisine food. Try the Thai soup or tomato *kofta*.

Confectionary

Kathleen's, several branches, including 12 Mirza Ghalib St, corner of Lord Sinha Rd.

Kookie Jar, Rawdon St. One of the best, though pricey.

Nahoum, Shop F20, New Market, T033-6526 9936. Good pastries, cakes, savouries. The original 1930s till and some fixtures still *in situ*.

Nepal Sweets, 16B Sarat Bose Rd. *Chandrakala*, almond *pista barfi*, mango *roshogolla*, *kheer mohan* (also savouries). Recommended.

Pure Milk Centre, near Rafi Ahmed Kidwai St/Ripon St corner. Good sweet 'curd' (*mishti doi*), usually sold out by lunchtime. Excellent hot *roshogollas*.

Kathi-rolls

Kathi-rolls (tender kebabs wrapped in *parathas*) are hard to beat. Try mutton/chicken egg roll (if you don't want raw onions and green chillis, order *'no piaaz e mirchi'*).

Brothers Snacks, 1 Humayun Pl, Newmarket. Safe, tasty bet with outdoor seats.

Rehmania and **Shiraz Golden Restaurant**, on opposite corners of Park St/AJC Bose Rd crossing. Muslim joints famed for their mutton rolls and kebabs.

Bars and clubs

Kolkata *p64, maps p66, p68, p70, p72*
Bars

The larger hotels have pleasant bars and upmarket restaurants serve alcohol. The top hotels are well stocked, luxurious but pricey. In Sudder St, **Fairlawn's** pleasant garden terrace is popular at dusk attracting anyone seeking a chilled beer. The clientele is quite mixed, fairy lights set the greenery glowing and it's perfect for a first night drink to acclimatize – but beware the below-average food and stiff charges for snacks. **Sunset Bar** in the **Lytton Hotel** nearby is also open to thirsty travellers, and has a not unpleasant pub ambience. **Super Pub Bar**, Sudder St, is always busy and sociable, but expect gruff service and check your change. The 9th floor bar **Blue and Beyond** at the Lindsay Hotel, has great views over New Market and Kolkata and some excellent Indian and Chinese food, plus OK Western dishes for those craving fish and chips. **Sam's Pub**, off Park St, is open later than most (last orders at 2330 on weekend nights) and still permits smoking in a curious indoor gazebo; football and cricket matches are shown on the flatscreen. 'Local' bars, open usually from 1100-2230, often lack atmosphere or have deafening live singing; some are positively men only – there is a seedy choice down **Dacres Lane**, just north of Esplanade. A friendlier place to hear live acts is the **Hotel Embassy Bar**, which accepts females; some vintage elements remain despite the plastic tabletops and veneer walls. Women are also welcome in the **Broadway Bar** at the Broadway Hotel (last orders 2230), where marble floors, polished retro seating, soft lighting, whirring fans and windows open to the street make it one of the best choices in the city. The bar at the **New Empire Cinema**, between New Market and Chowringhee, is pleasant, blue-lit and efficiently staffed. **Oly Pub**, 21 Park St, is an institution: very noisy, serves steak and eggs, no women allowed downstairs. Another classic is **Tripti's**, SP Mukerjee Rd (next to Netaji Bhavan metro), Mon-Sat 1100-2300, Sun 1100-2230. Established in 1935, Tripti's is styled like a canteen, no smoking but still smoke-stained, 1950s flooring and shuttered windows, expect rowdiness and cheap booze. It's on the 1st floor up hidden steps, look for the sign; take a wander round sprawling and atmospheric **Jadu Babu Bazar** to the rear while in the area.

Discos and nightclubs

At hotels: **Incognito** (Taj Bengal), closed Mon, understated, relaxed ambience, 30-plus crowd, good food, taped music, fussy dress codes. **Someplace Else** (Park). Pub, live bands play loud music to the same crowd each week. **Tantra** (Park). Taped music, large floor, young crowd, no shorts or flip-flops, cover charge. Next door **Roxy** is less popular, but has free entry and is more relaxed, with slouchy sofas upstairs. **Underground** (Hindusthan International). Good live band, young crowd, good sizzlers, pool tables. The club beneath **Ginger** restaurant (106 SP Mukerjee Rd, near JD Park metro) accommodates same-sex couples. **Shisha**, 22 Camac St, T033-2281 1313. Dark and stylish with a chilled atmosphere and DJ most nights, but the smoking bans means no more hookahs adding to the atmosphere. **Soho**, Ideal Plaza, 11/1 Sarat Bose Rd. Open until 0230 Fri and Sat (Rs 600 per couple on Sat). Becoming the place to be seen, with a curved bar, funky lighting, a good mix of Western and Hindi tunes and flatscreen TVs showing big sporting events.

Private clubs

Some are affiliated to a number of Indian and foreign clubs including Royal Overseas League, Travellers, St James's, National Liberal, Oxford and Cambridge universities. To use the facilities you need to be a member of these clubs, or the guest of a local member.
Bengal Club, 1/1 Russell St, T033-2226 6954. The former house of Lord Macaulay, has an excellent dining room.
Tollygunge Club, 120 DP Sasmal Rd, T033-2473 2316. Built on an old indigo plantation, 18-hole golf course, riding, tennis, pool, away from centre, atmosphere and location make up for average rooms and restaurant.

● Entertainment

Kolkata *p64, maps p66, p68, p70, p72*
The English-language dailies (*Telegraph*, *Times of India*, etc) carry a comprehensive list. *Cal Calling* is a monthly listings booklet available from **Oxford Book Shop**, Park St or **Sasha**, Mirza Ghalib St, Rs 45.

Cinema

A/c and comfortable cinemas showing English-language films are a good escape from the heat, and many are still very cheap. Check the newspapers for timings, programmes change every Fri. **Elite**, SN Banerjee Rd, and **New Empire Cinema**, New Market St, are conveniently close to Sudder St. **Nandan Complex**, AJC Bose Rd, T033-2223 1210, shows classics and art-house movies; the **Kolkata International Film Festival** is held here in Nov, an excellent event. Swish **Inox** multiplexes (www.inoxmovies.com) are scattered around town (Forum, City Centre); tickets for these are Rs 100-150 and can be booked by credit card over the phone. **Fame cinema**, www.famecinemas.com, Rs 100-250, in South City Mall is open 1000-0100, ticket line T4010-5555.

Dance, music, theatre and art

Regular performances at **Rabindra Sadan**, Cathedral Rd. Kala Mandir, 48 Shakespeare Sarani. **Gorky Sadan**, Gorky Terrace, near Minto Park. **Sisir Mancha**, 1/1 AJC Bose Rd. Some of these also hold art exhibitions as at **Academy of Fine Arts**, Cathedral Rd, and **Ramakrishna Mission**, Gol Park. **Seagull Arts and Media Centre**, 36C SP Mukherjee Rd, T033-2455 6492, www.seagullindia.com, holds regular photography exhibitions. You can see Bengali theatre of a high standard at **Biswaroopa**, 2A Raja Raj Kissen St, and **Star Theatre**, 79/34 Bidhan Sarani.

Performing arts

English-language productions staged by British Council and theatre clubs. **Sangeet Research Academy**, near Tollygunge Metro station, a national centre for training in Indian Classical music, stages free concert on Wed evenings. **Rabindra Bharati University**, 6/4 Dwarakanath Tagore Lane, holds performances, particularly during the winter, including singing, dancing and *jatras*. *Jatra* is community theatre, highly colourful and exaggerated

both in delivery and make-up, drawing for its subject romantic favourites from mythology or more up to date social, political and religious themes.

☺ Festivals and events

Kolkata *p64, maps p66, p68, p70, p72*
Jan Ganga Sagar Mela at Sagardwip, 105 km south of Kolkata, where the River Hugli joins the sea, draws thousands of Hindu pilgrims. See page 129.
Mar/Apr Holi (*Dol Purnima*) spring festival.
Jun-Jul Ratha Yatra at Mahesh, nearby.
Sep-Oct Durga Puja, Bengal's celebration of the goddess during **Dasara**.
Oct-Nov Diwali (*Kali Puja* in Bengal) is the festival of lights.
Dec Christmas. Numerous churches hold special services, including Midnight Mass, and the New Market takes on a new look in Dec as **Barra Din** (Big Day) approaches with temporary stalls selling trees and baubles. Other religious festivals are observed as elsewhere in India.

○ Shopping

Kolkata *p64, maps p66, p68, p70, p72*
Most shops open Mon-Fri 1000-1730 or later (some break for lunch), Sat 1000-1300. New Market stalls, and most other shops, are closed on Sun.

Art

Artists' Circle, 46 Circus Av, T033-2283 3176. Interesting exhibitions by emerging artists.
Centre Art Gallery, 87C Park St. Mainly works by Bengali artists.
Chemould Art Gallery, 12F Park St. One of the big names in contemporary art, and worth keeping an eye on.
CIMA, 2nd floor, Sunny Towers, 43 Ashutosh Chowdhury Av, T033-2485 8717, www.cimaartindia.com. Tue-Sat 1100-1900, closed Sun, Mon 1500-1900. The best

exhibition space in the city and the shop has a good stock in wall-hangings, metalwork, clothes, stoles, ornaments etc.
Galerie 88, 28B Shakespeare Sarani, www.galerie88.in. 1200-2000. Contemporary art.
Studio 21, 17/L Dover Terrace (off Ballygunge Phari), T033-2486 6735, studio21.gallery@gmail.com. A minimalist new space for emerging artists from all disciplines, art/photography exhibitions change regularly. Hard to find in a residential area, best accessed from Dover Lane (take 2nd turning on right then ask). Same opening hours as CIMA, to which the gallery is affiliated.

Books
College St, a wealth of second-hand pavement bookstalls along this street mainly for students but may reveal an interesting first edition for a keen collector (see page 74).
Crossword, Elgin Rd. Deservedly popular chain store, with 2 floors of books, CDs and films and a busy coffee shop.
Kolkata Book Fair, check venue with tourist office. End of Jan for a fortnight, stalls sell paperback fiction to antiquarian books.
Mirza Ghalib St. Has a string of small shops selling new, used and photocopied versions of current favourites. Bargaining required.
Oxford Book Shop, Park St. Huge selection of English titles, postcards and films, nice café upstairs where you can browse through titles. Excellent for books on Kolkata.
Seagull, 31A SP Mukherjee Rd. Amazing stock of art-related coffee-table books.
Starmark, top floor, Emami Centre, 3 Lord Sinha Rd, T033-2282 2617-9; also City Centre and South City Mall. Mon 1200-2030, Tue-Sun 1000-2030. The best selection of fiction in Kolkata, plus imported magazines, films.

Clothes and accessories
Ananda, 13 Russell St. Fancy saris.
Anokhi, Shop 209 Forum Shopping Mall, 10/3 Lala Lajpat Rai Sarani, near AJC Bose Rd. Beautiful block-print bed-linens, floaty bed-wear, scarves, accessories, clothes and more. Made in Jaipur, mid-range prices.

Ballyfabs Jute Shop, 2 Camac St. Daily 1130-1930, Sun 1230-2100. Unique, delightfully decorated bags in jute.
Biba, South City Mall, Prince Anwar Shar Rd, www.bibaindia.com; also has franchises in **Pantaloons** department stores. Chic cotton print dresses, tasteful *salwar*.
Fabindia, 16 Hindustan Park (also branches at Woodburn Park, near AJC Bose Rd, and City Centre Mall in Salt Lake). 1000-2030. Clothes, textiles, toiletries, rugs and home furnishings from fair-trade company. Well worth a visit.
Hotline Services, 7 Sudder St. Traveller wear, plus a range of scarves and wall-hangings.
Monapali, 15 Louden St. Designer *salwar*.
Ogaan, P545 Lake Rd Extension. High-quality clothes including swimwear and lingerie.
Ritu's Boutique, 46A Rafi Ahmed Kidwai Rd. *Kurtas* and saris.
Taj Bengal arcade. For pricey leather goods.

Government emporia
Government emporia are mainly in the town centre and are fixed price shops. Several at **Dakshinapan**, near Dhakuria Bridge, Mon-Fri 1030-1930, Sat 1030-1400, convenient, excellent selection of handloom and handicrafts. **Central Cottage Industries**, 7 JL Nehru Rd. **Kashmir Art**, 12 JL Nehru Rd. **Phulkari**, Punjab Emporium, 26B Camac St. **Rajasthali**, 30E JL Nehru Rd. **Tripura**, 58 JL Nehru Rd. **UP**, 12B Lindsay St.

Handicrafts and handloom
There are many handicraft shops around Newmarket St, selling batik prints, handloom, blockprints and embroidery, but starting prices are usually excessive so bargain hard. Shops listed below are all either fair trade-based or associated with self-help groups.
Ashalayam Handicrafts, 1st floor, 44 Mirza Ghalib St. Products made by street children who have been trained and given shelter by the **Don Bosco Ashalayam Project**. Proceeds are split between the artisans and the trust.
Bengal Home Industries Association, 11 Camac St. Good selection of printed

cotton (bedspreads, saris) and assorted knick-knacks. Relaxed, fixed price.

Calcutta Rescue Handicrafts, Fairlawn Hotel. Thu 1830-2000. Medical NGO sells great selection of cards, bags and trinkets made and embroidered by former patients.

Karma Kutir, 32 Ballygunge Place. Excellent embroidered clothes.

Karmyog, 12B Russell St. Gorgeous handcrafted paper products.

Sasha, 27 Mirza Ghalib St, T033-2252 1586, www.sashaworld.com. Mon-Sat 1000-1900, Sun 1000-0100. Attractive range of good quality, fair trade textiles, furnishings, ceramics, metalwork, etc but not cheap, welcome a/c.

Jewellery

Bepin Behari Ganguly St (Bow Bazar) is lined with mirrored jewellers' shops; **PC Chandra, BB Dutt, B Sirkar** are well known. Also many on Rash Behari Av. **Silver market** (Rupa Bajar) is off Mirza Ghalib St opposite Newmarket. Gold and silver prices are listed daily in the newspapers.

Markets

The **New Market**, Lindsay St, behind the original Hogg Market (largely rebuilt since a fire in 1985 and recently revamped), has more than 2500 shops. It used to be said that you could buy anything from a needle to an elephant (on order) in one of its stalls. Today it's still worth a visit; come early morning to watch it come alive. You will find mundane everyday necessities to exotic luxuries, from fragrant florists to gory meat stalls. Be prepared to deal with pestering basket-wallahs.

For conventional shopping try **Air-Conditioned Market**, Shakespeare Sarani, for imported food and toiletries; **The Forum**, Elgin Rd, has Anoki, Western clothing, cinema and restaurants; plus **City Centre**, Salt Lake, and **Planet M**, on Camac St. The newest to open is **South City Mall**, Prince Anwar Shar Rd, closest metro Rabindra Sarovar, open 1100-2030 for shopping (Body Shop,

Marks and Spencer, huge Spencers supermarket, etc), later for restaurants and cinema. On Free School St, **More** supermarket is convenient and well-stocked, Mon-Fri 0730-2200, weekends 1000-2100.

Kolkata has a number of **bazars**, each with a character of its own. In Bentinck St are Muslim tailors, Chinese shoemakers plus Indian sweetmeat shops and tea stalls. **Gariahat market** early in the morning attracts a diverse clientele (businessmen, academics, cooks) who come to select choice fresh fish. In **Shyambazar** the coconut market lasts from 0500 to 0700. **Burra Bazar** is a hectic wholesale fruit market held daily. The colourful **flower market** is on Jagannath Ghat on the river bank. The old **China Bazar** no longer exists although **Tiretta Bazar** area still retains its ethnic flavour; try an exceptional Chinese breakfast from a street stall.

Music
Music World, 18G Park St, T033-2217 0751. Sells a wide range of all genres.

Tailors
Garments can be skilfully copied around New Market and on Madge Lane. Tailors will try to overcharge foreigners as a matter of course.

▲ Activites and tours

Kolkata *p64, maps p66, p68, p70, p72*
Body and soul
Look out for adverts around Sudder St for informal yoga classes held on hotel rooftops.
Aurobindo Bhavan, 8 Shakespeare Sarani, T033-2282 3057. Informal drop-in classes for men and women (separate classes), 3 times a week. Phone for times.

Cricket
Occasional Test matches and One-Day Internationals at Eden Gardens, see page 69, 100,000 capacity; get tickets in advance.

Football

The season starts in May and continues through the monsoons. The club grounds are on the Maidan (try **East Bengal Football Club**, T033-2248 4642).

Golf

Royal Calcutta Golf Club, 18 Golf Club Rd, T033-2473 1352, founded in 1829, the oldest golf club in the world outside the UK. It moved to its present course in 1910 having taken the radical step of admitting women in 1886.

The Tollygunge Club, 120 Despran Sasmal Rd, T033-2473 5954. The course is on land that was once an indigo plantation.

Horse racing

Royal Calcutta Turf Club, T033-2229 1104. Racing takes place in the cool season (Nov to early Apr) and monsoon (Jul-Sep); tote, bookmakers available. The Derby is in the first week of Jan. The history of racing goes back to the time of Warren Hastings and the 1820s grandstand is especially handsome. It's a fun, cheap day out in the public stands, better still if you can access the members enclosure to get up close to the racehorses and enjoy a drink in the bar with antlers mounted on the wall.

Sightseeing tours

WBTDC tours, departure point is Tourism Centre, 3/2 BBD Bagh E, 1st floor, T033-2248 8271. Daily tours, 0830-1730, Rs 150 in non a/c bus, Rs 200 in a car for 4-5 passengers. Tour stops at: Eden Gardens, High Court, Writers' Building, Belur Math, Dakshineswar Kali Temple, Jain Temple, Netaji Bhavan, Kolkata Panorama and Esplanade, Victoria Memorial, St Paul's Cathedral and Kali Ghat. Entry fees not included. Private tour operators also offer city tours. Approved guides from **Govt of India Tourist Office**, T033-2582 5813.

Swimming

The **Hindustan International Hotel** pool is open to non-residents (Rs 300).

Tour operators

Best deals in air tickets to/from the East (through Bangkok) are offered by agents in the Sudder St area (about US$120).

Help Tourism, Sadananda Kothi (1st floor), 67A Kali Temple Rd, Kalighat, T033-2455 0917, www.helptourism.com. Wide variety of wildlife and adventure tours in Assam, Arunachal and North Bengal, with strong eco credentials and involvement of local communities. Recommended.

American Express, 21 Old Court House St, T033-2248 9491. **Mercury**, 43 JL Nehru Rd, T033-2288 3557/59. **Thomas Cook**, 19B Shakespeare Sarani, T033-2282 6719. **Travel Planners**, 7 Red Cross Pl, T033-2243 5138. Recommended.

Volunteer work

Many people come to Kolkata to work with one of the NGOs. The following organizations happily accept volunteers, though it's wise to contact them in advance.

Don Bosco Ashalayam Project, T033-2643 5037, www.ashalayam.org. Rehabilitates young homeless people by teaching skills.

Missionaries of Charity (Mother Teresa), The Mother House, 54A AJC Bose Rd, T033-2249 7115. The majority of volunteers work at one of the Mother Teresa homes. Induction/registration sessions are at 1500 on Mon, Wed and Fri in various languages.

⊖ Transport

Kolkata p64, maps p66, p68, p70, p72
Kolkata is at the eastern end of the Grand Trunk Rd (NH2). Many city centre roads become one way or change direction from 1400 to 2100 so expect tortuous detours.

Air

Enquiries T033-2511 8787. The spacious terminals are well organized if not state-of-the-art. There is adequate seating in the departure lounge as well as a few shops, drink dispenser and clean toilets.

A Reservation counter for rail (same-day travel only) and one for hotels are in the Arrivals hall. There are money changers at the exit of the International terminal.

For transport to town, pre-paid taxis (office closes at 2200) to the city centre cost about Rs 250 (de luxe cars, Rs 500-650). From the city centre to the airport costs the same or less if you bargain. The public bus is not recommended for arrival as it's a 400-m walk across the car park and under the flyover to the road. The nearest Metro station is at Dum Dum (Rs 6 to city centre); auto-rickshaws to the Metro cost about Rs 60. Transit passengers with onward flights may use the Airport Rest Rooms (some a/c, doubles, dorm, all good value).

Domestic For schedules and prices it's best to visit a 3rd-party booking site such as www.yatra.com or www.makemytrip.com. Airlines include: **Air India**, 50 Chowringhee Rd, T033-2282 2356, airport T033-2248 2354. **Jet Airways**, 18D Park St, T033-3989 3333, airport T033-2511 9894. **Indigo**, T033-4003 6208, www.go indigo.com; **Kingfisher**, T1800-180 0101, www.flykingfisher.com; and **Spicejet**, T1800-180 3333, www.spicejet.com.

International For international flights, see page 21. Airlines include: **Biman Bangladesh**, airport, T033-2511 8772. **Cathay Pacific**, 1 Middleton St, T033-2288 4312. **Druk Air**, 51 Tivoli Court, 1A Ballygunge Circular Rd T033- 2240 2419. **Emirates**, Trinity Tower, 83 Topsia Rd Sth, T033-4009 9555. **Gulf Air**, 230A AJC Bose Rd, T033-4006 3741, airport T033-2511 1612. **KLM**, 1 Middleton St, T033-2283 0151. **Kuwait Airways**, 230A AJC Bose Rd, T033- 2240 3575. **Lufthansa**, Tower 2, 8A, Millennium City, DN62, Sec V, Salt Lake, T033-4002 4200. **Singapore Airlines**, Tower 2, 9A, Millennium City, DN-62, Sector V, Salt Lake, T033 2367 5417. **Thai Airways**, 229 AJC Bose Rd, 8th floor, T033-2283 8865.

Bicycle
Bike hire is not easy; ask at your hotel if a staff bike is free. Spares are sold along Bentinck St, north of Chowringhee.

Bus
Local State transport services run throughout the city and suburbs from 0500-2030; usually overcrowded after 0830, but very cheap (minimum Rs 4 on big blue buses) and a good way to get around. Maroon minibuses (little more expensive, minimum Rs 5) cover major routes. South Bengal minibuses are bigger and will often stop on request.

Long distance An extensive hub and spoke bus operation from Kolkata allows cheap travel within West Bengal and beyond, but long bus journeys in this region are gruelling as roads are generally terrible, and are a last resort when trains are full. The tourist office, 3/2 BBD Bagh, has timetables. Advance bookings at computerized office of **Kolkata State Transport Corp (STC)**, Esplanade, T033-2248 1916. **Kolkata STC**: to **Balurghat**; **Digha**; **Farakka**; **Mayapur**; **Jalpaiguri**; **Cooch Behar**; **Malda**; **Siliguri**; 12 hrs; **Bankura**; **Bishnupur**; and **Purulia**. More comfortable a/c buses to Siliguri depart from Esplanade, Rs 550-700. **Orissa & Bihar STC**, Babu Ghat: to **Bokaro**; **Dhaka**, **Gaya**, **Puri**, 11 hrs. **Bhutan Govt**, **Phuntsholing** via Siliguri, 1900, 16 hrs.

To Bangladesh Private buses to **Dhaka**) can be booked from numerous agencies on Marquis St, from where they also depart.

Ferry
Local To cross the Hugli, between Haora station and Babu Ghat, Rs 4, except Sun. During festivals a ferry goes from Babu Ghat to Belur Math, 1 hr.

Long distance Shipping Corp of India, 1st floor, 13 Strand Rd (enter from Hare St), T033-2248 4921 (recorded information T033-2248 5420), 1000-1300 (for tickets), 1400-1745 (information only), operates a steamer to **Port Blair** in the Andamans. Some 3 or 4 sailings a month (66 hrs), Rs 1961 to Rs 7631 one way. For tickets go 4 days in advance, and be there by 0830; huge queue for 'bunk class'. See page 301.

Metro

The Metro is usually clean, efficient and punctual. The 16.5-km route from Dum Dum to Tollygunge runs 0700-2145, Sun 1400-2145, every 7-15 mins; fare Rs 4-8. Note that trains are sometimes longer than the platforms. There are women-only sections interspersed throughout the train.

Rickshaw

Hand-pulled rickshaws are used by the local people especially along the narrow congested lanes. Auto-rickshaws operate outside the city centre, especially as shuttle service to/from Metro stations along set routes. Auto-rickshaws from Sealdah station to Sudder St cost about Rs 60.

Taxi

Car hire with driver: **Everett**, 4 Government Pl North, T033-2248 7038; **Gainwell**, 8 Ho Chi Minh Sarani, T033-2454 5010; **Mercury**, 46 JL Nehru Rd, T033-2248 8377. Tourist taxis from **India Tourism** and WBTDC offices. Local taxis are yellow. Ambassadors: insist on the meter, then use conversion chart to calculate correct fare.

Train

Kolkata is served by 2 railway stations, **Haora** (Howrah is still used on timetables) and **Sealdah**. Haora station has a separate complex for platforms 18-21. Enquiries, Haora, T033-2638 7412/3542, 'New' Complex, T033-2660 2217, Sealdah, T033-2350 3535. Reservation, T138 (computerized). Foreign tourist quota is sold at both stations until 1400, at which point tickets go on general sale. Railway reservations, 6 Fairlie Place, BBD Bagh; 0800-1300, 1330-2000, Sun 0800-1400 (best to go early). At Fairlie Place, tourists are automatically told to go to the Foreign Tourist Counter to get Foreign Tourist Quota. It usually takes at least 30 mins. You will need to show your passport and an encashment or ATM receipt as well as the completed form. You can pay in US dollars, sterling or euros, but expect a poor exchange rate.

Trains listed depart from Haora (**H**), unless marked '(**S**)' for Sealdah (timings change every Apr and Oct). To **Allahabad**: see New Delhi. **Agra Fort**: *Jodhpur Exp 2307*, 2330, 20 hrs. **Bhubaneswar**: *Dhauli Exp 2821*, 0600, 7 hrs; *Falaknuma Exp 2703*, 0725, 6½ hrs; *Howrah Puri Exp 2837*, 2335, 7 hrs. **Chennai**: *Coromandel Exp 2841*, 1450, 26½ hrs; *Howrah Chennai Mail 2839*, 2345, 28 hrs. **Mumbai** (**CST**): *Gitanjali Exp 2860*, 1400, 31½ hrs (via **Nagpur**, 17½ hrs); *Howrah Mumbai Mail 2810*, 2015, 33 hrs (via **Nagpur**, 18 hrs); *Howrah Mumbai Mail 2321*, 2200, 37½ hrs (via **Gaya**, 7½ hrs). **Mumbai** (**Lokmanya Tilak**): *Jnaneswari SD Exp 2102*, 2255 (Mon, Wed, Thu, Sun), 31 hrs (via **Nagpur**, 17½ hrs). **Nagpur**: See Mumbai trains plus *Howrah Ahmedabad Exp 2834*, 2355, 19 hrs. **New Delhi** via **Gaya** and **Allahabad**: *Rajdhani Exp 2301*, 1645 (except Sun), 17 hrs; *Rajdhani Exp 2305*, 1405 (Sun), 20 hrs, via **Patna**; (**S**) *Rajdhani Exp 2313*, 1640 (daily), 18 hrs. **New Jalpaiguri** (**NJP**): (**S**) *Kanchenjunga Exp 5657*, 0645, 11½ hrs; (**S**) *Darjeeling Mail 2343*, 2205, 10 hrs; *Kamrup Exp 5959*, 1735, 12½ hrs. **Puri**: *Jagannath Exp 8409*, 1900, 9½ hrs; *Howrah Puri Exp 2837*, 2235, 9 hrs. **Ranchi**: *Howrah Hatia Exp 8615*, 2220, 9 hrs; *Howrah Shatabdi Exp 2019*, 0605 (except Sun), 7 hrs.

To Bangladesh It is now possible to travel direct to **Dhaka** on the newly revived *Moitree Express*, Sat and Sun 0710, from **Kolkata** (**Chitpur**) Terminal, 13 hrs, stops only at the border for customs and immigration.

Tram

Kolkata is the only Indian city to run a tram network. 0430-2300. 2nd-class carriage Rs 3.50-4, front '1st class' Rs 4-4.50, but no discernible difference. Many trams originate at **Esplanade depot** and it's a great way to see the city – ride route 1 to Belgachia through the heart of North Kolkata's heritage, or Route 26 from the **Gariahat** depot in the south all the way to Howrah, via Sealdah and College St.

● Directory

Kolkata *p64, maps p66, p68, p70, p72*
Banks There are 24-hr ATMs all over the
city centre. Money changers proliferate on
Sudder St. **Thomas Cook**, 4/A ground floor,
Park Mansions, Park St. **Cultural centres
and libraries** British Council Information
Centre, L&T Chambers, 16 Camac St,
T033-2282 5370. Good for UK newspapers,
reference books. Mon-Sat 1100-1900. **French
Association**, 217 AJC Bose Rd, T033-2281
5198. **Goethe Institut**, Max Mueller Bhavan,
8 Pramathesh Barua Sarani, T033-2486
6398, www.goethe.de/kolkata. Mon-Fri
0930-1730, Sat 1500-1700. **Embassies and
consulates** Bangladesh, 9 Bangabandhu,
Sheikh Mujib Sarani, T033-2290 5208/9,
www.bdhckolkata.org. **Germany**, 1 Hastings
Park Rd, T033-2479 1141-2, www.kalkutta.
diplo.de. **Myanmar**, 4th floor, Block D, White
House, 119 Park St, T033-2217 8273. **Nepal**,
1 National Library Av, T033-2456 1224,
nepalconsulate@dataone.in. **Netherlands**,
5 Rameshwar Shaw Rd, T033-2289 7020,
consulkolkata.netherlands@gmail.com.
Norway, 5B, Roudon St, T033-2287 9769.
Spain, 1 Taratolla Rd, T033-2469 5954.

Sri Lanka, 302A Centre Point, 28/2
Shakespeare Sarani, T9831-257401. **Thailand**,
18B Mandeville Gardens, T033-2440 7836,
rtcgkkt@eth.net. **UK**, 1A Ho-Chi-Minh Sarani,
T033-2288 5172-6, http://ukinindia.fco.gov.uk.
USA, 5/1 Ho-Chi-Minh Sarani, T033-3984
2400. **Internet** Many across the city; several
in Sudder St area. Standard charge is Rs 15
per hr. **Medical services** Apollo
Gleneagles Hospital, 5B Canel Circular Rd,
T033-2320 3040. **Wockhardt Medical
Centre**, 2/7 Sarat Bose Rd, T033-2475 4320,
www.wockhard hospitals.net, reliable
diagnostic centre. **Woodlands Hospital**,
8B Alipore Rd, T033-2456 7076-9. There
are many chemists around Lindsay St and
Newmarket. **Angel**, 151 Park St (24-hr).
Dey's, 6/2B Lindsay St. **Moonlight**, 180 SP
Mukherjee Rd (24-hr). **Post** Poste Restante
at GPO, 0800-2000, closed Sun and holidays.
Speed Post At major post offices including
airport and Park St. Book-post and packaging
is convenient at Free School Post Office,
Mon-Sat 1000-1730; parcel stitching service
Mon-Fri 1000-1500, Sat 1000-1400. **DHL &
Blue Dart**, Kanak Building, Middleton St,
24-hr counter T033-2288 1919.

Contents

Footprint features

West Bengal

At a glance

◉ **Getting around** Bagdogra airport for quick access to the hills. Or trains link Kolkata to Siliguri, which has jeeps to Darjeeling and Kalimpong. Never take a long-distance bus unless you have to.

◉ **Time required** A week for a good taste of both lowlands and highlands, plus a week for a trek around Darjeeling.

☼ **Weather** Getting very hot and sticky by Apr, though the hills remain cool and inviting.

✖ **When not to go** In the monsoon months, unless you crave the sight of rain.

★Don't miss ...
1 A peaceful weekend at Murshidabad, page 98.
2 A visit to a tea estate in Darjeeling and trekking in the spring, page 106.
3 Wednesday and Saturday market in Kalimpong, page 114.
4 Sunderbans Tiger Reserve, page 129.

This cultured corner of the sub-continent has added immeasurably to India's overall identity. The heritage of the great Hindu saint Ramakrishna, a rich literary tradition presided over by the ghost of Rabindranath Tagore and a wealth of unique festivals, not to mention the region's ingrained leftist leanings, all unite to make the most densely populated Indian state deliciously vibrant.

Travelling north takes you through a land that has been left wonderfully fertile by the ever-shifting River Gangas and run-off from the Himalaya. Intensely populated and cultivated, the area contains such treasures as the terracotta temples at Bishnupur, and Santiniketan, the placid rural oasis in which Tagore established his artistic university. Historic palaces and spectacular mosques crumble against a backdrop of village life in Murshidabad, the delightful former capital of the Nawabs of Bengal. Luminescent expanses of green paddies and clusters of banana trees trace the river north towards the Himalayan foothills, via the Sultanate monuments at Gaur and Pandua, and east to the one-horned rhinos in Jaldapara Park.

Synonymous with tea the world over, Darjeeling has always been a holiday destination, particularly during the summer months when the cool mountain air provides relief from the heat of the plains. With large Tibetan and Nepali populations, the hill stations have a very different feel: monasteries, prayer flags and steamed dumplings give a taste of the land and peoples that lie deeper in the Himalaya.

South of Kolkata, the sultry Sunderbans, a World Heritage Site, comprise 54 mangroved islands interwoven by streams, home to a large Bengal tiger population. Also in the south is Digha, which offers a surprisingly relaxing beach break on the Bay of Bengal, just a few hours away from Kolkata.

North of Kolkata

The plains north of Kolkata are home to the peaceful university town of Santiniketan, home of Tagore, and the 300-year-old terracotta temples of Bishnupur. The legacy of the Muslim nawabs lives on in the impressive ruins of Gaur and Pandua, while atmospheric Murshidabad provides an accessible blend of Bengali history and relaxation. ▸▸ *For listings, see pages 101-104.*

Bishnupur → *For listings, see pages 101-104. Colour map 2, C1.*

The warrior Malla Kings of Bengal ruled this area from Bishnupur for nearly two centuries, until the East India Company sold it to the Maharajah of Burdwan in 1805, for arrears of land revenue. The Mallas were great patrons of the arts and built uniquely ornamental terracotta temples. It is also where the Dhrupad style of classical Indian singing originated, and the legendary Bishnupur Gharana (School of Music) still resonates from this ancient past. Local handicrafts include silk, tassar, conch-shell and bell-metalware and the famous terracotta Bankura horse, Dokhra, and also slate statues and artefacts. Bengali sweetmeats and flavoured tobacco are local specialities.

Ins and outs → *Phone code: 03244. Population: 61,900.*

Getting there Buses from Kolkata and Durgapur drop passengers on the edge of town. The train station is 3 km out of town, from where a cycle-rickshaw to the Tourist Lodge costs Rs 20.

Getting around   The town is haphazardly clustered around the Pokabandh Lake; most visitors stay on College Road. It is possible to see all the temples listed by foot (and much more besides), but very easy to get lost in the intricate network of streets. Cycle rickshaws can be hired for Rs 100-150 for two hours.

Sights

There are more than two dozen temples in Bishnupur, mostly dedicated to Krishna and Radha. They are usually built of brick, but sometimes of laterite, and on a square plan with a gently curved roof imitating the Bengali thatched *chala* (hut). The terracotta tiles depict episodes from the *Ramayana* and *Mahabharata*, and also scenes from daily life. Inside, there is a *thakurbari* (sanctuary) and a *vedi* (platform) for the image, on one side. The upper storey has a gallery joined by one, five or even nine towers.

Most of the temples are concentrated within the fort, which was built later by Muslim rulers. Distances given are from the **Tourist Lodge**. The **Rasmancha** (500 m) is a unique Vishnu shrine with a pyramidal roof, built by Bir Hambir in 1600. It is illuminated at night by coloured floodlights. The well-preserved cannons, in particular the 4-m-long **Dalmadal** to the south of the Rasmancha, date back to the Mallas. Further south is **Jor Mandir** (1 km), a pair of hut-shaped temples with a single *sikhara* flanking a smaller diminutive temple with attractively ornamented panels, built in 1726 by Gopala Singha. The **Shyam Rai Temple** (1 km), perhaps the earliest example of the *pancharatna* (five towers), has a fine *sikhara* and dates from 1643. Each façade is triple arched and the terracotta panels show scenes from the *Ramayana*, the *Mahabharata* and Krishna's life. The large **Madan Mohan Temple** (3 km), with a white façade, was built of brick with terracotta panels in 1694 by King Durjan, while the 17th-century **Lalji** and **Madan Gopal** are built of laterite. The **Mrinmoyee Mandir** (3 km) has a clay idol of Durga dating from

AD 997, and in the courtyard a curiosity of nine trees growing together. Little remains of the Malla Kings' **Fort** (2.5 km). You can see the gate of laterite, with firing holes drilled in different directions and a 13th-century stone chariot. The water reservoirs are still there though the moat, once served by seven lakes, is partly dry.

Santiniketan → *For listings, see pages 101-104. Colour map 2, C1.*

Santiniketan, the 'Abode of Peace', is a welcome change from the hectic traffic, noise and dirt of Kolkata. Even a brief visit to the shady university campus, with its artistic heritage and its quiet, rural charm, makes a profound impression on most visitors, and is a must for aficionados of Bengal's greatest poet.

Ins and outs → *Phone code: 03463. Population: 65,700.*

Getting there The nearest railway station is Bolpur, which has trains from Kolkata's Haora and Sealdah stations. Cycle-rickshaws charge Rs 15-20 to Santiniketan, 3 km away. Local buses use a stand near the station. The road journey from Kolkata on the congested NH2 (213 km) can be very slow.

Getting around The Visva Bharati campus and Santiniketan's residential area are ideal for exploring on foot. The temples can be very difficult to find on foot in the maze of narrow streets. It is best to arrange a cycle-rickshaw for a tour, Rs 50 for 2½ hours.

Tourist information **Public Relations Office (PRO)** ⓘ *Vishva Bharati Office, T03463-252751, Thu-Tue 1000-1700.*

Santiniketan

Eating Ⓨ
Camelia Resort **1**

← Ramkinkar Sculptures

Sights

Vishva Bharati University ⓘ *closed Wed and Tue afternoon, sightseeing is permitted only after university hours: summer 1430-1700, winter 1415-1630 and during holidays 0700-1200, Rs 5, no photography, all compounds are subdivided by wire fences*, has an interesting history. The Maharishi Debendranath Tagore, father of Rabindranath Tagore, the Nobel Laureate, started an *ashram*, later named Santiniketan. In 1901 Rabindranath started an experimental place of learning with a classroom under the trees, and a group of five pupils. It went on to become the Vishva Bharati University in 1921. It now attracts students from all over the world and aspires to be a spiritual meeting ground in a serene, culturally rich and artistic environment. Open-air classes are still a feature of this unique university. Among the many *Bhavans* are those concentrating on fine art (Kala Bhavan) and music and dance (Sangit Bhavan). The **Uttarayan Complex** where the poet lived consists of several buildings in distinctive architectural styles. **Sadhana Prayer Hall**, where Brahmo prayers are held on Wednesday, was founded in 1863, see page 344. The unusual hall enclosed by stained-glass panels has a polished marble floor which is usually decorated with fresh *alpana* designs. **Chhatimtala**, where Maharishi Debendranath sat and meditated, is the site of special prayers at Convocation time. In keeping with its simplicity, graduates are presented with a twig with five leaves from the locally widespread *Saptaparni* trees.

Rabindra Bhavan ⓘ *Uttarayan complex, Thu-Mon 1030-1330 and 1400-1630, Tue 1030- 1330, no photography, bags may not be permitted, shoes must be removed before entering each building*, is a museum and research centre containing photographs, manuscripts and Tagore's personal belongings; the peripheral buildings also contain photos. The museum is well documented and very informative so allow at least an hour. The garden is delightful, particularly when the roses are blooming. **Kala Bhavan** ⓘ *Thu-Mon 1500-1700*, has a rich collection of 20th-century Indian art, particularly sculptures, murals and paintings by famous Bengali artists. **Nandan Museum** ⓘ *Thu-Mon 1000-1330 and 1400-1700, Tue 1000- 1330*, has a collection of terracotta, paintings and original tracings of Ajanta murals.

Surul (4 km), with its evocative village atmosphere and small terracotta temples with interesting panels on their façades, makes a pleasant trip. The *zamindari* 'Rajbari' with its durga shrine gives an impression of times past.

Ballavpur Deer Park (3 km) ⓘ *Thu-Tue 1000-1600*, is a reclaimed wooded area of rapidly eroding laterite *khowai* with spotted deer and winter migratory birds.

Around Santiniketan

Bakresvar, 58 km northwest of Santiniketan, is known for its medicinal sulphurous hot springs (separate bathing areas for men and women, though you may not fancy the tepid pools full of people doing laundry). There are seven major *kunds* (springs) from 36°C to 67°C, the hottest being Agnikunda (fire spring). Temples to Siva, Sakti, Kali and Vishnu make it a Hindu pilgrimage centre. The temples are modern and white tiled though the Kali temple is old and painted red. Allow five hours for the trip.

Murshidabad → *For listings, see pages 101-104. Colour map 2, B1. Phone code 03482. Population: 36,900.*

Named after Nawab Murshid Kuli Khan, a Diwan under Emperor Aurangzeb, Murshidabad became the capital of Bengal in 1705 and remained so up to the time of the battle of

Plassey. The town lies on the east bank of the Bhagirathi, a picturesque tributary of the Ganga, with imposing ruins scattered around and an enchanting time warp feel. A vibrant vegetable bazar takes place each morning beneath decaying columns left over from the days of the *nawabs*, and the town comes to life for the famed Muslim festival of **Muhurram** at the end of January. Come during the week to avoid the crowds.

Nizamat Kila on the river bank was the site of the old fort and encloses the Nawabs' Italianate **Hazarduari** ('1000 doors') **Palace** ⓘ *Sat-Thu 1000-1500, Rs 100, no photography*, built in 1837. It is now a splendid museum with a portrait gallery, library and circular durbar hall and contains a rare collection of old arms, curios, china and paintings. The large newer **Imambara** (1847) opposite, also Italianate in style, is under a continuous process of renovation and is worth exploring. The domed, square **Madina** (pavillion) with a veranda that stands nearby may be what remains of the original Imambara. There are numerous 18th-century monuments in the city which are best visited by cycle-rickshaw ⓘ *Rs 100 for 3 hrs*. Mir Jafar and his son Miran lived at **Jafaragunj Deorhi**, known as the traitor's gate. **Kat-gola** ⓘ *Rs 50*, the atmospheric garden palace of a rich Jain merchant, houses a collection of curios including Belgian glass mirror-balls and has an old Jain temple and boating 'lake' in the grounds. The **Palace of Jagat Sett**, one of the richest financiers of the 18th century, is 2 km from the Jafargung Cemetery to the north of the palace. The brick ruins of **Katra Masjid** (1723), modelled on the great mosque at Mecca and an important centre of learning, are outside the city to the east. It was built by Murshid Kuli Khan who lies buried under the staircase. **Moti Jheel** (Pearl Lake) and the ruins of **Begum Ghaseti's Palace** are 2 km south of the city. Only a mosque and a room remain. **Khosbagh** (Garden of Delight) ⓘ *across the river, easily accessible by bamboo ferries, Rs 1, 24-hr*, has three walled enclosures. It is recommended to hire a boat (Rs 200 from **Hotel Manjusha**) to journey upstream to Baranagar, three well-preserved terracotta temples in the Bangla style; drift back down and stop off at the Jain town of **Azimganj**.

Malda → *For listings, see pages 101-104. Colour map 2, B1. Phone code: 03512.*

Malda is a convenient and comfortable base from which to visit the atmospheric ruins of Gaur and Pandua, with plenty of banks and other amenities in the town centre. Now famous mainly for its large juicy Fajli mangoes, Malda was established around 1680 by the English, who bought an entire village from a local landlord and built it into a market town. **Malda Museum** (1937) has a collection of stone images, coins and inscriptions from Gaur and Pandua. The **market** behind the **Tourist Lodge** is fascinating. Old Malda, which lies at a confluence of rivers 4 km away, has the **Jami Masjid**, built in 1596 out of decorated brick and stone with some good carving on the entrance pillars. The 17-m **Nimasarai Tower** across the river dates from the same period, and has strange stones embedded on the outer surface, which may once have been used to display beheaded criminals.

Gaur and Pandua → *Colour map 2, B1.*

Gaur's situation on the banks of the River Ganga, yet within easy reach of the Rajmahal Hills with their fine black basalt, made it possible for gifted stonemasons to construct beautiful religious and secular buildings. Muslim monuments of the sultanate period are strewn around the quiet, deserted city. Pandua alternated with Gaur as a capital of Bengal between 1338 and 1500, when it was abandoned. Some of the ruins here show clearly how the Muslims made free use of material from Hindu temples near Malda.

Gaur

On the ancient site of Lakshanavati, Gaur was the capital of King Sasanka in the seventh century, followed by the Buddhist Pala kings. The city became famous as a centre of education and culture during the reign of the Hindu Sena kings in the 12th century. In the early 13th century it was invaded by Bhaktiar Khalji and then captured by the Afghan Fakhr-ud-din Dynasty in the 14th century. They plundered the temples to construct their own mosques and tombs. Gaur was sacked by Sher Shah Suri in 1537 and the city's population was wiped out by plague in 1575.

The remains of the embankments of the fort are to the south on the bank of the Bhagirati. The great golden mosque, **Bari Sona Masjid** or Baroduari (12-door), was built in 1526 and is an enormous rectangular stone-faced brick structure with a large open square in front. Fine marble carving is still visible on the remains of the minarets. Note the small Kali temple at the entrance.

Bangladesh can be seen from the **Dakhil Darwaza** (early 15th century), the main fort gateway with its five-storeyed towers. It was built of small red bricks embossed with terracotta decorations. The turrets and circular bastions produce a striking contrast of light and shade with decorative motifs of suns, rosettes, lamps and fretted borders. During the 15th century, a number of mosques and mausoleums were built in the new architectural style.

The **Firuz Minar** (Victory Tower), built by Sultan Firuz Shah in 1486, has a spiral staircase. The lower storeys are 12 sided while the upper are circular, with striking blue and white glazed tiles, used in addition to the terracotta and brick. The builders of the **Chika Mosque** ('Bat Mosque', early 15th century), near the Kadam Rasul, made free use of Hindu idols in its construction. The **Chamkati Mosque** (circa 1475) shows the vaulted ceiling of the veranda. Inside the southeast corner of the fort is the massive **Baisgazi Wall**, which enclosed the Old Palace with its *darbar*, harem, etc. **Kadam Rasul** (1513) is a domed building with a Bengali *chala* roof, which housed the relic of the Prophet, a footprint in stone. The two-storeyed **Lukochuri Darwaza** (Hide-and-Seek Gate, circa 1655) is in the later Mughal style.

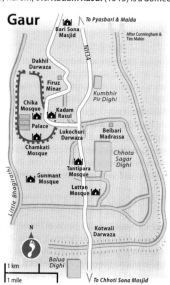

Gaur To Pyasbari & Malda · After Cunningham & Tim Makin · NH34 · Bari Sona Masjid · Dakhil Darwaza · Firuz Minar · Kumbhir Pir Dighi · Chika Mosque · Kadam Rasul · Palace · Lukochuri Darwaza · Belbari Madrassa · Chamkati Mosque · Chhota Sagar Dighi · *Little Bhagirathi* · Gunmant Mosque · Tantipara Mosque · Lattan Mosque · N · Kotwali Darwaza · 1 km / 1 mile · Balua Dighi · To Chhoti Sona Masjid

The **Tantipara Mosque** (circa 1475; *tanti*, weaver) has superbly decorated red brick with octagonal turrets and five entrance arches. The elegant **Lattan** (Painted) **Mosque** (1475), attributed to Yusuf Shah, was decorated with bands of blue, green, yellow and white glazed tiles. Some 2 km south, close to the Bangladeshi border, is the ruined **Chhoti Sona Masjid**, has a carved gate.

Ramkeli, not far from the Bari Sona Masjid, has the Madan Mohan Jiu Mandir and is of religious significance for followers of **Sri Chaitanya**, the 14th-century Bengali religious reformer. **Tamaltola** marks where he meditated under a tree and pilgrims come to see a footprint in stone.

To get here, take a bus for Mohodipur from near the **Tourist Lodge** in Malda, and ask to be dropped at Pyasbari (tea and snacks available). Stay on the narrow tarmac road and you won't get lost. Turn right from the NH34 for the site, which you can wander around for free. To return to Malda, stop a bus or share a taxi. Or arrange a half-day taxi hire through the tourist office in Malda (Rs 600).

Pandua

The old brick-paved road, nearly 4 m wide and about 10 km long, passes through the town and most of the monuments stand close to it. The **Adina Masjid** (1364-1374) ⓘ *free*, exemplifies Muslim architecture in medieval Bengal. Built by Sultan Sikander Shah and once comparable to the great eighth-century mosque at Damascus, it is sadly in a poor state of repair. The vast space enclosed by pillared aisles has an 88-arch screen around a quadrangle with the mosque. Influence of 12th-century Sena architecture is evident in the tall, ornate, tiered *sikhara* and trefoil arches and the remarkable absence of a large entrance gateway. Most of the substructure, and some pillars, was of basalt plundered from existing Hindu temples and palaces. A small doorway in the western back wall of the mosque, clearly taken from an earlier Vishnu temple, exhibits the stonemasons' skill and the exceptional metalwork of the time. The **Eklakhi Mausoleum**, built of brick (circa 1412), has a Hindu idol carved on its front lintel. The **Qutb Shahi Mosque** (also *Sona* or Golden Mosque) was built in 1582. Further along are the ruins of the 17th-century **Chhoti** and **Bari Dargahs**.

To get to the site, take a Siliguri or Raiganj bus from the **Tourist Lodge** in Malda and ask to be dropped at Pandua Bus Stand. The narrow tarmac road to the site, off the NH34, is easy to follow and gives a fascinating behind-the-scenes view of Bengali village life. Buses from Adina return to Malda.

ⓦ North of Kolkata listings

For Sleeping and Eating price codes and other relevant information, see Essentials pages 34-38.

ⓢ Sleeping

Bishnupur *p96*

D-E Tourist Lodge, end of College Rd, T03244-252013. Lovely clean and spacious rooms, a/c, Western toilets, balconies with view over garden, restaurant and bar. Run by West Bengal Tourist Board, small discount for single occupancy. Best option in town.
F Hotel Heritage, Chhinnamasta More, end of College Rd, T03244-254298. Range of rooms, some cleaner than others, a/c and non-a/c. Also dorms.
Other budget hotels in same area, though some can be quite seedy.

Santiniketan *p97, map p97*

There are a couple of cheap guesthouses within the campus; to arrange a stay (maximum 3 days) contact the Public Relations Office (PRO), T03463-252751.
C Camellia Resort, Prantik (3 km from campus), T03463-262043, www.camellia group.org. Clean but dull rooms (some a/c) on 3 floors around a central courtyard, good restaurant, beautiful large garden, pool, well located in open countryside but you need transport, rickshaws or car hire available, free transport to/from Bolpur station.
C-E Chhuti Holiday Resort, 241 Charupalli, Jamboni, T03463-252692, www.chhuti resort.com. Comfortable thatched rooms with bath, some a/c, good restaurant, innovative.

D-E Rangamati, Prabhat Sarani, Bhubandanga, Bolpur, T03463-252305. 22 decent rooms, some with balcony, dorm (Rs 150), restaurant (Indian and Chinese).

D-F Royal Bengal, Bhubandanga, Bolpur, T03463-257148. Clean and modern, all rooms with balcony and attached bath, dorm (Rs 200), soulless restaurant.

D-F Santiniketan Tourist Lodge (WBTDC), off main road, Bolpur, T03463-252699. Slightly faded rooms, varying sized a/c rooms, small non-a/c (**E**), 13-bed dorm (Rs 80), pleasant garden, poor food.

D-F Sathi, Bhubandanga Rd, Bolpur, T03463-254630. Some a/c, 3, 4 and 5-bedded rooms, best on 1st floor, terrace (front and back).

F-G Manasi Lodge, Santiniketan Rd, Bolpur, T03463-254200. Clean rooms, attached bath, lovely staff, popular courtyard restaurant.

G Nisa, opposite Mela Polo Ground, Bolpur, T03463-253101. Basic but clean rooms with fan, those at rear have balconies.

G Railway Retiring Rooms, Bolpur. 1 a/c, restaurant.

Murshidabad p98

F Ashoke Mahal, Omrahaganj, T03482-320855. Clean and pleasant, rear room 202 is the best with a balcony overlooking the river.

F Manjusha, by Hazarduari Palace, T03482-270321. The best location in town, with serene riverside setting for spotting dolphins, lush garden of flowers and fruit trees, charming manager can help with bike, rickshaw and boat hire, food (by arrangement) is a hit-and-miss. Rooms are simple but clean, with fans.

F Indrajit, near railway station, T03482-271858. Wide choice of rooms of all standards, friendly staff, truly excellent multi-cuisine restaurant plus bar.

F Sagnick, 77 Omrahaganj, T03482-271492. New hotel with some a/c rooms, check a few, some allow glimpses of the river. Tiny tiled bathrooms, TVs and keen staff.

G Youth hostels at Lalbagh and Murshidabad, reserve through Youth Services, 32/1 BBD Bagh S, Kolkata, T03482-280626. Very cheap.

Malda p99

D-G Continental Lodge, 22 KJ Sanyal Rd, by State Bus Stand, T03512-252388. Reasonable rooms, restaurant, friendly, views over town from public balcony.

E-G Tourist Lodge, NH34, T03512-266123. Reservations (Kolkata) T033-2248 8271. 13 rooms around courtyard (4 a/c) some with bath, a/c bar, restaurant, dorm (Rs 80).

F Chanakya, NH34, town centre, T03512-266620. Some a/c in the 22 rooms, restaurant, bar, clean, modern.

G Railway Retiring Rooms. A/c rooms and dorm, modernized, helpful staff. (South Indian platform snacks recommended.)

🍽 Eating

Bishnupur p96

♈ **Sree Hotel**, College Rd, beside Tagore statue, 0930-1500, 1800-2000. Bengali and South Indian food, excellent dosas, good value.

Santiniketan p97, map p97

♈♈ **Camelia Resort**, Prantik. Good food, wide choice, well priced.

♈♈ **Chhuti** (see Sleeping). Has restaurants but may require advance notice.

♈ **Kalor Dokan**, an institution since the time of Tagore, open all hours.

♈ **Maduram**, Santiniketan Rd, Bolpur. Highly recommended sweet shop.

♈ **Railway canteen**. Cheap and reliable.

✲ Festivals and events

Bishnupur p96

Aug Jhapan, in honour of the serpent goddess Manasa, dates from the 17th century. This regional harvest festival is linked with the fertility cult and is unique. Venomous snakes (cobras, pythons, vipers, kraits, flying snakes) are brought in baskets by snake-charmers who display amazing tricks.

Santiniketan *p97, map p97*
End Jan/early Feb Magh Mela, an agricultural and rural crafts fair at Sriniketan, marks the anniversary of the founding of Brahmo Samaj. **Vasanta Utsav** coincides with **Holi**. Programmes of dance, music and singing are held throughout the year, particularly good during festivals. **Late Dec** (check with Bengal TIC) **Poush Mela**, an important fair, coinciding with the village's **Foundation Day**. Folk performances include Santals dances and Baul songs. Bauls are Bengal's wandering minstrels, who are worshippers of Vishnu. They travel from village to village singing their songs, accompanied by a single string instrument, *ektara*, and a tiny drum. Tribal silver and Dhokra metal crafts make attractive buys.

Murshidabad *p98*
Late Dec (check with Bengal TIC) **Muharram**, a fair lasting a few days, which culminates in a 6-hr procession through the village.

O Shopping

Bishnupur *p96*
Cottage industries flourish in the different *paras* (quarters) each devoted to a specialized craft: pottery in Kamarpara, *sankha* (conch-shell); cutting in Sankharipara; and weaving, particularly Baluchari silk saris, in Tantipara. **Silk Khadi Seva Mandal**, Boltala, and **Terracotta Crafts**, 500 m from the Tourist Lodge, are recommended.

Santiniketan *p97, map p97*
The local embossed leather work is distinctive. **Suprabhat Women Handicrafts**, Prabhat Sarani, Bhuban Nagar, opposite **Tourist Lodge**, Bolpur, 0930-1300, 1700-1900. Excellent, creative embroidery (including

kantha), ready made or to order, crafted by local women.
Smaranika Handicraft Centre, opposite Bolpur Station. Interesting embroidery, jewellery and saris at fixed prices.
Subarnarekha, next to railway booking office in Santiniketan. Sells rare books.

Murshidabad *p98*
Woven and handblock-printed silk saris and bell-metal ware are the main local industries.

⊖ Transport

Bishnupur *p96*
Bus/rickshaw Cycle rickshaws are widely available. WBSTC buses from Esplanade to **Kolkata**, 5½ hrs on local roads. STC Super Express buses to **Durgapur** (1 hr).

Car hire Useful for exploring the surrounding area. Available from **Tourist Lodge**; **Kiron Homeo Hall**, Matukgunge.

Train Trains from Kolkata (**H**) to **Bankura**: *Rupasi Bangla Exp 2883*, 0600, 3½ hrs, *Howrah-Purulia Exp 2827*, 1645, 3½ hrs.

Santiniketan *p97, map p97*
Taxi Mainly cycle-rickshaws; taxis available.

Train Trains from **Kolkata** (**H**): *Ganadevata Exp 3017*, 0605, 2¾ hrs; *Shantiniketan Exp 3015*, 1010, 2½ hrs. From **Bolpur** to **Kolkata** (**H**): *Shantiniketan Exp 3016*, 1310, 2½ hrs; *Kanchenjunga Exp 5658* (**S**), 1611, 4 hrs, booking recommended (avoid station counter as the better university booking office, 0800-1400, has a daily quota of 50 reserved seats). Also trains to New Jalpaiguri (for Darjeeling) via Malda.

Murshidabad *p98*
Bus/train The train *Lalgola Passenger* from **Kolkata** (**S**) leaves 2300, 5½ hrs, daily. From Murshidabad, the *Bagirathi Mail*, 0620, takes

4 hrs back to **Sealdah**. Arriving from northern destinations, trains stop at New Farakka from where it's a 2-bus to **Berhampur**. Buses between Berhampur and Kolkata are painful. **Jeep/rickshaw** Jeeps from Berhampur local bus stand to **Lalbagh**, 40 mins, Rs 10; or shared auto-rickshaw, 30 mins, Rs 8. Then cycle-rickshaw to Hazarduari gate, Rs 10.

Malda *p99*

Bus/rickshaw Buses are cheap and rickshaws common. For **Gaur** and **Pandua**, buses, taxis (Rs 600 for half-day tour) and *tongas*. Bus to **Murshidabad**, 3-4 hrs, Rs 60. **Siliguri**, WBSTC Rocket buses 1700-2400, 6½ hrs. Buses to Kolkata not recommended.

Train To **New Jalpaiguri**: *Kanchenjunga Exp 5658*, 1330, 6 hrs. **Kolkata** (**S**): *Kanchenjunga Exp 5659* (AC/II), 1242, 8 hrs.

ⓘ Directory

Bishnupur *p96*
Banks State Bank of India changes foreign cash, ATM next door. **Internet** Several along College Rd. **Medical services** Sub-Division Hospital, near the Court. **Pharmacy** Kumar Medical Hall opposite Tagore statue, English spoken.

Santiniketan *p97, map p97*
Banks State Bank of India, Bolpur and Santiniketan. **Medical services** Pearson Memorial Hospital, Santiniketan.

Murshidabad *p98*
Banks Icici Bank, has ATM. **Internet** Dolphin Service Centre, T03482-270190. Only place with broadband, 1 computer, Rs 20 per hr, daily 1000-2330.

West Bengal Hills

The Himalayan foothills of northern West Bengal contain a wealth of trekking opportunities and hill stations in stunning locations including the region's prime tourist destination, Darjeeling. The old colonial summer retreat is surrounded by spectacular views and still draws plenty of visitors to enjoy cooler climes and a good cuppa. The area also holds one of the Indian one-horned rhino's last safe havens in the Jaldapara Wildlife Sanctuary.

In early 2008, tensions flared in the region over renewed demands for a separate Gorkha (ethnic Nepali) state to be carved out of West Bengal. Apparently galvanized by the success of Gorkha policeman Prashant Tamang in the Indian Idol TV talent contest, the protests resulted in strikes and road closures and occasional violence. Check on the situation before travelling.

▶▶ *For listings, see pages 116-128.*

Siliguri, Jaldapara and Gorumara → *For listings, see pages 116-128. Colour map 2, A1/A2.*

Surrounded by tea plantations, **Siliguri** (phone code: 0353) is a largely unattractive transport hub with busy main roads lined with shops, a couple of good markets and one of the largest stupas in India (100 ft) at nearby Salugara Monastery, 5 km away. The narrow-gauge steam toy train to Darjeeling starts from here during the tourist season (or a diesel train goes each morning at 0915); the town is an essential stepping-off point for travel into the hills and to a couple of national parks in the vicinity. Useful tourist information is available from **WBTDC** ① *1st floor, M4 Hill Cart Rd, T0353-251 1974, www.westbengaltourism.gov.in, Mon-Fri 1000-1730, also at NJP Station and airport, the Forest Development Corporation in the main office books the lodges in Jaldapara Wildlife Sanctuary. On the opposite side of Hill Cart Rd, the DGHC tourism office have little information but take bookings for their lodges in North Bengal T0353-518680, open Mon-Fri 0900-1700, Sat-Sun 0900-1300.*

The River Torsa flows through **Jaldapara Wildlife Sanctuary** ① *Rs 50, still camera Rs 50, video Rs 500, jeeps Rs 200.* It covers an area of 116 sq km (only 30 sq km is open to tourists) and is situated close to Phuntsholing in Bhutan. The riverine forests of sal, khair and sheeshu harbour the one-horned rhino, elephants, leopards, gaur (Indian bison), wild boar, several species of deer, and sloth bears. Ornithologists come to see crested and fishing eagles, and the rare Bengal florican. Trained elephants and vehicle safaris are available to take visitors around, and there is good accommodation in the form of tourist lodges which are bookable in Siliguri (see above). The best time to visit is from November to April, when forest cover is thinner and animals are easier to sight. About a 1000-strong population of the Toto tribe still maintain their traditions and customs in the village of Totopara, 30 km to the north of the sanctuary.

Located in the Dooars (meaning 'door' in Bengali and Assamese) region, 90 km from Siliguri, the **Gorumara National Park** ① *Rs 80/200 (sunset visit more expensive than at other times), still camera free, video Rs 300, car entrance Rs 60, guide Rs 60,* is an interesting diversion little visited by foreign tourists. Covering 85 sq km, the riverine grasslands and forests hide one-horned rhinos, gaur, leopard, elephants, deer and more than 200 species of bird. A few watchtowers give great views and the chance to spot elephants as they come to water. The park is closed from 15 June to 15 September.

For tens of thousands of visitors from Kolkata and the steamy plains, Darjeeling is a place to escape the summer heat. Built on a crescent-shaped ridge the town is surrounded by hills, which are thickly covered with coniferous forests and terraced tea gardens. The

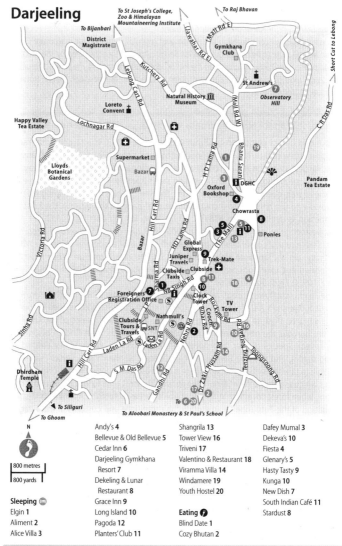

Darjeeling

Sleeping 🛏
Elgin 1
Aliment 2
Alice Villa 3
Andy's 4
Bellevue & Old Bellevue 5
Cedar Inn 6
Darjeeling Gymkhana
    Resort 7
Dekeling & Lunar
    Restaurant 8
Grace Inn 9
Long Island 10
Pagoda 12
Planters' Club 11
Shangrila 13
Tower View 16
Triveni 17
Valentino & Restaurant 18
Viramma Villa 14
Windamere 19
Youth Hostel 20

Eating 🍴
Blind Date 1
Cozy Bhutan 2
Dafey Mumal 3
Dekeva's 10
Fiesta 4
Glenary's 5
Hasty Tasty 9
Kunga 10
New Dish 7
South Indian Café 11
Stardust 8

Darjeeling Himalayan Railway – a mini miracle

For many people, the somewhat erratic narrow-gauge Toy Train between New Jalpaiguri and Darjeeling, with its 0.6-m gauge track, which used to be hauled by sparkling tank engines, is a rewarding experience. The brainchild of East Bengal Railway agent Franklyn Prestage, the train promised to improve access to the hills from the sweltering humidity of the Kolkata plains in the summer. Following the line of an earlier steam tramway, the name was changed to the Darjeeling Himalayan Railway Company (DHR) in 1881. It is a stunning achievement, winding its way up the hillside, often with brilliant views over the plains covering the 82 km with gradients of up to 1:19. At Ghoom it reaches 2438 m and then descends 305 m to Darjeeling. The DHR has been upgraded to a World Heritage Site and has newly refurbished carriages with cushioned seats and window curtains for the tourist trains. It is a must for steam buffs – despite derailments which are "swiftly dealt with and you are lifted back on the tracks within 20 minutes".

idyllic setting, the exhilarating air outside town, and stunning views of the Kangchenjunga (known as Khangchendzonga in Sikkim) range (when you can see through the clouds) attract plenty of trekkers too. Nevertheless, Darjeeling's modern reality is a crowded, noisy and in places shockingly dirty and polluted town. Between June and September the monsoons bring heavy downpours, sometimes causing landslides, but the air clears after mid-September. Winter evenings are cold enough to demand log fires and lots of warm clothing.

Ins and outs → *Phone code: 0354. Population: 107,500. Altitude: 2134 m.*

Getting there Bagdogra, near Siliguri, is Darjeeling's nearest airport, where jeeps and shared taxis tout for business. Trains connect New Jalpaiguri (NJP) with Kolkata and other major cities. The diesel 'toy train' runs from Siliguri/NJP in season but is very slow. Most people reach Darjeeling by jeep and arrive at the motor stand in the lower town, though some go to Clubside on The Mall, which is more convenient for most accommodation.

Getting around Most of Darjeeling's roads slope quite gently so it is easy to walk around the town. The lower and upper roads are linked by a series of connecting roads and steep steps. For sights away from the centre you need to hire a taxi. Be prepared for seasonal water shortages and frequent power cuts. After dark a torch is essential. ▸▸ *See Transport, page 126.*

Tourist information **WBTDC** ⓘ *Belle Vue, 1st floor, 1 Nehru Rd, T0354-225 4102, 1000-1700, off-season 1030-1600,* not much information available. Also at railway station, and at New Car Park, Laden La Road. **Darjeeling Gorkha Hill Council** (DGHC) ⓘ *Silver Fir (below Windamere), The Mall, T/F0354-225 5351.*

History

Darjeeling means region of the *dorje* (thunderbolt) and its official but rarely used spelling is Darjiling. The surrounding area once belonged to Sikkim, although parts were annexed from time to time by the Bhutanese and Nepalese. The East India Company returned the territory's sovereignty to the Rajas of Sikkim, which led to the British obtaining permission to gain the site of the hill station called Darjeeling in 1835, in return for an annual

Darjeeling tea gardens

An ancient Chinese legend suggests that 'tay', or tea, originated in India, although tea was known to have been grown in China around 2700 BC. It is a species of Camellia, Camellia thea. After 1833, when its monopoly on importing tea from China was abolished, the East India Company made attempts to grow tea in Assam using wild chai plants found growing there and later introduced it in Darjeeling and in the Nilgiri hills in the South. Today India is the largest producer of tea in the world. Assam grows over half and Darjeeling about a quarter of the nation's output. Once drunk only by the tribal people, it has now become India's national drink.

The old orthodox method of tea processing produces the aromatic lighter coloured liquor of the Golden Flowery Orange Pekoe in its most superior grade. The fresh leaves are dried by fans on withering troughs to reduce the moisture content and then rolled and pressed to express the juices which coat the leaves. These are left to ferment in a controlled environment to produce the desired aroma. Finally the leaves are dried by passing them through a heated drying chamber and then graded – the unbroken being the best quality, down to the fannings and dust. The more common crushing, tearing, curling (CTC) method produces tea which gives a much darker liquor.

Most of Darjeeling's tea is sold through auction houses, the largest centre being in Kolkata. Tea tasting and blending are skills which have developed over a long period of time and are highly prized. The industry provides vital employment in the hill areas and is an assured foreign exchange earner.

payment. It was practically uninhabited and thickly forested but soon grew into a popular health resort after a road and several houses were built and tea growing was introduced. The Bengal government escaped from the Kolkata heat to take up its official summer residence here. The upper reaches were originally occupied by the Europeans, who built houses with commanding views. Down the hillside on terraces sprawled the humbler huts and bazars of the Indian town.

Sights

In the pedestrianized centre of town, on the ridge, **Chowrasta** is the natural heart of Darjeeling and particularly atmospheric at dawn and dusk. The **Mahakal mandir** atop **Observatory Hill**, sacred to Siva, is a pleasant walk though the views of the mountains are obscured by tall trees. Sacred to both Hindus and Buddhists, the temple is active and colourful, with prayer flags tied to every tree and pole in the vicinity. Beware of the monkeys as they bite. Further along Jawahar Road West is **Shrubbery (Nightingale) Park**, a pleasant detour if still too early to visit the zoo. Views to the north are excellent from the renovated park, and every evening cultural shows take place here (information from the DGHC tourist office).

Padmaja Naidu Himalayan Zoological Park ① *daily 0830-1630 (summer), 0830-1600 (wineter) except Thu, Rs 100*, houses high-altitude wildlife including Himalayan black bears, Siberian tigers, Tibetan wolves and plenty of red pandas, as well as deer, a multitude of birds and the gorgeously marked rare clouded leopard. There are large enclosures over a section of the hillside, though at feeding time and during wet weather they retreat into their small cement enclosures giving the impression that they are restricted to their cells. There is a reasonably successful snow leopard breeding programme, with over 40 births since 1983, and it is the only Asian zoo to have successfully introduced red pandas into the wild. Entrance fees to the zoo also include the **Himalayan Mountaineering Institute** ① *T0354-227 0158, no photography, entrance is through the zoo on Jawahar Rd West*. Previously headed by the late Tenzing Norgay who shared the first climb of Everest in 1953, the Institute has trained up many a mountaineer and runs training courses during dry months of the year (see page 124). Within the complex, the Everest Museum traces the history of attempted climbs from 1857 and the Mountaineering Museum displays old equipment including that used on the historic Tenzing-Hillary climb.

The decaying **Natural History Museum** ① *Bishop Eric Benjamin Rd, 1000-1600, Rs 5*, has a large collection of fauna of the region and a certain charm if you enjoy. The **Tibetan Refugee Self-help Centre** ① *T0354-225 5938, thondup@cal.vsnl.net.in, Mon-Sat 0800-1700*, with its temple, school and hospital is north of town. From Chowrasta, take the lane to the right towards the viewpoint, and then walk down for about 30 minutes (ask around). After the Chinese invasion, thousands of Tibetan refugees settled in Darjeeling (many having accompanied the Dalai Lama) and the rehabilitation centre was set up in 1959 to enable them to continue to practise their skills and provide a sales outlet. You can watch them at work (carpet weaving, spinning, dyeing, woodwork, etc) during the season, when it is well worth a visit (closes for lunch). The shop sells fabulous woollen carpets (orders taken and posted, see Shopping), textiles, curios and jewellery, though not cheap to buy.

On the way to the refugee centre is the lovely **Bhutia Bustee Monastery**, which used to stand on Observatory Hill but was moved to its present position in 1861. Someone will show you around and point out gold-flecked murals that have been gorgeously restored. South of town, the **Aloobari Monastery**, on Tenzing Norgay Road, is open to visitors. Tibetan and Sikkimese handicrafts made by the monks are for sale.

Near the market are **Lloyds Botanical Gardens** ① *Mon-Sat 0600-1700*. These were laid out in 1878 on land given by Mr W Lloyd, owner of the Lloyd's Bank. They have a modest collection of Himalayan and Alpine flora including banks of azaleas and rhododendrons, magnolias, a good orchid house and a herbarium. It is a pleasant and quiet spot. **Victoria Falls**, which is only impressive in the monsoons, provides added interest to a three-hour nature trail. There are several tea gardens close to Darjeeling, but not all welcome visitors. One that does is the **Pattabong Estate** on the road towards Sikkim. Visit the **shrubbery**, behind Raj Bhawan on Birch Hill, for spectacular views of Kangchendzonga.

Around Darjeeling

① *Roads can get washed away during the monsoon and may remain in poor condition till Oct*. At **Ghoom**, altitude 2550 m, is the important Yiga-Choling Gompa, a Yellow-hat Buddhist Monastery. Built in 1875, it houses famous Buddhist scriptures (beautifully displayed) in an interior the colour of the surrounding forests. The austere monastery is a nice walk, at the end of Ghoom's main market street. Also worth visiting is the Sakyaguru Monastery, closer to the Darjeeling road, which has 95 monks. It is well recommended to make the 11-km journey to Ghoom by **steam train** taking 45 minutes. The little **Railway Museum** ① *Rs 20, daily 1000-1300 and 1400-1600, ticket from station and staff will unlock the gate*, outlines the history of the Darjeeling Himalayan Railway and has some interesting old photos. A few spruced up carriages offer a tourist-only ride in summer with a photo stop at Batasia (departing 1040, returning 1200, and again at 1320, returning 1440; but check times at the station or www.dhr.in, Rs 240); bookings must be made 90-days in advance, although it is possible to buy spare seats on the day from agents who have private counters set up at Darjeeling station. Alternatively, take the passenger steam train at 1015 (first class Rs 144; second class Rs 5), which goes to Kurseong via Ghoom, or the diesel train at 0915 (first class Rs 144; second class Rs 27), and return on foot or by jeep. (See also the Toy Train, page 126.) All pass through **Batasia Loop**, 5 km from Darjeeling on the way to Ghoom, which allows the narrow gauge rail to do a figure-of-eight loop. There's a war memorial here in a pleasant park with good mountain views.

The disused **Lebong Race Course**, 8 km from Darjeeling, was once the smallest and highest in the world and is still pleasant for a walk. It was started as a parade ground in 1885.

If the weather is clear, it is worth rising at 0400 to make the hour's journey for a breathtaking view of the sunrise on Kangchenjunga at **Tiger Hill** ① *jeeps from Darjeeling Rs 600*. Mount Everest (8846 m), 225 km away, is visible on a good day. The mass of jeeps and the crowds at sunrise disappear by mid-morning; it's a nice walk back from Tiger Hill (about two hours, 11 km) via Ghoom and the Japanese Peace Pagoda, where drumming between 1630-1900 is worth seeing.

Trekking around Darjeeling → *For listings, see pages 116-128.*

The trekking routes around Darjeeling are well established, having been popular for nearly 100 years. Walks lead in stages along safe tracks and through wooded hills up to altitudes of 3660 m. Trails pass through untouched nature filled with rhododendrons, magnolias, orchids and wild flowers, together with forests, meadows and small villages. All this to a backdrop of mountains stretching from Mount Everest to the Bhutan hills, including the third highest mountain in the world, **Khangchendzonga**. The best trekking seasons are April to May, when the magnolias and rhododendrons are in full bloom, and October to November. In spring there may be the occasional shower. In autumn the air is dry and the visibility excellent. In winter the lower altitude trails that link Rimbick with Jhepi (18 km) can be very attractive for birdwatchers. There is an extensive network of varied trails that link the hillside towns and villages. Agents in Darjeeling can organize four- to seven-day treks, providing guide, equipment and accommodation (see page 124).

In a bid to provide employment for local youth, the **West Bengal Forest and Wildlife Department** has stipulated that visitors must have a guide/porter in order to enter the Singalila National Park. Checks to this effect are made at the Manebhanjang checkpoint at the entrance to the park. If you haven't arranged a trek through an agent in Darjeeling, local guides can be hired in Manebhanjang for between Rs 300-500 per day (although paying more secures someone who speaks good English and has a better knowledge of local flora and fauna); porters are Rs 200-250. Entry fees for the park are also paid at the checkpoint (foreigners Rs 100, Indians Rs 20, still camera Rs 25, video camera Rs 100). If you prefer to go alone, it is possible (though a bit risky) to pay for a guide for the duration of your trek but not actually take the guide, just showing the payment receipt at the checkpoint to gain entry to the ridge (although further checkpoints on the way also have to be negotiated).

Singalila trek

The 160-km Singalila trek starts from the small border town of **Manebhanjang**, 26 km from Darjeeling. The journey to and from Darjeeling can be done by shared or private jeep in 1½ hours. Walking from Manebhanjang north to Sandakphu (rather than starting in Sandakphu and heading south) means you are always walking towards the most stunning views. If you have not arranged for transport to meet you at a particular point then it is entirely possible to travel back to Darjeeling from any roadhead by jeep, with services at least once daily, often three to four times daily.

Note Singalila is not an easy trek, several parts are very steep and tough. Even up to May, temperatures at night are freezing and it is essential to take plenty of warm clothes.

There are plenty of trekkers huts of varying standards and prices (on an organized trek these will have been booked for you) at Tonglu, Sandakphu, Phalut, Gorkhey, Molley, Rammam, Rimbick, Siri Khola and other villages. Although room is usually available, it's wise to book in advance during May/June and October when trails can be very busy. Any trekking agent in Darjeeling can arrange these bookings for a small fee. Private lodges, such as **Sherpa Lodge** in Rimbick and Rammam, and other trailside lodges in Meghma, Jaubari and Kalpokhri, are generally friendly, flexible and provide reasonable basic accommodation. Some places can prepare yak curry on request, and be sure to sample hot *chhang*, the local millet brew, served in a wooden keg and sipped through a bamboo straw.

Darjeeling treks

The entire area is a birdwatcher's paradise with over 600 species including orioles, minivets, flycatchers, finches, sunbirds, thrushes, piculets, falconets and Hoodson's Imperial pigeons. The mixed rhododendron, oak and conifer forests are particularly well preserved.

Day 1 To Tonglu (or Tumling) 1 km beyond Manebhanjang town you reach a rough stone paved track leading sharply up to the left. Tonglu (3030 m) is 11 km from this point if you follow the jeep track, slightly less if you take the frequent but very steep short cuts. Alternatively, head for Tumling, just the other side of the peak of the hill from Tonglu (you take the alternative road from Meghma and rejoin the main route 1 km after Tumling). There is a trekkers' hut at **Tonglu** with 24 beds and a fine view of the Khangchendzonga range. From here you can also see the plains of North Bengal and some valleys of Nepal in the distance. Closer to hand are the snow fed rivers, the Teesta in the east and Koshi in the west. You can also sleep in **Tumling** where **Shikhar Lodge** has simple basic and clean rooms, run by a local teacher's friendly family, "fabulous supper and breakfast" plus a lovely garden. There are tea shops at **Chitre** and at **Meghma**, which has an interesting monastery noted for its large collection of Buddhist statues; 108, according to locals. Ask at the tea house opposite to get in.

Day 2 To Jaubari and Gairibans A level walk along the ridge takes you past the long 'mani' wall to the Nepalese village of Jaubari; no visa is needed and good accommodation is available should you wish to spend a night in Nepal. After Jaubari the trail turns sharply to the right back into Indian territory and down through bamboo and rhododendron forests to the village of Gairibans in a forest clearing. You could carry on all the way to Sandakphu, a long hard day's hiking.

Day 3 To Sandakphu It is 14 km uphill to Sandakphu, with a lunch break in Kalpokhri with its attractive attractive 'black' lake surrounded by fir trees, about midway. Even in winter the lake never freezes. The last 3 km from Bhikebhanjang (tea shop) to Sandakphu are particularly steep; this section takes more than an hour but the views from the Singalila Ridge make it all worthwhile. **Sandakphu**, a small settlement located at 3636 m, is considered the finest viewpoint on the trek, and is the prime destination for most visitors. Located 57 km from Darjeeling, it is accessible by jeep (the same narrow bumpy track used by trekkers), which is how many Indian tourists make the journey during the season. A viewpoint 100 m above Sandakphu offers fantastic views, including the northern face of Everest (8846 m, 140 km away as the crow flies), Khangchendzonga (8598 m), Chomolhari, the highest peak in Bhutan, and numerous peaks such as Pandim that lie in Sikkim.

There are several trekkers' huts and lodges, each with a dining area, toilets and cookhouse. These vary widely in standards and price, some costing up to Rs 500 per person; it's worth seeing a few. The drive back to Manebhanjang by pre-arranged 4WD can take four hours along the very rough track, if you finish the trek here.

Day 4 Sandakphu to Phalut Phalut, 22 km from Sandakphu along an undulating jeepable track, is at the junction of Nepal, Sikkim and West Bengal. It offers even closer views of Khangchendzonga. It is best to avoid trekking here in May and June and mid-September to 25 October when large numbers of college trekking teams from West Bengal descend on the area. From Phalut it's possible to get a jeep back the way you came, via Sandakphu. Alternatively you can walk south for 4 km back towards **Bhikebhanjang** and then take a 16-km-long trail through fine forests of the Singalila National Park down to **Rimbick**.

Day 5 **Phalut to Rimbick** From Phalut, there is **Gorkhey**, with accommodation, and it's a further 3 km to the village of **Samanden**, hidden in a hanging valley. From Samanden, it is a 5-km walk to **Rammam** where there is a clean, comfortable **Sherpa Lodge** in a pleasant garden, recommended for friendly service and good food. Alternatively, the **Trekkers' Hut** is about 1 km before Rammam village. From Rammam it is a two-hour walk down to a couple of attractive trekkers' huts at **Siri Khola** and a further two hours to Rimbick. Again, this area has a wealth of birdlife. From Rimbick there are around three jeeps a day to take you back to Darjeeling (Rs 100, four or five hours).

Although Gorkhey, Phalut, Rammam and Rimbick lie just south of the border with Sikkim, entering Sikkim is not permitted on this route, though agents say this may change in future; ask in Darjeeling about the current situation.

Sabarkum via Ramman to Molley or Bijanbari

An alternative quieter trail links Sabarkum (7 km before Phalut on the main Sandakphu–Phalut trail) with Rammam, with a possible overnight halting stay at the **Trekkers' Hut** in **Molley**. Those with five days to spare can return by the **Rammam–Rimbick–Jhepi–Bijanbari** route (153 km). From Rammam you can cross by a suspension bridge over the Siri Khola River and follow the path up the valley, which leads to Dentam in Sikkim (entry into Sikkim is not permitted). This less well-trodden valley has rich birdlife (particularly kingfishers), and excellent views of undisturbed forest. From **Bijanbari** (762 m) it is possible to return to Darjeeling, 36 km away by jeep, or climb a further 2 km to Pulbazar and then return to Darjeeling, 16 km away. Those wishing only to go to Rimbick can get a jeep from there, or may return to Manebhanjang via Palmajua and Batasi (180 km), which takes one day.

Mirik → For listings, see pages 116-128.

Mirik, 49 km from Darjeeling, at an altitude of 1730 m, has forests of japonica, orange orchards, tea gardens and cardamom plantations. Its restful ambience, dramatic views and homely accommodation make it an appealing stop for a couple of days of relaxation. **Sumendu Lake**, with its 3.5 km cobbled promenade, offers boating, while **Krishannagar**, south of the lake, has a carpet weaving centre and the impressive **Bokar Gompa**, a 15-minute stroll from the main road. You can trek to **Kurseong** and **Sandakphu**, or less ambitiously, take a bus part way up the Darjeeling road and walk back through rolling tea estates, and little villages of flower-laden cottages.

Kurseong

Kurseong or 'Place of the White Orchid' east of Mirik, is a small town worthy of a couple of nights' pause on the way to/from Darjeeling. Surrounded by tea gardens and orange orchards (through which there is pleasant walking to be done), locals will sincerely tell you that they call Kurseong 'paradise'.

There are no grand sights in the town, but it is an interesting hike up to the ridge, via St Mary's hamlet (north of the market along Hill Cart Road). Shortcuts past quaint houses and the eerie Forestry College lead up to **St Mary's Well and Grotto**, which has fine views and a shrine with candles. Tracks through a young forest reach imposing Dow Hill School, established 1904, and either continue up and over the ridge to tiny Chetri Bustee, or bear right to the little **Forest Museum** at Dow Hill. Head back down via scenically located **Ani**

Gompa, housing a small community of nuns belonging to the Red Hat sect, and pass pretty cottages using footpaths. It's around a five-hour walk with stops; ask locals for directions, but double any time frame they give to destinations. Useful sketch maps can be provided by **Cochrane Place** (see listings, page 120), where it is also possible to arrange guided hikes tailored to match walkers' interests and stamina. In the town itself there's the narrow and crowded *chowk* market to explore, while a half-hour walk from the railway station brings you to **Eagle's Crag** (shadowed by the TV tower), an awesome vantage point in clear weather.

The **Makaibari Tea Estate**, 4 km from town, makes an interesting excursion. Dating from 1859 it is India's oldest tea garden, responsibly managed by charismatic Rajah Banerjee who has done much to support the community and initiate environmental and organic development on the estate. The highest price ever fetched at a tea auction was for Makaibari leaves when Rs 18,000 was paid for a kilogram in 2003. Nearby **Ambootia Tea Estate** also conduct factory visits, and from here there's a walk to an ancient Siva temple amid massive Rudraksh and Banyan trees. Kurseong is famed for its plethora of boarding schools. At **Tung** nearby, the St Alphonsus Social and Agricultural Centre, run by a Canadian Jesuit, is working with the local community through education, housing, agricultural, forestry and marketing projects. They welcome volunteers; contact ⓘ *SASAC, Tung, Darjeeling, West Bengal, T0354-234 2059, sasac@satyam.net.in*. The steam train to Darjeeling leaves every afternoon, supposedly at 1500.

Kalimpong → *For listings, see pages 116-128. Colour map 2, A2.*

Set in beautiful wooded mountain scenery with an unhurried air about it, Kalimpong was a meeting point of the once 'Three Closed Lands' on the trade route to Tibet, Bhutan and Nepal. Away from the crowded and scruffy centre near the motor stand, the town becomes more spaced out as mountain roads wind up the hillsides leading to monasteries, mission schools and orchid nurseries. Some say that the name is derived from *pong* (stronghold) of *kalon* (king's minister), or from *kalibong*, a plant fibre.

From Darjeeling, the 51-km journey (2½ hours) is through beautiful scenery. The road winds down through tea estates and then descends to 250 m at Tista where it crosses the river on a 'new' concrete bridge. 'Lovers' Meet' and 'View Point' give superb views of the Rangit and Tista rivers.

Ins and outs → *Population: 43,000. Altitude: 1250 m.*

Getting there Bagdogra is the nearest airport and New Jalpaiguri the nearest railhead. Buses and shared jeeps arrive from there at the Bazar Motor Stand in two to three hours. Getting around The centre is compact enough to be seen comfortably on foot. The surroundings are ideal for walking, though some may prefer transport to visit nearby sights. ▸▸ *See Transport, page 127.*

Sights

The traditional **market** at the 10th Mile has a great atmosphere. The *haat* here every Wednesday and Saturday draws colourful villagers who come to sell fruit, unfamiliar vegetables, traditional medicines, woollen cloth, yarn and much more. It is remarkably clean and laid back, a delight to explore. Unusual merchandise includes: curly young fern tops, bamboo shoots, dried mushrooms, fragrant spices, musk, *chaang* paraphernalia, large chunks of brown soap, and tiny chickens in baskets alongside gaudy posters.

There a number of monasteries in and around Kalimpong; the oldest of which, **Thongsa Gompa Bhutanese Monastery** (1692), 10th Mile, has been renovated. The **Tharpa Choling Monastery** (1922) has a library of Tibetan manuscripts and *thangkas*. Further north, is the **Tibetan Monastery** (Yellow Hat) at Tirpai. The **Pedong Bhutanese Monastery** (1837) near the old Bhutanese Damsang Fort at Algara (15 km away) holds ceremonial dances every February. South of town, at Durpin Dara, the highest point in Kalimpong with superb views, stands the **Ringkinpong Monastery** of Zang Dog Palri Phodrang. Unique outside Tibet, it has a school of Tibetan Medicine and is particularly interesting when prayers are being chanted. **Dr Graham's Homes** from town on Deolo Hill, www.drgrahamshomes.org, was started by the missionary Doctor John Anderson

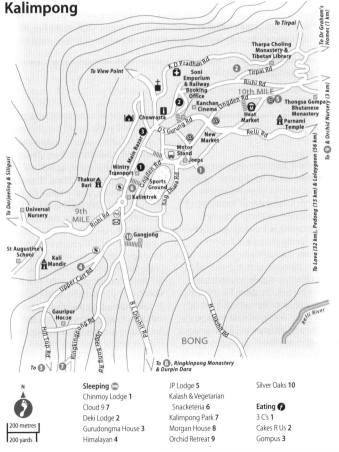

Kalimpong

Sleeping
Chinmoy Lodge 1
Cloud 9 7
Deki Lodge 2
Gurudongma House 3
Himalayan 4
JP Lodge 5
Kalash & Vegetarian
 Snacketeria 6
Kalimpong Park 7
Morgan House 8
Orchid Retreat 9

Silver Oaks 10

Eating
3 C's 1
Cakes R Us 2
Gompus 3

Graham in 1900 when he admitted six needy children. Now there are about 1000 pupils visitors are welcome to the school as well as the dairy, poultry and bakery projects.

Kalimpong excels in producing orchids, amaryllis, roses, cacti, dahlias and gladiol **Nurseries** include **Ganesh Mani Pradhan** on 12th Mile; **Universal** on 8th Mile; **Shanti Kun** on BL Dikshit Road; and **Himalayan** on East Main Road.

Walks

There are pleasant hikes along the Tista Road through rice fields to **Chitray Falls**, 9 km a three-hour walk to **Bhalu Khop** and a 1½-hour downhill walk from the motor stand to the Relli River. You can picnic on the river beaches at Tista Bazar and Kalijhora.

Further afield, scenic two- to three-hour treks are possible from **Lava** (32 km east monastery and weekly market on Tuesday), and **Lolaygaon** (southeast, 56 km by road vi a Lava), which has spectacular views of Kangchendzonga. Rhododendrons flower in Apri around this region. Both villages are accessible by public jeep from Kalimpong and have reasonably priced accommodation (bookable at the Forest Dept at WBTDC office in Siliguri, or www.wbfdc.com); walking between the two is a lovely trek of about 10 km.

◉ West Bengal Hills listings

For Sleeping and Eating price codes and other relevant information, see Essentials pages 34-38.

● Sleeping

Siliguri *p105*
Hill Cart Rd is officially Tenzing Norgay Rd.
A Cindrella, Sevoke Rd, '3rd mile' (out of town), T0353-254 7136, www.cindrella hotels.com. Comfortable a/c rooms, decent pool, competent vegetarian restaurant, internet, car hire, pick-up from airport, efficient. Drinks in the bar or on the roof terrace.
A Sinclairs, Pradhan Nagar, T0353-251 2440, www.sinclairshotels.com. Architecturally curious from the outside, a/c rooms are comfortable with flat-screen TVs although getting a bit worn. The restaurant and O2 bar are stylish with good food, small pool is disappointing, attentive and warm service. Some **AL** suites. Breakfast included.
C-E Conclave, Hill Cart Rd (opposite SNT bus stand), T0353-251 6144, www.hotelconclave. com. A newish hotel with good quality rooms, a/c, satellite TV, licensed bar, Eminent restaurant serving quality Indian/European food, intermittent internet, parking.
C-E The Tiara, Sevoke Rd (opposite the Gurudwara), T0353-243 6024,

thetiarahotel@hotmail.com. A 'boutique' hotel where ethnic mixes with kitsch (particularly in the lobby which has a plastic grotto, trees and fish pond). Top-floor rooms each styled with traditional designs and decor of NE Indian States (Sikkim, Orissa, Bihar, etc) and suitably priced at Rs 1575 for a double. Public areas are clean and shiny, and the non-a/c rooms great value for the decent standard (particularly the singles, Rs 400). Good restaurant, see Eating, page 121.
C-F Vinayak, Hill Cart Rd, T0353-243 1130. Clean rooms with bath, some a/c, good restaurant, look at a few rooms as some of the budget options are excellent value.
E-F Anjali Lodge, Nabin Sen Rd (next to the Gurudwara), off Sevoke Rd, T0353-252 2964. Institutional building, bright white paint throughout, large rooms with concrete floors have clean sheets, towels, soap, TV, cheaper without a/c (doubles Rs 700/500), some have balcony or there is spacious public balcony. Suspicious staff soon warm up. A good choice.
E-F Mainak (WBTDC), Hill Cart Rd (opposite main bus stand), T0353-251 2859, www.west bengaltourism.gov.in. Large and open 1970s-style hotel, 38 comfortable rooms (check a few, they vary), 14 a/c, and some

suites. Set back from the road in dusty gardens, with restaurant and bar, helpful staff. Be sure not to overlap with a wedding party; call ahead.

E-F Yatri Hotel, Hill Cart Rd (opposite main bus stand), T0353-251 4707, yatrihotel98@yahoo.com. Basic, cheap rooms with bath, restaurant serves good food. The dim and cosy bar next door is a friendly place to have an icy beer (Rs 80-120) or watch some sport.

F Hill View Hotel, Hill Cart Rd (opposite SNT bus stand), T0353-251 9951. Shabby old place, but about the only hotel in town with any character. Sadly, the wooden balcony only has views of the traffic on Hill Cart Rd. Manager is helpful and clean sheets are provided. Single rooms (Rs 150) share a common bath, doubles have private, little restaurant at rear.

G Railway Retiring Rooms, Siliguri Junction and New Jalpaiguri. 4 rooms and 6 dorm beds in each, good vegetarian snacks.

G Siliguri Lodge, Hill Cart Rd (near SNT bus stand), T0353-251 5290. Grotty exterior but clean sheets and relatively quiet, being set back from the road. Kind staff.

G Youth Hostel, Kangchenjunga Stadium, 130 beds.

Jaldapara and Gorumara *p105*

A Riverwood Forest Retreat, Gorumara, Dakshin Dhupjhora, www.riverwood retreat.com. This eco-friendly resort has lush surrounds, and some balconies have views of mountain peaks. Comfortable well-appointed rooms, attentive staff, no TVs or internet. Guided excursions into Gorumara, plus day treks, village visits and tea tourism (reasonably priced) can also be arranged.

C Hollong Forest Tourist Lodge, Hollong, 6 km from Madarihat, T03563-262228, book well in advance (3 months) either directly, or via the Tourist Bureau, Siliguri, T0353-251 1974. Built of timber on stilts deep inside the park. 6 rooms (all meals), the lodge is very popular and is en route to Phuntsholing in Bhutan. The only place where you can organize elephants rides (Rs 200).

D-F Madarihat Tourist Lodge, Madarihat. Outside the park boundaries, non-a/c double rooms are Rs 1400 or there's a dorm for Rs 400.

F Nilpara Forest Bungalow, Hasimara. 2 rooms, very basic, caretaker will prepare a simple meal if requested but take all provisions.

F Youth Hostel and Lodge, 4 km from Hasimara railway station, 18 km from Madarihat, at Baradabri. 3 rooms, 14 beds in 4 dorms, poor catering, reserve through DFO, Tourism Centre, Jalpaiguri, T03563-262239 or Kolkata, T033-2248 8271.

Darjeeling *p106, map p106*

Most hotels are within 2 km of the station and motor stand, a stiff walk uphill. Some top-end hotels include all meals and most offer discounts off season (Jul-Sep, Dec-Feb). Some charge extra for Christmas and New Year. Prices listed are for high season.

LL-AL Windamere, Observatory Hill, T0354-225 4041, www.windamerehotel.com. Enviable location, good views when clear, a true relic of the Raj. Spacious rooms and cottages (no phone or TV in some), beware those with dated bathrooms (limited hot water), terraces, chintzy and cluttered with memorabilia, coal fires (can be smoky), hotties in bed, pre-war piano favourites accompany tea. Lounge/bar is a characterful place for a drink, outside guests welcome for high tea (Rs 375) or beer (Rs 150). Full-board only.

AL The Elgin, HD Lama Rd, T0354-225 7226, www.elginhotels.com. Beautifully renovated colonial hotel, rooms are full of atmosphere with polished floors, fireplaces, nooks and crannies while being plush and well appointed, marble bathrooms. Photos, brass fittings and carpets give warmth to public spaces, lounge and bar area pleasantly like a country sitting room, tiered garden is small and flower-filled but looks onto a high fence. Annoyingly, there is no option but to take a package including all meals, and high tea is grossly overpriced for outside guests.

AL-A Cedar Inn, Dr Zakir Hussain Rd, T0354-225 4446, www.cedarinndarjeeling.com. Slightly out of town, but with great views and free shuttle service to town throughout the day. Family friendly, health club, lovely garden with wrought iron furniture. Wood panelled rooms are stylish and thoughtfully laid out (bathrooms a bit 1980s), public areas filled with enormous plants, bar newly renovated and restaurant welcoming and informal. Extension being added in same style as the original building, essential to book in advance.

A-B Darjeeling Gymkhana Resort, next to Gymkhana Club, T0354-225 4391, www.sunflower-hotels.com. Wood panelled rooms (all with fireplaces) are large and modern yet warm and welcoming. Nice location on Observatory Hill, club on doorstep for sports/activities, location. Particularly suited to families (4-bed rooms Rs 3500). Indian restaurant good, but its position in the central foyer means staff chatter can be irritating when you're in your room.

A-C Planters' Club, The Mall, T0354-225 4348. AKA the 'Darjeeling Club', this wooden building dates from 1868 and oozes history from the curved veranda and creaking balconies. New decor in VIP rooms is actually unattractive, a better choice are the 'super' doubles (Rs 1500) which are dated but have the Raj aura; huge fireplaces, white-painted furniture, bathrooms feel Victorian. Nice staff and a good place for an evening tipple (see listings, page 123).

A-F Viramma Villa, Jalapahar Rd (behind IG Bungalow), T0354-225 5357. New place in a nice location on the ridge with unimpeded valley views and a variety of spotless rooms, laminate or wood floors, homely and cheerfully furnished. Listed tariffs are high but while they are getting established huge discounts are available. Well worth popping in to see if you can negotiate a deal.

B Shangrila, 5 Nehru Rd, T0354-225 4149. A small and characterful hotel in a good spot near Chowrasta. Large rooms have been tastefully renovated in 2009, subtly lit,

flatscreen TVs, some with good views from the window seating. Swish new bathrooms, all double beds (no twins, 20% discount for single), 3 rooms have Victorian fireplaces. Excellent restaurant (see page 121).

B-D Old Main Bellevue Hotel, Chowrasta, T0354-225 4178, www.darjeelinghotel.co.uk. Rooms with character in the Heritage bungalow on the hill are atmospheric although not high-spec, clear aspect from the picnic tables in the charming garden. Doubles in a newer front building are over-priced for shabby carpets and unrenovated bathrooms.

C-E Bellevue, Chowrasta, T0354-225 4075, www.bellevuehotel-darjeeling.com. Wide range of rooms (Rs 650-1800) with bath and geysers, some large, bright and airy (eg rooms 35, 49), some with fireplaces or stoves, all have loads of character with old wooden fittings (though major renovations are planned). Genuinely friendly management. Very centrally located, and small rooftop with unparalleled K'dzonga view.

C-E Dekeling, 51 Gandhi Rd (the Mall), on Clubside, T0354-225 4159, www.dekeling.com. Homely rooms are noticeably warm, most have private bath (24-hr hot water), delightful lounge areas with stoves. Range of room tariffs (average Rs 1200), some attic front rooms with views, 2 doubles with shared bath are a bargain at Rs 650. Good restaurant, brilliant hosts, reserve ahead (1 month in advance in high season). Noisy when jeeps depart at 0400 for Tiger Hill with lots of hooting.

D-E Alice Villa, 41 HD Lama Rd, below DGHC Tourist Office, Chowrasta, T0354-225 4181, hotelalicevilla@yahoo.com. Large clean rooms (fireplace in some, bucket of coal cost extra) in an old bungalow are simple, with colonial charm, and fairly priced at Rs 825 (high season). Bathrooms newly tiled in pastel shades and soft furnishings in the covered terrace are bad taste. The modern wing at the rear is not so appealing. Checkout 1200.

)-F Grace Inn, 8/B Cooch Bihar Rd, 0354-225 8106, T(0)98326-15082, hegraceinn@sify.com. Some large, well-furnished rooms, much of the best at the back (with views), subtly lit restaurant with ambitious menu, cheerful staff. Worth stopping by on the way to backpacker places, as massive discounts are available (room with a geyser for Rs 300).

E Valentino, 6 Rockville Rd, T0354-225 2228. Clean rooms with a green theme are getting faded but with good mountain views (especially from upper storeys), central heating and 24-hr hot water, good Chinese restaurant, bar, excellent rooftop sundeck.

E-F Aliment, 40 Zakir Hussain Rd, T0354-225 5068, alimentweb@sify.com. Clean rooms vary in size and cheerfulness, pay more for TV and hot shower (available 1-hr per day as required), average food in social restaurant (beer Rs 70), internet (Rs 30 per hr), packed with travellers, good atmosphere, excellent library.

F Andy's, 102 Zakir Hussain Rd, 5 mins from Chowrasta past pony sheds towards TV tower, T0354-225 3125, T(0)94341-66968, www.andysguesthouse.biz. Airy rooms are notable for their cleanliness, upper floors with small shower or hot buckets provided. Bird's-eye views from rooftop, storage for trekkers, friendly and honest atmosphere, Mrs Gurung is informative and helpful. Discounts for single travellers, often full. No food.

F-G Long Island, Rockville Dham, near TV tower, T0354-225 2043, pritaya19@yahoo.com. Attractive exterior, clean basic rooms, some with private shower (hot water 0800-2000) or share communal bathroom. Appealingly quaint restaurant, quiet location, great views from rooftop and upper rooms. Run by friendly Nepali family. Recommended, single room rates, try to book ahead.

F-G Tower View, Rockville Dham, down the back of TV Tower, T0354-225 4452. Pleasant, clean rooms with toilet, shared hot shower, wood stove and dusty book collection in restaurant.

G Pagoda, 1 Upper Beechwood Rd, T0354-225 3498. Clean but basic rooms with period furniture in a characterful building, some with bath (limited free bucket hot water), peaceful, good value. Rooms at front better, though not much view from shared balcony. Away from the main backpacker scene and an easier walk from tranport links. Very friendly, small library.

G Triveni, 85 Dr Zakir Hussain Rd, T0354-225 3978, T(0)9932-345607. Well-kept basic box rooms with bath and hot bucket (Rs 10). Pleasant and low-key management, Triveni collects the overspill from the Aliment across the road. Good for solo travellers (Rs 125/100, with/without bath), 3-bed dorm (Rs 80), doubles Rs 250.

G Youth Hostel, Dr Zakir Hussain Rd, T0354-225 2290. Mainly cheap dorm beds, superb position on top of the ridge, no restaurant, trekking information available.

Trekking around Darjeeling *p110*

C Karmi Farm, Bijanbari, contact **Samsara Travel** in Darjeeling, T0354-225 6370, samsara@dte.vsnl.net.in. A haven of rural peace at Kolbong, which you may choose to use as a base, north of Bijanbari (access via Kaijali, 4WDs stop 20 mins' walk away, or it's 2-3 hrs by pony from Pulbazar). 7 doubles with bath, simple but spotless, superb food, US$20 includes food/porters.

F Teacher's Lodge, Jaubari. Excellent value. There is a large **Trekkers' Hut** at Gairibans with about 20 beds.

Mirik *p113*

AL-B Orange County Retreat, T0354-244 3612. Catering chiefly to Indian tourists, 12 stone cottages, plus a honeymoon suite. Plenty of views and nature. Arranges treks in the Singalila range.

A-D Jagjeet, T0354-224 3231, www.jagjeethotel.com. Large, well-furnished rooms, although cheaper ones are a bit musty. Good restaurant and bar.

D-F Ratnagiri, T0354-224 3243. Bright spotless rooms with great views, and a cute garden restaurant. Excellent choice.
E Tourist Lodge, T0354-224 3371. Huge wood-panelled rooms with balconies have excellent views and plenty of character, ignore the faded exterior.
F-G Lodge Ashirvad, T0354-224 3272. The best budget option, with 24-hr hot water in some rooms, rooftop with monastery views and a helpful owner.

Kurseong *p113*

B Cochrane Place, 132 Pankhabari Rd, Fatak, (2 km from Kurseong on the road to Mirik), T0354-233 0703, www.imperialchai.com. Rebuilt and recreated colonial home with de luxe rooms (all unique) crammed with antiques and atmosphere, the personal touch of the owner in evidence throughout. Passion fruits grow by balconies, the tiered garden is delightful (organic veg), spa/yoga/meditation and 'stick' massage are reasonably priced, superlative meals and tea menu (see page 122). Views of Kanchenjunga from some rooms. Newer annex is cheaper and simpler, still very comfortable with a chalet air. Lovely walking through tea gardens and villages nearby. Management are informative and interesting. Solar lighting being introduced, wheelchair access. Highly recommended.
D Makaibari Homestays, Makaibari, T033-2287 8560, www.makaibari.com. Villagers from the tea community provide all meals and a unique experience in their family homes, US$25 per day per couple, Western toilets.
D Tourist Lodge, Hill Cart Rd (1 km from station), T0354-234 4409. Gloomy corridors but some lovely wooden rooms (check a couple), good views, 24-hr hot water, heaters in winter, snack bar, decent bar (beer Rs 120) and restaurant. Car hire.
F Kurseong Palace, 11 Hill Cart Rd, T0354-234 5409, kurseong_palace@yahoo.com. Acceptable rooms with TV and carpets, hot water, nice staff.

Kalimpong *p114, map p115*

Hotels offer discounts during winter and monsoon; not all accept credit cards.
A Silver Oaks, Main Rd, T03552-255296, www.elginhotels.com. Beautiful rooms, some with fabulous views, good restaurant (own fruit and vegetables), pleasant terraced garden.
B Gurudongma House, Hill Top Rd, T03552-255204, www.gurudongma.com. Rooms in charming family house and cottage with meals, Alpine tents, gardens, personal service (collect from motor stand), book ahead. Also restored farmhouse at Samthar where you can enjoy country pleasures and wonderful food; contact **Gurudongma Tours and Treks**, gurutt@satyam.net.in.
B Himalayan, Upper Cart Rd, 10-min walk from town centre, T03552-255248, www.himalayan hotel.co.in. Stone-built characterful family home. 20 rooms (better upstairs) and 8 spacious suites in imaginatively designed 'cottages', lovely veranda, mountain views, attractive gardens, set menu meals, helpful management and almost too-attentive service.
B Orchid Retreat, Ganesh Villa, longish walk from town (4 km from the market), T03552-255389, theorchidretreat.com. In interesting orchid nursery, 6 rooms in traditional thatched cottages (built with local materials), hot water (no TV or phone), home-cooked meals (Rs 100-150), lovely terrace garden with special palm collection, personal attention, peaceful. No walk-ins, must book in advance.
B-C Kalimpong Park, Ringkingpong Rd, T03552-255304, www.indiamart.com/kalimpongparkhotel. Raj atmosphere aplenty in good-sized, airy rooms, **B** suites (some in older 2-storeyed house), good restaurant and bar, garden, pleasant peaceful location, knowledgeable owner.
B-C Morgan House, Singamari, Durpin Dara Hill, T03552-255384, 3 km from centre. Beautiful location, 7 rooms with bath (good views from upstairs), restaurant, bar, gardens.

D Crown Lodge, off Bag Dhara Rd, near Motor Stand, T03552-255846, slg_ramklg@sancharnet.in. 21 clean well-maintained rooms with bath, hot water, generator, very friendly and helpful, pleasant.

D-E Kalash, on main road above **Vegetarian Snacketeria**, T03552-259564. Spotless rooms over a great restaurant, but traffic noise can be a problem.

D-F JP Lodge, RC Mintry Rd, T03552-257457, www.jplodge.com. Clean comfortable rooms with charming staff, designated meditation space in a wood-panelled garret.

E Cloud 9, Ringkingpong Rd, T03552-259554. Clean attractive rooms, good multi-cuisine restaurant.

E-F Chinmoy Lodge, below Motor Stand, T03552-2256364. Set among quaint old buildings, with sweeping views from roof and cheery, freshly painted rooms.

E-G Deki Lodge, Tirpai Rd, uphill from Motor Stand, T03552-255095, www.geocities.com/dekilodge. Pristine rooms aimed at various budgets, cosy terrace restaurant with great views, kind and knowledgeable staff, a place with character.

🍴 Eating

Siliguri *p105*

🍴-🍴 Havelli, SS Market Complex, Hill Cart Rd, T0353-253 5013. Subtly lit, beige walls and wood sculptures prevail, more intimate than most. Multi-cuisine is high standard and the choices endless, including continental. Family atmosphere, open 1100-2230.

🍴-🍴 Tera, at **The Tiara Hotel**, 1st floor, Sevoke Rd, T0353-243 6024. An orderly restaurant with pleasing decor, tables with cloths and flowers, but a dominant TV screen. Mainly Indian cuisine, some Western breakfast choices, alcohol served.

🍴 Amit's Amardeep, 7 Sevoke Rd. Upstairs a/c, cheap youthful place with North Indian and Chinese, good biryani, friendly able staff. Open 0830-2230.

🍴 Jain Jaika Bhojnalaya, Shikha Deep Building (3rd floor), Sevoke Rd. Look for their red and white sign down a tiny alley (there's a lift). Sunny orange walls and a chequered floor, pure veg food, best as a breakfast option (excellent paratha and veg – other items on menu generally unavailable), opens at 0800-1530, 1830-2130.

🍴 Khana Khazana, Hill Cart Rd. Pleasant outdoor terrace plus indoor seating (fans), generous portions, South Indian is decent or there's tandoori, rolls, Chinese, veg/non, but lassis and shakes are average. Clean family atmosphere. Open 0700-2230.

🍴 Rasoi, Ganeshayan Building (2nd Fl), beside Sky Star Building, Sevoke Rd, T097758-802071. Pure veg food in a modern spacious environment, great for kebabs and South Indian (40 kinds of *dosa*), interesting *dhals*, plus some Chinese options. Open 1030-2230.

Darjeeling *p106, map p106*

Hotels with restaurants will usually serve non-residents. Several have bars.

🍴🍴 New Elgin, see **The Elgin Hotel**. Formal dining room with some character, OK meals, very pleasant service. Come for a slice of history rather than the food. Afternoon tea is very overpriced, better to just have a drink and enjoy the surroundings.

🍴🍴 Shangrila, see Sleeping. Darjeeling's chicest dining experience, contemporary decor mixed with tasteful Tibetan artefacts, and a wide menu of delicious multi-cuisine food plus bar. Gracious service, open later than most; recommended.

🍴🍴-🍴 Glenary's, Nehru Rd (the Mall), T0354-225 7554, glens_getaways@sancharnet.in. Modern tearoom with excellent confectionery and pastries, friendly, first class breakfast, Kalimpong cheese and wholemeal bread sold. Licensed restaurant upstairs is pricier but lively and with a good atmosphere, bar downstairs has local band on Sat (supposedly 1900-2200 but often finishes early). Speedy internet café (Rs 30 per hr).

⍓-⍓ Lunar, 51 Gandhi Rd, T0354-225 4194. Thoroughly delicious pure veg Indian dishes, and some decent sandwiches, pizzas and Chinese. Modern and informal, family environment, big windows for the view. Lassis are fragrant and creamy, service competent and kindly.

⍓-⍓ Valentino, closed for refurbishment at time of research, but renowned for their excellent Chinese and Continental menu.

⍓ Blind Date, top floor, Fancy Market, NB Singh Rd. Warm and friendly place always packed with locals, cheap Tibetan and Chinese mains, divine soups and clean kitchen in open view. A must.

⍓ Cozy Bhutan, Gandhi Rd. Bhutanese cuisine consists of lots of beef and pork, plus a few interesting veg options, mix of mild or spicy. Friendly and charismatic elderly lady in charge. Lowest ceilings in Darjeeling, darkened cubby holes are rather seedy. Open 0930-1930.

⍓ Dafey Mumal, Laden La Rd. Buzzing bar and acceptable Chinese and Tibetan meals.

⍓ Dekeva's, 52 Gandhi Rd, near club side. Nice little Tibetan place, cosy, local meals, fast food.

⍓ Fiesta, Chowrasta. Café-style restaurant serving a mainly Western menu. A bit faded, but a good spot to watch the world go by.

⍓ Hasty Tasty, Nehru Rd. Very good pure vegetarian Indian fast food, not the cheapest but worth it.

⍓ Kunga, Gandhi Rd. Cheerful unpretentious Tibetan joint, with great *momos* and huge backpacker-friendly breakfasts. But it's the range of fantastic soups that are most memorable. Has toilets. Open 0830-2030.

⍓ New Dish, JP Sharma Rd. Chinese. Adventurous menu, mainly Chinese (cheap), excellent chicken entrées, friendly staff. Open 0800-1930. Scruffy aquamarine mirrored walls, serves beer (Rs 75).

⍓ South Indian Café, Chowrasta. Indian. Very good vegetarian meals.

⍓ Stardust, Chowrasta. Basic range of North and South Indian dishes, pure vegetarian, great views from the terrace.

Mirik *p113*
Restaurants in the larger hotels are reliable, plus there are extremely cheap *dhabas* near the bus stand offering passable noodle dishes.

⍓ Samden, main road, Krishnanagar. Great Tibetan food in a quaint little restaurant.

Kurseong *p113*
⍓-⍓ Chai Country, at Cochrane Place (see Sleeping). A meal at Cochrane is not to be missed if in Kurseong. Food is gourmet and inventive, best are the Anglo-Indian dishes with a twist (*dhal* with mint, oyster mushrooms smoked with tea) otherwise African curry, veggie shepherd's pie and more; puddings are exquisite (baked mango). No liquor license.

⍓ Abhinandan Fast Food Corner, Naya Bazar (on way to Eagle's Crag). Cubby hole, with lampshades made of fishing basket traps and character, good veg rolls, thukpa, momos. Open 0900-2030.

⍓ Gorkha Bhancha Ghar, at the railway, opposite the platform. This specialist *bhancha ghar* (kitchen) serves up cheap and excellent Nepali food in clean surroundings, from 0700-1900.

⍓ Hill Top, 11 TN Rd, T(0)99331-29177. Good for Chinese and Tibetan in a cosy restaurant-cum-bar that makes a nod to Chinese decor. Cheap beer.

Kalimpong *p114, map p115*
Most restaurants shut at 2000. Local canteens behind the jeep stand dish out delicious *momos* and noodle soups at rock-bottom prices.

⍓ Gompus, Chowrasta (in hotel). Largely meat-based menu, good for Tibetan and Chinese, very popular, alcohol served.

⍓ 3C's (formerly **Glenary's**), Main Rd. Hangout for local youth, with Western food, good breakfasts, great pastries and decent coffee.

⍓ Cakes R Us, past DGTC on DB Giri Rd. Café-style offerings.

† Vegetarian Snacketeria, Main Rd, opposite Main Bazar. Tasty South and North Indian plus a wide choice of drinks.

🎧 Bars and entertainment

Darjeeling *p106, map p106*
English-language films show at the Inox cinema in Rink Mall, www.inoxmovies.com, T0354-225 7226. Seats from Rs 90-140. There are several great options for a *chota peg* in Raj-era surroundings. Try the **Planters' Club** bar (see Sleeping, page 118), among the moth-eaten animal trophies inside or out on the terrace (closes early around 2100), the **Windamere** (see Sleeping, page 117) for a cosy lounge-feel among knik-knaks, or the **Gymkhana Club** (see Activities, page 124) for billiards, worn leather seats, and bags of atmosphere. **Joey's Pub**, though housed in an unlikely looking heritage cottage, gathers a rowdy crowd every night for drinks in a true pub ambiance. Surprisingly good typical British bar snacks. Very social, open 0930-2300, beers Rs 90-95.

🎉 Festivals and events

Darjeeling *p106, map p106*
Apr/May Buddha Purnima/Jayanti celebrates the birth of the Buddha in the monasteries.

🛍 Shopping

Darjeeling *p106, map p106*
The markets are colourful and worth visiting.

Books
Greenland, Laden La Rd, up some steps near entrance to Prestige Hotel. Book swap.
Oxford Bookshop, Chowrasta. Good stock especially local interest, best in town, amiable staff.

Handicrafts
Local handicrafts sold widely include Buddhist *tankhas* (hand-painted scrolls surrounded by Chinese brocade), good wood carving, carpets, hand-woven cloth, jewellery, copper, brass and white metal religious curios such as prayer wheels, bowls and statues. Chowrasta shops are closed on Sun, Chowk Bazar and Middle Bazar on Thu.
Dorjee, Laden La Rd. **Eastern Arts**, Chowrasta. **H Mullick**, curios from Chowrasta, a cut above the rest.
Nepal Curios, Laden La Rd. **Tibetan Refugee Self-help Centre** (see page 109), hand-woven carpets in bold designs and colours (from US$360 including packaging, at least 6-month waiting list).

Photography
Das Studios, The Mall. Stationery, postcards, interesting black-and-white prints from Raj days; order from album (1-2 days).

Tea
Nathmull's, Laden La Rd (above GPO) and at Rink Mall, nathmulls@goldentips tea.com. An institution, vast selection (Rs 140-10,000 per kg), avoid fancy packs, knowledgeable owner.

Kalimpong *p114, map p115*
Handicrafts
Tibetan and Nepalese handicrafts and woven fabrics are particularly good. There is an abundance of shops on RC Mintry Rd.
Gangjong, Primtam Rd (ask at **Silver Oaks Hotel** for directions). Interesting paper factory.
Soni Emporium, near Motor Stand, Mani Link Rd. Specializes in Himalayan handicrafts.

🔺 Activities and tours

Siliguri and Jaldapara *p105*
Tour operators
Help Tourism (Association of Conservation & Tourism), 143 Hill Cart Rd (1st floor), T0353-253 5893, www.helptourism.com.

Recommended for eastern Himalaya and arranging homestays in villages around the tea gardens.

Shakul Pradan, T09749-391230. With 2-3 days advance notice, Shakul (who works for WBTDC) can arrange a package to Jaldapara, including elephant ride, jeep transport, private hotel in Madariat and all meals, for Rs1200 per person per day.

Darjeeling *p106, map p106*
Clubs
The old **Gymkhana Club**, T0354-225 2892, has good snooker tables, badminton, squash, tennis and roller skating (tie skates on with string). Temporary membership Rs 50 per day, up to Rs 55 for activities, excellent staff. The **Planters' Club**, The Mall, T0354-225 4348, the old Darjeeling Club, a relic of the Raj, membership (Rs 50 per day), allows use of pleasant colonial restaurant (buffet meals cost extra), bar, billiards, a bit run down but log fires, warm and friendly.

Mountaineering
Himalayan Mountaineering Institute, in the zoo compound, T0354-225 4087, www.himalayanmountaineeringinstitute. com. Office open Mon-Sat 1000-13000. Runs mountaineering training courses, from 'adventure' level (15-day, US$250, Nov-Dec and Apr-May), through basic (28-day, Mar-May and Sep-Nov) to advanced (28-day, Mar, May and Sep).

Riding
Pony rides are popular on the Mall starting at Chowrasta; also possible to do a scenic half-day ride to Ghoom – agree price in writing.

River rafting
On the Tista, a range of trips from 1½ hrs to 2-day camps with fishing (Rs 2500 for 6 or more, transport extra), contact DGHC (see below).

Tour operators
Clubside Tours & Travels, JP Sharma Rd, T0354-225 5123. Hotel booking, tours, treks, good jeep hire, air tickets for all domestic carriers.
DGHC, runs a variety of tours leaving from the tourist office, including to Mirik, Tiger Hill, Darjeeling town and surrounding areas. Price lists are available at the office.
Darjeeling Transport Corp, 30 Laden La Rd. Maruti vans, jeeps, Land Rovers and a few *sumos* are available. Prices vary according to the season so negotiate rates.
Juniper Tours, behind police island, New Car Park, Laden La Rd, T0354-225 2095, also Air India and Jet Airways agent.
Meghma Tours & Travels, 51 Gandhi Rd, T0354-228 9073, meghmatourstravels@ yahoo.co.in. A variety of day tours as well as trips into Sikkim.

Trekking agents
Clubside Tours & Travels, see Tour operators, above.
Himalayan Adventures, Das Studios, Nehru Rd, T0354-225 4090, dastrek@ aussiemail.com.au.
Himalayan Travels, 18 Gandhi Rd, T/F0354-225 2254, kkgurung@cal.vsnl.net.in. Long established, good for Sikkim and Singalila treks, tours to Bhutan (need 3-5 days' notice, US$180-240 per day depending on group size).
Trek-Mate, Singalila Arcade, Nehru Rd, T0354-225 6611, chagpori@satyam.net.in. Well-equipped, English-speaking guides, excellent service, recommended.

Kalimpong *p114, map p115*
DGAHC tourist office, DB Giri Rd, can advise on walking routes and rafting.
Gurudongma Tours & Travels, T03552-225204, www.gurudongma.com. High-quality, personalized treks, priced accordingly.

Border essentials: India–Nepal

Kakarbhitta, the Nepalese border town, has only basic accommodation. Visas cost US$30 to be paid in exact cash and you'll need two passport photos. From the border, buses depart 0300-2400, arriving the same evening at Kathmandu (595 km, 15-16 hours); the journey can be very tiring. From Kakarbhitta it is also possible to fly (seasonal) from Bhadrapur (34 km, with free transfer to airstrip) to Kathmandu with RNAC, Everest Air or Buddha Air (Nep Rs 1400, one hour). Alternatively, get a taxi to Biratnagar in Nepal (150 km) and fly from there to Kathmandu (US$99).

Kalimpong Village Tours, Mondo Challenge, Peepal Dhara, 8½ Mile, Rishi Rd, T0355-226 0026, T(0)9932-368974, www.kalimpong villagetour.wordpress.com. Gentle trekking on 1- to 3-day tours, taking in local culture and village life in the Koshyem region. Mondo Challenge are a not-for-profit organization. **Mintry Transport**, Main Rd. Jet Airways and Air India agent.

Siliguri *p105*
Help Tourism (Association of Conservation & Tourism), 143 Hill Cart Rd (1st floor), T0353-253 5893, helptour@shivanet.com. Travel agent. Recommended for Eastern Himalaya.

☉ Transport

Siliguri *p105*
Try to arrive at **Siliguri** or **NJP** in daylight (before 1900). Rickshaw drivers can be quite aggressive at NJP.

Air
Bagdogra airport, 13 km away, with tourist information counter and little else; security checks can be rigorous. Flights to **Kolkata**, **Delhi** and **Guwahati**. Air India, Hill Cart Rd (2nd floor, opposite Biswadeep Cinema), T0353-251 1495. Daily 1000-1700, closed Sun. Jet Airways, Vinayak Building, Hill Cart Rd, T0353-243 5876, airport T0353-255 1675, daily. Kingfisher, to **Delhi** daily and **Guwahati**, 3 times a week. Helicopter daily in fine weather to **Sikkim** (see page 144), depending on

demand. Transfer from the airport: STC buses to Darjeeling and Gangtok. Shared taxis to Darjeeling (Rs 1200), Gangtok (Rs 1600), Kalimpong (Rs 1200) and Siliguri (Rs 300).

Bus
Siliguri is on NH31, well connected with Darjeeling (80 km), Gangtok (114 km) and Kalimpong (54 km) and served by buses from WB, Assam, Bihar, Sikkim and Bhutan. **Tenzing Norgay Central Bus Terminus** (CBT) is on Hill Cart Rd, next to Siliguri Junction Railway Station.There are also many private operators just outside the CBT offering similar services. Bus to **Madarihat** (for Jaldapara) leaves from the CBT at 0700, 3 hrs, Rs 55; **Malda**, frequent buses from 0430-2300, 6 hrs, Rs 112; **Mirik**, 0730, 2-3 hrs, Rs 60. The WBSTC's overnight Rocket bus to **Kolkata**departs 1800, 1900 and 2000 from Hill Cart Rd, 12 hrs, Rs 215, but it's a tortuous journey on terrible roads. For greater comfort on a Volvo bus, try Gupta Tour & Travels, T0353-645 4077, departing for Kolkata at 2000. Ticket counter 13 in the CBT for buses to Assam: **Guwahati** at 1700, 12 hrs, Rs 250; **Tezpur** at 1400, 16 hrs, Rs 330. Buses to North Bengal go from the **Dooars Bus Stand** at the junction of Sevoke and Bidhan roads: **Kalimpong** 0700, 2-3 hrs, Rs 65. SNT Bus Station, is opposite CBT: **Gangtok**, buses leave regularly between 0730-1330, Rs 86-110, 5 hrs; de luxe private buses from CBT (separate ticket window), Rs 100.

    To Bhutan Bhutan Government buses, tickets from Counter 14 at CBT, 0700-1200.

To **Phuntsholing**: buses at 0720, 1200, 1400, 1500, Rs 75, 3-4 hrs. NBSTC buses run at 0700 and 1200, Rs 75.

To Nepal To **Kathmandu** buses (or more conveniently taxi or Land Rover, every 15 mins or so from opposite CBT) to **Panitanki** on the border (35 km, 1 hr); transfer to **Kakarbhitta** by cycle-rickshaw. See box, page 125. Tickets from **Tourist Services Agency**, Pradhan Nagar, Siliguri, T0353-253 1959, bytours@cal2. vsnl.net.in; Siliguri to Kakarbhitta (Rs 120); Kakarbhitta to Kathmandu/Pokhara (Nep Rs 520); also through tickets.

Jeep
Shared jeeps are the best way to get to and around the hills, as they leave more frequently and are faster than buses, and only a little more expensive. **Kalimpong**, from Sevoke Rd stand, 2½ hrs Rs 70/60; Gangtok, Sevoke Rd or outside CBT on Hill Cart Rd, 3½-4 hrs Rs 120; **Darjeeling**, from Hill Cart Rd, 3-3½ hrs, Rs 85-95; Kurseong, Hill Cart Rd (near Conclave Hotel), 1½ hrs, Rs 50. Jeeps leave from outside NJP for **Darjeeling** and **Gangtok**, at higher price and with some waiting while drivers tout for customers.

Train
Railway Enquiry at NJP, T0353-256 1555. **Siliguri Junction** and NJP, 5 km away, have tourist information. There are buses, tempos (Rs 10), cycle-rickshaws (Rs 40), trains and taxis (Rs 100) between the two. NJP has good connections to other major destinations in India. For long-distance rail journeys from NJP, first buy tickets at Siliguri (Computerized Reservations, Bidhan Rd near Stadium), 1000-1300, 1330-1700 (to avoid the queue go to Chief Reservations Officer at side of building), then go to NJP station for train. Porters demand Rs 50 for 2 cases.

To **Darjeeling**, the Toy Train, www.dhr.in, leaves from NJP, calling at Siliguri Junction on its way.

Daily diesel service leaves at 0900, 7½ hrs (0930, 7hrs from Siliguri); Rs 42 in 2nd class. New 1st class service to **Kurseong**, 0830 from NJP. Services are often disrupted by landslides during the rains, though the upper section from Kurseong (accessible by bus/jeep) continues to run; check beforehand. Take special care of luggage; thefts reported.

Steam trains run daily from Siliguri to **Sukna**, 0930, 40 mins, and on Sat and Sun to **Tindharia**, 0930, 2½ hrs.

From NJP to **Kolkata** (S): *Darjeeling Mail*, *2344*, 2000, 10 hrs. **Kolkata** (H): *Kamrup Exp*, *5960*, 1635, 14 hrs; *Kanchenjunga Exp, 5658* (AC/II), 0755, 11½ hrs. **New Delhi**: *NE Exp, 2505*, 1705, 26½ hrs; *Rajdhani Exp* (Mon, Wed, Thu, Fri, Sun), 2423, 1305, 21 hrs. From Kolkata (S) to Siliguri: *Darjeeling Mail*, *2343*, 2205, 10 hrs, connects with the Toy Train from NJP.

Jaldapara *p105*
Air
The nearest airport is Bagdogra (see page 107). Air India has daily connections with **Kolkata** (50 mins), **Guwahati** and **Delhi**. From airport, bus to Siliguri; then 4 hrs' scenic drive through tea gardens to Jaldapara (155 km).

Bus
Express buses from Kolkata to Madarihat or Siliguri to Park (128 km). Forest Department transport to Hollong inside the sanctuary.

Train
Hasimara station (18 km from park) has trains to **Siliguri Junction**: daily *Mahananda Exp 4083*, 0805, 2 hrs.

Darjeeling *p106, map p106*
Air
The nearest airport is Bagdogra (90 km), see Siliguri, above. Transfer by car takes 3 hrs. Pre-paid taxi counter to left of exit, around Rs 1200 (sharing possible). **Air India**, Belle Vue Hotel, Chowrasta, T0354-225 4230. Mon-Sat 1000-1700, Sun 1000-1300.

Bus
NH31 connects Darjeeling with other parts of India. Minibuses go from the main transport stand to nearby hill stations but run infrequently, are slower than jeeps, and not much cheaper. Services run to **Mirik** at 0825 and 1415, and to **Manebhanjang** at 1300. A comprehensive timetable is posted at the ticket counter beside the main stand.

Jeep
Shared jeep is the quickest and most convenient way of getting around the mountains. Jeeps leave regularly to local destinations, and if you pick a jeep that is already over half full, you won't be waiting long before you set off. During the high season it is well advised to book a day in advance (particularly to reserve seat No 1), The prices per person in a share jeep are: Rs 80 to **Siliguri** (2½ hrs via short cut); to **Gangtok** Rs 130; **Mirik** 2½ hrs, Rs 60; to **Kalimpong** 3 hrs, Rs 60-80. The journey to Kalimpong is stunning, along narrow ridges planted with tea bushes and past wooden villages teetering on precipices.

Motorbike
Enfields and other models can be rented from **Extreme Himalayas**, based in the internet café, 0830-2230, opposite Cyber Planet on Zakir Hussein Rd. Contact Gautam, T(0)9933-070013. Around Rs 350 per day.

Taxi
Easily available in the lower part of town.

Train
Diesel service to **New Jalpaiguri** (**NJP**) at 0915, 6-7 hrs (narrow gauge, see page 126), 90 km away. Darjeeling station also has some old steam engines. The narrow-gauge steam tourist train to **Ghoom** with a photo stop at Batasia Loop, departs 1040 and 1320 (sometimes other schedules during high season, check current schedules),

Rs 240 (see Ghoom Monastery, page 109). A passenger steam train also goes to Kurseong (Rs 10/144) via Ghoom (Rs 5/111), daily at 1015, taking 2 hrs.

Mirik *p113*
Access from Bagdogra airport (55 km), Darjeeling (50 km) and Siliguri (52 km). Buses and jeeps to and from other hill stations 0630-1800.

Kurseong *p113*
Jeep
51 km from Siliguri, off the main Darjeeling road, or via Pankhabari. Buses and jeeps to **Siliguri**, 1½ hrs and **Darjeeling**, 1 hr, leave from near the railway station; for **Mirik** jeeps leave from Pankhabari Rd.

Train
A diesel service leaves for Darjeeling 0900 and 1330 (often late), Rs 144/25, 3 hrs. The steam train runs to Darjeeling at 1000 and 1500, 3½ hrs. Ticket office, T0354-234 4700, open 0900-1100, 1400-1600.

Kalimpong *p114, map p115*
Air
Nearest airport is at Bagdogra, 80 km, 3-3½ hrs by car, Rs 1200 (see Siliguri); seat in shared taxi or bus, Rs 75. **Air India** and **Jet Airways**; bookings with **Mintry Transport**.

Bus
State and private buses use the Motor Stand. Several to **Siliguri**, 3 hrs; **Darjeeling**, 3½ hrs; **Gangtok**: 3½ hrs (very scenic). **Kolkata**, fast 'Rocket' buses.

Jeep
Shared jeeps depart 0630-1500, depending on demand; much quicker than buses. To **Darjeeling**, Rs 70 (Rs 50 on cramped back seat); **Siliguri** Rs 70/Rs 50; **Gangtok** Rs 120.

Train

The nearest mainline railhead is New Jalpaiguri (NJP), 67 km. Tickets from **Rly Out Agency**, next to Soni Emporium, Motor Stand. Computerized bookings and a small tourist quota for trains departing to NJP.

ⓘ Directory

Siliguri *p105*

Banks Several ATMs on Hill Cart and Sevoke roads; there's a convenient Axis Bank cashpoint opposite the CBT by Hotel Heritage. **Internet** Moulik, behind Vinayak, Hill Cart Rd, T0353-243 2312. **Net-N-Net**, 1st floor, off Hill Cart Rd opposite bus stand, handy and fast, requires photo ID, open 0930-2130 closed Sun. Rs 20 per hr. **Sai Raj**, Patel Rd, behind Khana Khazana, daily 1000-2230, Sun 1030-1400, Rs 20 per hr. **Medical services** Hospital, T0353-252 1920; North Bengal Clinic, T0353-242 0441. Recommended. **Post** GPO, Hospital Rd, Mon-Sat 0700-1900, Sun 1000-1400. **Useful contacts** Bhutan tourism, near railway station. Sikkim tourism, Hill Cart Rd.

Darjeeling *p106, map p106*

Banks There are many ATMs and exchange houses all over town. **Chemists** Frank Ross, Nehru Rd, Puri, Nehru Rd, above Keventer's. **Couriers** FedEx at Global Express, Robertson Rd, T0354-225 8706. Open Mon-Fri 0900-1700, Sat 0900-1300. **Internet** Compuset Centre, 14 Gandhi Rd, T0354-225 6415, compuset@yahoo.com. Fast connection, no skype, cheap printing, Rs 30 1 hr (min Rs 10), open 0800-2000 including Sun. Glenary's, the Mall, T0354-225 7554, speedy connection, Rs 30 per hr. **Medical services** Planters' Hospital, Nehru Rd, T0354-225 4327. Sadar Hospital, T0354-225 4218. Mariam Nursing Home, below Gymkhana Club, T0354-225 4328, has been recommended for its medical facilities. **Post** GPO, Laden La Rd. **Useful contacts** For Sikkim permits (free, take your passport) go to Office of the District Magistrate, Hill Cart Rd (down- hill from the motorstand), T0354-225 4233, Mon-Fir 1100-1300 and 1430-1600, then get form stamped again at FRO, Laden La Rd, T0354-225 4278, 0930-1700, and return to DM where the permit is issued; 2 hrs.

Kurseong *p113*

Banks SBI, has ATM, opposite station and another 500 m down Pankhabari Rd. **Internet** Cyber Planet, in Unique Sweet Market, open 1000-2030, Rs 25 per hr.

Kalimpong *p114, map p115*

Banks Banks don't change money; Emporium, Mani Link Rd, accepts Visa and Mastercard. **Medical services/post** There is a hospital and a post office near the police station.

South of Kolkata

To the south of Kolkata are the tidal estuary of the Hugli and the mangrove forests of the Sundarbans. Famous for their population of Bengal tigers, the Sundarbans reach into Bangladesh, but it's possible to take a day trip down to the mouth of the Hugli or boat trips into the Sundarbans themselves. ▸▸ *For listings, see page 130.*

Sagardwip

Ganga Sagar Mela is held in mid-January, attracting over 500,000 pilgrims each year who come to bathe and then visit the **Kapil Muni Temple**. The island has been devastated many times by cyclones. To get there catch a bus from Esplanade or take a taxi to Kakdwip and then take a ferry across to Kochuberia Ghat (Sagardwip). From there it is a 30-minute bus ride across island to where the Ganga meets the sea.

Sunderbans Tiger Reserve → *Colour map 2, C2.*

ⓘ *Permit required (maximum of 5 days) from the WBTDC in Kolkata, T033-2248 8271, where you can also book a package tour (take your passport). Alternatively, contact the Secretary, Department of Forests, G Block (top floor), Writers Building (top floor), T033-2221 5999. Best not to go at weekends, when Bengali tourists tend to take over and scare away any wildlife.*
Sunderbans (pronounced Soonder-buns) is named after the Sunderi trees. The mangrove swamps are said to be the largest estuarine forests in the world. Improved management is battling to halt the loss of mangrove cover as it is exploited for fuel. Most villagers depend on fishing and forestry, while local honey gatherers who are active in April and May are said to wear masks on the backs of their heads to frighten away tigers, which they believe only attack from the rear! You will notice large areas of *bheries* for aquaculture. Prawn fisheries are the most lucrative and co-operative efforts are being encouraged by the government.

The reserve, a World Heritage Site, preserves the habitat of about 300 Bengal tigers (*Panthera tigris*). They are bigger and richer in colour than elsewhere in South Asia and are thought to be able to survive on salt water (rainwater is the only fresh water in the park). Tigers here are strong swimmers and known to attack fishermen. Methods of improved management include providing permanent sources of fresh water for tigers by digging deep, monsoon-fed ponds, installing solar-powered lighting to scare them away from villages and electrifying dummy woodcutters. Although you are unlikely to see a tiger, there are spotted deer, wild boar, monkeys, snakes, fishing cats, water monitors, Olive Ridley sea turtles and a few large estuarine crocodiles here, particularly on Lothian Island and Chamta block.

The best season is September-March. Heavy rains and occasional cyclones in April/May and November/December can make visiting difficult. Take water, torch, mosquito repellent and be prepared for cool nights. You must be accompanied by armed forest rangers. Motor launches can be hired from Canning and Sonakhali (Basanti), but it is better to go down the narrow creeks in human-powered boats. You may be able to go ashore on bamboo jetties to walk in the fenced-in areas of the forest which have watchtowers (dawn to dusk only).

Digha → *Colour map 2, C1. 185 km from Kolkata.*

Digha was described by Warren Hastings visiting over 200 years ago as the 'Brighton of the East', though there is not a pebble for at least 2000 km. The casuarina-lined, firm wide beach is popular with Bengalis. The small **Chandaneswar Temple**, 10 km away, actually in Orissa, is an important Siva temple which can be reached by bus.

For Sleeping and Eating price codes and other relevant information, see Essentials pages 34-38.

⊜ Sleeping

Sagardwip *p129*

WBTDC runs 2-day boat trips with lodging on board (**L–C**) during **Ganga Sagar Mela**. You can also stay at the *dharamshala* for a donation. **F Youth Hostel**. Book via the Youth Services office in Kolkata, T033-2248 0626, ext 27.

Sunderbans Tiger Reserve *p129*

A few basic lodges are in Gosaba. One is in Pakhirala, the last village before Sajnekhali. **E Tourist Lodge**, Sajnekhali, contact through WBTDC, T033-2248 8271. Raised on pillars and fenced from wildlife, solar power, small basic rooms with mosquito nets (ask for linen), some Western toilets, hot water in buckets, 20-bed dorm (Rs 220), simple meals (poor choice but if you buy fish, chef will cook it), no alcohol. Book ahead; carry your permit.

Digha *p129*

There is plenty of choice to suit all budgets. **C Sea Coast**, T03220-266305. With some a/c rooms, this is the best 3-star option. **E-F Sea Hawk**, T03220-266235. Comfortable rooms, on 3 floors, some a/c. **E-F Tourist Lodge**, T03220-266255. Rooms on 3 floors, 4 a/c, 5-bed dorm (Rs 80), meals, bar.

▲ Activities and tours

Sunderbans Tiger Reserve *p129*

Sunderbans Jungle Camp, Bali village; book through **Help Tourism** in Kolkata (see page 89). 6 bungalows, in indigenous style with modern bathrooms, in one of India's best community tourism ventures, set up by a group of ex-poachers. Local fishermen supply fish and offer trips into mangrove forests; it's also a chance to interact with villagers and experience authentic folk performances.

WBTDC Tours: 2-day and 3-day trips (infrequent during monsoon, Jul-Sep), by coach from Kolkata then 'luxury' launch with onboard accommodation. Prices vary with standard of lodging: a 2-day tour costs Rs 2300 for 10-12 bed dorms to Rs 11,000 for a 2-person coupé; 5% tax is added. The launch is the only way to visit the Sunderbans during monsoon.

⊖ Transport

Sunderbans Tiger Reserve *p129*

Road and boat From Kolkata: CSTC bus from Babu Ghat, Strand Rd, to **Sonakhali** (first depart 0630 then hourly, Rs 36, 3½ hrs), then hire a **boat** to Sajnekhali (Rs 400-500, 3 hrs). Alternatively, from Basanti, take public ferry to **Gosaba** (1½ hrs, Rs 8), then travel across the island by flat-bed van rickshaw (5 km, 45 mins) which enables you to see interesting village life, and finally take a boat to Sajnekhali; recommended for at least one way. Lodge staff will arrange boat hire with park guide (about Rs 600 for 4 hrs, Rs 1000 for 8 hrs; boats can take 6-8 people). Since these are tidal waterways, boats are not always able to moor near the ghats, and during monsoons or bad weather they will not sail.

Train and boat Kolkata (Sealdah) to **Canning** (105 km) and then boat to Docghat where you can get a shared auto or bus to Sonakhali, where you get another boat. From Canning you can get a private boat direct to Sajnekhali Lodge (Rs 800 per day), but the journey is long and dependent on the tide.

Digha *p129*

Bus A/c luxury buses leave from Esplanade, taking 4 hrs (Rs 170). Public buses leave from Esplanade and Howrah and take 4½-5 hrs (Rs 75).

Train Direct train from Howrah on Sun, 2867A, 0755, 3½ hrs. From Mon-Sat trains depart Salimar (on west bank of Hugli south of Howrah) at 0800.

Contents

Footprint features

Sikkim

At a glance

⊖ **Getting around** Shared jeeps are cheap, fast and much more frequent than buses. Helicopter service from Bagdogra to Gangtok.

◉ **Time required** 1-2 days in and around Gangtok, 2 days for Yumthang Valley, minimum 4-5 days for West Sikkim.

☀ **Weather** Clear and warm in Sep, chilly Oct-Feb, warm and dry but often foggy from Mar until the start of the monsoon in late May/Jun. Best in Sep and Oct.

✕ **When not to go** The monsoon can cause havoc with road transport.

★ **Don't miss ...**
1 Tashi Viewpoint over the Kangchendzonga range, page 139.
2 Rumtek Monastery, page 139.
3 An early-morning walk at Pemayangtse Monastery, page 146.
4 Khecheopalri Lake and village homestays, page 147.
5 Distant valleys of Yumthang and Tsopta, pages 151 and 152.

Khangchendzonga, the third highest mountain in the world, dominates the skyline of Sikkim. The state is renowned as much for its wonderful wildlife and rich variety of plants and flowers as for its ethnically varied population. Sikkim's original inhabitants, the Lepchas, call the region Nye-mae-el, meaning 'Paradise'. To the later Bhutias it is Beymul Denjong, or the 'Hidden Valley of Rice'. The name Sikkim itself is commonly attributed to the Tsong word Su-khim, meaning 'New' or 'Happy House'. The monasteries of Rumtek and Pemayangtse are just two among a wealth of fascinating centres of Buddhism in the state.

Sikkim is an orchid-lovers' paradise, with 660 species found at altitudes as high as 3000 m. Organic farming and ecotourism are officially enshrined in government policy, and although trekking is less developed than in other parts of the Himalaya, the state is beginning to attract ramblers and trekkers in serious numbers.

You can stay a few days in Gangtok, making day trips to Rumtek and Phodong, then move on to Pelling or Yuksom, visiting Pemayangtse Monastery and Khecheopalri Lake, before continuing to Kalimpong or Darjeeling in West Bengal. Road journeys within Sikkim are very scenic, but numerous hairpin bends and unsealed sections can also make them extremely slow, so expect to travel at 10-40 kph. Conditions deteriorate considerably during the monsoon, which can sometimes make travel impossible.

Background → *Population: 540,500. Area: 7298 sq km.*

The land

Geography Sikkim nestles between the peaks of the eastern Himalaya, stretching only 112 km from south to north and 64 km from east to west. This small area contains a vast range of landscapes and habitats, from subtropical river valleys to snow-covered peaks. Despite comprising just 0.2% of India's landmass, Sikkim accounts for an astounding 26% of its biodiversity. The state encompasses the upper valley of the Tista River, a tributary of the Brahmaputra, the watershed of which forms the borders with Tibet and Nepal. In the east lies the Chumbi Valley, a tongue of Tibetan land separating Sikkim from Bhutan that gives the state its strategic and political sensitivity. The Sikkimese believe Khangchendzonga (known as Kanchenjunga in West Bengal, or the 'Five Treasures of the Great Snows'), at 8586 m, to be the repository of minerals, grains, salt, weapons and holy scriptures. On its west is the massive 31-km-long Zemu Glacier.

Climate In the lower valleys Sikkim's climate is subtropical. Above 1000 m, it is temperate, while the higher mountain tops are permanently under snow. Sikkim is one of the Himalaya's wettest regions, with most rain falling between mid-May and September.

History

From the 13th century Tibetans, like the Namgyal clan, immigrated to Sikkim. In 1642 Phuntsog Namgyal (1604-1670) became the Chogyal (king). With a social system based on Tibetan Lamaistic Buddhism, the land was split into 12 *dzongs* (fortified districts).

In the 18th century Sikkim lost land to Nepal, Bhutan and the British. When the Gurkhas of Nepal launched a campaign into Tibet and were defeated by the Chinese in 1791-1792, Sikkim won back its northern territories. The narrow Chumbi Valley, which separates Sikkim from Bhutan, remained with Tibet. When the British defeated Nepal in 1815, the southern part of the country was given back to Sikkim. However, in the next conflict with Nepal, Darjeeling was handed over to the British in return for their assistance. In 1848 the Terai region at the foot of the mountains was annexed by the British.

Nepalis migrated into Sikkim from the beginning of the 19th century, eventually becoming more numerous than the local inhabitants. This led to internal conflict also involving the British and the Tibetans. The British won the ensuing battles and declared Sikkim a Protectorate in 1890. The state was controlled by a British Political Officer who effectively stripped the *Gyalpos* of executive power. It was many years before the Sikkimese regained control.

Culture

Ethnic groups The Naong, Chang and Mon are believed to have inhabited Sikkim in prehistoric times. Each ethnic group has an impressive repertoire of folk songs and dances. The **Lepchas**, who call themselves Rongpas and claim to be the original inhabitants of Sikkim, may have come from Tibet well before the eighth century and brought Lamaistic Buddhism, which is still practised. They are now regarded as the indigenous peoples. They are deeply religious, peace loving and typically shy but cheerful. The government has reserved the Dzongu area in North and Central Sikkim for Lepchas, who now make up less than 10% of the population. For a long time, the Lepchas' main contact with the outside world was the market-place at Mangan, where they bartered oranges and cardamom. Their alphabet was only devised in the 18th century by the king.

Permits

Free **Inner Line Permits** (ILPs) are issued to foreigners to enter Sikkim for up to 15 days. Recent revisions to the rules stipulate that 30-day IPLs can now be granted on application – check to see whether this change is now actually in effect. 15-day ILPs are repeatedly renewable, allowing stays of up to three months. These allow visits to Gangtok, Rumtek, Phodong, Mangan, Rabangla, Namchi, Gezing, Pemayangtse, Pelling, Yuksam, Pakyong and Soreng. Contact an Indian mission abroad when applying for an Indian visa (enclosing two extra photos), or apply at any FRO (Foreigners' Registration Office) or the Sikkim Tourism Office in New Delhi, Kolkata, Siliguri or Darjeeling (check www.sikkim.gov.in for office details). The checkpoint at Rangpo, on the border with West Bengal, issues a 15-day permit for foreigners on entering Sikkim; processing time is just 10 minutes. Visas are extendable at the FRO in Gangtok (Yangthang Building, Kazi Rd, Gangtok, open daily 1000-1600) or by the Superintendent of Police in Namchi (south), Geyzing (west) and Mangan (north). On exiting Sikkim, it is not permitted to return for three months.

Certain areas in north and west Sikkim (Chungthang, Yumthang, Lachen, Chhangu, Dzongri) have been opened to groups of two to 20 travellers, on condition that travel is with a registered agency. The required Protected Areas Permits (PAP) can be arranged by most local travel agents; apply with photocopies of your passport (Indian visa and personal details pages), ILP and two photos.

The **Magar**, a minority group, are renowned as warriors and were involved in the coronation of Phuntsog Namgyal, the first Chogyal of Sikkim in 1642.

The **Bhotias** (meaning 'of Bhot/Tibet') or Bhutias entered Sikkim in the 13th century from Kham in Tibet. Many adapted to sedentary farming from pastoral nomadism and displaced the Lepchas. Some, however, retained their older lifestyle, and combined animal husbandry with trading over the Trans-Himalayan passes: Nathula (4392 m), Jelepla (4388 m), Donkiala (5520 m) and Kongrala (4809 m). Over the years the Bhutias have come into increased contact with the Lepcha and intermarried with them. Nearly every Bhutia family has one member who becomes a monk. Monasteries remain the repositories of Bhutia culture and festivals here are the principal social events. However, those who have visited Ladakh or Zanskar may find them architecturally and artistically a little disappointing. The Bhutias are famous for their weaving and are also skilled woodcarvers.

The **Newars** entered Sikkim in large numbers from Nepal in the 19th century. Skilled in metal and woodwork, they were granted the right by the Chogyal to mine copper and mint the Sikkimese coinage. Other Nepali groups followed. With high-altitude farming skills, they settled new lands and built houses directly on the ground unlike the Lepcha custom of building on stilts. The Newars were followed by the Chettris and other Nepali clans who introduced Hinduism, which became more popular as their numbers swelled.

Religion In Sikkim, as in Nepal, Hinduism and Buddhism have interacted and amalgamated so Himalayan Hinduism includes a pantheon of Buddhist *bodhisattvas* as well as Hindu deities. The animist tradition also retains a belief in evil spirits.

Buddhist **prayer flags** flutter in the breeze everywhere. The different types, such as wind, luck and victory, are printed with texts and symbols on coloured pieces of cloth and are tied to bamboo poles or trees. **Prayer wheels** carrying inscriptions (which should be turned clockwise) vary in size from small hand-held ones to vast drums which are installed by a monastery or *stupa*. Whitewashed masonry **chortens** (*stupas*) usually commemorate the Buddha or Bodhisattva, the structure symbolizing the elements (earth, water, fire, air, ether). The eight **lucky signs** appear as parasol, pot or vase, conch shell, banner, two fishes, lotus, knot of eternity and the wheel of law (Dharma Chakra). Bowls of **water** (Thing Duen Tsar) are offered in prayer from left to right during Buddhist worship. The gift of water from one who is free from greed and meanness is offered to quench thirsty spirits and to wash the feet, and represents flower (or welcome), incense, lamp, perfume and food.

Festivals Since the 22 major festivals are dictated by the agricultural cycle and the Hindu-Buddhist calendar, it is best to check dates with the Gangtok tourist office.

Jan/Feb Bumchu meaning 'sacred pot' is a 1-day festival at the monastery in Tashiding. The sacred pot is opened once a year and the water level within forecasts the prosperity of Sikkim in the coming year.

Feb/Mar Losar (Tibetan New Year) is celebrated for about a week at Tashiding. It is preceded by Lama dances in Rumtek.

Apr/May Buddha Purnima/Jayanti is the most sacred day in the Buddhist calendar, falling on the full moon of the lunar month of Vaishaaka. 'Buddha's birthday' is also the day he gained enlightenment and attained Nirvana.

Jun Saga Dawn, a Buddhist festival with huge religious processions round Gangtok. **Rumtek Chaams Dance festival** is held in commemoration of the 8 manifestations of Guru Padmasambhava, who established Buddhism in Tibet.

Aug/Sep Pang Lhabsol commemorates the consecration of Khangchendzonga as Sikkim's guardian deity; the Lepchas believe that the mountain is their birthplace. The masked warrior dance is especially spectacular; warriors wear traditional armour of helmets, swords and shields. Celebrations are held in Pemayangtse.

Sep/Oct Dasain is one of the most important Nepali festivals. It coincides with **Dasara** in North India, see page 40. On the first day barley seeds are planted in prayer rooms, invocations are made to Durga, and on the eighth day buffalo and goats are ritually sacrificed.

Dec Diwali (the Festival of Lights). **Kagyat Dances** performed by monks (especially at Enchey), with religious music and chanting, enact themes from Buddhist mythology and end with the burning of effigies made of flour, wood and paper. This symbolizes the exorcism of evil spirits and the ushering in of prosperity for the coming year. **Losoog** (**Namsoong** for Lepchas at Gangtok) is the Sikkimese New Year, also called **Sonam Losar**. Farmers celebrate their harvest and beginning of their new cropping calendar.

Modern Sikkim

In 1950, Sikkim became a Protectorate of India. In 1973 there were growing demands for accession to India by the local population, consisting mainly of Nepalis, and Sikkim was formally made an associate state. The Gyalpos lost their power as a result of the new democratic constitution and Sikkim became the 22nd state in the Union in 1975. Although there is no separatist movement, India's takeover and the abolition of the monarchy, supported by many of Nepali origin, is still resented by many Sikkimese who don't regard themselves as Indians. The state enjoys special tax and other privileges, partly because of its highly sensitive geopolitical location on the disputed border with China. In the 2009 general election the Sikkim Democratic Front (SDF), a party confined to Sikkim, won all 32 seats in the State Assembly.

Gangtok and around

→ Colour map 2, A2. Phone code: 03592.
Population: 55,200. Altitude: 1547 m.

Gangtok ('High Hill'), the capital of Sikkim, sits on a ridge overlooking the Ranipul River. The setting is spectacular with fine views of the Khangchendzonga range, but the town has lost some of its quaint charm with the mushrooming of concrete buildings along the national highway and the main road. The crowded Mahatma Gandhi Marg and the colourful bazars below it are where all the town's commercial activity is concentrated. Away from here, there are many serene areas and quiet alleys that remain virtually untouched. ▶ For listings, see pages 140-144.

Ins and outs

Getting there There is a small airport near Gangtok linked to Bagdogra airport (see page 125), 124 km away, by a regular helicopter service. Most visitors arrive from North Bengal by the attractive road following the Tista (NH31A), which is accessible all year except in very wet weather (mid-June to September) when there may be landslips. Permits and passports are checked at Rangpo where 15-day permits (extendable in Gangtok or district headquarters, see box, page 135) are available (passport and two photos required). SNT buses terminate at the Paljor Stadium Road stand, while jeeps from Siliguri/Bagdogra stop at Nam Nang jeep stand south of Gangtok, connected to the centre by a 10-minute ride in a shared minibus taxi. Jeeps for West Sikkim use the main jeep stand on NH31A just below the tourist office, while jeeps for destinations north leave from another stand near Vajra cinema (five-minute taxi ride north of centre). ▶ See Transport, page 144.

Getting around The busy hub around MG Marg, pedestrianized in the evening, is a

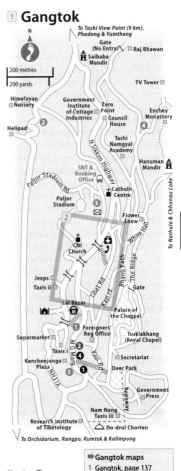

1 **Gangtok**

To Tashi View Point (9 km),
Phodong & Yumthang

Gate (No Entry) — Raj Bhawan
Saibaba Mandir
TV Tower
Himalayan Nursery
Government Institute of Cottage Industries
Zero Point
Enchey Monastery
Helipad
Council House
Tashi Namgyal Academy
N Sikkim Highway
SNT & Booking Office
Hanuman Mandir
Paljor Stadium Rd
Paljor Stadium
Catholic Centre
Flower Show
To Nathula & Chhangu Lake
CNI Church
White Hall
Jeeps
Taxis ii
Bhanu Path
The Ridge
Tibet Rd
Gate
Lal Bazar
Palace of the Chogyal
Foreigners' Reg Office
Supermarket
Tsuklakhang (Royal Chapel)
Taxis i
MG Marg
Secretariat
Kanchenjunga Plaza
Deer Park
NH31A
Government Press
Nam Nang Taxis iii
Ropeway
Research Institute of Tibetology
Do-drul Chorten
To Orchidarium, Rangpo, Rumtek & Kalimpong

Sleeping 🛏
Denzong Inn 1
Hidden Forest 2
Nor-khill 3
Siniolchu Lodge 4
Tashi Delek & Blue Poppy
Restaurant 5

Eating 🍴
China Palate 1
Taste of Tibet 4

Bars & clubs 🍷
Pub 25 2

15-minute walk from end to end. Away from the bazars, the town is pleasant for walking around (see Rajesh Verma's *Sikkim: A Guide and Handbook*, Rs 140). For excursions further afield you'll need to hire a jeep or taxi; rates are fixed and displayed on the back window.

Tourist information **Sikkim** ⓘ *MG Marg, Gangtok Bazar, T03592-221634, daily 0800-2000* Apply for permits here.

Sights

At the north end of town the **Government Institute of Cottage Industries** ⓘ *Mon-Sat 0900-1230 and 1330-1530, closed 2nd Sat of month*, produces a wide range of local handicrafts, including wool carpets, jackets, dolls, handmade paper, carved and painted wooden tables. Items are of high quality (and prices) but there's no parcel service for sending packages home.

Enchey Monastery is 3 km northeast of the main bazar. It's a pleasant walk that takes you past the small **flower garden** at Whitehall (orchids on show March-April). Originally built by the eighth Chogyal in the 1840s, the present building dates from 1909. Religious dances are held in August and December; see Festivals, page 136.

The **Palace of the Chogyal** is only open once a year in the last week of December for the **Pang Lhabsol Festival**. Below this is the **Tsuklakhang** or Royal Chapel, standing on a high ridge where royal marriages and coronations took place. This is the major place of worship and has a large and impressive collection of scriptures. The interior houses Buddha images and is lavishly decorated with woodcarving and murals. Visitors are welcome during Tibetan New Year but may not be permitted at other times; photography is prohibited.

Moving south along the road you pass the **Secretariat** complex on your left. Beyond this is the **Deer Park**, loosely modelled on the famous one at Sarnath, with a statue of the Buddha. From here a **ropeway** ⓘ *0930-1700, Rs 50 one way*, descends the hill to Deorali Bazar, near which is the unique **Namgyal Institute of Tibetology** ⓘ *Mon-Sat 1000-1600*, established in 1958 to promote research into Tibet and Mahayana Buddhism. The library maintains a large and important Buddhist collection with many fine *thangkas*, icons and art treasures on display. To the south, surrounded by 108 prayer wheels, the gold-topped **Do-drul** Chorten contains relics and a complete set

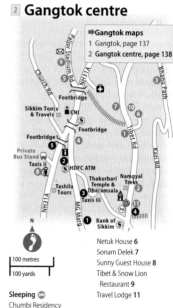

Gangtok centre

➡ **Gangtok maps**
1 Gangtok, page 137
2 Gangtok centre, page 138

Netuk House 6
Sonam Delek 7
Sunny Guest House 8
Tibet & Snow Lion
  Restaurant 9
Travel Lodge 11

Sleeping 🛏
Chumbi Residency
  & Tangerine 1
Kanchen Residency 10
Lhakpa 2
Mintokling Guest House 3
Modern Central Lodge 4
Mount Jopuno 5

Eating 🍴
Famous Roll Corner 3
Marwari & Gujarat Thali 4
Masala 1
Paradise 5
Rasoi/Blue Sheep 2

of holy texts. Nearby is a monastery for young lamas with large statues of the Buddha and Guru Padmasambhava.

Tashi Viewpoint via Enchey Monastery is 9 km away. Go early to watch the sun rise over the Khangchendzonga range. **Hanuman Tok**, a hill with a small temple, 8 km away, is another viewpoint.

Around Gangtok

Rumtek Monastery → *Colour map 2, A2. 24 km southwest of Gangtok. Phone code: 03592. Altitude: 1550 m. www.rumtek.org.*

Standing in one of the attractive lower valleys with fluttering prayer flags, the monastery is the headquarters of the Kagyu ('Black Hat') order of Tibetan Lamaistic Buddhism. The monks fled Tibet after the Chinese invasion, bringing with them whatever statues, *thangkas* and scriptures they could carry. At the invitation of the Chogyal they settled in Rumtek. The new monastery was built in the 1960s in the traditional style as a faithful copy of the Kagyu headquarters in Chhofuk, Tibet, with typical monastic paintings and intricate woodwork. The **Dharma Chakra Centre** houses the unique golden reliquary of the 16th Gyalwa Karmapa, who died in 1981.

Visitors are dropped at the gate at the bottom of a gentle uphill path; passports may be checked. A 20-minute walk past local houses and curio shops leads to the monastery. Outside, you may see pairs of monks chanting prayers in their quarters or catch some younger ones playing football in the field. The main hall is impressive but lacks Pemayangtse's atmosphere. Visitors are welcome but are asked not to disturb the monks during prayers (0400, 1800, except Sunday). In the adjacent building you can watch the wood-block printing of texts on handmade paper. The peace is broken when hordes of tourists arrive.

Fambong Lho Wildlife Reserve
ⓘ *25 km from Gangtok across the Ranipool Valley, Rs 5.*

A little beyond Rumtek, this reserve has serene jungle walks in the hills, with waterfalls, mountain views, orchids and wildlife (marten, fox, red panda, boar; even wolf and sloth bear). You are free to go on your own (though this is not advisable on some stretches) and can climb or walk for one to six days. There are log huts at Golitar and Tumin, Rs 50.

Saramsa Gardens→ *14 km south of Gangtok.*

The gardens contain more than 500 indigenous species in what is more like a botanical garden with large orchidariums. The best season is March to early May; you may be disappointed at other times. The road to Saramsa forks east off the NH31A a few kilometres south of **Tadong**, which has a couple of places with rooms and refreshments including the fairly modern **Tashi Tadong** and the **Daragaon**.

Kyongnosla Alpine Sanctuary→ *Altitude: 3200-4100 m. Permit required (see page 135).*

Located 31 km from Gangtok on the Nathula highway, which until 1962 was the main route for mule trains trading between Gangtok and Lhasa in Tibet, the sanctuary extends from the '15th Mile' check post to the ridges bordering Rongchu and Chhangu Lake. Among the junipers and silver firs the sanctuary harbours some rare ground orchids and rhododendrons and numerous medicinal plants including the *Panax pseudo-ginseng*. The best time to visit is April-August and October-November. The Himalayan marmot has been reintroduced here. Other mammals include goral, serow, red panda, Himalayan black bear, Tibetan fox and yellow-throated martens, together with very colourful pheasants.

Two easy treks lead to the Shiv Gufa (1 km from the road), where you can crawl into a tiny cave on your hands and knees to see a small Siva image and several tridents embedded in the soft floor, and to Kheding (4 km), while longer and more difficult ones to Simulakha, Namnang Lakha and Nakcho are very scenic. Trekkers with permits for Chhangu may return from Nakcho via the lake.

Chhangu (Tsomgo) Lake → *36 km from Gangtok. Altitude: 3774 m.*

The holy Chhangu Lake lies 5 km further along the precipitous Nathula road. Completely frozen in mid-winter, it's best to visit March-May and September to mid-December. There are excellent views of Khangchendzonga from the nearby ridge and superb sunsets, but the lake area is overcrowded and spoilt by snack kiosks and loud Hindi music. You can walk around the 1-km-long lake in about an hour. Permits are needed (apply with photo and passport a day ahead) or there are organized tours. If you go independently, allow six hours for the return trip; a jeep/minivan costs about Rs 800-1000.

⦿ Gangtok and around listings

For Sleeping and Eating price codes and other relevant information, see Essentials pages 34-38.

⦿ Sleeping

Gangtok *p137, maps p137 and p138*
Heating is essential in winter. Some budget hotels charge extra for heaters. Dogs bark at night so take some ear plugs. Discounts are available Jul-Aug and Dec-Jan.
L-AL Nor-khill, T03592-205637, www.elgin hotels.com. Beautiful rooms in an old palace, meals included, spacious public rooms, good views and gardens, exchange, curio shop, once excellent but standards are slipping.
AL-A Tashi Delek, MG Marg, T03592-202991, www.hoteltashidelek.com. 46 rooms and some suites (better on top floors) with lots of clutter and attractive *objets d'art*, excellent restaurant (see Eating, page 142), bar, exchange, airlines counter, terrace garden with enthralling views, friendly service. Pricey but recommended, it's a Gangtok institution.
A-B Chumbi Residency, Tibet Rd, T03592-226618, www.sikkiminfo.net/chumbi. Modern hotel decked out with traditional Tibetan furniture, plenty of marble, good rooms with old fashioned but perfectly adequate bathrooms, clean and quiet,

dynamic manager. Good restaurant (see Eating, page 142).
A-B Netuk House, Tibet Rd, T03592-202374, netukhouse@gamil.com. 12 comfortable rooms built and decorated in the Himalayan style in an extension to a traditional family home, varying layouts so check a few, only 2 with double rather than twin beds. Excellent Sikkimese food (extra Rs 1000 per day for all meals), quiet location, mountain views from the huge shared terrace, friendly, excellent service. Significant discounts possible at quiet times, otherwise it is overpriced albeit charming. Down a side lane, sign obscured by foliage.
A-C Tibet (Dalai Lama Trust), PS Rd, T03592-202523, www.hoteltibetgangtok.com. 34 rooms, good views from those at rear, restaurant, bar, exchange, Tibetan books and crafts for sale, very pleasant, peaceful and charming (but some critical reports).
B-D Sonam Delek, Tibet Rd, T03592-202566, www.hotelsonamdelek.com. Balconied rooms with bath, best choice for views of the mountains, pleasant restaurant (great local food), terrace garden.
C Hidden Forest, 2 km from centre in Middle Sichey, T03592-205197, www.hiddenforest retreat.org. 12 spacious, timber-floored rooms

in the home of a forest officer and his family, set in a 3-acre nursery full of orchids and medicinal plants, with paths leading into the surrounding forest, homegrown organic food served in cozy dining room, a unique choice. Recommended.

C Mintokling Guest House, Bhanu Path, T/F03592-204226, www.mintokling@com. Prettily decorated rooms with bath, timber-floored on 2nd storey or carpets on ground/1st, among working veg gardens, flowers, lawns and prayer flags, good restaurant, charming Sikkimese owner. Recommended, book in advance through the website as often full.

D-E Denzong Inn, near Kanchenjunga Bazar, T03592-202692, denzonginn@rediffmail.com. Set in an interesting complex with faint Chinese-mafia feel, 24 rooms and good if slightly threadbare suites (**C**). Some rooms on the terrace come with proper green baize card tables, and Chinese restaurant isn't bad.

D-E Sunny Guest House, by jeep stand on NH31A, T03592-202179, www.sunnyguesthouse.com. Pleasantly old-school rooms with bath, TV, carpets, super K'dzonga views from top floor, forgettable room service. Handy location means now walking up hills with luggage.

D-F Travel Lodge, Tibet Rd, T03592-203858, travellodge.gangtok@gmail.com. Decent modern hotel, with rooms at the front that are spacious and light. Can get a good deal on smaller side rooms, a good step up from backpacker places but at budget prices. All have reliable geysers and TV; affable staff.

E Mount Jopuno (Sikkim Tourism), PS Rd, T03592-203502. Out of 12 rooms, 4 de luxe (**C**), good restaurant and service, eager young staff (at Institute of Hotel Management).

E-F Kanchen Residency, Tibet Rd, T(0)92325-13781, kanchenresidency@indiatimes.com. Great mountain views from front-facing l arge rooms, carpets, new bathrooms though some damp patches appearing. Cheaper side rooms, also older and shabbier, some rooms have squat toilets. Discounts possible.

E-F Siniolchu Lodge, near Enchey Monastery, T03592-202074. Good views, 24 rooms on 3 floors up a hillside, some with bath and heating, restaurant, bar, tours.

F-G Modern Central Lodge, MG Marg, T03592-204670, www.modern-hospitality. com. Simple, clean and colourful rooms with bath, best in front on upper floors, a bit noisy, great lounge packed with books on Sikkim, basic but good restaurant, good jeep tours (long-established, using high standard accommodation), very friendly and helpful.

G Lhakpa, Tibet Rd, T03592-223002. Cheap rooms, some with bath, even cheaper dorm, restaurant (excellent Chinese), views.

Rumtek Monastery *p139*

A Bamboo Resort, Sajong Village, T0353-220 2049, www.sikkim.ch. Gorgeous views of the mountains, set on the edge of paddy fields, with 10 large comfortable bedrooms in different colour themes. The Swiss owner has created a wonderful retreat, with meditation, massage, creative workshops, and a library to relax guests. Organic food is delicious, half-board. Recommended.

A Martam Village Resort, Gangkha, Upper Martam, 5 km from the monastery, T03592-203314. Overlooking the valley, 11 pleasant, traditional-style thatched cottages with large picture windows, good meals. Recommended.

B Shambhala Mountain Resort, 500 m before the monastery, T03592- 252241, parekh.house@gems.net.in. Set in the grounds of a large estate. 31 cottages in traditional tribal styles, or comfortable rooms in main building, most with good views from balconies, vegetarian restaurant (wide choice), bar, exchange, pick-up from Siliguri arranged.

F Sungay, near monastery gate. Basic rooms in old guest house, cleanish shared toilet, friendly.

Kyongnosla Alpine Sanctuary *p139*

F Log Huts, 2 rooms in each at Kyongnosla and Lamnang Lakha. You must apply for a permit (Rs 5) to Chief Wildlife Warden, Sikkim Forest Dept, Deorali, Sikkim 737102, to enter the sanctuary.

⑦ Eating

Gangtok *p137, maps p137 and p138*
Lightly spiced Sikkimese meat and vegetable dishes are usually eaten with noodles or rice. *Churpi* is a local yak milk curd cheese.

℗ Blue Poppy, Tashi Delek (see Sleeping). International. Good meals at Rs 450 (Sikkimese recommended, order in advance) though the restaurant itself is soulless.

℗ Snow Lion, in Hotel Tibet (see Sleeping). Good Tibetan and Sikkimese in elaborately decorated room, but service can be glacial and vegetarian meals may come with flecks of meat.

℗ Tangerine, in Chumbi Residency (see Sleeping). Down in the bowels of the hotel, this appealing split-level restaurant has a mix of Thai cushions and standard seating, and a nice little terrace for drinks. Sikkim dishes are good (seasonal availability) and there is a diverse menu of Indian, Chinese, continental plus some Thai mains.

℗ Taste of Tibet, MG Marg. The better of 2 similarly named places, serving excellent Tibetan soups and noodles to an accompaniment of whatever internet radio channel happens to be tuned in.

℗-℗ Masala, MG Marg under Karma Hotel, T03592-20484, www.masalatherestaurant.in. Funkily decorated and fastidiously clean, serving pure vegetarian Indian (paneer is their strength) and Chinese. Intimate and cosy, serves alcohol. Open 0800-2230.

℗ Baker's Cafe, branches dotted around town (including MG Marg). Reliable for pastries and authentic brown bread.

℗ China Palate, Star Cinema Building, MG Rd. Excellent value Chinese in a laid-back place with a bar, open 1030-2030.

℗ Famous Roll Corner, New Market, Lal Bazar Bridge, T(0)97759-52175. Delicious, fast and famous rolls are spicy or not, depending on your choice of sauce.

℗ Hotel Paradise, National Highway (by footbridge near Sikkim Tourism). Open

0730-2130 for cheap and filling *thalis* in a functional canteen environment, veg/egg/ fish start at Rs 35 with good variety of dishes.

℗ Marwari & Gujarati Thali (Jain Restaurant), Tibet Rd. Utterly delicious thalis, that are endlessly refilled for Rs 50, a taste sensation. Plus great momos and competent staff. Open 0700-2100.

℗ Rasoi (AKA Blue Sheep), MG Marg (by the Tourist Office). Wonderful South Indian breakfast items and a broad spectrum of multi-cuisine items, served in an airy, clean, smart family restaurant. Creamy thick lassis and juices are particularly notable. Opens at 0830, gets very busy at night.

⑦ Bars and clubs

Gangtok *p137, maps p137 and p138*
Bars in most restaurants serve local spirits distilled at Rangpo: brandy, rum, whiskey and liqueurs. *Chhang* is the unofficial national drink. A bamboo mug (*thungba*) is filled with fermented millet through which boiled water is allowed to percolate; the drink is sipped through a bamboo straw. You can enjoy this mildly intoxicating pleasant drink for over an hour simply by adding hot water. More conventional alcoholic drinks are available at Gangtok's numerous Wine Shops.

Live & Loud, Sonam Gyatso Marg, Tibet Rd. Continental café-style ambiance on the balconies overlooking the street, and fun live music at weekends.

Pub 25, Naya Bazar, T03592-205324. Spacious with comfy leather seating, this smart but uninspired new bar has a large selection of cocktails/shooters etc and a good food menu (including Israeli and Italian dishes), music is inoffensive. Pricier than some. Smoking section upstairs.

The terrace at the hotel **Tashi Delek** has exceptional views and is recommended for a sunset beer (Rs 75).

⊙ Shopping

Gangtok *p137, maps p137 and p138*
Books
Good Books, down steps off MG Marg near Gandhi statue. Lots of choice including many local interest titles.

Handicrafts
Traditional crafts include carpets, *thangkas*, traditional jewellery, shirts, boots and fur caps and woodcarvings.
Charitrust Handicrafts, Tibet Hotel. Modest collection, good quality, books on Tibet.
Handcrafts Centre, Zero Point. Mon-Sat 0930-1230, 1300-1530. Artisans can be seen at work.

Markets
Lal Bazar (Haat on Sun, closed Thu) is an interesting walk down the steps off MG Marg. It winds up at Kanchenjunga Shopping Plaza, an uninspiring concrete edifice, but selling some unusual local fruit and vegetables and yak's milk cheese fresh and dried (skewered on string).

⊛ Festivals and events

Rumtek Monastery *p139*
Feb Special colourful **Losar** dances are held 2 days before the Tibetan New Year (check date). Arrive 3 days earlier to see rehearsals without masks, *pujas* and ceremonies are held during this period.
Jun The important **Rumtekchaam** is performed on the 10th day of the 5th month of the Tibetan calendar; masked dancers present 8 manifestations of the Guru Rimpoche. Tours in Jul-Aug from Gangtok.

▲ Activities and tours

Gangtok *p137, maps p137 and p138*
Mountaineering
Himalayan Mountaineering Institute, based in Darjeeling, see page 124.

River rafting
Rafting trips are arranged by the **Department of Tourism**, and private travel agents, on the Tista River (from Dikchu or Singtam, 1-hr drive from Gangtok) and the Rangit River (from Melli Bazar, 4 km from Tista Bridge, which has a **Wayside Inn** for refreshments, or **Rishi**). 1-day trips cost US$45, 2-day US$70, some Grade II-III rapids. A 2-hr ride is ideal for the beginner; wonderful scenery.

Tour operators
Tours of Gangtok are arranged from the Tourist Information Centre, T03592-221634, open daily 0800-2000. **Morning tour:** Government Institute of Cottage Industries, Deer Park, Chorten, Research Institute of Tibetology, Orchid Sanctuary and Enchey Monastery. In season daily 0930-1230, Rs 45.
Afternoon tour: Orchidarium and Rumtek Monastery, 1400/1430-1700, Rs 55. Tours of **Phodong:** Rs 70 (more expensive by car).
West Sikkim: Requires a minimum 16. Fri at 1030 returning Sun 1600 (2 nights), Rs 600.

Some companies offer tours before the season opens, eg to North Sikkim in Jan/Feb when roads and trekking routes may be closed. To support ecologically responsible tourism, contact **Ecotourism Society of Sikkim (ECOSS)**, T03592-228211, www.sikkim info.net/ecoss/, for a list of approved tour operators. Most agents help to arrange Protected Area Permits for trekkers.
Modern Treks & Tours, MG Marg, T03592-204670, moderntreks@hotmail.com. Quality tour operator, good for North Sikkim where their accommodation is the best on offer.
Namgyal Treks and Tours, 75 Tibet Rd, T03592-223701, www.namgyaltreks.net. Experienced, well organized.
Singalila, NH31A, opposite petrol pump, T03592-221556, singalila@hotmail.com. Arranges coach tours and river rafting.
Yuksom Tours and Treks, Borong House (above Telephone Exchange), T03592-226822, www.yuksom-tours.com. Professional, well-equipped treks at the higher end of the market with great food, car hire Rs 1500-2500 per day.

⊖ Transport

Gangtok *p137, maps p137 and p138*
Air The nearest main airport is Bagdogra (124 km away), see page 125. **Air India**, above Green Hotel, MG Marg, T03592-223354, www.airindia.com, 1000-1300, 1400-1600; **Jet Airways**, RNC, MG Marg, T03592-223556, www.jetairways.com.

To get to Gangtok: taxi Rs 1500, 4-5 hrs; or get bus/shared taxi to Siliguri and change to jeep for Gangtok (Rs 130, 4 hrs). A daily government 5-seater helicopter (Gangtok T03592-281372, Bagdogra T0353-2512646, 2698036) runs between Bagdogra and Gangtok; unreliable since heavy cloud or rain prevents flights, but is an excellent option (Rs 2000 each way, 45 mins, 10 kg luggage) with mesmerizing views.

Bus SNT (Sikkim Nationalized Transport) Bus Stand, NH31A, 0900-1300, 1400-1600. Private buses from **West Point Taxi Stand**, NH31A, T03592-202858. Some only operate in the high season. Buy tickets 24 hrs in advance; hotels can help. Journeys cost between Rs 65-95. To **Rumtek**, 1600 1 hr; to **Namchi**, 0730 (4½ hrs); **Namok, Phodong, Chungthang, Mangan**, 0700 (return 1500); **Pelling** via **Gezing**, 0700 (5 hrs); **Jorethang**, 0700. North Bengal service to **Kalimpong**, 75 km, 0715 (4-4½ hrs); to **Siliguri** (5 hrs), 0630-1330 (4½-5 hrs).

Taxi/jeep Shared taxis (Rs 10) run along NH31A, stopping at marked taxi stops. Charter taxis charge fixed, relatively high rates around town. Rates for sightseeing negotiable; around Rs 1500 per day for travel outside Sikkim, Rs 1200 within Sikkim; plus night halt Rs 200. Tourist office has a list of official rates.

There are several jeep stands in the city. Most useful to travellers is the main private bus and jeep stand on NH31A, office hours 0600-1800, T03592-2203 862. Advisable to book a day in advance. For South Sikkim: to **Ravangla**, 0700, 0745, 1230 and 1430, 3 hrs, Rs 80; several to **Namchi**, between 0700-1500, 3 hrs, Rs 90; and **Jorethang**, every

30 mins between 0630-1600, 3 hrs, Rs 100. To West Sikkim: **Gezing**, 0700, 1200, 1230 and 1300, 4 hrs, Rs 120; **Pelling**, 0700, 1230 and 1300, 4½ hrs, Rs 150; **Yuksom**, 0700 and 1300, 5½ hrs, Rs 150, via **Tashiding**, 4 hrs, Rs 130. Lal Bazar jeep stand is the hub for East Sikkim: **Rumtek**, Rs 35; Nam Nang Jeep Stand, Rs 10 taxi ride south from MG Marg (for North Bengal). North Jeep Stand: for Mangan, Rs 100. Share jeeps leave on a fixed schedule, most departing early morning; much quicker and more frequent than buses to most destinations.

Train Nearest mainline railhead is NJP. Computerized Bookings, SNT Compound, 0800-1400 (till 1100 on Sun). NJP Enquiries, T0353-269 1555.

Rumtek Monastery *p139*
Bus From **Gangtok** about 1600 (1 hr) along a steep narrow road, returns about 0800.
Jeep Shared jeep: Rs 25 each; last return to Gangtok 1300. **Rumtek** to **Pemayangtse**, 4 hrs.
Taxi Taxi from Gangtok, Rs 300 (return Rs 500, 1½-hr wait).

❶ Directory

Gangtok *p137, maps p137 and p138*
Banks 1000-1400, Sat 1000-1200 (difficult to get exchange). **State Bank of India**, MG Marg. **State Bank of Sikkim**, Tibet Rd. Several ATMs on MG Marg, including UTI, HDFC.
Internet Omni Cafe (1st floor) above Panorama Photo Studio, T03592-220329. Open 0830-2000 daily, Rs 25 per hr, clean and pleasant with a café but only 3 pcs. Several others on Tibet Rd and MG Marg, Rs 30 per hr.
Medical services STNM Hospital, Stadium Rd, opposite Hotel Mayur, T03592-222944.
Post GPO, Stadium Rd, Mon-Fri 0900-1700, Sun 1000-1400, has reliable parcel service.
Useful numbers Ambulance: T03592-231137. Fire: T03592- 222001. Police: T03592-202033.

South and West Sikkim

This enchanting region contains the essence of Sikkim: plunging rice terraces, thundering rivers, Buddhist monasteries etched against the sky, and the ever-brooding presence of Mount Khangchendzonga. ➤➤ *For listings, see pages 147-150.*

Jorethang

For travellers, the market town of Jorethang on the Sikkimese border is chiefly a transport hub for destinations in south/west Sikkim and West Bengal. Darjeeling is just 30 km away, but to enter Sikkim via Jorethang (bypassing Gangtok altogether) it is necessary to obtain permission in advance as the border post does not issue permits. There is not much to see in the grid-pattern town itself; a stroll east along the riverbed from the suspension bridge brings you to a colourful hybrid temple with shady pagodas, and the market is a good place to stock up on food supplies. Near the bridge is the SNT bus station, opposite which is a **tourist information centre** ① *daily 0830-2000*, where keen staff proffer a couple of brochures. The three jeep stands, plus hotels and bars, are in the street behind and beyond the tourist office. There's an ATM machine (State Bank of India) on Street 1, opposite the Walk In Hotel.

Ravangla and Maenam Sanctuary → *Altitude: 2155-3260 m.*

Ravangla (Rabongla), 65 km southwest of Gangtok, is a small village whose timber-fronted main street retains a strong frontier flavour and serves as the gateway to one of Sikkim's best day hikes. The 12-km trek through the sanctuary to **Maenam Peak** (3260 m), which dominates the town, takes about three hours. The sanctuary harbours red panda, civet, blood pheasant and black eagle, and is most beautiful when the magnolia and rhododendron are in bloom in April-May. **Bhaledunga**, another 30-minute hike along the ridge, on the steep cliff edge above the Tista, juts out in the shape of a cockerel's head.

Towering above it on the 'wish-fulfilling hill' of Samdruptse is a 45-m statue of Guru Padmasambhava, the patron saint of Sikkim who spread Buddhism to Tibet in the ninth century. Resplendent in copper and a coat of bronze paint, the **statue** ① *0700-1700, free*, can be seen from Darjeeling, around 40 km away. A ropeway from Namchi is planned; otherwise take a taxi, Rs 250 return. Not to be outdone, a 33-m statue of Siva is rising on another hill outside Namchi, which is supposed to be completed in 2010.

The administrative headquarters of West Sikkim, **Gezing** (Gayzing, Gyalshing), 105 km west of Gangtok, is at the crossroads of bus routes and has a busy market with food stalls, shops, a few hotels (none recommended) but little else to detain visitors.

Tashiding

Forty kilometres north of Gezing is the gold-topped **Tashiding monastery**, built in 1716, which stands on a conical hill between the Rathong and Rangit rivers on a spot consecrated by Guru Rimpoche. The most sacred *chorten* in Sikkim is here, even the sight of it brings blessing and washes away sins. It contains relics of the Buddha, and stands in a field of many *stupas* surrounded by *mani* walls. You will see numerous stones with high-class carvings of *mantras* around the monastery, made on site by a prolific artisan. Following the track beyond the *stupa* field brings you to a small cemetery where cremations are performed, and continuing down (beware of leeches) is an area designated for 'burial of dissenters' who are left in wooden boxes while their clothes and possessions are thrown down the hillside.

The main *gompa* has been refurbished and all the frescos repainted; these particularly fine murals are intricate and expansive, with Tantric motifs. Pilgrims attend the **Bumchu Festival** in February/March to drink water from the sacred pot which has never run dry for over 300 years. Below the monastery is the small **Tshchu Phur Cave** where Guru Rinpoche meditated; follow the trail on the left of the main steps to the monastery until you see a small building, opposite which is a painting on the rocks. Carry a torch if you plan to crawl into the cave.

Pemayangtse → *112 km west of Gangtok. 72 km from Darjeeling. Altitude: 2085 m.*

A full-day trip by car from Gangtok, along a very scenic road, Pemayangtse (Perfect Sublime Lotus) was built during the reign of the third Chogyal Chador Namgyal in 1705. It is about 7 km from Gezing, above the main road to Pelling.

The awe-inspiring **monastery** ⓘ *0700-1600, Rs 10, good guided tours, 0700-1000 and 1400-1600 (if closed, ask for key), no photography inside,* Sikkim's second oldest, is near the start of the Dzongri trek. For many, the monastery is the highlight of their visit to Sikkim; it certainly has an aura about it. Take an early morning walk to the rear of the monastery to see a breathtaking sunrise in perfect peace. The walls and ceiling of the large *Dukhang* (prayer hall) have numerous *thangkas* and wall paintings, and there is an exceptional collection of religious artworks including an exquisite wooden sculpture on the top floor depicting the heavenly palace of Guru Rimpoche, the *Santhokpalri*, which was believed to have been revealed in a dream. The old stone and wood buildings to the side are the monks' quarters. According to tradition the monks have been recruited from Sikkim's leading families as this is the headquarters of the Nyingmapa sect. Annual *chaam* dances are held in late February and in September.

The **Denjong Padma Choeling Academy** (**DPCA**), set up to educate needy children, runs several projects, such as crafts and dairy, and welcomes volunteers, who can also learn about Buddhism and local culture. The meditation centre offers courses and can accommodate visitors for a small charge and volunteers for free at the new hostel (see below); a rewarding experience. Volunteers can spend up to six weeks during March-December. Contact Jules Stewart, London, T0207-229 4774, jjulesstewart@aol.com.

Rabdanste, the ruined palace of the 17th- to 18th-century capital of Sikkim, is along the Gezing-bound track from the monastery, 3 km from Pelling. From the main road, turn left just before the white sign 'Gezing 6 km', cross the archery field and turn right behind the hill (road branches off just below Pemanyangtse). Follow the narrow rocky track for 500 m to reach the palace.

Pelling → *2 km from the monastery and 9 km by road from Gezing.*

Pelling sits on a ridge with good views of the mountains. The rather bleak little town has three areas linked by a winding road, Upper and Middle with views and hotels, and Lower Pelling with banks and other services. Upper Pelling is expanding rapidly with new hotels springing up to accommodate honeymooners from Kolkata, and makes the most convenient base for visits to Pemayangtse. You can also visit the **Sanga Choelling Monastery** (circa 1697), possibly the oldest in Sikkim, which has some colourful mural paintings. The hilltop monastery is about 3 km along a fairly steep track through thick woods (about 30 minutes). The area is excellent for walking.

The **Sikkim Tourist Centre** ⓘ *Upper Pelling, near Garuda, T03595-250855,* is helpful.

Khecheopalri Lake and Yuksom

A road west of the Pelling–Yuksom road leads to this tranquil lake where the clear waters reflect the surrounding densely wooded slopes of the hills with a monastery above; Lepchas believe that birds remove any leaf that floats down. Prayer flags flutter around the lake and it is particularly moving when leaflamps are floated with special prayers at dusk. The sanctity of the lake may be attributed to its shape in the form of a foot (symbolizing the Buddha's footprint), which can be seen from the surrounding hills. The lake itself is not visually astonishing, but walks in the surrounding hills are rewarding and a night or two can easily be spent here. There are staggering views from the tiny hamlet by the *gompa* on the ridge (accessed by the footpath in the car park, just ask for the *gompa*) where homestays are available. You can trek from Pelling to Yuksom via the lake without a permit in two days, a beautiful journey.

Yuksom (Yuksam), 42 km north from Pelling by jeepable road, is where the first Chogyal was crowned in 1641, thus establishing the kingdom of Sikkim. The wooden altar and stone throne stand beside Nabrugang *chorten*, with lovely wall paintings and an enormous prayer wheel, in a beautifully peaceful pine forest. During **Buddha Purnima** (the Buddha's birthday) in late April and May, women from the local community gather mid-morning to sing and pray in a low-key yet moving ceremony. Below Nabrugang, past pretty houses, **Kathok Lake** is a small green pool though the reflection of the prayer flags that surround it are photogenic, and the monastery of the same name nearby is worth the short uphill walk.

Although most people are in Yuksom because it is the starting point for the Gocha La trek, the village makes a quiet and relaxing base for a few days' stay, with several day walks leading out from the centre. It's a 45-minute climb to the attractive **hermit's retreat** at **Dhubdi** (circa 1700) above the village. A rewarding three-hour hike leads to **Hongri Monastery**, about halfway to Tashiding, mainly following a stone trail. Descending the path between the Yangri Gang and Panathang hotels, it is 45 minutes to a wooden bridge over the Phamrong Khola which has deliciously icy pools (accessed from the other side). The trail continues to Tsong village, with a sweet homestay in the first cottage in Lower Tsong (Rs 100 per night, three beds, contact Tara Chetri T(0)9775-816745) and onwards up the steep hill to the plain stone-slab monastery. It's a perfect picnic spot, with stone tables among the mossy *chortens* and glorious views. From here, it is another three to four hours' walk to Tashiding.

◉ South and West Sikkim listings

For Sleeping and Eating price codes and other relevant information, see Essentials pages 34-38.

◉ Sleeping

Jorethang *p145*
F Hotel Namgyal, near SNT bus station, T03595-276852. Best choice in town with simple rooms (doubles only, Rs 450), typically slab-floored with walls painted split colours. Fans, TVs, hot water in garish bathrooms. Best at the back, where they have windows as well as balconies. Decent restaurant and cheap beer.

F-G Hotel Janta, near tourist information, T03595-276104. Basic place but fills up fast, only 7 rooms, dorm beds for Rs 100 and single-person discounts (to Rs 300). Restaurant is cosy, with good *thukpa* and momos, well-stocked bar.

Ravangla *p139*
A Kewzing homestays, Kewzing village, 8 km towards Legship, T03595-260141, T094348-65154, ktdc@sikkimfoundation.org. A community-driven programme allows guests to stay in family homes in a quiet Bhutia village. Rooms vary widely, some better value

than others, and there is a maximum 2-night stay in any house to ensure even distribution of income. A rare and fascinating insight into traditional rural life. Rates include all meals and guide; cultural programme extra Rs 1000.

C-E Mt Narsing Village Resort, 15th Mile (bookable through Yuksom Tours & Treks, see page 143). Two rooms in a bungalow (**E**) situated in a delightfully flower-filled garden, with incredible views over the terraced valley slopes to a monastery. Plus an isolated annex, 1 km from the main road, which is more luxurious. Quaint rooms are carpeted, homely, with simple bamboo furniture and modern bathrooms (geysers). Good meals are served in the open-sided restaurant.

D-F Maenamla, Kewzing Rd, T03595-263861, maenamla@hotmail.com. Smartest choice in town, with carpeted rooms, clean baths, hot water from geyser, friendly and welcoming.

F Melody, Ralang Rd, T03595-260817. Basic but charming rooms with wooden floors, clean, friendly.

Tashiding p145

D-G Yatri Niwas, by monastery gate (250 m south of jeep stand), T(0)9832-623654. Brand new and with teething problems (running water not guaranteed) therefore generous discounts possible. 4 rooms are tasteful and comfortable (pay more for wood walls and parquet floors), or dorm beds for Rs 150. Pleasant gardens.

G Blue Bird, main market (50 m uphill from jeep stand), T03595-243248. Very basic old-school rooms, single/double/dorm, all share a bath (hot water if there is electricity), run by a kind Bengali family. Restaurant below is by far the best place to eat.

G Dhakkar Tashiding Lodge, 200 m down from jeep stand, T03595-243249. Large concrete rooms with great views from the back, 3 or 4 beds, best of the shared bathrooms in town.

G Mt Siniolchu, main market (50 m beyond Blue Bird), T03595-243211. Friendly, 5 clean rooms (3 big and beautiful ones on upper floor), shared bath, hot water.

Pemayangtse p146

A Mount Pandim, 15-min walk below monastery, T03593-250756, www.elgin hotels.com. Sparkling bright rooms with bath, some with beautiful mountain views, in freshly renovated and upmarket lodge.

Pelling p146

Power and water cuts can last 4 hrs or more and dogs often bark all night. Several **G** in Upper Pelling, with excellent views if you can overlook the often dubious cleanliness. Best is **Kabur**, T03595-258504, with a terrace restaurant and internet. With over 30 places to choose from, and hotel building going on unchecked, the following are recommended.

D-E Sikkim Tourist Centre, Upper Pelling, near Jeep Stand, T03595-258556. Simple rooms, some with views, cheaper on roadside, rooftop restaurant (cooking excellent but service limited; only snacks after 1400), tours.

E Norbu Ghang, Main Rd, T03595-250566. Rooms with bath, better views from those away from road, views from the terrace are superb. Restaurant.

E-F Haven, Khecheopalri Rd, Middle Pelling, T03595-258238. Clean doubles with hot running water.

G Garuda, Upper Pelling, near bus stop, T03595-250614. Rooms in basic lodge with bath, hot water (heaters Rs 100-150), dorm, restaurant (breakfast on rooftop, mountain views), internet, backpackers' favourite.

G Sisters Family Guest House, near Garuda, T03595-250569. 8 simple clean rooms, shared bath (bucket hot water). Friendly, great food.

Khecheopalri Lake p147

A couple of families take in guests at homestays in the small village on the ridge (25 mins' walk up the hill, left up the path by the car park near the lake). Highly recommended for a relaxing interlude with stunning mountain views.

G Pilgrims' Lodge, on the edge of the lake. Enterprising Mr Tenang provides Sikkimese porridge and millet bread (and much more), and leads short circular hikes around the lodge.

G Trekkers Hut, 400 m before the lake on the left. Simple rooms and friendly staff provide food, information and a bonfire at night.

Yuksom *p147*

For **E** homestays in the village contact **Khang- chendzonga Conservation Committee**, T03595-241211, www.kcc sikkim.org. Highly recommended, with meals and activities included.
A-B Yuksom Residency, Main Rd, T03595-241277. Huge new construction out of keeping with the village around, white marble predominates and terrace lit-up at night. Rooms are huge and well appointed (especially the **AL** suite with parquet flooring), furnishings high quality rather than rustic, flat-screen TVs, lots of light and some with good views. Gift-shop has some nice jewellery, restaurant a bit stiff.
D Tashigang, T03595-241202, hoteltashigang @rediffmail.com. Intimate rooms with lovely views (some with balcony), wooden floors, striped bedspreads and simple tasteful furnishings. Aging in a good way. Marble and tile bathrooms, some **C** suites, everything clean and polished. Own vegetable patch and restaurant (see Eating, below), peaceful garden. Very welcoming and staff are on the ball.
E-F Hotel Pemathang, Main Rd, T03595-241221, T(0)90020-90180, kinzongbhutia@ yahoo.com. Quietly chic reception with lavish flowers, but most rooms big and blank, carpeted, paint already getting shabby. However, the 2 back doubles (Rs 700) with balconies and view of Kabur peak are nice, others share a balcony.
E-F Hotel Yangrigang, Main Rd, T03595-241217, yan13jan@yahoo.com. The main backpacker hub, with an acceptable restaurant and internet facilities (Rs 60 per hr) as well as good standard rooms (doubles Rs 400-500) mostly with twin beds, bigger and better views upstairs (Rs 700-800), geysers and comfy beds. Manager is informative and pleasant. Treks easily arranged from here.
G Dragon, Main Rd, T03595-241290, T(0)9733-244759. Friendly and sociable guesthouse with clean small rooms (shared bath, hot water unreliable). Nice outdoor area, and good for a snug beer/meal in the family kitchen.
G Pemalingpa Cottage, just below Tashigang Hotel. Lovely little homestay, basic, only 2 rooms one of which is delightfully rustic and sunny. Outside toilet, hot buckets provided, family make every effort to make guests welcome. Highly recommended.

🍴 Eating

Pelling *p146*

Don't miss local *chhang* brewed in the area.
Ⱡ **Alpine**, Khecheopalri Rd (below **Garuda**, see Sleeping). Chinese, Kashmiri especially good. Yellow, wooden cottage run by friendly Ladakhi lady.
Ⱡ **Mock-Too**, Upper Pelling opposite **Sikkim Tourist Centre** (see Activities and tours, below). Excellent fresh snacks including *momos*, paratha and samosas.

Yuksom *p147*

A 2000 curfew is imposed by the police in Yuksom, when all activities move indoors – get your food order in early.
ⱠⱠ **Tashigang** (see Sleeping, above). Cheery hotel restaurant is unpretentious, with delicious Sikkimese specialities (seasonal) such as nettle soup and wild fern curry. Other more typically Indian dishes also available. Ingredients come from their vegetable garden or surrounding countryside. Recommended.
Ⱡ **Gupta's**, on the main street, attracts travellers to its social outdoor seating area, and does surprisingly good quesadillas and pizza, as well as *thali* (no refills) and yak's cheese *momos*. Next door, **Yak** is of a similar ilk and with friendlier owners.

⛰ Activities and tours

Pelling *p146*

Help Tourism, Sikkim Tourist Centre, T03595-250855. Good information and tours.

Yuksom p147

Most people arrange their trek in Gangtok/
Darjeeling; US$25-40 per person per day,
depending on service. There's a growing trend
for agents to tag on extra group members
(picked up in Yuksom) who get a greatly
discounted price. While this works well for
some parties, it can leave a sour taste for those
who are funding the majority of the trip.
**Khangchendzonga Conservation Committee
(KCC)**, see Sleeping. Helps arrange trekking
guides and porters. Agents arrange permits
with 2 days' notice, saving a trip to Gangtok.

⊖ Transport

Buses can be crowded, especially during **Pujas**
and **Diwali**. Quicker, more convenient jeeps
run to/from Gangtok and between all main
towns in the west, often leaving early morning;
check locally for current times. If no jeep is
going directly to your destination, it may be
best to go to Gezing, Jorethang or Namchi,
which have frequent services in all directions.
Direct jeeps leave from all three towns for
Siliguri, 4-5 hrs, and **Darjeeling**, 2-3 hrs.

Jorethang p145

The SNT bus stand has services to: **Siliguri**,
0930, Rs 71; **Gangtok**, 1230, Rs 72; **Rangpo**,
1230, Rs 45; **Namchi**, 0830, 1200 and 1600, Rs
20; **Soreng**, 1400, Rs 20; **Pelling**, 1500, Rs 50;
Ravangla, 1200, Rs 45; **Teesta**, 0930, Rs 32.
    There are 3 jeep stands in Jorethang, close
together on the south side of town near the
Tourism Office. The main stand serves: **Siliguri**,
departures between 0700-1600, Rs 90, 2½ hrs;
Gangtok, from 0700-1600, Rs 100, 3 hrs;
Karkabita (for Nepal), 0730, 0830, 0930 and
1330, 4 hrs, Rs 130; **Kalimpong**, 0900-1430,
Rs 60, 1½ hrs and **Gezing**, regular service, 2 hrs,
Rs 55. The block slightly uphill behind the main
stand has jeeps for: **Tashiding**, 1½ hrs, Rs 70
and **Yuksom**, 3 hrs, Rs 90, from 1200-1500.
Closer to the Tourism Office, jeeps for:
Darjeeling, from 0800-1530, 2 hrs, Rs 90
and **Namchi**, 0600-1100, 45 mins, Rs 25.

Tashiding p145

Several jeeps from **Gezing** via **Legship**, and
from **Yuksom** (early morning). To **Jorethang**,
0700 & 0800, 1½ hrs, Rs 70; **Gangtok**, 0630
and 0700, 3½ hrs, via **Ravangla**,1½ hrs, Rs 50;
Yuksom, 1100 and 1300, 1 hr, Rs 50; **Gezing**,
1½ hrs, 0730, Rs 60. Tashiding is a day's trek
from **Pemayangtse** or **Yuksom** (allow 7 hrs).

Pemayangtse p146

From **Gezing**: bus or shared jeep to
monastery, 1000-1430, Rs 15-20. From
Pelling, taxi Rs 50 one way, easy walk back.

Pelling p146

To **Gezing** reasonably frequent jeeps (Rs 20)
or walk along steep downhill track, 1-2 hrs.
To **Khecheopalri Lake**: last bus at 1400, or
you can walk 5 hrs (part very steep; last 3 hrs
follows road, with short cuts). Buses and
shared jeeps to **Yuksom** (until 1500, 3 hrs),
Damthang, **Gangtok** (4 hrs); **Darjeeling** via
Jorethang, tickets from stand opposite **Hotel
Garuda**, Rs 180. **Siliguri**: SNT bus 0700; tickets
sold at provision store next to **Hotel Pelling**
where bus starts, and stops uphill at jeep
stand near **Garuda** hotel.

Khecheopalri Lake p147

From **Pelling**: jeep share, 1½ hrs; to
Tashiding (3 options): **1)** 0700 bus to Gezing,
then jeep. **2)** Bus to Yuksom 1500 (irregular)
from 'junction', 10 km from lake, overnight
in Yuksom, then bus at 0700 (or jeep) to
Tashiding, 1 hr. **3)** Hitch a lift on the Pelling to
Tashiding jeep, which passes the 'junction'at
about 1400 (try sitting on top of jeep to enjoy
the beautiful scenery).

Yuksom p147

Shared jeeps leave from near Gupta's
restaurant, buy ticket a day ahead in season.
To **Pelling**, 0630, 2½ hrs, Rs 60; **Gezing**, 0630,
3 hrs, Rs 60; **Jorethang**, 0630, 3½ hrs, Rs 90
via **Tashiding**, 1 hr, Rs 60; **Gangtok**, 0630 and
1300, 5 hrs, Rs 160; **Pelling**, 0630, 2½ hrs, Rs 60.
To reach **Khecheopalri Lake**, private hire only.

North Sikkim

You'll need to join an organized tour to explore the outposts of the Yumthang and Tsopta valleys, where traditional Lepcha and Bhotia villages huddle beneath mountains that rear steeply towards Tibet. The scenery is spectacular, though the road well travelled – particularly by Indian tourists. Expect to be restricted in your movements and spend long days in a jeep. May to July is the best time to see primula and other alpine flowers in bloom in the high-altitude meadows. ►► *For listings, see page 153.*

Phodong → *Colour map 2, A2.*

The renovated early 18th-century monastery of Phodong is 1.5 km above the north Sikkim Highway, about 2 km before Phodong village. The track is accessible by jeep, and tours to North Sikkim usually include a visit to the monastery on the way back down to Gangtok. Otherwise, it is a pleasant walk up to the *gompa* where friendly monks show you around; there are especially beautiful frescoes and wall paintings. A further hike of 2 km takes you to picturesque **Labrang** monastery of the Nyingmapa sect, unique in that it retains its original structure undamaged by time or fire. Below the track nearby is the ruined palace of **Tumlong**, the capital of Sikkim for most of the 19th century.

☾ *The Singhik Viewpoint is a worthwhile stop before Phodong, with an unusual aspect on the Kangchendzonga range if skies are clear.*

Phodong to Chumthang

In addition to several police checkpoints, the road beyond Phodong passes through some mildly attractive villages, fluffy forested slopes, and past dramatic waterfalls on the way to bustling **Mangan**, the district headquarters, and then **Singhik**. In both places there are perfectly acceptable lodges with good views and a friendly welcome to the rare independent traveller who stops here (though Mangan has more opportunities for decent eating and transport connections). Beyond Singhik, permits are required for foreign tourists which travel agents arrange in Gangtok, along with vehicle, driver and accommodation, as part of a tour. The road and the Tista River part at Chumthang, dominated by a hydroelectric project, with one track leading northeast to the Yumthang Valley and the other northwest to Tsopta Valley.

Yumthang Valley → *Colour map 2, A2. 135 km north of Gangtok.*

Lachung sits among spectacular mountain scenery at 2400 m and acts as a gateway to the increasingly popular Yumthang Valley. Still run on the traditional democratic Dzomsa system, the village is a stronghold of Bhotia culture, though the daily influx of tourists from Gangtok and the rapid construction of lodges to accommodate them has begun to take its toll. Hotels, most over three storeys high, have started to dominate the series of small villages which make up Lachung. The central point is Faka Bazar by the suspension bridge, worth crossing to visit pretty **Lachung Monastery** (open mornings/evenings only) up the opposite hillside in Sharchog village; shortcuts past patches of cultivation and neat pastel-hued homes reach the monastery in about 30 minutes. The paintings of demons and the Wheel of Life in the porch are particularly dramatic, and a path behind the *gompa* climbs up for gorgeous views back down the valley.

The road north to Yumthang passes through the **Shingba Rhododendron Sanctuary**, which has 24 of the 40 rhododendron species found in Sikkim, along with attractive aconites, gentians, poppies, saxifrages, potentillas and primulas. May-July is the best time to see these and other high-altitude alpine flowers growing in the wild.

The valley slopes of **Yumthang**, the 'Valley of the Flowers', are surrounded by imposing snow-clad mountains. Glaciers flow down slopes forested with fir towards the milky turquoise water of Lachung River and, in summertime, the valley floor is indeed carpeted with purple primulas. This is the official end-point for foreigners, and a place where all jeep tours stop for a photo opportunity. A few minutes' walk from the refreshments stalls on the main road are unappealing sulphur hot springs; from here a stone path leads into a lovely hour's walk through the rhododendron forests. It is (unofficially) possible, and usually offered (for an additional charge), to continue for a further hour along the rough road to Samdong (Tibetan, meaning 'bridge'). It is a dramatic drive with views above the pink rocky riverbed and pale khaki-coloured valley walls, to a closer encounter with snowy peaks. Indians tourists can carry on further to Zero Point, but the final halting point for foreigners is signalled by impromptu noodle and liquor stands.

Tsopta Valley

The Bhotia village of **Lachen**, 122 km from Gangtok, is the chief overnight stop when visiting the stark landscape of the Tsopta (Chopta) Valley. Lachen straggles along one edge of the road along the steep river valley, surrounded by thick alpine forests. The 2000-strong population are known as Lachenpas, and traditionally were yak-herders. An unmetalled road follows the river from Lachen, up the mountainside past ponies, yaks and rhododendron cover to the more interesting village of Thangu 30 km north, where accommodation is also available. On the edge of **Thangu** (altitude 4260 m) potato, cabbage and spinach are cultivated from the arid land, men and women sharing the workload in the fields. Traditional sturdy wooden dwellings and dry stone walls demarcate the land and the scent of smouldering pine prevails. The wide river valley beyond the village has spectacular views towards the mountains and Tibet. It is a seasonal grazing ground for yaks, here grow Jatamasi plants which is used to make incense. Foreign tourists spend a couple of hours wandering the valley floor, covered in wild flowers in summer, while Indian tourists can continue up to Gurudongmar Lake (foreigners need a special permit from the Home Affairs Office in Delhi for this, which is not guaranteed).

Thangu is the starting point for the gruelling trek to **Green Lake** (altitude 5120 m) which takes around 14 days in total. Special permits are necessary that require at least six weeks to arrange – they are expensive, as is the entire venture as all supplies and equipment have be carried. The high cost means that tourist numbers are few. Much of the trek goes through thick spruce and fir forests, as well as the huge variety of rhododendron species for which the region is famed.

For Sleeping and Eating price codes and other relevant information, see Essentials pages 34-38.

➲ Sleeping

Phodong *p151*

F Yak and Yeti, T03595-260884. Quiet and clean. Some rooms with toilet, hot water in buckets, but meals are pricey. Recommended.

Lachung *p151*

The tour agents determine where you stay in North Sikkim. Try to specify a certain hotel if you don't wish to leave it up to chance, and the cost will be built into the tour accordingly. Particularly nice options are listed below, in descending order of price and comfortableness, but all hotels are of a higher standard than budget travellers will be accustomed to.

Taagsing Retreat (AKA Modern Residency), Singring, www.modernresidency.com. Lachung's most comfortable accommodation is a striking bottle-green pagoda on the southern edge of the village. The 22 Sikkimese-styled rooms are arranged on several levels, with balconies and great views. Pure veg restaurant serves buffet meals, plus there's a meditation hall, bar, library and little museum. Staff are lovely. Tours booked through Modern Treks & Tours, Gangtok (see page 143).

Golden Fish, Main Rd, Singring, T03592-214852, www.hotelgoldenfishitgo.com. This very clean and warm option has friendly, relaxed and efficient staff. Excellent food is prepared and high standards maintained. The 2010 season will see new suites with TVs. Can book a package through the website.

Season House, up the hill, Singring, T(0)9434-449042. Quaint rooms in the old log cabin or brand new ones in the chalet, excellent bathrooms. Quietly efficient staff and good food. At the highest point on the road, save for the Rimpoche's residence next door, so fabulous views from the terrace.

Sela Inn, Faka Bazar, T03592-214808. Older and shabbier, this well-established welcoming place has an atmospheric restaurant and is closer to any 'action' in town.

Sonam In Lodge, Main Rd, Singring, T03592-214830. Run by a charming family who speak little English, cosy simple rooms in an old-style wooden building are Rs 300, hot buckets provided.

⊖ Transport

Phodong and Mangan *p151*

From Gangtok, take a bus to the start of the jeep track, 0800 (2 hrs), Rs 35; return bus, 1500. Jeeps travel up to **Labrang** monastery. Jeeps to **Mangan** leave in the early morning and it is advisable to book at least 2 days in advance.

Trekking in Sikkim

Trekking is the biggest draw of Sikkim for many foreign tourists, and no previous experience is necessary as most treks are at 2000-3800 m. The trail to Dzongri (three to four days) or on to Gocha La (8-9 days) is the most popular and climbs to nearly 5000 m, but there are plenty of day trails on clear paths that are less physically taxing. An added attraction is that dzos (a cross between a cow and a yak) can carry your gear instead of porters, though they are slower. The trekking routes also pass through villages that give an insight into the tribal people's lifestyle. With this area coming under threat from pollution by rubbish left by trekkers, be sure to choose a trekking agency that enforces good environmental practices; ECOSS in Gangtok (see page 143) and the KCC in Yuksom (see page 150) can point you in the right direction.

▶▶ *For listings, see pages 140-144, 147-150 and 153.*

Ins and outs

Best time to visit March to late May and October to early December. April is best for flowers. **Leeches** can be a problem in the wet season below 2000 m.

Permits Foreigners must be in a group of at least two before applying for a trekking permit. Approved trekking agents can assist with applications. Areas open to foreigners include the Khangchendzonga Biosphere Reserve near Yuksom (permits can be arranged in a morning, from either Gangtok or Yuksom), the Lachung and Yumthang valleys in North Sikkim (very expensive, 6 weeks' processing time) and Chhangu in East Sikkim (one-day). The **KCC** in Yuksom can arrange guides (Rs 300-400 a day), cook (Rs 250), porter (Rs 100), and yak/pony (Rs 150), and book trekkers' huts (Rs 50 per head).

Maps and guidebooks *Sikkim: A Guide and Handbook*, by **Rajesh Verma**, updated annually, introduces the state and has descriptions of treks, with trekking profiles. The **U 502** sheets for Sikkim are *NG 45-3* and *NG 45-4*. PP Karan published a map at the scale of 1:150,000 in 1969 (US$3, available from the Program Director of Geography, George Mason University, Fairfax, VA 22030, US). A very detailed map is *Sikkim Himalaya* (Swiss Alpine Club) – Huber 1:50,000, £16.

Khangchendzonga National Park

ⓘ *Rs 180 (5 days), Rs 50 for each extra day, camera Rs 10, porter Rs 5, pack animal Rs 5, camping Rs 25 per tent, trekkers' hut Rs 50 per person, Tsokha Hut Rs 75 per bed.*

The park offers trekking routes through picturesque terraced fields of barley, past fruit orchards to lush green forests of pines, oak, chestnut, rhododendrons, giant magnolias, then to high passes crossing fast mountain streams and rugged terrain. Animals in the park include Himalayan brown bear, black bear, the endangered musk deer, flying squirrel, Tibetan antelope, wild ass and Himalayan wild goat. The red panda lives mostly on treetops at 3000-4000 m. There are about 600 species of bird.

The Khangchendzonga trek falls within the newly designated national park, from which all forms of industry and agriculture have been officially banished. The park office in **Yuksom**, about 100 m below the trekkers' huts, has interesting exhibits and helpful staff.

The classic trekking route goes from **Yuksom to Gocha La** (variously spelt Goecha La and Gochela). This eight- to nine-day trek includes some magnificent scenery around Khangchendzonga, and there are excellent views as you travel up the Ratong Chu River to the amphitheatre of peaks at the head of the valley. These include Kokthang (6150 m), Ratong (6683 m), Kabru Dome (6604 m), Forked Peak (6116 m) and the pyramid of Pandim (6720 m) past which the trail runs.

Trekkers' huts (F), in picturesque places at Yuksom, Tsokha and Dzongri, are fairly clean with basic toilets. Bring sleeping bags; meals are cooked by a caretaker.

Day 1 Yuksom to Tsokha An eight-hour climb to the growing village of Tsokha, settled by Tibetan refugees. The first half of the climb passes through dense semi-tropical forests and across the Prek Chu on a suspension bridge. A steep climb of two hours leads first to **Bakhim** (2740 m), which has a tea stall, a forest bungalow and good views. The track goes through silver fir and magnolia to Tsokha (2950 m), the last village on the trek. Trekkers' hut and campsite at Tsokha.

Day 2 Tsokha to Dzongri Mixed temperate forests give way to rhododendron. **Phedang** is less than three hours up the track. Pandim, Narsingh and Joponu peaks are clearly visible, and a further hour's climb takes the track above the rhododendrons to a ridge. A gentle descent leads to Dzongri (4030 m, 8 km from Bakhim). There is a trekkers' hut and campsite. Dzongri attracts pilgrims to its *chortens* holding Buddhist relics. From exposed and windswept hillsides nearby are good panoramic views of the surrounding mountains and of spectacular sunrises or sunsets on Khangchendzonga.

Day 3 Dzongri to Thangshing A trail through dwarf rhododendron and juniper climbs the ridge for 5 km. Pandim is immediately ahead. A steep drop descends to the Prek Chu again, crossed by a bridge, followed by a gentle climb to Thangshing (3900 m). The southern ridge of Khangchendzonga is ahead. There is a trekkers' hut and campsite.

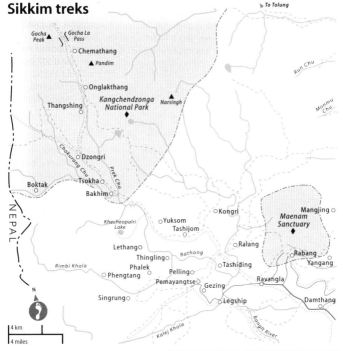

Sikkim treks

Day 4 Thangshing to Samity Lake The track leads through juniper scrub to a steeper section up a lateral moraine, followed by the drop down to the glacial and holy Samity Lake. The surrounding moraines give superb views of Khangchendzonga and other major peaks. You can't camp at the lake; a new campsite is 1 km away at Lammuney.

Day 5 To Zemathang and Gocha La and return The climb up to Zemathang (4800 m) and Gocha La (4900 m) gives views up to the sheer face of the eastern wall of Khangchendzonga. It is a vigorous walk to reach the pass, but equally impressive views can be gained from nearby slopes. Sometimes guides stop before the official 'Gocha La' viewpoint, be wary of this and ask the advice of other trekkers that you meet on the way. Much of the walk is on rough moraine.

Day 6 Samity Lake to Thangshing Return to Thangshing. This is only a two-hour walk, so it is possible to take it gently and make a diversion to the former yak grazing grounds of Lam Pokhari Lake (3900 m) above Thangshing. The area is rich in medicinal plants, and you may see some rare high-altitude birds and blue sheep.

Days 7 and 8 Thangshing to Tsokha The return route can be made by a lower track, avoiding Dzongri. Dense rhododendrons flank the right bank of the Prek Chu, rich in birdlife. Day 7 ends in Tsokha village. The next morning you retrace your steps to Yuksom.

Other treks in Sikkim

It's possible to trek from town to town, if you're prepared to do a lot of road walking and ask villagers to show you short cuts. One of the best circuits, for up to seven days but also enjoyable in smaller sections, begins from Pelling or Pemayangtse, descending through terraced fields to the Rimbi Khola river, then climbing up to Khecheopalri Lake. From here you can easily reach Yuksom in a day, then continue on to Tashiding, and either return to Pemayangtse or climb eastwards towards Kewzing and Ravangla.

Contents

Footprint features

Northeastern Hill States

At a glance

⊖ **Getting around** Flights and trains to most of the state capitals; buses, jeeps or car hire elsewhere.

◉ **Time required** 2-3 days for Kaziranga; 3 days for Shillong and Cherrapunji; a week each for eastern and western Arunachal; a week or more to explore tribal Nagaland.

☼ **Weather** Wet and humid most of the year, especially in Jul which produces extraordinary downpours; Dec-Mar can be cold.

✖ **When not to go** In the monsoon, unless you crave the sight of rain.

The Northeast is a true frontier region. It has more than 2000 km of border with Bhutan, China, Myanmar (Burma) and Bangladesh and is connected to the rest of India by a narrow 20-km-wide corridor of land – aptly coined the 'chicken neck' by locals. One of the most ethnically and linguistically diverse regions in Asia, each of the seven northeastern states has its distinct culture and tradition.

Arunachal Pradesh, only recently opened to visitors, is home to fascinating tribal cultures and the Buddhist enclave of the majestic Tawang Valley – more like Tibet than India. To its south, Assam, the most densely populated and largest of the states, occupies the scenic lowlands of the Brahmaputra Valley and attracts visitors to some of India's best national parks. Meghalaya's beautiful hills have the dubious distinction of being the wettest region in the world, as well as one of the friendliest. The little-visited four southeastern states of the region – Nagaland, Manipur, Mizoram and Tripura – make up a fascinating area, hilly, remote, and a zone where the tribal cultures of South and Southeast Asia intertwine.

The Northeast has been a politically sensitive region since Independence. Insurgency in places continues to surface making travel in some areas unsafe. Arunachal Pradesh, most of Assam, Meghalaya, Tripura and Mizoram are largely free of problems. Nevertheless, advice on travel to these and the other states should be sought locally. Permits are required for Arunachal Pradesh, Mizoram, Nagaland and Manipur.

Assam

→ Population: 26.6 million. Area: 78,438 sq km.

The lush valley of the Brahmaputra, one of the world's great rivers, provides the setting for Assam's culturally rich and diverse communities. Although it is tea that has put the state on the world map, the fertile river valley is home to generations of rice farmers, and tribal populations continue to have a significant presence. A highlight of any visit is Kaziranga National Park, where the population of Asian one-horned rhinos has been steadily increasing over recent years meaning that sightings are virtually guaranteed. ▸▸ *For listings, see pages 170-181.*

The land

Geography Assam stretches nearly 800 km from east to west, the length of the broad floor of the Brahmaputra Valley. The Himalaya to the north and the Shillong Plateau to the south can be clearly seen. The state is dominated by the unpredictable Brahmaputra, constantly changing course to create new sandbanks, and encasing Majuli, the largest riverine island on earth. Earthquakes are common; one in 1950 was estimated as the fifth biggest earthquake ever recorded.

Climate Unless you really want to see rain, avoid the monsoon. Assam is in one of the wettest monsoon belts in the world. Even the central Brahmaputra Valley, protected by the rain shadow of the Shillong Plateau, has over 1600 mm of annual rainfall. The rest of the Assam Valley has up to 3200 mm a year, mostly between May and September. Although summer temperatures are high, from December to February it can be cold, especially at night.

History

The Ahoms, a Shan ruling tribe, arrived in the area in the early 13th century, deposed the ruler and established the kingdom of Assam with its capital in Sibsagar. They later inter-mixed with Aryan stock and also with existing indigenous peoples (Morans, Chutiyas) and most converted to Hinduism. The Mughals made several attempts to invade without success, but the Burmese finally invaded Assam at the end of the 18th century and held it almost continuously until it was ceded to the East India Company in 1826. The British administered it in name until 1947 though many areas were beyond their effective control.

People

Nearly 90% of the people continue to live in rural areas. The ethnic origin of the Assamese varies from Mongoloid tribes to those of directly Indian stock. There has been a steady flow of Muslim settlers from Bengal since the late 19th century. The predominant language is Assamese, similar to Bengali although harder to pronounce. In Assamese, 'how are you?' is *'Apni kene koya?'* and 'good' is *'bahal'.*

Modern Assam

The Assam Valley is in a strategically sensitive corridor for India, lying close to the Chinese frontier. Its sensitivity has been increased by the tension between local Assamese and immigrant groups. The failure of the AGP (Assam Gana Parishad) to hold its alliance together and to control the violence that has become endemic through Assam contributed to its downfall. Congress returned to power in the 2006 elections under Chief Minister Tarun Gogoi, a lawyer and long serving member of the Lok Sabha, and won seven of the 14 Lok Sabha seats in 2009. The state has suffered a long-running

Permits for visiting the Northeast

Visitors to Assam, Meghalaya and Tripura do not need permits but may need to register on arrival and departure at the airport. Foreigners visiting Arunachal Pradesh, Nagaland, Manipur and Mizoram can apply for **Restricted Area Permits (RAPs)** from the **Ministry of Home Affairs** (Foreigners Division, Lok Nayak Bhavan, Khan Market, New Delhi 110003, T011-2461 1430). Send two photos and allow up to six weeks; success is by no means guaranteed, particularly for Manipur. Groups of four and married couples stand a better chance. Indians require **Inner Line Permits (ILPs)** from the Ministry of Home Affairs.

In **Kolkata** RAPs are issued at the **Foreigners Regional Registration Officer (FRRO)** (237A AJC Bose Rd, T033-2283 7034, Mon-Fri 1000-1730 but come between 1100-1400); ask for the Officer in Charge. It takes one to two days for permits to be issued, or if you are lucky it can be the same day. The cost is at the discretion of the FRRO (Arunachal, US$200 for four people). At the FRRO, it is

necessary to apply as a group of four for each of the restricted states; however, a married couple (with an original marriage certificate in English) can enter **Nagaland** as a pair. Permits are valid for a maximum of 10 days for Nagaland and Arunachal, a maximum of four days for **Manipur**. It is necessary to bring a copy of your confirmed return flight ticket to Manipur when applying for the RAP.

Local travel agents can help and save you some bureaucratic hassle. They can obtain permits within a few days, and even supply by fax or email, with a commission charge of around Rs 1000. This is especially worthwhile for **Arunachal Pradesh**, as agents can now obtain permits for individual travellers, at a cost of around US$100 plus commission, valid up to 30 days. (See listings under each state for tour agents who can help.) Itanagar, Ziro, Along, Pasighat, Miao, Namdapha, Tipi and Bhalukpong are all open to tourists. Mizoram travel agents can arrange permits for individuals, Rs 500, the process takes at least 10 days.

---

low-intensity conflict and in late 2006 and early 2007 a number of bombings occurred in the capital Guwahati. The most troubled area is still the beautiful Cachar Hills in the south, and it is not recommended to visit this region in particular. Seek advice from your consulate and local tour agencies before travelling.

Guwahati → *For listings, see pages 170-181. Colour map 2, B4.*

Despite its commanding position on the south bank of the mighty Brahmaputra, it is easy to forget that Guwahati is a riverside town, the waterside having little impact on people's lives. The main entrance point for visitors to the northeastern states, the city retains a relaxed and friendly atmosphere. Paltan Bazar, where most visitors arrive, is very busy and crowded as are the narrower streets and markets of Fancy Bazar to the west.

Ins and outs → *Phone code: 0361. Population: 808,000.*

Getting there LBG airport (23 km) has flights from Kolkata, Delhi, Bagdogra and airports throughout the Northeast. Assam State Transport (AST) runs a coach to the city for Rs 80 (look out for their representative at the arrivals gate); pre-paid taxis cost Rs 355. Some 1150 km from Kolkata, Guwahati is at the junction of NH31, 37 and 40, and is well

connected by road to all major centres of the northeast. The railway station is in the central Paltan Bazar, while most state and private buses arrive immediately to its south.
▶▶ See Transport, page 178.

Getting around It is easy to walk around the two main commercial areas of Paltan and Pan (pronounced *Paan*) Bazars, which have most of the hotels and restaurants. Red minibuses or canters are cheap and very efficient around the city (conductors call out the stops), whereas auto-rickshaws need hard bargaining. Political incidents in the city mean there is a visible military presence. Carry a torch when walking at night; large holes in the pavement lie in wait to plunge unwary travellers straight down into the sewers.

Tourist information Information booths for Assam and Meghalaya are at the airport, with useful maps; not always open. **Assam Tourism** ① *Directorate, Station Rd, T0361-254 7102,*

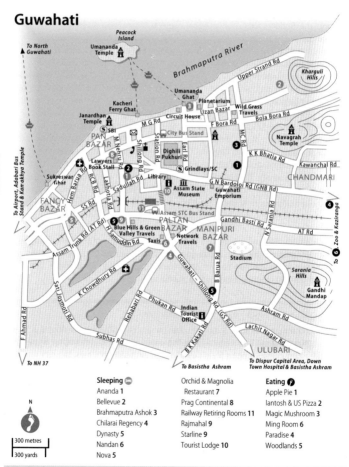

Guwahati

Sleeping
Ananda **1**
Bellevue **2**
Brahmaputra Ashok **3**
Chilarai Regency **4**
Dynasty **5**
Nandan **6**
Nova **5**
Orchid & Magnolia
  Restaurant **7**
Prag Continental **8**
Railway Retiring Rooms **11**
Rajmahal **9**
Starline **9**
Tourist Lodge **10**

Eating
Apple Pie **1**
Iantosh & US Pizza **2**
Magic Mushroom **3**
Ming Room **6**
Paradise **4**
Woodlands **5**

N
300 metres
300 yards

www.assamtourism.org. **Assam Tourism Development Corporation (ASTDC)** ⓘ *B Barua Rd, T0361-245 4421, astdcorpn@sancharnet.in.* Counters at airport and railway station.

History

Guwahati, on the site of the ancient capital of a succession of local chieftains, was once known as Pragjyotishpur ('City of Astrology'). The **Navagrah** ('nine planets') **Temple** on a hill here was the ancient centre of astronomy and astrology. It was also a centre of learning and a place of Hindu pilgrimage. In the seventh century, Hiuen Tsang described its beautiful mountains, forests and wildlife. Today it is the business capital while **Dispur**, the 'Capital Area', is just to the south.

Sights

The 10th-century **Janardhan Temple**, in the heart of the city, was rebuilt in the 17th century. The Buddha image here uniquely blends Hindu and Buddhist features. The **Umananda** (Siva) **Temple** ⓘ *Peacock Island in the Brahmaputra, can be reached by ferry, Rs 10, 0930-1615*, was built by an Ahom king in 1594, in the belief that Uma, Siva's consort, had stayed there. The wooded island is peaceful and the hazy little village pleasant for a wander; ask the priests about the rare golden langurs that live here. **Assam State Museum** ⓘ *Tue-Sun 1000-1615 (Nov-Mar), 1000-1700 (Apr-Oct), closed 2nd and 4th Sat of the month, Rs 2, photography with permission*, covers epigraphy, sculpture and natural history. The sections on village life, crafts and ethnography are particularly interesting. This small, well-lit museum is thoughtfully displayed, with some information in English, and is informative on the neighbouring cultures. **Srimata Sankaradeva Kalakshetra** ⓘ *Panjabari, on road to Narangi, Tue-Sun 0800-2200, Rs 10, bus No 8*, is a cultural complex set up to serve as a centre for Assamese dance, drama, music, fine arts and literature ('a theme park of Assamese life'). It features a museum, theatre, artists' village and heritage park. **Assam State Zoo and Botanical Gardens** ⓘ *off Zoo Rd, 6 km southwest of the city, Rs 50, cameras Rs 70*, is a cheap way to get up close to one-horned rhinos, snow leopards, tigers and snakes for those who don't want to take their chances at Kaziranga or other national parks.

Excursions from Guwahati

Kamakhya Temple, 7 km west, is believed to be an old Khasi sacrificial site on Nilachal Hill. A centre for Tantric Hinduism and Sakti worship, rebuilt in 1665 after the 10th-century temple was destroyed by a Brahmin convert to Islam. It typifies Assamese temple architecture with its distinctive beehive-shape *sikhara* (spire), the nymph motifs and the long turtleback hall. The dark sanctum contains the creative part of the goddess which is said to have fallen here, see page 75, and pilgrims enter to touch the wet *yoni* of Kamakhya (Sakti). Western visitors are allowed into the sanctum but should be prepared for the highly charged atmosphere and to walk barefoot on a floor sodden with the sacrificial blood of a goat. Ask for Hemen Sarma, a knowledgeable resident Brahmin, on entering the complex. No Bengali will leave Assam without visiting this temple, hence queues can be immense (a donation to the priests of Rs 500 will grant instant access, or go at dawn to be first in line). ▸▸ *See Festivals, page 176.*

Further up the hill is a smaller temple and a viewpoint with panoramic views of the Brahmaputra. It can be visited by bus from MG Road (towards Adabari Bus Stand); ask to be dropped near Kamakhya. From here take a canter (red minibus) from AT Road to the temple or walk up the steep and slippery rocky path at the back of the hill. An intense and memorable outing.

Basistha Ashram, 12 km south of Guwahati, is believed to be sage Basistha's (Vasistha) hermitage. It is a scenic spot with three mountain streams nearby.

North Guwahati is a sleepy town across Saraighat Bridge, which can be reached by any ferry from the *ghat*. The **Digheswari Temple** is worth a visit. Take a rickshaw from the other bank, an auto-rickshaw or a shared four-wheeler.

Around Guwahati

Hajo, a friendly and peaceful town, 34 km across the river, produces bell-metal work and is sacred to three religions. **Hayagriba Madhab Hindu temple** is said to contain a Buddhist relic. Some believe this is where the Buddha attained Nirvana. Its hilltop location is more spectacular than the temple itself. The main street behind the tank stocked with fish leads to an old **Ganesh temple** after 2 km; a friendly priest might allow you in. Hajo is also sacred to Muslims; the **Pao Mecca Mosque**, 3 km further, built by Pir Ghiasuddin Aulia is supposed to have a *pao* (quarter) of the sanctity of Mecca. Take a bus from Adabari Bus Stand, which drops you off at the Hindu temple (one hour, last return at 1600 but very crowded; you may have to travel on the roof).

The small village of **Sualkuchi**, on the north bank of the Brahmaputra, is famous for silk production from non mulberry leaf-fed worms, hence its unique natural colour. Every household is involved with weaving of *muga*, *endi* or *pat* silk; prices are 30% cheaper than in Guwahati. Take the ferry from Guwahati or a bus from Hajo (20 minutes).

Pabitora is a small wildlife sanctuary a two-hour drive from Guwahati (60 km), on the border of Nagaon and Kamrup districts; rhinos can be found here. **Madan Kamdev**, 45 km north of Guwahati, has been called Assam's Khajuraho due to the dozen or so erotic sculptures that adorn the walls. The temples which may date from the 11th to 12th centuries, possibly reconstructed in the 18th, are believed to be associated with tantric practices. The principal shrine to Uma-Mahesvara (Siva-Parvati) is still in use and the setting, surrounded by fields and nature, is picturesque. Buses from Guwahati go to Baihata on NH31, 4 km from the site; rickshaws transfer visitors from there.

Manas National Park → *For listings, see pages 170-181.* *Colour map 2, A3.*

A World Heritage Site and one of India's most beautiful sanctuaries, Manas lies in the Himalayan foothills, southeast of the river Manas, on the Assam-Bhutan border. Over half the area is covered with tall grass and patches of deciduous woodland. This changes to dense semi-evergreen forest in the upper reaches and to conifer on the hills towards Bhutan.

Ins and outs

Manas has two ranges; the main range is entered from Bansbari village and the eastern range from Koklabari village, both have offices which issue permits to the park. Charges for entry and camera are similar to Kaziranga (see below). Jeeps are available to rent for around Rs 1000 per day, you can walk or cycle, and sometimes elephant safaris are possible.

Pick up provisions beforehand. Use the Bansbari gate with a Forest Range Office to get to Mathanguri inside the park (20 km, 30 minutes). Book a car or taxi for the return trip. If you travel around dawn (0500) and before (1600) you may see some wildlife. Travel is not allowed after sunset. The maximum temperature in summer is 35°C, minimum 18°C; the winter maximum is 24°C, minimum 7°C. Annual rainfall is 4100 mm. The best season is November- March. Take something warm, a hat and shoes for wading through slippery streams.

Background

Manas, with a buffer zone of 2800 sq km (including two other far-flung sanctuaries) and a core area of 391 sq km, was demarcated in 1977-1978 when the preservation programme Project Tiger was launched. At the last count there were more than 80 tigers. Until 2005, Manas was the hideaway of Bodo rebels and poachers and generally deemed unsafe for visiting tourists and with the tiger population in steep decline, labelled as a UNESCO 'World Heritage Site in Danger'. This has been turned around since the creation of a separate 'Bodoland' in northwest Assam and the park is becoming a model for eco-tourism and community involvement, particularly in the Eastern Range which is managed by **Manas Maozigendri Ecotourism Society** (MMES).

Sights

The forests are home to most of the larger animals found in Kaziranga, most common being wild buffalo, swamp deer, hog deer, sambar and elephant. Some 22 of the animal and bird species are on the endangered list of the IUCN including the rare capped and golden langur, which can be seen among the flowering trees, mostly on the Bhutan side. There are also pigmy hog, hispid hare, slow loris, clouded leopard, rhino and tiger. The sanctuary is rich in birdlife (over 400 species), and attracts migratory flocks of redstarts, forktails, mergansers and ruddy shelduck. The eastern range is famed for its huge population of Bengal floricans, which are best spotted December-March. Otters are frequently seen in the Manas River.

Kaziranga National Park → *For listings, see pages 170-181. Colour map 2, A5.*

Kaziranga was declared a game sanctuary in 1916 to save the Indian greater one-horned rhino and became a national park in 1974. It is now a World Heritage Site. In a beautiful setting on the banks of the Brahmaputra, and with the Karbi Anglong Hills to the south, the 430-sq-km park combines elephant grass mixed with thorny rattan cane, areas of semi-evergreen forest and shallow swamps.

Ins and outs

Guwahati is 215 km from Kohora, the main entry point to Kaziranga on the NH37. Park roads open 0800-1100, 1400-1630. Foreigners Rs 250. Camera fees change regularly: currently Rs 50, video, Rs 500. There's a 25% discount on fees after three consecutive days. Summer maximum 35°C, minimum 18°C; Winter maximum 24°C, minimum 7°C. Annual rainfall 2300 mm, heavy in summer. The best season is mid-November to the end of April (December and January are best for birds). The park is closed mid-April to mid-October during monsoons. Wear cotton clothing but take a jacket. ▸▸ *See Transport, page 179.*

Entry into the park is by private vehicle, hired jeep or trained elephants. Although elephants cover less ground than motor vehicles, they can get a lot closer to the wildlife, particularly rhinos and buffalo. **Elephant rides** ① *book the night before through the Forest Range Officer, foreigners Rs 1000, Indians Rs 120, plus jeep transfer from town, Rs 120,* carry four people and get mixed reports; the consensus seems to be that they are less enjoyable when demand is heavy. The viewing posts just inside the park may offer quieter viewing. **Jeeps** for five or six people can be hired from the **Department of Tourism** in Kaziranga or private agents. Government jeeps cost Rs 700 (Rs 120 per person in a shared vehicle) for three hours; private ones Rs 900-1000 for 50 km or 2½ hours. A car or jeep must be accompanied by a Forest Department Guard (Rs 50), who can give directions as well as spot wildlife. Cars and jeeps pay a road toll, Rs 150. Total price per jeep is Rs 920-1220.

Sights

The **rhino** population is over 1800 here and they are guaranteed to be seen in the marshes and grasslands. Despite Kaziranga's status as a national park, poachers still manage to kill the animal for its horn, which is used in Chinese and Tibetan medicine. The park also has over 1000 wild buffalo, sambar, swamp deer (over 500), hog deer, wild pig, hoolock gibbon, elephant (1246 in 2004), python and tiger (89 at last count in 2000), the only predator of the one-horned rhino. There is a rich variety of shallow-water fowl including egrets, pond herons, river terns, black-necked stork, fishing eagles and adjutant storks, pelicans and the rare Bengal florican. There are otters and dolphins in the river.

There are four road routes for visiting the park: the **Central Range** (Kohora, Daflang, Foliomari) is the the most visited as it is full of big mammals; the **Western Range** (Baguri, Monabeel, Bimoli, Kanchanjuri) has the highest rhinoceros density but tall elephant grass makes visibility difficult; the **Eastern Range** (Agortoli, Sohola, Rangamatia) has good possibilities for seeing wildlife, but at a distance; the **Burhapahar Range**, furthest west, has only recently become accessible. Keep receipts as fees are valid for several trips in one day.

Panbari Forest Reserve, 12 km from Kaziranga, has hoolock gibbons and a good variety of birdlife. Contact the Forest Office in Guwahati, for permission to visit.

Tezpur and around → For listings, see pages 170-181. Colour map 2, A4. Phone code: 03712.

Tezpur, on the north bank of the Brahmaputra, 180 km northeast of Guwahati, is the site of Assam's first tea plantations. The **Tourist Lodge** ⓘ *Jenkins Rd, T03712-221016, Mon-Sat 1000-1615; closed every 2nd and 4th Sat of the month*, has a brochure and can sketch out a map of town. The town's ancient origins can be seen at **Da Parbatia**, 5 km west, which has the entrance gate of an early Gupta-style temple. In Tezpur's centre, **Chitralekha Udyan** (Cole Park) ⓘ *Rs 10, camera Rs 20, boat Rs 10, 0900-2000*, was created after an earthquake revealed ancient remains and is now a pleasant park around a lake that is lit up at night; some of the slabs of friezes and sculpture unearthed are on display outside the **museum** ⓘ *at the Dak Bungalow, near the Tourist Lodge*. The **Station Club**, opposite the District Commissioner's office, is one of Assam's oldest planters' clubs dating from 1875, with period furniture and a bar worthy of a drink if you can find a member to invite you. Otherwise they are happy to let you look around, although only the card tables, billards and tennis courts remain. A nice spot for sunset is **Agrigarh** ⓘ *Rs 10, 0800-1930*, a 1-km stroll past Ganesh Ghat, with hilltop views over the Brahmaputra and the town. Climb the lookout tower to catch the breeze and be on the same level as circling birds of prey. Possibly the largest Siva linga in India is found inside **Mahabhairab Mandir**, a Rs 10 rickshaw ride from the centre, which has a nightly *puja* at around 1830.

An interesting excursion is to take a Guwahati-bound bus, get off at the bridge over the Brahmaputra, then negotiate with a boatman to take you to the river's confluence with the Bhoreli for some river **dolphin watching**. Some hotels, **Luit**, for example, offer such trips. It involves a 30-minute rickshaw ride, Rs 150, followed by boat hire, around Rs 1000.

The 76-sq-km **Orang National Park** ⓘ *66 km northwest of Tezpur, foreigners Rs 250*, is often called a miniature Kaziranga. It has similar flora and fauna, though viewing is not as rewarding. This is compensated by its peaceful and intimate atmosphere, especially if staying inside the park. Arriving by car is best from Tezpur, though buses between Guwahati and Tezpur go via Orang village. From the village, it is a 15-km dusty track to the park.

Nameri National Park ⓘ *40 km north of Tezpur, on the Arunachal border, entry and camera fees are similar to Kaziranga*, is on the river Jia Bhoreli and covers 210 sq km. It is

Plantation labour

Today Assam produces over half of India's tea. Old colonial tea planters' bungalows surrounded by neat rows of emerald green tea bushes dominate the landscape, particularly in Upper Assam. After an early experiment using imported Chinese labourers ended in near mutiny, the British began the mass recruitment of Adivasis from the Choto Nagpur Plateau, Andhra Pradesh and Orissa. They have been assimilated into Assamese society but are recognized as a separate 'tea tribe' with a language, customs and dances that remain unique. One of the largest groups of organized labour in India today, they enjoy benefits undreamed of by other workers including free health care, education and subsidized food. The lifestyle of the plantation, hardly changed since the Raj, has been tarnished lately by the rise of insurgency, with tea companies being targeted for extortion and kidnapping.

home to tigers (26 in 2006), elephants, Indian bison, barking and hog deer, as well as 300 bird species, including about 20 endangered white-winged wood ducks. Flora includes evergreens, bamboo and some open grassland. Buses/*sumos* travelling between Tezpur and Tawang can drop travellers off at Hatigate on the main road. From here, it is 2.5 km down a track to the **Eco Camp** (see Sleeping, page 172), a recommended overnight stop and good place to arrange visits to the park. There are no roads; you can trek within the park with a forest guide and take a boat ride on the river. The best time to visit is October-April.

Bhalukpong, 20 km west of Nameri, is on the Assam-Arunachal border en route to Tawang. This nondescript village is surrounded by the forests of **Pakhui Game Sanctuary**, a mass of ferns, moss and orchids, with a hot spring, orchid garden and good fishing. You can camp (take your own tent) on the picturesque bank of the River Jia Bhoreli or stay in the government tourist cottages overlooking the river. Jeeps and buses from Tezpur all pass through Bhalukpong en route to Tawang.

Northeast Assam → For listings, see pages 170-181.

Jorhat → Colour map 2, A5.

Jorhat is one of Assam's major tea centres with a **Tea Festival** held in November. It's a relatively orderly town with good facilities but there are no historical sites nearby – most people only stop here because it is convenient for visiting Majuli Island to the north. The main commercial street, Gar-Ali, runs south (about 1 km from the railway station) down to AT Road where the bus stands are located to the west. Parallel to Gar-Ali (one block west) is MG Road, where you will find the **Assam Tourism office**, some cheap lodges and a miniature one-room **museum** ① *inside the Post Graduate Training College, Mon-Sat 0930-1700, free*, displaying Ahom artefacts and curvaceous Krishnas minus his flute. During the first week of February, **horse races** are held at the 1876 **Gymkhana Club** ① *Club Rd North, T0376-221 1303, office open 0800-1600*, where there is also an 18-hole golf course, tennis, billiards and a bar with ancient staff, piano and pictures of England.

Majuli Island → Colour map 2, A5.

Majuli Island is one of the largest river islands in the world, though constantly changing, and currently around 650 sq km. The flooding of the Brahmaputra River means that at times Majuli is reduced to a cluster of islands, some as small as a hut top. Roads keep shifting but villagers adapt to re-routing by building cost-effective bamboo bridges. Cut off from the mainland to the south about 400 years ago, it is served by ferries from Jorhat, but it can still be accessed from North Lakhimpur by road during summer. The island is essentially a flat expanse of paddy fields and sky with very little motorized traffic, making it a peaceful place for cycling or exploring **Mishing villages** (where homes are built on stilts, not only to avoid flood-risk but also because it is believed to be more hygienic).

On the first Wednesday of the month **Gimnur Polo** (in February-March), the colourful Mishing festival of Ali-Ai-Lvigang is celebrated. See www.majulitourism.com, or contact Majuli's tourism officer (Jyoti Narayan Sarma, T(0)9435-657282) for festival dates. Majuli is also a birdwatchers' paradise.

At the forefront of Assamese Vaishnava culture, the island is an important centre for arts, crafts and science. Work is in progress to declare it a World Heritage Site. The *satras* (monasteries) here, inspired by the 15th-century saint Sankardeva and his disciple Madhavdeva, are worth visiting – particularly those to the east of Kamalabari. They are essentially small, self-sufficient villages where Vishnu is worshipped through regular performances of dance dramas at the temples. Out of 64 *satras*, 22 remain, the others have fallen victim to erosion by the Brahmaputra. A useful sketch map showing the location of the *satras* is available from **La Masion de Ananda** (see Sleeping, page 174).

Satras in and around **Kamalabari** and **Garamur** can be visited on foot, but others require a bicycle or rickshaw. **Auniati**, 5 km west of Kamalabari, is home to 450 monks and has a little museum with old manuscripts, utensils, jewellery and silver of the Ahom kings (entrance Rs 50). **Bengenatti**, east of Uttar Kamalabari, is a centre for performing arts and tribal dance forms. Others worth visiting are **Nauten Kamalabari** and **Dekhinpat**. Colourful traditional masks are still made at **Natun Chamaguri**, 12 km east of Kamalabari, and a visit is recommended.

Hollong Park Gibbon Sanctuary
ⓘ *16 km from Majuli Island, Rs 250 per person (4 hrs' viewing), includes an armed guide.*
The sanctuary at **Bhalowguri** was designated in 1998, but is scarcely visited by tourists. The low-key nature of the operation is a big part of the appeal, and few leave disappointed, although dense forest growth makes the gibbons hard to spot. Viewing the wild elephants requires an overnight stay in the specially constructed hut on stilts with two rooms, bring supplies (contact District Forest Officer in Jorhat, T0376-232 0008). To reach the park, 18 km south of Jorhat, catch a bus from the top of MG Road in Jorhat and go via Mariani by auto.

Sibsagar and around
District headquarters of the largest tea and oil producing area in the Northeast, **Sibsagar** was the Ahom capital for two centuries. There are several royal tanks. Daupadi (the Ahom King's wife) built the huge tank in the centre of town and its three temples in 1734. On the east bank there is a birdwatching tower and a library. The tower of the Siva Dol on its bank is one of the tallest Siva temples in India, and a fascinating place to witness **Sivaratri** (celebrated in early March).

The **Joysagar** at **Rangpur**, 5 km away, and the three temples on its bank date from 1697. **Kareng Ghar**, 5 km away, is a seven-storeyed palace, three floors of which are underground. Nearby, the two-storied oval **Rang Ghar** was the royal sports pavilion where elephant fights and games took place – said to be the oldest amphitheatre in Asia. Take a bus from BG Rd Bali Ghat in Sibsagar (Rs 5, 20 minutes); then cycle-rickshaw (Rs 15).

The burning bush

As well as rhinos and tea, Assam is the home of the world's hottest chilli. The Naga Jalokia chilli, which grows naturally in the northeast, has been tested to have a firepower of 855,000 Scoville Heat Units, meaning that one drop of its juice would need diluting that many times in order to be rendered neutral. This makes it more than twice as hot as the previous titleholder, the Mexican red savina Habanero, though whether your mouth and stomach would notice the difference is debatable: anything above 5000 SHUs is considered super-hot.

Dibrugarh, Tinsukia and Borajan Reserve Forest

Much of the town of **Dibrugarh** was destroyed during the 1950 earthquake, only a few old buildings remain on the main streets. The new town on the Brahmaputra is surrounded by tea estates, where a couple of delightful old tea-planters bungalows are available for guests to soak up some Raj nostalgia. Dibrugarh is a convenient stop when setting off for (or returning from) eastern and central Arunachal Pradesh as transport connections are good and hotels are comfortable. **Tinsukia**, a major transport junction in the Northeast, is convenient for visiting the nearby Dibru-Saikhowa National Park and the **Borajan Reserve Forest** ① *5 km from Tinsukia*. The reserve consists of a small (500 sq m) patch of forest, which is home to five species of primate (Hoolock gibbon, capped langur, slow loris, stump tailed macaque and common macaque), though not all are easy to spot.

Dibru-Saikhowa National Park

① *Foreigners, Rs 250. Contact DFO, Rangagora Rd, Tinsukia, T0374-233 1472, for day visits.*
A national park since March 1999, on the southern flood plain of the Brahmaputra near Tinsukia, this is largely a semi-wet evergreen forest. The 340-sq-km core area is within a large biosphere reserve and provides a refuge for endangered species such as tiger, leopard, leopard cat, clouded leopard and elephant, though sightings are rare. The real draw is the rich birdlife, which includes the very rare white-winged wood duck, best spotted during a dawn boat ride. Silky brown dolphins are more commonly seen at sunset while wild horses congregate on the western edges of the park. The best time to visit is November-March. Temperatures range from 6-36°C. Average annual rainfall is 2300-3600 mm.

Entry points are at **Guijan** on the southern edge of the park, and **Dhola** (near Saikhowa Ghat) in the north, both accessible by auto-rickshaw/jeep from Tinsukia. Arrival from Guijan is easier as a boat across the river takes you to the Range Office at the park entrance. If you cross from Dhola, the Range Office is 5 km into the park at Narbarmora; in either case it is best to notify your arrival beforehand. If stopping overnight to get an early start the only options are two simple eco-camps on the riverbank at Guijan.

Margherita → *Colour map 2, A6.*

Margherita, the constituency of the present chief minister, is on the Dihing River at the foot of the Patkoi Range and was named by Italian railway engineers in the late 19th century after the Queen of Italy. The town is surrounded by tea estates and is the headquarters of Coal India Ltd. The last of the steam railway engines in Assam is still operating.

Ledo → *Colour map 2, A6.*

The small coal mining town of Ledo, 6 km northwest of Margherita, was the headquarters of Northern Combat Area Command during the Second World War and is the start of the 470-km **Stilwell Road**. Named after General Joseph Stilwell, the road was the most ambitious and costly engineering project of the war, US$137 million at the time. Once a two-lane bitumen highway linking Ledo with Myitkyina in North Burma, through the Pangso Pass, and with Kunming in China, it is now closed beyond Nampong in Arunachal Pradesh. A sign, 6 km west of Ledo, commemorates the 'Road to Mandalay' but there is little else remaining.

◉ Assam listings

For Sleeping and Eating price codes and other relevant information, see Essentials pages 34-38.

◉ Sleeping

Guwahati *p161, map p162*
Hotel staff often speak little English. There are some budget hotels at Sadullah and M Nehru Rd crossing; those in Paltan Bazar are often full by the afternoon. Most medium-priced hotels have some a/c rooms and tend to serve Indian meals only. You may need to complete 4 copies of the hotel registration slip and then register with the police soon after arrival. Most hotels outside Guwahati require photocopies of passport ID and the visa page.
AL-A Dynasty, SS Rd, T0361-251 6021, www.hoteldynastyindia.com. 68 comfortable rooms, excellent restaurants serve Indian and Chinese food.
A Brahmaputra Ashok, MG Rd, T0361-254 1064, www.theashokgroup.com. 49 rooms (the riverside ones are best), central a/c, TV, bamboo and cane furniture, good restaurant, credit cards, good travel agency.
A-C Nandan, GS Rd, Paltan Bazar, T0361-254 0855, www.hotelnandan.com. The 55 clean rooms don't quite match up to the stylish frontage and feel a bit 1970s, some a/c, expensive suites, restaurants, decent bar.
B Rajmahal, Paltan Bazar (near bus stand), T0361-254 9141, www.rajmahalhotel.com. 80 rooms conveniently located, good value, excellent restaurant, pool not that appealing (non-residents Rs 75 for 45 mins).

B-C Prag Continental, M Nehru Rd, Pan Bazar, T0361-254 0850. 62 rooms, some a/c, terrace restaurants, **Continental Café**.
C-D Bellevue, MG Rd, on river front opposite Raj Bhawan, T0361-254 0847. Not the plushest in town, but quiet and with great elevated views over the river. 45 rooms, restaurant (continental recommended).
C-D Chilarai Regency, HP Brahmachari Rd, Paltan Bazar, T0361-263 9748. Some of the 44 large rooms have a/c. Bar, exchange.
C-D Nova, SS Rd, Fancy Bazar, T0361-251 1464. Clean but fusty rooms with dated bathrooms (**C** a/c, much brighter), delicious if utilitarian **Natraj** restaurant (Indian, Chinese) has slow service (room service quicker), yet pleasant, friendly and helpful.
D-E Starline, Md Shah Rd, Paltan Bazar, T0361-251 8541. Of the 74 clean rooms, 12 have a/c with hot water 24 hrs. Chinese/ Indian restaurant, polite and helpful staff.
F Tourist Lodge (Assam Tourism), close to railway station, T0361-254 4475. 25 clean simple rooms with nets, toilets and balcony, canteen, staff speak English and are friendly, tourist information (1000-1700). Great value except for single persons who have to pay the price of a room (Rs 440).
F-G Orchid, B Barua Rd, opposite stadium, T0361-254 4471. Set back from road in own compound, 23 clean rooms, 5 a/c, hot water in buckets, excellent **Magnolia** restaurant.
F-G Suradevi, MLN Rd, Panbazar, T0361-254 5050. Basic bearable rooms are cheap, but suffer from light pollution from the corridors and are noisy. Good restaurant.

G Ananda, M Nehru Rd, T0361-254 4832. Rock-bottom prices for small dark rooms but pleasant, vegetarian dining hall. The old-style Assam House at the front is cute at night, the RCC at the rear is a blank block.

G Railway Retiring Rooms. Some a/c rooms, small dorm, book at Enquiry Counter.

Manas National Park *p164*
If you arrive late at Barpeta Rd you will need to spend the night there.

B-D Manas Jungle Camp, Koklabari, T03666-268052, www.helptourism.com, www.manas100.com. 4 basic ethnic cottages at the boundary of the park, a chance to see the work of MMES and visit the handicraft workshop at a Bodo village nearby.

D Bansbari Lodge, at the park entrance, www.assambengalnavigation.com. Simple but comfy huts have tea gardens on one side and the jungle on the other. All 16 twin rooms have hot showers, plus attractive gardens, a library and delicious meals.

E-G Manas Guest House, Durgabari Rd, Barpeta Rd, T03666-260935. The best choice in town, clean, cheap and recommended for good service and helpful staff.

F Mathanguri Forest Lodges, on hill overlooking Manas River. Very simple but clean and well maintained, the lodges are within the park and enjoy staggering views. The erosion of land by the Beki River is threatening the upper bungalow, which is the nicer of the 2. Camping possible. Cook available but bring provisions (from Barpeta Rd). Book well in advance through the Field Director's Office, Main Rd, Barpeta Rd, T03666-261413.

Kaziranga National Park *p165*
New lodges are springing up around Kaziranga as quickly as the elephant grass. The government-run **Tourist Complex**, 1 km south of the main gate in Kohora village, has perfectly adequate options, while a few other places stand out for their eco-awareness and tastefulness. Good discounts are available off-season – but the park itself is closed.

LL Diphlu River Lodge, 15 km west of Kohora, T0361-260 2223, www.diphlu riverlodge.com. Utterly chic luxury with a rustic slant, 12 Mishing-style huts, connected by bamboo walkway, surround rice paddies with a prime location on the edge of the national park. Rooms are furnished in a colonial theme from natural materials, bathrooms are inspired, 2 verandas for lounging, and the staff all faultless. Once inside the peaceful enclave everything is included in the price (apart from alcohol) – limitless visits to Kaziranga, walks with naturalists, picnics, meals, visits to Mishing villages. Come here for peace and serenity.

AL-A Iora, Bogorijuri, Kohora, T03776-262411/2, www.kazirangasafari.com. Stark white building out of keeping with the wildlife vibe, but the only place with a swimming pool. Rooms are contemporary, fitted out with stone, wood and woven cane and a sprinkling of southeast Asian aesthetics. Glass walk-in shower, elegant bar and restaurant.

C Jupuri Ghar, Kaziranga Tourist Complex, Kohora, T(0)9435-196377, jupuri@gmail.com. Peaceful setting on a slope above tea gardens and paddies, these new thatched cottages have cane furniture and woven walls, a/c and terraces onto the garden. Pleasant open restaurant, attractive tribal decorations, BYO until they get a license. Also bookable through **Network Travels**, see page 177.

C Wild Grass, 1.5 km from NH37, 5.5 km from Kohora, ask for Kaziranga IB Bus Stop, 400 m north of resort, T03776-262085, T(0)9954-416945, www.oldassam.com. Unpretentious and relaxing, with a lovely location, 18 spotless rooms in 2 lofty chalets, wooden floors, cane furniture, can get very cold in winter. Great meals (Rs 450 for 2 people) and service, beautiful walks through forests and tea plantations, excellent guided tours, pickup from Guwahati for groups, cultural shows in the evenings by the campfire of Assamese dancing. Half price May-Oct.

E Aranya Tourist Lodge, Tourist Complex, T03776-262429. White paint and marble predominate the 24 large rooms with bath (hot water) and good balcony. A/c is Rs 150 extra, simple garden, **Rhino Restaurant**, bar (slow service).

E Dhansree Resort, Kohora, T03776-262501. A variety of rooms and cottages with brick-red exteriors and thatch, fans and geysers. Incongruous water features and use of paint mar the pleasant garden, but nicely located among tea trees.

F Bonani, Tourist Complex, T03776-262423. 5 breezy white rooms with fans, nets, wicker furniture and large bathrooms (geysers) are good value. Much nicer on the upper level.

G Bonashree, Tourist Complex, T03776-262423. Cheaper still, 9 rooms, a large veranda lends some old-world charm, pleasant garden, but often full. Hot buckets available.

G Kunjaban Dormitory, Tourist Complex, T03776-262423. Linen optional (Rs 25), 12- or 3-bed rooms (Rs 25-50). Safe and secure, but no hot buckets.

Tezpur and around p166

LL Wild Mahseer, Addabarie Tea Estate, near Balipara, T(0)9435-197650, www.oldassam.com. In a world of its own, this pristine heritage bungalow sits among 9 ha of gardens and trees on the edge of a working tea garden. Rooms are luxurious yet homely with huge beds and bathrooms in modern colonial style, and every inch taken care of. Absorbing library, tea-tasting café and 3 (cheaper) bungalows in the grounds, Delicious Anglo-Indian food, warm and entertaining hosts.

C-E Centre Point, Main Rd (opposite the police station), Tezpur, T03712-232359, hotelcentrepoint.tezpur@gmail.com. Spanking new hotel with fresh linen and plumped up pillows, plain but pleasing decor and TVs. Cheaper rooms have hot water by the bucket, staff are eager to please and **Tiffin Restaurant** is good. Recommended, if you can deal with false windows and bad acoustics.

D-G Eco Camp, Nameri National Park, Sonitpur, T(0)9854-019932, or contact **Network Travels**, see page 177. 11 thatched-cottage tents with bath, brightly furnished

with local fabrics, set among jungle trees around a grassy lawn. 6 bunk beds in the bamboo dorm (Rs 160), wash block, sunny little restaurant. A friendly and special place, worth spending a couple of nights.

D-F Luit, Ranu Singh Rd, 200 m from bus stand, Tezpur, T03712-222083, hotel_luit@ rediffmail.com. Set back from the main road, this retro hotel has large but average rooms in new wing (Rs 700), some a/c (Rs 1200) and some bargain-basic rooms in the old wing (Rs 300), restaurant, bar.

E Durba, KK Rd, Tezpur, T03712-224276. Clean rooms with TV, **Appayam** restaurant.

E-F Basant, Main Rd, Tezpur, T03712-230831, T(0)9401-278499. Good, clean paintwork and sheets, well-maintained rooms all with TV (doubles Rs 350/400/780, cold water/hot water/ac), recommended to phone ahead. Singles are small but totally acceptable. Soulless restaurant on the top floor.

E-F Tourist Lodge, Jenkins Rd (opposite Chitralekha Udyan), Tezpur, T03712-221016. Budget non-a/c rooms for Rs 330, newly refurbed a/c Rs 550. All twin bed with attached bath. Book ahead, there are only 10 rooms. Cheap simple restaurant.

E-G Tourist Lodge, Bhalukpong, T03782-234037. 10 raised cottages with octagonal bedrooms, or 4 airy rooms sharing a terrace (good value) look out across the Jia Bhoroli River to Nameri and Pakhuya parks. Work is underway to turn the watch-tower into a restaurant. Can arrange local transport to visit Nameri. (The private guesthouse **Kunki Resort** next door is not nearly as appealing, but there if the lodge is full.)

F Bungalows, Orang National Park. Reservations: Divisional Forest Officer, Barpeta Rd, T03666-261413. A new lodge at the entrance to the park at Silbari, and another 1 km inside the park at Satsimulu, overlooking swampy grasslands where animal spotting is possible. Bring your own provisions; the cook/guide will prepare your food.

G Parajit, Main Rd, Tezpur, T03712-220565. Decent budget rooms have pink walls, clean furnishings and squat toilets in a bungalow with a bit of soul. Often full, ring ahead. Good restaurant has cheap *thalis*, 1100-1530 and 1930-2100.

Jorhat *p167*

A few hotels and the Tourist Lodge are on MG Rd and a more salubrious cluster (all pretty similar) is found on Solicitor Rd (off AT Rd) near the ASTC bus station. Some old planter's bungalows languish in the tea estates on the outskirts of town, far from the madding crowd.

A Thengal Manor, 15 km southeast of Jorhat, T0376-230 4673, www.welcomeheritage hotels.com. Thengal feels regal with its white portico, marble-topped tables and antique furnishings. Rooms are elegant rather than luxurious, meals Anglo-Indian around the immense dining table, and staff incredibly kind. After bringing bed-tea, they throw open the shuttered windows to let in the morning sun. The immaculate grounds contain ponds, vegetable gardens, and the family mausoleum. Excellent tea tours should be pre-arranged. Half-board.

B Burrah Sahib's Bungalow and **Mistry Sahib's Bungalow**, contact as for **Thengal Manor**, above. The joy of these 2 properties is in their location deep in the heart of tea country, in sweeping time-warp gardens, the air heavy with nostalgia. Recent refurbishment has mingled gloriously period furniture with ill-matched ceramics and artworks, but the wide verandas and strolls through the plantations compensate. Guests can use the golf course nearby, and swimming pools are planned.

C MD's Continental, MD House, Marwari Patty (off AT Rd), T0376-230 0430, mdscontinental@gmail.com. This new hotel has tastefully furnished rooms, the theme Asian throughout with wooden floors, contemporary art and luxury bathrooms. Restaurant is slick and very reasonably priced, lounge-bar is more of a bistro (imported liquor), MD's sweets on the ground floor the best in town. Staff extremely professional.

D-E Dilip, Solicitor Rd, T0376-332 1610. Clean, friendly, with reliable hot water.

D-E Paradise, Solicitor Rd, T0376-332 1521. Decent restaurant but dismal bar, 31 1970s rooms, 9 a/c, hot water, laundry and exchange. Jet Airways and Air India offices on the upper floors.

E Woodland Cottage, BG Rd (off MG Rd), T0376-232 2786. This Assamese-style bungalow has character, though rooms are faded, there's a patio out front with plants and murals which is good for morning tea. Hot running water, some rooms a/c, their nearby restaurant brings room service.

F Janata Paradise, Solicitor Rd, T0376-232 0610. Homely rooms and homely atmosphere, a decent cheap restaurant and handy location make this a good choice.

F Prashaanti Tourist Lodge, MG Rd, T0376-232 1579. Spotless twin-bed rooms with essential mosquito nets are great value (single Rs 210, double Rs 330, room 101 has best balcony), though a planned refurbishment will add a/c and hike the price. 24-hr hot water. Brand new men-only dorm (Rs 100) and bar out the back. Assam Tourism in the same building with very helpful staff.

G Palace, MG Rd, T0376-232 3891. Small budget lodge, rooms have tiny attached bath, TV and plug-in mosquito deterrents. Charming owner will let you sample his home-made pickles. Cluttered rooftop but no balconies.

Majuli Island *p167*

C-E Mou Chapori, near Neematighat, Jorhat, contact Bibhuti Borah, T(0)9854-335242 or **Rhino Travels** (see page 177), www.mou chaporiresort.com. When the river is high (May-Sep) a boat leaves from Nimatighat to the island (Rs 50), during the dry season Mou Chapori is accessible by land. Cottages and huts are sadly heavier on painted plywood than bamboo but it's a good location and the price includes horse riding, boating, table tennis. Also a houseboat where guests can sleep (Rs 2000). Good place to spend the day (Rs 25), or camp on the sandy shores if you have a tent. Staff couldn't be nicer. Guided trips to Majuli arranged. Try local fish in the little restaurant.

G Circuit House, Garamur, T03775-274439. Twin-bed rooms, very basic but have mosquito nets and attached bath, decent food and bed tea. Foreigners should phone ahead, or write a letter of application on arrival at the SDO's office next door.

G Garamur Satra, Garamur, T(0)9435-466539. 4 rooms. Bedding and nets provided.

G La Maison de Ananda and **Do:ni Po:lo**, Garamur, T03775-274768, T(0)9425-205539, danny002in@yahoo.com. A Mishing-style stilt house designed by a French architect who fell in love with Majuli, La Maison is quaint, made entirely of bamboo and yet very comfortable (sleeps 3 people). **Do:ni Po:lo** next door has a dorm with 2 doubles and 2 single beds, clean linen, blankets and nets, lit by pinpricks of light through the woven walls. A further 2 rooms have twin beds. Clean Indian-style toilet out the back and hot bucket on request. Bicycles/motorbikes to rent, Rs 50/300 per day. Both places have relaxing verandas and are managed by local fixer Danny Gam. Lovely family atmosphere.

G Nautum Kamalabari Guest House, Kamalabari (8 km from Garmur), T03775-273302. Spartan and no hot water but incredibly cheap.

G Uttar Kamalabari Guest House, Kamalabari, Majuli Island, T(0)9435-823352. Very basic, bring own bedding and leave a donation, you may try to reserve by asking to call Dulal Saikia (the head priest) to the phone, then ring back after 10 mins.

Sibsagar *p168*

D-E Siddhartha, BG Rd, T03772-224281. 29 rooms some with a/c, restaurant, bar, modern.

D-F Brahmaputra, BG Rd, T03772-222200. 48 rooms, restaurant, limited English but helpful, clean.

G Tourist Lodge, near Siva Dol, T03772-222394. Helpful tourist office, 6 clean rooms, often full, call in advance it's a real bargain.

Dibrugarh and Borajan Reserve Forest *p169*

B Chowkidinghee Chang Bungalow (aka Jalannagar South Bungalow), off Mancotta Rd, 1.5 km from Dibrugarh. A truly charming indulgence in colonial history, this managers' bungalow on the edge of a tea estate has gloriously period rooms opening out onto enormous screened verandas with white cane furniture. Built on stilts to avoid floods and wild animals. Shiny wood floors throughout, there's a Victorian fireplace in the sitting-cum-dining room, both bedrooms are en suite and have dressing rooms. An additional room downstairs is not nearly as attractive. The proximity of the road is the only thing to gripe about. Bring your own alcohol.

B Mancotta Chang Bungalow, off Mancotta Rd, Milan Nagar, 5 km from Dibrugarh. Another heritage planter's bungalow on stilts exudes the same ambiance but is larger, with 2 fabulous colonial bedrooms on the upper level, 2 modern rooms downstairs (walk through the patio doors in the morning to enjoy the garden) and a separate bungalow with a post-war feel that sleeps 2 singles. In the upstairs rooms chintzy curtains, brass fittings, Seypoy prints and plenty of tumblers and brandy glasses make drinks on the veranda more attractive than the satellite TV. Bathrooms have enamel claw-footed tubs. Horse riding, tea tours and more are arranged by **Purvi Discovery** who also take the bookings (see Activities and tours).

D Hotel Natraj, HS Rd, T0373-232 7275. Recently remodelled, clean tiled rooms have comfortable beds, tonal furnishings and excellent bathrooms. 24-hr hot water, a/c, TV. Reasonable bar (with special deals) and though the restaurant is soulless the food is delicious. Breakfast included.

D-F Indsurya, RKB Path, Dibrugarh, T0373-232 6322. A short walk from the station, the grim frontage of the Indsurya hides good-value rooms which are clean

and comfy. The attractive lobby sports an impressive wooden rhino and plenty of wicker furniture. It's often full so call ahead.
E Hotel Devika, Puja Ghat, off AT Rd, T0373-232 5956, www.hoteldevika.com. Rooms at the front are best with Western toilets and good light, TV, clean. Corridors have plants and the building has some character. Decent discounts available, staff very obliging. Hot water by the bucket.
G Asha Lodge, AT Rd (at intersection with HS Rd), T0373-232 0053. As basic as it gets, rooms are grim but the cheapest around. The dusty wooden veranda is good for watching the street-life below.

Tinsukia and Dibru-Saikhowa National Park *p169*
D Banashree Eco-camp, Guijan, near Tinsukia, T(0)9954-594940, www.naturehunt.com. Owned by charismatic poacher-turned-ecologist, Benu, the **Banashree** provides good food and guiding in the national park. Simple stilt huts are a bit overpriced for plywood and grubby toilets however, and mosquitoes are nasty – insist on a net. Right on the banks of the Dibru River, erosion has caused the surrounding tea gardens to start sliding into the water in a most picturesque way. Adjacent **Wave Ecotourism** has wicker stilt huts.
E Highway, AT Rd, T0374-233 5383, 500 m from New Tinsukia station. Modern, 20 rooms, some a/c, vegetarian restaurant.
F President, Station Rd, T0374-233 8789, computer2@sancharnet.in. Basic, noisy rooms with attached bath, pay more for TV, average vegetarian restaurant, very handy for the station and kind staff.
G Retiring Rooms, New Tinsukia Station. Very basic vegetarian food, budget beds.

🍴 Eating

Guwahati *p161, map p162*
Assamese *thalis* including rice, fish and vegetable curry, often cooked with mustard. Try vegetarian *kharoli* (mashed mustard seeds)

with *omita khar* (papaya cooked with burnt 'bark' of the banana plant). Larger hotels, including **Bellevue** and **Rajmahal**, serve continental food and have bars.
ﾹﾹﾹ Dynasty (see Sleeping). Chinese. Recommended.
ﾹﾹ Ming Room, Rajgarh Rd, near Chandmari Flyover. Very good Chinese.
ﾹ Apple Pie, MC Rd. Pastries, ice creams.
ﾹ Hits Cafeteria, near Central School, Khanapara, T0361-230 0090. Out in the suburbs, great lunch and dinner.
ﾹ Iantosh, near Donbosco School, Panbazar, T0361-254 7770. Huge selection of Indian (rolls, biryani, veg or non-veg) and Chinese dishes, in a pleasant bar-stool environment. Free delivery and ice cream. The fairly authentic **US Pizza** joint next door has some great deals on unlimited pizza, plus salad, garlic bread and brownie for Rs 150 (1100-1800).
ﾹ Magic Mushroom, MC Rd. International. Clean, good quality, varied menu, psychedelic decor, very friendly and helpful owner.
ﾹ Paradise, GNB Rd, Chandmari, T0361-254 6904. Closes 1530-1800. Assamese. Great *thalis* (Rs 55), very clean and friendly, cycle rickshaw from station, Rs 10.
ﾹ Station restaurant. Good omelettes.
ﾹ Woodlands, AT Rd (older branch on GS Rd). Indian vegetarian. Clean, a/c, specializes in lunch and dinner *thalis* (Rs 40).

Tezpur *p166*
ﾹ Chinese Villa, NC Rd, T03712-232726. Magnificent *momos* and a whole host of other delicacies in a high-rise block that also incorporates an Indian restaurant on the upper level and excellent south Indian snacks and *lassis* on the ground floor.
ﾹ Madras Hotel, off Main Rd. Decent *dosas*, *idli* and other south Indian delights provide welcome spice after the relative blandness of Assamese cooking. Basic, busy but under-staffed, and smoky from the kitchen fires.

Jorhat *p167*
On Majuli Island, food is available at simple eateries. Carry drinking water.

Ⅱ-Ⅰ **Beijing Banquet**, MG Rd, near Tourist Lodge. Exciting variety for pork eaters and a usefully descriptive menu. The starkly square room is warmed by bright orange walls and passable Chinese *objets d'art*. Generous combo-meals are great value for Rs 100.
Ⅰ **Canteen**, State Bus Stand. Cheap, does good *roti* breakfasts. Toilets.
Ⅰ **Food Hut**, MG Rd, next to **Beijing Banquet**. Simple eatery serving a delicious 8-dish Assamese *thali*; also pigeon and duck.
Ⅰ **Woodlands**, BG Rd (between MG Rd and Gar-Ali), T0376-232 7653. Open 0930-2130. Veg and non-veg, good *thalis* and some welcome south Indian dishes. Small, popular and efficient.

Dibrugarh *p169*
Ⅰ **Asha Refreshment Lodge**, AT Rd (by intersection with HS Rd). Seriously cheap food, *channa dal* is especially nourishing and salads fresh. The family room behind the curtains is much more pleasant than the murky main room.
Ⅰ **Garden Treat**, beside the flyover, Mancotta Rd, T0373-232 4140. Open 1100-2100. Despite the proximity of the flyover this garden haven is lovely for eating great-value fish with mustard, under a sun umbrella. There are several continental dishes alongside the Indian and Chinese. Has an old-world charm though the building is actually modern.
Ⅰ **H2O**, 1st floor, Amrit Mansion, RNC Path, T0373-232 1759. Closes 2200. More about having a drink than eating – it's hard to see your food in the almost pitch blackness. Modern and a bit trendy; disco lights.
Ⅰ **Momo Hut**, Gar-Ali (opposite Eley Cinema). Rolls, chow meins, basic Indian, and one of few places that can rustle up a veg *momo* not just pork or chicken.
Ⅰ **Payash Sweets & Restaurant**, 1st floor, City Tower, HS Rd, T0373-232 4076. An excellent veg restaurant hidden up a flight of stairs in the shopping mall, popular with local youth. *Lassis* are cheap and frothy, huge *dosas*, plenty of great Chinese, interesting

paneers dishes and fluffy pizzas. *Marwari thali* is delicious. Staff efficient and low-key.
Ⅰ **Swagat Family Restaurant**, HS Rd (at the junction with AT Rd). Staggering numbers of staff milling around despite it always being busy. Rudimentary downstairs room is good for breakfast (*subji puri* Rs 10, opens at 0630) while the sunny yellow and blue restaurant upstairs is livelier at lunch and dinner and serves Chinese and North Indian food.

Tinsukia *p169*
Ⅰ **Payash Sweets & Restaurant**, has 2 branches in Tinsukia, one of which is fortuitously close to the AST Bus Stand.

☻ Festivals and events

Guwahati *p161, map p162*
Jan Magh Bihu and; **Mid-Apr** Rongali Bihu, are week-long festivities celebrated with singing and dancing. **Jun** Ambubachi marks the end of Mother Earth's menstrual cycle with a fair at Kamakhya Temple.
Sep The Manasa Festival honours the Snake goddess. You can watch devotees dancing and entering into trances from galleries on the hillside.
26-28 Dec The Assam Tea Festival is celebrated with events in various places.

O Shopping

Guwahati *p161, map p162*
Silk and handicrafts
Muga, pat and *endi* silks, hats, bamboo and cane baskets, flutes, drums and pipes are typical of the area. Guide prices: silk per metre: *muga* Rs 400+ (saris Rs 4000+), *pat* Rs 250 (saris Rs 2000+), *endi* Rs 150-300. *Pat mikhala* and *shador*, Rs 1500, *endi* shawls Rs 300+. Bargain in **Pan Bazar** and **Fancy Bazar**. Also try: **Assam, Ambari**, for silks, bamboo, wood, brass and ceramics; **Assam Co-op Silk House**, HB Rd, Pan Bazar, for pure silk

tems; **Khadi Gramudyog**, near Guwahati
Emporium; **Manipur**, Paltan Bazar;
Purbashree, GNB Rd. Traditional crafts;
Tantuja, Ulubari. Bengal handloom.

Jorhat *p167*
People's Bookstore, Plaza Market, 37 Gar-Ali,
T0376-232 1419. Daily 0830-2030, Sun
lunchbreak 1300-1700. Surprisingly good
selection of modern fiction, plus popular
classics (Rs 60), magazines and newspapers.

Dibrugarh *p169*
Art Fed, just off Mancotta Rd, Thanachorali.
Mon-Sat 1000-1900. Attractive *Muga* silks
shawls, *Jhapi* wall decorations, and silk saris/
half saris with golden Assamese thread designs.

🏔 Activities and tours

Guwahati *p161, map p162*
Assam Bengal Navigation, 1st floor, Mandovi
Apartments, GNB Rd, Ambari, Guwahati,
T0361-260 2223, www.assambengal
navigation.com. Sister concern to **Jungle
Travels** (see below) runs 7- or 10-day cruises
along the Brahmaputra aboard the charming
RV Charaidew and *RV Sukapha*, both with
12 en suite cabins, nostalgic saloon bar and
quintessential sundeck; *Sukapha* also has a
small Ayurvedic spa. Land excursions visit the
national parks, villages, historical sites and
provide opportunities to barbecue on the
islands of the mighty river. From Jul-Sep, the
Charaidew moves to the Hooghly for 7-day
cruises between Kolkata and Jangipur. The
company also runs **Bansbari Lodge** in Manas
National Park and **Diphlu River Lodge**, a new
luxurious resort in Kaziranga National Park
(see Sleeping).
Assam Tourism, Tourist Lodge, Station Rd,
T0361-254 7102. City: Basistha Ashram, Zoo,
Museum, Kamakhya Temple, Govt Sales
Emporium. Open 0900-1500. Rs 90. Tue,
Sun (minimum 10). River cruises: from near
Janardhan Temple, winter 1500, 1600; summer
1600, 1700, 1 hr, Rs 50. Kaziranga: Nov-Apr,

departs 0900, arrives 1600, return 1600 on
following day, Rs 600, foreigners Rs 1250
(inclusive) allows only from 1500 to 1000
(on next day) in the park. Separate morning
buses, depart 0700, 5½ hrs. Shillong: departs
0700, Rs 255 (tiring, as the windy hill roads
take 3½ hrs each way). Private companies
(see below) may be more reliable.
Help Tourism, www.helptourism.com.
Based in Kolkata/Siliguri, but with a field
office in Guwahati. Award-winning eco-tours,
maximizing the involvement of local people.
Homestays and simple camps in rural areas,
generally booked as part of a package.
Good for trips to Namdapha, central and
eastern Arunachal, as well as Assam.
Jungle Travels India, 1st floor, Mandovi
Apartments, GNB Rd, Ambari, Guwahati, T0361-
260 2223, www.jungletravels india.com. Wildlife,
heritage, tribal, tea, and other tours around
Assam, Arunachal and Sikkim. Top-notch
service from experienced and friendly staff.
Network Travels, 17 Paltan Bazar,
GS Rd, T0361-273 9630, www.north-east-
tourism.com. Imaginative tours including
river cruises, good for airline ticketing
and buses, efficient and reliable.
Rhino Travels, M Nehru Rd, T0361-254 0061.
For visiting game reserves and Shillong.
Also recommended for permits to visit
other northeast states.
Traveland, 1st floor, **Brahmaputra Ashok**,
MG Rd, T0361-254 1064, rchaliha@
hotmail.com. Knowledgeable and helpful.
Wild Grass, Barua Bhavan, 107 MC Rd, Uzan
Bazar, T0361-254 6827, www.oldassam.com.
Very helpful, knowledgeable, efficient. Highly
recommended for good value wildlife, tribal
tours and Arunachal (can get a permit in
5 days), free travel advice on phone (Nov-Apr).

Kaziranga National Park *p165*
Assam Tourism offers a 2-day tour, also see
Wild Grass; both under Guwahati, above.

Tezpur and around *p166*
Adiytya Tours & Travels, SC Rd, Tezpur,
T03712-232018, T(0)9854-000103,

adiytyatours4731@rediffmail.com. Good for car hire up to Tawang (fleet of 12 vehicles) and do package tours to Arunachal.
Anand Air Travels, MC Rd, Tezpur, T03712-222109. For flight tickets, Mon-Sat 0900-1900, Sun until 1600.
Assam Anglers' Association, T03712-220004, assamangling@yahoo.com, operates a strict 'catch-record-release' system to conserve the golden mahseer.
Eco camp, Potasali, T03714-244246. Organizes whitewater rafting and mahseer fishing on the Bhoreli. Rafting, for fishing or nature watching, for 2 people on rubber rafts, Rs 650 per day, Rs 300 transport to/from raft.

Jorhat *p167*
Assam Tourism, Prashaati Tourist Lodge, MG Rd, T0376-232 1579, www.assamtourism.org, www.assamtourismonline.com. Helpful staff provide advice on transport and accommodation, decent map and pamphlets.

Dibrugarh *p169*
Purvi Discovery, T0373-230 1120, www.purviweb.com, www.assamtea tourism.com. Tours around the Northeast states with very professional service and attention to detail. Experienced in tours to Namdapha and around Arunachal. Managers of the Chowkidinghee and Mancotta Chang bunglows – a great base for the horse riding, kayaking, tea tours or cookery classes on offer. The un-signed office is located in the lane behind the Radha Krishna temple, Medical College area, Rs 20 in a cycle rickshaw from Dibrugarh centre.

⊖ Transport

Guwahati *p161, map p162*
Air
Information T0361-245 2859. **Air India**, Ganeshguri, T0361-226 4425; airport, T0361-284 0279, www.airindia.com. 2 daily to **Kolkata** and one to **Delhi**, **Agartala**, **Bagdogra**, **Imphal**, **Lilabari**. Jet Airways,

Panchvati, GNB Rd, T0361-266 2202, airport T0361-284 0130, www.jetairways.com, to **Bagdogra**, **Delhi**, **Imphal**, **Kolkata**. Also flights with Kingfisher, T3300 8888, www.flyking fisher.com, **Indigo**, www.goindigo.com, and Spicejet, T1800-180 3333, www.spicejet.com.

A helicopter service is run by **Meghalaya Transport Corp**, T0364-222 3129, to **Shillong**, Mon-Sat, Rs 945, on to **Tura** on Mon, Tue, Wed, Fri, Rs1985; tickets at airport.

Bus
Between 2400-0500 buses are not allowed to enter the city, but taxis are. Red minibus 'canters' or 'Omni taxis' cover main roads, but are prone to accidents.
Long distance Private coaches (and taxis) operate from Paltan Bazar, with waiting rooms, left-luggage, snack bars. Operators: **Assam Valley**, T0361-254 6133, **Blue Hill**, T0361-252 0604, **Green Valley**, T0361-254 2852, and others have buses to all the hill states.

Assam STC Stand, Paltan Bazar, T0361-254 4709. Left luggage, Rs 3 per day. Reservations 0630-1230, 1330-1700. Meghalaya STC, T0361-254 7668. Buses to: **Aizawl** (11 hrs); **Imphal** (579 km); **Itanagar** (11 hrs); **Jorhat via Kohora (for Kaziranga)** (6 hrs); **Kaziranga** and Upper Assam: bus for **Tinsukia** and **Digboi** (0700 a/c; 0730), halt at Wild Grass Resorts after 4 hrs. **Kohima** 2000, 2015, 2030 (13 hrs); **Shillong** (103 km) hourly, 0600-1700 (3½ hrs); **Silchar** 1730; **Siliguri**; **Tezpur** every 30 mins (3½ hrs).

City Bus Stand, Station Rd (north end): to **Hajo** (1½ hrs).

Adabari Bus Stand, AT Rd (4 km west of centre) reached by 'canters' from MG Rd, has buses to **Hajo**, **Orang** and **Nalbari**.

Ferry
To **North Guwahati** from MG Rd Ferry Ghat. To **Peacock Island**: Rs 10 each way. 0930-1630.

Rickshaw
From Paltan Bazar to Fancy Bazar Rs 35, Fancy Bazar to Navagraha Temple Rs 50.

Taxi

Sightseeing Rs 100 per hr (excluding petrol); Guwahati Taxis, Paltan Bazar, near Police Station; **Green Valley**, Silpukhuri, T0361-254 2852, cars/jeeps Rs 1100 per day plus overnight Rs 150. **Traveland**, 1st floor, Brahmaputra Ashok, MG Rd, T0361-254 1064. Reliable and efficient. **Chandana**, Goswami Villa, Zoo Narengi Rd, T0361-255 7870, has Tata Sumo (a/c), Rs 1500 per day.

From Paltan Bazar to **Shillong**, Rs 1100, shared taxis fill up quickly when trains arrive.

Train

Station has snack bars, chemists, tourist information, left luggage (trunks and suitcases only), on showing ticket. Enquiries: T0361-254 0330. Reservations: 100 m north of the station on Station Rd, T0361-254 1799, 0800-1330, 1400-2000; Foreign Tourists, Counter 3, where great patience is needed. To **Kolkata** (H): *Kanchenjunga Exp 5658*, 2230, 21½ hrs (via **New Jalpaiguri**, 9 hrs); *Kamrup Exp 5960*, 0745, 23½; *Saraighat Exp 2346*, 1245, 17 hrs (via **New Jalpaiguri**, 7 hrs). To **Delhi** (ND): *Rajdhani Exp 2423/5*, 0705, 28 hrs; *North East Exp 2505*, 0945, 34 hrs. To **Dibrugarh** via Dimapur: *Rajdhani Exp 2436*, 1830, 11 hrs; *Brahmaputra Mail 4056*, 1445, 13 hrs; *Kamrup Exp 5959*, 1630, 14½ hrs.

Manas National Park *p164*

Buses travel on a good fair weather road between Guwahati and Barpeta Rd but no further; taxis charge, Rs 600-800 per journey. The nearest train station is at Barpeta Rd (40 km) with trains to **Guwahati** and **Kolkata**.

Kaziranga National Park *p165*
Air

Nearest airport is at Jorhat (88 km), see page 180. Foreign tourists must use Guwahati's Borjhar airport, see page 161.

Bus/car

Best to ask **Wild Grass** if they have a vehicle going from Guwahati, or confirm timings of private buses. ASTC buses between Guwahati and Jorhat via **Kohora** stopping at **Nagaon** (30 mins, where you can stop overnight); departs 0900, 1000, 1100, 1230, 5-6 hrs. Private buses: **Green Valley** (office behind bus station) coaches depart Guwahati for Tinsukia and Digboi, 0700 and 0730; lunch stop at **Wild Grass Resorts**, after 4 hrs. **Guwahati**: a/c bus from Dibrugarh stops at resort for lunch; leaves at 1330. **Kaziranga Forest Lodge** has 10 seats reserved on the Express coach between Golaghat and Guwahati. **Assam Tourism bus**, depart 0930 from **Bonashree Lodge**, arrive Guwahati 1600. From **Shillong** get a Jorhat bus and switch at **Jorabat** for Kaziranga.

Train

Furkating (75 km) has the nearest station with trains from **Guwahati** and **Dibrugarh**; buses via **Golaghat**.

Tezpur and around *p166*
Air

Saloni Airport is to the north of Tezpur: Air India, T03712-231657, www.airindia.com, flies to/from **Kolkata**.

Bus/taxi

Frequent buses to/from **Guwahati** 0500-1330, Rs 80-90, luxury bus Rs 110-130 (4½-5 hrs); **Kaziranga** from 0600 until 1400 (2 hrs). Daily to **Dibrugarh**, 0615-1230, luxury at 0800 (7 hrs) via **Jorhat**; **Itanagar** at 1000 and 1215, Rs 130-150 (4½ hrs); **North Lakhimpur**, between 0545-1300, Rs 110 (5-6 hrs); **Tawang** (14 hrs). To **Nameri**, take a Bomdila-bound bus/*sumo* and get off at Hatigate, from where its 2.5 km to the Eco-camp. Taxi to **Orang/Nameri**, Rs 600 plus petrol.

Sumos

ASTC, T(0)9435-080318, T(0)9864-182449, and several private companies with offices near the bus stand run *sumos* to **Tawang** and destinations in between, leaving at 0530, 12-14 hrs, pickup from hotel.

Train

The train station is 1 km past the main bus stand at Jhaj Ghat. Irregular services to **Guwahati** take 10 hrs, much better to take a bus. Trains also run from Rangapara to North Lakimpur, via Tezpur.

Jorhat *p167*
Air

Jorhat has the main airport 7 km from town with airlines coach or autos for transfer. Private taxis Rs 100 to town or Rs 600 to Kaziranga. To **Kolkata** with Air India, T0376-232 1521, airport, T0376-234 0294, www.airindia.com; Jet Airlines, Hotel Paradise, T0376-232 5652, airport, T0376-234 0881, www.jetairways.com; and **Kingfisher**, www.flykingfisher.com. **Air India**, to **Bangalore**, Thu and Sun, and **Guwahati**.

Bus

ASTC Stand on AT Rd, T0376-232 0009, office open 0600-2130. Buses to **Guwahati**, 0600, 0700, 0740, 0900, 1245 (a/c) and 1445 (7 hrs, Rs 210-245), via **Kaziranga** (2 hrs, Rs 50); frequent services to **Tezpur** from 0600-1430 (3 hrs, Rs 75); **Sibsagar** (3 hrs, Rs 30); **Dibrugarh** (5 hrs, Rs 80). Private buses leave from outside ASTC, ticket booths are nearby and prices slightly higher. Local services (to Nimatighat, Rs 10, and elsewhere) leave from the public bus stand at the north end of MG Rd.

Train

Station (3 km southeast of bus stand) has no toilets. To **Guwahati**: *Jan Shatabdi Exp 2068*, Mon-Sat 1355, 6 hrs, via Lumding, narrow gauge to **Haflong**: 0715, 4½ hrs – beautiful route but tourists are discouraged; **Haflong Tourist Lodge** is occupied by the army.

Majuli Island *p167*
Bus/rickshaw

Bus from Jorhat (public bus stand, junction of MG and AT Rds) to **Nimatighat** (13 km north, Rs 10); allow 1 hr. Buses/shared buses meet incoming ferries at the *ghat*. To hire an auto-rickshaw Rs 150. During the dry months,

North Lakhimpur is accessible by road; buses or shared taxis take about 6 hrs from Majuli.

Ferry

Government ferry from **Nimatighat**, 0930, 1030, 1400, return 0730, 0830, 1330 and 1500. Confirm schedule, as they change seasonally, as does crossing time as boats have to circumnavigate sand bars, but going to Majuli about 1½ hrs, coming back is longer as it's upstream. The ferries can carry up to 2 cars. Buses run from the *ghat* in Majuli to **Kamalabari** (about 5 km) and **Garamur** (8.5 km, Rs 10).

Sibsagar *p168*

Nearest airport: Jorhat (60 km). Nearest railway station: Simaluguri (20 km). Regular buses to **Guwahati**, **Kaziranga**, **Simaluguri**.

Dibrugarh *p169*
Air

The airport is 16 km from town. Air India, T0373-230 0114, airport, T0373-238 2777, www.airindia.com, to **Kolkata**, Tue-Thu, Sun. Jetlite to **Kolkata** daily except Sun, and **Delhi** daily. Also flights to **Guwahati** with Kingfisher, Jetlite and Air India. Pawan Hans helicopters go to **Arunachal** daily, T(0)9435-734407, T(0)9436-051250.

Bus

Private Bus Stand on AT Rd services to **Guwahati** (Rs 300), **Tezpur** (Rs 210), **Itanagar** (Rs 370) and places in between, 0700-1800 but not to fixed schedules.

AST Bus Stand is on Mancotta Rd, Chowkidinghee, with buses to **Guwahati**, **Jorhat**, **Tinsukia**. They often go and pick up more passengers from AT Rd (in front of the Asha Hotel) before leaving town.

Train

To **Guwahati** (continuing to **New Delhi**): *Brahamaputra Mail 4055*, 2245, 13½ hrs; *Rajdhani Exp 2423A*, Thu, 2015, 10 hrs *Kamrup Exp 5660*, 1800, 13½ hrs (continues to **NJP** and **Kolkata** (**H**) in further 24 hrs). Local *BG Pass* to **Ledo** (via Tinsukia) Sun-Fri 0700, 1600.

Tinsukia *p169*

Bus/train

ASTC Bus Stand on AT Rd; private buses from top end of Rangagora Rd. To **Jorhat**, Rs 80. It's a Rs 5 rickshaw ride between the ASTC stand and the old train station, from where passenger trains run to **Jorhat** daily (except Sat) at 1450 (5 hrs, Rs 50), and a fast shuttle goes to **Guwahati** daily at 1615 (14 hrs, Rs 240) calling at **New Tinsukia** station at 1700. The 2 train stations are 3 km apart. New Tinsukia has most of the long-distance trains, to **Guwahati** (continuing to **New Delhi**) *Brahamaputra Mail*, daily at 0025 (12 hrs), *Rajdhani Exp*, daily at 2120 (9 hrs) continues to **Delhi**, *Kamrup Exp 5960* (AC/II), daily at 1740 (12 hrs), continues to **NJP** and **Kolkata** (**H**).

● Directory

Guwahati *p161, map p162*

Banks United Bank of India, HB Rd, Pan Bazar. ATM and TCs, minimum Rs 50 commission. Grindlays/SC Bank, Dighali Pukhari, GNB/Earl Rds, Mon-Fri 1000-1500, Sat 1000-1230. ATM plus TCs, commission 1% or Rs 100 but quick and efficient. **Internet** Sangita Communications, Anuradha Cinema Complex, GNB Rd, 0830-2000. **Medical services** Ambulance: T0361-266 5114. Down Town Hospital, GS Rd, Dispur, T0361-233 6906/233 1003, by far the best. **Post** GPO (entrance on Shillong Rd) with *Speed Post* (7 days). Counter 1 for evaluation and 14 for stamps, then basement for franking. **CTO**: in Pan Bazar. **Useful contacts** Fire: T0361-254 0222. **Police**: T100.

Kaziranga National Park *p165*

Bank State Bank of India, ATM, 400 m east of the Tourist Complex gate. **Internet** Pharmacy to the right of the gate to the Tourist Complex has 1 computer, Rs 80 per hr. **Post** In the Tourist Complex. **Useful contacts** The Wildlife Society has a library of books and magazines and may show wildlife films to groups. **Range Officer**, T03776-226 2423. **Director**, Tourist Complex, Bokakhat, T03776-268095.

Tezpur *p166*

Banks United Bank of India and Federal Bank, Main Rd, both have ATMs. **Internet** Animit Cyber Cafe, Gopal Agarwalla Complex, Main Rd, T03712-230482, has new computers, daily 0930-2030. **Net Com**, Main Rd, Rs 20 per hr, daily 0930-2100.

Jorhat *p167*

Banks State Bank of India, AT Rd has ATM and exchanges TCs (show proof of purchase). **Internet** Relax, Plaza Market (opposite Bata), Gar Ali, Rs 20, daily 1000-2130, Sun 1100-1400 and 1700-2100. Trisho, Solicitor Rd (Biman Barua Rd), new keyboards, Rs 20 per hr, daily 0930-2100, Sun 1400-2100.

Majuli Island *p167*

Bank United Bank of India, Kamalabari, has ATM. **Internet** Mice, Garamur, has slow connection and only 1 computer, Rs 40 per hr, 0700-1900. Kamalabari has a couple of cybercafés.

Dibrugarh *p169*

Bank State Bank of India, ATM at the Railway Station. **Internet** Jig N Joy, City Tower, HS Rd, T0373-232 7554. Fast connection in clean, cool cubicles, Rs 20 per hr, staff speak English, printing and CD burning, daily 0930-1900, Sun 0900-1300.

Meghalaya

→ *Population: 2.3 million. Area: 22,500 sq km.*

Meghalaya ('abode of the clouds'), with its pine-clad hills, beautiful lakes, high waterfalls and huge caverns, has been called the 'Scotland of the East' because of the similarity of climate, terrain and scenery. The wettest region in the world, between May and September the rain comes down like waterfalls as the warm monsoon air is forced up over the hills. Home to the Garo, Khasi and Jaintia tribes, the hill state retains an untouched feel. There are traditional Khasi villages near Shillong with views into Bangladesh. Entry permits are required (see box, page 161). ▸▸ *For listings, see pages 186-188.*

Background

The land Much of the plateau is made up of the same ancient granite as found in peninsular India; its south facing slope, overlooking Bangladesh, is very steep. The hills rise to heights just under 2000 m, which makes it pleasantly cool but it is also one of the wettest places on the earth (Mawsynram has received more than 20 m of rainfall in one year). Much is still densely forested. Shillong is the only important town; 80% of the people live in villages. Compact and isolated, Meghalaya's rolling plateau lies in a severe earthquake belt. In 1897, Shillong was entirely destroyed in an earthquake.

Government The hill state was created on 21 January 1972. Since 1980 the Congress Party has dominated Lok Sabha elections, but it has never won more than 25 of the 60 State Assembly seats. The Hill Peoples Union, despite being a minority, has claimed the largest number of seats, but once again the Congress won both Lok Sabha seats in the 2008 elections.

History The Khasi, Jaintia and Garo tribes each had their own small kingdoms until the 19th century when the British annexed them. The Garos, originally from Tibet, were animists. The Khasis are believed to be Austro-Asiatic. Jaintias are Mongolian and similar to the Shans of Burma. They believed in the universal presence of god and so built no temples. The dead were commemorated by erecting monoliths and groups of these can be seen in Khasi villages in central Meghalaya between Shillong and Cherrapunjee. In the 19th century many Jaintias were converted to Christianity by missionaries, although they continued many of their old traditions.

People Meghalaya is divided into three distinct areas, the Garo, Khasi and Jaintia Hills, each with its own language, culture and particular customs. All three tribes are matrilineal, passing down wealth and property through the female line, with the youngest daughter taking the responsibility of caring for the parents.

Shillong → *For listings, see pages 186-188. Colour map 2, B4.*

Situated among pine-clad hills and lakes, Shillong retains a measure of its colonial past particularly around Ward Lake. Elsewhere in town, unattractive newer buildings have encroached upon open spaces and Shillong's trade-mark mists are being replaced by smog.

Ins and outs → *Phone code: 0364. Population: 132,900. Altitude: 1496 m.*

Tourist information **India Tourism** ⓘ *GS Rd, Police Bazar, T0364-222 5632, 1000-1700*, free map. **Meghalaya Tourism** ⓘ *opposite Meghalaya Bus Stand, Jail Rd, T0364-222 6220*. **Directorate of Tourism** ⓘ *Nokrek Building, 3rd Meghalaya Secretariat, Lower Lachaumiere, T0364-222 6054, www.meghalayatourism.com, 0700-1800*. Very helpful.

Sights

The horseshoe-shaped **Ward Lake** ⓘ *closed Tue*, is popular for boating. It is near Raj Bhavan and is a two-minute walk from Police Bazar. Behind it is the **Botanical Garden** ⓘ *0900-1700*. The **Butterfly Museum** ⓘ *1000-1600*, is in a private house between Police Bazar and Wahingdoh, where butterflies are bred for conservation and sale. The golf course, amid pines, is ideal for an early-morning walk. **Tee & Putt** provides excellent freshly brewed coffee. **Bara Bazar** is well worth a visit to see authentic local colour. It attracts tribal people, mainly women, who come to buy and sell produce – vegetables, spices, pots, baskets, chickens and even bows and arrows. Small stalls sell real Khasi food.

Shillong

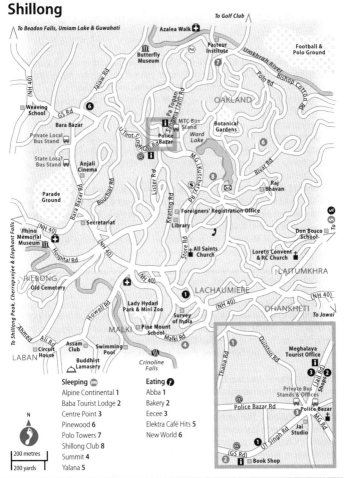

Sleeping 🛏
Alpine Continental 1
Baba Tourist Lodge 2
Centre Point 3
Pinewood 6
Polo Towers 7
Shillong Club 8
Summit 4
Yalana 5

Eating 🍴
Abba 1
Bakery 2
Eecee 3
Elektra Café Hits 5
New World 6

N

200 metres
200 yards

The Archery Stakes

The Archery Stakes, unique to Shillong, take place Monday to Saturday. Members of different clubs shoot more than 500 arrows at a tiny cylindrical bamboo target for four minutes. The punters count the number that stick and anyone who has guessed the last two digits of the number of arrows that stick is rewarded with an 80:1 win. A second shoot takes place an hour later when the odds are 6:1 but if you correctly forecast both results the odds are as high as 4500:1.

Naturally, the bookies are the best-dressed men in town. Start times of the event vary but it's usually around 1530-1600 (ask locally in the morning), and to find the exact field, go to the Polo Ground and ask. There are bookies' shops all over town and elsewhere in the state; bets are even placed as far off as Kolkata and Mumbai. The Stakes were legalized only in 1983 when the state government realized that it could raise a hefty 40% tax on the daily money-spinner.

Just over 1 km away is **Lady Hydari Park** ① 0830-1630, Rs 2, camera Rs 10, video Rs 1000, which is designed like a Japanese garden, where you will see the pine native to the area – *Pinus khasiana*. It is well laid out with its **Forest Museum** and **Mini Zoo**.

The nearby **Crinoline Waterfalls** has a swimming pool surrounded by orchids, potted bonsais and a rock pool with reeds and water lilies. At Lumparing, Laban, the Buddhist **Lamasery** near the Assam Club is interesting but be prepared for a steep climb.

Shillong Peak (10 km, 1960 m) is 3 km from the Cherrapunjee Road, commanding spectacular views. **Laitkor Peak** is on the same ridge, 3 km from the Shillong–Jowai Road, and is under Air Force control; visitors have to report at the barrier. Buses drop you at the appropriate junction.

Elephant Falls (12 km), off the Cherrapunjee Road, is a picturesque spot with two high waterfalls. You can walk down to the lowest pool and get a good view, though the falls themselves are less impressive between November and May. The attractive **Umiam Lake** (Barapani), 16 km, offers fishing and boating.

Rhino Memorial Museum, Hospital Road, in a striking building, has a good tribal collection with a bizarre mix of military paraphernalia.

Around Shillong → For listings, see pages 186-188.

Mawsynram → 55 km from Shillong.

Mawjymbuin Cave has water dripping from a breast-shaped stone on to what looks like a Siva lingam. The rainfall record in Mawsynram has beaten that of Cherrapunjee with over 20 m in one year. Take a bus from Bara Bazar in Shillong at 1400. It takes three hours (Rs 20). **Jakrem**, 64 km away, has hot springs. Buses leave Shillong at 1400, taking three hours.

Cherrapunjee → Colour map 2, B4. Altitude: 1300 m.

The old administrative headquarters of the Khasis, picturesque Cherrapunjee (also known as Shora) is a pleasant, quiet town spread out along a ridge with gravestones dotting the surrounding hillocks. The best time to visit for spectacular views is during the drier months of October to January. The heat and humidity can be oppressive much of the year. By March it is hazy most days and you should expect the odd torrential downpour. It once held the record as the wettest place on earth, but nearby **Mawsynram** has surpassed this. On average it still gets 11,500 mm annually.

The colourful **Ka lewbah Sohrarim market** is held every eight days and attracts hordes of Khasi tribespeople. The local orange flower honey is sold from a house (clearly signposted) just below Cherra Bazar (about 100 m on the road; avoid plastic bottles). Surprisingly, a variety of banana here actually contains seeds.

Nohkalikai Falls, reputedly the world's fourth highest, is 5 km away, near Sohrarim. A vendor sells good orange flower honey. **Montana Tourism**, Cherra Bazar, arranges group tours (US$10). Limestone caves nearby include Krem Mawmluh (4503 m) with a five river passage and Krem Phyllut (1003 m) at **Mawsmai**, with a large fossil passage and two stream ways. Mawsmai also has high waterfalls in the wet season.

The most astonishing sight around Cherrapunjee and a must-see of the Northeast are a series of living **root-bridges** found near Mawshamok. Here, Khasi tribespeople have trained the roots of the *ficus elastica* rubber tree into robust bridges, spanning streams that become raging torrents in the monsoon. It takes 15-20 years for the bridges to become strong enough to support the crossing of people and goods between the villages, but they last for several centuries – getting sturdier as they age. There is an excellent eco-friendly resort (see Sleeping, page 186) that can provide sketch maps for the challenging treks to the bridges. From the resort, a day-trek entails a very steep 45-minute descent to the tangled mass of a 'single' root-bridge, well worth the effort and pain of the ascent back up. Or it is possible to overnight at **Nogriat** village, 11 km away through the dense forest, where there is a four-room guesthouse (Rs 200 per person, meals Rs 50). This trek involves descending 3000 steps to reach several root-bridges including the extraordinary Umshiang 'double-decker' model, and plenty of up-and-down hills to Nogriat. Also when in Cherrapunjee, check when the Shora eighth-day market is next occurring, a vivid affair attended by pipe-smoking villagers.

Jainta Hills

Jowai, 64 km southeast of Shillong on NH44, is the headquarters of the Jaintia Hills, circled by the Myntdu River. The market, full of tribal women, is especially colourful. From Shillong cars take 2½ hours, buses a little longer. **Nartiang**, 55 km from Shillong, is a scenic spot famed for its monoliths, which were raised in tribute to Jainta kings. It is only 12 km from Jowai and accessible by public transport, although vehicles are crammed way beyond capacity.

Syndai, 40 km south, has many caves used by ancient warriors as hide-outs, such as Krem Sweep with a vast chamber. India's longest (6381 m) and deepest (106.8 m) Eocene Age cave with cataracts and falls is **Krem Um-Lawan**, 60 km southeast of Jowai near **Lumshnong**.

Tura

The centre of the West Garo Hills District, Tura, 220 km southwest of Guwahati, sits at the foot of the jungle-clad 1457 m Nokrek Peak. It is a spread-out town with a slow pace of life. Tura Bazar is dominated by the new supermarket, a red-and-white mini shopping mall, with an underground car park. The small fruit and vegetable market in the basement is well organized. A museum-cum-cultural complex is planned 200 m west of **Orchid Lodge**. Weekly tribal markets are held in surrounding villages and the **Wangala dance festival**, with great ceremonial drumming, occurs in November after the harvest.

Nokrek Peak can be reached by a 5-km trek, but involves rock climbing, so is best not attempted alone. **Nokrek National Park** is 55 km away. Jeeps from Tura Bazar cost Rs 1150-1500 for the round trip (daily rate). Ask the tourist office for a guide. **Naphak Lake**, 112 km, near the Simsang River is good for fishing and birdwatching.

Siju → *Colour map 2, B3.*

Southeast of Tura just below the town, with others nearby, is one of India's longest caves (4.8 km) with a fine river passage. Groups of at least four are needed for caving so look out on noticeboards. It is more enjoyable and cheaper to travel this way. Bus to Baghmara 45 km, 1½ hours; from there to Tura, leaves at 0900.

⊙ Meghalaya listings

For Sleeping and Eating price codes and other relevant information, see Essentials pages 34-38.

⊜ Sleeping

Shillong *p182, map p183*

A-C Centre Point, GS Rd, Police Bazar, T0364-222 5210, www.centrepointshillong.com. 24 comfortable modern rooms with views, good restaurant (Indian, Chinese), **Cloud Nine Pub** has bands at the weekends.

A-C Tripura Castle, Cleve Colony, T0364-250 1111, www.tripuraroyalheritage. The first heritage hotel in the northeast, with 10 art deco-style rooms with brass fireplaces, tea lounge, holistic therapy. It was the summer residence of the maharajahs of Tripura.

B Polo Towers, Polo Grounds, Oakland Rd, T0364-222 2341, www.hotelpolotowers.com. 50 well-appointed rooms, exchange (cash), modern and efficient, popular bar Sat nights.

C Alpine Continental, Thana-Quinton Rd, T0364-222 0991, alpineshillong@hotmail.com. 41 comfortable rooms and suites, hot water (0730-1030), reasonable restaurant, small cosy bar, exchange (cash, TCs), terrace garden, prompt room service.

C-D Pinewood, Rita Rd, near Raj Bhavan, T0364-222 3146. Well located and an atmospheric Raj relic, 40 old-fashioned rooms (needing a coat of paint), **A** suites, best in nostalgic old bungalow, spacious grounds, restaurants, bar, exchange, golf.

C-D Shillong Club, MG Rd (near Ward Lake), T0364-222 5533, resi@hotmail.com. Best to book ahead, 18 rooms in a charming 'colonial' club, Indian restaurant, bar, tennis, billiards.

C-D Summit, Sikandra, 23 Lachaumiere (south of NH between Dhankheti and Malki), T0364-222 6216, fmh_sikandra@hotmail.com. On the edge of town, this hotel has character and well-furnished, clean comfortable rooms. Great service and good food, family atmosphere.

E-F Baba Tourist Lodge, GS Rd, T0364-221 1285. Basic, friendly, clean, restaurant, 27 rooms of which the singles are microscopic.

F Yalana, Main Rd, Laitumkrah (near Don Bosco), T0364-221 1240. Comfortable hotel, 17 rooms, good restaurant, very friendly.

Cherrapunjee *p184*

D-F Cherrapunji Holiday Resort, Laitkkynsew village, T03637-244 218/9, T(0)9436-115925, www.cherrapunjee.com. Lovely hosts and an idyllic setting make this little resort particularly enchanting. Double tents are Rs 500, or spacious simple rooms are Rs 1150-1250 plus 20% tax. Plenty of help is given for lone trekkers, experienced guides lead river canyoning expeditions (best Oct-Feb), there's a host of birdlife, plus natural swimming pools to cool off in. Highly recommended.

Tura *p185*

C-F Rikman Continental, Tura Bazar, T03651-220744, rikman_tura@hotmail.com. 16 clean rooms, bath, restaurant.

D-E Orchid Lodge (MTDC), New Tura (4 km from Tura Bazar), city bus to Dakopgre stops outside, or auto-rickshaw (Rs 50; Rs 70 at night), T03651-242394, T(0)9856-221160. Dorm (Rs 100), 7 rooms, TV (variable reception despite a giant satellite dish), dining hall meals at set times, tourist office (tours of Siju, Balpakram).

Siju *p186*

G Tourist Lodge (MTDC), T03639-222141. Take your own provisions, a chowkidar will cook for you. Another at Baghmara, T03651-232394.

🍴 Eating

Shillong *p182, map p183*
Try a local pork dish, *dohkhleh* (minced brains with onion and spices) with *jadoh* (rice flavoured with turmeric or pig's blood) and *saag* (greens) with spicy *tung tap* (hot chutney made with dried fish) at places in Bara Bazar and a stall behind Centre Point.
† Abba, Malki Point and GS Rd. Closed Sun. Delicious Chinese.
† Bakery, GS Rd. Serves pizzas and fast food. Recommended.
† Eecee, near bus Stand, Police Bazar. Western. Good restaurant and great cakes.
† Elektra Café Hits, Nazareth Hospital, Laitumkhra. International. Excellent breakfast and lunch. Also has delicious chocolate cake.
† New World, GS Rd. Good Chinese.

Cherrapunjee *p184*
Cherra Bazar has a few eateries.
† Orchid Restaurant, opposite the falls. Serves good food.

🎭 Entertainment

Shillong *p182, map p183*
Shillong is known for its retro music scene and weekend nights see rock bands perform at the cavernous **Cloud Nine Pub** at Centrepoint Hotel. Blues music on Wed, courtesy of Lou Majaw and his aging band. Entrance Rs 200. Better bars at **Pinewood**, **Polo Towers** and **Shillong Club** for more atmosphere. *Kiad*, the local rice wine, is popular in roadside bars.

🎉 Festivals and events

Shillong *p182, map p183*
4-5 Feb Roots Festival Unlimited, a folk event at Orchid Lake Resort, Umiam, Barapani, 20-min drive from Shillong, www.rootfestival.co.in.
6 Feb Jammin' is a Bob Marley festival that attracts a few thousand, usually held at the Orchid Lake Resort, tickets Rs 50-100.

24 May Bob Dylan Festival, at the State Central Library Auditorium, Rs 100-1000.

🛍 Shopping

Shillong *p182, map p183*
You can get handwoven shawls, canework, Khasi jewellery, handicrafts, orange flower honey. **Govt Emporia** are on Jail Rd and GS Rd. In **Bara Bazar**, tribal women sell attractive Khasi silver, gold and amber jewellery.

🏔 Activities and tours

Shillong *p182, map p183*
Golf
Golf Club, T0364-222 3071. 19-holes, clubs for hire; the wettest, and also one of the most beautiful, 'natural' courses in the world.

Swimming
Club near Crinoline Waterfalls, 0600-1630 (women 1100-1200, 1400-1500).

Tour operators
Blue Hill Travels, Police Bazar. Very helpful.
Cultural Pursuits, Hotel Pegasus Crown, T0364-2550753, www.culturalpursuits.com. Eco-adventure tours of Assam, Meghalaya.
Meghalaya Adventurers, Hotel Centre Point, T0364-222 5210. Offers cave tours. Visitors may contact Patricia Mukkim, a local teacher-cum-journalist, T0364-223 0593, patria@technologist.com. She is well informed about local culture and history.
Meghalaya Tourism, T0364-222 6220, www.meghalayatourism.com. Tourist Information Centre, Police Bazar, local tours stopping a few mins at most sights (2½ hrs at Umiam Lake). 0830-1530, Rs 120. Cherrapunjee, Nohkalikai Falls, Mawsmai cave (torch essential) and falls: 0745-1630 (15-20 mins at each place). Rs 200. Tours only occur when there are sufficient numbers, so Sundays are the safest bet. Recommended and good value, especially for solo travellers.

Natural Ways, Hawakhana, Tura, T(0)9863-091278, somuingty@yahoo.co.in. Adventure tours in the Garo Hills.

Water sports
Umiam Lake (16 km), waterskiing, boating and fishing.

⊖ Transport

Shillong *p182, map p183*
Air Transport to Guwahati Airport (127 km): taxi, Rs 700 (3 hrs), nearly double for departures after 1100, or hourly bus, Rs 50. Air India flies daily except Tue at 1155 to **Kolkata** and **Dimapur**. Bookings through Sheba Travels, Police Bazar, T0364-222 7222, which also runs an airport coach.

Meghalaya Helicopter, Meghalaya Transport Corporation (MTC) Bus Stand, T0364-222 3129, 1000-1600, flies to **Guwahati**, Rs 945 (Mon-Sat) and **Tura** (Mon, Wed, Fri), maximum 10 kg baggage, but poor safety record. Tickets from MTC Bus Stand, Jail Rd.

Bus Meghalaya TC, Jail Rd, T0364-222 3200. To **Guwahati**, frequent, 0600-1700, 3½ hrs; **Silchar**, 2100, 11½ hrs. Also from stands near Anjali Cinema, Bara Bazar to towns in Meghalaya. Private bus companies have offices/booths around Police Bazar for long-distance connections in the Northeast.

Taxi Metered, yellow-top taxis pick up passengers to share rides. Flag one down and hop in if it is going your way; short hops, eg Police Bazar to Laitumkhrah, Rs 10. **MTDC** taxis at Pinewood Ashok or the tourist office. Sightseeing, Rs 1800 (8 hrs, 100 km).

For long-distance: **Tourist Taxi Association**, Police Bazar, T(0)94361-16824, share taxi to **Guwahati**, Rs 125 each, 3 hrs.

Train Guwahati (103 km) is the nearest railhead. Tickets from **MTC Bus Stand**, T0364-222 3200. 0600-1100, 1300-1600.

Cherrapunjee *p184*
Bus From **Shillong** (Bara Bazar), to Cherrapunjee, 1½ hrs; **Mawmluh**, 2 hrs.

Taxi From Cherra Bazar for **Nohkalikai Falls**, **Krem Mawmluh** and views over the plains of Bangladesh, Rs 300; also share taxis. Meghalaya Tourism in Shillong, runs tours.

Tura *p185*
Air Helicopter services to/from **Shillong** and **Guwahati**.

Bus To **Baghmara** 106 km (for Siju, none direct), 1300, 4-5 hrs, along the Bangladesh border. Buy tickets the day before from booth near **MTC Bus Stand**, Tura Bazar; ask your hotel to buy your ticket for a small fee. Private buses to **Guwahati** (8 hrs), **Shillong** (12 hrs, night bus arrives at 0400), **Siliguri** from Tura Bazar. Booking offices are easy to find.

❶ Directory

Shillong *p182, map p183*
Banks State Bank of India, MG Rd, 1st floor. Mon-Fri 1130-1400. **Indian Overseas Bank**, GS Rd (Police Bazar end). Both currency and TCs. **Internet** On GS Rd and Police Bazar Rd. **Medical services** Ambulance, T0364-222 4100. **Civil Hospital**, GS Rd, T0364-222 3889. Nazareth Hospital, Laitumukhrah, T0364-222 4052. Chemist in Police Bazar. **Post** GPO, GS Rd, Police Bazar. **Useful contacts** Foreigners' Registration Office, Lachumiere near the State Museum.

Arunachal Pradesh

→ *Population: 1.1 million. Area: 84,000 sq km.*
This is Northeast India's largest and most remote state. The Tawang Monastery, birthplace of the sixth Dalai Lama and surrounded by awesome mountainscapes, is a major attraction, along with the rich tribal heritage throughout the state. In the east, the forests canopies of Namdapha National Park shelter elephant, clouded leopard, snow leopard, tiger, Himalayan black bear, red panda and musk deer. ⇢ *For listings, see pages 193-196.*

The land

On the Northeast frontier of India, Arunachal Pradesh is India's least densely populated state with just 13 people per sq km. It stretches from the foothills of the eastern Himalaya to their permanently snow-capped peaks to the north. The Brahmaputra, known here as the Siang River, enters the state from China and flows through a deeply cut valley. Stretching from the Himalaya to the steamy plains of the Brahmaputra valley, Arunachal Pradesh has an extraordinary range of forests from the Alpine to the subtropical – from rhododendrons to orchids, reeds and bamboo. It is an orchid lover's paradise with over 550 species identified.

Climate

Bomdila (2500 m) and Tawang (3500 m) are exceptionally cold between October and March with temperatures in Tawang dropping as low as -12°C. However, clear skies are most likely October to December, and it is also when many flowers are in bloom.

History

The entire region had remained isolated since 1873 when the British stopped free movement. After 1947 Arunachal became part of the North East Frontier Agency (NEFA). Its strategic significance was demonstrated by the Chinese invasion in 1962, and the Indian government subsequently broke up the Agency giving statehood to all the territories surrounding Assam. Arunachal became the 24th state in 1987, though China continues to argue that until the international border between it and India are agreed some of the territory remains disputed. At the same time the state is disputing its southern border with Assam, and in April 2001 the state government lodged a petition with India's Supreme Court against the government of Assam for 'large-scale encroachment' on its territory. Having long borders with China and Myanmar, it is a truly frontier State. The state was opened to tourists in 1995 with the first foreigners being given permission to trek only as recently as 1998. Congress won both Lok Sabha seats in 2009.

Culture

The Arunachali people are the state's greatest attraction. In the capital Itanagar you may even see Nishi warriors wearing hornbill feathers in their caps, carrying bearskin bags and their knives in monkey-skin scabbards.

A great diversity of the tribal people speak over 60 different dialects. Most have an oral tradition of recording their historic and cultural past by memorizing verses handed down through generations. Some Buddhist tribes have, however, maintained written records, largely recording their religious history. Some tribes worship Donyi and Polo, the Sun and Moon gods.

Itanagar-Naharlagun → For listings, see pages 193-196. Colour map 2, A5.

Itanagar, the new capital, and Naharlagun, the old town 10 km away, together provide the capital's administrative offices. Itanagar, sited between two hills, has the governor's residence on one and a new Buddhist temple on the other, with shops, bazar, traditional huts and more recent earthquake-proof wooden-framed buildings in between. The capital has been identified as Mayapur, the 11th-century capital of the Jitari Dynasty.

Ins and outs → *Phone code: 0360. Population: 61,900.*

Getting there and around Visitors arriving at Lilabari or North Lakhimpur in Assam take two hours by bus (or a little less by taxi) to Itanagar, calling at Naharlagun Bus Station before climbing up along a scenic road to the new capital. Regular buses run from Guwahati and Shillong. Frequent buses run between Itanagar and Naharalagun from 0600 until 2000. Cycle-rickshaws only available in Naharlagun. ▶▶ See Transport, page 196.

Tourist information India Tourism ⓘ *Sector 'C', Itanagar, T0360-221 2949/221 8739, helpful.* Arunachal Pradesh Tourism ⓘ *Naharlagun, T0360-224 1752, www.arunachaltourism.com.*

Sights

The yellow-roofed **Buddhist temple** stands in well-kept gardens on a hilltop with good views. The **Gyaker Sinyi** (Ganga Sekhi Lake), 6 km, is reached by a rough road through forests of bamboo and tree ferns. On reaching the foot of the hill, walk across a bamboo bridge, up steps cut on the hillside to reach a ridge overlooking the forest lake. The brick fort (14th-15th century) is believed to have been built by King Ramachandra. In Naharlagun, the **Polo Park** is on top of a ridge with interesting botanical specimens including the cane thicket, which looks like palm, as well as a small **zoo**.

Jawaharlal Nehru Museum ⓘ *Tue-Sun, Rs 50,* has good coverage of tribal people: a collection of art, wood carvings, musical instruments and religious objects. The first floor has archaeological finds from Malinthan, Itafort, Noksaparbat and others.

Western Arunachal Pradesh → For listings, see pages 193-196. Colour map 2, A4.

The whole journey, from Tezpur in Assam (the nearest airport) to Tawang, is spectacular, passing waterfalls, terraced paddy fields, alpine forests and mountain streams. The road north crosses the border at **Bhalukpong** (see page 167), and continues towards Bomdila passing through low wooded slopes for about 60 km. On the bank of the Bhoreli River in the upper plains is **Tipi**, with the Orchid Research Centre and a glasshouse with 500 species of orchids. From there the road rises sharply to reach Bomdila.

Ins and outs

For those not travelling with a hired jeep, **ASTC** buses or **Tata** *sumo* services ply between Tezpur and Tawang (in winter, buses only make it as far as Dirang). *Sumos* are far preferable, though more expensive: they are significantly quicker and can negotiate the narrow, terrifying roads far better. To take the journey in one go means a gruelling 12-14 hours, better to do this coming back rather than going up. When breaking the journey at Bomdila or Dirang, try to book onward *sumo* tickets in advance and ask for 'number 1 seat' for best views and comfort. Coming back down from Tawang, the best seats are reserved days in advance so again do some forward planning. Check travel conditions locally (Sela Pass is frequently closed by snow) and, if in a private vehicle, don't travel after dark as visibility on the narrow mountain roads can be very poor at night.

Bomdila → *Colour map 2, A4. Altitude: 2530 m.*

On a clear day, Bomdila has marvellous views of the snow-capped mountains. There's a craft centre, apple and cherry orchards, three Buddhist *gompas* and a museum. Transport links are good, there is internet connection and hotels are generally more comfortable than those in Dirang, but it is a sprawling rather unattractive place. Buses leave from the bus stand in the lower part of town and *sumos* from the main bazar, 2 km up the hill and therefore more convenient for hotels. **Himalayan Holiday** in the market has some basic tourist information.

Dirang → *Colour map 2, A4.*

About an hour's drive after Bomdila, the road cuts through the miniature village of Old Dirang and continues another 5 km to larger (newer) Dirang, which has a few guesthouses and simple places to eat. It is a more appealing stop than Bomdila when breaking the journey to Tawang, though make sure you book an onward ticket in advance. A day can easily be spent walking to tiny peaceful villages nearby. The obvious attraction is the old village, huddled around the confluence of two rivers, where a population of some 1200 Monpa tribespeople inhabit traditional stone dwellings with slatted wooden upper levels and woven roofs. One of the morning *sumos* to Bomdila can drop you off at the ancient three-storey **Khatsikpa Gompa** atop a small ridge, from where it's a steep walk past *stupas* and *mani* walls down to the village. Here, women walk along knitting, men carrry woven *shingrong* baskets from head-straps and kids run around with babies tied on their backs. Across the main bridge, a sign points the way to the plain stacked stones of **Dirang Dzong** (generally locked), one of several *dzongs* in the district from where Tibetan officials collected taxes. An hour or so is sufficient to explore the pathways of the village, and then it's an easy walk back to New Dirang following the road along the river, criss-crossing a couple of bridges on the way.

From the central crossroads in New Dirang, the turning signed to the Yak Research Centre leads into a 2-km uphill tramp to lovely **Yewang** village. The track forks but both lead to the village: the new track to the right is quicker, but it's nice to turn left and walk through the first cluster of homes surrounded by terracing and agriculture before reaching the beautiful *gompa* at the highest point of Yewang. The forested foothills begin in earnest from here, while the village trickles down the hillside below among fields of yellow mustard flowers, pink peas, millet, cabbage or corn – depending on the season.

To Tawang → *Colour map 2, A4.*

After passing through the pretty Dirang Valley shrouded in pine woods, the route snakes past lonely army camps and teetering villages to the **Sela Pass** which at 4215 m presents a far starker view. The successor to Lama Guru Rimpoche has been found in a village nearby. Stop a while here above the clouds, along one of the highest motorable roads in the world, with views of a high-altitude lake and graphite peaks streaked with snow. **Jaswantpur**, 13 km from the pass, has the *samadhi* to the brave Jawan (soldier), Jaswant Singh, which commemorates how he, his fiancé and her friend valiantly held up the advancing Chinese army in 1962 for three days before laying down their lives. Drivers along this road, many of them ex-army personnel, stop to pay their respects at the poignant memorial.

The road then descends alongside a river before emerging on the edge of Tawang Valley, where the folded foothills are of an unimaginable scale, plunging and twisting towards

Tibet. Numerous tiny hamlets and golden *gompas* speckle the near-vertical slopes opposite the improbably large village of **Jang**, 42 km before Tawang. Houses here are checkerboard Assamese-style or Monpa cubes, and many older Monpa wear a densely woven black yak-wool skullcap, the tentacles of which channel rainwater away from the wearer's face. After crossing the river, the old village of **Lhou** is especially atmospheric (worth a visit if using private transport) before the final 18 km to Tawang township.

Tawang → *Colour map 2, A4. Phone code: 03794. Population: 4600.*
Although set in breathtakingly dramatic scenery at 3500 m, the town of Tawang itself is not immediately attractive. The prayer wheels in the Old Market square, overlooked by a mini *gompa* and flower-laden balconies, have charm and two Tibetan-style gates are beautifully maintained. Most people are here to see the **monastery**, birthplace of the sixth Dalai Lama, and the second largest Buddhist monastery in the world (after Lhasa). Dating originally from 1681, it houses around 450 *lamas* belonging to the Gelugpa (Reformed) Sect of Mahayana Buddhist monks. Buddhism arrived in the area with Padmasambhava in the eighth century but the local Monpas were converted to the Tantric Buddhist cult only after the establishment of the monastery here by Merag Lama in the 17th century. During renovations in the 1990s, the main building was completely rebuilt. The lofty prayer hall, containing a 5.5-m-high golden Buddha heaped with silky prayer scarves, sees monks gather at 0500 and again at 0715 for worship (observers welcome) after which the young trainees go to the monastic school next door. It generally takes 15-20 years for the *lamas* to complete their doctorates in Buddhist philosophy, though the current Dalai Lama was just 25 when he finished. The **museum** ① *opened on request, Rs 20, cameras Rs 20*, contains a wealth of treasures, including 700-year-old sculptures, numerous *thangkas* and priceless manuscripts. These, and other precious objects left in storage, are soon to be properly displayed in a new two-storey building.

Exiting via the south gate of the monastery complex takes you down a grassy ridge, strung with small *chortens* and *mani* walls, for some excellent views. Visible on a ridge northeast from the monastery is the **Gyamgong Ani Gompa**, home to some three dozen nuns who are studying there, a 1½-hour walk down and up a steep ravine (only advisable in dry weather).

Lake District
Just above Tawang beyond the monastery is the Lake District, an exceptionally beautiful area with many high-altitude lakes, including the tranquil Sangeshar Lake where a dance sequence from the film *Koyla* was shot. After a fork and an army outpost, the road continues towards **Klemta**, just a few kilometres from the Indian border. There are a few scattered monasteries and a shrine to all faiths at the spot where Guru Nanak rested as he trekked into Tibet, 500 years ago. **Ptso**, 25 km from Tawang, has a small cabin by a lake which is used by the military. To explore this area you'll have to hire a jeep and guide, carry snacks and drinks, and be prepared for steep, treacherous mountain roads. It is all worth it for the breathtaking mountain scenery.

Gorsam Chorten
This immense *chorten* (*stupa*) is 105 km from Tawang, near Jimithang, where there are some simple places to stay. The setting is amazing, and the road little travelled by foreigners. A few public *sumos* run to the village each week, taking two to three hours; book ahead with an agent in Tawang or hire a vehicle.

Ziro → *Colour map 2, A5. 150 km north of Itanagar. Altitude: 1475 m.*

Ziro lies in a picturesque level valley of the Apatani plateau, surrounded by pine-covered mountains. The Apatani tribals who live in small, densely populated villages have evolved a sophisticated system of irrigated paddy cultivation. You can also visit Nisi **tribal settlements**. There are daily buses from Itanagar (200 km away) and Lilabari (100 km).

Parasuram Kund → *Colour map 2, A6.*

This lake in Eastern Arunachal attracts thousands of pilgrims at **Makar Sankranti** (mid-January) who come to the fair and to take a holy bath. It's possible to stay at the spartan **Government Tourist Lodge** (contact Dy Commissioner, Tezu, well in advance). From Tinsukia, launch along the Brahmaputra (1½ hours) to Sadiya Ghat, there are buses to Parasuram Kund.

Namdapha National Park → *Colour map 2, A6.*

ⓘ *Permit required from Project Tiger Office in Miao, T03807-222249, where you can also book the Deban Guesthouse. Porters can be hired in Miao. Stock up on food and provisions. Entry to the park is in Deban, 25 km away. Most people visit on a pre-arranged tour (minimum of 2 people, Rs 4000-6000 per day). For independent transport, see page 196. Malaria is prevalent inside the park and leeches are voracious, take precautions. Waterproofs are essential year-round. The best season is Oct-Apr, as the monsoon rains make rivers and pathways impassable.*
Namdapha encompasses a range of altitudes from 200 m to 4500 m, from the low-lying flood plains to the snow-capped mountain of Daphabum. The sheer size and spread of the park is astonishing, its dense forest stretches over the Myanmar border in the far east and large tracts are unexplored except by the native Lisu people, whose settlements are a week's walk away from Miao. It is unique as it is home to four members of the cat family: tiger, leopard, snow leopard and clouded leopard, although it is extremely rare to see any of them. There are also elephants, Hoolock gibbons, butterflies, sambhar, deer, gaur, goral and wild hogs and a rich birdlife (especially hornbills). Expect to be on foot most of the time, in any case, as the 'road' is completely overgrown. The variety of vegetation is as fascinating as the fauna, and many people rate Namdapha as the best national park in India.

◉ Arunachal Pradesh listings

For Sleeping and Eating price codes and other relevant information, see Essentials pages 34-38.

◉ Sleeping

Itanagar-Naharlagun *p190*
Try to reserve rooms in advance. Some hotels seriously hike their prices Sep-Jan.
B Donyi-Polo Ashok, Sector C, Itanagar, T0360-221 2627. Arunachal's most upmarket hotel, in a decaying concrete building with 20 rooms, 2 a/c suites and average restaurant.
D Arun Subansiri, Zero Point, Itanagar, T0360-221 2806. Comfortable, large and modest rooms, hot shower, 1200 check-out.

G Youth Hostel, Naharlagun. Basic, 60 beds.

Bomdila *p191*
B-D Siphiyang Phong, T03782-222286, hotelsiphiyangphong@rediffmail.com. Pleasant but pricey, all rooms have hot water and TV. Restaurant is cheery with checked tablecloths and plenty of bamboo panelling. Travel desk T03782-223676.
F-G Tourist Lodge and **La**, are other options.

Dirang *p191*
B-D Heritage Pemaling, 1.5 km out of the village, T03780-242615, T(0)9436-877274. Standard/de luxe rooms are frumpy but clean with new tiled bathrooms, the only

real difference being the valley views from the de luxe. Suites (Rs 3000 plus tax) are much more attractive in a chintz-and-wicker way, with large bathroom and balcony. Restaurant for residents only.

E Dirang Resort, IB Rd, T03780-242352, dirangresorts@yahoo.co.in. Modern Western bathrooms (geysers), separate sitting area, wooden floors and balcony, lace in the windows and cobwebbed pink walls – but you can hear something scratching about in the roof and the staff are dazed and vacant.

E Dirang Tourist Lodge, next to **Heritage Pemaling**, T03780-242175, www.himalayan-holidays.com. Spacious clean rooms, attached bath with geyser, and great views down over the river and Dirang. Only 4 rooms so booking necessary, Rs 750 per room (single or double). Meals provided, but give advance warning.

E Maa Laxmi, Leiky Complex, Main Market, T03780-242372, T(0)9435-083105. This basement hotel has 6 uninspiring rooms with attached (squat) toilets, bright blue paint and kitchen sinks. Beds are wide but you would expect clean sheets for the price.

E-F Moon, Main Rd, T03780-242438. Upstairs 4-bed room has a decent bathroom with geyser, but others share a smelly common bath (hot bucket available). Rooms have clean sheets and paintwork, hard beds, and nothing more.

F-G Dreamland, Main Rd, T03780-242296. 3 simple twin rooms in a family home (sharing their basic clean bathroom), potted plants aplenty, plenty of bedding provided although beds are hard. Beer in the little restaurant is appealing, but avoid the food. Hot buckets Rs 20.

Tawang *p192*

Apart from dormitory beds (men only), single travellers to Tawang will have to pay the price of a double room. There are plenty of lodges clustered around the Old Market area, where *sumos* terminate.

B-C Tenzin Guest House, 6 km from Tawang village by road, or a 45-min hike up footpaths (as is the monastery directly above), T03794-200095. A modern concrete house with 4 spotless rooms upstairs, bit overpriced,

but certainly comfortable. The setting is peaceful and attractive.

C-D Tawang Inn, Nehru Market, T03794-224096. The highest-spec rooms in town, particularly in terms of bathrooms. Carpets, attractive furnishings, thick pillows, TV, heaters, lots of wood and cane. 6 **B** suites. Ask for a room with a view.

D-E Tourist Hut, Nehru Market, T03794-222739, T(0)9436-051291. The best value in Tawang, 7 rooms are new with heaters, towels, laminate floors, and plenty of colourfully clashing patterns and blankets – preferable on the 1st floor. A range of prices, pay more for TV or front-facing view, kind management willing to negotiate. Recommended.

F Tourist Lodge, 200 m (signed) from jeep stand in the Old Market, T03794-222359. A lodge with 20 well-furnished but poorly maintained rooms, but they do have heaters and hot water. Contact the Deputy Commissioner to make reservations.

F-G Nefa, Nefa Complex, Nehru Market, T03794-222419. Double rooms are gloomy and old-fashioned while the staff are young and jolly. Men can stay in the 4-bed dorm.

Ziro *p193*

D-E Blue Pine, T03788-224812. Most people's 1st choice, other places are closer to town.

G Circuit House, reservations through Mr Sadhana Deori, Deputy Commissioner, Lower Subansiri District, T03788-224255. 8 rooms.

Namdapha National Park *p193*

There is a simple government lodge at Miao.

B Camp Namdapha, across the river from Deban Rest House. Picturesque location, offers 10 bamboo huts and log cabins as well as tented accommodation. Guides, porters and all meals are included in the price, booked as part of a tour.

G Deban Forest Rest House. Advance bookings through Field Director's office in Miao, T03807-223126. Basic clean rooms with mosquito nets and a dorm, bath, caretaker-cook. Ethnic bamboo huts overlooking the Noa Dihing River are more expensive.

🍴 Eating

Dirang *p191*

⭑ **Dipak Sweets & Snacks**, Main Rd. Open 0600-1900. Excelllent *chola* with samosa or *puris* in the morning. One of few places open after noon on Thu.

† **Hotel Raj**, Main Rd. Open 0600-1800. Good *dal baht* (Rs 40) and *thukpa* (Rs 30).

† **Hotel Samaroh**, Main Rd. Cheap and busy, rice meals/chow mein/greasy rolls are tasty. Veg and non-veg.

Tawang *p192*

In Nehru Market, a small bakery sells substantial muffins and pastries.

⭑-† **Hotel Tawang View**, Nehru Market, T03794-223009. Open 0830-2100. Probably the best restaurant in town, with a huge vegetarian and non-vegetarian menu, most of which is actually available (unlike other places). Indian dishes particularly recommended. Red walls, coloured bulbs, plastic flowers, and the occasional drunk local.

† **Dragon Restaurant**, Old Market, T03794-224475. Open 0700-2030. Delicious Chinese and Tibetan staples take a while to prepare and meat is rarely available, quite cosy surrounds with fairy lights. Look for the Chinese lanterns outside.

🎉 Festivals and events

Tawang *p192*

Feb/Mar Losar is celebrated for 8-15 days in western Arunachal.

Oct/Nov Buddha Mahatsova has cultural programmes, monastic and tribal dances, over 3 days.

🛍 Shopping

Itanagar-Naharlagun *p190*

The cotton textiles available here are colourful and are beautifully patterned. You can also get wooden masks and figures, cane belts and caps. **Handicrafts Centres** have shawls, *thangkas*, handloom, wood carvings, cane and bamboo work and carpets; you can watch tribal craftsmen trimming, cutting and weaving cane. **Bomdila** is good for handwoven Monpa carpets.

🏔 Activities and tours

Itanagar-Naharlagun *p190*

Arunachal Travels, Itanagar, agents for Air India.

Duyu Tamo, T(0)9436-044905, duyutours@yahoo.com. Tamo is from the Apatani tribe, and is hence a good choice for a tour from Ziro-Pasighat. He works in conjunction with Help Tourism, and can also arrange/dispatch permits for independent travellers in Arunachal.

Himalayan Holidays, APST Rd, Ganga, Itanagar, T0360-221 8534, www.himalayan-holidays.com.

Nature Expeditions India, Gurgaon, T0124-236 8601, www.himalaya-india.com.

Bomdila *p191*

Dawa Tsering, based between Bomdila and Dirang, T(0)9436-676225, dawaap@yahoo.com. Trustworthy and informative Dawa arranges treks and tours with a cultural slant, visiting villages, camping and homestays, and can swiftly arrange permits for Arunachal.

Himalayan Holidays, ABC Buildings, Main Market, T03782-222017, www.himalayan-holidays.com. Useful for booking *sumo* tickets in advance.

Tawang *p192*

Arunachal Tourism, at the Tourist Lodge, Old Market, T03794-222359. Has a couple of interesting pamphlets.

Himalayan Holidays, Old Market, T03794-223151, T(0)94362-48216, www.himalayan-holidays.com. Open 0500-1930. Organizes tours and jeep hire, good for booking advance *sumo* tickets back to Tezpur.

Tribal Discovery (same office as Himalayan), Old Market, T03794-223151, T(0)9436-045075, davidsongtom@yahoo.com. Reasonable prices on tours to tribal villages, the monastery, nunneries, etc. Vehicle hire (including petrol) for a day at the Lakes is Rs 2500.

⊖ Transport

Itanagar-Naharlagun p190
Air The nearest airport is Lilabari in Assam, 57 km from Naharlagun, 67 km from Itanagar, which has twice weekly flights to **Guwahati**. Transfer by bus. **Air India**, T03752- 223725, www.airindia.com, to/from **Kolkata** twice a week. **Kingfisher**, www.flykingfisher.com, twice weekly to **Kolkata** and **Guwahati**.

There is a **helipad** at Naharlagun, T0360-2245261, with weekly connections to towns in Arunachal, and daily (except Sun) to **Guwahati** or **Dibrugarh**.

Bus APST from Naharlagun Bus Station. **Guwahati** (381 km, 8 hrs, Rs 135); **Shillong** (481 km, Rs 170); **Ziro** (6 hrs); **North Lakhimpur**; **Bomdila** (Mon, Thu, 12 hrs). **Blue Hills** overnight coach to **Guwahati** (11½ hrs). Enquiries: T0360-2244221.
Taxi Naharlagun/Itanagar, Rs 170 plus fuel; Rs 25 (shared taxi).

Train The nearest railhead is North Lakhimpur in Assam, 50 km from Naharlagun and 60 km from Itanagar; **Harmoti station** is 23 km from Naharlagun. **Railway Out Agency**, Naharlagun bus station, T0360-224 4209. Nearest railheads for the bigger towns: **Along**: Silapathar; **Tezu**: Tinsukia; **Namdapha**: Margherita.

Bomdila, Dirang and Tawang p191 and 192
Air There is a **helipad**, T(0)9435-734407, T(0)9436-051250, 40 km from Tawang, with twice-weekly flights to **Guwahati**.

Bus ASTC buses run between Tezpur and Tawang when weather conditions permit;

if there is too much snow they terminate at Dirang. The narrow and twisting road means *sumos* are recommended over the bus.
Tezpur–Tawang (12-14 hrs, depart 0530, Rs 400); **Tezpur–Bomdila** (5½ hrs, Rs 180); **Bomdila–Dirang** (1½ hrs, Rs 80); **Bomdila–Tawang** (6-7 hrs, 0530, Rs 280); **Dirang–Tawang** (6½ hrs, 0830, Rs 280). *Sumos* pick up from hotels in all towns.

Use the contacts below to book seats in advance. In Tezpur: **ASTC Sumo Service**, T(0)9435-080318, T(0)9864-182449. In Bomdila: **Gourab**, T(0)9436-236055, or **Himalyan Holidays**, T03782-222017. In Dirang: **Dream Destination**, T03780-242737, **Dirang Valley Tours**, T03780-242560, or **Himalyan Holidays**, T03780-242464. In Tawang: **Himalyan Holidays**, T03794-223151, or **Pine Ridge**, T03794-222306.

Namdapha National Park p193
Air Dibrugarh (160 km) has the nearest airport (direct flights to/from **Kolkata**).

Bus/taxi Irregular state buses from Dibrugarh go to **Miao**, via **Margherita** (64 km). A taxi from Dibrugarh costs Rs 3000 one-way, you can also hire taxis in Margherita.

Train The nearest local railhead is Margherita. The nearest mainline railhead is Dibrugarh.

ⓘ Directory

Itanagar-Naharlagun p190
Banks/post There are banks and post offices. **Medical services** RK Mission Hospital, T0360-221 8780.

Tawang p192
Banks SBI, near the Old Market has ATM. **Internet** Dofain Cyber Cafe, Rs 50 per hr, new PCs, open winter 0930-1800, till 2000 summer. Monyul Cyber Cafe, Rs 50 per hr, efficient, winter 0830-1730, till 2000 summer.

Nagaland

→ *Population: 2 million. Area: 16,579 sq km.*
Nagaland, the narrow strip of mountain territory, has a long border with Myanmar (Burma) to the east. There are green valleys with meandering streams, high mountains with deep gorges and a rich variety of wildlife and flora. ▶▶ *For listings, see page 199. For entry permits, see box, page 161.*

History

The British reached peace with the Nagas at the end of the 19th century and found them useful allies in the war against the Japanese, who advanced as far as Kohima before finally retreating from the region. After Indian Independence, Nagaland became a separate state on 1 December 1963. A separatist movement for full Independence continues, as the 1975 Shillong Accord was rejected. A series of month-to-month ceasefires in effect during the 1990s came to a drastic end in 2004, when insurgents attacked the railway station in Dimapur. As elsewhere in the Northeast, check with your consulate before travelling to Nagaland, and avoid travelling at night. The Nagaland People's Front won the single Lok Sabha seat in 2009.

Culture

Tribal groups Nagaland is almost entirely inhabited by 16 groups of the Tibeto-Burmese tribes – among them are the Angamis, Aos, Konyaks, Kukis, Lothas, Semas and Wanchus, collectively known as the **Nagas**. There are many tribal languages spoken: Angami, Ao, Chang are a few. The Nagas were once head hunters and were known for their fierceness and the regular raids they made on Assam and Burma. The warring tribes believed that since the enemy's animated soul (*yaha* in Wanchu dialect) was to be found at the nape of the neck, it could only be set free once beheaded. However, since the spiritual soul, *mio*, resided in the head and brought good fortune, enemy heads (and those of dead comrades) were prized as they could add to a community's own store of dead ancestors. The hilltop villages are protected by stone walls. The *morung*, a meeting house, acts as a boys' dormitory, and is used for storing weapons and once displayed the prizes of war (enemy heads). The huge sacred drum stands by each *morung* is a hollowed-out tree trunk resembling a buffalo head. Some believe that the Nagas' ancestors came from the seafaring nation of Sumatra and retain this link in legends, village drums and ceremonial jewellery, which uses shells.

Festivals When it comes to festivals Nagaland leads the party, with all 16 tribes enjoying their own ceremonies, feasts and dancing throughout the year. However, the big event is the **Hornbill Festival** in the first week of December. Originally orchestrated by the government as a cultural *mêlée* to attract tourists from India and abroad, the festival has taken on a life of its own and it's worth planning a trip to Nagaland around it. Tribes rival with each other to put on the most memorable display, clad in fabulous traditional dress, and as well as the prevalent tribal music recent years have also seen a rock festival take place. Handicrafts and food stalls, distinctive to each tribe, give both locals and tourists a chance to sample different styles of home-cooking and local brews.

Religion Today 90% of the Nagas are Christians. Originally, although they revered natural spirits, the Nagas believed in a single overseeing superforce, and hence incorporated the Christian Gospel into their cosmology quite readily. The Bible was translated into many of the Naga dialects (nearly every village has a church), yet many old customs have been retained. There are also remains of the Hindu Kingdom of the Kacharis at Dimapur near the present capital Kohima, which was destroyed by the Assamese Ahoms in the 16th century.

Crafts The ancient craft of weaving on portable looms is still practised by the women. The strips of colourful cloth are stitched together to produce shawls in different patterns which distinguish each tribe. Ao warriors wear the red and black striped shawl with a central white band embroidered with symbols.

Kohima → Colour map 2, B5. Phone code: 0370. Population: 78,600. Altitude: 1500 m.

The British-built town of Kohima lies in the valley between higher hills, alongside the immaculately kept war cemetery. Kohima attracted world attention during the Second World War because it was here that the Japanese advance was halted by the British and Indian forces. The original Angami Kohima village is set on a hill above overlooking the Main Bazar. There may be a strong military presence in town.

The **Second World War Cemetery** is in a beautiful setting, with well-maintained lawns where rose bushes bloom. Two tall crosses stand out at the lowest and highest points. The stone markers each have a polished bronze plaque with epitaphs commemorating the men who fell here, to halt "the invasion of India by the forces of Japan in April 1944" by the British 14th Army under General William Slim. The cherry tree, which was used by Japanese soldiers as a snipers' post, was destroyed; what grew from the old stump marks the limit of the enemy advance. At the base of the Second Division lower cross, near the main entrance, are the lines: "When you go home/Tell them of us and say/For your tomorrow/We gave our today."

Three kilometres away by road, the striking red-roofed **Cathedral of Reconciliation** (1995) overlooks the cemetery from a hill. Part funded by the Japanese government, representatives from both sides of the conflict attended the inauguration.

The **Main Bazar** attracts colourful tribal women who come to buy and sell their produce. The vast **Kohima Village** (Bara Basti) has a traditional Naga ceremonial gateway carved with motifs of guns, warriors and symbols of prosperity, though the 20th century has had its impact. The traditional Naga house here has crossed horns on the gables, carved heads to signify the status of the family, huge baskets to hold the grain in front of the house and a trough where rice beer is made for the community.

Nagaland State Museum ⓘ *Bayavu Hill Colony, 1.5 km from centre, Mon-Sat 0930-1430, closed 2nd Sat of the month,* has a collection of anthropological exhibits of the different Naga tribes. The basement has birds and animals of the Northeastern Hill states.

Around Kohima

Khonoma is an authentic tribal village, 20 km southwest, with a proud past, and is surrounded by extensive terraces for rice cultivation. Another 20 km along the same road takes you to **Dzulekie**, at 2134 m, with attractive waterfalls and trout streams in a deep rocky gorge. There is a Tourist Rest House and Cottages. Trek to **Jopfu Peak**, at 3043 m, which is 15 km south, between November and March for clear mountain views. **Dzukou Valley**, at 2438 m, 15 km further south, is best from June to September for its colourful rhododendrons, lilies and meadow flowers. A new campsite should be ready on the Jakhama route.

Dimapur → Colour map 2, B5.

Dimapur, on the edge of the plains northwest of Kohima, is the railhead and has Nagaland's only airport. Busy and crowded, it is the state's main commercial and trading centre.

This was the old capital of the Kacharis (13th-16th century) and the **Kachari relics**, including a huge brick-built arch, are 1 km from the NST Bus Station. Nearby are 30 huge mushroom-shaped carved megaliths believed to represent the fertility cult. Visit **Chumukedima** old village on a hill above town, or trek to the **Triple Falls** at Seithekima.

Nagaland listings

For Sleeping and Eating price codes and other relevant information, see Essentials pages 34-38.

Sleeping

Kohima *p198*
D Japfu Ashok (ITDC), PR Hill, T0370-224 0211, hoteljapfu@yahoo.co.in. 27 large heated rooms in motel arrangement, satellite TV, restaurants.
F Pine, Phool Bazar, T0370-224 3129. 7 rooms.
G Bonanza Lodge, opposite main bus stand. Friendly and helpful, but limited English. Some rooms come with a private bath.

Dimapur *p198*
D-E Tragopan, Circular Rd near Overbridge, T03862-230351. Some of the 22 rooms have a/c, some **C** suites, all have TV and hot water (in the mornings), restaurant, library, internet.
G Tourist Lodge, near Nagaland bus station, T03862-226335. Doubles, dorm, tourist office.

Eating

Kohima *p198*
Local dishes are simple but may include water snails, eels, silkworm curry, hornet larvae or fermented fish.
† Dimori Cove, 13 km on NH39 to Manipur. The eatery has a small swimming pool, good views.
† Naga, Secretariat. Japanese. Pleasant, lively.

Festivals and events

Kohima *p198*
The different tribes celebrate their special festivals when priests perform ceremonies followed by dancing, singing and drinking.
Feb Sekrenyi is celebrated by Angamis for 10 days when all work in the fields ceases.
Apr Konyak Aoling, a 6-day 'New Year' festival marking the beginning of spring.
May Ao Moatsu, 6-day festival marking the beginning of the growing season.

Dec Hornbill Festival, when all tribes gather in Kisama to display traditional sports and dance.

Shopping

Kohima *p198*
Warm, colourful Naga shawls are excellent. Also get beads, shoulder bags, decorative spears, table mats, wood carvings and bamboo baskets.

Activities and tours

Kohima *p198*
Nagaland Tourism, Raj Bhavan Rd, T0370-2254 3124. 5-day cultural, trekking and tribal tours.

Transport

Kohima *p198*
Air/train The nearest airport and railhead is at Dimapur; buses (Rs 50, 3 hrs) from Kohima.
Bus Blue Hills luxury coaches go to capitals in the Northeast; Green Hills, for bookings.
Taxi Nagaland State Transport (NST), T0370-222 2265. From **Dimapur**, Rs 500, shared Rs 100.

Dimapur *p198*
Air Airport is 5 km from town. Air India, T03862-229366; airport, T03862-242441, www.airindia.com. To **Kolkata** daily.
Bus From Golaghat Rd to **Guwahati** 292 km (10-11 hrs), **Imphal** 142 km (5-6 hrs); from Nagaland Bus Stand to **Kohima** hourly, 3 hrs.
Train Enquiries: T131. To **Delhi**: *Brahmaputra Mail 4055*, daily 0540, 48 hrs; *Rajdhani Exp 2435*, Tue, Sat 0125, 19 hrs. **Dibrugarh**: *Kamrup Exp 5959*, 2145, 8½ hrs. *Brahmaputra Mail 4056*, 2005, 8½ hrs; *Rajdhani Exp 2424*, except Mon and Fri, 2245, 6 hrs. **Guwahati**: *Rajdhani 2435*, Tue and Sat, 0125, 5½ hrs; *Jan Shatabdi Exp 2068*, except Sun 1615, 4½ hrs; *Brahmaputra Mail 4055*, 0540, 6 hrs; plus some slower trains.

Manipur

→ *Population: 2.4 million. Area: 22,327 sq km.*

The former princely state of Manipur, the 'land of jewels', bordering Myanmar, has a low-lying basin in its centre surrounded by hills that rise to over 2000 m. The reedy Lake Loktak, the largest freshwater lake in the Northeast, and the flat-bottomed basin and river valleys that drain into it, add to the beauty of the land. It is the land of graceful Rasa dances, of the famous Women's market in Imphal, of rare orchids and the endangered thamin, the brow-antlered deer. Note that at the time of research the FCO advised against all travel to Manipur. ▸▸ *For listings, see pages 202-203.*

History

Manipur has always been quite independent of its neighbouring tribal areas. It was often invaded from Burma but also enjoyed long periods of relatively stable government. At the end of the Indo-Burmese War in 1826 it was brought into India by the Treaty of Yandabo, British sovereignty being recognized in 1891. In 1939 a remarkable women's social revolt ('Nupilan' from '*nupi*', meaning women, and '*lan*', war) led to government action against monopolistic traders. The contemporary party Nisha Bandh consists of an all-women patrol that seeks to keep the streets safe at night. The role of women traders can be seen most colourfully in the women's market in Imphal. During the Second World War, Imphal was occupied by the Japanese. After Indian Independence Manipur became a Union Territory and achieved statehood in 1972. Congress won both Lok Sabha seats in 2009.

People

The majority of the population are Vaishnavite Hindus. They belong to the *Meithe* tribe and are related to the *Shans* of Burma, who live in the valleys. The 20 or so hill tribes who constitute about a third of the population are Christian. Like the Nagas, the Manipuris have a reputation for being great warriors, still practising their skills of wrestling, sword fighting and martial arts. Most wars were fought across the border in Burma. They are also keen on sport, and polo, which is said to have originated in Manipur, is the principal sport.

Dance, drama and music

The ancient musical forms of the valley dwellers are closely connected to the worship of Vishnu, expressed in Manipuri dancing. The *Rasa* dances performed at every ceremony are characterized by graceful and restrained movements and delicate hand gestures. The ornate costumes worn by the veiled women are glittering and colourful; the stiff, heavy skirts barely move. The *Sankirtana* dance often precedes the *Rasa*. It is usually performed by men and is vigorous, rhythmic and athletic, and they play on the *pung* (drums) and cymbals while they dance. The tribal ritual dances, some of which are performed by priests and priestesses before deities, may end in a trance. Others can last several days, observing a strict form and accompanied by the drone of a bowed instrument, *pana*. *Thang-ta* is a skilful martial art performed to beating drums, and is practised by both sexes dressed in black.

Political developments

Troubled by a variety of internal conflicts since the late 1980s and with separatist movements voicing open dissent with rule from New Delhi, Manipur's State Assembly has had an unsettled recent history. One recent bone of contention is the Tipaimukh Dam, a

500 mw hydro- and flood-protection project that has stirred up strong opposition from some quarters in Manipur and across the border in Bangladesh. The foundation stone for the project was laid in December 2006.

Democracy is very popular, with over 90% of the electorate turning out to vote in recent elections, but it has not produced stability. In the February 2007 elections the Indian National Congress under Chief Minister Okram Ibobi Singh won half the 60 seats, but it is too early to judge whether the long-running disturbances in the state will be resolved. Be sure to find out about the current situation before travelling to Manipur.

Imphal → *For listings, see pages 202-203. Colour map 2, B5.*

The capital Imphal (from *yumpham*, meaning homestead) lies in the heart of an oval-shaped valley cut through by narrow rivers and surrounded by forested hills. The city has the large open space of the Polo Ground but is otherwise not particularly attractive. Due to its location it has become a principal export route for Myanmar's illegal drugs.

Ins and outs → *Phone code: 0385. Population: 217,300.*

Getting there and around The airport is 8 km south of the city with taxis and autos available for transfers. Bus travel is tiring due to the long distances involved. The dusty centre and the Ima Market are easy to cover on foot. Auto- and cycle-rickshaws can take you to places beyond the centre. ▶▶ *See Transport, page 203.*

Tourist information India Tourism ⓘ *Old Lambulane, Jail Rd, T0385-222 1131, closed Sat-Sun, airport desk opens for flights.* **Manipur Tourism** ⓘ *Hotel Imphal, T0385-222 0802, manipur@x400.nicgw.nic.in, Mon-Sat 0900-1630, closed 2nd Sat of the month.* **Meghalaya Tourism** ⓘ *Hotel Imphal, T0385-222 0459.*

Sights

The **Shri Govindaji Temple** to Krishna with two golden domes adjoins the royal palace. This **Vaishnavite centre** with shrines to Vishnu, Balaram, Krishna and Jagannath has regular performances of ceremonial dancing; Manipuri dancing originated here in Imphal. Overlooking the university, the historic **Palace of Langthaband**, with its ceremonial houses and temples, stands on the hills among formally planted pine and jack-fruit trees, 8 km along the Indo-Burma road.

Khwairamband Bazar (Ima Market) ⓘ *0700-1900*, in the town centre, is the largest women's bazar anywhere in the country, some say in Asia. It is an excellent place for handicrafts, handloom goods, jewellery and cosmetics as well as fish, vegetables, pickles, orange honey and other foodstuffs. As many as 3000 women gather here every day. It represents a form of family work-sharing: while younger mothers stay at home to look after children, the older women and grandmothers come to the market. The women do not bargain and will be offended if you try to pick through fruit or vegetables, as they take great pride in serving only the best quality at a fair price. Their own union helps to maintain the bazar and is a potent political force.

The **war cemeteries** are managed by the Commonwealth War Graves Commission, one on the Imphal–Dimapur NH39 and the other on the Imphal–Ukhrul Road. They are beautifully maintained and serenely peaceful sites.

The **Konghampat Orchidarium** ⓘ *12 km along the NH39, best time to visit Apr-May*, set up by the Forest Department, has over 120 species of orchids including some rare ones.

The **Manipur State Museum** ⓘ *near the Polo Ground, T0385-222 0709, Tue-Sun 1000-1630*, has a collection of art (including portraits), archaeology, natural history, geology, old arms, costumes and textiles. **Matua Museum** is a private collection of art, textiles and manuscripts to preserve the identity of Manipuri culture.

Around Imphal

Moirang, 45 km from Imphal, on Loktak Lake, is noted for its early Manipuri folk culture and the traditional folk dance form. The temple to the forest god, known as Thankgjing, has robes of the 12th-century Moirang kings and holds a ritual dance festival each summer. During the Second World War Moirang was the headquarters of the Indian National Army (INA) for a short time, and their flag was raised in the palace grounds as a symbol of national independence for the first time on 12 April 1944. There is an INA memorial and a war museum. You can stay on **Sendra Island** in Loktak Lake, see Sleeping, below.

Keibul Lamjao National Park → *For listings, see page 202-203. Colour map 2, B5.*

The park, covering 25 sq km, is the only floating sanctuary of its kind. It has a small population of thamin (Sangai), the endangered brow-antlered deer. The sanctuary was set up in 1977 on Loktak Lake when the swamps, the natural habitat of the thamin, were reclaimed for cultivation resulting in the near extinction of this 'dancing deer'. The thamin feed on mats of floating humus covered with grass and *phumdi* reeds until the rainy season when they move to the hills. You can travel through the creeks on small boats. There is also a viewing tower on Babet Ching hillock. Other wildlife include hog deer, wild boar, panther, fishing cat and water birds.

Travel restrictions for foreigners apply, and permits are granted only for Imphal and a few neighbouring attractions. The nearest airport and railway are at Dimapur, 32 km from Imphal. The best time to visit is between December and May. Temperatures range from 41°C to 0°C and annual rainfall is 1280 mm.

⚫ Manipur listings

For Sleeping and Eating price codes and other relevant information, see Essentials pages 34-38.

⚫ Sleeping

Imphal *p201*
D Anand Continental, Khoyathong Rd, T0385-222 3422. Good rooms with bath, TV.
D Imphal, Dimapur Rd, T0385-222 0459, manipur@x400.nicgw.nic.in. Run by the tourist department, 60 large rooms in an imposing white edifice, some a/c, modern facilities, pleasant gardens, restaurant.
E-F Excellency, Airport Rd, T0385-222 5401. Varied rooms, some a/c, restaurant.
G Sendra Tourist Home, on Sendra Island, contact the Department of Tourism, in Imphal,

T0385-222 0802. A very peaceful spot with lovely views of the lake where fishermen, who live on islands of floating weeds, use nets to farm fish and *singhara* (water chestnut). Cheap beds, small restaurant.
G Youth Hostel, Khuman Lampak, T0385-222 3423. Dorm (Rs 30).

Keibul Lamjao National Park *p202*
Forest Lodges at Phubala and Sendra.

⚫ Eating

Imphal *p201*
Manipur is a 'dry' state. In hotel restaurants, try *iromba*, the Manipuri savoury dish of fish,

vegetables and bamboo shoots and the sweet *Kabok* made with molasses and rice. Govindaji Temple prepares local dishes with advance notice. ⍾ **Sangam** and **Welcome** are good cheap options.

⊙ Entertainment

Imphal *p201*
Cultural shows with Manipuri dancing can be seen at **Rupmahal**, BT Rd, and at **Kala Academy**.

⊛ Festivals and events

Imphal *p201*
Feb-Mar Yaosang on full moon night, boys and girls dance the Thabal Chongba and sing in a circle in the moonlight. A festival in **May-Jun** is held in honour of forest gods. **Sep** Heikru Hitongba is mainly non religious, when there are boat races along a 16-m wide moat in narrow boats with large numbers of rowers.

⛰ Activities and tours

Imphal *p201*
Manipur Tourism, www.manipur.nic.in/tourism.htm. Tours to Sri Govindaji Temple, Bishnupur, INA Memorial, Moirang, KL National Park and the Loktak Lake, depart from **Hotel Imphal**, Sun 0800.
Seven Sisters, North AOC, T0385-222 8778. For touring the region.

⊖ Transport

Imphal *p201*
Air
Taxi to town, Rs 150. **Air India**, MG Av, T0385-222 0999, airport T0385- 222 0888, www.airindia.com: **Kolkata**, daily (some via **Aizwal**); **Delhi**, **Guwahati**, **Jorhat**, **Silchar**, 2-3 times weekly. **Jet Airways**, Hotel Nirmala, MG Av, T0385-244 1546, airport T2455054, www.jetairways.com, to **Guwahati**, Tue, Wed; **Kolkata** (via Guwahati), Tue, Wed (via Jorhat), Thu, Sun. **Indigo**, www.goindigo.in, flies daily to **Delhi** and **Kolkata**.

Bus
Buses connect Dimapur (215 km) the nearest railhead, with **Imphal** (8 hrs), Rs 60; share taxi Rs 250. Daily private buses (some a/c) for **Guwahati** (579 km), 24 hrs, via Silchar (198 km) to **Shillong**, through: Blue Hills, MG Av, T0385-222 6443. **Manipur Golden Travels**, MG Av, T0385-222 1332. **Kangleipak**, T0385-222 2131.

Taxi
Tourist taxis from the Tourist Information Centre.

⊙ Directory

Imphal *p201*
Banks Banks in Bazar, Thangal Bazar and MG Av. **Medical services** Hospitals at Porompat and Lamphalpat. **Post** There is a GPO.

Mizoram

→ *Population: 891,100. Area 21,000 sq km.*
The southernmost of the Northeastern Hill States, Mizoram lies between Myanmar (Burma) and Bangladesh. Until 1972 it was known as the Lushai Hills, a district of Assam. The six or so parallel north–south ranges of hills, which rise to an altitude of over 2000 m, are covered in dense forests of bamboo and wild banana. At the bottom of the deep gorges the rivers run in narrow ribbons.
➡ *For listings, see page 205. For entry permits, see page 161; the state government also issues permits.*

Culture

Tribal groups 'Mizo' is derived from *mi* (man) and *zo* (highland), a collective name given by their neighbours to a number of tribes that settled in the area. The different groups of tribal people are thought to have originally come from northwest China in the seventh century, gradually travelled southwards and reached this area less than 300 years ago. The Mizos were animists, believing in good and evil spirits of the woodland. Mizo villages perch on top of the ridges with the chief's house and the *zawlbuk* (bachelors' dormitory) in the centre. Built on steep slopes, houses often have front doors at street level while the backs stand precariously on stilts. Every home proudly displays orchids and pots of geranium, begonia and balsam. More than 1000 varieties of medicinal plants grow wild.

Religion The raiding of British tea plantations up until the end of the 19th century led to the introduction of Inner Line Permits, which restricted movement of people but gave free access to missionaries, who carried out their religious duties and introduced literacy (which is exceptionally high in this state, the language having adopted the Roman script). Most Mizos are Christian converts and have a strong tradition of Western choral singing. The mainly nomadic Chakmas along the western border practise a religion which combines Hinduism, Buddhism and animism. Some even claim descent from one of the lost tribes of Israel. A few Kukis who were once headhunters, and Chins, have converted to Judaism.

Economy

Rice and maize, supplemented by shifting cultivation, supports 75% of the population. There are no mineral resources exploited yet and no large-scale industries though the government has sponsored some light industrial development in Aizawl. Handicrafts and handwoven textiles predominate.

Aizawl → *Colour map 2, B5/C5. Phone code: 0389. Population: 229,700. Altitude: 1132 m.*

The road from Silchar comes upon the isolated capital Aizawl (pronounced Eye-jull), built along a central ridge and several surrounding spurs. White-painted churches stand out above the residential buildings that cling precariously to the hillsides.

Bara Bazar, the main shopping centre, is on the other side of the central ridge. The steep Zion Street is lined with stalls selling garments and Mizo CDs. In the main market people gather in their traditional costumes to sell produce from farms and homesteads including river crab in little wicker baskets.

At the **Weaving Centre** you can watch women at their looms weaving traditional shawls which are for sale. **Luangmual Handicrafts Centre**, 7 km away, has a *khumbeu* ceremonial bamboo hat made using waterproof wild *hnahthial* leaves.

Mizoram State Museum ① *McDonald's Hill, Rs 5, Mon-Fri 1100-1600*, is small but has an interesting collection of historical relics, ancient costumes and traditional implements.

Champhai

Champhai, on the Indo-Myanmar border and known as the fruit bowl of the Northeast, is worth a visit for its stunning location and sense of history (if your permit allows a visit here).

◉ Mizoram listings

For Sleeping and Eating price codes and other relevant information, see Essentials pages 34-38.

😴 Sleeping

Aizawl *p204*
E Ahimsa, Zarkawt, T0389-234 1133.
Comfortable rooms, restaurant.
E Ritz, Bara Bazar, Chaltlang, T0389-232 3358.
Comfortable rooms, all with bath and cable TV, de luxe or standard options, good restaurant.
F Tourist Lodge, Chaltlang, T0389-234 1083. 14 large but tired rooms, good restaurant, good views and lovely staff.

🍴 Eating

Aizawl *p204*
There's cheap local Mizo food at Bara Bazar.
Ⴅ Labyrinth, Chandmari. Cheap Chinese and Indian food.

✺ Festivals and events

Aizawl *p204*
Early Mar Chapchar Kut, a traditional spring festival marking the end of **Jhumming** is celebrated with singing dancing and feasting. **Cheraw** is performed by nimble-footed girls who dance in and out of bamboo poles, clapped together by teams of young men. Similar dances are performed in Myanmar, Thailand and the Philippines.

⛰ Activities and tours

Aizawl *p204*
Directorate of Tourism, Treasury Sq, T0389-2333475, http://mizotourism.nic.in/home.htm.

Omega Travels, Zodin Sq, T0389-232 3548, omegatravels89@yahoo.co.in. Mon-Sat 1000-1700. Helpful agents, can arrange permits costing Rs 500 for 1-4 people. Email a scan of passport and visa; permits take 10 days.

🚍 Transport

Aizawl *p204*
Air New Langpui Airport (37 km north); for tickets and bus transfer contact **Quality Travels**, Chandmari, T0389-234 1265. **Air India**, T0389-234 1265, airport T0389-234 4733, www.airindia.com, and **Kingfisher**, www.flykingfisher.com, fly to **Kolkata** and **Guwahati**, daily with some flights via Imphal. Travellers from the rest of the Northeast usually arrive by bus via Silchar to the north.
Bus The major operator in the state is Mizoram State Transport. It runs buses to **Silchar**, 180 km (9 hrs), Rs 150, which is the nearest railhead; the 4WD *sumos*, however, are quicker and not too pricey. Private buses to **Guwahati** via Silchar and Shillong, Rs 280.
Taxi Rs 200 for 2 hrs' sightseeing in town.

ⓘ Directory

Aizawl *p204*
Bank State Bank of India. **Medical services** Civil Hospital, T0389-232 2318, Presbyterian Hospital, Durtland (7 km), T0389-236 1185. **Post** GPO, Treasury Sq.

Tripura

→ *Population: 3.19 million. Area: 10,492 sq km.*

Still extensively forested, the tiny former Hindu Princely State of Tripura managed to retain a large degree of independence through much of the last millennium until it joined India in 1949. Partition and the 1971 creation of Bangladesh resulted in the influx of huge numbers of Bengali refugees, and although the tribal population still retain centuries-old practices they are now very much in the minority. For many years, travel here was deemed unsafe as tribal insurgents violently pursued their goals, but now successful government incentives and stricter border controls mean that this little-visited enclave is open for easy exploration. Impressive sights are few, but not far between, and the pretty villages and rolling scenery make for a relaxing if low-key few days. The tourist trail in Tripura is as yet virtually untrodden, and this is the chief pleasure in a visit to this unique and mellow state. ▸▸ *For listings, see pages 209-212.*

The land

Covering just under 10,500 sq km, Tripura is almost surrounded on the north, west and south by Bangladesh. The north falls into four valleys, separated by hills rising to just under 1000 m. The more open land of the south is forested with hardwoods, including sal and teak, and 77% of the state is covered by trees. Parts of Tripura receive more than 4000 mm of annual rainfall.

History

Tripura is believed to have existed in the times of the epic *Mahabharata*. Historically, it was ruled by the Manikyas of Indo-Mongolian origin from the 14th century. Since Tripura was constantly feuding with her neighbours, particularly the Nawabs of Bengal, the British offered help to the maharaja and established a protectorate, separating the princely state from tribal lands outside the control of the Hindu rajas. The Manikyas ruled continuously right up to 15 October 1949 when Tripura acceded to India. It became a full state in 1972. In the 1930s, Maharaja Bir Bikram made his kingdom more accessible by opening an airport. Rabindranath Tagore based his play *Visarjan* and novel *Rajasri* on the legends of the Manikyas. The CPI(M) won both Lok Sabha seats in 2009.

Culture

The tribes of Tripura now make up just 31% of the population, and, although some distinctive customs have been retained, there has been much interchange between the predominant Bengali culture and indigenous traditions. A typical tribal welcome involves building a bamboo arch, garlanding the honoured guest while wafting incense, and this is now something seen in all Tripuri special occasions (such as marriages) regardless of peoples' ethnic roots. You may notice brightly coloured parasols in the village pond which are put there in honour of dead ancestors. An invitation into someone's home could be a chance to try *gudok*, a preparation of green and wild vegetables boiled without oil and very healthy.

There is a high degree of literacy in the state, estimated at 84%, almost equal between the genders. And despite its small size it has no less than 100 daily newspapers (six in English) and numerous weekly and monthly publications.

Modern Tripura

Economy Rice is the main crop while rubber has gained importance (the state is now second only to Kerala in production). Tea, coffee beans, bamboo, pineapples and oranges are important cash crops. Sugar cane, mustard, potatoes and pulses are also grown. In recent years the Indian government has encouraged small industries and weaving, carpentry, pottery and basket making are common. Tripura suffers from the continuing failure of Bangladesh and India to agree a trade and travel treaty, which would allow goods to be taken in transit across Bangladesh. This adds hugely to the time and cost of transport to Kolkata, still a major market for Tripura goods, and lorries can take two weeks to make a journey that could take two days by the direct route. This, coupled with the strength of the workers' and merchants' unions, means that the cost of living is high even in comparison to Delhi and Mumbai.

Government The state's democratic process operates under severe constraints. Politically motivated killings and kidnappings are becoming a thing of the past, as the government tries to control rebel factions. Of Tripura's 856-km border, 640 km has been fenced and this has had a great impact on movement of insurgents. The 60 member state assembly is controlled by the Left Front, and autonomous district councils operate in many areas.

Agartala → *For listings, see pages 209-212. Colour map 2, C4.*

A small and pleasant city, Agartala is noticeably green with many little backstreets of simple bungalows nurturing spindly betel-nut trees and banana plants in their gardens. The city centre is generally free from heavy traffic and comes to life with hundreds of cycle rickshaws during rush hours. The city's red brick official buildings contrast with the British preference for white paint, still obvious on some important structures, notably the maharaja's palace.

Ins and outs → *Phone code: 0381. Population: 189,300. Altitude: 1280 m.*

Getting there The most convenient way to get to Agartala is by air, with connections to Kolkata and Guwahati taking under an hour. Foreigners must register their arrival at the airport. Transfer to the centre of town by taxi (Rs 225) or auto (Rs 95). Buses from Guwahati take about 20 hours or the train involves a change at Lumding in Assam, then chair-car onward to Agartala. The border with Bangladesh, just 2 km from Agartala, is convenient for anyone with a visa to get to Dhaka, which is three hours by road and three hours by train.

Getting around The centre can be covered on foot, otherwise cycle-rickshaws are Rs 5 for short distances. There may be a strong military presence in town, although they show little interest in foreign tourists. ▶▶ *See Transport, page 211.*

Tourist information Tourist office ① *Ujjayant Palace, East Wing, T0381-222 5930, www.tripura.nic.in.* **Bangladesh Visa Office** ① *2 km north of the centre, Mon-Fri 1000-1200,* for applications. Six-month visas cost about US$46 for UK nationals ; US$23 for nationals of USA and Australia.

Climate Summer maximum 35°C, minimum 24°C. Winter maximum 27°C, minimum 13°C. Annual rainfall: 2240 mm, June-August. Best time to visit: September-March.

Sights

The airport road from the north of town leads to the **Ujjayanta Palace** ① *grounds open daily, 1700-1830, Rs 3, cameras free, no video allowed.* Built by Maharaja Radha Kishore Manikya in 1901, it stands amid large well-kept Mughal gardens with pools and floodlit musical fountains. Close up, the white paintwork is crumbling and water-stained but the grand marble staircase, imposing central dome and arched hallways still impress. The vast palace has magnificent tiled floors, a carved wooden ceiling in the Chinese room and beautifully crafted front doors. Now the State Legislature, it is normally closed to visitors, but you may ask to look around when the Assembly is not in session. The State Museum is destined to be re-homed here when the Assembly moves to a new building, but this is still some way off. Good views of the palace lit up at night can be had from the **Sri Laxminarayan temple** to the right of the main (south) entrance. The late 19th-century **Jagannath temple** across an artificial lake to the west of the palace, rises to a striking orange four-storeyed *sikhara*.

Tripura Government Museum ⓘ *HG Basak Rd, Mon-Sat 1000-1300 and 1400-1700, closed on public holidays, Rs 2, cameras free*, has a small but well-displayed collection of delicate stone images from the temples of Udaipur, eighth- to 10th-century Buddhist sculptures from Pilak (rather weathered), and ancient figurines (some dating from 2500 BC) which show the elaborate hairstyles of the Sunga Period. On the upper level, there are examples of Bengali *kantha* embroidery, tribal weaving and jewellery, and interesting portraits of the maharajahs – look for the last maharajah's coronation procession from the Ujjayanta Palace, in 1928.

The **Temple of Chaturdasa Devata**, 8 km east, near Old Agartala, is dedicated to 14 gods and goddesses, represented by their heads only. It combines the Bengali Bankura style with a Buddhist *stupa*-type structure. In July, **Kharchi Puja**, which has evolved from a tribal festival, attracts worshippers from all over Tripura.

North of Agartala → *For listings, see pages 209-212.*

Travelling outside Agartala is easy, with various one- to six-day tours organized by the tourism department and regular bus or jeep connections between towns. One section of the Agartala–Assam Highway is still heavily guarded by military forces and vehicles travel in convoy. Seek advice before travelling north through the state.

Unakoti and Kailashahar → *Colour map 2, B4.*

Ten kilometres from the friendly town of Kailashahar, **Unakoti** is the site of the largest bas-relief sculpture in India. Buses from Kailashahar drop off on the main road 1 km from the site but finding transport back can be difficult; auto-rickshaws will do a round trip. The seventh-century rock carvings are cut vertically into the hillside, the largest being an impressive 10-m-high depiction of Siva. The style is unusual, reminiscent of statues in South America more than representations of the Hindu pantheon. It is a quiet and peaceful place, unless you come during the **mela** (March/April). **Kailashahar** has a good market.

Jampui Hills

Some 220 km from Agartala, the Jampui Hills are a serene and forested area good for walking and tasting tribal culture. Between October and December the orange groves are heavy with fruit, while the famed orchids bloom between March and May. Very much off the foreign tourist trail, it's a worthy excursion if travelling into Tripura from the north.

South of Agartala → *For listings, see pages 209-212.*

Sepahijala Wildlife Sanctuary
ⓘ *24 km from Agartala, 0800-1600.*
The sanctuary has a botanical garden, small zoo and a boating lake and is a unique home to the spectacled monkey. The zoo is beautifully kept and new enclosures provide a more natural habitat. There are tigers, lions, cheetahs, bears and a rhino; the spectacle monkeys

live in the trees above while the lake attracts migrating birds. Elephant rides are offered too. It may be possible to visit a rubber plantation and watch the processing on a trip. Buses and jeeps from Agartala take about 30 minutes, and a couple of tourist lodges have cottages bookable through the Wildlife Warden, T0381-236 1225/7.

Udaipur *Colour map 2, C4.*

The **Tripura Sundari Temple**, 57 km south from Agartala, near the ancient capital Udaipur, was built on Dhanisagar Hill in the mid-16th century. The Matabari is believed to be one of the 51 holy *pithasthans* mentioned in the *Tantras*, where the Mother Goddess is served by red-robed priests. The pond behind has huge turtles which are delighted to be fed. A large fair is held during **Diwali** in October/November. Other temples of interest, in various states of atmospheric decrepitude, are the Jagannath Mandir and the Bhubaneswari Mandir. There is a good lodge. Buses and jeeps from Agartala take about one hour.

Neermahal

Some 53 km southeast of Agartala, this water-palace in the middle of Rudrasagar Lake was built in 1930 by the late maharaja. The striking white and red fairytale castle with towers, kiosks, pavilions and bridges is fun to explore although the interiors are empty. Boats take passengers from the litter-strewn shore (Rs 15 for 10 people or Rs 150 to hire the whole boat) throughout the day. It is particularly beautiful illuminated at night, and on Saturdays and Sundays there is a **son et lumière show** ⓘ *1745-1845, Rs 35 includes boat ride and entrance, commentary in Bengali,* the highlight of which is witnessing the palace become floodlit, perfectly reflected in the still waters, as you journey across. The lake itself attracts migratory birds. Sunset across the water is marred somewhat by the chimney of a brick factory.

Pilak

The eighth- to ninth-century archaeological remains of Buddhist and Hindu statutory at Pilak are distinctly underwhelming. That said, the nearby village of **Jolaibari** has a pleasant tourist lodge and active nightmarket, and the walk through the paddies and villages to the sites is rewarding in itself. About 1.5 km beyond the village (signed off the main road) is the **Shyamsundar** *stupa*; the cross-shaped brick base is all that remains, lined with terracotta tiles of frolicking people and animals. Another 2 km brings you to weathered stone images of Avolokiteshwar and Narasimhha, where further excavations are still unearthing intricate metal and stone artefacts.

◉ Tripura listings

For Sleeping and Eating price codes and other relevant information, see Essentials pages 34-38.

◉ Sleeping

Agartala *p207*

Most **D-E** have some a/c rooms, book in advance if you have somewhere particular in mind as rooms fill up quickly. Checkout times are almost always 1200.

D Ginger, Airport Rd, T0381-230 3333. Super new rooms are unquestionably the best in town and the standard far superior to others in this price range. The downside is being on the edge of town in a bit of a wilderness, though autos are cheap to the centre.
D-E City Centre, Madhyapara Rd, off HGB Road, T0381-238 5270/1, jaininn_pvtltd@ hotmail.com. Well-equipped large a/c rooms are worth patient haggling over, as huge

reductions are possible. Marble floors are cooling, everything works and management are attentive without being overly so. The restaurant, however, disappoints.
D-E Rajdhani, BK Rd (northeast of Ujjayanta Palace), T0381-222 3387. 27 clean rooms with bath plus **C** suites, car hire, but no longer the "first lift in Tripura!" Alcohol allowed only in the rooms. Staff speak good English.
D-E Welcome Palace, HGB Rd, T0381-231 4940, bantob@sancharnet.in. A very comfortable hotel with delightful staff and a range of a/c rooms, the cheapest (doubles Rs 700/900) get booked up fast so call ahead. Front desk can help with car hire and ticketing. The **Kurry Klub** restaurant is excellent.
D-F Overseas Mansion, HGB Rd, T0381-238 2783, hotel_overseas@yahoo.co.in. Check a few rooms, as paintwork and condition is variable. It's not luxury but at Rs 350 for a non-a/c double (same room for a/c, but with the unit switched on) this is better value than most and usually has vacancies.
D-F Radha International, 54 Central Rd, T/F0381-238 4530. A good choice, non-a/c singles in particular are a real bargain although they are tiny. It's relatively new and hasn't had time to degenerate too much. All rooms have TV and private bath.
D-F Somraj Regency, HGB Rd, 2nd floor Swasti Bazaar, T0381-238 2069. Rooms (basic double Rs 450) are nothing special, but it's close at hand if the **Welcome Palace** is full.
G Hotel Sagarita, Sakuntala Rd, T0381-238 0838. Only 8 rooms, 2 doubles, 6 singles, this very Indian option is clean and cheerfully painted. Very little English spoken, but good collection of useful contact numbers for car hire and services. All rooms have bath (hot bucket), fans and nets.
G Minakshi, Hawkers Corner, Khushbagan (near Museum), T0381-238 5810. Budget-basic old rooms have TV, mosquito nets and screens, attached bath, powerful fans and are cleaned daily. Staff are pleasantly eccentric. Simple fish and veg Indian meals prepared in the tiny 'restaurant'.

Kailashahar *p208*
F-G Unakoti Tourist Lodge, T03824-223635. Literally a stone's throw from the Bangladeshi border (fence-views from your window), this friendly and decent place has double rooms only (non-a/c Rs 220, a/c Rs 330).

Jampui Hills *p208*
G Eden Tourist Lodge, Vanghmun, T03824-238252. A simple place that's good value and clean, as is typical of Tripura's government accommodation.

Sepahijala Wildlife Sanctuary *p208*
G Forest Bungalow, contact Chief Conservator of Forests, Agartala, T0381-222 3779. In well-kept gardens above the lake, meals provided.

Udaipur *p209*
All of Udaipur's accommodation is found in the centre of town, 1 km from the bus/jeep stand.
E-G Gouri Hotel, Central Rd, T03821-222419. Clean and simple rooms plus a couple of pricier a/c doubles.
F-G Gomati Yatriniwas, T03821-223478. Government lodge with passable rooms should you decide to stop the night.

Neermahal *p209*
F-G Sagarmahal Tourist Lodge, on the lake, 1 km from Melagarh village, book through **Tripura Tourism**, T0381-222 5930, or just turn up. The majority of the comfortable rooms (a/c or non a/c) overlook the lake, as does the dorm. However, rooms in the new block have no views but are modern and superior. The restaurant serves generous and cheap meals (though salt-heavy), and staff are lovely.

Pilak *p209*
G Pilak Tourist Lodge, Jolaibari, T03823-263863. Newly decorated rooms are large (so are bathrooms) with wooden furniture, clean curtains, balconies, mosquito nets and old-style concrete floors. They are great value but directly on the road. The last room on the 1st floor is best, with lots of light coming

through the many windows. Scary dorms. The manager will offer pricey trips to the sights on his motorbike. No meals, food available in the small village.

🍴 Eating

Agartala *p207*
Restaurants in Agartala (or anywhere else in Tripura) are not permitted to serve liquor. There is a lack of decent street food in town.
🍴 **Bawarchi Kolkata**, 4 Mantri Bari Rd, T0381-222 6892. Open 1300-2200. The a/c restaurant at the back serves Indian veg and non-veg staples, plus chowmeins, tandoori and prawn dishes. The roll counter at the front is very cheap with a fast turnover on delicious egg/*paneer* (and other) rolls.
🍴 **Invitation Restaurant**, off Sakuntala Rd (down a tiny alley, opposite **Sagarita Hotel**), T0381-238 1447. Open 0900-2130. Pure veg food, south and north Indian, this clean and simple sit-down place is good for *thalis* (Rs 65) and *lassis*. Onion added on demand.
🍴 **Kurry Klub, Welcome Palace** (see Sleeping). Open 0630-2200. Offers a/c and salubrious surroundings, with a hotch-potch of art on the walls and mellow lighting. Excellent Indian and Chinese food comes in generous portions, nicely presented, but takes time to prepare. *Lassis* are fluid but deliciously fragrant. Western breakfast available, and it's one of few places to open early.
🍴 **Rajdharbar**, Rajdhani Hotel (see Sleeping). The clean and shiny glass tables don't really gel with the cave-effect decor (fake rock walls, plastic flowers and bamboo bridges) but the view towards the palace from the 5th floor is awesome (go during daylight) and the multi-cuisine menu appetizing.
🍴 **Shankar**, NSCB Rd. Interesting Bengali dishes in a canteen environment. Completely dead by 2000 and in an area without streetlights, it's best to go during the day.

Neermahal *p209*
Superb Bengali snacks and sweets are sold along the road and simple clean restaurants serve good meals (Rs 25-40).

🛍 Shopping

Agartala *p207*
Most shops are closed on Sun and only work a half-day on Sat (1000-1400). **Craft-Ex** and nearby **Tripura Cottage Industries** (daily 0900-2000) on Akhaura Rd have some lovely woven basketwares, stools and attractive wooden carvings in among the twee religious portraits etched on bamboo. All are made in Tripura. Exquisitely woven rush mats (Rs 200-490) and baskets are on sale at the wholesale market on NS Rd.

🔺 Activities and tours

Agartala *p207*
Tripura Tourism, main office at Palace Compound, T0381-222 5930, Mon-Sat 1000-1700, Sun 1500-1700; also at airport, T0381-234 2393, 0730-1830. Active in promoting their tours, although the only actual activity tends to be during Bengali holidays. Tours are good value, ranging from 1-7 days. The palace branch can book any of the 27 tourist lodges throughout Tripura.

🚍 Transport

Agartala *p207*
Air
Airport transfer, 13 km: taxi, Rs 225; auto-rickshaw, Rs 95. Flights to **Kolkata**, and **Guwahati** with **Air India**, Palace Compound, T0381-232 5470, airport, T0381-234 2020, www.airindia.com; **Jet Airways**, www.jetairways.com; **Indigo**, www.goindigo.in; and **Kingfisher**, www.flykingfisher.com.

Bus

Travelling around Agartala is easy. North-bound buses within the state leave from the Motor Stand on Motor Stand Rd, along with *sumos*. The south-bound station has bus and jeep connections to **Neermahal**, **Udaipur** and all other southerly destinations, just turn up as departures are consistent from 0600 until around 1600. Jeeps are faster and a bit more expensive.

The new **International Bus Stand** is on HG Hospital Rd, where buses leave for **Bangladesh** daily at 1200 (booking counter opens at 1030, Rs 1000 through to Kolkata).

In the same building is the TRTC office (0530-1900) with daily buses to **Guwahati** (1130, 20 hrs, Rs 424/500 for non or a/c) via **Shillong** and **Silchar** (0600, 13 hrs, Rs 137). There are private buses, also from the International terminal, to **Guwahati** (2 leave at 0600, 7 leave at 1200, Rs 475-495) and **Silchar** (1 at 0600, 12 hrs, Rs 250).

Car/taxi

Tourist taxi from Directorate of Information, about Rs 700 per day, T0381-222 2419. Car hire also possible from agents around town (clustered around Durga Bari Road). The **Welcome Palace** charge Rs 600 per day for an Indica car, plus Rs 6 per km.

Train

Agartalans are proud of their gleaming new railway station (5 km south) completed in 2008 and modelled on the Ujjayanta Palace. Computerized bookings at the station or office opposite the International bus station, T0381- 232 5533, Mon-Fri 0800-1945, Sun 0800-1345. 3 trains per day link with **Lumding** (8 hrs), **Dharmanagar** and **Silchar** (16 hrs) but, as these are only chair-car, the bus might be the more comfortable option. If travelling north to **Kalaishahar**, it's much quicker to take the train than the bus. From Lumding, it's a sleeper car on to **Guwahati**.

Construction is underway to complete the line, south to Sabroom, by 2011.

Kailashahar *p208*

To **Agartala** trains are quicker (3 per day, 3 hrs, Rs 36) than the bus (8 hrs, with army escort) and leave from Kumarghat. Frequent shared rickshaws cover the 20 km between Kailashahar and Kumarghat, Rs 20.

Udaipur *p209*

The bus and jeep stand are adjacent to each other, about 1 km from the town centre. Jeeps tend to run more frequently to **Jolaibari**, **Amarpur**, **Neermahal** and all nearby towns and villages. Autos are readily available to take you to the sights of **Udaipur**. If not staying overnight and in need of depositing luggage while you go sightseeing, the bus ticketing men have a safe room where they will store bags (till 1800).

Neermahal *p209*

Jeeps and buses drop off in the village of Melagarh. It's a Rs 10 rickshaw ride or 15-min walk to cover the 1.5 km to the lake.

Pilak *p209*

Between 0600-0800 5 buses leave Jolaibari (just north of the Tourist Lodge) for **Agartala**, others at 1200, 1300 and 1500 (Rs 48) stopping at **Udaipur** (2 hrs). Jeeps leave when full from the same place.

⊙ Directory

Agartala *p207*

Bank State Bank of India, HG Basak Rd.
Internet Netzone and Tabbu, 6 Sakuntala Rd, opposite each other and both with fast connections for Rs 20 per hr, daily 0700-2100.
Medical services GB Hospital, Kunjaban.
Post GPO: Chowmohani.

Contents

Footprint features

At a glance

◉ **Getting around** Flights to Bhubaneswar. Trains run up and down the coast; buses or car hire to explore the tribal lands.

◉ **Time required** Minimum 3 days for the Mahanadi Delta; 2-3 days for Similipal NP; 5 days for the south and a tribal safari.

◐ **Weather** Hot year round; dry in Dec and Jan, heavy rain from Jun-Sep.

⊗ **When not to go** Avoid the Orissa monsoon (Jun-Sep), one of India's wettest.

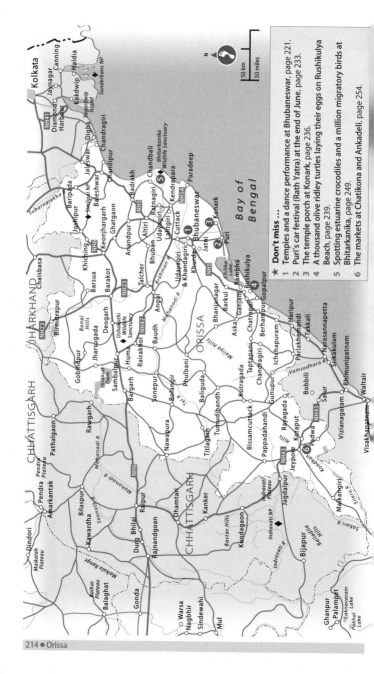

Don't miss ...

★

1 Temples and a dance performance at Bhubaneswar, page 221.

2 Puri's car festival (Rath Yatra) at the end of June, page 233.

3 The temple porch at Konark, page 236.

4 A thousand olive ridley turtles laying their eggs on Rushikulya Beach, page 239.

5 Spotting estuarine crocodiles and a million migratory birds at Bhitarkanika, page 249.

6 The markets at Chatikona and Ankadeli, page 254.

Orissa played host to one of the richest periods in Indian temple construction, most strikingly preserved in the magnificent Sun Temple of Konark, which acted as a beacon for sailors for nearly a millennium. Its intricately carved, sensual sculptures continue to mesmerize modern-day travellers, while the great and architecturally astonishing temples of Bhubaneswar and Puri draw pilgrims in their millions from across India – climaxing each summer with the electrifying Rath Yatra festival. Meanwhile, holidaymakers from Kolkata have enjoyed Puri's broad and sandy beaches for years and backpackers find rest and respite in the shady cafés and mellow guesthouses.

More than 2000 years ago, the fertile delta on which the modern capital Bhubaneswar stands witnessed one of the most significant battles of India's history, when the Emperor Asoka, having massacred his Kalingan opponents, converted to Buddhism and laid the foundations for one of the great empires of world history.

Inland, Orissa's beautiful hills, home to the Adivasis (tribal peoples), are among the least densely populated and most densely forested regions of India. Beneath them lie rich resources of iron ore, coal, bauxite and other minerals, but despite some mining activity much of the interior retains its remote charm. Weekly *haats* (markets) draw tribal communities together in a medley of colour, ornamentation and palm wine, reinforcing a culture and tradition that predates most others of the subcontinent.

Orissa has been experiencing outbreaks of communal violence in recent years, with violent clashes between Hindus and Christians, particularly in western districts. For the time being, 'tribal tourism' is avoiding certain areas; check the situation with the tourist office before you travel.

The land

Geography Near the coast it is easy to get the impression that Orissa is nothing but a flat alluvial plain composed of mile after mile of paddy fields. The coastline has shifted significantly in the last 2000 years as the land has risen relative to sea level, leaving the shallow Chilika Lake, which with an area of 1100 sq km is Asia's largest brackish lake, cut off from the sea; the lake now maintains its salinity levels by means of a man-made channel.

Inland, the alluvial soils give way to the ancient rocks of peninsular India, some of which bear huge iron ore resources. Until recently the densely forested hills were made inhospitable both by the difficulty of clearing the forest and by the devastating prevalence of malaria. Dense deciduous *sal* forest, peopled only by tribal groups living in isolation, dominated the landscape, and shifting cultivation was widely practised. Much of the forest has now been severely thinned and cultivation has spread up many of the valleys, but there remain remote and sparsely populated areas and roads that rarely see traffic, and the scenic rewards for the slowness of parts of the journey are great. The lakes to the south of Koraput in the 3000-million-year-old hills are particularly striking.

Climate Lying just south of the Tropic of Cancer, Orissa is very warm throughout the year, though the hills are sufficiently high to bring a welcome coolness. January and February are dry, but showers increase through the spring and the monsoon from June to September is one of the wettest in India; travelling in this period is best avoided. Coastal districts are particularly at risk from cyclones in October and November. The most recent of these was the catastrophic cyclone of October 1999 which caused the death of over 8000 people, and an estimated three million cattle, as well as inflicting massive damage to villages, forests and agricultural land.

History

Coastal Orissa formed a part of the ancient kingdom of Kalinga, which grew wealthy through trading, extending its colonial influence as far afield as modern Indonesia from the port of Kalinganagar as early as the fourth century BC. The Mauryan Emperor Asoka crushed the Kalingan Kingdom at Dhauligiri in 262 BC, but after experiencing the horrors of war and the accompanying bloodshed he converted to Buddhism. He preached the philosophy of peace, and while Buddhism flowered, his tolerance allowed Jainism and Hinduism to continue. After Asoka, the first century BC King Kharavela, a fervent Jain, built up a vast empire, recorded in the remarkable Udayagiri caves near Bhubaneswar. After Kharavela, separate political territories emerged in the north and centre of the region. Maritime trade flourished and Buddhism became popular again.

The greatest period of temple building in Bhubaneswar coincided with the Kesaris (6th-11th century), and then the Ganga Dynasty (11th-15th century), who were responsible for the Jagannath Temple in Puri (circa 1100) and the Sun Temple at Konark (circa 1250).

Orissa resisted the annexation of her territory by Muslims. After a short period of Afghan rule, the powerful Mughals arrived as conquerors in 1592 and during their reign destroyed many of the Bhubaneswar temples. It was their violent disruption of temple life in Puri and Bhubaneswar that later led the Brahmins to ban all non-Hindus from the precincts of the Lingaraj and Jagannath temples. The Mughals were followed by the Marathas in 1751.

In 1765 after Clive's win at Plassey, parts of Orissa, Bihar and Bengal were acquired by the East India Company with further gains in Cuttack and Puri at the beginning of the following century. Thus, by 1803, British rule extended over the whole region.

Culture

Tribal groups Orissa has the third highest concentration of tribals in India. The tribal population, nearly 25% of the total, live mainly in the Koraput, Kandhamal, Sundargarh and Mayurbhanj districts. Some 62 **Adivasi** ('ancient inhabitants') or tribal groups live in remote hill regions of the state, some virtually untouched by modern civilization, and so have kept their tribal traditions alive. Each has a distinct language and pattern of social and religious customs. They are not economically advanced and literacy is low. However, the tribal groups have highly developed artistic ability, as seen in their body paintings, ornaments, weaving and wall paintings. Music and dance also form an integral part of life-cycle ceremonies and seasonal festivals. They are remarkable in having maintained their distinct identities in a hostile and exploitative environment. There has been a new interest in their rich heritage and the Tourism Department is keen to promote visits to tribal areas, see page 254. (Suggested reading: Norman Lewis, *A Goddess in the Stones*.)

The **Khonds**, the most numerous (about 100,000), live mainly in the west and speak Kuvi, a Dravidian language, and Kui. They used to practise human Meriah sacrifice (now replaced by animal sacrifice), offering the blood to their supreme goddess represented by a piece of wood or stone, to ensure fertility of the soil. They use bows and arrows to protect themselves against wild animals.

The **Santals**, the second most numerous group, come from the northern districts of Mayurbhanj and Balasore. In the northwestern industrial belt, they have abandoned their aboriginal lifestyle to work in the steel mills. They belong to 12 patrilineal clans (*paris* or *sibs*) and speak Santali, one of the oldest languages in India. Santals believe that evil spirits in trees, forests and rivers have to be appeased by magic. The women practice witchcraft while the *ojhas* are the medicine men. Music and dance are an integral part of their daily life, especially in festivals during October-November and March-April.

In the southern districts, especially in Koraput, there are about 6000 **Bondos** ('naked people') of Tibeto-Burmese origin. They live isolated on high hills, growing rice by shifting cultivation and keeping domesticated cows and goats, and can only be seen when they come to trade in local markets. Bondo women are noticeable for their striking bead, brass and silver necklaces, and their shaved heads, decorated with plaits of palmyra leaves.

The **Saoras**, another major tribe, mostly live in hilly areas of Parlakhemundi (Gajapati district) and Gunupur (Rayagada district). Saoras live in *birindas* (extended families), descended from a common ancestor, under a headman who is helped by a religious leader. The shamans are able to communicate with watchful deified ancestors. Village houses of mud and stone walls are raised on plinths with high wooden platforms inside to store grain. The walls are decorated with remarkable paintings; traditional designs now incorporate hunters on aeroplanes and bicycles.

The **Koya** who live in villages in clearings in the middle of dense forest are distinguished by their headgear made of bison horn.

Dance, drama and music The region's magnificent temple sculpture gave rise to a classical dance form, **Odissi**, which shadows the postures, expressions and lyrical qualities of the carved figures. The dance was a ritual offering performed in the *nata mandirs* by the *maharis* (temple dancers) resplendent in their costume and jewellery. The subject is often Jayadev's *Gita Govinda* (12th century), which explores the depths of Krishna's love for Radha, the dancer expressing the sensual and the devotional.

The **folk dances** usually performed during festivals take various forms: day-long *Danda Nata*, the traditional fishermen's dance; *Chaitighoda* which requires a horse

Orissan temples

Orissan temples are graced by a tall, curvilinear tower, the *deul* (pronounced *day-ool*) or *rekha deul*, and a much lower, more open structure or porch in front of the entrance to the tower, the *jagamohana*. The dark interior of the sanctuary is designed to allow only a glimpse of the presiding deity and to enable priests to conduct ritual worship. A dancing hall (*nata mandir*) and a hall of offering (*bhoga mandir*) were often added in later temples.

The square plan of the sanctuary tower and the porch are broken vertically by the inward curving form of the main tower. Each exterior face of the sanctuary tower is divided by vertical, flat-faced projections (*rathas*).

Some Orissan architects likened the structure of the temple to that of the human body, and the names given to the vertical sections correspond to main parts of the body.

1 The platform (*pishta*) Early temples had no platform. In highly developed temples (eg Surya temple at Konark), the platform may be more than 3 m high.

2 The lower storey (*bada*) relates to the lower limbs. In early temples this was divided into three parts, the base (the foot), above which was a perpendicular section corresponding to the shin. This was topped by a set of mouldings. In some mature temples the scale of this section was greatly elongated and was itself then divided into five layers.

3 The upper storey (*gandi*, or human trunk) is a curvilinear spire in the case of the sanctuary, or a pyramidal roof in the case of the porch.

4 The head (*mastaka*) with crowning features. Divided into a series of elements, the 'head' or *mastaka* of the sanctuary developed over time. The 'neck' (*beki*) – a recessed cylindrical portion – is surmounted by the skull, *amla*. This is represented by a symbolic fruit, the *amalaka*. On the *amla* rests a 'water pot', an auspicious symbol, then on top of all comes the sacred weapon of the deity.

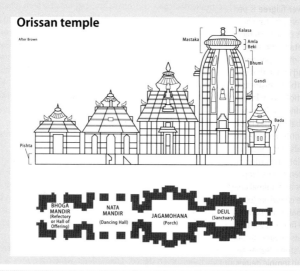

dummy; the battle dance called *Paika Nritya*; and *Chhau*, the dance-drama reminiscent of Orissa's martial past. There are also tribal dances performed in colourful costumes with distinctive headgear made of animal horns and shells, to the accompaniment of string instruments, flutes and drums.

Food and drink Rice forms the staple food, wheat taking second place. Meals include lightly spiced side dishes of vegetables and pulses, chutneys and pickles. Fresh seafood, especially prawns and the flat *pomfret* fish, are common in coastal areas. Try *mahura* or *saga bhaja* (fried mustard or spinach leaves), *dahi baigono* (aubergines cooked with yoghurt) or the festive *besara* (vegetables cooked with mustard seed paste).

Orissa is particularly noted for its milk sweets – *rasamalai, khiramohan, rajbhoga, rabidi, chhenapodapitha* and *kalakanda*. *Khiri* is prepared with milk and rice, semolina or vermicelli while special *pithas* are often filled with sweetened coconut.

Art and architecture

The temples of Bhubaneswar, along with those of Puri and Konark, represent a remarkably full record of the development of Orissan architecture from the seventh to the 13th century. Although some of the temples have suffered structural damage many are virtually intact and some are still in everyday use; centres of active pilgrimage, worship and faith.

Crafts

Stone carving has been highly developed in Orissa for more than 2000 years. The artistry that can be seen in early sculptures and the superb carvings on Orissan temples in Bhubaneswar, Puri and Konark is kept alive by modern craftsmen. They produce beautiful figures, bowls or plates carved out of soft soapstone, hard *kochila* or multicoloured serpentine from Khiching. Orissa also has a tradition of **hornwork** in Parlakhemundi and Cuttack, buffalo horn being carved into the typical small flat figures of animals and birds.

Silver filigree is perhaps one of the most distinctive and exquisite works of the Cuttack jewellers who turn fine silver wire into beautiful, fragile objects with floral patterns. The metal used is close to sterling silver and is drawn through finer and finer holes to make the wire.

Metalwork is popular. Craftsmen use brass (alloy of copper and zinc) and bell-metal (alloy of copper and tin) to produce small figurines, vases and plates. The tribal metal casting in the *dhokra* style by the *cire perdue* (lost-wax) process is found in Dhenkanal and Mayurbhanj districts. A clay core of the basic shape is covered by fine wax 'threads' before the whole is enclosed in a shell of straw and clay and then baked in a tiny charcoal fire. At the firing, molten metal is poured in, to displace the melting wax. Similar casting is done by tribal peoples in Bihar, Madhya Pradesh, Manipur and West Bengal.

Brightly coloured **woodcarvings** of the deities in the Jagannath temple, and figures of animals and birds make attractive gifts. **Ivory** inlay (now replaced by plastic) was traditionally carried out for rich patrons of the Puri temple, and also for making illustrated wooden covers for palm leaf manuscripts. The tradition of using **papier-mâché** masks of deities and animal characters to tell stories from the epics also comes from Orissa.

The *chitrakars* (picture makers), particularly from the village of Raghurajpur, 12 km from Puri, **paint** the *pattachitras* on specially prepared cloth, coated with earth to stiffen it and finally finished with lacquer after painting, producing pictures and attractive playing cards. Old sets of *ganjapa* cards consisted of 96 discs. The vibrant colours traditionally came from earth, stone, leaves and flowers. The best *chitrakars* are those allowed the honour to paint the Puri temple deities and their 'cars' each year. They are also commissioned by the rich to produce fine temple murals and manuscripts on paper and palmleaf. However, what are usually available in the bazars are cruder examples for pilgrims to take home.

Finds of the 16th century reveal how illustrated manuscripts were produced by holding an iron stylus stationary while moving a **palm leaf** underneath. It was a technique that helped to give the Oriya script its rounded form. The leaves were first prepared by drying, boiling, drying again, and then flattening them before coating with powdered shell. After inscribing, the grooves were rubbed with soot or powdered charcoal, while colour was added with a brush. The leaves were then stacked and strung together and placed between decorative wooden covers. The *pattachitra* artists in Raghurajpur have also revived this art form.

Pipli, a small town about 20 km southwest of Bhubaneswar, is well known for its **appliqué** work using brightly coloured embroidered cloth, probably originally designed for use in the Jagannath temple. The roadside stalls sell items for the house and garden – parasols, cushion covers, wall hangings – using striking animal, bird and flower patterns on a backcloth. Unfortunately, mass production has resulted in the loss of attention to detail of the original fine Pipli work, which picked out the motifs by cleverly stuffing sections of the pattern. Today, the best pieces of work are usually sent away to be sold in the government emporia in Bhubaneswar, Delhi and Kolkata.

Textile weaving has been a tradition throughout Orissa for generations and thousands are still employed in this cottage industry. It is one of the few regions in India producing **ikat**, the technique of resist-dyeing the warp or weft thread, or both, before weaving, so that the fabric that emerges from the loom has a delicate enmeshed pattern. The favourite designs include rows of flowers, birds and animals, using either *tussar* or cotton yarn. **Berhampur**, **Sambalpur**, **Mayurbhanj** and **Nuapatna** all produce silk and cotton *ikat* saris. Some also produce tapestry, bedspreads and embroidered fabric.

Crafts villages While some (for example, Raghurajpur and Pipli) are used to passing tourists, others are rarely visited by foreigners. It is worth visiting to see craftsmen at work and perhaps buy their goods. In **Raghurajpur** (reached via Chandapur, 10 km from Puri on the Bhubaneswar road), you can watch artists painting *pattachitras* in bright folk-art style or etching palm leaves (see *chitrakars* above). Sadly, the village has now been reduced to a sales exercise. **Pipli**, on the Bhubaneswar-Puri Road, specializes in appliqué work, **Balakati**, 10 km from Bhubaneswar, in bell-metal, while there is a community of Tibetan carpet weavers at **Chandragiri** near the Taptapani Hot Springs in tribal country. Adjacent to the Buddhist site of **Lalitgiri** is a stone-carvers' village. Master-weavers work at their looms in **Nuapatna** and **Maniabandha**, 100 km from Bhubaneswar, and in the narrow streets next to the temple at **Berhampur**. **Cuttack** remains famous for silver filigree work.

Modern Orissa

Political power in Orissa has alternated between the Congress and Opposition parties, most recently the BJD (the Biju Janata Dal, named after its former leader Biju Patnaik), which in alliance with the BJP won an overwhelming majority in the Assembly elections of February 2000. Chief Minister Naveen Patnaik, the son of Biju Patnaik, has held a range of ministerial posts in both state and central governments and has a strong reputation for integrity. In the 2009 State Assembly elections the BJD won 109 of the 147 seats. The BJP won seven, and the Congress 26. In the Lok Sabha elections the BJD won 14 of the 21 seats.

Bhubaneswar and around

Set on the edge of the lush green rice fields of the Mahanadi Delta, the pleasantly broad but increasingly crowded streets of the planned town of Bhubaneswar offer a striking contrast to the architectural legacy of its period of greatness over a thousand years ago. Named after 'The Lord of the Universe', Bhubaneswar still has some 500 of the original '7000' temples that once surrounded Bindusagar Tank. The graceful towers of those that remain, complemented by the extraordinary fineness of the stone carving, cluster by the lakeside away from the rushing traffic and often set among lovely gardens. ▸▸ *For listings, see pages 229-232.*

Bhubaneswar → *For listings, see pages 229-232. Colour map 3, A6.*

Ins and outs → *Phone code: 0674. Population: 647,300.*

Getting there The airport, served by direct flights from Delhi, Mumbai and Kolkata, is 4 km from the centre. Trains on the main Kolkata–Chennai line stop at Bhubaneswar station, from where many hotels are within walking distance. The New Bus Stand is 6 km northwest of town. Buses for Konark and Puri can be boarded by the State Museum.

Getting around The temples are a long walk from the modern centre and most hotels so it is best to hire a rickshaw to reach them. Once you're there it's easy enough to explore the old city on foot. ▸▸ *See Transport, page 231.*

Tourist information **Orissa Tourism** ⓘ *behind Panthanivas Hotel, Lewis Rd, T0674-243 2382, www.orissatourism,gov.in; also has a small office at the station (closes 2100),* provides good information and can book hotels. In an adjacent building, **Orissa Tourism Development Corp- oration (OTDC)** ⓘ *T0674-243 1515,* runs daily tours. **Government of India Tourism** ⓘ *B-21, BJB Nagar, T0674-243 2203, itobbs@ori.nic.in,* is helpful but in an obscure location.

History

Several sites testify to the importance of the Bhubaneswar region far earlier than the seventh to 11th centuries, when the Kalinga kings ruled over the area. Both Jain and Buddhist shrines give clear evidence of important settlements around Bhubaneswar in the first two centuries BC. The remains of a ruined moated city, Sisupalgarh (opposite the Dhauligiri battlefield and Asokan edicts), show that it was occupied from the beginning of the third century BC to the middle of the fourth century AD and the pottery shows Roman influence. Bhubaneswar is the capital of Orissa, chosen in 1948 in place of Cuttack partly because it was the ancient capital of the Kalinga Empire.

Temples

Parsuramesvara Temple The seventh-century temple, though small, is highly decorated, and is the best preserved of the early Bhubaneswar temples. The rectangular porch and the stepped roof indicate an early date. Even so, the porch was probably built after the sanctuary itself, as suggested by the rather crude junction between the two. In the early period the masonry was kept in place by weight and balance alone. Other features include the carving of a goddess and two sea monsters on the lintel over the sanctuary door.

The temple marks an important stage in the development of Hindu power at the expense of Buddhism in seventh-century Orissa, illustrated by the frequent representation of **Lakulisa**, the priest responsible for Hindu proselytism. He is sculpted in Buddha-like form, and often surrounded by disciples. Note also, the distinctive *chaitya*

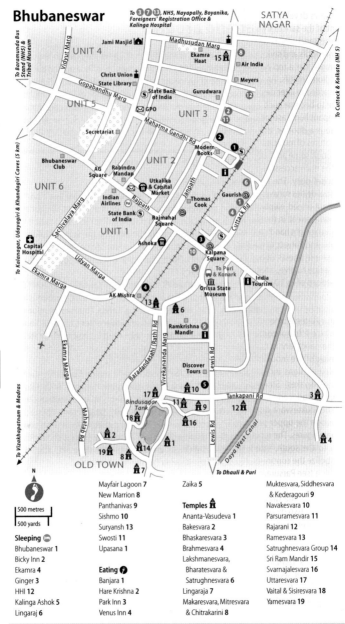

windows developed earlier in Buddhist *chaitya* halls, as at Ajanta. There are two on the front of the sanctuary tower.

The sanctuary is divided horizontally and vertically into three sections. The carvings show motifs and styles that were to reach their full flowering in later temples. The base, for example, has a top moulding (close to the ground) decorated with scrolls, birds, humans and floral motifs. At about eye level, the mouldings are distinctive. The recessed frieze (discarded in later designs) is embossed with early examples of the amorous couples that were to become such a prominent feature of the Konark temple, interspersed with *vyalas* (rampant lions) astride crouching elephants. In addition to the main entrance to the porch there is a door on the south side and four latticed windows. The vigorous and graceful sculptures of musicians and dancers on each side of the western doorway are outstanding, although some are badly weathered.

The main accessory deities are placed in niches on each side of the sanctuary housing the principal deity. The Parsurameshvara Temple was dedicated to Siva; only two of the three original deities survive. On the south of the sanctuary, at eye level in the middle of the tower, is the four-armed elephant-headed Ganesh, his trunk curled towards a bowl of *laddus*, his favourite sweet. In the southern niche is Karttikeya (Subrahmanya) with a peacock, carrying a fruit in his right hand and a spear in his left. The lintel above Karttikeya illustrates the marriage of Siva and Parvati; to their right are Agni (Fire), the kneeling Brahma, and Surya (Sun).

Temple priests will approach you for donations; these are not compulsory, but if you do decide to give, a token Rs 10 is sufficient. Visitor books may be proffered which show donations of Rs 1000; these are surely forged, don't feel pressured.

Muktesvara Temple Beautifully decorated with outstanding carvings, this late 10th-century temple belongs to the end of the first phase of temple building. Although it still has the three-fold horizontal division of the lower storey, a feature of the early period, the plan of the sanctuary is now divided into the five-sectioned form. Also, the platform here consists of five mouldings, as in later temples.

New designs include graceful female figures and pilasters carved with *nagas* and *naginis* (snakes). Strikingly, the porch has a new and more dramatic layered form. Ketu, too, is introduced as the ninth planet and Ganesh is joined by his mount, the mouse.

The Muktesvara displays the unique *torana* (gateway arch) dated at about AD 900; although the upper portion is restored, the original skill can still be seen in the graceful female figures. The rectangular tank at its east end, used by priests and devotees, and the well to the south, into which women still toss coins in the hope of curing infertility, symbolize the continued holiness of the site. On the door frame of the well is the figure of Lakulisa (see Parsuramesvara, above).

The *chaitya* windows carved on the sanctuary tower show the finest examples of the *bho* motif – the grinning face of a lion with beaded tassels emerging from its mouth, flanked by two dwarves. Notice the monkey scenes on the outer frame of the diamond-shaped lattice windows on the north and south walls.

Siddhesvara Temple Immediately to the northwest of the Muktesvara is the later Siddhesvara Temple. It shows the mature Orissan temple form almost complete. The vertical lower section is divided into five parts and the *amla* on top of the sanctuary is supported by four squatting figures. However, the overall effect is comparatively plain, as sculptures marked out on the rock were never executed.

Kederagouri Temple The Kederagouri Temple to the south is probably of the late 10th century but it is built in the *khakhara* form (see Vaital Deul, below), and has been substantially repaired. The porch was rebuilt in the early 20th century but still has a few original sculptures of real merit. Note the girl shown leaning against a post with a bird perched on it, on the south face of the eastern projection of the sanctuary. On the western projection is an equally beautiful sculpture of a girl removing her anklets.

Rajarani Temple ⓘ *0600-1800, foreigners Rs100, video camera Rs 25.* The entrance to the early 11th-century temple is 300 m east of the main road, set back from the road. It no longer has an image of the deity in the sanctuary and is out of use. The main tower is surrounded by four miniature copies, giving the sanctuary a near-circular appearance.

The *jagmohana* (porch) is plain although it has the mature style of a pyramidal roof. Many carvings are unfinished but give an insight into the method of cutting the stone into sections ('blocking out') followed by rough shaping ('boasted'), to be finished by the master sculptor. The finished work in the main sanctuary is impressive.

Perhaps the best-preserved features of the temple are the **Dikpalas** (Guardians of the eight cardinal directions) who protect the central shrine from every quarter. They are placed in pairs about 3 m above ground level, in the lower section of the main tower.

Starting from the left (south) of the porch they appear in the following order:

1 Facing east, **Indra**, the guardian of the east, holds a thunderbolt and an elephant goad, and his vehicle is the elephant.

2 At right angles to Indra, facing south, is the pot-bellied and bearded **Agni**, god of fire, riding a ram, guarding the southeast.

3 Moving a few metres along the wall, on the far side of the projection, is the south-facing **Yama**, holding a staff and a noose, with his vehicle the buffalo. The skull on his staff is a Tantric symbol.

4 Again at right angles to Yama is the west-facing **Nirritti**, guardian of the southwest. Nirritti, the god of misery, holds a severed head and a sword over the lying figure of a man.

5 Again facing west, but on the north side of the sanctuary's central projection, is the guardian of the west, **Varuna**. He holds the noose symbolizing fate in his left hand. His vehicle is the sea creature *makara*.

6 At right angles to Varuna, facing north, is **Vayu** (meaning 'wind'), guardian of the northwest. He holds a fluttering banner, and his vehicle is the deer.

7 The last pair of guardians are on the further side of the central projection, on the north and east facing sides respectively. First is **Kubera**, guardian of the north (pot-bellied to symbolize prosperity), placed above seven jars of precious stones. He has a horse.

8 **Ishana**, guardian of the northeast, symbolizing fecundity, is shown as was customary, with an erect phallus and accompanied by an emaciated figure.

Brahmesvara Temple The temple (built in 1060) is still in use today. Entering from the north you pass through the two enclosure walls, the inner forming a compact surround for the temple complex, raised on a platform. Facing you is a well-oiled image

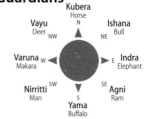

Dikpalas: the Directional Guardians

of Lakshmi, covered in cloth, with incense sticks burning in front. The sanctuary itself houses a Siva *linga*. There are minor shrines in each corner of the compound.

The sanctuary tower has a five-fold vertical division, typical of the later temples. The *pabhaga* (base) and the *varanda* (top of the wall) have rich carvings. The lower section of the wall is decorated alternately by miniature *khakhara* style 'temples', sculptures of rampant lions, while the central niches of the miniature temple carvings at the corners of the lower section have Dikpalas. In the corresponding spaces of the upper section are miniatures of the normal temple sanctuary towers, and graceful secular figures, including erotic couples.

Satrughnesvara Group The **Lakshmanesvara**, **Bharatesvara** and **Satrughnesvara** temples are almost certainly the oldest in Bhubaneswar, dating from the late sixth century. The southernmost temple in the group has been rebuilt by the Archaeological Department of Orissa. Only the cores of these three temple are now visible.

Vaital Temple A major feature of this small, late eighth-century temple is its form. Seen from the road the semi-cylindrical shape in section of the *deul* is immediately obvious. Its *khakhara* style derives, as Percy Brown says, from the shape of the *gopurams* of Dravida temples in South India, taken originally from the Buddhist *chaitya* halls. Another striking feature is the temple's tantric associations, marked by its presiding deity, Chamunda (a terrible form of Durga). Durga herself appears on the north face of the *bada* as the eight-armed *Mahishasuramardini* (slayer of the buffalo demon) holding a snake, bow, shield, sword, trident, thunderbolt and an arrow, piercing the neck of the demon.

Outside, on the east face of the *deul*, the lower of the two *chaitya* windows has a beautifully carved figure of the sun god Surya, with Usha (Dawn) and Pratyusha shooting arrows on either side of him while Aruna (also Dawn) drives a chariot in front. It has a certain incongruity in view of the image within the sanctum itself. The upper *chaitya* window has a 10-armed Nataraja, or dancing Siva.

Further evidence of the tantric basis of the temple comes from the stone post to which sacrifices were tethered, just in front of the *jagamohana*. The figure of Chamunda in the central niche is extremely difficult to see without artificial light, though very early-morning sun penetrates the gloom of the interior. The most chilling of the other figures is that of a male on the north wall "rising from the ground after filling his skull-cup with the blood of a person whose severed head lies on the right; on the pedestal is an offering of two more heads".

Lingaraja Temple Along with the Jagannatha Temple at Puri, the Lingaraja Temple (AD 1000), built 100 years earlier, represents the peak of achievement of the Orissan middle period. Non-Hindus are not allowed inside but you can get a view from a special platform outside the north perimeter wall (donations sought), or from the roof of the hospital on the west side where no one will hassle for donations. Early morning and late afternoon are best for photography.

Even from a distance the sanctuary's 54-m-high *Sri Mandir* (tower) dominates the landscape. It is one of the four main buildings in the temple compound, with several subsidiary shrines. To the left of the tower is the *Jagamohana* (pillared porch), then the *Nata Mandir* (dancing hall) and finally the *Bhoga Mandir* (hall of offering). The latter two were added a century after the sanctuary and the porch.

The monumental tower, which rises in a distinctive curve, is 17 m sq in plan with projecting faces. The *amla* head with a pot-shaped pinnacle carrying the trident of Siva is supported by four mythical gryphons. The middle section has vertical lines of miniature towers sculpted in sharp relief on a background of horizontal mouldings. The massive protruding sculpture of a lion crushing an elephant on each side is a common symbol in Orissan architecture.

Ananta-Vasudeva Temple This is a hive of practical as well as spiritual activity in the mornings, when temple priests prepare kilos of rice, hoist pottery urns to-and-fro, chop mountains of vegetables and wash pots in time for the 1030 meal. It's a worthwhile halting point to absorb the charged smoky atmosphere as pilgrims amass.

Other sights
Orissa State Museum ⓘ *Gautam Nagar, Tue-Sun 1000-1700 (last entry 1630), closed government holidays, foreigners Rs 50, Indians Rs 5, camera Rs 100*, has archaeological exhibits including a collection of copper plates, coins, sculptures, musical instruments and rare palm leaf manuscripts; good anthropological section. Allow an hour or two.

The **Tribal Museum of Man** ⓘ *CRP Sq, northwest of town, off NH5 on bus route, Tue-Sun 1000-1700, free*, has a collection of tribal dress, weapons, musical instruments and jewellery, and is worth visiting if you are planning to travel on to tribal regions. Five short documentaries explain tribal life and interesting reconstructions of typical houses are found to the rear of the building.

North of town, the Government Regional Plant Resource Centre, **Ekamra Kanan** ⓘ *Nayapally, Mar-Oct 0800-2000, Nov-Feb 0900-1900, Rs 5*, has a large rose garden, woods, flowerbeds and a large lake which attracts migratory birds. It also boasts a Cactus Garden with over 550 species of cacti and succulents, one of the largest collections in India.

Heading out on the subsidiary road from Bhubaneswar to Cuttack, the medieval regional capital, is **Nandan Kanan** ⓘ *20 km east, Tue-Sun 0800-1700, summer 0730-1730, foreigners Rs 100, Indians Rs 10, camera Rs 5, video Rs 500; cable car across the lake, Rs 22, last return 1600; safari Rs 15*, where the zoo and botanical garden are surrounded by dense forest. There are tigers, including rare white ones, lion and white tiger safaris, rhinos, panthers, leopards, wildfowl and reptiles in their natural surroundings. It has also succeeded in breeding black panthers and *gharials* in captivity. The botanical gardens with its cactus house and rosarium are across the lake; much of it is derelict. **Shradhanjali Restaurant** near the entrance serves good *thalis* and snacks.

Udayagiri and Khandagiri caves → *For listings, see pages 229-232. Colour map 3, A6.*

The caves, 6 km west of Bhubaneswar, on the two low hills of Udayagiri and Khandagiri, date from the time of Jain occupation of the region, at least the second century BC. A narrow valley winds between the hills, the route of an early Buddhist pilgrim track leading to a *stupa* which probably stood on the present site of Bhubaneswar. The coarse-grained sandstone which forms Khandagiri ('broken hill') and Udayagiri ('hill of the sunrise') rises nearly 40 m above the surrounding lateritic and infertile plain. The crumbling nature of the sandstone into which the caves were dug has exposed them to severe damage, moderately repaired by the Archaeological Survey of India.

Ins and outs

Getting there The caves are very easy to visit by car, bus, rickshaw (Rs 250 return, includes waiting) or bicycle from Bhubaneswar, but the area can get very crowded. Allow at least three hours for the round trip.

Getting around Heading straight up the ramp at Udayagiri will take you round the caves in reverse number order, better to head round the path to the right first. Some with sculptures are protected by wire-meshed gates. The most significant are described below.

Tourist information 0800-1800. Udayagiri costs Rs100, video Rs 25. Khandagiri is free.

History

The Jain caves are among the earliest in India. Furthermore, some of the rock inscriptions found above the Hati Gumpha (Elephant Cave, No 14) and elsewhere, speak of the Chedi

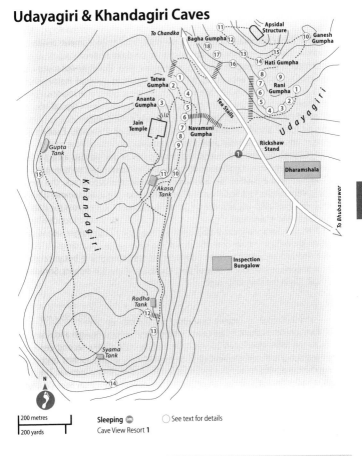

Udayagiri & Khandagiri Caves

To Chandka

Apsidal Structure

Bagha Gumpha 12

Ganesh Gumpha

Hati Gumpha 14

Rani Gumpha

Tatwa Gumpha

Ananta Gumpha

Jain Temple

Navamuni Gumpha

Tea Stalls

Udayagiri

Rickshaw Stand

Gupta Tank

Khandagiri

Akasa Tank

Dharamshala

To Bhubaneswar

Inspection Bungalow

Radha Tank

Syama Tank

N

200 metres
200 yards

Sleeping ⬤
Cave View Resort **1**

◯ See text for details

Dynasty who ruled over Kalinga from their capital, probably at Sisupalgarh, 9 km southeast of Khandagiri.

Kharavela, according to his own record, extended his rule across a large part of North, Central and South India. At home he made great efforts to improve canals, rebuild his capital city of Kalinganagara, and also to excavate some of the caves at Udayagiri-Khandagiri. Probably all the caves now visible were constructed during the 150 years before Christ. Designed for the ascetic life of Jain monks, they simply provided dry shelter, with no concessions to any form of comfort. Too low to stand in, the cells are no more than cramped sleeping compartments.

Although the Jains did not enjoy royal patronage after the fall of Kharavela's Dynasty, Jain occupation was continuous throughout successive Buddhist and Hindu periods in the region. The Parsvanatha temple on top of Khandagiri was built in the early 19th century, while the Hindu temple dates from the 1970s.

Udayagiri

Cave 1 The **Rani Gumpha**, on the path to the right, is the largest and most impressive of the caves. It is a double-storeyed monastery cut on three sides of a quadrangle with fine wall friezes and some pillars that have been restored. The right wing of the lower storey has pilasters at the entrance to the cell and the arches are beautifully carved with religious and royal scenes while the main central wing celebrates the king's victory march. There are two small guard rooms with decorative outer walls. In the upper storey, the doorway arches to the cells are ornately carved; auspicious Jain symbols (snake and lotus) appear among vivid secular friezes of a woman's abduction, an elopement, and a duel between a man and a woman.

Cave 10 **Ganesh Gumpha**, about 50 m from the top of the hill, guarded by Ganesh statues, has friezes illustrating the Sanskrit love story of Udayan and Bassavadatta. From Cave 10 head up the path to the left, where an **apsidal structure** was unearthed in 1958. It is very similar to a Buddhist *chaitya* hall in plan and it was almost certainly a place of worship used by Jain monks. From here, there are stupendous views of Bhubaneswar and Khandagiri.

Cave 12 **Bagha Gumpha** is carved bizarrely into the shape of a tiger's open mouth, an inscription showing it to have been the cave of the town judge.

Cave 14 The last important cave on Udayagiri, the **Hati Gumpha** (Elephant Cave), has the most important inscription, that of King Kharavela. Protected by a masonry shelter since 1902, it is in the Magadhi script.

Khandagiri

Caves 1 and 2 Known as **Tatowa Gumpha** from the parrots carved above their door arches. Two sentries in *dhotis* guard Cave 1 which bears the name **Kusuma**. Modern steps lead up to the more elaborately carved Cave 2 on the left. On the back of the cell are Brahmi inscriptions in red pigment (first century BC to first century AD), obscured by modern Orissan graffiti.

Cave 3 **Ananta Gumpha**, at the top of the flight of steps, named after the two serpents on the door arches, has some very interesting reliefs using unique motifs, though the protective glass makes them hard to see. On the back wall of the cell, among the various symbols is the *svastika*, auspicious to the Jains.

Cave 7 **Navamuni Gumpha**, named after the nine Tirthankaras (*munis*) carved on the back and right walls, was originally a residential cell. On the back wall of the original right hand cell are seven Tirthankaras in high relief including Parsvanatha under a seven-hooded canopy, and Risabanatha with a halo, seated on a bull.

There are lovely carvings of Digambara Jains on the back wall of the shrine with a corrugated iron roof half way up to the Jain temple at the top, from where there are excellent views.

Dhauli

The horrors of the Kalinga war at Dhauli led Asoka to acknowledge the value of Buddhist teachings. The two 'Kalinga Edicts' differ from others which expound Buddhist principles. The rock edicts at the bottom of the hill (circa 260 BC) give detailed instructions to Asoka's administrators to rule his subjects with gentleness and fairness. "…You are in charge of many thousand living beings. You should gain the affection of men. All men are my children, and as I desire for my children that they obtain welfare and happiness both in this world and next, the same do I desire for all men …". Above the inscription you can see the front of an elephant carved out of an enormous rock. Unfortunately, the edict is difficult to see clearly behind its protective cage.

Now the rock edicts are almost ignored by the bus loads of tourists who are taken on up the hill to the Buddhist **Peace Pagoda**. Known as the **Shanti Stupa**, the pagoda was built in the early 1970s by the Japan Buddha Sangha and Kalinga Nippon Buddha Sangha. The old Hindu temple of Lord Dhavaleswar which was reconstructed in 1972 is also on the hilltop here.

◉ Bhubaneswar listings

For Sleeping and Eating price codes and other relevant information, see Essentials pages 34-38.

◉ Sleeping

Bhubaneswar *p221, map p222*

LL-L Mayfair Lagoon, 8B Jaydev Vihar, Nayapalli, 5 km from centre, T0674-236 0101, www.mayfairhotels.com. Low-level expansive palace-style hotel with attractive cottages and rooms set around lagoon, 5-star facilities, very stylish yet quite kitsch. Friendly efficient staff, pickup included. Recommended for a fun splash-out.

LL-AL HHI, 112 Kharvel Nagar, Janpath, T0674-253 1465, www.hhihotels.com. With tastefully furnished rooms in cool mellow tones, the HHI fancies itself as boutique. The pool is tempting, restaurants chic, and the lounge bar has evening music. In the centre of town (unlike other high-end options), sizeable discounts available.

L-AL The New Marrion, 6 Janpath, opposite Sri Ram Mandir, T0674-238 0850,

www.hotelnewmarrion.com. Spacious rooms and overpriced suites boast peculiar decor, go for the cheaper rooms as the higher range merely have hot balconies overlooking the cloudy pool. Huge discounts negotiable. Food options excellent (**Mirch Masala** for Indian, **Bling** for Mexican/Western/good coffee), and an Irish-themed sports bar.

AL Swosti, 103 Janpath, T0674-253 5771, www.swosti.com. 60 a/c rooms (little difference between standard and de luxe), restaurant with some Orissan specialities, small comfy bar, overpriced compared to those out of town but good discounts if you hint.

AL-A Sishmo, 86/A1 Gautam Nagar, T0674-243 3600/5, www.hotelsishmo.com. Well-run but in need of freshening up, with 72 comfortable a/c rooms, some getting musty and threadbare, facilities include health club and tiny pool that is supposedly being renovated, decent restaurant and bar is worn but cosy, checkout 1200.

AL-A Suryansh, P1 Jaydev Vihar, near Kalinga Hospital, Nandan Kanan Rd, T0674-230 3300, www.suryanshhotels.com. New and spruce rooms aren't huge but they're comfortable and well appointed, good restaurants (Rs 250 lunch buffet excellent, dinner à la carte) and a fresh and friendly bar (happy hour 1400-1900). Rooftop pool a bit disappointing, but gym is well equipped.

A Kalinga Ashok, Gautam Nagar, T0674-243 1055, www.hotelkalingaashok.com. 32 large clean rooms but getting jaded (especially the bathrooms, ones overlooking the lawn are preferable, all a/c, TV, restaurant and coffee shop. Sizeable discounts available.

C Ginger, Jayadev Nihar, Nayapali, T0674-230 3933, www.gingerhotels.com. By far the best value in this range, with sleek modern rooms and fantastic service. Amenities, TV and technology all state of the art; downsides are the barren surroundings, distance into town and buffet meals rather than à la carte. Great discounts if you book online.

C Panthanivas, Lewis Rd, T0674-243 2515, www.panthanivas.com. Clean, spacious rooms but some getting a bit tatty (same price single or double), hot bath, all a/c, average restaurant, punitive 0800 check out, tourist office at the rear.

C-D Bicky Inn, 61 Janpath, T0674-253 6435. 26 small, but well-kept rooms, mostly a/c, Indian-style hotel, rooftop restaurant.

D-E Bhubaneswar, Cuttack Rd, T0674-231 3245. Generally clean and good value but staff could be more helpful. 42 rooms with bath, some a/c, some decrepit, always busy.

E Ekamra, Kalpana Sq, T0674-231 1732. Simple, grubby rooms, though clean linen, cheap singles, restaurant, internet café below. Mainly used by Indian workers.

E-F Lingaraj, Old Station Bazar, T0674-231 3565. Basic clean rooms, dorm.

E-F Upasana, Cuttack Rd, behind Bhubaneswar, T0674-231 4144. 20 fresh clean rooms, some a/c, with all-important mosquito mesh on windows, away from

main road so quieter, decent room service, friendly, 24-hr checkout. Cheaper non-a/c rooms at back are a bargain for clean linens and TV. Recommended.

Udayagiri and Khandagiri caves
p226, map p227
D-E Cave View Resort, T0674-247 2288. 5 rooms.

❼ Eating

Bhubaneswar *p221, map p222*
🍴🍴🍴 **Deep Down South**, The New Marrion (see Sleeping). An excellent, almost trendy choice for unusual South Indian: try tomato/chilly sponge *dosa*, or mint/*dhania*/gunpowder *dosa*, or safer ground is the delicious *rava masala dosa*. Good *lassis* too.

🍴🍴🍴 **Mayfair Lagoon** (see Sleeping). Pleasant restaurants include outdoor truck stop-style. Great Western fast food and sweets.

🍴🍴🍴 **Swosti** (see Sleeping). Varied menu. Dimly lit, generous, local specialities to advance order.

🍴🍴 **Banjara**, Station Sq. Good lunch/dinner.

🍴🍴 **Hare Krishna**, Lalchand Complex, Janpath, T0674-250 3188. Strict vegetarian. Upstairs, a/c, smart, tasty food.

🍴🍴 **Park Inn**, Rajpath. Dim but unthreatening place for a beer (Rs 90-120) with a wide menu of Indian and Chinese veg/non dishes.

🍴 **New Ganguram Sweets**, various locations around town. Delicious sweets and snacks.

🍴 **Venus Inn**, 217 Bapuji Nagar (1st floor), T0674-253 1738. Clean and friendly, with decor that hints at temple architecture, subtle lighting and a/c. Best for South Indian vegetarian, *uttapams*, breakfasts and *dosas*. Recommended.

🍴 **The Zaika**, Lewis Rd. Open 1100-1500 and 1900-2230. Hygienic and delicious food (Indian and Chinese), handy if you are staying in the Tourist Lodge.

🎭 Entertainment

Bhubaneswar *p221, map p222*
Programmes of Odissi and folk dances and folk drama are staged regularly and are worth seeking out. Schedules are irregular so call to see what's on. **Rabindra Mandap**, near GPO, T0674-251 7677, and **Jayadeva Bhavan** (State Information Centre) near bus stand, T0674-253 0794.

🎉 Festivals and events

Bhubaneswar *p221, map p222*
26 Jan-1 Feb Tribal Fair attended by groups from different regions – excellent performances and crafts exhibitions over 7 days.
Mar/Apr Asokashtami, the **Lingaraja Car Festival**. The image of Siva is drawn on a chariot from the Lingaraja Temple to visit the Ramesvara Temple for 4 days.

🛍 Shopping

Bhubaneswar *p221, map p222*
Some shops close on Thu and take a long lunch break. Market Building shops display prices but ask for a discount. The main street-market area is closed on Mon.
Boyanika, West Market. Recommended for saris and Orissan handloom fabrics.
Ekamra Haat, Madhusudan Marg. One-stop market for Orissan handicrafts and textiles.
Meyers, Janpath. The award-winning weavers have recently opened a fancy new store selling typical Orissan saris.
Utkalika, East Tower. Sells Orissa handloom and handicrafts.

Books
AK Mishra, 209 Bapuji Nagar, T0674-253 3349. Mon-Sat 1000-1400 and 1600-2100. Biggest and best bookshop in town, lots of fiction and not too jumbled.
Modern Book Co, Station Sq. Mon-Sat

0930-1400 and 1630-2100. Reasonable selection of novels.

🏔 Activities and tours

Bhubaneswar *p221, map p222*
Discover Tours, 463 Lewis Rd, T0674-2430477, T(0)9437-111230, www.orissa discover.com. For special interest tours (cultural, treks, wildlife parks and ethnological). Sarat Acharya and Bijaya Pattnaik are excellent guides and have won awards from the Regional Tourist Board. Tours organized even at short notice, though ask ahead for full service. Recommended.
OTDC, T0674-243 1515, runs various tours by 'luxury' coach from Transport Unit, behind **Panthanivas**. Ask about special tours to Chilika Lake. They will also pick up/drop off at hotels. To Nandankanan, Khandagiri, Udaigiri, Dhauli and museum with good guide (Tue-Sun 0900-1730, Rs 150, Rs 200 a/c). To Pipli, Konark and Puri (0900-1800, Rs 180/250, plus entry fee to Konark). To Puri and Satapada (0830-1800, Rs 175). To Barkul and Narayani (0830-1800, Rs 175). A new OTDC enterprise is the 'Hop On Hop Off' a/c bus which takes in city or heritage sights on a single ticket, 0830-2030, passing through designated stops at half-hourly intervals – pick up a route map from the OTDC office.

🚌 Transport

Bhubaneswar *p221, map p222*
Air
Airport 4 km. Taxi transfer, Rs 100 through **OTDC**. From airport Rs 100-150.
Air India, Rajpath, T0674-253 0533, airport, T06274-534472, www.airindia.com, daily to **Delhi**, **Kolkata**, **Chennai**, **Bangalore** (**Bengaluru**), **Mumbai** and **Hyderabad**. Indigo, www.goindigo.in, Kingfisher, www.flykingfisher.com, and Jetlite, www.jetlite.com, also cover these routes. Kingfisher flies to **Raipur**.

Bus

Local City buses are cheap and cover major routes but avoid evening rush hour.
Long distance New Bus Stand is at Baramunda on the NH5 (6 km from centre) where there are auto-rickshaws for transfer. Enquiries T0674-235 4695, private bus enquiries T0674-235 4769. Some long-distance buses go through the city first, stopping at the Old Bus Stand, off Rajpath. Regular buses to **Puri** and **Konark** (both 1½-3 hrs) pick up passengers from outside the museum on Lewis Rd. Most are very full, but usually thin out at Pipli. Buses to **Cuttack** (1 hr) stop on the opposite side of the road.

Taxi

Tourist taxis, unmetered. **OTDC (Transport)** T0674-243 1515, and private operators have a/c and non a/c cars for full and half day sightseeing. Cars Rs 600, a/c, Rs 800, for 8 hrs or 80 km. A round trip by car visiting Konark and Puri from Bhubaneswar takes 6-8 hrs. Allow at least 1 hr for Konark.

Train

Reservations, T0674-253 2350; enquiries, T0674-253 2233. Computerized booking hall is in separate building opposite the station. Auto- and cycle-rickshaws for transfer. **Chennai**: *Coromandal Exp 2841*, 2140, 21 hrs; *Howrah Chennai Mail 2839*, 0635, 25½ hrs. **Kolkata (H)**: *Shatabdi 2074*, 0620, 6½ hrs, except Sun; *Dhauli Exp 2822*, 1315, 7 hrs; *Coromandal Exp 2842*, 0500, 7½ hrs;

Falaknuma Exp 2704, 1055, 8½ hrs; *Howrah Mail 2840*, 2040, 7½ hrs; *Jagannath Exp 8410*, 0015, 8 hrs; *East Coast Exp 8646*, 0740, 8½ hrs, *Puri Howrah Exp 2838*, 2145, 7½ hrs. **Mumbai (CST)**: *Konark Exp 1020*, 1515, 37½ hrs. **Koraput**: *Hirakhand Exp 8447*, 2000, 16 hrs. **Secunderabad**: *Falaknuma Exp 2703*, 1405, 20 hrs; *Konark Exp 1020*, 1515, 21 hrs; *East Coast Exp 8645*, 1940, 23 hrs; *Visakha Exp 7015*, 0835, 23 hrs. **New Delhi**: *Purushottam Exp 2801*, 2325, 30 hrs; *Utkal Exp 8477*, 2250, 40 hrs, both go via **Mughal Sarai (Varanasi)**.

⊙ Directory

Bhubaneswar *p221, map p222*
Banks State Bank of India, Rajpath, by Police Station. ATM and exchange on 1st floor, sterling, US$ cash and TCs (closed Sun). **ICICI**, near Shree Raj Talkies, Janpath, and **Thomas Cook**, 130 Ashok Nagar, Janpath, for over the counter exchange. There are many ATMs on Janpath and around Kalpana Square, and also by the main entrance to the railway station. **Internet** Gaurish Internet, Cuttack Rd (opposite petrol station), daily 0900-2230, new and fast. Also at **Ekamra Hotel** and on Kalpana Sq (noisy location but quick).
Medical services Capital Hospital, Unit 6, T0674-239 0688; **Kalinga Hospital**, Nandan Kanan Rd, T0674-230 0570/230 1227, private hospital. **Post** GPO, Sachivalaya Marg.
Useful contacts Foreigners' Registration Office, Sahid Nagar, T0674-254 0555.

Footprint Mini Atlas
Northeast India

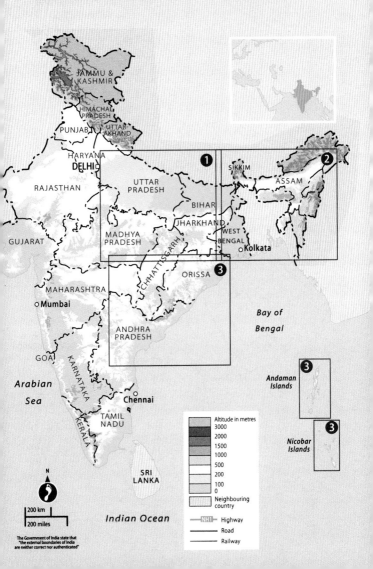

The Government of India state that "the external boundaries of India are neither correct nor authenticated"

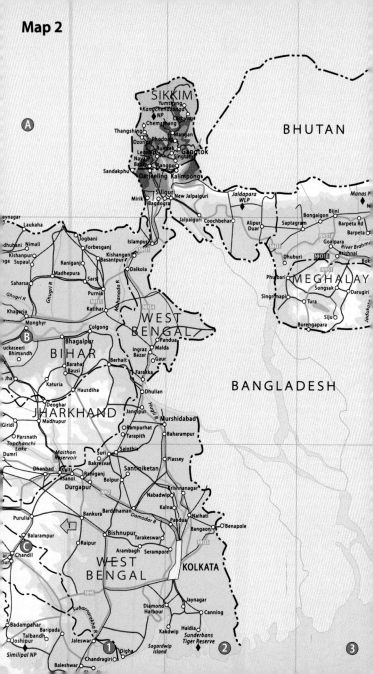

Map 3

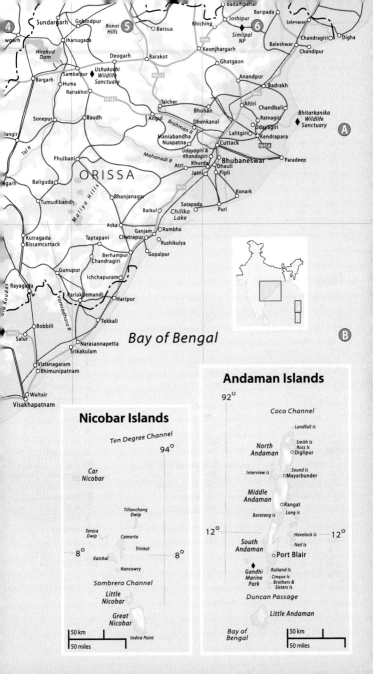

Index

Map symbols

▢	Capital city	
○	Other city, town	
	International border	
	Regional border	
⊖	Customs	
	Contours (approx)	
▲	Mountain, volcano	
⇌	Mountain pass	
	Escarpment	
	Glacier	
	Salt flat	
	Rocks	
	Seasonal marshland	
	Beach, sandbank	
⦚	Waterfall	
	Reef	
═══	Motorway	
───	Main road	
───	Minor road	
━━━	Track	
┄┄┄	Footpath	
───	Railway	
	Railway with station	
✈	Airport	
🚌	Bus station	
Ⓜ	Metro station	

- - - -	Cable car
	Funicular
	Ferry
	Pedestrianized street
⫩ ⫩	Tunnel
→	One way-street
	Steps
⇌	Bridge
	Fortified wall
	Park, garden, stadium
	Sleeping
	Eating
	Bars & clubs
	Building
	Sight
	Cathedral, church
	Chinese temple
	Hindu temple
	Meru
	Mosque
	Stupa
	Synagogue
	Tourist office
🏛	Museum
✉	Post office
	Police

Ⓢ	Bank
@	Internet
♪	Telephone
	Market
	Medical services
Ⓟ	Parking
	Petrol
	Golf
	Archaeological site
	National park, wildlife reserve
	Viewing point
	Campsite
	Refuge, lodge
	Castle, fort
	Diving
	Deciduous, coniferous, palm trees
	Mangrove
	Hide
	Vineyard, winery
	Distillery
	Shipwreck
✕	Historic battlefield
	Related map

The Southeast

The Southeast encompasses Puri, one of the four holiest pilgrimage centres for Hindus, and Konark, which Mark Twain described as one of the wonders of the world. The Irrawady dolphins and flamingos of Chillika figure prominently in brochures, and the lake is an easy and rewarding excursion from Puri (particularly for birdwatchers) with some attractive places to stay overnight. ▸▸ *For listings, see pages 240-245.*

Puri → *For listings, see pages 240-245. Colour map 3, A6.*

Puri's tourist guesthouses cater to the flocks of Kolkata holidaymakers who take advantage of the highly revered Jagannath Temple and the long sandy beach to combine

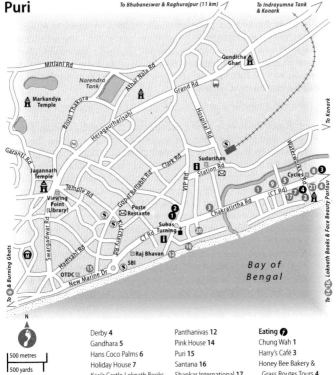

Puri

To Bhubaneswar & Raghurajpur (11 km)

To Indrayumna Tank & Konark

N

500 metres
500 yards

Bay of Bengal

To Konark

Sleeping 🛏
Arya Palace 1
Baywatch Residency 2
Chanakya BNR 3

Derby 4
Gandhara 5
Hans Coco Palms 6
Holiday House 7
Kasi's Castle, Loknath Books
  & Tanuja Tribe Tour 7
Lotus 8
Love & Life 9
Mayfair Beach Resort 10

Panthanivas 12
Pink House 14
Puri 15
Santana 16
Shankar International 17
Sun Row Cottage &
  Internet 5
Youth Hostel 20
Z 21

Eating 🍴
Chung Wah 1
Harry's Café 3
Honey Bee Bakery &
  Grass Routes Tours 4
Peace 4
Wild Grass 2
Xanadu Garden 4

pilgrimage with relaxation. The massive curvilinear temple tower dominates the skyline, and the otherwise sleepy town seethes with life during the **Rath Yatra** (Car Festival) in June/July. Yet for most of the year Puri feels like an out of season backwater where quiet shady lanes and prettily painted houses merge into the built-up beach-front and animated market areas on the west side of town.

Ins and outs → *Phone code: 06752. Population: 157,600.*

Getting there The railway station is about 1 km from the main hotels and the bus stand, 500 m north of it, on Grand Road. Cycle-rickshaws tout for business all across town.

Getting around It is well worth renting a bike or motorbike to visit the temple, bazar and explore the coast if you don't wish to hire a rickshaw. Places on CT Road have bikes (Rs 30 per day), mopeds (Rs 120-150) or motorbikes (Rs 200-250) for hire. ▶▶ *See Transport, page 244.*

▶▶ *See Transport, page 244.*

Tourist information **Orissa Tourism** ⓘ *Station Rd, T06752-222664, Mon-Sat 1000-1700*, with a museum above. There is also a tourist counter at the railway station, T06752-223536.

History

The Sabaras, an Adivasi tribal group who predated the Dravidians and Aryans, were believed to have inhabited the thickly wooded area around Puri. Some believe that this was Dantapura, which once held the holy Buddhist Tooth relic. According to Murray, in Japan and Sri Lanka, the **Tooth Festival** of Buddha was celebrated with three chariots and the similarity with the **Rath Yatra** at Puri further strengthens the theory that the deities here evolved from Buddhist symbols.

Sights

Jagannath Mandir This temple is the major attraction of Puri and, for Hindus, to remain here for three days and three nights is considered particularly rewarding. The temple attracts thousands on feast days and particularly during **Rath Yatra**. Non-Hindus are not allowed inside this temple. The fact that in the eyes of Jagannath (Lord of the Universe), there are no caste distinctions, has made Puri a very popular destination with the devout. The wooden figures of the three deities, **Jagannath**, **Balabhadra** and **Subhadra**, stand in the sanctuary garlanded and decorated by the priests. The extraordinary form that Jagannath takes is believed to be the unfinished work of the craftsman god Viswakarma, who in anger left this portrayal of Lord Vishnu incomplete. Small wooden replicas of the three images are available around the temple. There are vantage points for viewing the temple; for example, the roof of Raghunandan Library (closed Sundays) opposite the main entrance to the east or from the Jaga Balia Lodge nearby. A small donation is expected in return.

The temple is referred to by some as the white pagoda (the Konark Temple being the black pagoda) and was completed in the late 12th century. The original temple built in the Kalinga style consisted of the **deul** (sanctuary) and the **jagamohan** (audience hall) in front of it. It was only in the 14th or 15th century that the **nata mandir** (dance hall) and the **bhoga mandir** (hall of offerings) were added in alignment in the style of other Orissan temples. The *nata mandir* is unusual in that it has 16 pillars in four rows to support the large ceiling. The site is a virtual 200 m sq enclosed within an outer wall 6 m high. Within is another concentric wall which may have acted as fortification, inside which stands the tallest temple in Orissa, 65 m high, crowned by the wheel of Vishnu and a flag. On the higher ground in the enclosure are 30 small shrines, much in the Buddhist *stupa* tradition. Pilgrims are expected to visit at least three of these smaller temples before proceeding to the main temple. The outer wall has the main **Lion entrance**. On this east side there is an intricately carved

Rath Yatra

Traditionally the only occasion on which non-Hindus and Hindus of low caste can set eyes on one of India's most beloved deities, Lord Jagannath's 'car festival' brings Puri's streets to life in an extraordinary frenzy of colour and noise. Shaped like a temple sanctuary and brightly decorated, Lord Jagannath's car is the largest; 13 m tall, it has 16 wheels each 2 m in diameter. Loud gongs announce the boarding of the deities onto the chariots with the arrival of the Raja of Puri accompanied by bedecked elephants. With a golden broom and sprinkling holy water, the raja fulfils his role as the 'sweeper of the gods', symbolizing that all castes are equal before God. The procession is led by Balabhadra's car, followed by Subhadra's with Lord Jagannath's bringing up the rear, about 4000 people are needed to draw each chariot. The 3-km journey to Gundicha Ghar, Lord Jagannath's birthplace, may take as much as 24 hours.

During the week away, the deities are dressed in new garments daily and treated to special *podapitha* (rice cakes) before they return with a similar procession nine days later. The ceremonies and the fairs attract more than 500,000 devotees to Puri each year. In the past some were said to have thrown themselves under the massive wheels to die a blessed death. Certainly accidental deaths often happened – Westerners who first saw the spectacle in the 18th century mistook such instances for human sacrifices. Fortunately, stricter security these days means that fewer devotees are crushed to death beneath the heavy wheels. After the festival, the *raths* are broken up and bits are sold to pilgrims as relics.

Rath Yatra is due to fall on 13 July 2010 and 3 July 2011.

10-m-high free-standing stone pillar with a small figure of Aruna, the 'charioteer of the sun'. This once stood in front of the *nata mandira* at Konark, see page 237. To the left of the main entrance is the temple kitchen which daily prepares 56 varieties of food making up the *bhogas*, which are offered to the deities five times a day; the *mahaprasada* is then distributed from the Ananda Bazar to thousands. At festival times as many as 250,000 are served daily. The temple is supposed to be a self-sufficient community, served by 6000 priests and over 10,000 others who depend on it for their livelihood. The four sacred *tanks* in Puri provide thousands of pilgrims with the opportunity to take a holy dip. The **Narendra Tank** is particularly famous since the deities are taken there during the Snana Yatra.

Gundicha Ghar The terminus of the **Rath Yatra**, where the deities from the Jagannath Temple spend a week, is open to Hindus only. It shows the unique and ingenious way wrought-iron framework supported the laterite lintels of the massive temples.

The beach The long stretch of Puri's golden beach is shallow enough to walk out a long distance. Sunrise is particularly striking. The currents can be treacherous at times. Take great care and avoid swimming out too far. The best hotels have a stretch of fairly clean sand. The customary *nolia*, fisherman-turned-lifeguard in a distinctive conical hat, may be hired for either half or a full day, at a small price. The fishing villages along the coast east of CT Road are worth visiting particularly at sunrise or sunset when the fishing boats are coming and going, but be prepared to pick your way carefully.

Konark (Konarak) is one of the most vivid architectural treasures of Hindu India and is a World Heritage Site. It no longer stands as a landmark on the seashore since the land has risen and the sea is now 2 km away. Though much of it now lies in ruins, the porch is still magnificent. Be forewarned that the high volume of tourist traffic inevitably means that levels of 'hassle' increase proportionally.

Ins and outs → Phone code: 06758.

Getting there and around The 35-km drive from Puri (small toll charged) through attractive scenery passes a Turtle Research Centre off the Marine Drive after 10 km and through coastal villages with beautifully decorated houses including Chaitan, a stone carvers' hamlet. The energetic can cycle to Konark and bring the bike back on the bus. The site itself is very compact and can only be seen on foot. ➤ See Transport, page 245.

Tourist information Archaeological Survey and government-approved **guides** conduct tours of less than an hour. Unofficial guides will press their services (about Rs 60), but can be unreliable.

History

The Sun Temple was built by King Langula Narasimha Deva in the 13th century, although there may have been an older ninth-century temple on the same site. Built of *khondalite*, it is said to have taken 1200 masons 16 years to complete. It was only in 1901

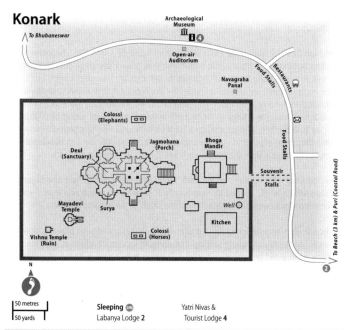

Konark

To Bhubaneswar

Archaeological Museum

Open-air Auditorium

Navagraha Panal

Food Stalls

Restaurants

Colossi (Elephants)

Deul (Sanctuary)

Jagmohana (Porch)

Bhoga Mandir

Food Stalls

Surya

Mayadevi Temple

Souvenir Stalls

Well

Kitchen

Vishnu Temple (Ruin)

Colossi (Horses)

To Beach (3 km) & Puri (Coastal Road)

N

50 metres
50 yards

Sleeping
Labanya Lodge **2**

Yatri Nivas &
Tourist Lodge **4**

that the first tentative steps were taken to reclaim the ruins of the temple from the encroaching sand. By that stage not only had the sanctuary or *deul* collapsed but a number of the statues had been removed, many in the 1830s by the Hindu Raja of Khurda, who wanted them to decorate temples he was building in his own fort, 100 km away, and at Puri. There has been substantial renovation, some of it protective and some replacing fallen stonework and sculptures.

The site

① *0600-1800, foreigners, Rs 250, video Rs 25. Official guides, Rs 100 per hr.*
The **Surya Temple** is set back 180 m from the road and is reached by a wide laterite path. The sanctuary has no deity for worship, so shoes may be worn. The exception is the small structure in the northeast corner of the site which houses the old *Navagraha* (nine planets) doorway arch, removed from the temple. The path to the temple is lined with beggars, as in major centres of Hindu pilgrimage.

Temple compound The temple presents its most imposing aspect from the steps of the *bhoga mandira* (refectory) at the eastern end of the complex, an isolated hall with pillars raised on a richly decorated platform guarded by a pair of stone lions; some believe this may have been a *nata mandira* (dancing hall). To its west is an open space leading to the porch (*jagamohana*) which rises magnificently to its original height of 39 m. The massive lower section of the original *deul* (sanctuary) was once over 60 m tall.

From the south wall you can see that the temple was built in the form of a war chariot. Twelve pairs of great wheels were sculpted on either side of the temple platform. In front of the eastern entrance a team of seven horses were shown straining to pull the chariot towards the dawn. In Hindu mythology the Sun god traverses the sky in a chariot drawn by seven horses, each representing a day of the week. The 12 pairs of wheels may have symbolized the 12 months of the year, and the eight spokes in each wheel, the divisions of the day into eight *prahars*. Each wheel also functions as a working sundial.

The sculptures The walls of the *bhoga mandir* are covered by carvings, but as Debala Mitra writes, they are of "mediocre quality". The platform gives an excellent view of the whole east front of the main temple with its porch doorway, and the large, remarkably vivid carvings on the terraces of its pyramidal roof, unique in Orissan architecture.

The sculptures draw for their subject from every aspect of life – dancers, musicians, figures from mythology, scenes of love and war, of court life, hunting, elephant fights. Since the temple was conceived to reflect a rounded picture of life and since *mithuna* or union in love is a part of that, a significant section of the sculpture is erotic art. Konark is unusual in that the carvings are found both on the outer and inner surfaces.

The porch roof is divided into three tiers, separated by terraces. Above the bottom and middle tiers is a series of musicians vividly captured in a variety of rhythmic poses playing drums, cymbals and *vinas*. On the bottom tier at either end of the central segments are dramatic sculptures of Siva as the awe-inspiring Bhairava. The top of the porch is crowned with the flattened spheres typical of Orissan temples.

The *upana* (plinth), a few centimetres high, runs right round the base of the temple, and is decorated with a variety of friezes – elephants (estimated at over 1700, and each different), including wild elephants being trapped, military marches, hunting, journeys, and a variety of other animals including crocodiles and a giraffe.

The platform is divided into the same five horizontal layers that characterize the temple itself. These are richly decorated with creepers and scrolls, and end with tiny motifs of *chaitya* windows. Along the lower mouldings are spaced miniature temple-like façades (*khakhara-mundis*) which contain niches. Set into these are figures, often of young women – caressing a bird, washing hair, playing the *vina*. The slabs between have a variety of carvings – some are erotic, some are *nagas* or *naginis*, each with a human head but with the tail of a snake.

The middle of the platform has three horizontal mouldings at about eye level. Above this, the *upper jangha* is richly sculpted, sometimes with religious scenes such as *Mahishasuramardini* (Durga as the goddess of destruction) and *Jagannatha*, enshrined in a temple. Other sculptures show royal courts or simple family scenes. Along the top of the platform is the veranda, consisting of two mouldings separated by a narrow recess. Though severely damaged, these are decorated with friezes.

From the platform you will see the intricately carved eight-spoked wheels, each shown with its axle, a decorated hub and an axle pin. Floral motifs, creepers and the widely shown *chaitya* windows cover the stonework. Medallions with gods such as Surya and Vishnu, erotic figures, nobles and animals all add life to the structure.

Sanctum sanctorum Although the *jagmohana* is now the dominant building of the complex, the scale of the sanctuary is still evident. The climb up the outer walls allows you to see at close quarters the remarkable chlorite statues of Surya, on the outer north, west and south walls. The large grey-green statues stand in sharp contrast with the surrounding yellowish-orange *khondalite* stone. Surya stands on a chariot drawn by his seven horses, lashed by Aruna, the charioteer, surrounded by two four-armed gods, a pot-bellied Brahma on the right and possibly Vishnu on the left. Below them are possibly four wives of Surya.

The sanctuary itself is currently inaccessible – a new stairway has been in the pipeline since at least 2003. The main feature inside is the chlorite platform at the western end of the 10-m-sq room intended for the presiding deity. This image from the pedestal was moved to the Jagannath Temple complex in Puri. The platform that remains is nonetheless outstanding; some carvings almost certainly show the king, the donor of the temple, accompanied by priests. The hollows on top of the platform's eastern edge resulted from the placing of pots over a long period.

The Colossi Originally each of the three staircases to the porch was guarded by a pair of colossi – rampant lions on top of a crouching elephant to the east, decorated elephants to the north, and war horses to the south. The last two pairs have been remounted a short distance from their original sites. The lions have been put in front of the eastern steps up to the *Bhoga mandira* near the entrance.

Archaeological Museum
ⓘ *Near Yatri Nivas, Sat-Thu 1000-1700, Rs 5.*
This museum has a small collection including many important pieces from the Sun Temple complex. Occasional lectures and films are shown. Archaeological Survey publications can be bought here.

Chilika Lake → *For listings, see pages 240-245. Colour map 3, A5.*

ⓘ *Boats from Barkul, Rambha and Satapada, 1 hr, around Rs 60. Nalabana birdwatching trip, Rs 120, 4 hrs. Book the night before, pay 0730 on the day and wait until the boat is full.*

Chilika is the largest brackish water lake in Asia (1100 sq km) stretching across the Khurdha, Puri and Ganjam districts, and forms an enormous lagoon as it is joined to the Bay of Bengal with a narrow mouth, a sandy ridge separating it from the sea.

The lake is the habitat of the rare Irrawaddy dolphin (particularly around Satapada), as well as being the winter home of migratory birds, some flying great distances from Iran, Central Asia and Siberia. During the winter months, from November to February, you can watch white-bellied sea eagles, ospreys, golden plovers, sandpipers, flamingos, shovellers, pelicans and gulls. The lake attracts fishermen who come in search of prawn, mackerel and crab. Some ornithologists blame the growth in prawn farming, as well as the increasing discharge from rivers, silting and salinity, for reduced bird numbers. The large **Nalabana Island** (Reed Island) sanctuary is at times below water. Human activity is also threatening the dolphins, currently numbering around 140, who meet their deaths in the propellers of motorized boats shockingly frequently.

The **Kalijai Temple** stands on one of the tiny rock islands. It gets very crowded at weekends. **Satapada**, on the other side of the lake, has a tourism complex.

Rushikulya

This is the only one of the three nesting sites in Orissa where it is currently possible and permitted to view the *arribada* (mass nesting) of olive ridley sea turtles. **Gahirmatha** in the north (at Bhitarkanika Wildlife Sanctuary) is a restricted area while the beach at Devi has become the 'lost arribada' with no turtles having appeared for several seasons. The beach at Rushikulya is found to the north of the river; the nearest place to stay is the government lodge in **Rambha** (20 km, book ahead), otherwise Gopalpur is conveniently close.

The phenomenon begins in November when the turtles, from as far away as South America and the Pacific, arrive in their *lakhs* to reproduce. Over the next few months they feed and mate (which takes place on the surface of the water, clearly visible) before coming ashore to nest around the middle of February. Peak nesting occurs at night, and it is an awesome sight to see the females traversing the beach in the early-morning mists. Six to eight weeks later, the eggs begin to hatch (around the first week of April) and the hatchlings make their way to the sea to take their chances with the fishing trawlers' nets and natural predators. Only about one in every 1000 will survive.

Gopalpur-on-Sea → *Phone code: 0680.*

Gopalpur was an ancient sea port from which early settlers from Kalinga sailed as far as Java, Bali and Sumatra. Then it was a port for the export of Aska sugar and 'coolie' labour to the Assam tea gardens. Later still it became a popular seaside resort for the British offering a beautiful sandy beach. Today, however, it has a rather faded feeling and appearance although tourists from West Bengal come in droves during the winter months. Sand dunes, groves of coconut and casuarinas separate the fringes of the small town from the beach, while the backwaters, creeks and lagoons give some variety. A red and white **lighthouse** ⓘ *1630-1730, Rs 10*, opens to visitors briefly each afternoon; there are good views but photography is not allowed. Gopalpur is a quiet retreat and a suitable base from which to visit Rushikulya, but sunbathing on the public beach is ill-advised and certainly not relaxing, making one or two days most people's limit.

For Sleeping and Eating price codes and other relevant information, see Essentials pages 34-38.

◉ Sleeping

Puri *p233, map p233*

Avoid arriving at your hotel by rickshaw as commission will be added to the room rate. Instead, get down nearby and walk. Most backpackers stay in hotels on **CT Rd** towards the fishing village at the eastern end. Domestic visitors prefer the seaside resorts along **Marine Drive**. Most check out at 0800 and several have a 2200 curfew. Check before staying out late. Some hotels will arrange pickup from the station.

AL Hans Coco Palms, Swargdwar, off New Marine Dr, T06752-230038, www.hanshotels.com. 40 good sea-facing a/c rooms with balconies/terraces, palm-filled restaurant, pleasant garden, good pool, friendly staff, knowledgeable manager, book ahead in season. Recommended.

AL Mayfair Beach Resort, CT Rd, T06752-227800, mayfair1@sancharnet.in. Very well run, 34 well-furnished a/c cottages and rooms, some with sea view, rampant tropical garden, good pool (residents only), clean section of beach, decent restaurants, friendly staff. Recommended.

A-C Chanakya BNR, CT Rd, T06752-222063, chanakyabnrpuri@hotmail.com. This slice of history is being extensively refurbished, fortunately in an appropriately old-world style. Spacious a/c rooms have dark wood furniture, cream trimmings and a colonial feel, with the bonus of trendy bathrooms. Best on the 1st floor with fabulous wide verandas overlooking sea, siestas encouraged (quiet hours 1400-1600), claim to serve the best continental food, billiards, croquet, and the swimming pool/health club/spa are due for completion end-Aug 2009.

C-E Panthanivas (OTDC), CT Rd, T06752-222740, www.panthanivas.com. 48 rooms including 3 **B** suites, a few a/c, rooms in old

block run down, better in newer block, tour booking, pleasant garden with beach access.

D-E Puri, Marine Parade, T06752-222114, www.purihotel.in. Institutional hotel on seafront that is an institution in itself for Bengali family holidaymakers, thus quieter during the week. Wide choice (including 9- and 10-bed rooms), clean, some a/c, vegetarian restaurant. In the 'Indian' part of Puri, killer views from the top floors. 24-hr checkout.

D-E Samudra, CT Rd, T06752-222705, hsamudra@yahoo.co.in. 52 decent clean rooms, all with breezy sea-facing balconies, better at front on higher floors with sea view, TV, restaurant, friendly staff.

D-E Shankar International, CT Rd, T06752-222696. Indian-style hotel set around lawn, 30 rooms with beach views, plus 6 cottages, small but clean, restaurant.

E Gandhara, CT Rd, T06752-224117, www.hotelgandhara.com. Clean, comfortable rooms (some a/c) amid lovely gardens, quiet at the back, are good value and dorms are cheap. Friendly staff and impeccable service, but stringent security, restaurant, popular. Free pickup from the bus or railway station.

E-F Arya Palace, CT Rd, T06752-232688, neeraj21jain@indiatimes.com. 32 rooms (some a/c) in new hotel, clean and airy, hot bath, TV, generous discounts when quiet.

E-F Z, CT Rd, T06752-222554, www.zhotel india.com. 12 spacious rooms have minimal furniture, some with clean shared bath. 2 rooms have wonderful balconies, but if you don't manage to reserve one of these it's not really worth the price. The dorms are great value though at Rs 100, and very clean. In an old mansion, with a huge terrace and lots of sociable areas (movie/games room), solar-powered, popular.

E-G Lotus, CT Rd, T06752-223852. Quite clean, 9 simple rooms (mostly **G**), good restaurant, **Harry's Café**.

E-G Love & Life, CT Rd, T06752-224433, loveandlife@hotmail.com. Good-value rooms in 3-storey, airy building but much better are the cottages at rear, theoretical hot water, nets, dorm (Rs 50), the eccentric staff soon warm up. The kind of place people stay for a while.

F Baywatch Residency, CT Rd, T06752-226133. Close to the beach but out of 'the scene', most rooms have an extra seating area and TV. Ones at the front are preferable, ask for clean linen. Compared to others nearby, you get much more for your money.

F Holiday House, CT Rd, T06752-223782, hhflourish@yahoo.co.in. The blank outside hides reasonable, good-sized rooms, better sea-facing (prices rise with altitude!), not a backpackers' hangout, restaurant has Orissan food and more.

F-G Derby, CT Rd, T06752-223961. Deservedly popular, 10 rooms with squat toilets, clean sheets and towels on request. Rooms onto the pretty garden are a bit pricier but better furnished and larger, the adjacent restaurant is good and the rooftops are relaxing.

F-G Sun Row Cottage, CT Rd, T06752-223259, chitaranjan@hotmail.com. Set around small, colourful garden, 10 simple rooms in double cottages have little terraces, excellent restaurant, long-stay discounts. A bargain.

G Kasi's Castle, CT Rd, T06752-224522. Only 7 spotless rooms (book ahead) with attached bath in friendly family house, good choice but not much light and lacking spaces to relax.

G Pink House, CT Rd, T06752-222253. 15 basic rooms, some 3-5 bedded, only 1 with inside bath (hot buckets available). The only guesthouse directly on beach, very friendly, popular with long-stayers, beach shack restaurant will provide service to the room. Recommended.

G Santana, CT Rd, at the end of the fishing village, T06752-223491. Simple rooms in friendly, secure hotel, popular with Japanese visitors.

G Youth Hostel, CT Rd, T06752-222424. Separate, though somewhat dishevelled male and female dorms, some 2-3 bedded, camping, good Indian meals.

Konark *p236, map p236*

C-F Yatri Nivas and **Tourist Lodge** (OTDC), T06758-236820. Good-value, clean rooms with nets, some 4-bedded, some a/c with geyser and TV, pleasant gardens, restaurant, free cultural programme on weekend evenings during season. Check-out 1200.

G Labanya Lodge, away from temple, T06758-236824, labanyalodge1@rediffmail.com. Most popular of the budget lodges. 13 musty rooms, mostly with attached bath, cycle hire, travel.

Chilika Lake *p239*

To stay in an attractive campsite by the lake, contact **Grass Routes** (see page 244).

C-E Panthanivas (OTDC), 1 km from road end, Barkul, T06756-220488, www.panthanivas.com. 35 small recently renovated rooms in a lovely lakeside setting, some a/c, bar, restaurant, tourist office, boating complex, 0800 checkout, busy during weekends and holidays.

C-G Panthanivas (OTDC), Rambha, T06810-278346, www.panthanivas.com. 18 rooms or cottages, some a/c, dorm beds Rs 150, nice gardens, half rate for day visitors 0900-1700. Checkout 1200.

D-F Yatri Nivas, Satapada, on the north side of the lake, closest to Puri, T06752-262077. Attractive location, decent rooms. 1st floor rooms have balconies and the best views. Checkout 0900.

G Shree Khrishna Lodge, Barkul (500 m from **Panthanivas**), T06756-221195. Simple, clean rooms, some with bath.

Gopalpur-on-Sea *p239*

Discounts of 30% can often be negotiated, but during high season (Oct-Dec, and 20-30 Jan) hotels are busy with Bengali tourists.

A Swosti Palm Resort, southern end of the beach close to the lighthouse, T0680-224 2455, palmresort@swosti.com. Renovated with 29 decent rooms around a small garden; the restaurant is a bit gloomy and there's no pool but the bar and atmosphere are relaxing. The most luxurious choice in Gopalpur.

D Song of the Sea, next to lighthouse, T0680-224 2347. Clean, light and airy rooms in family-run hotel, peaceful location, simple restaurant. The best rooms are at the front on 1st floor with sea view, pleasant though pricey.

D-E Sea Pearl, beachfront, T0680-224 2556. Cheaper non-a/c rooms are fairly basic (Rs 600) but some are sea facing (others face the building next door), it's better on the upper levels. All have baths and TV. Checkout 0900.

E-F Green Park, one block back from the beach, T0680-224 2016, greenpark016@ yahoo.com. 17 clean rooms (some a/c), simple Indian-style hotel, best with sea view, 24-hr check out. No restaurant or bar.

E-F Hotel Kalinga, behind *Sea Pearl*, T0680-224 2067. Spotless rooms in a very well-maintained family-run hotel, some with TV, clean bath (hot bucket) and linen, simple but excellent food, nice terraces overlooking sea (though no private balconies). Posters adorn the highly colourful walls. Checkout 0900.

F Plaza Millennium, at the north end of the beach, T0680-224 2647, T(0)9853-921325. Large breezy rooms have appalling murals and curtains, but clean bathrooms; there's a good 1st-floor option with a huge sea-facing balcony (Rs 400) that can sleep 4. Checkout 0900.

F Sea Side Breeze, T0680-224 2075. Right on the beach, 14 clean freshly painted rooms, 12 of which face the sea. Food on order and the bathrooms are decent (hot bucket), but some of the world's lumpiest pillows. Staff are accommodating without being ingratiating, it's ideal for backpackers.

F-G Heaven Spot, Rewu St, T0680-224 3274. 5 small, basic but clean rooms with attached bath, away from beach, serves as a base.

G Rosalin, beachfront, T0680-224 2367. Very basic rooms with attached bath around a scrubby littered garden. Strictly for those on a tight budget, it's friendly but prepare for mosquitoes. **Shining Dew** restaurant next door is hot and boxy.

❼ Eating

Puri *p233, map p233*
Puri's signature dish is the *mahaprasad* of rice, dahl, vegetables and sweet prepared by 400 cooks at the Jagannath Temple. It can be bought at the Anand Bazar in the temple complex, or you can in theory have it delivered to your hotel. There is an abundance of fresh fish; ensure all is fresh and thoroughly cooked. Hotels expect advance notice from non-residents.

Fresh cheap local fish is grilled at numerous stalls along Marine Drive every evening, but the proximity of the burning ghats might be off-putting.

❬❬ Chung Wah, Hotel Lee Garden, VIP Rd. Very good Chinese in a bustling environment, efficient and highly recommended, cooling a/c.

❬❬-❬ Peace, CT Rd. Friendly garden café, a pleasant place to relax. Outdoor seating is usually packed with Westerners, the muesli fruit curd is the biggest you'll ever see and this alone attracts a keen following. Interesting fish dishes and Japanese pretenders.

❬❬-❬ Wild Grass, VIP Rd, T06752-229293. Extremely pleasant open-air restaurant with rustic theme, lots of plants and wicker-work to relax among. Some Orissan specialities, the tomato *khata*, *tandoori* prawn and veg *jaikema* are particularly good. Friendly and not to be missed.

❬❬-❬ Xanadu Garden, CT Rd, T06752-227897. The vast breakfast menu covers any requirement, and for other times there's everything from burgers to *gado-gado*. Pretty at night with fairy lights and the obligatory Orissan mirrored lampshades, sand beneath your feet and painted palm trunks. Recommended for fish.

❬ Harry's Café, CT Rd. Pure vegetarian (no onion or garlic) South Indian. Good *thalis* and snacks.

Honey Bee Bakery and Pizzeria, CT Rd, T06752-320479. Best for fresh bread, muffins and great coffee in a clean and chilled environment, no hint of staff resting on their laurels.

Konark *p236, map p236*
There are plenty of places serving *thalis* and snacks.
Sun Temple Hotel. Good choice among the many basic eating places lining the road opposite the temple entrance. Friendly service, everything cooked fresh, and the breakfast *parathas* are fantastic.

Gopalpur-on-Sea *p239*
Super-cheap stalls opposite **Sea Shell** serve chow mein and *parathas*.
Krishna, by **Sea Pearl Hotel** (see Sleeping). Opens at 0800, last food orders at 2200. Like much of Gopalpur, **Krishna** is painted Sprite-green. Clean and friendly with just a couple of tables, they do cheap Indian meals, Western breakfasts, and good fish, prawn and calamari.
Naz restaurant, opposite **Krishna**. Similar in appearance and even cheaper, but with less variety.
Sea Shell, beachfront. Umbrellas and stiff breezes enhance its air of a decaying British seaside snack stall, but the Chinese and Indian meals are reasonable and can be enjoyed with a beer.

⊕ Entertainment

Puri *p233, map p233*
Top hotels and resorts have bars. Classical *Odissi* dance, folk dances and drama which are always performed for festivals are also staged from time to time and are worth seeking out.

⊛ Festivals and events

Puri *p233, map p233*
Mid-Apr 21-day **Chandan Yatra** coincides with the **Hindu New Year** when images of Jagannath, his brother and sister are taken out in boats on the Narendra Tank. *Chandan* is the sandal paste used to anoint the deities. **Snana Yatra**, which follows, marks the ritual bathing of the deities on a special barge. For 15 days the gods are kept out of sight, when worshippers may only pray before *pattachitras* (paintings). Every few years new images of the deities are carved from specially selected trees and the old ones are secretly buried by the temple priests.
Jun Rath Yatra, see box, page 235.
Nov Beach Festival, a week of cultural shows, crafts and food stalls.

Konark *p236, map p236*
Feb Honouring the Sun god; pilgrims flock here from evening to sunrise.
19-21 Feb A dance festival is run by a private organization headed by Guru Ganga Dharpradhan.
1-5 Dec Classical dance festival at the open-air auditorium opposite Yatri Nivas.

○ Shopping

Puri *p233, map p233*
Visit the vast **bazar** around the Jagannath Temple, along Bada Danda and Swargadwara, but you have to bargain. **Pathuria Sahi** is the stone carvers' quarter and **Raghurajpur** (12 km) produces *pattachitras* and etchings on palm leaf, see page 219.

Books
Loknath, CT Rd. Second-hand books or sale/exchange, library (Rs 7 per day), postcards.

Handicrafts

Stone carvings, papier-mâché masks, painted wood figures, paintings, appliqué and hornwork all make good buys.
Akbar, CT Rd. Cheap painted cards.
Odissi, Dolamandap Sahi. Handlooms.
Sudarshan, Station Rd. Stone carving, where you can also watch masons at work carving out images of deities.
Sun Crafts, Tinikonia Bagicha.
Utkalika and **Crafts Complex**, Mochi Sahi Sq.
Weavers' Co-op Society, Grand Rd.
For handlooms.

▲ Activities and tours

Puri *p233, map p233*

The tourist office has a list of government-approved tour companies. Almost every hotel on CT Rd has a travel office, but for 'tribal tours' it's worth paying more to go with a conscientious agency.
Grass Routes, CT Rd, T(0)9437-029698/ T(0)9437-022663, www.grassroutes journeys.com. Offers a fascinating selection of outings in and around Puri, Claire and her husband are keenly promoting responsible tourism. Cooking classes go via the market to learning Orissan dishes in a family home, or excursions further afield visit tribal areas. Trips to Chilika Lake need 24-hrs' notice so the camping spot can be set up. Not cheap, but recommended.
Heritage Tours, Mayfair Beach Resort, T06752-223656. Expensive yet moral enterprise, offering a variety of tours. A good benchmark for comparing prices, but more importantly – 'tribal tourism' is taken seriously. Well-established and friendly.
OTDC, T06752-223526, full-day tours (except Mon, entry fees extra) to Konark, Dhauli, Bhubaneswar, Khandagiri, Udayagiri and Nandankanan Zoo. It is a long day, 0630-1830, Rs 170. Chilika Lake (Satapada), 0730-1730, Rs 130. Half-day tours also available.
Tanuja Tribe Tour, Tanuja Complex, CT Rd, T06752-220717, tanujatribetour@yahoo.com.

Reputable agency with pleasant guides, not as pricey as some.

Gopalpur-on-Sea *p239*

Sagar Tours & Travels, Beach Rd, T0680-224 2963, T(0)9437-127548. Provides cheap car and driver hire at Rs 500 per day, and can sort out train/bus tickets.

⊖ Transport

Puri *p233, map p233*
Air

Bhubaneswar, 60 km, is the nearest airport (see page 231). Prepaid taxi to Puri from the airport Rs 600, 1-1½ hrs.

Bicycle and motorcycle

Hiring a bike or a motorbike is a good option for exploring the coast. There are several outlets on CT Rd. Cycles costs around Rs 30 per day. Motorbikes around Rs 200-250 per day, moped Rs 120-150.

Bus

Enquiries, T06752-224461. The huge, open bus stand on Grand Rd runs regular buses to **Bhubaneswar** and **Konark**. Minibuses are faster. There are also services to **Cuttack**, **Visakhapatnam** and **Kolkata**.

Rickshaw

Cycle-rickshaws available all over town. From the bus stand to CT Rd costs Rs 25; from the railway station Rs 15. To avoid commission being added to room price, ask to be dropped off at the **BNR Hotel** and walk along CT Rd to your hotel.

Taxi

Tourist taxis from larger hotels, CT Rd agencies, and taxi stand, T06752-222161; Rs 700 per 8 hrs or 80 km. To **Bhubaneswar** around Rs 600.

Train

Enquiry, T131. **Kolkata** (**H**): *Jagannath Exp 8410*, 2230, 10 hrs; *Puri Howrah Exp 2838*, 2005,

9 hrs. **New Delhi**: *Purushottam Exp 2801*, 2145, 32½ hrs; *Utkal Exp 8477*, 2125, 41 hrs. **Guwahati (H)**: *Guwahati Exp 5639*, 1410 (Sat only), 32 hrs via **New Jalpaiguri**, 24 hrs.

Konark *p236, map p236*
Bus
OTDC 'luxury' coach or ordinary, very crowded bus from **Puri** (1½ hrs) and **Bhubaneswar** (up to 3 hrs).

Taxi
Prepaid taxi from Bhubaneswar airport costs Rs 600.

Chilika Lake *p239*
Chilika Lake is easiest to reach by road (NH5) from Barkul, 6 km south of Balugaon or Rambha at the south end of the lake.

Bus
Buses from **Bhubaneswar** and **Berhampur**. Satapada at the northern end can only be reached via **Puri**.

Ferry
OTDC motor launches are available from **Barkul**, **Rambha** and **Satapada** although during the week it may not be cost effective. Dolphin-watching is the main focus of boats from Satapada. Private country boats are also available at Barkul and Rambha.

Train
Slow passenger trains on the Chennai–Kolkata line stop at **Balugaon**, **Chilika**, **Khallikote** and **Rambha**.

Gopalpur-on-Sea *p239*
Bus
There are regular private buses from the New Bus Stand, **Berhampur** (Rs 6, 30 min).

❶ Directory

Puri *p233, map p233*
Banks Allahabad Bank, Temple Rd is best for changing cash. Other exchanges on CT Rd. Several ATMs on Grand Rd, CT Rd and at the railway station. **Internet** Nanako, near Sun Row Cottage on CT Rd. **Medical services** District HQ Hospital, T06752-222062. **TB Hospital**, Red Cross Rd, T06752-222094. **Post** GPO on Kutchery Rd. PCOs and internet on CT Rd.

Konark *p236, map p236*
Post Sub Post Office, near Panthanivas.

Chilika Lake *p239*
There is a post office, a government dispensary and a tourist office at Barkul, T06756-220855.

The Northeast

It is possible to visit several places of historic and religious interest in the north of Orissa in three to seven days, as well as to see outstandingly beautiful scenery and the Similipal National Park. Some of the accommodation is excellent value (particularly at Chandipur), though in places it is very basic. ▸ *For listings, see pages 251-253.*

Cuttack → *For listings, see pages 251-253. Colour map 3, A6. Phone code: 0671. Population: 535,100.*

Cuttack occupies an important strategic position in relation to the network of canals in the region. Situated at the head of the Mahanadi delta and surrounded by the great river and its tributary the Kathjuri, the town is almost an island, its crowded streets and bazars clustered up towards its western end. **Orissa Tourism** ① *Arunodaya Market Building, Link Rd, T0671-231 2225*, and **Railway Station Counter** ① *T0671-261 0507*, both have helpful staff.

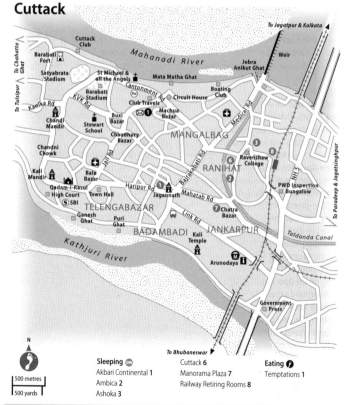

Cuttack

N

500 metres
500 yards

Sleeping	Cuttack 6	Eating
Akbari Continental 1	Manorama Plaza 7	Temptations 1
Ambica 2	Railway Retiring Rooms 8	
Ashoka 3		

Cuttack is one of Orissa's oldest cities and its medieval capital. It was founded by Nrupat Kesari (ruled 920-935). It remained the administrative centre until the end of the British Raj and was the state capital until 1956. The ancient **stone embankment** to the south was built in the 11th century by the Kesari ruler to protect the town from flooding by the Kathjuri River. It still stands as a reminder of the engineering skills practised 900 years ago. The **Qadam-i-Rasul** (Kadam Rasul) in the centre of the old city, visited as a shrine by both Muslims and Hindus, has three 18th-century mosques with beautiful domes and a music gallery. The shrines contain relics of the Prophet Mohammad; the prophet's footprint is carved on a circular stone. The famous silver filigree shops are in Balu Bazar.

To the northwest the blue granite 13th-century **Barabati Fort** is being excavated by the Archaeological Survey. Its wide moat and gateway remain but the nine-storeyed palace has disappeared. Probably built by a Ganga ruler, it was in Marhatta hands when it was taken by the British in 1803. Close to the fort is the vast **Barabati Stadium** where major sporting and cultural events are held. The **Church of St Michael and all the Angels** (CNI) by the river, typical of Raj-style church buildings, is worth a visit.

Ratnagiri, Udayagiri and Lalitgiri → *For listings, see pages 251-253. Colour map 3, A6.*

The beautiful hills and rice-growing lands are home to remarkable Buddhist remains of the Vajrayana sect, set in an idyllic landscape surrounded by green fields. The excavations at the three sites have revealed Buddhist *stupas*, monasteries, sculptures and Buddha images.

Ins and outs

Getting there and around The sites can all be visited in a day from Cuttack or Bhubaneswar by car. If you go by bus you will need to stay overnight (there is a government tourist lodge). Rickshaws can be hired at Patharajpur. ▸▸ *See Transport, page 253.*

Tourist information Entry to each site costs US$2 for foreigners.

Ratnagiri → *70 km from Cuttack, 115 km from Bhubaneswar.*

ⓘ *Museums open Sat-Thu 1000-1700.*

Ratnagiri, the site of the 'Jewel Hill', on the bank of River Keluo, has produced the best finds. The extensive remains show excellent sculptural skill combining different coloured stones, from blue-green chlorite to the purple-red garnets encrusted in brownish silver khondalite. The finds include three monasteries (two quadrangular), eight temples and several *stupas* believed to date from the seventh century. The largest monastery (No 1) is 55 m sq with a surrounding veranda with 60 pillars built around a courtyard entered through a carved gateway. At one end a shrine has a khondalite Buddha image and remnants of about 24 cells for monks which were built of brick but had stone door frames. Look for the intricate carving on the doorway of the back porch wall: a dancer stamping her feet; a royal lady with her arm around a maid; a woman meditating. The seventh-century University of Pushpagiri may have flourished here; Hiuen Tsang, the Chinese traveller, after his visit in AD 639 described it as one of Orissa's two Buddhist centres of learning. Four galleries display fine sculptural figures dating from the ninth to the 10th centuries, terracotta and ivory objects, inscribed copper plates and miniature bronzes produced by the lost-wax process.

Udayagiri → *10 km south of Ratnagiri.*

Excavations by the Archaeological Department have unearthed better preserved carvings including the door jambs to the sanctum. The monastery, within a large compound, has

Turtles in peril

It is estimated that the coast of Orissa attracts 300,000-800,000 olive ridley turtles (*Lepidochelys olivacea*) to its beaches each year to lay their eggs. Sea turtles are believed to return to nest where they hatched so the mysterious cycle continues. They arrive at night, for a fortnight around the full moon from November to May, with a spectacular *arribadas* (from the Portuguese, meaning 'the coming') in February, when record numbers find their way from the Indian Ocean or from Australia, via the Pacific. They lay their eggs in nests excavated in the sand, a safe distance above the waterline and shed a salty 'tear' afterwards. The eggs hatch about two months later. Incubation temperature deciding the sex; clutches are male around 24-26°C and female around 30-32°C, mixed when temperatures are in between.

The 10-km stretch of Gahirmatha beach attracts the vastest numbers, but Rushikulya further south is the only place where it is permitted to observe this natural phenomenon. The nesting beach at Paradeep is long gone, a consequence of the development of Damra Port with its inevitable ship canals and bright lights that disorientate the juvenile turtles. But the biggest threat is the nets of the trawler boats, which sweep up anything in their path. Legislation prohibiting trawlers from near-shore waters is almost never implemented, and hundreds of thousands of turtles have met their deaths in the last 10 years. Organizations working to improve the situation include www.greenpeace india.org and www.atree.org.

18 cells with a veranda arranged around a courtyard. The 3-m Lokesvar Buddha image here has an eighth-century inscription on it. Further up the hill, fragments of sculpture have been excavated among the ruins.

Lalitgiri

The site about 3 km south of Bandareswar village was first excavated in 1985. Large architectural remains including a 20-m-high apsidal temple have been found together with sculptures and decorated door jambs. A stone platform with inscriptions dates this site closer to the second century although Kushana Brahmi inscriptions on an underlying brick *stupa* suggest Buddhist occupation around the first century BC. Three caskets were also found, two of which contained stone, silver and gold caskets with preserved relics inside. The caretaker will open the small museum. There is a stone-carvers' village at the base of Lalitgiri which traces its connections back to ancient times and produces excellent sculpture.

The coast → *For listings, see pages 251-253.*

Paradeep → *Colour map 3, A6. 94 km from Cuttack on the NH5A.*
Paradeep is a port at the mouth of the Mahanadi River. Some 2500 years ago Orissan sailors regularly set sail for Indonesia and mainland Southeast Asia from this point. The harbour is base to 1600 colourfully painted fishing trawlers, which are an amazing sight but it is largely these that are affecting the olive ridley turtles so adversely (see box, above). Visitors today find they can't escape industrial pollution here – "a layer of black dust settles on every surface in no time". There are a few overnight options and regular buses arrive from Cuttack and Bhubaneswar, should you decide to make the unusual choice of a detour to Paradeep.

Bhitarkanika Wildlife Sanctuary → *Colour map 3, A6.*

ⓘ *55 km from Bhadrak on NH5. Mail/express trains stop at Bhadrak. Foreigners Rs 1000 per day, plus boat transport of around Rs 2000. Entry is easiest from Chandbali, entry permits from the Assistant Conservator of Forests, T06786-220372, 0600-1800, though it is also possible from Rajnagar or Gupti. Tour operators in Puri or Bhubaneswar can make all the arrangements but need prior notice – otherwise try for a permit on the day with a local agent (try Sanjog Travels, Chandbali, T06786-220495). Best time to visit: Nov-Feb.*

Virtually every species of mangrove is found in the forests in the Bhitarkanika Sanctuary, but their swamps are better known for estuarine crocodiles, water monitors, cobras and the endangered olive ridley sea turtles (see box, page 248). The 10-km stretch of beach at **Gahirmatha** is a protected marine sanctuary that attracts thousands of nesting turtles each year, but for tourists it's off-limits due to the nearby missile-testing site on the **Wheeler Islands**. Onshore wildlife includes rhesus monkeys, wild boar and deer, plus many species of migratory and resident birds (storks, herons, kingfisher, ducks, eagles and more).

The creeks and waterways are negotiated by motorboat, with stop-offs at **Dangamar Island** to view immense estuarine crocodiles and **Bagagahana Island** to see the multitude of nesting storks. In any case, expect to see the various beasts in their natural environment on mud-banks and in trees when navigating the sanctuary. Tours usually finish up with a visit to an almost-too picture-perfect typical Orissan village. There is accommodation in the forest rest houses or a couple of comfortable lodges nearby (see Sleeping, page 251). Like all Orissa's national parks, Bhitarkanika is prohibitively expensive for many travellers but most visitors leave feeling satisfied with the wildlife sightings and overall experience.

Baleshwar → *Colour map 3, A6.*

Northeast from Bhubaneswar, this medieval maritime trading port was first established by the British in 1642 with subsequent competition from the French who called it *Farasidinga* and the Dutch *Dinamardinga*. Ruins of **Dutch tombs** can still be seen and traces of **canals**, up which ocean-going ships were hauled inland. The **Khirachora Gopinath Temple** is at Remuna (9 km) and **Panchalingesvar Temple**, 30 km away. **Orissa Tourism** ⓘ *Panthanivas Hotel, Police Line, T06782-262048.*

Chandipur → *Colour map 3, A6.*

On the coast 16 km from Balashwar, Chandipur has one of Orissa's finest beaches. The tide recedes 5 km daily and the dunes and casuarina groves make it particularly attractive and a pleasant, quiet stopping place. When the tide is in scores of fisherfolk trawl for small fish along the coast. About 3 km north of the **Panthanivas Hotel** is the fishing harbour at **Balarama Gadi** where fresh fish can be bought daily. The occasional explosions that can be heard come from the missile testing site nearby, which is on the road to Baleshwar.

Mayurbhanj District → *For listings, see pages 251-253.*

The district is thickly forested with hills, waterfalls and streams and is home to abundant wildlife, which can best be seen at Similipal National Park. There are prehistoric sites at Kuchai and Kuliana. The historic sites are Khiching, Baripada and Haripur, where the Bhanja rulers have left their mark. The area produces excellent tussar silk, carvings in multi-coloured translucent serpentine stone (from Khiching) and tribal metal casting of toys and cult images. The tribal people have enriched the culture of the district particularly with their traditional dances. Accommodation throughout the district is very basic.

Haripur → *16 km southeast of Baripada.*

Haripur was founded by Maharaja Harihar in 1400 as the capital of the Bhanja Dynasty. A later king built the magnificent **Rasikaraya Temple** which, though now in ruins, is a unique example of a brick-built Orissan temple. The area is still fascinating as it has several more historic buildings nearby. The ruins of Ranihamsapur, the inner apartment of the queen, is to the north of the courtyard while the remains of the Durbar Hall with its beautiful sculptured stone columns and arches is to the east. The brick **Radhamohan Temple** and 14th-century **Jagannath Temple** are interesting architecturally although the deities were moved and are now worshipped nearby in **Pratapapur**.

Baripada → *Colour map 3, A6.*

The district headquarters has a **museum** ⓘ *Tue-Sun 0700-1200 summer, 1000-1700 winter, closed holidays*, to the east of town with a small collection of stone sculpture, coins and inscriptions. **Chhau dance festival**, known as **Chaitra Parba**, is held in mid-April; the **Rath Yatra** in July is unique because the chariot carrying *Subhadra* is drawn by women. **Tourist office** ⓘ *Baghra Rd, near the bus stand, T06792-252710*. **Tiger Reserve Office** ⓘ *Bhanjpur (2 km), T06792-252593, simitig@dte.vsnl.net.in.*

Similipal National Park → *Colour map 3, A6.*

ⓘ *320 km from Bhubaneswar, entry for day visitors 0600-1200; those with reservations 0600-1400. All must leave before sunset. Foreigners Rs 1000 per day, plus vehicle and trekking charge; camera Rs 100 for 3 days, video camera Rs 10,000 per day. Malaria prophylaxis is strongly recommended. Entry is from Pithabata, near Baripada (NH5), or Jashipur (NH6). Entry permits from the Range Officer, Pithabata Check Gate or the Assistant Conservator of Forests, Khairi, Jashipur, T06797-232474. Some tour operators in Bhubaneswar can make all the arrangements (eg Discover Tours) but need 4 weeks' notice – otherwise try for a permit on the day with a local agent (eg Ambika in Baripada). Best time to visit: Nov to Feb (park open 1 Nov-15 Jun); May to Jun can be very hot. Temperature, 45-50°C. Rainfall, 2000 mm.*

Similipal is Orissa's principal wildlife sanctuary covering 2750 sq km at the heart of which is one of the country's earliest tiger reserves. The area has majestic sal forests interspersed with rosewood and flowering trees, as well as broad expanses of grassland, waterfalls, gorges and river valleys. The landscape is actually the main draw these days, as the core area to which visitors are permitted access is very small and consequently much trampled. Sightings of big beasts are rare, and many recent visitors have been disappointed.

The 42 species of animals include tiger (101), elephant (565), leopard (119), wolf, chital, sambar, deer, gaur and flying squirrel. There are over 230 species of birds including mynahs, parakeet and peacocks. Visitors are allowed to go to the waterfalls, the **Chahala woodland** and **Nawana Valley**, in the core area, on the dedicated forest road. The **Barehipani waterfall**, with a drop of 400 m, and the **Joranda Falls**, 150 m, are both very impressive as are the **Bachhurichara grassland** where you might see a herd of elephants and the 1158 m peak of Meghasani. However, most of the larger wildlife prefer to remain further inside the core area which does not allow visitors.

Open jeeps or Tata *sumos* (more comfortable, though enclosed) are the usual choice of vehicle inside the park (Rs 1200-1500 for up to five passengers). Jeep hire can be arranged through the Forest Office in Jashipur, **Baripada Tourist Office**, or **Ambika** in Baripada (see Sleeping, page 251) which can also arrange accommodation. Logging disturbance and dense vegetation make viewing difficult and is further hindered by visitors who ignore the signs asking for silence, and there is an increasing problem of litter in the park.

Khiching → *Colour map 3, A6. 20 km west of Joshipur along the NH6.*

The capital of the Bhanja rulers in the 10th to the 11th century, a visit to Khiching can be combined with an excursion to Similipal from Chandipur. The local deity Kichakesvari, once the family goddess of the Mayurbhanj royal family, has a temple built entirely of chlorite slabs. The reconstructed 20th-century temple, which has fine carvings, is believed to have used the traditional temple building skills which date back to the eighth century. Nearby there are a number of other temples built in the Kalinga style, some of which are still in use.

◉ The Northeast listings

For Sleeping and Eating price codes and other relevant information, see Essentials pages 34-38.

⊕ Sleeping

Cuttack *p246, map p246*

C Akbari Continental, Haripur Rd, Dolmundai, T0671-242 3251. 60 rooms, central a/c, hot bath with tubs, balconies view of garden obscured by ugly extension, inefficient reception, all a bit tatty for the price.
D-F Manorama Plaza, Mahatab Rd, T0671-233 1681. Most of the 54 clean and reasonable, though small, rooms have a/c. Restaurant, travel desk, bizarre birdsong doorbells.
E-F Ashoka, Ice Factory Rd, College Sq, T0671-264 7509. 50 clean rooms, half a/c with hot bath, chaotic reception but rooms OK once allocated. Restaurant, taxi service.
E-G Ambica, Pilgrim Rd, College Sq, T0671-261 0137, hotelambica@yahoo.com. Range of rooms from a/c to cheap singles with shared bath, clean and simple, friendly manager, vegetarian restaurant, close to railway. Breakfast and bed-tea included.
G Cuttack, College Rd, T0671-261 0766. Basic, but serviceable, some with bath.
G Railway Retiring Rooms. 4 rooms (1 a/c), cheap dorm.

Bhitarkanika Wildlife Sanctuary *p249*

D-F Aranyanivas, Chandbali, T06786-220397, www.visitorissa.org. Handy location for arranging visits to the sanctuary, this small and pleasant lodge (7 rooms) has garden surrounds and a decent cheap restaurant.
F-G Forest Lodges, Ekakula, Gupti and Dangamala. Reserve and pay in advance

through the Divisional Forest Officer in Rajnagar, T06729-272460. Bring your own food supplies.

Baleshwar *p249*

C-E Torrento, Januganj, 4 km from centre near NH5, T06782-263481. 28 rooms, some a/c, good restaurant, exchange, health club.
E-G Swarnachuda, Sahadev Khunta (close to bus stand), T06782-262657. Wide range of rooms with bath, some a/c, restaurant/bar.
G Railway Retiring Rooms. A/c and non a/c rooms, dorm (Rs 30).

Chandipur *p249*

Some hotels are reluctant to accept foreigners.
D-F Panthanivas (OTDC), on beach, T06782-270051, www.panthanivas.com. 41 rooms, some a/c and **C** suites, dorm, nets, internet, decent food, helpful staff, newer block better, ample mosquitoes and cockroaches in old block nearer beach. Tours including Similipal (minimum 10 people). Checkout 0800.
E-G Chandipur, T06782-270030. Small, simple rooms with attached bath, clean linen, nets.

Baripada *p250*

E-G Sibapriya, Traffic Sq, T06792-255138. 20 rooms, "best in town" but non a/c rooms grubby, a/c better, restaurant.
F-G Ambika, Roxy Rd, T06792-252557. 10 reasonable a/c rooms, helpful staff, decent restaurant, tours of Similipal, good value.
F-G Mahapatra, opposite bus stand, T06792-255226. Bit grubby, 8 simple rooms, some a/c, balconies overlook the bus stand.
G Ganesh Bhavan, Main Market, T06792-252784. 32 basic rooms, some with bath.

Simililpal National Park *p250*
D-F Aranyanivas (OTDC), at Lulung (3 km from Pithabata Gate), reserve at Baripada Tourist Office, T06792-252710, or www.panth anivas.com. 8 non-a/c double rooms, 2 dorms with 12 beds each (Rs 200), only restaurant inside park, completely run on solar power.
D-F Panthasala, outside the park area, 35 km from Baripada towards Jashipur, has 4 doubles. Reservations as for **Aranyanivas**.
E Forest Rest Houses, the booking process is complicated and all food should be taken with you. Most rooms have several beds and cost Rs 200-400 per head if full, otherwise it can work out to be expensive. Maximum stay is 3 nights. Those at **Chahala** (an old hunting lodge, 35 km from Jashipur), **Nomana** (60 km), **Joranda** (72 km) and **Barehpani** (with view of waterfall, 52 km) must be booked through Field Director, Similipal Tiger Reserve Office, PO Bhanjpur, Baripada, 757002 Orissa, T06792-252593. Write enclosing an SAE (minimum 30 days, maximum 60 days before date of stay) and include names of group members, sex, age, nationality, visa/passport details. You will hear about method of advance payment. Rest houses at **Badampahar** (16 km from Jashipur), **Gudgudia** (25 km) and **Jamuani** (25 km), though not in the core area can be reserved in person up to 10 days in advance from DFO, Karanjia, Jashipur, T06796-220226. Reservation counter open daily 1000-1330.

Khiching *p251*
E-F Inspection Bungalow, contact Executive Engineer, PO Baripada.
E-F Revenue Rest Shed, PO Khiching, contact District Magistrate, PO Baripada.

🍴 Eating

Cuttack *p246, map p246*
Outside the better hotels there are few decent eateries. In the evenings street stalls set up around Buxi Bazar for cheap bites.
🍴 **Temptations**, near Buxi Bazar. Best ice creams in town, also reasonable pizzas.

🎭 Entertainment

Cuttack *p246, map p246*
You can try a makeshift pedalo on the Mahanadi River. **Mahanadi Boating Club** (2 men, a few chairs and an umbrella), on the Ring Rd, charges Rs 15 per person per 30 mins. Power boats cost Rs 550 per hr.

🛍 Shopping

Cuttack *p246, map p246*
Utkalika, Jail Rd. Very good selection of textiles and handicrafts including horn and brass objects and jewellery. The famous silver filigree shops are in **Nayasarak** and **Balu Bazar**.

⛰ Activities and tours

Cuttack *p246, map p246*
Club Travels, Mani Sahu Chowk, Buxi Bazar, T0671-230 4999.

🚌 Transport

Cuttack *p246, map p246*
Bus Long-distance buses stop at the bus stand in Link Rd. Services to all points in Orissa from the main bus stand in Badambari. Regular services to **Bhubaneswar**. Also state transport to major towns in **Andhra Pradesh**, **Chhattisgarh**, **Madhya Pradesh** and **West Bengal** (including Kolkata).
Taxi At the railway station and some hotels. Full-day trip to **Lalitgiri**, **Ratnagiri** and **Udayagiri** (excluding entrance fees), Rs 600-800, depending on bargaining skills.
Train East of town, Enquiries T131.
Bhubaneswar and **Puri**: Several express and passenger trains, but timings can be unreliable, so quicker to take bus. **Chennai**: *Coromandal Exp 2841*, 2040, 21½ hrs; *Howrah Madras Mail 2839*, 0550, 26½ hrs. **Kolkata** (**H**): *Shatabdi 2074*, 0645, 6 hrs, except Sun; *Dhauli Exp 2822*, 1340, 7 hrs; *Coromandal Exp 2842*, 0530,

6½ hrs; *Falaknuma Exp 2704*, 1130, 7 hrs; *Jagannath Exp 8410*, 0100, 7½ hrs; *East Coast Exp 8646*, 0820, 8 hrs. **New Delhi**: *Purushottam Exp 2801*, 0015, 30½ hrs. **Secunderabad**: *Falaknuma Exp 2703*, 1318, 21½ hrs; *East Coast Exp 8645*, 1840, 24 hrs.

Ratnagiri, Udayagiri and Lalitgiri *p247*
A day excursion from Cuttack or Bhubaneswar is possible by car (Rs 800). Get to Chandikhol on NH5 (43 km), with some roadside eating places, and turn right on NH5A (towards Paradeep) and then take the first turn left (at '12 km', before Patharajpur). Udayagiri is 1.5 km west of the road (8 km from NH5A) and Ratnagiri, 10 km further north. Return to the NH5A and continue towards Paradeep passing the Patharajpur **Panthasala** (Rest House) on the right. Turn right (south) at 20 km for Lalitgiri, 5 km away. Alternatively, buses from Cuttack stop at Chandikhol where you can hire a car for a 85-km return journey. Or take another bus to Patharajpur, hire a rickshaw and visit the first 2 sites.

Baleshwar *p249*
Bus The stand at Sahadevkhunta Rd has services to major towns, but few to **Chandipur**.
Train Written 'Balasore' in timetables, the railway station is 500 m from bus stand, on the main Chennai–Kolkata line. There are frequent trains to **Bhubaneswar**: best is *Dhauli Exp 2821*, 0920, 4 hrs. **Chennai**: *Coromandel Exp 2841*, 1805, 24 hrs; *Howrah Madras Mail 2839*, 0305, 29 hrs. **Kolkata** (**H**): *Shatabdi 2074*, 0910, 4 hrs, except Sun; *Coromandel Exp 2842*, 0805, 4 hrs; *Falaknuma Exp 2704*, 1355, 4 hrs; *East Coast Exp 8646*, 1120, 4½ hrs. **New Delhi**: *Rajdhani Exp 2421*, 1410 (Wed, Sat, Sun), 21 hrs; *Rajdhani Exp 2443*, 1200 (Mon, Fri), 22½ hrs; *Purushottam Exp 2801*, 0230, 27 hrs; *Utkal Exp 8477*, 0155, 37 hrs. **Puri**: *Jagannath Exp 8409*, 2300, 5½ hrs; *Purushottam Exp 2802*, 0010, 5½ hrs. **Secunderabad**: *Falaknuma Exp 2703*, 1035, 23½ hrs; *East Coast Exp 8645*, 1545, 27 hrs.

Chandipur *p249*
There are only 4-5 buses per day to/from **Baleshwar** (20 km, with the nearest railhead). Ask at Panthanivas for approximate timings. Ask for Rs 200 for a taxi to/from **Baleshwar**.

Baripada *p250*
Private and government buses serve the region's main towns. You can hire a jeep to visit Similipal. Ask at **Ambica** (see page 251) or tourist office. The nearest train stations are at Baleshwar (Balasore) and Tata Nagar.

Similipal National Park *p250*
The road from Baripada is via Lulung, 30 km west, which has a regular bus service. The nearest train stations on the Southeastern Railways are at Tatanagar and Balasore.

Khiching *p251*
Regular buses from Baripada, 150 km. Nearest train station is 96 km away, but it is better to get down at Balasore, 210 km, which has a fast service on the Southeast Railway.

🌐 **Directory**

Cuttack *p246, map p246*
Banks State Bank of India, near High Court, sterling and US$ TCs and cash exchange. Forex on 1st floor. **Internet** Jail Rd next to cinema. Good connection, Rs 25 per hr. **Medical services** Christian Mission Hospital, recommended. Private clinics on Medical Rd.

Baleshwar *p249*
Banks State Bank of India, Branch, near ITT, 3 km from railway station; the only bank authorized to deal in foreign exchange between Cuttack and Kolkata; come prepared.

Baripada *p250*
There is a district hospital, post office and shops selling local handicrafts and handloom.
Banks Nearest foreign exchange is at Baleshwar. The Central Co-op Bank paints a list of its top 10 defaulters on the wall outside!

Western Orissa

Settled in ancient times, Ptolemy's text of the second century refers to this area as a diamond trading centre. In the eighth century King Indrabhuti became a Buddhist and a preacher of the Vajrayana sect. ›› *For listings, see pages 258-261.*

Tribal areas → *For listings, see pages 258-261. Colour map 6, A5/B5.*

Orissa's rich tribal heritage has survived among the hills and forests across the districts of Koraput, Kandhamal, Kalahandi, Ganjam, Keonjhar, Dhenkanal and Mayurbhanj (see page 217). The state government is actively promoting tourism in some of these areas, however, at the time of writing, only the southwestern areas were accessible due to disturbances between Hindus and Christians in northwest and central regions.

It is best to book a tour at least a month ahead to allow time to get permits to visit tribal territories. Without permits, tours are restricted to roadside villages where development programmes are already changing traditional values and in some cases the influx of tourism has created a disappointing 'circus' effect, with demands of money for photos, dances and sweets for the children. With permits and a guide, it is possible to visit the more isolated villages, do some trekking and spend nights camping in picturesque locations. Individual visitors face difficulties from the local police, so it is best to take a guide in any instance. Always seek out the village chief for permission to enter a village.

Photography is prohibited in Bondo and Dongariya territories. Permission should always be asked before taking photographs of tribal people. Respect their privacy should they decline. Walking around settlements with a video camera is not appreciated.

Transport is usually by car (a/c ups the tour price but is necessary during the hotter months) or jeep. Foreign exchange is only available in Sunubeda so it's best to change money in advance, although there are ATMs in larger towns.

Tribal markets

Typical 'social interest' tours offered by travel agents include a number of tribal villages with a chance to attend fascinating markets and witness 'cultural' dances. Some of the tribes seen in these areas include Dongariya Kondhs, Dhurubas, Parajas, Koyas, Bondos and Gadabas. In Koraput District, **Ramgiri**, 70 km southwest of Jeypore, has a picturesque Tuesday market where Kondh people come to sell fresh vegetables and baskets and to buy salt. **Chatikona** brings Kondh women to the colourful Wednesday market where they sell beedi leaves and large almond-flavoured seeds. **Ankadeli**, 70 km southwest of Jeypore, has a tourist-heavy Thursday market where Bondo women, clad entirely in bead, sell handloom fabric (Rs 200), lengths of coloured beads, metal jewellery (don't be tempted to purchase one of their antique neck-rings) and exquisite woven grass bracelets. The later you stay, the busier it gets. **Nandapur**, 44 km south of Koraput, has a huge Thursday *haat* where trading in livestock, saris, vegetables and the local alcohol takes place on either side of the National Highway. Jeypore (see page 256) in particular has some good accommodation. Sleeping and eating are also available at **Laxmipur**, **Rayagada** and **Baliguda** (see page 258).

Ganjam District, south of Chilika Lake, takes its name from the Persian *'Ganj – Am'*, meaning 'granary of the world' – a testimony to its agricultural fertility. Still largely covered in dense forest, it was settled in prehistoric times and came under the influence of Emperor Asoka's rule. The handicrafts of the region include brass and bell-metal ware, hornwork, wood carvings, silks and carpets.

Ganjam

Ganjam used to be the District Headquarters, but the administration was moved to Chatrapur because of its unhealthy location. Its chief interest is the small East India Company **fort** and a Christian **cemetery** at the north end of town, near a large factory between the main road and the sea. An interesting excursion inland takes you to **Aska** (52 km) and **Bhanjanagar** (85 km).

Berhampur

A trading centre for silk fabric, Berhampur is the district's major commercial town. The **Thakurani**, **Jagannath** and **Nilakanthesvar Siva temples** ① *near DIG Residence, Tue-Sun 0700-1400 (summer), 1000-1700 (winter), closed government holidays*, are all worth visiting. Berhampur is also a good place to shop for silks. The **museum** has a collection of sculpture, anthropological and natural history specimens; no photos are permitted. **Tourist office** ① *New Bus Stand, 1st floor, T0680-228 0226*. **Railway station counter** ① *T0680-220 3870*.

Taptapani

Water from the very hot sulphur springs discovered at Taptapani in a forest setting, 50 km from Berhampur, is channelled to a pool for bathing. There is a shrine to goddess Kandhi inside the original *kund* (pool) as it is believed to cure infertility – tribal women come to the hot water pool near the **Panthanivas** hotel to try to pick up a seed pod from the mud at the bottom. Direct buses leave from Berhampur, 50 km away, and Bhubaneswar, 240 km away.

Chandragiri

In the tribal hills, 32 km south of Taptapani, Tibetan carpet weavers have settled in a refugee colony at Chandragiri. The temple and Buddhist prayer flags lend a distinctive atmosphere. You can watch weavers and craftsmen at work; good prices.

Jaugada → *35 km north of Berhampur.*

Jaugada in the Malati Hills is famous for one of Asoka's '**Kalinga Edicts**' (see Dhauli, page 229), which was discovered at the beginning of the 19th century, but the shelter was built only in 1975. Emperor Asoka's doctrine of conquest through love instead of the sword and his declaration "All men are my children" appears here. Sadly, some parts of the inscriptions have now disappeared. The old fort (circa sixth century) contains stone images of the five *Pandavas*, which are worshipped in the Guptesvar Temple. Jaugada is reached by a jeep road from Purusottampur which has buses from Berhampur.

Buguda, a few kilometres away, has the Viranchinarayan Temple with its beautifully carved wooden *Jagamohan* and murals depicting stories from the epic *Ramayana*. Also, close by, **Buddhakhol** has Buddhist sculptures as well as shrines to Siva.

Koraput District → *For listings, see pages 258-261.*

Jeypore → *Phone code: 06854.*

Jeypore itself is unspoilt by tourism and is surrounded by incredibly beautiful scenery. There is a derelict fort and palace, to which entrance is sadly forbidden, and an interesting market, which remains bustling until 2200. A good range of accommodation and friendly locals make it an excellent base for a few days. It is possible to organize your own tour from Jeypore and reportedly easier to get permits to visit tribal areas in Koraput rather than in Bhubaneswar. Most people stay in Jeypore on Wednesdays in order to visit **Ankadeli market** the next morning; it's a glorious 75-km drive through the rolling hills, past brown rivers and glassy reservoirs. One of the world's oldest terracing systems creeps up the shallow valleys between hills wooded with cashew and mango trees, the undergrowth thick with coffee and black pepper plants. Tribal women working in the paddies add splashes of colour to a landscape already made vibrant by emerald and gold crops against the tangerine earth.

Koraput

Koraput is another useful base for visiting the tribal areas. **Orissa Tourism** ① *Raipur-Visakhapatnam Rd, T06852-250318, Mon-Sat 1000-1700*, can help arrange car hire. The elevated **Jagannath Temple** admits non-Hindus (unlike the temple in Puri) and is an interesting place to lunch (see Eating, page 260). Note the painting ceilings inside the main building. Further up the hill, there is a worthwhile **Tribal Museum** ① *daily 1000-2130, donation*, where you can purchase the *Tribes of Koraput* booklet (Rs 90), which is a valuable introduction to the region. Displays include tribal jewellery, weaving, cultivation methods and some illuminating maps of the area. The **Orissa Coffee Planters' Association**, around 20 km from Koraput, is happy to show visitors around the plantation which has fruits and spices as well as coffee.

Kotapad → *46 km northwest of Jeypore on N43.*

The clean area of weavers' houses in Kotapad has large pots of cotton and tussore silk soaking in natural dyes, while skeins hang drying. Weavers are happy to show you work in progress. The Co-op ensures even pricing; a 3-m shawl costs Rs 350-600. It is worth seeking out award winner Jagabandhu Samarth. As the word gets around that there are visitors in town, weavers will find you to show you their pieces but there is no pressure to buy.

Sambalpur and around → *Colour map 3, A5. Phone code: 0663.*

Sambalpur is a pleasant, small town with a number of decent hotels and a few restaurants grouped in the centre. The presiding deity Samalesvari, to whom a temple was built here by the Chauhans in the mid-16th century, probably accounts for the town's name. The district is famous for its textiles, particularly its tie-dye ikat work. **Orissa Tourism** ① *Panthanivas, T0663-241 1118*, has helpful staff and can help plan excursions. **Railway counter** ① *Khetrajpur, T0663-252 1661.* Tours are often cancelled due to lack of passengers.

The villages and the countryside are pleasant in themselves and you might consider visiting **Baragarh**, 1½ hours, and **Barpali**, three hours' drive, with a guide, if you are interested in weaving. **Sonepur**, a lively small town with a colourful market square and temple, is particularly rewarding. A scenic road from Sambalpur along the Mahanadi River ends in a footpath down across the wide sandbank over half the river in the dry season. Small boats ferry passengers across the remainder.

Debjharan Sanctuary has been recently created and developed as a picnic spot in forest situated 35 km south of Sambalpur, 5 km east of the NH6. There is a small waterfall and a dam with waterhole at Chaura Asi Mal and a Forest Rest House. Taxis from Sambalpur cost Rs 300-400 for a return day trip.

Ushakothi Wildlife Sanctuary → *Colour map 3, A5. 48 km east of Sambalpur on the NH6.*
Ushakothi is densely forested and covers 130 sq km. The sanctuary has wild elephant, leopard, tiger, bison, wild boar and chital (barking deer). The best time to visit is from November to June, at night. Take a guide with search lights and see the wildlife from the watchtowers sited near watering points to which the animals come. Open hooded jeeps are recommended. Permits to visit, and guides, can be obtained from the Forest Range Officer, PO Badrama. The **Forest Rest House**, Badrama, 3 km away, is very basic with no electricity.

Hirakud Dam → *Colour map 3, A4.*
The Mahanadi created enormous problems every year through devastating floods of the delta region and in order to combat these the Hirakud Dam was built about 20 km northwest of Sambalpur. The key section is a 1100-m-long masonry dam, with a further earth dam of over 3500 m. One of the longest mainstream dams in the world, it is over 60 m high and drains an area twice the size of Sri Lanka. Since its completion in 1957 there have been no serious floods in the Mahanadi delta and it allows the irrigation of vast areas of high-quality land. You get an excellent view from the revolving tower, Gandhi Minar, at one end of the dam. Contact the Deputy Superintendent of Police, Security Force, Hirakud before visiting. There are regular buses from Sambalpur.

Debrigarh Wildlife Sanctuary
This sanctuary adjoins Hirakud Lake, around 50 km from Sambalpur. With an area of 347 sq km, the dry deciduous forest is home to tiger, leopard, sloth bear, chital, sambar, nilgai and a number of resident and migratory birds. Muggar crocodiles and freshwater turtles are among the reptiles present. Entry to the sanctuary is at Dhodrokusum, with a watchtower at Pathedurga. There are basic **Forest Rest Houses** at Dhodrokusum and Dechua, or a **Tourist Cottage** at Chaurasimal. The best season to visit is from October to May. For permission and guides, contact DFO (Wildlife), Motijharan, T0663-240 2741. For information contact Chief Wildlife Warden (Orissa), Bhubaneswar, cwlwob@hotmail.com.

Huma → *About 32 km south of Sambalpur.*
Huma has a famous **Leaning Temple**, on the bank of the Mahanadi, dedicated to Lord Siva. The temple leans southwards but the pinnacle is vertical. The colourful Kudo fish, which are easily seen from January to June, are believed to belong to Siva so are never caught by fishermen; visitors may feed them grain. Country boats are available for hire. There are regular buses from Sambalpur to Huma Chowk, then walk 2 km to the temple.

Sundargarh District
To the north of Sambalpur is Sundargarh District. In the tribal heartland, it is an area of undulating hills with the richest deposits of mineral wealth in the state. Cave paintings are evidence of the existence of early man. Once relatively untouched by modern civilization, the district was chosen for the siting of the first public sector steel plant at Rourkela. The route from Sambalpur to Rourkela runs north, 192 km, passing through some glorious scenery. The Brahmani flows along a wide rocky and sandy bed, a torrent

in the monsoon, with forested hills on either side. A large industrial town girdled by a range of hills and encircled by rivers, **Rourkela** has a major steel plant and fertilizer complex, both of which may be visited with permission from the PRO. There are banks, post offices, shops and hospitals.

◉ Western Orissa listings

For Sleeping and Eating price codes and other relevant information, see Essentials pages 34-38.

◉ Sleeping

Tribal areas *p254*
Rayagada
C-E Hotel Sai International, JK Rd, T06856-225554/5. The best rooms around, but on a limb on the edge of town. Multi-cuisine restaurant is nothing special, but there's a bar and travel desk that can help with car rental. Non-a/c rooms are Rs 700 and have hot water by the bucket, or Rs 1200 for a room with geyser and a/c. Staff are well meaning but a little confused.
E-G Jyoti Mahal, Convent Rd, T06856-223015. Decent and friendly, 25 reasonably sized rooms with bath, good restaurant.
F-G Swagath, New Colony, T06856-222208. 44 clean rooms, good local-style restaurant.

Laxmipur
F-G Hotel Konark, green building by Ambedkar Chowk. Good *thalis*, friendly young English-speaking owner. Decent lunch stop.

Baliguda
Baliguda is basically a one-street town, a quiet, friendly place with a slow pace of life.
G Santosh, off Main Rd. 16 rooms, best on the 1st floor with attached bath.

Berhampur *p255*
Few visitors stay overnight. However, if arriving late, the following are adequate:
D-F Kameswari, close to railway station on Station Rd, T0680-221 1283, radhahotelbam@ rediffmail.com. 28 rooms, 7 a/c.
E-G Hotel Radha, near the Old Bus Stand, T0680-222 2341. Some a/c in the 45 rooms.

F-G Gitanjali, close to the railway station, T0680-220 4822.
F-G Udipi, near the Old Bus Stand, T0680-222 2196.
G Puspa, Gatekeeper's Sq, 1.5 km from the New Bus Stand, T0680-222 1117. Basic.

Taptapani *p255*
B-E Tourist Lodge, Padamari, T06816-255031. For breaking the journey in a place where there's literally nothing to do but relax, this is ideal. Variety of simple accommodation – 12 rooms, 5 tents, log cabins and a tree-house furnished entirely from woven reeds. The 2 de luxe suites in the main cottage have gigantic wet rooms and, although the Roman baths aren't that appealing, the low-lit barn-like rooms are tastefully so. Hillview Restaurant is OK, breakfast included. Irritating 0800 checkout.

Jeypore *p256*
B-D Hello Jeypore, East Octroi Check Post, NH43, 2 km from centre, T06854-223 1127, www.hotelhellojeypore.com. Comfortable, well-furnished a/c rooms some overlooking garden (roadside is noisy), hot power shower though bathrooms are jaded and a re-fit is scheduled, TV, efficient service, restaurant or dinner in the garden (try *alu raita*, veg much better than non-veg, plenty of Chinese). Smoky blue-lit bar gets busy or drinks on the lawn at reasonable prices. Of the mid-range options it has the best atmosphere in town, but it's still relatively overpriced.
D Mani Krishna, MG Rd, T/F06854-231139, www.hotelmanikrishna.com. Modern a/c rooms are spacious and nicely fitted-out, all with balconies some of which see the sunset over the ramshackle roofs of Jeypore. Bathrooms are the best in town, good manage-

ment, but lacking any character or space to relax. Restaurant and alcohol via room service.

D Sai Krishna, MG Rd, T06854-230253/5, www.hotelsaikrishna.com. Next door to the Mani, in the same tall mirrored edifice, and not much to choose between the 2. De luxe rooms are not worth the extra money, standard and club rooms suffice. There's a bar and restaurant, underground car park, and eager staff. Central location is good for exploring town.

F-G Madhumati, NKT Rd, T06854-241377, hotelmadhumati@yahoo.com. 30 large rooms (shortly to be renovated), some a/c but non-a/c are a steal at Rs 300, TV, mosquitoes, hot water, good restaurant, bar only has strong beer, very helpful manager. Attractive location next to the palace. Definitely the best budget choice in town.

G Shankar Hotel, Main Rd, T06854-233150. Basic grim doubles, the de luxe ones get booked out quickly, some cheap rooms (Rs 80) with common bath (but "not for ladies"), noisy yet friendly.

Koraput p256

F-G Athithi Bhavan, Gundicha Chowk, T06852-250610. At the base of the temple and managed by the Jagannath Temple Trust, non-a/c (Rs 200) and a/c rooms (Rs 400) with bath have TV and are clean and attractively painted with faux chalk designs on terracotta. The whole building is light and airy and characterful. Temple *thalis* available in the restaurant.

G Ambica Heavens, T06852-251136. Bearable rooms with bath, TV, quieter at back.

Sambalpur p256

D-E Panthanivas (OTDC), Brook's Hill, end of VSS Marg, T0663-241 1282, www.panth anivas.com. Despite all having balconies, few of the 34 rooms (clean linen, 12 a/c with TV) have decent views. Restaurant, bar. Checkout 0800.

D-F Saket, T0663-240 2345. Some a/c in 30 decent, clean rooms with hot bath, TV, restaurant.

D-F Sheela Towers, VSS Marg, T0663-240 3111. The 41 smallish rooms are clean and comfortable, TV, 2 restaurants.

E-G Uphar, T0663-240 3078. Slightly cheaper sister concern of **Uphar Palace**.

E-G Uphar Palace, T0663-240 0519. 29 good clean rooms with bath, some a/c, TV, 2 restaurants (good South Indian).

G Rani Lodge, next to **Uphar Palace**, T0663-252 2173. Clean, simple rooms with bath, nets, early-morning mosque noise.

Hirakud Dam p257

E Ashok Nivas. Good guesthouse.

Sundagarh District p257

B Mayfair Garden, Panposh Rd, 3 km from Rourkela, T0661-252 0001, rkl_mayfair@ sancharnet.in. Touted as a 'farm resort', 18 comfortable rooms, decent restaurant, pool.

D-F Panthanivas (OTDC), Sector 5, 2 km from Rourkela, T0661-264 3280, www.panthanivas.com. 31 rooms, some a/c or good value non-a/c for Rs 450, restaurant/bar. Checkout 0800.

E Radhika, Bisra Rd, opposite railway station, Rourkela, T0661-251 0300. Reasonably clean, 60 large rooms, helpful staff.

❼ Eating

Jeypore p256

There are also restaurants in the hotels listed, as well as plenty as pure veg eateries close to the bus station on Main Rd.

🍴 **Aroma**, Hello Jeypore Hotel (see Sleeping). The restaurant is quiet and a/c but shame about the huge projector screen dominating the lawn.

🍴 **Bhagwan Restaurant**, MG Rd, T06854-232616, above Lokesh Parlour. Open 1030-1500 and 1800-2230. Standard veg (Rs 30-70) and non-veg (Rs 70-120) Indian meals, conveniently located in the centre of town near the main market.

Koraput *p256*

⊌ **Jungle Restaurant**, at the Tribal Museum. Open till 2200. Has cheap offerings on a shady patio surrounded by foliage.

⊌ **Jagannath Temple**. Serves a filling and tasty *thali* and is popular with families. Make a donation of Rs 25 on entering the temple then join the queues. Meals eaten off leaves with the hands cross-legged on the stone floor.

▲ Activities and tours

Jeypore *p256*
Discover Tours (see page 231) and Grass Routes (see page 244) are recommended. **Perfect Travels**, Rajmahal Chowk, T06854-242 1856. Car and driver, Rs 1200 per day. **Travel Care**, Sardar Patel Marg, T06854-2422291. For tours write to Mr Pujari 4-6 weeks in advance with a photocopy of the relevant passport pages.

Sambalpur *p256*
Providing jeeps and taxis for sightseeing: **Nalini Travels**, Buddharaja, near flyover; **Swati Travels**, near Ashoka Talkies.

⊖ Transport

Berhampur *p255*
Bus The Old and New Bus Stands are about 3 km from the railway station, 2 km from each other. Government buses use the **Old Bus Stand**, private buses (which are more regular and reliable) the **New Bus Stand** and cover major towns in Orissa and neighbouring states. Several buses to **Bhubaneswar** a day, Rs 80, 4 hrs on a good road.

Train Berhampur, sometimes referred to as **Brahmapur** in timetables, is on the main Chennai–Kolkata line, enquiries T131. **Chennai**: *Coromandel Exp 2841*, 2400, 18 hrs; *Howrah Madras Mail 2839*, 0910, 19½ hrs. **Kolkata** (**H**) via **Bhubaneswar**: *Coromandel Exp 2842*, 0205,

10 hrs; *Falaknuma Exp 2704*, 0800, 10½ hrs; *East Coast Exp 8646*,, 0430, 12½ hrs. **Secunderabad**: *Falaknuma Exp 2703*, 1645, 17 hrs; *Konark Exp 1020*, 1755, 18 hrs; *East Coast Exp 8645*, 2230, 20 hrs; *Visakha Exp 7015*, 1105, 21½ hrs.

Jeypore *p256*
Bus Government buses, T06854-233181, 0700-2200, run to nearby cities, you can book tickets in advance (a good idea if wanting to travel by more comfortable high-tech rather than ordinary service). Frequent bus service to **Koraput** between 0400-2300 (1 hr, Rs 13). Also 5 buses per day to **Sambalpur** (15 hrs, Rs 300), **Bhubaneswar** (20 hrs, a/c Rs 410, non-a/c Rs 300) and **Visakhapatanam** (6 hrs, a/c Rs 140). Buses leave from next to the government stand, T(0)9437-373180, and go to neighbouring villages, enquire about times. For **Ankedelli market** a bus leaves at 0700, returning 1400. Private buses also to **Bhubaneswar** (1800, Rs 330), **Raipur** (1900, 2000, 2100, Rs 280) and **Berhampur** (1830, 1930, Rs 170-200).

Car If travelling by car from the coast, make sure the car can manage the hill roads and the driver isn't worried about entering tribal areas.

Train The train station is 7 km away. A daily train connects with **Vishakhapatnam**. From **Vizag**, *Kirandol Exp*, 0745, 8 hrs. Superb views for first 3 hrs uphill then down to Araku Valley; 2nd class is full of firewood and farm produce and best avoided. From the north, travel to Vizianagaram station, and then by bus or taxi.

Koraput *p256*
Koraput has more passenger trains connecting it than Jeypore, which is mainly used for goods and mineral transportation. Trains to **Bhubaneswar**: *Hirakhand Exp 8448*, 1825, 16 hrs. From Bhubaneswar, *Hirakhand Exp 8447*, 2000, 16 hrs. **Kolkata** (**H**): *Koraput Howrah Exp 8006*, 0645, 25 hrs, via **Sambalpur**, 12 hrs.

Sambalpur *p256*

Bus Sambalpur has 2 bus stands, one for government buses, the other for private buses near Laxmi Talkies. Both are within a short cycle-rickshaw ride from VSS Marg, though the latter has more regular services to major towns in the area.

Jeep/taxi Jeep/taxi hire is the easiest way to visit wildlife sanctuaries. Contact the tourist office for tours. Return jeeps to **Debjharan**, Rs 300-400; to **Ushakothi** (1600-0400), Rs 500.

Train There are 2 stations: Sambalpur and Sambalpur Rd, both 2-3 km from hotels on VSS Marg. **Kolkata** (**H**): *Koraput Howrah Exp 8006*, 1815, 13 hrs. **Puri** (via **Bhubaneswar**): *Tapaswini Exp 8451*, 2250, 9½ hrs (7½ hrs).

Sundagarh District *p257*

Bus Rourkela's **New Bus Stand** is in walking distance of Bisra Rd hotels; turn right and right again. Buses to all major destinations.

Train Rourkela's train station is a minute's walk from Bisra Rd and hotels. **Kolkata** (**H**): *Howrah Maiil 2809*, 2305, 7 hrs; *Azad Hind Exp 2129*, 2120, 6½ hrs. **Mumbai** (**CST**): *Gitanjali Exp 2860*, 2015, 26 hrs. **Patna**: *South Bihar Link Exp 3287*, 1510, 18 hrs. **Puri** via **Bhubaneswar** (all stop at Balasore and Cuttack): *Tapaswini Exp 8451*, 1920, 12½ hrs (10 hrs).

● Directory

Berhampur *p255*

There is a **Christian Mission Hospital**, post offices and shops. **Bank** State Bank of India, Main Branch, State Bank Rd, changes foreign cash and TCs.

Jeypore *p256*

Bank State Bank of India, has ATM at Main Road branch, and behind the Private Bus Stand. **Internet** SJRM, Main Rd (opposite the government hospital), daily 0900-1400 and 1500-2200, speedy connection and new computers, Rs 15 per hr. Other internet places are dotted around town, including opposite the Hotel Madhumati. **Post** Main Rd.

Koraput *p256*

Bank State Bank of India, has ATMs by the bus and railway stations.

Sambalpur *p256*

Bank State Bank of India, near Collectorate, for foreign exchange. **Post** Main post office, near Collectorate. Several internet cafés on VSS Marg, Rs 20-25 per hr.

Contents

Northwest of Kolkata

At a glance

⊖ **Getting around** Be ultra-aware
of your personal safety: kidnappings,
robberies and highway hold-ups
are by no means rare. Book a/c
accommodation on trains, and
restrict road travel to daylight hours.

◉ **Time required** Allow 2 days
to 'feel' Bodh Gaya; Varanasi can
take 3 days or 3 months.

☽ **Weather** It is hot all year round
on the Ganges plains.

✕ **When not to go** The height of
summer can be punishing.

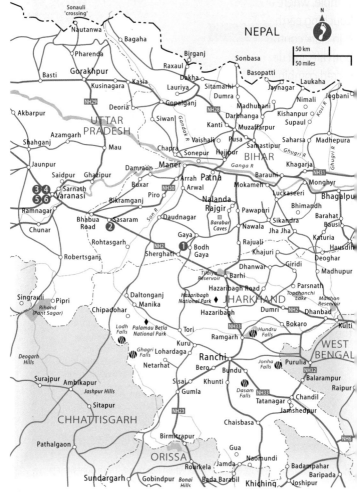

At Bodh Gaya – the most important of Buddhism's four pilgrimage sites – the Gautama Buddha attained supreme Enlightenment. It is a place that calls pilgrims and travellers alike, and a centre for Vipasana meditation with an atmosphere that mixes the heady India of the plains with the tranquil mood of a Himalayan outpost. Buddhism's legacy is powerfully visible in the architecture of the Mahabodhi Temple, where an immense gold-painted image of the Buddha in 'touching earth pose' is reputed to be at least 1000 years old.

In stark contrast to mellow Bodh Gaya, Varanasi pulsates with both life and death. It encapsulates India: all that is wonderful and sacred combined with all that is dark and mysterious. The great river Ganga Ma – regarded by Hindus as the physical and spiritual life source of the country – draws millions of pilgrims to the bathing ghats at Varanasi every year, making them buzz with activity each dawn and dusk. The burning funeral pyres cast ashes on the Brahmin priests and tribespeople who come to perform purifying rites, just as they have from time immemorial. For Varanasi is thought to be the oldest living city on earth.

Otherwise known as Benares or Kashi (City of Light), there are 1500 temples, shrines and palaces towering over the ghats or hiding in the teeming, confusing alleyways. Arrival at the station, finding the hotel of your choice, or trying to negotiate boat hire is almost always fraught, but nothing can detract from the intensely spiritual atmosphere that pervades the old city and the waterfront at all times.

Gaya and Bodh Gaya

An enclave of Buddhism in the dusty Hindu state of Bihar, Bodh Gaya is a must for anyone with even a passing interest in the teachings of Siddhartha .Temples abound, built by various Asian countries, each in a unique Buddhist style. Access to Bodh Gaya is via the town of Gaya, where fans of a Passage to India can make a day trip to the Barabar Caves (a journey that can be almost as arduous as that in the novel). In recent years, the state of Bihar has acquired an unfortunate – now almost proverbial – reputation for crime and banditry. Travellers should be aware that this is one of India's poorest regions, and strictly avoid travelling by night on rural roads. That said, Bodh Gaya and Gaya are well used to tourists, and those who adopt the necessary precautions have no problems in travelling around this corner of Bihar. ▸▸ *For listings, see pages 271-273.*

Gaya ▸ *For listings, see pages 271-273.*
Colour map 1, B5.

Gaya, on slightly raised ground in the valley between two hills, was blessed by Vishnu with the power to absolve all temporal sins. Its many sacred shrines attract Hindus at Pitrapaksh Tarpan (September-October), when prayers are offered for the dead before pilgrims take a dip in the seasonal holy River Phalgu. Cremations take place on funeral pyres in the burning ghats along the river. **Tourist office** ⓘ *Bihar, Gaya Junction Railway Station Main Hall, T0631-2402155, 0600-2100.*

Sights ▸ *Phone code: 0631. Population: 383,200.*
There are several old Buddhist temples and monastery remains around Gaya. In the centre of the town is the **Vishnupad Temple**, which is supposed to have been built over Vishnu's footprint, imprinted on a rock set in a silver basin. The 30-m-high temple has eight rows of beautifully carved pillars supporting the *mandapa* (pavilion), which were refurbished in 1787. Only Hindus are permitted into the sanctum and temple grounds which has the *Akshayabat* (the immortal banyan tree under which the Buddha is believed to have meditated for six years), where the final *puja* for the dead takes place. Brahmayoni Hill, 1 km southwest, with its 1000 stone steps, which lead to a vantage point for viewing both Gaya and Bodh Gaya.

Gaya

To Patna & Barabar Caves

Station Rd
Swala Rd
Gandhi Chowk
Swarajpuri Rd
Mora Rd
Dak Banglow Rd
Narayan Marg
Fruit & Vegetable
ATM
To Dobhi
Gandhi Maidan
Buses to Patna, Ranchi & Hazaribagh
Auto-rickshaws to Bodh Gaya
Rajendra Ashram
Chand Chhora
Phalgu River
To Buses to Rajgir
N
500 metres
500 yards
Vishnupad Temple
To Bodh Gaya

Sleeping
Ajatsatru 1
Akash 2
Railway Retiring Rooms 3
Royal Surya 4
Siddhartha International 5
Vishnu International 6

Eating
Saas Bahu Biryani 1

Monastic University for the Buddhist world

It is assumed that the Gupta emperors were responsible for Nalanda's first monasteries. In the seventh century Hiuen-Tsang spent 12 years, both as a student and a teacher, at Nalanda which once had over 3000 teachers and philosophers. The monks were supported by 200 villages, and a library of nine million manuscripts attracted men from countries as far flung as Java, Sumatra, Korea, Japan and China. Great honour was attached to a Nalanda student and admission was restricted with seven or eight out of 10 applicants failing to gain a place.

I-Tsing, another Chinese scholar, arrived here in AD 673 and also kept detailed records, describing the severe lifestyle of the monks. The divisions of the day were measured by a water clock, and the syllabus involved the study of Buddhist and Brahmanical scriptures, logic, meta-physics, medicine and Sanskrit grammar.

The university flourished until 1199 when the Afghan Bhaktiar Khalji sacked it, burning, pillaging and driving the surviving residents into hiding. It was the end of living Buddhism in India until the modern revival.

The **Surya Temple** at **Deo**, 20 km away, dedicated to the Sun God, attracts large crowds in November when **Chhatt Puja** is celebrated.

Around Gaya

Barabar Caves are 35 km north. The 22 km rough track leading to the caves in the impressive granite hill turns east off the main road to Patna at **Belagunj** (30 minutes from Gaya, two hours from Patna) where buses and trains stop. From here allow four hours to walk up. It is only safe to go in daylight and not alone; a solitary sadhu is inclined to jump out at you from nowhere! Alternatively you can squeeze into one of the infrequent local buses which navigate the track as far as 'Dheia' (ask for the conductor for Barabar), leaving a one-hour walk to the caves. Enquire about safety at Belagunj Police Station first as the area is prone to banditry.

The best option is to hire a 4WD from Bodh Gaya (Rs 1200-1500, check with tourist office). Collection from Gaya available.

The whale-backed quartzite gneiss hill stands in wild and rugged country. Inscriptions reveal that, on instructions from Asoka, four chambers were excavated, cut and chiselled to a high polish by the stonemasons, as retreats for ascetics who belonged to a sect related to Jainism. Percy Brown pointed out that the extraordinary caves, particularly the *Lomas Rishi* and the *Sudama*, are exact copies of ordinary beehive shaped huts built with bamboo, wood and thatch. The barrel-vaulted chamber inside the *Sudama* is 10 m long, 6 m wide and 3.5 m high which through a doorway leads to a circular cell of 6 m diameter. The most impressive craftsmanship is seen on the façade of the *Lomas Rishi* which replicates the horseshoe shaped gable end of a wooden structure with two lunettes which have very fine carvings of lattice-work and rows of elephants paying homage to Buddhist stupas. Excavation is incomplete as there was a possibility of the cave collapsing. There is also a Siva temple on the Siddheshwar peak.

There is accommodation by the caves (Rs 250) but it is not advisable to stay overnight. Bring plenty of bottled water with you as it is not sold at Barabar.

The caves inspired the setting of EM Forster's A Passage to India. *They date from the third century BC and are the earliest examples of rock-cut sanctuaries.*

At **Nagarjuna Hill** there are three further rock-cut sanctuaries, 1 km northeast from Barabar. The *Gopi* (Milkmaid's) cave having the largest chamber. Inscriptions date these to about 50 years after the excavations at Barabar.

Bodh Gaya → *For listings, see pages 271-273. Colour map 1, B5.*

Bodh Gaya, a quiet town near the river Niranjana (Phalgu), is one of the holiest Buddhist pilgrimage centres. It was under the Bo tree here that Gautama, the prince, attained enlightenment to become the Buddha.

Ins and outs → *Phone code: 0631. Population: 30,900.*

Getting there Travel in daylight only, for your own safety. Buses run from Gaya, Patna, Nalanda and Rajgir. » *See Transport, page 273, for further details.*

Getting around The hotels, temple and monasteries are a few minutes' walk from the bus stand.

Tourist information Tourist office ① *Bihar, corner of Bodhgaya Rd and Temple St, T0631-2200672.*

The site

Bodh Gaya was 'lost' for centuries until rediscovered by Burmese Buddhists in 1877 which led to restoration work by the British. UNESCO declared the Mahabodhi Temple complex as a World Heritage Site in 2002. The event was to be marked by the arrival of a 152-m-high bronze statue, the highest in the world, but political unrest in the region led to the project being relocated to Kushinagar, Uttar Pradesh.

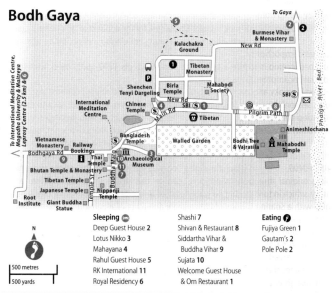

Bodh Gaya

Sleeping
Deep Guest House 2
Lotus Nikko 3
Mahayana 4
Rahul Guest House 5
RK International 11
Royal Residency 6

Shashi 7
Shivan & Restaurant 8
Siddartha Vihar &
  Buddha Vihar 9
Sujata 10
Welcome Guest House
  & Om Restaurant 1

Eating
Fujiya Green 1
Gautam's 2
Pole Pole 2

500 metres
500 yards

Border essentials: India–Nepal

To Nepal STRCs and private buses run daily from Harding Park Bus Stand to Raxaul (5-7 hours, Rs 60). However, timings are difficult and the buses packed and uncomfortable. Night buses reach the border early in the morning. Morning buses from Patna connect with the night bus to Kathmandu. Either way you have an overnight bus journey, unless you stay at Birganj – an unenviable option, though there are two modest hotels. **Raxaul** has little to offer; **Ajanta**, Ashram Road, has rooms with bath. In Raxaul the *tempo* stand is south of the railway line and the Immigration and Customs office. You can cross the border to **Birganj** by rickshaw/*tempo* (15-20 minutes). In Birganj the *tempo* stand and Bus Park are in Adarsh Nagar, to the south of town. In the morning, buses depart from the bus stand east of the clock tower. To **Tandi Bazar** (4 hours, for **Chitwan**, Rs 60), **Pokhara** (11-12 hours, Rs 90) and **Kathmandu** (11-12 hours, Rs 95). Even Express buses are slow and packed. Tourist minibuses are the only moderately comfortable option. You need an exit stamp in Raxaul from the Indian Immigration office (round the corner, and across the road from the Customs office), which is a great hassle. You may need customs clearance first. After crossing the border you need to get an entry stamp from the Nepalese Immigration counter (open early morning to late evening). Occasionally an unjustified additional fee is demanded for 'extras', eg registration card, or a 'visa' fee in US dollars.

From Nepal When travelling to India via Patna it is best to stay overnight in **Hetauda** and catch the 0530 bus to Birganj (three hours); go to the bus stand at 0500 to get a seat. At **Birganj**, walk or get a (pricey) horse-drawn rickshaw to the *auto-tempo* stand at the second crossroads. From there travel to Raxaul. Remember to get an exit stamp from Nepalese Immigration before crossing the border and an entry stamp from Indian Immigration in Raxaul.

Lamas, Rimpoches and Buddhists from all over the world assemble here during the *monlam* (December/January) when the area north of the bus station resembles a medieval encampment with tents serving as informal restaurants and accommodation. The food is smoky and there are long waits, but it is atmospheric and full of colour. The 'tourist season' draws to a close at the end of February when many restaurants close and meditation courses stop running. Unfortunately the air can get heavily polluted, partly due to badly serviced buses, making a walk along the road rather unpleasant.

Mahabodhi Temple
ⓘ *0500-2100.*
Asoka's original shrine near the Bodhi tree was replaced by this temple in the second century, which in turn went through several alterations. The temple on a high and broad plinth, with a soaring 54-m-high pyramidal spire with a square cross-section and four smaller spires, houses a gilded image of the Enlightened Buddha. The smaller spires may have been added when Burmese Buddhists attempted extensive rebuilding in the 14th century. An ornately carved stone railing in bas relief surrounds the temple on three sides and several carved Buddhist stupas depict tales from the Buddha's early life. Unlike earlier circular railings this had to conform to the quadrangle of the temple structure. Its height of 2 m, its lighter proportions and the quality of the carving dates it to the Sunga period

(early first century BC). The lotus pond where the Buddha may have bathed is to the south. To the north is the *Chankramana*, a raised platform (first century) with lotus flowers carved on it, which marks the consecrated promenade used by the Buddha while meditating. Numerous attempts to restore the temple have obscured the original. The candle-lit evening ceremony is worth attending.

The original Bodhi tree (pipal or *Ficus religiosa*) was supposedly destroyed by Asoka before he was converted, and others which replaced it also died. The present tree behind the temple is believed to come from the original stock – Prince Mahinda carried a sapling from the sacred Bo tree to Sri Lanka when he went to spread Buddhism there. This in turn produced a sapling which was brought back to Bodh Gaya. The red sandstone slab, the **Vajrasila**, under the tree marks the place where Gautama sat in meditation. Today, pilgrims tie pieces of coloured cloth on its branches when they come to pray. To the west of the Mahabodhi Temple complex there is a pretty walled garden, with fabulous champagne palms (*Hyophorbe lagenicaulis*) lining the paths.

The **Archaeological Museum Bodh Gaya** ① *T0631-2200739, Mon-Sat 1000-1700, Rs 2*, behind the walled garden, houses the stone railings which once enclosed the Bodhi tree. The carved sandstone and granite pillars, Sunga (second to first century BC and early medieval sixth to seventh century AD respectively), make a visit worthwhile.

Animeshlochana is another sacred spot where the Buddha stood to gaze in gratitude at the Bodhi tree for a week, after his Enlightenment. The temple also attracts Hindu pilgrims since the Buddha is considered to be one of the *avatars* or incarnations of Vishnu.

Other temples

Pilgrims from many lands have built their own temples. You can start at the giant 21 m stone **Buddha statue** at the end of Temple Road, which was unveiled by the Dalai Lama in 1989. The modern two-storey, spotless **Japanese Temple** ① *0700-1200, 1400-1800*, next door, with beautiful polished marble floors has gold images of the Buddha. The **Tibetan Temple and Monastery** next to this (1938) is ornately painted and has a *Dharma Chakra* (Wheel of Law) which must be turned three times when praying for forgiveness of sins. A large 2-m metal ceremonial drum in red and gold is also on display. Opposite is the **Nipponji Temple** complex with a free clinic, monastery and a Peace Bell (rung from 0600-1200 and at 1700). Returning to the Mahabodhi Temple you will pass the colourful **Bhutan Temple** protected by carved Himalayan deities, a glittering pagoda-style **Thai Temple** and a **Bangladesh Temple**. The **Chinese Temple** houses an enormous, revolving ceremonial prayer drum.

Teaching centres

Magadha University, an international centre for studies in history, culture and philosophy, is about 3 km from the Mahabodhi Temple. The **Tibetan Medical and Astro Institute** carries out research and gives advice. **Meditation courses**, varying from a week to a month during the winter, follow both the Mahayana and Hinanyana traditions; enquire at the Burmese, Tibetan and Thai monasteries. **Insight Meditation** ① *www.insightmeditation.org*, runs retreats during January and February in the Thai monastery. The **International Meditation Centre** ① *contact via Woodland Rd, Denbury, Devon, UK, TQ12 6DY, T0631-220 0707*, opposite the Thai monastery, also holds courses throughout the year. The **Root Institute** ① *off the Magadha University Rd, T0631-220 0714*, opposite the Thai monastery, is involved in community self-help schemes and gives popular short introductory courses.

Sasaram → *Colour map 3, B5.*

ⓘ *This Muslim site, between Gaya and Varanasi, is well worth a visit. The tombs are a short rickshaw ride from the railway station, which has left luggage (Rs 10).*

Sher Shah Suri, who was responsible for the tombs, asked the master-builder Aliwal Khan to build a tomb for his father **Hasan Khan** around 1535. This later inspired the building of the impressive second tomb for Sher Shah himself. The first imitated the octagonal structure and walled enclosure of the earlier Lodi tombs but was rather plain. What followed, however, was extraordinary not only in scale, but also in its conception. **Sher Shah's mausoleum** ⓘ *Mar-Jul 0700-1800, Aug-Feb 0800-1700, Rs 100*, 500 m away, was set in a large artificial lake so it appears to float. A modern redbrick gateway opposite the Dak Bungalow leads down to the tombs. You enter it by a causeway after going through a guard room on the north bank (originally visitors approached by barge from the ghat on the east side). The grounds and lake provide a relaxing break, though travellers report a certain amount of hassle from local youth.

⊕ Gaya and Bodh Gaya listings

For Sleeping and Eating price codes and other relevant information, see Essentials pages 34-38.

⬤ Sleeping

Gaya *p266, map p266*
Mostly very basic with non a/c rooms, clustered around the train station. Frequent power cuts.
B-D Siddhartha International, off Station Rd, T0631-243 6243, www.rajgir-residency.com. Modern, great food, but noisy and overpriced. Rooms are either a/c or with balcony, not both.
E-F Ajatsatru, opposite railway station, T0631-243 4584. Range of rooms with bath (hot water), some gloomy and noisy, 24-hr checkout. Popular ground floor restaurant.
E-F Royal Surya, Dak Banglow Rd, T0631-242 3730, hotelroyalsurya@rediffmail.com. Spacious, bright rooms, 24-hr checkout, affable staff. Generator, but no a/c during power cut.
E-F Vishnu International, Swarajpuri Rd, T0631-222 4422. New building with large public balcony and an all-important generator. Noisy.
F-G Akash, in the alley opposite the station, T0631-222 2205. Rooms with bath, TV and air cooler around Islamic-style courtyard, bucket hot water, the best bottom-rung option in town. Dorm beds on terrace available but not recommended (Rs 75).

G Railway Retiring Rooms, at Gaya Junction. 6 rooms, 2 a/c, dorm Rs 50 (not for women).

Bodh Gaya *p268, map p268*
Simple budget hotels often quote higher rates so bargain. Good off-season discounts are available.
A Lotus Nikko Hotel, behind walled garden, T0631-220 0700, www.lotusnikkohotels.com. 62 clean and spacious renovated rooms with a/c, those on 1st floor preferable. Good location in pretty grounds.
A The Royal Residency, Dumahan Rd, T0631-220 0124, www.theroyalresidency.net. 64 rooms, central a/c, Wi-Fi internet, most luxurious in town.
A-B Sujata, Buddha Marg, past the Bangladesh Temple, T0631-220 0481, www.sujatahotel.com. Large and lovely rooms, Japanese bath (20 people, Rs 6000/4 hrs), soulless restaurant. Suitable for large groups.
B R.K. International, Buddha Marg Rd, T0631-220 1247, rk_international2008@ yahoo.com. New, 22 spacious clean rooms, a/c, hot water, overlooking Thai Temple. Curious mural above check-in desk.
C Shashi, Buddha Marg, T0631-220 0459. Small, clean rooms, restaurant. Good discounts off season.
C-D Mahayana, Main Rd, T0631-220 0756, mahayanagt@yahoo.com. Huge bright rooms

in an airy building with courtyards, peaceful vibe and charming staff, a good choice. The Dalai Lama stayed here during his visit to Bodh Gaya in 1998.

E-G Siddartha Vihar, Bodhgaya Rd, T0631-220 0445. Decent a/c rooms with balconies in a quirky circular building; next door **Buddha Vihar** (Bihar Tourism) has very cheap dorm beds.

F Root Institute, Magadha University Rd, T0631-220 0714, www.rootinstitute.com. Rooms in a peaceful rural setting, shared or private bath, excellent food, meditation halls and library.

F-G Rahul Guest House, behind Kalachakra Ground, T0631-220 0709. Clean and cheery rooms, plus a good terrace, in a super-peaceful location.

G Deep Guest House, next to Burmese Monastery, near Sujata Bridge, T0631-220 0463, deepguesthouse@yahoo.com. Clean rooms, friendly staff, roof terrace in high season, peaceful atmosphere.

G Shiva, opposite temple, T0631-220 0425. Basic rooms, some with bath, friendly, good restaurant downstairs.

G Welcome Guest House, above Om restaurant on Main Rd, T0631-220 0377. Caters to backpackers, good central location, internet café downstairs. Very cheap dorm beds (Rs 50).

Monasteries

Some monasteries provide spartan accommodation primarily for pilgrims; contact the monk in charge. They expect guests to conform to certain rules of conduct.

G Bhutan Monastery, Buddha Rd, T0631-220 0710. 18 rooms in guesthouses, shared facilities.

G Burmese Vihar, Gaya Rd. Simple rooms (some newer) with nets, dorm, no fan, garden (eat at **Pole Pole** opposite).

G Tibetan Monastery, Temple Rd, T943-020 0476. 10 rooms, shared bath.

Sasaram *p271*

It is advisable to avoid staying overnight here.
F Shilpa Deluxe, GT Rd, T06184-222 3305. 15 rooms, dirty, staff have TV on loud non-stop.
F Youth Hostel.
Station Refreshment Room for breakfast and simple thalis, fairly clean, "nice waiters at least try to chase the rats"!

⊘ Eating

Gaya *p266, map p266*
❅ **Saas Bahu Biryani Restaurant**, Swarajpuri Rd, decent cheap food, friendly staff, a/c and non-a/c options.
❅ **Sujata**, opposite train station in Ajatsatru Hotel. Popular, large menu, cheap but good basic food. Tandoor after 1930.

Bodh Gaya *p268, map p268*
Most tent restaurants operate in winter only.
❅ **Café Om**, decent Western fare draws in every backpacker in town.
❅ **Fujiya Green**, near Kalachakra Ground. Extensive vegetarian/non-vegetarian menu, specializes in Tibetan but it has every continent covered. Attractive interior lives up to the name, friendly service.
❅ **Gautam's**, opposite Burmese Vihar, for apple strudel and cinnamon rolls. Mostly closed off season.
❅ **Lotus Nikko**, good a/c restaurant serving tasty food.
❅ **Pole Pole**, tent opposite Burmese Vihar. Clean, excellent management, good though not exceptional food. Chocolate chip cookies made to order.
❅ **Shiva**, diagonally opposite entrance to temple. Decent Japanese food and simple Western.
❅ **Siam Thai**, next to Chinese Temple. Authentic Thai cuisine, plush interior. Recommended.

⊖ Transport

Gaya *p266, map p266*
Bus
Long distance From Stand across the river: to **Rajgir**; from Gandhi Maidan Bus Stand: **Patna**, **Ranchi** and **Hazaribagh**. To **Bodh Gaya**: buses from the station, but very crowded. Crammed '6-seater' auto-rickshaws leave from station (Rs 10) and from main auto stand opposite the market (Rs 8). After 1800 only private auto-rickshaws are available: bargain hard, Rs 100-150. A cycle-rickshaw from the station to main auto stand is Rs 8-10.

Rickshaw
Auto- and cycle-rickshaws are easily available.

Train
Gaya is on the Grand Chord line of the Delhi-Kolkata section of Eastern Railway. Gaya Junction Railway Station, enquiries and reservations: T0631-243 2031, 0900-1600. **Delhi (ND)**: *Rajdhani Exp 2301*, 2222, except Sun, 11½ hrs; *Rajdhani Exp 2421*, 2253, Wed, Sat, Sun, 11½ hrs; *Purushottam Exp 2801*, 1415, 15 hrs;. **Kolkata (H)**: *Howrah Exp 2308*, 2035, 7½ hrs; *Kalka-Howrah Mail 2312*, 2342, 7½ hrs; *Rajdhani Exp 2302*, 0429, except Sat, 5½ hrs; plus others. **Patna**: *Palamau Exp 3347*, 0240, 2½ hrs; *Hatia Patna Exp 8624*, 0400, 2½ hrs; *Hatia Patna Exp 8626*, 1305, 2½ hrs. **Varanasi**: *Doon Exp 3009*, 0515, 5 hrs; *Poorva Exp 2381*, 1457, Wed, Thu, Sun, 3½ hrs;

plus lots that arrive/depart in middle of night, and others that go to Mughal Sarai, with transfer by auto-rickshaw to Varanasi.

Bodh Gaya *p268, map p268*
Patna has the nearest airport, while Gaya (16 km) has the nearest train station. Computerized train bookings next to the Tourist Office, Mon-Sat 0800-1400. Auto-rickshaws take 30 mins to Gaya; the last shared one leaves 1800, then private hire (Rs 50-100) until 2100.

Sasaram *p271*
Train to **Gaya**, *Doon Exp 3009*, 1908, 2 hrs. From **Gaya**, 0607, 1½ hrs; to **Varanasi**, 0755, 3½ hrs; from **Varanasi**: 1620, 2½ hrs.

⊕ Directory

Gaya *p266, map p266*
Banks State Bank of India ATMs, at station and next to market. **Post** Station Rd and GB Rd. Warning from travellers whose mail/parcels were pilfered here. **Internet** North end of Swarajpuri Rd, short cycle-rickshaw ride from train station.

Bodh Gaya *p268, map p268*
Banks State Bank of India has an ATM on Main Rd, and changes cash, TCs, Mon-Fri 1030-1430, Sat 1030-1230. **Post** T0631-240 0742. Mon-Fri 1000-1530, Sat 1000-1230. **Internet** Several options in the town centre.

Varanasi and around

→ *Colour map 3, B4. Phone code: 0542. Population: over 1.3 million.*

Perhaps the holiest of India's cities, Varanasi defies easy description. A highly congested maze of narrow alleys winding behind its waterfront ghats, at once highly sacred yet physically often far from clean. As an image, an idea and a symbol of Hinduism's central realities, the city draws pilgrims from around the world, to worship, to meditate, and above all to bathe. It is a place to be born and a place to die. In the cold mists of a winter's dawn, you can see life and death laid bare. For an outside observer it can be an uncomfortable, albeit unmissable experience, juxtaposing the inner philosophical mysteries of Hinduism with the practical complications of living literally and metaphorically on the edge.

More holy places surround Varanasi: Sarnath, one of Buddhism's major centres, Jaunpur, a city with a strong Islamic history, and Allahabad, a sacred place for Hindus due to its position at the confluence of the Ganja and Yamuna rivers. ▸▸ *For listings, see pages 281-288.*

Varanasi → For listings, see pages 281-288. Colour map 1, B4.

The city's focus extends from Raj Ghat in the north, to Assi Ghat in the south. At dawn the riverbank's stone steps begin to hum with activity. Early risers immerse themselves in the water as they face the rising sun, boatmen wait expectantly on the waterside, pilgrims flock to the temples, flower sellers do brisk business, astrologers prepare to read palms and horoscopes while families carry the dead to their last rites by the holy river. A few steps away from the ghats, motorbikers speed through the lanes past wandering *sadhus*, hopeful beggars, curious visitors and wandering cows, while packs of stray dogs scavenge among the piles of rubbish.

Ins and outs

Getting there Several airlines link Varanasi with Delhi, Khajuraho, Kathmandu, Mumbai and other cities. From Babatpur airport, 22 km away, there is an unreliable airport bus to the Air India office in the Cantonment area. Better to take a taxi from the prepaid booth. Most long-distance buses arrive at the bus stand near the crossroads 500 m northeast of the Junction Station. Most trains stop at the Junction Station near the Cantonment, about 6 km northwest of the Old City and the budget hotels. Some trains (eg Delhi–Kolkata *Rajdhani* and *Expresses* to New Jalpaiguri and Guwahati) do not pass through Varanasi itself but stop at Mughal Sarai, 27 km away, which is easily accessible by rail or road from Varanasi. Shared jeeps cost Rs 20 between the two stations, or a taxi is Rs 200.

Getting around The only way to really see the heart of the Old City is on foot, though no visit is complete without an early-morning boat trip along the ghats. Varanasi is quite spread out: the university to the south is nearly 7 km from the spacious Cantonment area and the Junction Station to the north. Around town, cycle-rickshaws are common, while autos are usually shared. Buses are hopelessly crowded so you might consider hiring a bike. Unmetered taxis are best for longer sightseeing trips. The city has some of the disadvantages of pilgrimage centres, notably rickshaw drivers who seem determined to extort as much as possible from unsuspecting visitors. Arrival at the station and finding your hotel of choice can be stressful, don't believe touts who tell you it is closed or full – such things rarely change in Varanasi. ▸▸ *See Transport, page 286.*

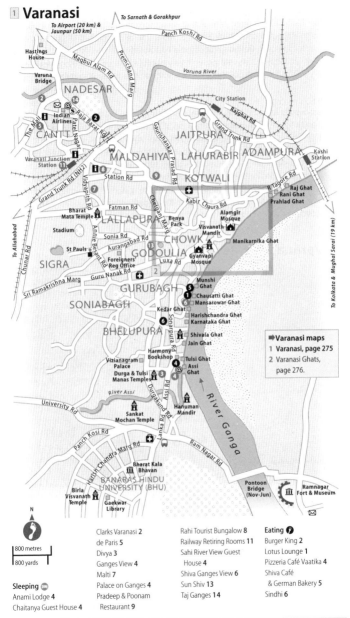

Varanasi

To Sarnath & Gorakhpur

To Airport (20 km) & Jaunpur (50 km)

Panch Koshi Rd

Hastings House

Maqbul Alam Rd

Premchand Marg

Varuna River

Varuna Bridge

NADESAR

The Mall

Raja Bazar Rd

Patel Nagar

Indian Airlines

CANTT

City Station

Raighat Rd

JAITPURA

Grand Trunk Rd

ADAMPURA

Kashi Station

Varanasi Junction Station

MALDAHIYA

LAHURABIR

Station Rd

Gaurishankar Prasad Rd

KOTWALI

R Tagore Rd

Raj Ghat
Rani Ghat
Prahlad Ghat

Grand Trunk Rd (NH2)

Vidyapith Rd

Kabir Chaura Rd

Chetganj Marg

Alamgir Mosque

Fatman Rd

Benya Park

Visvanath Mandir

Bharat Mata Temple

LALLAPURA

Manikarnika Ghat

Stadium

Sonia Rd

Aurangabad Rd

CHOWK

GODOULIA

Gyanvapi Mosque

St Pauls

Annie Besant Rd

Foreigners Reg Office

Luxa Rd

To Allahabad

Chunar Rd

Sri Ramakrishna Marg

Guru Nanak Rd

GURUBAGH

Munshi Ghat

Chausatti Ghat
Mansarowar Ghat

SONIABAGH

Kedar Ghat

Sonapura Rd

Harishchandra Ghat
Karnataka Ghat

BHELUPURA

Shivala Ghat
Jain Ghat

Harmony Bookshop

Vizianagram Palace

Durga & Tulsi Manas Temples

Tulsi Ghat
Assi Ghat

River Assi

University Rd

Sankat Mochan Temple

Durgakund Rd

Assi Rd

Lanka Rd

Hanuman Mandir

River Ganga

Panch Kosi Rd

Harish Chandra Marg Rd

Bharat Kala Bhavan

Ram Nagar Rd

BANARAS HINDU UNIVERSITY (BHU)

Birla Visvanath Temple

Gaekwar Library

Pontoon Bridge (Nov-Jun)

Ramnagar Fort & Museum

➡ Varanasi maps
1 Varanasi, page 275
2 Varanasi Ghats, page 276.

N

800 metres
800 yards

Sleeping
Anami Lodge 4
Chaitanya Guest House 4

Clarks Varanasi 2
de Paris 5
Divya 3
Ganges View 4
Malti 7
Palace on Ganges 4
Pradeep & Poonam
Restaurant 9

Rahi Tourist Bungalow 8
Railway Retiring Rooms 11
Sahi River View Guest
House 4
Shiva Ganges View 6
Sun Shiv 13
Taj Ganges 14

Eating
Burger King 2
Lotus Lounge 1
Pizzeria Café Vaatika 4
Shiva Café
& German Bakery 5
Sindhi 6

Tourist information **Uttar Pradesh Tourist Bungalow** ① *Parade Kothi, T0542-220 6638, Mon-Sat 1000-1700*, is very helpful, Japanese spoken. **Tourist Information Counter** ① *Junction Railway Station, near 'Enquiry', T0542-250 6670, 0600-2000*, provides helpful maps and information. **Government of India Tourist Office** ① *The Mall, Cantt, T/F0542-222 6378, Mon-Sat 0900-1730*, is well run, with very helpful manager and staff; guides available, about Rs 450 (half day), Rs 600 (full day) depending on group size. Also at Babatpur Airport.

History

Varanasi derives its name from two streams, the Varuna to the north and the Assi, a small trickle, on the south. **Banaras** is a corruption of Varanasi but it is also called **Kashi** ('City of Light') by Hindus. As one of the seven sacred cities of Hinduism, see page 336, it attracts well over one million pilgrims while about 50,000 Brahmins are permanent residents. The Jains too consider it holy because three *tirthankars* (seventh Suarsvanath, 11th Shyeyanshnath, 23rd Parsvanath) were born here.

Varanasi is said to combine the virtues of all other places of pilgrimage, and anyone dying within the area marked by the **Panch Kosi Road** is transported straight to heaven. Some devout Hindus move to Varanasi to end their days and have their ashes scattered in

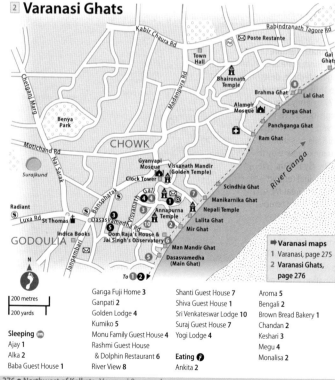

Varanasi Ghats

	Ganga Fuji Home **3**	Shanti Guest House **7**	Aroma **5**
	Ganpati **2**	Shiva Guest House **1**	Bengali **2**
200 metres	Golden Lodge **4**	Sri Venkateswar Lodge **10**	Brown Bread Bakery **1**
200 yards	Kumiko **5**	Suraj Guest House **7**	Chandan **2**
	Monu Family Guest House **4**	Yogi Lodge **4**	Keshari **3**
Sleeping 🛏	Rashmi Guest House		Megu **4**
Ajay **1**	& Dolphin Restaurant **6**	**Eating** 🍴	Monalisa **2**
Alka **2**	River View **8**	Ankita **2**	
Baba Guest House **1**			

Varanasi maps
1 Varanasi, page 275
2 Varanasi Ghats, page 276

the holy Ganga. Every pilgrim, in addition to visiting the holy sites, must make a circuit of the Panch Kosi Road which runs outside and round the sacred territory of Varanasi. This starts at Manikarnika Ghat, runs along the waterfront to Assi Ghat, then round the outskirts in a large semi-circle to Barna Ghat. The 58-km route is lined with trees and shrines and the pilgrimage is supposed to take six days, each day's walk finishing in a small village, equipped with temples and *dharamshalas*.

Varanasi was probably an important town by the seventh century BC when Babylon and Nineveh were at the peak of their power. The Buddha visited it in 500 BC and it was mentioned in both the *Mahabharata* and the *Ramayana*. It became a centre of culture, education, commerce and craftsmanship but was raided by **Mahmud of Ghazni**'s army in 1033 and by Qutb-ud-din Ghuri in 1194. **Ala-ud-din Khalji**, the King of Delhi (1294-1316), destroyed temples and built mosques on their sites. The Muslim influence was strong so even in the 18th century the city was known briefly as Mohammadabad. Despite its early foundation hardly any building dates before the 17th century, and few are more than 200 years old.

The city stands as the chief centre of Sanskrit learning in North India. Sanskrit, the oldest of the Indo-European languages, used for Hindu ritual has been sustained here long after it ceased to be a living language elsewhere. The **Banaras Hindu University** has over 150,000 rare manuscripts. Hindu devotional movements flourished here, especially in the 15th century under Ramananda, and **Kabir**, one of India's greatest poets, lived in the city. It was here that **Tulsi Das** translated the *Ramayana* from Sanskrit into Hindi.

Old Centre

Visvanath Temple (1777) has been the main Siva temple in Varanasi for over 1000 years. Only Hindus are allowed into the temple and there is stiff security by the entrances. The original temple, destroyed in the 12th century, was replaced by a mosque. It was rebuilt in the 16th, and again destroyed within a century. The present **'Golden' temple** was built in 1777 by Ahilya Bai of Indore. The gold plating on the roof was provided by Maharaja Ranjit Singh in 1835. Its pointed spires are typically North Indian in style and the exterior is finely carved. The 18th-century **Annapurna Temple** (*anna* food; *purna* filled) nearby, built by Baji Rao I, has shrines dedicated to Siva, Ganesh, Hanuman and Surya. Ask for directions as you make your way through the maze of alleys around the temples.

The **Gyan Kup** (Well of Knowledge) next door is said to contain the Siva lingam from the original temple – the well is protected by a stone screen and canopy. The **Gyanvapi Mosque** (Great Mosque of Aurangzeb), with 71-m-high minarets, shows evidence of the original Hindu temple, in the foundations, the columns and at the rear.

The 17th-century **Alamgir Mosque** (Beni Madhav ka Darera), impressively situated on Panchganga Ghat, was Aurangzeb's smaller mosque. It was built on the original Vishnu temple of the Marathas, parts of which were used in its construction. Two minarets are missing – one fell and killed some people and the other was taken down by the government as a precaution. You can climb to the top of the mosque for fantastic views (donation expected); again, bags are prohibited and you may be searched.

Back lanes

The maze of narrow lanes, or *galis*, along the ghats through the old quarters, exude the smells and sounds of this holy city. They are fascinating to stroll through though easy to get lost in. Some find it too over-powering. Near the Town Hall (1845), built by the Maharaja of Vizianagram, is the **Kotwali** (Police Station) with the Temple of **Bhaironath**, built by Baji Rao II in 1825. The image inside is believed to be of the Kotwal

(Superintendent) who rides on a ghostly dog. Stalls sell sugar dogs to be offered to the image. In the temple garden of **Gopal Mandir** near the Kotwali is a small hut in which Tulsi Das is said to have composed the *Binaya Patrika* poem.

The **Bhelupura Temple** with a museum marks the birthplace of the 23rd Jain Tirthankar **Parsvanath** who preached non-violence. The **Durga Temple** (18th-century), to the south along Durga Kund Road, was built in the Nagara style. It is painted red with ochre and has the typical five spires (symbolizing the elements) merging into one (Brahma). Non-Hindus may view from the rooftop nearby. Next door, in a peaceful garden, the **Tulsi Manas Temple** (1964) in white marble commemorates the medieval poet Tulsi Das. It has walls engraved with verses and scenes from the *Ramcharitmanas*, composed in a Hindi dialect, instead of the conventional Sanskrit, and is open to all (closed 1130-1530). Good views from the second floor of 'Disneyland-style' animated show. **Bharat Mata Temple**, south of Varanasi Junction Station, has a relief map of 'Mother India' in marble.

Riverfront

The hundred and more **ghats** on the river are the main attraction for visitors to Varanasi. Visit them at first light before sunrise (0430 in summer, 0600 in winter) when Hindu pilgrims come to bathe in the sacred Ganga, facing the rising sun, or at dusk when synchronized *pujas* are performed, culminating in leaf-boat lamps being floated down the river, usually from 1800. Large crowds gather at Mir Dasasvamedha (Main) Ghat and Mir Ghat every night, or there's a more low-key affair at Assi Ghat. Start the river trip at Dasasvamedha Ghat where you can hire a boat quite cheaply especially if you can share, bargain to about Rs 100-150 per hour for two to eight people, at dawn. You may go either upstream (south) towards Harishchandra Ghat or downstream to Manikarnika Ghat. You may prefer to have a boat on the river at sunset and watch the lamps floated on the river, or go in the afternoon at a fraction of the price quoted at dawn. For photographs, visit the riverside between 0700-0900. The foggy sunshine early in the morning often clears to produce a beautiful light. **Note** Photography is not permitted at the burning ghats but travellers are told that it is allowed and then a large fine is demanded. Other scams involve conmen collecting 'donations' to provide wood for burning the poor.

Kite flying is a popular pastime, as elsewhere in India, especially all along the riverbank. The serious competitors endeavour to bring down other flyers' kites and so fortify their twine by coating it with a mix of crushed light bulbs and flour paste to make it razor sharp. The quieter ghats, eg Panchganga, are good for watching the fun – boys in their boats on the river scramble to retrieve downed kites as trophies that can be re-used even though the kites themselves are very cheap.

Dasasvamedha Ghat Commonly called 'Main Ghat', Dasasvamedha means the 'Place of Ten Horse Sacrifices' performed here by Brahma, God of Creation. Some believe that in the age of the gods when the world was in chaos, Divodasa was appointed King of Kashi by Brahma. He accepted, on condition that all the gods would leave Varanasi. Even Siva was forced to leave but Brahma set the test for Divodasa, confident that he would get the complex ceremony wrong, allowing the gods back into the city. However, the ritual was performed flawlessly, and the ghat has thus become one of the holiest, especially at eclipses. Bathing here is regarded as being almost as meritorious as making the sacrifice.

Moving south You will pass **Munshi Ghat**, where some of the city's sizeable Muslim population (25%) come to bathe. The river has no religious significance for them. Close by is

Darbhanga Ghat where the mansion had a hand-operated cable lift. Professional washermen work at the **Dhobi Ghat**; there is religious merit in having your clothes washed in the Ganga. Brahmins have their own washermen to avoid caste pollution. The municipality has built separate washing facilities away from the ghat.

Narad Ghat and **Chauki Ghat** are held sacred since the Buddha received enlightenment here under a *peepul* tree. Those who bathe together at Narad, supposedly go home and quarrel! The pink water tower here is for storing Ganga water. High water levels are recorded at **Raj Ghat**. The flood levels are difficult to imagine when the river is at its lowest in January and February. **Mansarovar Ghat** leads to ruins of several temples around a lake. **Kedar Ghat** is named after Kedarnath, a pilgrimage site in the Uttarakhand, with a Bengali temple nearby.

The **Harishchandra Ghat** is particularly holy and is dedicated to King Harishchandra. It is now the most sacred *smashan* or cremation ghat although Manikarnika is more popular. Behind the ghat is a *gopuram* of a Dravidian-style temple. The **Karnataka Ghat** is one of many regional ghats which are attended by priests who know the local languages, castes, customs and festivals.

The **Hanuman Ghat** is where Vallabha, the leader of a revivalist Krishna bhakti cult, was born in the late 15th century. **Shivala Ghat** (Kali Ghat) is privately owned by the ex-ruler of Varanasi. **Chet Singh's Fort**, Shivala, stands behind the ghat. The fort, the old palace of the Maharajas, is where the British imprisoned him but he escaped by climbing down to the river and swimming away. **Anandamayi Ghat** is named after the Bengali saint Anandamayi Ma (died 1982) who received 'enlightenment' at 17 and spent her life teaching and in charitable work. **Jain Ghat** is near the birthplace of Tirthankar Shyeyanshnath. **Tulsi Ghat** commemorates the great saint-poet Tulsi Das who lived here (see Tulsi Manas Temple, page 278). Furthest upstream is the **Assi Ghat**, where the River Assi meets the Ganga, one of the five that pilgrims should bathe from in a day. The order is Assi, Dasasvamedha, Barnasangam, Panchganga and Manikarnika. Upstream on the east bank is the Ramnagar Fort, the Maharaja of Varanasi's residence (see page 281). Here the boat will turn to take you back to Dasasvamedha Ghat.

Moving north Leaving from Dasasvamedha Ghat, you will pass the following: **Man Mandir Ghat** ① *normally 0930-1730 but if you enquire locally you may be able to get in at dawn or dusk, Rs 100 foreigners, Rs 5 Indians*, built by Maharajah Man Singh of Amber in 1600 and one of the oldest in Varanasi. The palace was restored in the last century with brick and plaster. The beautiful stone balcony on the northeast corner gives an indication of how the original looked. Maharaja Jai Singh of Jaipur converted the palace into an **observatory** in 1710. Like its counterparts in Delhi, Jaipur and Ujjain, the observatory contains a fascinating collection of instruments built of brick, cement and stone. The most striking of these, at the entrance, is the Bhittiyantra, or wall quadrant, over 3 m high and just under 3 m broad and in the same plane as the line of longitude. Similarly placed is the Samratyantra which is designed to slope upwards pointing at the Pole Star. From the top of the Chakra Yantra there is a superb view of the ghats and the town. Near the entrance to the observatory is a small **Siva Temple** whose shrine is a lingam immersed in water. During droughts, water is added to the cistern to make it overflow for good luck.

The **Dom Raja's House** is next door, flanked by painted tigers. The *doms* are the 'Untouchables' of Varanasi and are integral to the cremation ceremony. As Untouchables they can handle the corpse, a ritually polluting act for Hindus. They also supply the flame from the temple for the funeral pyre. Their presence is essential and also lucrative since there are fees for the various services they provide. The Dom Raja is the hereditary title of the leader of these Untouchables. You can climb up through the astronomical observatory (which is overrun by monkeys) to the **Raja Dom's Palace** – a guide will take you round the court room, and on to the roof which has the best view of the river.

Mir Ghat leads to a sacred well; widows who dedicate themselves to prayer are fed and clothed here. Then comes **Lalita Ghat** with the distinctive Nepalese-style temple with a golden roof above and a Ganga *mandir* at water level. Above **Manikarnika Ghat** is a well into which Siva's dead wife Sati's earring is supposed to have fallen when Siva was carrying her after she committed suicide (see page 339). The Brahmins managed to find the jewel from the earring (*manikarnika*) and returned it to Siva who blessed the place. Offerings of *bilva* flowers, milk, sandalwood and sweetmeats are thrown into the tank where pilgrims come to bathe. Between the well and the ghat is *Charanpaduka*, a stone slab with Vishnu's footprint. Boatmen may try to persuade you to leave a 'private' offering to perform a *puja* (a ploy to increasing their earnings).

The adjoining **Jalasayin Ghat** is the principal burning ghat of the city. The expensive scented sandalwood which the rich alone can afford is used sparingly; usually not more than 2 kg. You may see floating bundles covered in white cloth; children, and those dying of 'high fever', or smallpox in the past, are not cremated but put into the river. This avoids injuring Sitala the goddess of smallpox.

Scindia Ghat, originally built in 1830, was so large that it collapsed. **Ram Ghat** was built by the Maharaja of Jaipur. Five rivers are supposed to meet at the magnificent **Panchganga Ghat** – the Ganga, Sarasvati, Gyana, Kirana and Dhutpapa. The stone column can hold around 1000 lamps at festivals. The impressive flights of stone steps run up to the Alamgir Mosque (see page 277). At **Gai Ghat** there is a statue of a sacred cow while at **Trilochana Ghat** there is a temple to Siva in his form as the 'Three-eyed' (*Trilochana*); two turrets stand out of the water. **Raj Ghat** is the last on the boat journey. Excavations have revealed a site of a city from the eighth century BC on a grassy mound nearby. Raj Ghat was where the river was forded until bridges were built.

Other sights

Varanasi is famous for ornamental brasswork, silk weaving and for its glass beads, exported all over the world. *Zari* work, whether embroidered or woven, once used silver or gold thread but is now done with gilded copper or brass. You can watch weavers at work in Piti Kothi, the Muslim area inland from Raj Ghat. The significance of **silk** in India's traditional life is deep-rooted. Silk was considered a pure fabric, most appropriate for use on ceremonial and religious occasions. Its lustre, softness and richness of natural colour gave it precedence over all other fabrics. White or natural coloured silk was worn by the Brahmins and others who were 'twice born'. Women wore bright colours and the darker hues were reserved for the lowest caste in the formal hierarchy, few of whom could afford it. Silk garments were worn for ceremonials such as births and marriages, and offerings of finely woven silks were made to deities in temples. This concept of purity may have given impetus to the growth of silk-weaving centres around ancient temple towns such as Kanchipuram, Varanasi, Bhubaneswar and Ujjain, a tradition that is kept alive today.

Banaras Hindu University (**BHU**), to the south of the city, is one of the largest campus universities in India and enjoys a pleasant, relaxed atmosphere. Founded at the turn of the 19th century, it was originally intended for the study of Sanskrit, Indian art, music and culture. The **New Visvanath Temple** (1966), one of the tallest in India, is in the university semicircle and was financed by the Birla family. It was planned by Madan Mohan Malaviya

(1862-1942), chancellor of the university, who believed in Hinduism without caste distinctions. The marble Siva temple modelled on the old Visvanath Temple, is open to all.

Bharat Kala Bhavan ① *BHU, T0542-230 7621, Mon-Sat 1100-1630, closed holidays, foreigners Rs 100, Indians Rs 10, camera Rs 20 (lockers at entrance)*, exhibits include sculptures from Mathura and Sarnath, excellent Mughal miniature paintings and Benarasi brocades.

Across the river in a dramatic setting on the edge of narrow crowded streets is the run-down 17th-century **Ramnagar Fort**, the former home of the Maharaja of Varanasi. The ferry costs Rs 10 return, or there are rickshaws from the main gate of BHU which cross a bone-jarring pontoon bridge to the fort (under water June to October), Rs 10 each way, or take a boat back or else walk over the pontoon bridge. The **museum** ① *T0542-233 9322, 1000-1700, Rs 16*, has palanquins, elephant *howdahs* and headdresses, costumes, arms and furniture gathering dust. Look out for the amazing locally made astrological clock and peer inside the impressive Durbar Hall, cunningly designed to remain cool in the summer heat, with lifesize portraits lining one wall. Nearby Ramnagar village has *Ramlila* performances during Dasara (October to November) and has some quieter backalleys which make for a relaxing hour's wandering.

● Varanasi and around listings

For Sleeping and Eating price codes and other relevant information, see Essentials pages 34-38.

● Sleeping

Varanasi *p274, maps p275 and p276*
Off-season discounts are available in Jun and Jul. Be prepared for power cuts and carry a torch at night. Some rickshaw drivers insist on taking you to hotels where they get a commission. Hotels on the riverfront can be difficult to locate, particularly at night when walking along the minor ghats is not advisable. Auto- and cycle-rickshaws cannot go down the narrow lanes of the old city, which are a confusing maze on first arrival. Local people will often show you the way but may expect a commission from the hotel, thus increasing the rate you pay. Most **E** hotels have rooms with TV and attached baths. Rooms with river view are worth the extra. Staying in the Cantonment area can be more comfortable and better value for money but it means missing out on the atmosphere of the city.

LL-L Taj Ganges, Nadesar Palace Ground, T0542-250 3001, www.tajhotels.com. 130 rooms, good restaurants (spotless kitchen), pool, top-class facilities, busy, but efficient service, taxis from here overcharge.

AL Clarks Varanasi, The Mall, T0542-250 1011. In a quiet location with good facilities, pool (non-residents, Rs 300 includes food), buffet-based restaurant with expensive drinks, beginning to feel a little outdated but discounts available.

A Palace on Ganges, B-1/158 Assi Ghat, T0542-231 5050, www.palaceonganges.com. Rooms are decorated in the style of a different Indian state or city, in a converted old palace. Restaurant with live Indian classical music plus a small rooftop dining area. The most luxurious hotel on the banks of the Ganga, but some rooms are getting faded.

A Rashmi Guest House, Manmandir Ghat, T0542-240 2778, www.palaceonriver.com. This modern tower is excellently located close to Main Ghat, rooms are clean and modern, a good place for families. The rooftop restaurant is reliable and hygienic. A/c, hot water, TV, advisable to book in advance.

A-B Ganges View, Assi Ghat, T0542-231 3218, hotelgangesview@yahoo.com. Old patrician home converted into welcoming guesthouse with a tastefully decorated range of small rooms, very pleasant atmosphere, interesting clientele (artists and academics), lovely riverside verandas, vegetarian food (restaurant for guests only). Deservedly popular and certainly unique, so book ahead.

B Shiva Ganges View, Mansarovar Ghat, near Andhara Ashram, T0542-245 0063, www.varanasiguesthouse.com. In a British-built old family house, 8 large spotless rooms have high ceilings, multiple windows, mosquito nets and coolers – but strange furniture and clashing decor. Great views from the front upstairs rooms, which share a balcony. The owner is very chatty.

B-D Pradeep, Jagatganj, T0542-220 4963, www.hotelpradeep.com. Clean rooms, most a/c, but near noisy junction. Excellent and very attractive roof top bar/restaurant with real lawn, friendly staff, recommended.

C Hotel de Paris, 15 The Mall, T0542-250 5131, hoteldeparis@indiananetwork.com. Fairly basic but spacious rooms in 100-year-old palace, very well-kept lawns, not bad value.

C-D Divya, behind Assi Ghat, T0542-231 1305, www.hoteldivya.com. Newish clean rooms meeting all standards, those without a/c have air coolers, close to Assi Ghat but not directly on the river, good mid-range choice. Attached **Yafah** restaurant has kitchens on view and Middle Eastern dishes as well as good salads and Indian staples.

D-E Malti, 31/3 Vidyapith Rd, T0542-222 3878, www.hotelmalti.com. Simple rooms, some a/c with balcony, restaurant. Avoids early-morning heat and includes transport to/from ghat north of Alamgir mosque, not bad value and handy for the station.

D-F Ganga Fuji Home, D7/21 Shakarkand Gali, near Golden Temple, T0542-239 7333. Clean rooms, some de luxe a/c, some with common bath, very friendly family, a/c **Nirmala** restaurant on rooftop restaurant with exceptional city views, entertainment 1930 every night, serves beer.

D-G Alka, Mir Ghat, T0542-240 1681, www.hotelalkavns.com. Wide variety of spotless rooms in a modern building, prime riverside location, often full, book

ahead. Handy access down to the ghats from the pleasant courtyard.

E Sun Shiv, D 54/16-D Ravi Niketan, Jaddumandi Rd (off Aurangabad Rd), T0542-241 0468, hotelsunshiv@rediffmail.com. 16 modest but charming rooms with balconies in unusual, art deco-inspired 1960s family house, room service, quiet, no commission to rickshaws. Highly engaging, multilingual owner.

E-F Chaitanya Guest House, B1/158-A, Assi Ghat, T0542-231 3686. A cosy family place with only 4 rooms, in an old building with moulded ceilings, coloured glass windows and tiny terrace at the front. Sadly views are over a car park rather than the Ganges. Rooms with a/c cost more, or air coolers in summer.

E-F Ganpati, next to **Alka** on Mir Ghat, T0542-239 0059, www.ganpatiguest house.com. Atmospheric old building, rooms range from cubby-holes to spacious, private or shared baths, no a/c. Great views from rooftop, very good restaurant, but reports of unpleasant staff.

E-G Rahi Tourist Bungalow (UP Tourism), off Parade Kothi, opposite railway station, T0542-220 8413. A/c and air-cooled rooms and dorm (Rs 120) in barrack-style 2-storey building, restaurant, bar, shady veranda, pleasant garden, simple, clean and efficient, very helpful tourist office.

E-G Sahi River View Guest House, Assi Ghat, T0542-236 6730, sahi_rvgh@sify.com. 12 rooms of all standards, great views from balcony and rooftop, food from spotless kitchen, free local and received calls, owner eager to please, no commission.

F-G Ajay, near Munshi Ghat, T0542-245 0970, ajayguesthousebns@yahoo.co.in. Rooms on several levels, all with bath, clean enough, good service, easy to find if arriving late at night.

F-G River View, Brahma Ghat, T(0)9415-697507, hotel_riverview@hotmail.com. 9 rooms (more underway) in peaceful, clean and friendly hotel, away from tourist scene but still ghat-side, some with bath, TV, air cooler, great views (watch dawn from front rooms), cute breezy restaurant, discounts on longer stay. Ask to be picked up from GPO.

F-G Sri Venkateswar Lodge, D5/64 Dasaswamedh, T0542-239 2357. Very clean rooms in calm, well-run hotel, all water solar heated, strictly no alcohol or drugs, an Indian rather than backpacker vibe.

G Anami Lodge, B1/60, Assi Ghat, T0542-231 4951, anami_lodge@yahoo.com. A good budget hotel on Assi Ghat, with cramped doubles and more roomy singles. Clean sheets but awful pillows, fresh paint, piping hot water and nice management, no hassle. Rooms at the front have decent views.

G Baba Guest House, D20/15 Munshi Ghat, T0542-245 5452, babaguesthouse@ yahoo.com. Basic, freshly painted rooms, some with bath, down, huge Korean menu, food served in downstairs café, when it's too hot to use there's a rooftop restaurant.

G Golden Lodge, D8/35 Kalika Lane, near Golden Temple, T0542-239 8788. Small clean rooms have character, 3 on roof, 24-hr hot water, enthusiastic proprietor, a/c restaurant (**Fagin's**), free washing machine.

G Kumiko, riverside near Dasasvamedha Ghat, T0542-309 1356, kumiko_house@ hotmail.com. Rooms and dorm, breakfast and dinner, Japanese spoken, friendly and quirky owners. Very welcoming. Recommended.

G Monu Family Guest House, D8/4 Kalika Ghat near Golden Temple, T(0)9335-668877. Sweet, atmospheric and a bargain, music lessons and language courses available.

G Railway Retiring Rooms, Varanasi Junction. Some a/c rooms and dorm.

G Shanti Guest House, 8/129 Garwasi Tola, near Manikarnika Ghat, T0542-239 2568. Rooms vary, open-air dorm, 24-hr rooftop restaurant serving tasty food, free boat trips twice a day, motorbike hire.

G Shiva Guest House, D20/14 Munshi Ghat, T0542-245 2108, shiva_guest_house@hot mail.com. 17 simple, clean rooms, some with

hot bath, rooftop restaurant (good food, great views), family-run, friendly. Recommended.

G Suraj Guest House, Lalita Ghat near Nepali Temple, T0542-239 8560. Tucked away behind a tiny temple, quaint simple rooms owned by eccentric family, extremely cheap, nice vibe.

G Yogi Lodge, D8/29 Kalika Gali, near Golden Temple, T0542-240 4224, yogilodge @yahoo.com. Simple rooms, shared bath, dorm (Rs 60), meals on roof terrace or in pleasant courtyard, open kitchen, internet, friendly staff, recommended.

🍴 Eating

Varanasi *p274, maps p275 and p276*
Restaurants outside hotels tend to be vegetarian and are not allowed to serve alcohol (though a couple do). Dry days are on the 1st and 7th of each month, and on some public holidays. Many tourist-oriented eateries are on **Bengali Tola** (large alley running from Main Ghat to Assi Ghat), and there are some excellent and cheap South Indian places at its southern end.

🍴 **Poonam**, Pradeep Hotel (see Sleeping). Good variety of fabulous Indian dishes, served by professional staff in classy surroundings. **Eden** restaurant on the roof is equally good – and has a garden.

🍴-🍴 **Brown Bread Bakery**, Tripura Bhairavi (near Golden Temple), T0542-645 0232. Excellent salads and unusually diverse menu in attractive *haveli* setting with cushions for lounging and live sitar music in evening. The service is abominable, however, and food comes in long drawn-out stages – never expect to eat all together. Always, busy, nonetheless.

🍴-🍴 **Dolphin**, on the rooftop of **Rashmi Guest House** (see Sleeping). Huge menu, plenty of mutton, fish and chicken, food is tasty and covers more continents. The breeze is welcome or there's a/c indoors for summertime. Indifferent staff, but beer (Rs 150) ensures it's busy.

♔-♔ **Lotus Lounge**, Mansarovar Ghat, T(0)9838-567717. Top spot for Ganga views from chilled-out terrace, prices are reasonable for inventive Asian and Western dishes, interesting salads and decent breakfasts. A perfect place if you need to get away from the bustle, plus a clean toilet.

♔-♔ **Ganga Fuji** (see Sleeping). Reasonable, safe food, tempered down for Western palate, live classical music in the evenings, helpful and friendly owner, popular. Recommended for ambiance and hospitality.

♔ **Alka** (see Sleeping). Good veg food from a hygienic kitchen in lovely surroundings. **Ganpati**, next door, has a rooftop restaurant with sublime views and courtyard with Mediterranean feel, both serving quality food.

♔ **Ankita**, Bengali Tola, near Pandey Ghat. The usual tourist menu but the environment is more cheerful than most with a mix of colourful patterns, fairy lights and a mash-up of iconography on the walls.

♔ **Aroma**, Dasasvamedha Rd, Godoulia, T0542-326 4564. Bland pastel decor and low ceilings but a clean a/c environment off the tourist circuit, best for south Indian meals. Free delivery 0800-2200 on orders over Rs 200.

♔ **Bengali Restaurant**, Bengali Tola. The lighting is warm in this cosy hideaway, and the tomato kofta and sumptuous *lassis* are memorable.

♔ **Burger King**, Nai Bazar, Cantt (next to Taj Ganges). Vegetarian only. Not a branch of the international chain. Good veggie cheese burger, ice creams, also chow meins, soups, no seats but recommended if waiting for the train.

♔ **Chandan**, Bengali Tola. Popular for breakfasts (good coffee and real toast), evening meals, and great shakshuka.

♔ **Keshari**, D14/8 Teri Neem, Godoulia (off Dasasvamedha Rd), T0542-240 1472. Excellent vegetarian *thalis* plus north and south Indian dishes and Chinese, "the longest menu in town", efficient service. Highly recommended.

♔ **Megu**, Kalika Lane near Golden Temple. Specializes in Japanese food, popular.

♔ **Monalisa**, Bengali Tola. Western favourites, always busy, nice atmosphere.

♔ **Pizzeria Café Vaatika**, Assi Ghat. Wonderful shady terrace on the Ganga, friendly staff, Italian and Indian food, excellent coffee. A perfect place to relax.

♔ **Shiva Café and German Bakery**, Bengali Tola near Naraol Ghat. Very popular, especially for breakfasts which are excellent (proper porridge). Spartan decor on the ground floor but the 2nd storey is a bit jazzier with low seating and a Nepali-theme, plus the staff are delightful.

♔ **Sindhi**, Bhelupura, next to Lalita Cinema. Excellent Indian vegetarian, difficult for foreigners to get fully sugared Indian *chai*.

⊕ Entertainment

Varanasi *p274, maps p275 and p276*
Clarks Cultural Centre, Peshwa Palace, Raj Ghat, in an old Brahmin refectory, enquire at **Clarks Varanasi**, The Mall, T0542-250 1011. Evening entertainment organized on request for groups, begins at sunset with *Ganga aarti* with floating of lamps, performance of music and dance; US$80-100 including pickup from hotel 1730, return 2030. At dawn, witness prayers with chanting and singing; provides a vantage point for photographs.

⊕ Festivals and events

Varanasi *p274, maps p275 and p276*
Feb Ganga Water Rally, organized by UP Tourism, is an international and national kayak get-together from Allahabad to Chunar Fort. A 40-km race from Chunar to Varanasi takes place on the final day. Also **International Yoga Week**.
Late Feb/early Mar 3 days at Sivaratri, festival of Dhrupad music attracts performers from near and far, beginners and stars, in a very congenial atmosphere, a wonderful experience, many *naga babas* (naked *sadhus*) set up camp on ghats.
Mar/Apr Holi is celebrated with great fervour.

station on the left as you exit. Be extra careful with your possessions on trains bound for Varanasi as theft is common.

Most trains stop at the **Junction** (or **Cantonment**) **Station**, T0542-234 8031 or 131, with 24-hr left luggage; to reach a Cantonment hotel on foot, use the back exit. Can be very crowded; use a retiring room if you have a long wait. **Mughal Sarai** station, T0542-225 5703, has the **Delhi/Kolkata** *Rajdhani Exp* (though some go via Patna); see below. Get your tickets (preferably a day in advance) from the **Foreign Tourist Assistance** inside the main hall which is very helpful and efficient, passport required (0800-2200, Sun 0800-1400). When it is closed use the computerized railway reservations (0800-1400, 1430-2000). **Agra Fort**: *Marudhar Exp 4853/4863*, 1720/1830, 12½/11¼ hrs (book ahead); or go to Tundla from Mughal Sarai Station (see below). **Allahabad**: *Mahanagari Exp 1094*, 1130, 3½ hrs; *Sarnath Exp 4260*, 1230, 2¾ hrs; *Kamayani Exp 1072*, 1550, 3¾ hrs. **Chennai**: *Ganga-Kaveri Exp 2670*, 2025, Mon, Wed, 48 hrs, reserve early. **Dehra Dun**: *Doon Exp 3009*, 1040, 24 hrs, book in advance (no tourist quota); *Janta Exp 4265*, 0830, 24 hrs; *Varanasi Dehra Dun Exp 4265*, 0830, 24¼ hrs, no a/c class. **Gaya**: *Dehra Dun Exp 3010*, 1615, 5¼ hrs; *Chauri Chaura Exp 5004*, 0025, 6 hrs. **Gorakhpur** (for Nepal): *Krishak Exp 5002*, 1630, 5½ hrs; *Manduadih Gorakhpur Exp 5104A*, 0550, 5¼ hrs; **Jaunpur**: *Sutlej Doon Exp 3307*, 0640 1¼ hr; *Farakka Exp 3483*, 1230, 50 mins. **Kanpur**: *Neelanchal Exp 8475*, 0742, Mon, Wed, Sat, 7¼ hrs; **Kolkata** (**H**): *Amritsar- Howrah Mail 3006*, 1650, 14¾ hrs; *Doon Exp 3010*, 1615, 14¾ hrs. **Lucknow**: *Varuna Exp 4227*, 0455, 5 hrs; *Kashi-Visvanath Exp 4257*, 1345, 6½ hrs. **Mahoba** (for **Khajuraho**): *Bundelkhand Exp 1108*, 1330, 12¼ hrs (onward bus, 0600). **Satna** (for **Khajuraho**): *Satna Mahanagari Exp 1094*, 1145, 6½ hrs (from Satna, bumpy bus next day, 5 hrs). **Mumbai** (**CST**): *Varanasi Lokmanya Tilak Exp 1066*, 2025, Tue, Thu, Sun, 25¾ hrs. **New Delhi**: *Lichchavi Exp 5205*, 1500, 13½ hrs; *Shramjeevi Exp 2401*, 1520, 14¼ hrs.

Mughal Sarai Station (with retiring rooms and left luggage). Take a connecting train from Varanasi (45 mins), or allow plenty of time as you need to cross the Ganga and there are huge jams. Best to take a taxi from Varanasi as buses are not dependable and a rickshaw would feel very vulnerable next to the speeding juggernauts. Mughal Sarai has several trains to **Gaya**; a good one is *Purushottam Exp 2802*, 1030, 3 hrs. Also to: **Kolkata** (**H**): *Rajdhani Exp 2302/2422*, 0235, 8-10 hrs; *Kalka Howrah Mail 2312*, 2030, 10½ hrs. **New Delhi**: *Poorva Exp 2381/2303*, 1910/2045, Wed, Thu, Sun, 13/11½ hrs; *Neelanchal Exp 8475*, 0655, Mon, Wed, Sat, 14½ hrs; *Rajdhani Exp 2301/5*, 0050, 9¼ hrs. **New Jalpaiguri** (for **Darjeeling**): *Mahananda Exp 4084*, 2120, 18½ hrs; *NE Exp 2506*, 1835, 16 hrs and to **Guwahati**, 24¼ hrs.

Transport to Nepal
See box, page 269, for border crossing. Payment for Nepalese visa at border in cash only. Try to carry exactly US$30 (other currencies not accepted), as money changers at the border give terrible exchange rates. It is illegal to carry Rs 500 and Rs 1000 notes into Nepal.

To **Kathmandu**, the journey requires an overnight stay near the border plus about 20 hrs on the road so can be tiring. **UP Roadways** buses go via **Gorakhpur** to **Sonauli**, depart 4 or 5 times per day, check at bus stand for timings, 9-10 hrs, Rs 130; from Sonauli, 0600. Private buses (agents near UP **Tourist Bungalow**, around Bengali Tola/Assi Ghat and opposite railway station), often demand inclusive fares for hotel stay; you may prefer to opt for their de luxe buses to the border. Well organized bus service by **Paul Travels**, T0542-220 8137, near **Tourist Bungalow**, Rs 600; departs 0830, reaches **Sonauli** 1830, overnight in "horrific" dorms on Nepali side, next morning depart 0830 for **Kathmandu** (10-11 hrs). Also possible to buy tickets direct to **Chitwan National Park** and **Pokhara** (both Rs 600).

❶ Directory

Varanasi *p274, maps p275 and p276*

Banks Most banks refuse to change money. Travellers are often stopped and asked for 'change'. State Bank of India at Hotel Kashika (Mon-Fri 1000-1400) T0542-234 3742, and Godoulia (near Indica Books), takes approximately 1 hr, changes Visa, TCs. Also at Clarks Varanasi and at airport. Radiant Services, D48/139A Misir Pokhra (by Mazda Cinema), Luxa Rd, Godoulia, T0542-235 8852. Daily 0700-2200, changes TCs and 36 currencies, has a 24-hr counter at Shanti Guest House, T0542-239 2017, and Cantt Office, above Union Bank of India, on the Mall, T0542-251 1052. Shops changing money offer a poor rate. **Internet** Many along Bengali Tola and around Assi Ghat, about Rs 30 per hr. **Medical services** Ambulance: T0542-233 3723. Heritage Hospital, Lanka (near BHU main entrance), T0542-236 8888. Private hospital, out-patients 0830-2000. Many hotels, even budget ones, have a doctor on call. **Post** Head Post Office: Bisheshwarganj (parcel packing outside). Post office in Cantt, Mon-Sat 1000-1800. A man offers to 'help' get a parcel posted for a fee (Rs 100), but you can do this yourself. Also a small post office on Bengali Tola. Couriers: City Airlinkers, Cantt, T0542-234 4214. **Useful contacts** Fire: T101, T0542-232 2888. Police: T100. Foreigners' Registration Office: Sidh Giri Bagh (not easy to find), T0542-241 1968.

Contents

At a glance

⊖ **Getting around** Slow government ferries run to an erratic timetable from Port Blair; private charters preferable. Bikes and motorbikes, auto-ricks and taxis for hire on the larger islands.

◉ **Time required** 1 week.

☀ **Weather** Tropical, with temperatures never higher than 32°C.

✕ **When not to go** Monsoon mid-May to mid-Sep.

Andaman & Nicobar Islands

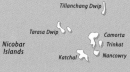

★ **Don't miss ...**
1 Port Blair's Cellular Jail and
  Ross Island, pages 295 and 298.
2 Havelock Island, page 303.
3 Saddle Peak National Park,
  North Andaman, page 311.
4 Butler Bay, Little Andaman, page 314.

The Andaman and Nicobar Islands were, until the tsunami in December 2004, a little-known chain of tropical islands in the Bay of Bengal. Thickly wooded with rainforest and tropical trees, edged by mangrove swamps and pristine palm-fringed, white-sand beaches and coral reefs, these remote islands easily rival the likes of the Maldives or the Caribbean in terms of natural beauty. Fortunately, five-star all-inclusive resorts have not taken hold on these remote islands, although joining the hammocks and wood cabins are some resorts with all the creature comforts.

The sparkling clear water makes it one of the best places in the world to explore the seabed; rare species – dugong and marine turtles – as well as tropical fish and coral reefs are a big attraction. Birdwatchers are also in paradise with 242 species recorded, including the grey teal. The canopied rainforests harbour 3000 species of plant including mangroves, ferns, orchids, palms, climbers and tropical fruits. Of the 58 species of mammal and 83 reptiles, many are endemic, as the islands are isolated.

The islands' aboriginal tribal people are of special interest to anthropologists. Some, such as the Jarawas and Sentinelese in the Andamans, have remained isolated and hostile to outsiders even up to the late 20th century. Others, the Great Andamanese for example, have interacted with non-tribal settlers for decades and now there are very few left. The Indian government keeps the Primitive Tribal Reserve Areas out of bounds.

The tsunami damaged parts of this paradise; the southern chain of islands, the Nicobars, was badly hit resulting in many deaths. Only the southernmost island in the Andamans – Little Andaman – was substantially affected. Parts of the Andamans are accessible to foreigners, the Nicobars are off-limits.

The land

Geography The Andaman and Nicobar group comprises about 300 islands formed by a submarine mountain range which divides the Bay of Bengal from the Andaman Sea. The islands lie between latitudes 6° to 14° north (about level with Chennai and longitudes 92-94° east, a span of 725 km). The land rises to 730 m (Saddle Peak), formed mainly of limestones, sandstones and clays. The Andamans are separated from the Nicobars by a 90-m-deep 150-km strait. The Andamans group has 204 islands (26 inhabited) with its three main islands of North, Middle and South, which are separated by mangrove-fringed islets, together called Great Andaman. The Nicobar Islands comprise 12 inhabited and seven uninhabited islands including three groups: Car Nicobar in the north, Camorta and Nancowry in the middle and the largest, Great Nicobar, in the south.

Climate Tropical, with temperatures of 20-32°C. Annual rainfall is 2540 mm. Monsoon seasons are usually May to mid-September, and November to mid-December (though the first may arrive as early as mid-April, bringing heavy rain on most days). The best time to visit is end November to mid-April. The climate has no extremes, the main contrasts coming with the arrival of the monsoons and tropical storms.

History

Lying on the trade route between Burma and India the islands appeared on Ptolemy's second-century map and were also recorded by the Chinese traveller I-Tsing in the seventh century. At the end of the 17th century the Marathas established a base there to attack the trading British, Dutch and Portuguese ships. Dutch pirates and French Jesuits had made contact with the islands before the Danish East India Company made attempts to evangelize the islands in the mid-18th century. The reputation of ferocity attributed to the Nicobarese may have been partly due to Malay pirates who attacked and killed sailors of any trading vessel that came ashore (some anthropologists believe that in spite of common belief, the aboriginals themselves were not cannibals). The first British attempt to occupy the islands was made in 1788 when the governor general of India sent Lieutenant Blair (whose name was given to the first port) and, although the first convicts were sent there in 1794, it was abandoned within a couple of years.

After the 'First War of Independence' (the 'Mutiny') in 1857, the British gained control of most of the islands and used them as a penal colony for its prisoners (who until then had been sent to Sumatra) right up to Indian Independence, with a short break from 1942-1945 when the Japanese occupied Port Blair, Ross Island and the Nicobar Islands. However, political prisoners were sent in large numbers only after the completion of the Cellular Jail in 1906. Each revolt on the mainland resulted in the transportation of people from various parts of India, hence the presence of Bengalis, Malayans and Burmese among others. Subhas Chandra Bose, the Indian Nationalist, first raised the Indian tricolour here in 1943.

Culture

Sir Arthur Conan Doyle in 1890 described the islanders as "perhaps … the smallest race upon this earth … fierce, morose and intractable". In the mid-19th century, the British guessed the tribal population was around 5000 but the number has been steadily dwindling. Today most of the inhabitants are Indians, Burmese and Malays – some being descendants of the criminals who were taken there. Since the 1950s, refugees from East Pakistan (Bangladesh), Burma and Indian emigrants from Guyana have settled on the

Tribals of Andaman and Nicobar

One story goes that the monkey god Hanuman stopped in the Andamans on his way to Lanka in search of Sita (see page 332), giving the islands his name. They have been inhabited by Aboriginal tribes (some Negrito) for thousands of years but remained unexplored because anyone attempting to land would be attacked. Today there are only a few Andamanese (who once inhabited the Great Andamans), some Onges in Little Andaman (who traditionally painted their naked bodies), the fierce Jarawas on South Andaman and the Sentinelese on North Sentinel. Car Nicobar (Carnic) is inhabited by mongoloid Nicobarese, the most numerous groups. Shompens, who may have been of pre-Dravidian stock, live on Great Nicobar.

The islanders hunted wild pigs, fished with nets and caught turtles with harpoons from dug-out canoes, they used iron for arrowheads and metal from wrecks for harpoons. Some tribes made pottery but the Andamanese particularly were exceptional since they had not discovered the art of fire-making.

The Anthropological Survey of India and the Andaman Administration have been jointly trying to establish friendly contact with the Jarawas and Sentinelese since the 1960s. They consistently repelled groups of explorers with poisoned arrows. More recently, some Sentinelese have picked up coconuts (which do not grow on their island) that were left on the beach as a gesture of friendship by anthropologists. In January 1991, Indian anthropologists succeeded in landing on North Sentinel and in February, a few Sentinelese boarded a lifeboat to accept gifts of coconuts. Study groups have made regular visits, removing most of their clothes in order to be accepted. The 400 or so Sentinelese do not appear to have a hierarchical social structure; they are naked, painting their bodies with chalk and ochre and wearing bead and bone ornaments. The Jarawas remain in the Tribal Reserve set aside to the west of the Andaman Trunk Road, all along the South and Middle Andamans.

main islands to be followed more recently by Tamils from Sri Lanka. The largest concentration is around the capital, Port Blair, with the majority of tribal people (about 15% of the population) living in the Nicobars.

Hindi, Bengali, Tamil, Malayalam and English are spoken. The Andamanese language does not resemble any other; it uses prefixes and suffixes to indicate the function of a word and is extraordinary in using simply two concepts of number, 'one' and 'greater than one'.

Modern Andaman and Nicobar

Economy Before the tsunami, tourism was rapidly becoming the islands' most important industry and the runway at the airport was extended in 2003. Forests represent an important resource. The government has divided 40% of the forests into Primitive Tribal Reserve areas which are only open to Indian visitors with permits, and the remaining 60% as Protected Areas set aside for timber for export as plywoods, hardwoods and matchwoods (a Swedish multinational owns extensive logging rights). Rubber and mahogany have been planted in addition to teak and rosewood which are commercially in demand. Fishing – lobsters, prawns and sea fish – and agriculture are also important, with rice a staple food crop.

Government As a Union Territory the Andaman and Nicobar Islands have a lieutenant governor, Shri Nagendra Nath Jha, a retired member of the Indian Foreign Service and member of the BJP's National Executive since 1994.

Tsunami

In December 2004, following the powerful earthquake off the coast of Indonesia, devastating tidal waves hit many countries. In this region, the aboriginal tribals living on the Nicobar Islands bore the brunt of the casualties. The official human fatalities are daunting: 8000 died in the Nicobars alone, and 80 died on Little Andaman. But this published death toll is contested by aid agencies, who say it is likely that more than half the archipelago's population of 35,000 were lost to the waves. As with all the countries affected, tourism is being encouraged as a direct way of spurring the economic revival that is needed to fund the relief effort and visitor permits are being issued to the Andamans, but the Nicobars, long closed to tourism to protect their tribal cultures, remain so. Of the 572 islands, Car Nicobar was the worst affected. Elsewhere, Little Andaman's two resorts were razed, and many businesses have let go of staff, but hotels are open and operating. Port Blair, the Andaman capital, was unscathed. Havelock Island, the government's prime focus for tourism, was not badly damaged, and the corals around Ritchie's Archipelago are all mostly intact and marine life abundant – so there's still good reason, besides those humanitarian, to visit.

Ins and outs

Getting there

Foreigners with tourist visas for India are allowed a maximum stay of 30 days on arrival at Port Blair, the capital, by air or sea, but may not visit tribal reserve areas or restricted islands including Nicobar. Permits are theoretically extendable, in Port Blair, for a stay of 15 days but only when your initial period of approval is about to expire. However, since the Mumbai terror attacks in 2008, getting an extension is no longer a matter of course and you will need to check the current situation on arrival – extensions are at the discretion of the Deputy Commissioner. Permits are issued on arrival; but be warned – if you cannot show a return ticket, authorities will only issue a 15-day permit (which can then be extended in Port Blair for another 15 days). Permits are checked on all embarking and disembarking ferries. Foreigners are permitted to visit and stay overnight in Port Blair, Havelock, Long Island, Neil Island, entire islands of South and Middle Andaman (excluding tribal reserve), Baratang, Rangat, Mayabunder, Diglipur, North Passage Island, Little Andaman Island (excluding tribal reserve), and all islands in Mahatma Gandhi Marine National Park except Boat, Hobay, Twin Island, Tarmugli, Malay and Pluto Island. You can also visit Jolly Buoy, Red Skin, South Cinque, Mount Harriet and Madhuban, Ross Island, Narcondam, Interview, Brother, Sister and Barren Island during the daytime. In practice, requests to visit remote islands such as Barren, North Passage and Narcondam, which have recently been opened to tourists, are often refused even though ships sail to them. Some dive companies arrange overnight stays as part of a course. Indians may visit the Andamans and Nicobars without a permit but must obtain a permit for restricted areas. See also http://tourism.andaman.nic.in. ▸▸ *For Transport, see page 301.*

Getting around

Hiring a scooter is the most enjoyable and practical way to visit places around Port Blair (recommended particularly for trips to Wandoor, Chiriya Tapu, Mount Harriet and Corbyn's Cove). Buses cover sights and towns on the limited road network. Inter-island ferries sail to coastal towns and islands, which are far more relaxing than the capital.

Port Blair and around

→ *Colour map 3, C6. Phone code: 03192. Population: 100,200.*
Port Blair, the capital, about 1200 km from Kolkata and Chennai, has only a handful of sights. The small town has changed in the last 30 years from one that received a ship from the mainland once a month if the weather permitted to a place connected by several daily flights from Chennai, Kolkata and Delhi. It has a hospital, shops, schools and colleges and a few museums, in addition to hotels and water sports facilities. ▸▸ *For listings, see pages 299-302. See also South Andaman map, page 304.*

Ins and outs

Getting there Veer Savarkar airport, 3 km south of Port Blair, has flights from Kolkata and Chennai. You can get an auto-rickshaw into town for Rs 30-50 if you bargain, or leave the airport compound and take a bus. Ships from the mainland dock at Haddo Jetty where you can get taxis but they invariably overcharge.

Getting around As Port Blair is very small, you can easily see the sights in a couple of days. Aberdeen Bazar in the town centre has most of the budget hotels, the bus station, shops and offices and is easily walkable although hilly.

Tourist information **Government of India Tourism** ⓘ *2nd floor (above Super Shoppe), 189 Junglighat Main Rd (VIP Rd), T03192-233006.* Enthusiastic and knowledgeable. **Directorate of Tourism** ⓘ *opposite Air India office, T03192-232694, http://tourism. andaman.nic.in, daily 0830-1300, 1400-1700; airport, open at flight times, T03192-232414.* Books accommodation and tours, trips to Ross Island and harbour cruises (1500-1700), Rs 75, depart from the Watersports Complex). **Andaman and Nicobar Islands Integrated Development Corporation (ANIIDCO)** ⓘ *New Marine Dry Docks (1st gate after Phoenix jetty), T03192-32098; airport T03192-232414,* runs **Tourist Home Complex** Haddo Hill, and screens films about the islands.

Sights

North of Aberdeen Jetty, the **Cellular Jail** (1886-1906) ⓘ *Tue-Sun 0900-1230, 1330-1615, Rs 5, camera Rs 10, video camera, Rs 50, allow 1 hr,* was originally built by the British to house dangerous criminals and could hold 698 solitary prisoners in small narrow cells. Subsequently, until 1938, it was used to incarcerate Indian freedom fighters. The Japanese used it to hold their prisoners of war during their occupation from 1942 to 1945. Three of the original seven wings, which extended from the central guard tower in a star-shape, survive. The jail was renovated in 1998 and is well maintained and the gardens flower-filled. The **museum** displays photographs and lists of 'convicts' held. There is a 'death house' with gallows and implements used in torture. Entering the cells gives an impression of the conditions within the prison in the early 1900s. There is a well-presented **son et lumière show** ⓘ *Mon, Wed and Fri at 1845, Rs 20, in English,* on prison life. Recommended.

   Chatham Saw Mill ⓘ *Mon-Sat 0630-1430 (arrive 0830 to arrive to avoid lunch break), allow 1½ hrs, no photography,* is one of the oldest in Asia, employing 1000 workers. Tours take you through the different processes of turning logs into 'seasoned' planks. For tours, report to the Security Office just outside the main gate. The **Forest Museum** ⓘ *0800-1200, 1430-1700,* here has unusual local woods including red paduk, satin and marble woods. It shows how different wood is used in the timber industry and methods of lumbering/finishing.

Port Blair

To Bamboo Flats

Chatham Island

Chatham Jetty

Chatham Saw Mill

To Hope Town & Bamboo Flats

To Kolkata, Chennai & Vishakapatnam

Haddo Jetty

HADDO

Foreshore Rd

Forest Museum

Mini Zoo

Panipath Rd

Wildlife Warden

Sagar Tours

Foreshore Rd

Phoenix Jetty

Docks

Ferry Bookings

Marine Museum

DELANIPUR

BUNIYADABAD

Anthropological Museum

Syriar

Moulana Azad Rd

Wine Shop

PREMNAGAR

PWD Of

MIDD

District Industries Centre

GOALGHAR

Railway Reservatic

Mini Bay

N

100 metres

100 yards

Junglighat Jetty

To Airport, Sippighat, Wandoor, Rangat & the North

JUNGLIGHAT

The **Mini Zoo** ⓘ *Tue-Sun 0800-1700*, has a small, uninspiring collection in some very old wooden cages with a few specimens of unusual island fauna including a sea crocodile farm. **Marine Museum** ⓘ *opposite Andaman Teal House, Tue-Sun 0830-1200, 1400-1700, Rs 10, camera Rs 20, video camera Rs 40, allow 30 mins*, has a collection of corals and shells and a display of 350 species of marine life. The **Zonal Anthropological Museum** ⓘ *Fri-Wed 0900-1300, 1330-1630, Rs 10*, is worth a visit; it has a small but interesting collection of photographs of 'exploratory expeditions' to visit the islanders and their dwellings. Woven baskets, pottery, bows and arrows, and other beautifully crafted artefacts are on display.

Viper Island, near Haddo Wharf at the mouth of the harbour, is where convicts were interned before the Cellular Jail was built.

Although the only beach close to Port Blair, **Corbyn's Cove**, 5 km from Port Blair, is only busy at weekends. The water is warm with gentle surf but the palm-fringed white sand beach is not as clean as others.

South Andaman

An easy bus or scooter ride away from Port Blair is **Wandoor**, an attractive beach made more interesting by the vast hulks of skeleton trees that were deposited by the tsunami. The beach gets very busy at weekends, particularly Sundays. The jetty at Wandoor is the place to rent private boats to **Cinque Island** which has spectacular snorkelling and diving; boats should cost around Rs 500-1000 plus Rs 50 for permission.

Chiriya Tapu, 28 km from Port Blair at the southern tip of South Andaman, is only an hour by road. Popular for birdwatching, it has excellent beaches with good snorkelling. From the bus stop, which has some tea shops, a track past the **Forest Guest House** (not possible to stay here) leads to the first beach. Continue along the trail through the forest for 20 minutes (several smaller trails are ideal for birdwatching), until you reach a second beach with very good corals 50 m out; at low tide you can walk a long way. The corals are not so spectacular along the coastline, but there is a large range of fish.

Mount Harriet is good for either a morning or a whole day trip but make an early start to avoid the heat. A path through the forest starts by the derelict water viaduct in Hope Town, which joins the surfaced road near the top. Allow 1½ hours to the top. Alternatively, the bus from the jetty stops in Hope Town near the viaduct, or will drop you at the start of the road up the hill with a 4-km walk from here. Near the top of the road lie the ruins of the chief commissioner's bungalow, abandoned in 1942. It is also possible to ride a scooter to the top but you will pass the **Forest Check Post** ① *Rs 10, scooter Rs 10, camera Rs 25,* where national park fees are charged. Taking the forest path on foot avoids the check post and fees. From Mount Harriet, a signpost marks the 2-km **nature trail**, which is easy to follow to **Black Rocks**, the spot where prisoners were pushed to their death.

Ross Island was originally developed under the British as the Residence of the Chief Commissioner and administrative headquarters. During the Second World War, it was occupied by the Japanese whose legacy is an ugly complex of concrete bunkers, still intact. The rest of the buildings on the island are ruins with spotted deer living peacefully among them. In many cases the walls are only still standing because of the climbing trees. However, the church in the centre and the Subalterns' club are impressive. The small **museum** ① *Thu- Tue dawn-dusk, Rs 10, foreigners must sign a registration book, allow 2 hrs, boat charter Rs 1000,* by the cafeteria has interesting old photos. The island is still under the jurisdiction of the Indian Navy and swimming is not allowed despite the clear enticing waters by the jetty.

About 30 km southwest of Port Blair, the **Mahatma Gandhi Marine National Park** protects some exceptional coral beds and underwater life. Covering an area of 280 sq km, the park comprises 15 uninhabited tropical islands dense with forest and with mangrove shores interrupting the aquamarine waters. Several species of exotic birds and plants thrive on the land while underwater lurk turtles, sharks and barracuda. The rich marine life includes angelfish, green parrot, yellow butterfly, black surgeon, blue damsel fish, silver jacks, squirrel, clown fish and sweetlips as well as sea cucumbers, sea anemones, starfish and a variety of shells – cowries, turbots, conches and the rarer giant clam, up to a 1 m wide. There are many beautiful corals – brain, finger, mushroom and antler – their colours derived from the algae that thrive in the living coral. Coral and shell collecting is strictly forbidden.

Popular islands to visit are Grub, Redskin, Jolly Buoy (requires a permit, obtainable from **Directorate of Tourism**), Pluto, Boat Island, with Tarmugli to the west, Kalapahar or Rutland to the east and the Twins to the south.

For Sleeping and Eating price codes and other relevant information, see Essentials pages 34-38.

◉ **Sleeping**

Port Blair and around *p295, map p296*
Most hotels offer significant discounts Apr-Sep, while prices rise significantly during peak times (Dec-Jan). The prices listed here reflect standard prices during the Oct-end Mar season.

AL Fortune Resort Bay Island, Marine Hill, 2 km, T03192-234101, www.fortunehotels.in. Colonial-style hotel with 48 a/c rooms (a little disappointing – not all have sea view, which costs more), some small replica local huts, cool open bar and a/c restaurant, good gardens but poor tennis court, unappealing sea water pool, far from beach but excellent view across harbour entrance. B&B, half or full board.

A-B Peerless Resort, Corbyn's Cove (4 km), set back from beach, T03192-233461, ppbeachin@sancharnet.in. 48 rooms, 4 cottages, pleasant and airy, well-kept mature gardens, tennis, beach nearby (take own snorkelling equipment), dive centre, excellent service, warm atmosphere, free airport transfer but need taxis to town (by day, wait on the beach for one to pass).

B-D Megapode Nest, Haddo Hill, www.niva link.com/megapodenest. 25 good a/c rooms, short walk from restaurant, large terrace, very peaceful. Includes breakfast and airport transfer.

B-E Hornbill Nest, 10 mins' walk from Corbyn's Cove, T03192-246042, hornbillresort @rediffmail.com. Clean rooms, some on hillside overlooking sea, central open-air lounge and restaurant, transport difficult (stop a returning empty taxi), best for those wanting a cheap shared room near the beach.

D-F Abhishek, Goalghar, T03192-233565, hotelabhishek@hotmail.com. Inconvenient location. Friendly, helpful management, good restaurant and bar, snorkel equipment for hire, free transfer (usually meets flights).

E Raja Monsoon Villa, 9 RP Rd, opposite Jama Masjid, T(0)9474-226394. Clean spacious rooms, good bathrooms and furniture, TVs, in a new building. Best on the 2nd floor, which is really breezy and has good views over town. Recommended. Discounts possible.

E-F Amina, Aberdeen Bazar (opposite Ganesh Temple), T(0)9933-258703, www.a2r2s4.com, Run by a lovely couple with good English, 4 spotless rooms are good value but rather cramped, as are bathrooms. Colourfully decorated and with clean furniture.

E-F Andaman Teal House, Delanipur, book through **Director of Tourism**, T03192-232694. Good views, 27 clean rooms with bath, non-a/c doubles good value, comfortable wicker furniture, spacious lounge-restaurant.

E-F Azad, Aberdeen Bazar, T03192-242646, The choice of most budget tourists, weathered walls but clean enough rooms with attached baths. Singles, small doubles or a/c, all with TV.

E-F Sai Residency, near Lighthouse Building, T03192-212737. Small clean rooms with TV, fresh sheets, some with a/c, 1 has a balcony. Handy for the jetty. From the main road follow the sign for **Sagarika Guesthouse**.

F ANIIDCO Tourist Home Complex, Haddo Hill, T03192-32380. Central. Restaurant, bar and gardens with superb views of the port and Phoenix Bay.

F Jai Mathi, 78 Moulana Azad Rd, T03192-230836. Large rooms, generally clean but variable standard, bucket hot water. Better on the upper floors as lower levels have long-stay gangs of friendly (but noisy) local workers. Not for lone women, bar, helpful staff.

F Shah and Shah, near Aberdeen Bazar, T03192-233696, shahnshahrediff@mail.com. 23 large rooms are rather shabby; benefits are the huge 1st-floor balcony, helpful owner, and proximity to bus station and ferry.

G Kavitha, Aberdeen Bazar, above **Ananda** restaurant, T03192-233762. Often has room when all others full (at time of ship arrive/depart) probably because it is rock-bottom basic. The majority of the 24 rooms are windowless with scuffed walls, but have fans. One of few places to offer a single-room rate.

South Andaman *p297*
There are excellent camping spots with fresh water in **Chiriya Tapu**, set back from Munda Pahar Beach. The trail continues through the forest to a couple of smaller beaches.

⊕ Eating

Port Blair and around *p295, map p296*
South Indian cuisine is prevalent and seafood is excellent. Recommended is local fish fry (spiced tuna or mackerel chunks), especially for trips out of Port Blair. Larger hotels have a wide selection, but meals (most ingredients imported from the mainland) can be expensive. There are several juice bars between the bus stand and clock tower. Government Guest Houses are open to non-residents.

♥♥ **New Lighthouse**, by Aberdeen Jetty. Wide choice of Indian and Chinese dishes in an open-air café, but the reason to come is for the fish – which everyone does at some point when in Port Blair. The evening barbecue has excellent tandoori fish, and lobster and crab come highly recommended. The cosy upstairs seating area serves up cold beer.

♥ **Ananda Restaurant**, Aberdeen Bazar, T03192-244041. Mon-Fri 1000-1830, Sat 1000-1400. Western breakfasts, soups, veg and non-veg; sweets or ice cream for dessert.

♥ **Annapurna**, Aberdeen Bazar. Open 0730-2200. Clean and a/c, always busy with families. Wide selection of vegetarian Indian, good Chinese dishes, but *lassis* disappointing.

♥ **Anurod Bakery**, towards Teal House. Good cakes, snacks and cornflakes.

♥ **Hotel Katta Bomman**, Aberdeen Bazar, T03192-221394. 0630-2200. Excellent South Indian *dosas*, *idli*, etc, from a plastic tray in a cheerful café. Food is fiery. Good fruit juices.

♥ **New India Café**, next to **Hotel Jaimathi**. Good South Indian breakfasts, in a somewhat shabby environment. Great food and prices.

♥ **Teal Bakery**, by bus stand. Good fruit cakes.
♥ **Tourist Home Complex**, Haddo. Indian. Excellent *thali* lunches, try the chicken dishes.

♬ Bars and clubs

Port Blair and around *p295, map p296*
A nice place for a drink is the airy terrace of the Nico Bar at **Fortune Bay Island**, under the soaring roof, with great views and larger-than-life ancestor statues as decoration (beer Rs 135). **Peerless Beach Resort** and **Tourist Home Complex** have decent bars, and Purple Bar at the **Sun Sea Resort** has a back room with some atmosphere and cheap beer. There are several cheap local bars around Aberdeen Bazar.

✹ Festivals and events

Port Blair and around *p295, map p296*
Dec/Jan Island Tourism Festival for 15 days, with music and dancing from all over India and focusing on local crafts, culture and food.

⃝ Shopping

Port Blair and around *p295, map p296*
Local curio shops are by the clock tower and opposite the post office. Tailors sell hammocks. **District Industries Centre**, Middle Point, near tourist office, Mon-Sat 0900-2000. Selection of souvenirs in wood and shell (the government limit collection of shells), good for jewellery.

▲ Activities and tours

Port Blair and around *p295, map p296*
Diving
Foreign tourists generally head to Havelock for diving safaris and courses (see page 307).

Swimming

Swimming is excellent off the uninhabited islands that tourists may visit for the day in Mahatma Gandhi National Park. The sea at Corbyn's Cove is not as clean as it should be.

Tour operators

Island Travel, Aberdeen Bazar, T03192-233358. Air India/Alliance Air/Jet Airways agents. Good excursions and car hire.
Shompen Travels, 2 Middle Pt, T03192-232360. Mon-Sat 0830-2100. Tours of Port Blair and the islands, can book tickets to Havelock, etc (Rs 150 commission, take your permit).

⊖ Transport

Port Blair and around *p295, map p296*
Make sure you confirm reservations. Problems can occur from mid-Apr to mid-May and during the Tourism Festival.

Air

Air India flies daily from **Kolkata** and **Chennai**, plus Jet Airways, Kingfisher and Indigo fly from **Chennai**. The new extended runway may permit flights to/from **Delhi**. Transport to town: frequent buses pass the airport entrance (Rs 5-6). Autos should charge Rs 30 per person; agree fare first. Some hotels send taxis. Flights are best booked a few weeks in advance (earlier for Apr-May). However, due to stricter enforcement of the 30-day stay regulations, officials may find you a seat to fly out even at the last moment. If stuck, try for tickets from Island Travels, Jet Airways or Air India, and ask to be placed on the priority waiting list. You can also request your international carrier to get Andamans' tickets, preferably months ahead. Reconfirm on arrival in India, and after you get to Port Blair. Avoid mid-Apr when the summer holiday rush starts. **Air India**, G55 Middle Pt, behind PO, T03192-234744. **Jet Airways**, 189 Main Rd, Junglighat, T03192-236922.

Bicycle

Hire from shops between Aberdeen Bazar and the bus stop (about Rs 5 per hr) but you need to be very fit to manage the hilly island.

Bus

Local State buses leave from the bus station near Aberdeen Bazar, T03192-232278. Computerized tickets are issued 0600-1900. There is a regular service to villages and districts. From Port Blair, buses go to **Wandoor Jetty** hourly 0530-1800, last returning at 1830 (1 hr). To **Corbyn Junction** buses every 30 mins (Rs 5), change to an auto (Rs 20) for the last 2 km to the cove. To **Chiriya Tapu** buses leave at 0500, 0730, 1030, 1200 (1 hr) but often late; returns 10 mins after arrivals; last at 1900.
Long distance Bus is the quickest to the far north, and the only way of reaching **Diglipur** (which involves crossing 3 creeks by ferry transfer) the same night (0400, 0430, 10 hrs, Rs 170), via **Baratang**. Others to **Mayabunder** (0500, 0945, 8 hrs, Rs 130) miss the last ferry to **Kalighat** (1630) which connects to Diglipur. Direct buses to **Rangat** (crossing 2 creeks by ferry transfer) leave at 0545 and 1145 (7 hrs, Rs 95). Private buses, to **Rangat** daily at 1100 (6-7 hrs, Rs1 30-180), and **Mayabunder**, often noisy video bus. Buy tickets a day ahead from agents around the bus stand.

Ferry

Most inter-island and harbour ferries operate from Phoenix Bay Jetty. Sailings appear in the *Daily Telegrams* newspaper (or ring Shipping Corp of India for times, T03192-233347). There are 2 decks and some snacks available on board. Daily to **Havelock**, at 0600, 1230 and (irregularly) 1400 (Rs 195); journey time is 2½ hrs if direct, or 4½ hrs if the boat goes via **Neil Island**. The Line Ferry leaves Port Blair at 0700 on Mon, Wed and Sat calling at **Neil**, **Havelock**, **Strait Island**, **Long Island** and **Rangat** (Rs 80, 7-8 hrs). To **Diglipur** via Aerial Bay Jetty, Tue evening and Fri morning,

14 hrs. **Little Andaman** (Hut Bay), daily at 0600 (Rs 25/70, 6-7 hrs). There are also less frequent services to **Narcondam** and **Barren**.

Boats to **Ross Island** daily except Wed, 0830, 1000,1230, tickets Rs 75 bought from the Directorate of Tourism. From Chatham Jetty to Bamboo Flats and Dundas Pt, hourly, 0600-2025 (2 hrs).

Mainland ferries These sail between Haddo Jetty, Port Blair and **Kolkata** (66 hrs) and **Chennai** (60 hrs) running to a schedule of sorts 3 to 4 times a month. Also **Vishakapatnam** (56 hrs) once a month. For immigration formalities, see page 294. Tentative schedules for the month are usually available at the end of the previous month; times of departure and arrival appear about a week before in the local papers. Last-minute changes are made depending on weather conditions and tides. Tickets are issued 7 days ahead but are not sold on the day of sailing. They can be difficult to get. Foreigners often stand a better chance than Indians, as there is a separate foreign quota available from booking office at Phoenix Jetty. Apply with 3 photos. The Directorate of Tourism has a tourist quota of 12 bunk-class berths for each sailing from Port Blair to **Kolkata** and **Chennai**. Put your name down well in advance. A few days before sailing, collect a form which entitles you to claim a berth from the Shipping Corporation of India a day or so before tickets go on public sale. End Apr/start May, 50% of tickets are reserved for the 'teachers' sailings' and finding a ticket out becomes almost impossible.

Ships vary, but prices per person are: De luxe Cabin (2 beds, shower), Rs 7631; 1st/A Class (4 bunks, shower), Rs 6341; 2nd Class (for 6), Rs 5031; Bunk Class, Rs 1961. The ships are 25 to 65 years old! Meals are available but it's a good idea to carry some snacks. A kiosk sells biscuits, cigarettes, mineral water, soft drinks. Disembarkation can be chaotic and a free-for-all.

Motorbike

TSG (TS Guruswamy), Moulana Azad Rd, T03192-232894. GDM, T03192-232999, further up the same road, has good Kinetic Hondas, Rs 150 per day. Check insurance papers.

Rickshaw and taxi

Taxis charge Rs 20 within town, Rs 100 for Corbyn's Bay and Haddo Jetty. They may refuse to use meters and are overpriced. Give autos Rs 10 for central areas of town, Rs 20 if it's a bit further; to the airport should be Rs 30.

Train

Railway Reservations Office, near Secretariat, T03192-233042, 0800-1230, 1300-1400. Supposedly separate queues for **Kolkata** and **Chennai**, but a total free-for-all in a small building – best avoided. Buy tickets in advance on the mainland if possible.

Directory

Port Blair and around *p295, map p296*
Banks Credit cards are not accepted at many places in the Andamans. Make sure you have plenty of cash before leaving Port Blair – as yet there are no cash facilities on other islands. **State Bank of India**, opposite bus station, open 0900-1300, Sat 0900-1100, has ATM. ATMs also at Aberdeen Bazar. TCs and currency can be changed at **Island Travels**, Aberdeen Bazar, and at larger resorts. **Internet** Networld, near the clock tower, Aberdeen Bazar, T03192-242459. Best connection, printing, CD burning, Rs 30 per hr, open 0900-2100, closed during Fri prayers (1130-1400). Also **Singh Internet**, near Katta Bomman restaurant, Aberdeen Bazar, Mon-Sat 0830-2130, Rs 30 per hr. **Medical services** Hospital, T03192-232102. **Post** GPO, Mon-Fri 0900-1700. **Useful contacts** Fire, T03192-232101. **Police**, T03192-233077. **Chief Conservator of Forests**, T03192-233321; **Deputy**, T03192-232816.

Ritchie's Archipelago

→ Colour map 3, C6.

The archipelago lies 20-40 km off the east coast of South Andaman and Baratang. Most of the islands are inhabited, but only three are open to foreign visitors: Havelock, Neil and Long Island. They are the focus of the government's tourist effort and can be reached by regular ferry service between Port Blair (Phoenix Jetty) and Rangat Bay (Nimbutala Jetty).
►► *For listings, see pages 305-308.*

Havelock Island

This beautiful island with pristine white beaches is the government's principal centre for tourist development outside Port Blair. The **tourist office** ① *a short walk from the jetty, daily 0900-1630*, has a map. It is the island most visited by foreigners and for good reason – the long stretch of beach from the jetty at Village No 1 down to No 5 beach is unquestionably one of the most beautiful in the whole archipelago. New hotels, restaurants and amenities are appearing at a rapid rate, some of which are insensitively landscaped and of an inappropriate scale for the small island. Yet, despite its popularity, you can easily – as anywhere in the Andamans – escape from other visitors and find your own private strip of sand for the day.

It is a fairly tough cycle ride (otherwise take a bus/auto) along the road to **Radhanagar Beach** (No 7), a dramatic curved bay with a beautiful lagoon at the far end. Narrow **Elephant Beach** can be reached by a jungle trek (not possible in wet conditions) and is a popular choice for snorkellers and novice divers who come by boat; note that mornings can be quite crowded. The **lighthouse**, near to Elephant Beach, is also an excellent spot for snorkelling. Sand flies can be a real nuisance on some of the beaches, notably No 7.

A week-long **Mela**, marking the birth of Subhas Chandra Bose, is held in January with special Bengali cultural programmes.

Neil Island

Neil is the smallest island in the Andamans that tourists are permitted to stay on. Lushly forested, it is very relaxed and attracts far fewer visitors than Havelock. **Bharatpur** (No 4) is the best beach for swimming although parts look onto the jetty. Good snorkelling is easily accessible from the shore, along a reef that begins at the jetty and stretches west along the coast to Beach No 1. Bicycles are for hire from resorts or in the village, and interesting half-day trips include the **Natural Bridge** on the southwest tip of the island (a pleasant spot to watch the sunset) and **Sitapur** in the east (Beach No 5). At Sitapur a beautiful curve of bay finishes at limestones caves where Hawabill birds (unique to the Andamans) construct their 'edible' nests. The tiny island of **Chota Neil** is visible from the beach; it is possible to arrange snorkelling trips through resorts or **Green Heaven** restaurant. Shops sell decent provisions but not tents or hammocks (camping is not permitted on the beaches).

Long Island

Another beautiful island, its main beach, **Lalaji**, is pristine. It is a two-hour walk through woods or by boat (Rs 200). The beach is lined with coconut trees and cattle steal any food left lying about. The drinking water from the well near the beach is of suspect quality. There are a couple of places to stay and getting around is by either bike or foot, there are no proper roads; two to three days is usually enough time to spend on the small island.

South Andaman & Ritchie's Archipelago

To Mayabunder

Middle Andaman

Jarawa Tribal Reserve (No Public Access)

Dharmapur
Nimbutala
Rangat
Amkunj Beach
Rangat Bay

Parkinson Island

Long Island

Jetty

North Button Island

Gandhi Ghat

Homfray's Strait

North Passage Island

Middle Button Island

Spike Island

Uttara

Outram Island

Cape Bluff

Kadamtala

Jetty

Strait Island

South Button Island

H Lawrence Island

Inglis Island

South Andaman

Baratang

Wilson Island

Inglis Island

Middle Andaman Strait

Peel Island

Tadma Bay

J Lawrence Island

Pitman Island

Elephant Beach

No 3
No 5

Kyd Island

Radhnagar Beach

No 7

Havelock Island

Ritchie's Archipelago

Jetty

Mount Campbell
Mount Harriet National Park

Neil Island

Jetty

Mount Harriet (365m)
Madhuban

Sir Hugh Rose Island

Bamboo Flats

Hope Town

Port Blair
Ross Island

Jarawa Tribal Reserve (No Public Access)

Viper Island & Tiny Island

Mahatma Gandhi Marine National Park (Wandoor)

Gharacharma

Husainabad

Wandoor

Sippighat

Tarmugli Island

Redskin Island

Hobay Island

Chiriya Tapu

Boat Island

Jolly Buoy Island

Rutland Island

To Cinque Islands

N

5 km
5 miles

For Sleeping and Eating price codes and other relevant information, see Essentials pages 34-38.

⊛ Sleeping

Havelock Island *p303, map p304*
Beach camping is not allowed on the island.
LL-AL Barefoot at Havelock, Beach No 7, T03192-236008, www.barefootindia.com. Encircled by dense rainforest and tall mahua trees, yet just off the 2-km white-sand beach. 9 small, bamboo, Nicobari cottages on stilts with nets, 8 a/c Andaman villas, 1 and 4-bed cottage, all of an ecologically sensitive design. **Mahua** restaurant is good (see Eating). Price includes breakfast. The tour operator **Barefoot Scuba** organizes jungle treks, kayaking, diving and snorkelling.
A Wild Orchid, Vijaynagar, Beach No 5, T03192-282472, www.wildorchidandaman. com. Thai-style cottages, non-a/c or a/c, delightful verandas, a short walk along a jungle path to the lovely beach with sun- loungers (Rs 100 for non-residents, includes towel, coconut and mineral water), luxuriant gardens, **Red Snapper** restaurant and bar. Breakfast included. Benny and Lynda are accomplished hosts, and often organize parties at either **Wild Orchid** or **Emerald Gecko**.
B Symphony Palms, Govindanagar, Beach No 3, T03192-214315, www.symphonypalms havelock.com. A total of 100 wood/concrete chalets arranged in rows facing each other, 80 of which scar the landscape across the road while the other 20 are at least beach-side although at right angles to the sea. Interiors are comfortable and tastefully fitted out, with stone floors, a/c, TV, good bathrooms and big double beds (no twins). For those who require a more conventional room for the night.
C-E Pristine Beach Resort, Beach No 3, T03192-82344, alexpristinebeach@ hotmail.com. Long-standing camp on one of the best stretches of beach, though some

rumours say it will close summer 2009 (check on arrival). Huts are overpriced due to popularity, all have attached baths, some are duplex with bamboo furniture. Sociable place for a beer.
C-F Emerald Gecko, Vijaynagar, Beach No 5, T03192-282170, www.emerald-gecko.com. Same owners as **Wild Orchid** and same high standards but a more rustic vibe. Good-value huts are bamboo-chic, with white sheets, box mosquito nets, shared washrooms. 6 bungalows have sand-floored bathrooms open to the elements, while 5 split-level lodges have reed blinds and great upstairs verandas.
C-G Barefoot Scuba, Beach No 3. Comfortable palm and bamboo bungalows, some duplex with terraces onto the sea, are more attractive than most with rush walls, towelling dressing gowns and soft mattresses. Clientele mainly divers on packages, but some budget 'chicken huts' (Rs 100, just a mattress) are cute and clean and a good choice. **Café del Mar** restaurant is average, though the proportions generous.
F Sea View, Beach No 3, T03192-282442. Simple new little bamboo huts, all with baths and front terraces. Unimaginatively arranged in a little garden but nice thatched restaurant on the beach. 16 huts in all planned.
F-G Green Valley, Village No 5, T(0)9933-298075. Blue wicker huts are nicely spaced out among a grove of betel trees, clean shared baths, cheap and well maintained. **Smita** restaurant opposite is OK and the family very friendly. Downside is that it's not beach-side.
G Smile Garden, Beach No 2, T(0)9933-210073. One of the nicer budget options with a hippyish vibe, very simple huts are attractively arranged around a little garden, with raised beds, mosquito nets, and nothing else (not even fans). It's 20 m past a local fishing family's home to the beach. Lovely staff and only Rs 120 (high season) or Rs 50 (low). Arrival is marred by the mirror-glass monstrosity of Kapil's hotel across the road.

Neil Island *p303, map p304*

Two new, more upmarket resorts are planned for next season on Neil, enquire at **Wild Orchid** (see Sleeping) and **Dive India** (see Activities tours, page 307) on Havelock for information.
D-E Hawabill Nest, T03192-82630, T(0)9434-291002. Government accommodation, in the village rather than next to the beach. Simple, spotless rooms with a/c (Rs 800) with hot shower although only has running water 0600-0700 and 1800-1900. Clean 4-bed dorms (Rs 150), TV room and dining room. Reservations, Secretariat, Director of Tourism, Port Blair, T03192-232694.
D-G Pearl Park, Laxmanpur Beach, T03192-282510/233880, pearlpark_2002@yahoo.co.in. The furthest camp to stay, basic huts share an unpleasant common toilet, more expensive and spacious ones have private baths, plus some (unappealing) concrete chalets. Nevertheless, it is a lovely setting among lush gardens, close to the beach with sunset views and good snorkelling (a dugong is often spotted here). Food, however, is average and staff lacklustre.
E-G Coco-N-Huts Beach Resort, Neil Kendra, T03192-282528, srikudvt@yahoo.com. Decent, mostly tiny huts (wicker, no unsightly concrete), some 2-storey, set out among palm trees, next to a nice patch of mangrove/beach although the end of the jetty is visible in distance. Central circular restaurant. New huts being added for next season.
E-G Tango Beach Resort, Laxmanpur Beach (No 1), T(0)9434-270454, www.tangobeach resort.in. Rather grotty huts have nets but no fans, however, the blank concrete chalets are fairly new and clean. 2 Nicobari-style huts are large and lack furnishings, with squat toilets. Jungle atmosphere among the towering trees, direct access to the beach with good snorkelling. Decent meals.
F-G A-N-D Beach Resort, Bharatpur, T(0)9474-238770. New and well-managed, these are the nicest huts on Neil with clean sheets, nets, little terraces, some with private

bath otherwise the common bathroom is very acceptable. Cheaper rooms have no fans. Handy for the village and owner is delightful. Adjacent Bharatpur beach is the best on Neil for swimming, the downside is that it's adjacent to the jetty.

Long Island *p303, map p304*

E-F Blue Planet, T03192-278573, www.blue planetandamans.com. Attractive huts, variety of prices and amenities, encircle a good restaurant, 2 mins from a lovely beach. The owners also have a campsite near the jetty.
G Forest Dept Guest House, on path uphill to the left from jetty, simple but cheap. Must book ahead from the Directorate of Tourism in Port Blair.

🍴 Eating

Havelock Island *p303, map p304*

Near Jetty in Village No 1 and at Village No 3 there are several basic places serving excellent grilled fish, vegetable and rice dishes.
₹₹₹-₹₹ Mahua, Beach No 7, T(0)9474-204725. Open 1230-2100. On the upper level of a thatched circular hut to catch the breeze, with white cushioned seating around low tables. Serves excellent Italian food, expensive but of a high standard and the chic and tasteful surroundings make it perfect for a special occasion.
₹₹ Barefoot Brasserie, by the jetty. Due to open summer 2009. Bakery downstairs and Italian and Indian menu upstairs.
₹₹-₹ Blackbeard's Bistro, Emerald Gecko (see Sleeping). Authentic Bengali and delicious continental dishes, good standard but not too highly priced, alcohol available and excellent breakfasts (get there by 1000).
₹₹-₹ Eco Villa, Beach No 2. German bakery and Western-orientated menu, lovely beach-side setting, recommended for authentic pizzas and chicken burgers.

Full Moon, Island Vinnie's, Beach No 3, T(0)9932-082204. Full Moon is relocating in Oct 2009 beneath palm trees by the beach. Some of the island's best food and suitably priced: grilled fish, delicious *dhal*, excellent salads and thoughtful breakfasts. Mellow atmosphere and good management have attracted a local following.

Gita's, Govindanagar, Village No 3. Good for cheap generous *thalis*, including *puri* and *channa* (but not spicy, ask for pickle), plenty to cater for Israeli tourists.

World Class Restaurant, Beach No 3. The best of the roadside eateries, reliable breakfasts, excellent cheap juice, usual wide menu, always busy.

Neil Island *p303, map p304*

Green Heaven, on the road to Tango. Open from 0800 till folks leave. Most people's top choice, it's a bit pricier but excellent food in generous portions. Grilled fish (try coconut), seafood, pasta, Western breakfasts.

Blue Sea, Ramnagar No 3, east of the market. Open till 2230. A simple thatched gazebo in a grassy garden, fresh seafood, chilled out staff, a good place to rest on a bike ride.

Chand, by the market in the village, does great chickpea *dhal*, egg rolls and *vadais*, plus a whole host of items aimed at tourist palates.

◎ Shopping

Havelock Island *p303, map p304*
Village No 3 has a good fruit and vegetable market. Memento t-shirts are a popular purchase (Rs 40-50), plus there's an (un-named) clothes shop just south of village No 3 with a good selection of women's clothes, bags and accessories. Coconut and shell jewellery is crafted by **Anupam Eco Arts World**, Village No 3. Waxing/threading and other hair treatments are available at **Sneha**

Beauty Parlour, Village No 3, near Big Bazar on the road to Radhanagar. Open 0930-1230 and 1530-1830.

▲ Activities and tours

Havelock Island *p303, map p304*
Dive operators
Almost all foreign tourists choose to do diving from Havelock, which is closer to the best dive sites, and has competitive prices and experienced instructors. Most operations shut during monsoon (31 May-1 Aug).
Andaman Bubbles, T03192-282140 www.andamanbubbles.com.
Barefoot Scuba, Beach No 3 and Beach No 7, www.diveandamans.com. Promotes 'eco-friendly tourism'. Digital equipment, PADI courses, high standards and the only dive shop in the world to employ an elephant. However, swimming with Rajan the rescue-elephant, who's become something of a celebrity, is costly at around Rs 10,000 per person.
Dive India, Island Vinnie's, Beach No 3, www.islandvinnie.com. Excellent standards and great staff. Customers are always happy.
Dive India, Havelock Tourist Services, Village No 3. Helpful Nafisa organizes snorkelling and fishing trips, and is a good source of information about ferries and buses.

⊖ Transport

Havelock Island *p303, map p304*
Auto-rickshaws Autos for hire from the jetty to Beach No 3, 5 Rs 30-50; to No 7 around Rs 150.

Bicycle hire Bikes and scooters available from Jetty, No 3, and from most hotels/camps. Bikes Rs 35-50 per day; scooters, Rs 120; motorbikes, Rs 150.

Bus Regular service from Jetty (No 1) all the way to **Radhanagar Beach** (No 7), via Village No 3; hourly, 0730-1130, 1330-1630; from No 7, 0830-1200, 1430-1730 (Rs 10-15, 20 mins). Avoid being swamped by school children at 0800 and 1500.

Ferry Getting a ticket out of Havelock can be traumatic, with long queues and only last-minute availability at the office. Paying someone Rs 50 commission to obtain your ticket for you is recommended. There are 2-4 boats to **Port Blair** daily, the fastest at 1615 (2½ hrs, Rs 195). Boats to **Neil Island** on Tue, Thu, Sun at 1000, Fri at 1500 (1½ hrs, Rs 195), carry on to Port Blair (4 hrs). **Line Ferry** on Mon, Wed, Fri, Sat to **Long Island** and **Rangat** at 1000. Check all timings – internet cafés have copies of latest schedules.

Neil Island *p303, map p304*
Ferry Boats leave to **Port Blair** daily at 0830, others on Mon, Wed at 1630, Tue 1130, Thu-Sun 1300 and Thu, Sat, Sun 1415 (2 hrs, Rs 195). To **Havelock Island**: Mon, Wed, Sat at 0900, Tue, Thu, Sat, Sun at 1415 (no boat on Fri, 1½-2 hrs, Rs 195). The **Line Ferry** connects with **Long Island** and **Rangat** Mon, Wed, Fri, Sat at 0900. There are no problems with purchasing tickets at Neil, just pay on board the ferry.

Long Island *p303, map p304*
Ferry Usually 5 boats a week from **Port Blair**, Phoenix Bay Jetty, via **Havelock Island**.

❶ Directory

Havelock Island *p303, map p304*
Bank An ATM machine is supposed to be in operation by Oct 2009. **Internet** Havelock Tourist Services, Village No 3 (open 0830-1300 and 1600- 2000) and **Lord Corner**, near Island Vinnie's (open 0830-2230), all connections are very slow on Havelock, Rs 2 per min, CD/DVD burning. **Medical services** Medical centre at Village No 3.

Middle and North Andamans

→ *Colour map 3, C6.*

The Andaman Trunk Road is the only road to the north from Port Blair. Since it passes through the restricted Jarawa tribal reserve, it is not possible to drive along this yourself; however, there are daily buses to Rangat and Mayabunder. The bumpy journey takes you past beautiful landscape and involves two ferry crossings. Occasionally the more adventurous Jarawas hitch a lift on the bus to the edge of the reserve. The route runs through some spectacular forest but sadly, despite controls, there has already been a lot of selective clearance of hardwoods. ▸▸ *For listings, see pages 311-313.*

Middle Andaman → *For listings, see pages 311-313.*

Rangat
Rangat is a small transit town with a few acceptable lodges. The main reason travellers spend a night here is in order to catch the Line Ferry to other islands, which leaves four times per week. **Amkunj Beach**, 8 km away, has little shade left but there is good snorkelling off the rocks at the top end of the beach. From Rangat, take any bus heading for Nimbutala or Mayabunder up to the fork for Rangat Bay, then walk 1 km along track to right just after the helipad.

There is a good sandy beach, ideal for swimming, across the road from **Hawksbill Nest**. However, the beach is a wildlife sanctuary where turtles nest between November to April and permission is needed from the Forest Department at Rangat or Mayabunder, or from the Beat Officer at Betapur, 4 km north of **Hawksbill Nest**; a permit costs Rs 10 per day. Those caught on the beach without permission are promised "an unpleasant experience".

Mayabunder → *157 km by sea from Port Blair.*
Mayabunder is the administrative centre for the Middle and North Andamans. All amenities are situated along a single road which runs along the brow of a ridge sticking out into the bay; the port is at the north end. An especially nice guesthouse (see page 311) and great value local fish and prawns add to the appeal of Mayabunder as a place to relax for a couple of days. You can visit the black sand **Karmateng Beach**, 25 minutes away by bus. A shallow sandy slope over 1 km long, with a few rocks at the north end, it is not so good for snorkelling or swimming, as it is exposed and the sea is choppy. Sandflies can be a real problem if there is no wind. A short distance from Karmateng is another idyllic beach popular with foreign tourists at **Gujinala**. You need permission from the Forest Office in Mayabunder or from Beat Officer at Karmateng. There are several islands in the bay opposite the jetty which can be reached by *dunghy*; ask fishermen to take you and expect to pay Rs 200 for a boat charter for several hours. All offer safe beaches for swimming but there is no good coral.

Avis Island and around
This tiny island is just east of Mayabunder but its ownership is disputed between the Forestry Department and The Coconut Society of Mayabunder. To visit, get permission from Forest Office in Mayabunder, and charter a *dunghy* (Sea and Sand guesthouse, see page 311, can arrange a boat). There is a lovely coral sand beach; it makes a great day trip (take a packed lunch) with good snorkelling – and no sandflies. Also enquire about permission to visit **Curlew Island**, **Rayhill Island**, **Sound Island**, **Interview Island** and

Mohanpur on the eastern coast of North Andaman. Tourists are encouraged to destroy any illegal deer traps they find.

Interview Island

Interview Island is home to wild elephants and now has a protected forest. Day visits can in theory be organized from Mayabunder, 20 km away. You may be able to stay overnight at the **Forest Department Guest House** with three rooms; contact the Forest Office in Mayabunder. The island can only be visited in a private boat.

Barren Island

Across to the east from Middle Andaman, Barren has India's only active volcano, which erupted in 1991 causing widespread destruction of the island's ecosystem. Smoky fire belches from the side of the crater. It is only possible to visit on a day trip with no landings permitted; the tourist office in Port Blair runs excursions which are popular.

North Andaman → For listings, see pages 311-313.

Kalighat

It is a small settlement at the point where the creek becomes too shallow for the ferry to go any further. Of no particular interest, it still makes a very pleasant and peaceful stopover between Port Blair and the north. You can cross the river by the mangrove footbridge and follow the path up into the forest which is good for birdwatching. Sadly you also get a good impression of how many hardwoods are being logged. You can (with some effort; little English spoken) take a bus to the beach at Ramnagar (11 km). Better still, hire a bicycle for Rs 5 per hour and enjoy a very pleasant push, ride, free-wheel, with a refreshing swim at the end as a reward.

Diglipur

Previously known as Port Cornwallis, Diglipur is the most northerly commercial centre that foreigners can visit. There is a good market and shops; a special **Mela** is held January/February, which attracts many traders.

Aerial Bay

The small fishing village is the last peaceful location before returning to Port

North Andaman

Blair. Most of the fish is taken to the market in Diglipur. Buses between Kalipur and Diglipur stop at Ariel Bay.

Smith and Ross islands
From Aerial Bay, you can visit tiny Smith and Ross islands just north, connected to one another by a white sandbar. You need permission (Rs 500 for foreigners) from the Range Officer, opposite the jetty entrance. This permit plus hire of a *dunghy* (Rs 600, 40 minutes crossing) make it an expensive day-trip, but it is worth doing. Smith Island, the larger of the two, has sun-loungers and wicker huts providing a bit of shade. Take your own food and water.

Saddle Peak National Park and Kalipur
Theoretically 'Lamia Bay Permits' for Saddle Peak and Lamia Bay are available from the Beat Officer in Lamia Bay. However, the path from Lamia Bay to Saddle Peak is very overgrown. **Kalipur**, a few kilometres south of Aerial Bay, is an interesting little place with a **Yatri Niwas** and some simple huts. There is a beach at Kalipur with Saddle Peak as an impressive backdrop; the sand is volcanic, however, and sandflies are a problem.

Lamia Bay has a pebble beach south of Kalipur which you can walk to. From the bus stop the road leads straight onto a path which is easy to follow (30 minutes). It is possible to camp under a small, round palm-leaf shelter. To the north, there are small bays strewn with large eroded boulders, while the beaches to the south lead towards Saddle Peak, 4.5 km away.

Despite the relatively short distance to **Saddle Peak** (730 m), the rocky beach, the steep climb, the thick forest and the heat, mean that you need a whole day for the trek, starting early in the morning after camping in Lamia Bay. Don't attempt the whole trip in a day from Aerial Bay.

Narcondam Island
East of North Andaman, this is the most remote island in the group. An extinct craterless volcano, it is covered in luxuriant forest (home to the Narcondam hornbill) and was declared a sanctuary in 1977. It is a birdwatchers' paradise though permission to visit is very hard to get and only 24-hour stops are allowed. There are occasional sailings from Aerial Bay.

◉ Middle and North Andamans listings

For Sleeping and Eating price codes and other relevant information, see Essentials pages 34-38.

◉ Sleeping

Rangat *p309*
E Hawksbill Nest, Cuthbert Bay, 18 km from Rangat (buses to Mayabunder go past, ask for Yatri Niwas). Book ahead at Secretariat, Director of Tourism, Port Blair, T03192-282603. 8 clean sea-facing rooms (Rs 250, better views on 1st floor), 2 a/c (Rs 400) 4-bed dorms (Rs 75).

E-F Hotel Avis, town centre. Simple rooms with (Rs 600) or without (Rs 300) a/c, no food available.
F Chandra Mohan Lodge, on outskirts of town. Blue wooden building, run-down, but friendly staff.

Mayabunder *p309*
E-G Sea and Sand, in town, T03192-273454, T(0)9434-287040. Run by a delightful Burmese couple, this gem of a guesthouse makes a visit to Mayabunder worthwhile.

The food is excellent, served in a cute cosy restaurant with cold beer and outdoor seating. Up a hill with great views of the mangroves and the ocean, rather than beachside. Shabby older rooms go for Rs 250, or 2 new (soon to be 4) are bright, spacious, with TV and hot water (Rs 550-650).
E Swiftlet Nest, 10 km from Mayabunder, away from the beach, contact Port Blair Directorate of Tourism, T03192-232694, overlooking paddy fields (forest not cleared at the beach). 10 good rooms, 4 a/c, dorm, 'manager absent' but good food, helpful staff.
F Dhanalakshmi and **Lakshmi Narayan** Small, dirty rooms.

As a last resort, the **Jetty Waiting Rooms** provide some shelter and canteen food.

Kalighat *p310*
There are a few hotels near the jetty.
F PWD Rest House, on a hill, 2 mins' walk from jetty (book ahead in Port Blair). 2 rooms, friendly housekeeper, excellent veg *thalis*.

Diglipur *p310*
G Drua, 15 rooms, unhelpful manager.
G Laxmi, 4 clean rooms with common bath (Rs 120), friendly, helpful. Recommended.
G Sports Stadium, with clean, spacious, guarded area for travellers with immaculate toilets and showers. Recommended.

Aerial Bay *p310*
F PWD Rest House, high up on a hill (book ahead in Port Blair). 2 rooms, often full.

Saddle Peak National Park and Kalipur *p311*
E-F Turtle Resort, Kalipur, book through Directorate of Tourism in Port Blair T03192-232694. Passable rooms, some a/c, dorm, poor food, rather unhelpful staff. Very peaceful, on a hillock overlooking paddy fields with thick forests leading up to the Saddle Peak National Park to the south, the views are magnificent.
F-G Pristine Beach Resort, Kalipur, T(0)9332-925089. Nestled in the jungle

a short walk from the beach, 6 stilt huts (outside bathroom) are very reasonably priced. Can provide snorkelling equipment.

🍴 Eating

Rangat *p309*
🍴 **Annapurna**, on corner of vegetable market (from bus stand, turn left opposite **Krishna Hotel**, the right and left again). Good food.
🍴 **Darbar Bakery**, near bus stand (on right, at start of road to **PWD Rest House**).
🍴 **Nisha** dhaba next to the bus stand, OK *dosas* and *parathas*.
There are also a few *dhabas* at Nimbutala Jetty (from where the Line Ferry departs) which serves up a better breakfast (omelette) than you find in town.

Kalighat *p310*
🍴 **Viji** has OK food, with a bakery, next door.

Diglipur *p310*
Plenty of snack bars; fresh fruit in the market.

Aerial Bay *p310*
Excellent fish is sold near harbour gates; larger fish (tuna, barracuda) in the afternoon (Rs 20-30 per kg). A few shops sell basic provisions and there is a small market by the bus stand.
🍴 **Mohan**. The owner speaks some English and is helpful, will prepare excellent fish dishes for you, good *thalis*, selection of drinks.

⊖ Transport

Rangat *p309*
Bus To **Mayabunder** 0600, connects with ferry to Kalighat at 0930, later bus at 1145 (2½-3 hrs); to **Port Blair**, daily, 0800, 0900 (Rs 95); 2 ferry crossings (at Nilambur and Gandhi Ghat), takes up to 8 hrs depending on bus connections, ie whether your bus goes on this ferry and/or if bus is waiting on other side at Nilambur. Expect the experience to be very bumpy and over-crowded.

Ferry The jetty is at **Rangat Bay** (Nimbutala), 7 km from town. The Line Ferry goes to **Port Blair** on Mon, Wed, Sat at 2000 and on Fri at 1400 (Rs 80, 7-8 hrs), via Long Island, Strait Island, Havelock and Neil Island. Tickets can be bought on board same day if there is space, but better to buy day before at the ticket office in Rangat. Boats from Mangrove Jetty go to **Long Island**; **Mayabunder**, 3 per week, 3 hrs.

Mayabunder *p309*
Bus **Port Blair**, depart 0600, tickets sold from 1500 the day before, at bus station (2 km from jetty). **Rangat**: local bus, 0830-1700 (2½-3 hrs). Also private buses. **Karmateng**: many for beach, 0715-1700 (return bus approximately 35 mins after these times). To **Diglipur**, 3 hrs.

Ferry For **Diglipur**: local ferry to Kalighat, or inter-island ferry from Port Blair calls en route to Aerial Bay every 11-12 days. **Kalighat**: small sea ferry daily, 0930, 1445, 2½ hrs (Rs 3), is very crowded, with little shade. Private *dunghies* leave at dawn; they can carry 20 people (Rs 25 each) and the occasional scooter; a charter costs Rs 400. **Port Blair**: check outside Assistant Commissioner's office near police station for schedules.

Kalighat *p310*
Bus To **Diglipur**: regular local service (45 mins), 0630, 0800, 1030, 1130, 1400, connect with ferry from Mayabunder.

Ferry To **Mayabunder** daily, 0500, 1230, 2 hrs (Rs 3), can get very crowded and virtually no shade; also *dunghy*, 0600, 2 hrs (Rs 15); or charter a *dunghy* at any time for about Rs 300 (the rate for a full boat).

Diglipur *p310*
Bus Buses to all the surrounding villages and beaches. Regular service to **Kalighat**, 45 mins (last at 1900) and **Aerial Bay** (30 mins) which has the occasional boat to **Port Blair**.

Aerial Bay *p310*
Bus It is not possible to reach Port Blair by bus in 1 day, the furthest you can hope to get is Rangat. Private and public buses to **Diglipur** and **Kalipur**, approximately every hour.

Ferry To **Mayabunder** and **Port Blair** (2 sailings a month). The jetty ticket office is not always sure when the next boat is due; better to contact the coastguard tower who have radio contact with Port Blair (no telephone connection with South Andaman). Fare: bunk Rs 47, deck Rs 27 (cabins for government officials only); Indian canteen meals. Tickets go on sale the day before departure at the Tehsildar's office, next to **Diglipur Rest House**; to avoid a long wait there, buy on the boat, though you may sometimes have to pay more, and only get a deck ticket.

Saddle Peak National Park *p311*
Bus Buses between **Diglipur** and **Kalipur**, via **Aerial Bay**. From Kalipur: departs 1230, 1330, 1530, 1740, 2015; to Aerial Bay, 25 mins, Rs 2.

❶ Directory

Rangat *p309*
Bank State Bank of India, by the bus stand.
Post Opposite the Police Station.

Little Andaman

→ *Colour map 3, C6.*

This large island lies 120 km south of Port Blair across the Duncan Passage, six hours on a boat. The main village, **Hut Bay** to the southeast, is 1 km away from the jetty. Heavily deforested during the 1960s and 1970s, much of the island is dominated by betel, red palm and banana plantations which are scenic enough. There were two resorts, both were razed during the tsunami, which pretty much destroyed tourism on Little Andaman for a few years. Now, a small string of guesthouses has grown up 500 m away from the jetty in Hut Bay although they are not on foreign tourists' agenda. The attraction, particularly for surfers, is the large and beautiful beach at **Butler Bay**, around 20 km from the jetty, where it is possible (although not officially permitted) to camp or put up hammocks. If you do make the trip, take plenty of water; food is available in the village a half hour's walk away. Bicycles, but not motorbikes, are available for touring the island to visit an attractive waterfall. There are no facilities for hiring snorkelling equipment, so bring your own. Be aware that the area is notorious for mosquitoes and sandflies and malaria is a real problem.

A fast boat leaves from Port Blair for Little Andaman daily at 0600, returning at 1300 (Rs 25/55 depending on class).

Nicobar Islands

→ *Colour map 3, C6.*

The names given by travellers and sailors from the east and the west all referred to these islands as the 'Land of the Naked' (Nicobar is derived from the Tamil word *nakkavaram*). The islands, which lay on the trade route to the Far East, were visited in the 11th century by the seafaring Cholas during the rule of King Rajendra I who attempted to extend his rule here. Before the British used the Nicobars as a penal territory in the late 19th century, European missionaries (particularly the Danish) made converts during the 17th and 18th centuries but few survived the difficulties of the climate and most died of fever within a year.

The islands, including **Katchal** with a large rubber plantation, **Nancowry** harbour, **Indira Point**, India's southernmost tip and **Campbell Bay** (Great Nicobar), are closed to foreign visitors; **Car Nicobar** to the north can be visited by Indians with a permit. The significant tribal population live in distinctive huts, which look like large thatched domes that are raised on stilts about 2 m high and are entered through the floor. The Nicobarese enjoy wrestling, fishing, swimming and canoeing but are best known for their love of music. Villages still participate in competitions of traditional unaccompanied singing and dancing which mark every festivity.

Contents

Footprint features

Background

History

The first village communities in South Asia grew up on the arid western fringes of the Indus Plains 10,000 years ago. Over the following generations successive waves of settlers – sometimes bringing goods for trade, sometimes armies to conquer territory and sometimes nothing more than domesticated animals and families in search of land and peace – moved across the Indus and into India. They left an indelible mark on the landscape and culture of all the countries of modern South Asia.

The first settlers
A site at Mehrgarh, where the Indus Plains meet the dry Baluchistan Hills in modern Pakistan, has revealed evidence of agricultural settlement as early as 8500 BC. By 3500 BC agriculture had spread throughout the Indus Plains and in the thousand years following there were independent settled villages well to the east of the Indus. Between 3000 BC and 2500 BC many new settlements sprang up in the heartland of what became the Indus Valley civilization.

Most cultural, religious and political developments during that period owed more to local development than to external influence, although India had extensive contacts with other regions, notably with Mesopotamia. At its height the Indus Valley civilization covered as great an area as Egypt or Mesopotamia. However, the culture that developed was distinctively South Asian. Speculation continues to surround the nature of the language, which is still untranslated.

India from 2000 BC to the Mauryas
In about 2000 BC Moenjo Daro, widely presumed to be the capital of the Indus Valley Civilization, became deserted and within the next 250 years the entire Indus Valley civilization disintegrated. The causes remain uncertain: the violent arrival of new waves of Aryan immigrants (a theory no one now accepts), increasing desertification of the already semi-arid landscape, a shift in the course of the Indus and internal political decay have each been suggested as instrumental in its downfall. Whatever the causes, some features of Indus Valley culture were carried on by succeeding generations.

Probably from about 1500 BC northern India entered the Vedic period. Aryan settlers moved southeast towards the Ganga valley. Classes of rulers (*rajas*) and priests (*brahmins*) began to emerge. Grouped into tribes, conflict was common. In one battle of this period a confederacy of tribes known as the Bharatas defeated another grouping of 10 tribes. They gave their name to the region to the east of the Indus which is the official name for India today – Bharat.

The centre of population and of culture shifted east from the banks of the Indus to the land between the rivers Yamuna and Ganga, the *doab* (pronounced *doe-ahb*, literally 'two waters'). This region became the heart of emerging Aryan culture, which, from 1500 BC onwards, laid the literary and religious foundations of what ultimately became Hinduism, spreading to embrace the whole of India.

The Vedas The first fruit of this development was the Rig Veda, the first of four Vedas, composed, collected and passed on orally by Brahmin priests. While some scholars date the oral origins as early as the beginning of the second millennium BC, the date of 1300 BC to about 1000 BC still seems more probable. In the later Vedic period, from about 1000 BC to 600 BC, the Sama, Yajur and Artha Vedas show that the Indo-Aryans developed a clear sense of the Ganga-Yamuna *doab* as 'their' territory.

From the sixth to the third centuries BC the region from the foothills of the Himalaya across the Ganga plains to the edge of the Peninsula was governed under a variety of kingdoms or Mahajanapadhas – 'great states'. Trade gave rise to the birth of towns in the Ganga plains themselves, many of which have remained occupied to the present. Varanasi (Benaras) is perhaps the most famous example, but a trade route was established that ran from Taxila (20 km from modern Islamabad in Pakistan) to Rajgir 1500 km away in what is now Bihar. It was into these kingdoms of the Himalayan foothills and north plains that Mahavir, founder of Jainism, and the Buddha were born.

The Mauryas
Within a year of the retreat of Alexander the Great from the Indus in 326 BC, **Chandragupta Maurya** established the first indigenous empire to exercise control over much of the subcontinent. Under his successors, that control was extended to all but the extreme south of peninsular India.

The centre of political power had shifted east into wetter, more densely forested but also more fertile regions. The Mauryans had their base in the region known as Magadh (now Bihar) and their capital at Pataliputra, near modern Patna. Their power was based on massive military force and a highly efficient, centralized administration.

The greatest of the Mauryan emperors, **Asoka** took power in 272 BC. He inherited a full-blown empire, but extended it further by defeating the Kalingans in modern Orissa, before turning his back on war and preaching the virtues of pacifism, see page 229. Asoka's empire stretched from Afghanistan to Assam and from the Himalaya to Mysore.

The state maintained itself by raising revenue from taxation – on everything, from agriculture, to gambling and prostitution. He decreed that 'no waste land should be occupied and not a tree cut down' without permission because all were potential sources of revenue for the state. The *sudras* (lowest of Hindu castes) were used as free labour for clearing forest and cultivating new land.

Asoka (described on the edicts as 'the Beloved of the Gods, of Gracious Countenance') left a series of inscriptions on pillars and rocks across the subcontinent. Over most of India these inscriptions were written in *Prakrit*, using the *Brahmi* script, although in the northwest they were in Greek using the *Kharoshti* script. They were unintelligible for over 2000 years after the decline of the empire until James Prinsep deciphered the Brahmi script in 1837. Through the edicts Asoka urged all people to follow the code of **dhamma** or dharma – translated by the Indian historian Romila Thapar as 'morality, piety, virtue and social order'. He established a special force of *dhamma* officers to try to enforce the code, which encouraged toleration, non-violence, respect for priests and those in authority and for human dignity.

However, Romila Thapar suggests that the failure to develop any sense of national consciousness, coupled with the massive demands of a highly paid bureaucracy and army, proved beyond the abilities of Asoka's successors to sustain. Within 50 years of Asoka's death in 232 BC the Mauryan Empire had disintegrated and with it the whole structure and spirit of its government.

A period of fragmentation: 185 BC to AD 300
Beyond the Mauryan Empire other kingdoms had survived in South India. The Satavahanas dominated the central Deccan for over 300 years from about 50 BC. Further south in

what is now Tamil Nadu, the early kingdoms of the Cholas and the Pandiyas gave a glimpse of both power and cultural development that was to flower over 1000 years later. In the centuries following the break up of the Mauryan Empire these kingdoms were in the forefront of developing overseas trade, especially with Greece and Rome. Internal trade also flourished and Indian carried goods to China and Southeast Asia.

The classical period – the Gupta Empire: AD 319-467

Although the political power of Chandra Gupta and his successors never approached that of his unrelated namesake nearly 650 years before him, the Gupta Empire which was established with his coronation in AD 319 produced developments in every field of Indian culture. Their influence has been felt profoundly across South Asia to the present.

Geographically the Guptas originated in the same Magadhan region that had given rise to the Mauryan Empire. Extending their power by strategic marriage alliances, Chandra Gupta's empire of Magadh was extended by his son, Samudra Gupta, who took power in AD 335, across North India. He also marched as far south as Kanchipuram in modern Tamil Nadu, but the heartland of the Gupta Empire remained the plains of the Ganga.

Chandra Gupta II reigned for 39 years from AD 376 and was a great patron of the arts. Political power was much less centralized than under the Mauryans and as Thapar points out, collection of land revenue was deputed to officers who were entitled to keep a share of the revenue, rather than to highly paid bureaucrats. Trade with Southeast Asia, Arabia and China all added to royal wealth.

That wealth was distributed to the arts on an unprecedented scale. Some went to religious foundations, such as the Buddhist monastery at Ajanta, which produced some of its finest murals during the Gupta period. But Hindu institutions also benefited and some of the most important features of modern Hinduism date from this time. The sacrifices of Vedic worship were given up in favour of personal devotional worship, known as bhakti. Tantrism, both in its Buddhist and Hindu forms, with its emphasis on the female life force and worship of the Mother Goddess, developed. The focus of worship was towards a personalized and monotheistic deity, represented in the form of either Siva or Vishnu. The myths of Vishnu's incarnations arose in this period.

The Brahmins, the priestly caste who were in the key position to mediate change, refocused earlier literature to give shape to the emerging religious philosophy. In their hands the *Mahabharata* and the *Ramayana* were transformed from secular epics to religious stories. The excellence of contemporary sculpture both reflected and contributed to an increase in image worship and the growing role of temples as centres of devotion.

The spread of Islamic power – the Delhi Sultanate

From about AD 1000 the external attacks which inflicted most damage on Rajput wealth and power came increasingly from the Arabs and Turks. Mahmud of Ghazni raided the Punjab virtually every year between 1000 and 1026, attracted both by the agricultural surpluses and the enormous wealth in cash, golden images and jewellery of North India's temples which drew him back every year. He sacked the wealthy centres of Mathura (UP) in 1017, Thanesar (Haryana) in 1011, Somnath (Gujarat) in 1024 and Kannauj (UP). He died in 1030, to the Hindus just another *mlechchha* ('impure' or sullied one), as had been the Huns and the Sakas before him, soon to be forgotten. Such raids were never taken seriously as a long-term threat by kings further east and as the Rajputs often feuded among themselves the northwest plains became an attractive prey.

Muslim political power was heralded by the raids of Mu'izzu'd Din and his defeat of massive Rajput forces at the Second Battle of Tarain in 1192. Mu'izzu'd Din left his deputy, Qutb u'd Din Aibak, to hold the territorial gains from his base at Indraprastha. Mu'izzu'd Din made further successful raids in the 1190s, inflicting crushing defeats on Hindu opponents from Gwalior to Benaras. The foundations were then laid for the first extended period of such power, which came under the Delhi sultans.

Qutb u'd Din Aibak took Lahore in 1206, although it was his lieutenant **Iltutmish** who really established control from Delhi in 1211. Qutb u'd Din Aibak consolidated Muslim dominion by an even-handed policy of conciliation and patronage. In Delhi he converted the old Hindu stronghold of Qila Rai Pithora into his Muslim capital and began several magnificent building projects, including the Quwwat-ul-Islam mosque and the Qutb Minar, a victory tower. Iltutmish was a Turkish slave – a *Mamluk* – and the Sultanate continued to look west for its leadership and inspiration. However, the possibility of continuing control from outside India was destroyed by the crushing raids of **Genghis Khan** through Central Asia and from 1222 Iltutmish ruled from Delhi completely independently of outside authority. He annexed Sind in 1228 and all the territory east to Bengal by 1230.

A succession of dynasties followed, drawing on refugees from Genghis Khan's raids and from still further to the west to strengthen the leadership. In 1290 the first dynasty was succeeded by the Khaljis, which in turn gave way to the Tughluqs in 1320. **Mohammad bin Tughluq** (ruled 1324-1351) was described by the Moorish traveller Ibn Batuta as 'a man who above all others is fond of making presents and shedding blood'. Despite its periodic brutality, this period marked a turning point in Muslim government in India, as Turkish Mamluks gave way to government by Indian Muslims and their Hindu allies. The Delhi sultans were open to local influences and employed Hindus in their administration. In the mid-14th century their capital, Delhi, was one of the leading cities of the contemporary world but in 1398 their control came to an abrupt end with the arrival of the Mongol Timur.

Timur's limp caused him to be called Timur-i-leng (Timur the Lame, known to the west as Tamburlaine). This self-styled 'Scourge of God' was illiterate, a devout Muslim, an outstanding chess player and a patron of the arts. Five years before his arrival in India he had taken Baghdad and three years before that he had ravaged Russia, devastating land and pillaging villages. India had not been in such danger from Mongols since Genghis Khan had arrived on the same stretch of the Indus 200 years before.

After Timur, it took nearly 50 years for the Delhi Kingdom to become more than a local headquarters. The revival was slow and fitful. The last Tughluqs were succeeded by an undistinguished line of Sayyids, who began as Timur's deputies who were essentially Afghan soldier/administrators. They later called themselves sultans and Lodi kings (1451-1526) and moved their capital to Agra. Nominally they controlled an area from Punjab to Bihar but they were, in fact, in the hands of a group of factious nobles.

The Mughal Empire

In North India it is the impact of the Mughal rule that is most strikingly evident today. The descendants of conquerors, with the blood of both Tamburlaine (Timur) and Genghis Khan in their veins, they came to dominate Indian politics from Babur's victory near Delhi in 1526 to Aurangzeb's death in 1707. Their legacy was not only some of the most magnificent architecture in the world, but a profound impact on the culture, society and future politics of South Asia.

Babur (the tiger) Founder of the Mughal Dynasty, Babur was born in Russian Turkestan on 15 February 1483, the fifth direct descendant on the male side of Timur and 13th on the female side from Genghis Khan. He established the Mughal Empire by leading his cavalry and artillery forces to a stupendous victory over the combined armies of Ibrahim Lodi, last ruler of the Delhi Sultanate and the Hindu Raja of Gwalior, at **Panipat**, 80 km north of Delhi, in 1526. When he died four years later, the Empire was still far from secured, but he had not only laid the foundations of political and military power but had also begun to establish courtly traditions of poetry, literature and art which became the hallmark of subsequent Mughal rulers.

Babur, used to Persian gardens and cool Afghan hills, was unimpressed by what he saw of India. In his autobiography he wrote: "Hindustan is a country that has few pleasures to recommend it. The people are not handsome. They have no idea of the charms of friendly society, of frankly mixing together, or of familiar intercourse. They have no genius, no comprehension of mind, no politeness of manner, no kindness or fellow-feeling, no ingenuity or mechanical invention in planning or executing their handicraft works, no skill or knowledge in design or architecture; they have no horses, no good flesh, no grapes or musk melons, no good fruits, no ice or cold water, no good food or bread in their bazars, no baths or colleges, no candles, no torches, not a candlestick."

Babur's depressing catalogue was the view of a disenchanted outsider. Within two generations the Mughals had become fully at home in their Indian environment and brought some radical changes. Babur was charismatic. He ruled by keeping the loyalty of his military chiefs, giving them control of large areas of territory.

Humayun However, their strength posed a problem for Humayun, his successor. Almost immediately after Babur's death Humayun was forced to retreat from Delhi through Sind with his pregnant wife. His son Akbar, who was to become the greatest of the Mughal emperors, was born at Umarkot in Sindh, modern Pakistan, during this period of exile, on 23 November 1542.

Akbar Akbar was only 13 when he took the throne in 1556. The next 44 years were one of the most remarkable periods of South Asian history, paralleled by the Elizabethan period in England, where Queen Elizabeth I ruled from 1558 to 1603. Although Akbar inherited the throne, it was he who really created the empire. He also gave it many of its distinguishing features.

Through his marriage to a Hindu princess he ensured that Hindus were given honoured positions in government, as well as respect for their religious beliefs and practices. He sustained a passionate interest in art and literature, matched by a determination to create monuments to his empire's political power and he laid the foundations for an artistic and architectural tradition which developed a totally distinctive Indian style. This emerged from the separate elements of Iranian and Indian traditions by a constant process of blending and originality of which he was the chief patron.

But these achievements were only possible because of his political and military gifts. From 1556 until his 18th birthday in 1560, Akbar was served by a prince regent, Bairam Khan. However, already at the age of 15 he had conquered Ajmer and large areas of Central India. Chittor and Ranthambore fell to him in 1567-1568, bringing most of what is now Rajasthan under his control. This opened the door south to Gujarat.

Afghans continued to cause his empire difficulties, including Daud Karrani, who declared independence in East India in 1574. That threat to Mughal power was finally crushed with Karrani's death in 1576. Bengal was far from the last of his conquests. He brought Kabul back under Mughal control in the 1580s and established a presence from Kashmir, Sind and Baluchistan in the north and west, to the Godavari River on the border of modern Andhra Pradesh in the south.

Akbar deliberately widened his power base by incorporating Rajput princes into the administrative structure and giving them extensive rights in the revenue from land. He abolished the hated tax on non-Muslims (*jizya*) – ultimately reinstated by his strictly orthodox great grandson Aurangzeb – and ceased levying taxes on Hindus who went on pilgrimage. He also ended the practice of forcible conversion to Islam.

Artistic treasures abound from Akbar's court – paintings, jewellery, weapons – often bringing together material and skills from across the known world. Akbar's eclecticism had a political purpose, for he was trying to build a focus of loyalty beyond that of caste, social group, region or religion. Like Roman emperors before him, he deliberately cultivated a new religion in which the emperor himself attained divinity, hoping thereby to give the empire a legitimacy which would last. While his religion disappeared with his death, the legitimacy of the Mughals survived another 200 years, long after their real power had almost disappeared.

Jahangir Akbar died of a stomach illness in 1605. He was succeeded by his son, Prince Salim, who inherited the throne as Emperor Jahangir ('world seizer'). He added little to the territory of the empire, consolidating the Mughals' hold on the Himalayan foothills and parts of central India but restricting his innovative energies to pushing back frontiers of art rather than of land. He commissioned works of art and literature, many of which directly recorded life in the Mughal court. Hunting scenes were not just romanticized accounts of rural life, but conveyed the real dangers of hunting lions or tigers; implements, furniture, tools and weapons were made with lavish care and often exquisite design.

From early youth Jahangir had shown an artistic temperament, but he also became addicted to alcohol and then to opium. In his autobiography, he wrote: "I had not drunk until I was 18, except in the time of my infancy two or three times my mother and wet nurses gave it by way of infantile remedy, mixed with water and rose water to take away a cough ... years later a gunner said that if I would take a glass of wine it would drive away the feeling of being tired and heavy ... After that I took to drinking wine... until wine made from grapes ceased to intoxicate me and I took to drinking arrack (local spirits). By degrees my potions rose to 20 cups of doubly distilled spirits, 14 during the daytime and the remainder at night."

Nur Jahan Jahangir's favourite wife, Nur Jahan, brought her own artistic gifts. Born the daughter of an Iranian nobleman, she had been brought to the Mughal court along with her family as a child and moved to Bengal as the wife of Sher Afgan. She made rapid progress after her first husband's accidental death in 1607, which caused her to move from Bengal to be a lady in waiting for one of Akbar's widows.

At the Mughal court in 1611, she met Jahangir. Mutually enraptured, they were married in May. Jahangir gave her the title Nur Mahal (Light of the Palace), soon increased to Nur Jahan (Light of the World). Aged 34, she was strikingly beautiful and had an astonishing reputation for physical skill and intellectual wit. She was a crack shot with a gun, highly artistic, determined yet philanthropic. Throughout her life Jahangir was so captivated by her that he flouted Muslim convention by minting coins bearing her image.

By 1622 Nur Jahan effectively controlled the empire. She commissioned and supervised the building in Agra of one of the Mughal world's most beautiful buildings, the

I'timad ud-Daula ('Pillar of government'), as a tomb for her father and mother. Her father, **Ghiyas Beg**, had risen to become one of Jahangir's most trusted advisers and Nur Jahan was determined to ensure that their memory was honoured. She was less successful in her wish to deny the succession after Jahangir's death at the age of 58 to Prince Khurram. Acceding to the throne in 1628, he took the title of Shah Jahan (*Ruler of the World*) and in the next 30 years his reign represented the height of Mughal power.

Shah Jahan The Mughal Empire was under attack in the Deccan and the northwest when Shah Jahan became Emperor. He tried to re-establish and extend Mughal authority in both regions by a combination of military campaigns and skilled diplomacy. Akbar's craftsmen had already carved outstandingly beautiful *jalis* for the tomb of Salim Chishti in Fatehpur Sikri, but Shah Jahan developed the form further. Undoubtedly the finest tribute to these skills is found in the Taj Mahal, the tribute to his beloved wife Mumtaz Mahal, who died giving birth to her fourteenth child in 1631.

Aurangzeb The need to expand the area under Mughal control was felt even more strongly by Aurangzeb ('*The jewel in the throne*') than by his predecessors. He had shown his intellectual gifts in his grandfather Jahangir's court when held hostage to guarantee Shah Jahan's good behaviour, learning Arabic, Persian, Turkish and Hindi. When he seized power at the age of 40, he needed all his political and military skills to hold on to an unwieldy empire that was in permanent danger of collapse from its own size.

Aurangzeb realized that the resources of the territory he inherited from Shah Jahan were not enough. One response was to push south, while maintaining his hold on the east and north. Initially he maintained his alliances with the Rajputs in the west, which had been a crucial element in Mughal strategy. In 1678 he claimed absolute rights over Jodhpur and went to war with the Rajput clans at the same time embarking on a policy of outright Islamisation. However, for the remaining 39 years of his reign he was forced to struggle continuously to sustain his power.

The East India Company and the rise of British power

The British were unique among the foreign rulers of India in coming by sea rather than through the northwest and in coming first for trade rather than for military conquest. The ports that they established – Madras, Bombay and Calcutta – became completely new centres of political, economic and social activity. Before them Indian empires had controlled their territories from the land. The British dictated the emerging shape of the economy by controlling sea-borne trade. From the middle of the 19th century railways transformed the economic and political structure of South Asia and it was those three centres of British political control, along with the late addition of Delhi, which became the foci of economic development and political change.

The East India Company in Madras and Bengal

In its first 90 years of contact with South Asia after the Company set up its first trading post at **Masulipatnam**, on the east coast of India, it had depended almost entirely on trade for its profits. However, in 1701, only 11 years after a British settlement was first established at Calcutta, the Company was given rights to land revenue in Bengal.

The Company was accepted and sometimes welcomed, partly because it offered to bolster the inadequate revenues of the Mughals by exchanging silver bullion for the cloth it bought. However, in the south the Company moved further towards consolidating its political base. Wars between South India's regional factions gave the Company the chance to extend their influence by making alliances and offering support to some of these factions in their struggles, which were complicated by the extension to Indian soil of the European contest for power between the French and the British.

Robert Clive The British established control over both Bengal and Southeast India in the middle of the 17th century. Robert Clive, in alliance with a collection of disaffected Hindu landowners and Muslim soldiers, defeated the new Nawab of Bengal, the 20-year-old Siraj-ud-Daula, in June 1757 at **Plassey** (Palashi), about 100 km north of Calcutta.

Hastings and Cornwallis The essential features of British control were mapped out in the next quarter of a century through the work of **Warren Hastings**, Governor-General from 1774 until 1785 and **Lord Cornwallis** who succeeded and remained in charge until 1793. Cornwallis was responsible for putting Europeans in charge of all the higher levels of revenue collection and administration and for introducing government by the rule of law, making even government officers subject to the courts.

The decline of Muslim power

The extension of East India Company power in the Mughal periphery of India's south and east took place against a background of the rising power of Sivaji and his Marathas.

Sivaji and the Marathas Sivaji was the son of a Hindu who had served as a small-scale chief in the Muslim-ruled state of Bijapur. The weakness of Bijapur encouraged Sivaji to extend his father's area of control and he led a rebellion. The Bijapur general Afzal Khan, sent to put it down, agreed to meet Sivaji in private to reach a settlement. In an act which is still remembered by both Muslims and Marathas, Sivaji embraced him with steel claws attached to his fingers and tore him apart. It was the start of a campaign which took Maratha power as far south as Madurai and to the doors of Delhi and Calcutta.

Although Sivaji himself died in 1680, Aurangzeb never fully came to terms with the rising power of the Marathas, though he did end their ambitions to form an empire of their own. While the Maratha confederacy was able to threaten Delhi within 50 years of Aurangzeb's death, by the early 19th century it had dissolved into five independent states, with whom the British ultimately dealt separately.

Nor was Aurangzeb able to create any wide sense of identity with the Mughals as a legitimate popular power. Instead, under the influence of Sunni Muslim theologians, he retreated into insistence on Islamic purity. He imposed Islamic law, the *sharia*, promoted only Muslims to positions of power and authority, tried to replace Hindu administrators and revenue collectors with Muslims, and reimposed the *jizya* tax on all non-Muslims. By the time of his death in 1707 the empire no longer had either the broadness of spirit or the physical means to survive.

Bahadur Shah The decline was postponed briefly by the five-year reign of Aurangzeb's son. Sixty-three when he acceded to the throne, Bahadur Shah restored some of its faded fortunes. He made agreements with the Marathas and the Rajputs and defeated the Sikhs in Punjab before taking the last Sikh guru into his service. Nine emperors succeeded Aurangzeb between his death and the exile of the last Mughal ruler in 1858. It was no accident that it was in that year that the British ended the rule of its East India Company and decreed India to be its Indian empire.

Mohammad Shah remained in his capital of Delhi, resigning himself to enjoying what Carey Welch has called "the conventional triad of joys: the wine was excellent, as were the women and for him the song was especially rewarding". The idyll was rudely shattered by the invasion of **Nadir Shah** in 1739, an Iranian marauder who slaughtered thousands in Delhi and stole priceless Mughal treasures, including the Peacock Throne.

The East India Company's push for power

Alliances   In the century and a half that followed the death of Aurangzeb, the British East India Company extended its economic and political influence into the heart of India. As the Mughal Empire lost its power India fell into many smaller states. The Company undertook to protect the rulers of several of these states from external attack by stationing British troops in their territory. In exchange for this service the rulers paid subsidies to the Company. The British extended their territory through the 18th century as successive regional powers were annexed and brought under direct Company rule.

Progress to direct British control was uneven and often opposed. The Sikhs in Punjab, the Marathas in the west and the Mysore sultans in the south, fiercely contested British advances. **Haidar Ali** and **Tipu Sultan**, who had built a wealthy kingdom in the Mysore region, resisted attempts to incorporate them. Tipu was finally killed in 1799 at the battle of Srirangapatnam, an island fort in the Kaveri River just north of Mysore, where Arthur Wellesley, later the Duke of Wellington, began to make his military reputation.

The Marathas were not defeated until the 1816-1818 war. Even then the defeat owed as much to internal fighting as to the power of the British-led army. Only the northwest of the subcontinent remained beyond British control until well into the 19th century. Thus in 1799 **Ranjit Singh** was able to set up a Sikh state in Punjab, surviving until the late 1830s despite the extension of British control over much of the rest of India.

In 1818 India's economy was in ruins and its political structures destroyed. Irrigation and road systems had fallen into decay and gangs terrorized the countryside. Thugs and dacoits controlled much of rural areas in Central India and often robbed and murdered even on town outskirts. The stability of the Mughal period had long since passed. From 1818 to 1857 there was a succession of local and uncoordinated revolts in different parts of India. Some were bought off, some put down by military force.

A period of reforms

While existing political systems were collapsing, the first half of the 1800s was also a time of radical social change in territories governed by the East India Company. **Lord William Bentinck** became governor-general at a time when England was undergoing major reform. In 1828 he banned the burning of widows on the funeral pyres of their husbands (**sati**) and then moved to suppress **thuggee** (the ritual murder and robbery carried out in the name of the goddess Kali). But his most far reaching change was to introduce education in English.

From the late 1830s massive new engineering projects began to be taken up; first canals, then railways. The innovations stimulated change and change contributed to the growing unease with the British presence. The development of the telegraph, railways and new roads, three universities and the extension of massive new canal irrigation projects in North India seemed to threaten traditional society, a risk increased by the annexation of Indian states to bring them under direct British rule. The most important of these was Oudh.

The Rebellion

Out of the growing discontent and widespread economic difficulties came the Rebellion or 'Mutiny' of 1857. On 10 May 1857 troops in Meerut, 70 km northeast of Delhi, mutinied.

They reached Delhi the next day, where **Bahadur Shah**, the last Mughal Emperor, took sides with the mutineers. Troops in Lucknow joined the rebellion and for three months Lucknow and other cities in the north were under siege. Appalling scenes of butchery and reprisals marked the struggle, only put down by troops from outside.

The Period of Empire

The 1857 rebellion marked the end not only of the Mughal Empire but also of the East India Company, for the British government in London took overall control in 1858. Yet within 30 years a movement for self government had begun and there were the first signs of a demand among the new Western-educated elite that political rights be awarded to match the sense of Indian national identity.

Indian National Congress Established in 1885, this was the first all-India political institution and was to become the key vehicle of demands for independence. However, the educated Muslim elite of what is now Uttar Pradesh saw a threat to Muslim rights, power and identity in the emergence of democratic institutions which gave Hindus, with their built-in natural majority, significant advantages. Sir Sayyid Ahmad Khan, who had founded a Muslim University at Aligarh in 1877, advised Muslims against joining the Congress, seeing it as a vehicle for Hindu, and especially Bengali, nationalism.

The Muslim League The educated Muslim community of North India remained deeply suspicious of the Congress, making up less than 8% of those attending its conferences between 1900-1920. Muslims from UP created the All-India Muslim League in 1906. However, the demands of the Muslim League were not always opposed to those of the Congress. In 1916 it concluded the Lucknow Pact with the Congress, in which the Congress won Muslim support for self-government, in exchange for the recognition that there would be separate constituencies for Muslims. The nature of the future independent India was still far from clear, however. The British conceded the principle of self-government in 1918, but they already fell far short of heightened Indian expectations.

Mahatma Gandhi Into a tense atmosphere Mohandas Karamchand Gandhi returned to India in 1915 after 20 years practising as a lawyer in South Africa. He arrived as the government of India was being given new powers by the British parliament to try political cases without a jury and to give provincial governments the right to imprison politicians without trial. In opposition to this legislation Gandhi proposed to call a *hartal*, when all activity would cease for a day, a form of protest still in widespread use. Such protests took place across India, often accompanied by riots.

On 13 April 1919 a huge gathering took place in the enclosed space of Jallianwala Bagh in Amritsar. It had been prohibited by the government and General Dyer ordered troops to fire on the people without warning, killing 379 and injuring at least a further 1200. It marked the turning point in relations with Britain and the rise of Gandhi to the key position of leadership in the struggle for complete independence.

The thrust for Independence Through the 1920s Gandhi developed concepts and political programmes that were to become the hallmark of India's Independence struggle.

Mahatma Gandhi

Mohandas Karamchand Ghandi, a Westernized, English-educated lawyer, had lived outside India from his youth to middle age. He preached the general acceptance of some of the doctrines he had grown to respect in his childhood, which stemmed from deep Indian traditions – notably *ahimsa*, or non-violence. On his return the Bengali Nobel Laureate poet, Rabindranath Tagore, had dubbed him 'Mahatma' – Great Soul. From 1921 he gave up his Western style of dress and adopted the hand spun *dhoti* worn by poor Indian villagers. Yet, he was also fiercely critical of many aspects of traditional Hindu society. He preached against the discrimination of the caste system which still dominated life for the overwhelming majority of Hindus. Often despised by the British in India, his death at the hands of an extreme Hindu chauvinist in January 1948 was a final testimony to the ambiguity of his achievements: successful in contributing so much to achieving India's Independence, yet failing to resolve some of the bitter communal legacies which he gave his life to overcome.

Ultimately political Independence was to be achieved not by violent rebellion but by *satyagraha* – a 'truth force' which implied a willingness to suffer through non-violent resistance to injustice.

In 1930 the Congress declared that 26 January would be Independence Day – still celebrated as Republic Day in India today. Mohammad Iqbal, the Leader of the Muslim League, took the opportunity of his address to the League in the same year to suggest the formation of a Muslim state within an Indian Federation. Also in 1930 a Muslim student in Cambridge, **Chaudhuri Rahmat Ali**, coined a name for the new Muslim state **PAKISTAN**. The letters were to stand 'P' for Punjab, 'A' for Afghania, 'K' for Kashmir, 'S' for Sind with the suffix '*stan*', Persian for country. The idea still had little real shape however and waited on developments of the late 1930s and 1940s to bear fruit.

By the end of the Second World War the positions of the Muslim League, now under the leadership of **Mohammad Ali Jinnah** and the Congress led by **Jawaharlal Nehru**, were irreconcilable. While major questions of the definition of separate territories for a Muslim and non-Muslim state remained to be answered, it was clear to General Wavell, the British Viceroy through the last years of the war, that there was no alternative but to accept that independence would have to be given on the basis of separate states.

Independence and Partition

One of the main difficulties for the Muslims was that they made up only a fifth of the total population were scattered throughout India. It was therefore impossible to define a simple territorial division which would provide a state to match Jinnah's claim of a '*two-nation theory*'. On 20 February 1947, the British Labour Government announced its decision to replace Lord Wavell as Viceroy with Lord Mountbatten, who was to oversee the transfer of power to new independent governments. It set a deadline of June 1948 for British withdrawal. The announcement of a firm date made the Indian politicians even less willing to compromise and the resulting division satisfied no one.

Independence arrived on 15 August for India and the 14 August for Pakistan because Indian astrologers deemed the 15th to be the most auspicious moment. Several key Princely States had still not decided firmly to which country they would accede. Kashmir was the most important of these, with results that have lasted to the present day.

Modern India

India, with an estimated 1.17 billion people, is the second most populated country in the world after China. That population size reflects the long history of human occupation and the fact that an astonishingly high proportion of India's land is relatively fertile. About 60% of India's surface area is cultivated today, compared with 10% in China and 20% in the United States.

Although the birth rate has fallen steadily over the last 40 years, initially death rates fell faster and the rate of population increase has continued to be nearly 2% – or 18 million – a year. Today over 320 million people live in towns and cities.

Politics and institutions

When India became independent on 15 August 1947 it faced three immediate crises. Partition left it with a bitter struggle between Muslims on one side and Hindus and Sikhs on the other which threatened to tear the new country into pieces at birth. An estimated 13 million people migrated between the two new countries of India and Pakistan.

In the years since Independence, striking political achievements have been made. With the two-year exception of 1975-1977, when Mrs Gandhi imposed a state of emergency in which all political activity was banned, India has sustained a democratic system in the face of tremendous pressures. The general elections of May 2004 saw the Congress Party return as the largest single party, with 220 of the 540 Lok Sabha seats. They managed to forge alliances with some of the smaller parties and thus formed the new United Progressive Alliance government under the prime ministership not of the Congress Party's leader, Sonia Gandhi, but of ex-finance minister, Manmohan Singh.

The constitution

Establishing itself as a sovereign democratic republic, the Indian parliament accepted Nehru's advocacy of a secular constitution. The president is formally vested with all executive powers exercised under the authority of the prime minister.

Parliament has a lower house (the *Lok Sabha* – House of the people) and an upper house (the *Rajya Sabha* – Council of States). The former is made up of directly elected representatives from the 543 parliamentary constituencies (plus two nominated members from the Anglo-Indian community), the latter of a mixture of members elected by an electoral college and of nominated members.

India's federal constitution devolves certain powers to elected state assemblies. Each state has a governor who acts as its official head. Many states also have two chambers, the upper generally called the Rajya Sabha and the lower (often called the Vidhan Sabha) being of directly elected representatives. In practice many of the state assemblies have had a totally different political complexion from that of the Lok Sabha. Regional parties have played a far more prominent role, though in many states central government has effectively dictated both the leadership and policy of state assemblies.

States and Union Territories Union territories are administered by the president 'acting to such an extent as he thinks fit'. In practice Union territories have varying forms of self-government. Pondicherry has a legislative Assembly and Council of Ministers. The 69th

Amendment to the Constitution in 1991 provided for a legislative assembly and council of ministers for Delhi, elections for which were held in December 1993. The Assemblies of Union Territories have more restricted powers of legislation than full states. Some Union Territories – Dadra and Nagar Haveli, Daman and Diu, all of which separated from Goa in 1987 when Goa achieved full statehood – Andaman and Nicobar Islands and Lakshadweep have elected bodies known as Pradesh Councils.

Secularism One of the key features of India's constitution is its secular principle. Some see the commitment to a secular constitution as having been under increasing challenge from the Hindu nationalism of the Bharatiya Janata Party, the BJP.

The judiciary India's Supreme Court has similar but somewhat weaker powers to those of the United States. The judiciary has remained effectively independent of the government except under the Emergency between 1975-1977.

The civil service India continued to use the small but highly professional administrative service inherited from the British period. Renamed the Indian Administrative Service (IAS), it continues to exercise remarkable influence across the country. The administration of many aspects of central and regional government is in the hands of this elite body, who act largely by the constitutional rules which bind them as servants of the state. Many Indians accept the continuing efficiency and high calibre of the top ranking officers in the administration while believing that the bureaucratic system as a whole has been overtaken by widespread corruption.

The police India's police service is divided into a series of groups, numbering nearly one million. While the top ranks of the Indian Police Service are comparable to the IAS, lower levels are extremely poorly trained and very low paid. In addition to the domestic police force there are special groups: the Border Security Force, Central Reserve Police and others. They may be armed with modern weapons and are called in for special duties.

The armed forces Unlike its immediate neighbours Pakistan and Bangladesh, India has never had military rule. It has around one million men in the army, one of the largest armed forces in the world. Although they have remained out of politics the army has been used increasingly frequently to put down civil unrest especially in Kashmir.

The Congress Party The Congress won overall majorities in seven of the 10 general elections held before the 1996 election, although in no election did the Congress obtain more than 50% of the popular vote. In 1998 its popular support completely disappeared in some regions and fell below 30% nationally and in the elections of September-October 1999 Sonia Gandhi, Rajiv Gandhi's Italian-born widow, failed to achieve the much vaunted revival in the Party's fortunes. Through 2001 into 2002 a change began with the BJP losing power in state assemblies in the north and becoming increasingly unpopular nationally, and the Congress picking up a wide measure of support, culminating in their victory in the May 2004 general election, when Sonia Gandhi nominated Manmohan Singh as prime minister.

Non-Congress parties Political activity outside the Congress can seem bewilderingly complex. There are no genuinely national parties. The only alternative governments to the Congress have been formed by coalitions of regional and ideologically based parties. Parties of the left – Communist and Socialist – have never broken out of their narrow regional bases. The **Communist Party of India** split into two factions in 1964, with the Communist Party of India Marxist (**CPM**) ultimately taking power in West Bengal and Kerala. In the 1960s the **Swatantra Party** (a liberal party) made some ground nationally, opposing the economic centralization and state control supported by the Congress.

At the right of the political spectrum, the **Jan Sangh** was seen as a party of right wing Hindu nationalism with a concentrated but significant base in parts of the north, especially among higher castes and merchant communities. The most organized political force outside the Congress, the Jan Sangh merged with the **Janata Party** for the elections of 1977. After the collapse of that government it re-formed itself as the **Bharatiya Janata Party (BJP)**. In 1990-1991 it developed a powerful campaign focusing on reviving Hindu identity against the minorities. The elections of 1991 showed it to be the most powerful single challenger to the Congress in North India. In the decade that followed it became the most powerful single party across northern India and established a series of footholds and alliances in the South. Elsewhere a succession of regional parties dominated politics in several key states, including Tamil Nadu and Andhra Pradesh in the south and West Bengal and Bihar in the east.

Recent developments By mid-2001 the gloss had worn off the popularity of the BJP and it had suffered a series of scandals, but the prime minister had kept the core of the government together. In July 2001 Pakistan's military ruler General Pervez Musharraf visited New Delhi and Agra for talks at the Indian Government's invitation, but they ended in a shambles.

The attacks on New York and Washington on 11 September and the US-led 'War on Terror' has had major repercussions in India and Pakistan. While the Taliban's rapid defeat brought a new government to power in Afghanistan, strongly supported by India, the Kashmir dispute between India and Pakistan deepened. Both India and Pakistan sought political advantage from the war on terror, and when a terrorist attack was launched on the Indian parliament on 13 December 2001 the Indian government pushed massive reinforcements to the Pakistan border from Gujarat and Rajasthan to Kashmir. India demanded that President Musharraf close down all camps and organizations which India claimed were the source of the attacks in Delhi and Kashmir. Although President Musharraf closed down *Lashkar e Taiba* and *Jaish e Mohammad*, two of the most feared groups operating openly in Pakistan, cross-border firing intensified along the Line of Control in Kashmir and attacks in Kashmir continued. On 16 May 2002 terrorists launched a devastating attack on an army camp in Jammu, killing at least 20 people, and Sonia Gandhi demanded that the Government translate rhetoric into action. After the change of government in May 2004, however, things have improved dramatically, with the new Indian prime minister seeming to enjoy a genuinely warm rapport with Pakistan's Pervez Musharraf. Progress over the following three years was slow and was complicated by the continuing unrest in Pakistan itself and the challenge of apparently renewed support for the Taliban in some of its border regions. Work continues, however, on resolving the Kashmir problem.

The 2009 elections saw the **United Progressive Alliance** (UPA) led by the Indian National Congress form the new government. This meant Manmohan Singh became the first prime minister since Nehru to be re-elected after completing a full five-year term. In West Bengal, which had been led by a democratically elected Communist government for over 30 years, the tide turned to the UPA. The Left Front won just 15 of the 42 Lok Sabha seats. Assam and Arunachal also carried a UPA majority, while Sikkim saw a win by the Sikkim Democratic Front.

Culture

Language

The graffiti written on the walls of any Indian city bear witness to the number of major languages spoken across the country, many with their own distinct scripts. In all the states of North and West India an Indo-Aryan language – the easternmost group of the Indo-European family – is predominant. Sir William Jones, the great 19th-century scholar, discovered the close links between Sanskrit (the basis of nearly all North Indian languages) German and Greek. He showed that they all must have originated in the common heartland of Central Asia, being carried west, south and east by the nomadic tribes who shaped so much of the following history of both Europe and Asia.

Sanskrit As the pastoralists from Central Asia moved into South Asia from 2000 BC onwards, the Indo-Aryan languages they spoke were gradually modified. Sanskrit developed from this process, emerging as the dominant classical language of India by the sixth century BC, when it was classified in the grammar of **Panini**. It remained the language of the educated until about AD 1000, though it had ceased to be in common use several centuries earlier.

Hindi and Urdu The Muslims brought Persian into South Asia as the language of the rulers, where it became the language of the numerically tiny but politically powerful elite. The most striking example of Muslim influence on the earlier Indo-European languages is that of the two most important languages of India and Pakistan, Hindi and Urdu respectively. Most of the other modern North Indian languages were not written until the 16th century or after. Hindi developed into the language of the heartland of Hindu culture, stretching from Punjab to Bihar and from the foothills of the Himalaya to the marchlands of central India.

Bengali At the east end of the Ganga plains Hindi gives way to Bengali (Bangla), the language today of over 50 million people in India, as well as more than 115 million in Bangladesh. Linguistically it is close to both Assamese and Oriya.

Scripts

It is impossible to spend even a short time in India or the other countries of South Asia without coming across several of the different scripts that are used. The earliest ancestor of scripts in use today was **Brahmi**, in which Asoka's famous inscriptions were written in the third century BC. Written from left to right, a separate symbol represented each different sound.

Devanagari For around 1000 years the major script of northern India has been the Nagari or Devanagari, which means literally the script of the 'city of the gods'. Hindi, Nepali and Marathi join Sanskrit in their use of Devanagari. The Muslim rulers developed a right to left script based on Persian and Arabic.

Numerals Many of the Indian alphabets have their own notation for numerals. This is not without irony, for what in the Western world are called 'Arabic' numerals are in fact of Indian origin. In some parts of South Asia local numerical symbols are still in use, but by and large you will find that the Arabic number symbols familiar in Europe and the West are common.

Architecture

Over the 4000 years since the Indus Valley civilization flourished, art and architecture have developed with a remarkable continuity through successive regional and religious influences and styles. The Buddhist art and architecture of the third century BC left few remains, but the stylistic influence on early Hindu architecture was profound. From the sixth century AD the first Hindu religious buildings to have survived into the modern period were constructed in South and East India.

Hindu temple buildings

The principles of religious building were laid down by priests in the *Sastras*. Every aspect of Hindu, Jain and Buddhist religious building is identified with conceptions of the structure of the universe. This applies as much to the process of building – the timing of which must be undertaken at astrologically propitious times – as to the formal layout of the buildings. The cardinal directions of north, south, east and west are the basic fix on which buildings are planned. George Michell suggests that in addition to the cardinal directions, number is also critical to the design of the religious building. The key to the ultimate scale of the building is derived from the measurements of the sanctuary at its heart. Indian temples were nearly always built according to philosophical understandings of the universe. This cosmology, of an infinite number of universes, isolated from each other in space, proceeds by imagining various possibilities as to its nature. Its centre is seen as dominated by **Mount Meru** which keeps earth and heaven apart. The concept of *separation* is crucial to Hindu thought and social practice. Continents, rivers and oceans occupy concentric rings around the mountain, while the stars encircle the mountain in another plane. Humans live on the continent of **Jambudvipa**, characterized by the rose apple tree (*jambu*). For more information on temple architecture specific to the South, see Footprint's *South India*.

Mandalas The Sastras show plans of this continent, organized in concentric rings and entered at the cardinal points. This type of diagram was known as a **mandala**. Such a geometric scheme could be subdivided into almost limitless small compartments, each of which could be designated as having special properties or be devoted to a particular deity. The centre of the mandala would be the seat of the major god; they provided the ground rules for the building of stupas and temples across India and gave the key to the symbolic meaning attached to every aspect of religious buildings.

Temple design The focal point of the temple, its sanctuary, was the home of the presiding deity, the 'womb-chamber' (*garbhagriha*). A series of doorways, in large temples leading through a succession of buildings, allowed the worshipper to move towards the final encounter with the deity to obtain *darshan* – a sight of the god. Both Buddhist and Hindu worship encourage the worshipper to walk clockwise around the shrine, performing *pradakshina*.

The elevations are symbolic representations of the home of the gods. Mountain peaks such as Kailasa are common names for the most prominent of the towers. In North and East Indian temples the tallest of these towers rises above the *garbagriha* itself, symbolizing the meeting of earth and heaven in the person of the enshrined deity. In later South Indian temples the gateways to the temple come to overpower the central tower. In both, the basic structure is usually richly embellished with sculpture. When first built

The story of Rama

Under Brahmin influence, Rama was transformed from the human prince of the early versions into the divine figure of the final story. Rama, the 'jewel of the solar kings', became deified as an incarnation of Vishnu. The story tells how Rama was banished from his father's kingdom. In a journey with his wife, Sita, and helper and friend, Hanuman (the monkey-faced God depicted in many Indian temples, shrines and posters), Rama fought the king **Ravana**, changed in late versions into a demon. Rama's rescue of Sita was interpreted as the Aryan triumph over the barbarians. The epic is seen as South Asia's first literary poem and is recited in all Hindu communities.

Ravana, demon king of Lanka

this would usually have been plastered and painted and often covered in gems. In contrast to the extraordinary profusion of colour and life on the outside, the interior is dark and cramped but here it is believed, lies the true centre of divine power.

Muslim religious architecture

Although the Muslims adapted many Hindu features, they also brought totally new forms. Their most outstanding contribution, dominating the architecture of many North Indian cities, are the mosques and tomb complexes (*dargah*). The use of brickwork was widespread and they brought with them from Persia the principle of constructing the true arch. Muslim architects succeeded in producing a variety of domed structures, often incorporating distinctively Hindu features such as the surmounting finial. By the end of the great period of Muslim building in 1707, the Muslims had added magnificent forts and palaces to their religious structures, a statement of power as well as of aesthetic taste.

European buildings

Nearly two centuries of architectural stagnation and decline followed the demise of Mughal power. The Portuguese built a series of remarkable churches in Goa that owed nothing to local traditions and everything to Baroque developments in Europe. Not until the end of the Victorian period, when British imperial ambitions were at their height, did the British colonial impact on public rather than domestic architecture begin to be felt. Fierce arguments divided British architects as to the merits of indigenous design. The ultimate plan for New Delhi was carried out by men who had little time for Hindu architecture and believed themselves to be on a civilizing mission. Others at the end of the 19th century wanted to recapture and enhance a tradition for which they had great respect. They have left a series of buildings, both in formerly British ruled territory and in the Princely States, which illustrate this concern through the development of what became known as the Indo-Saracenic style.

In the immediate aftermath of the colonial period, Independent India set about trying to establish a break from the immediately imperial past, but was uncertain how to achieve it. In the event foreign architects were commissioned for major developments, such as Le Corbusier's design for Chandigarh and Louis Kahn's buildings in Dhaka and Ahmadabad. The latter, a centre for training and experiment, contains a number of new buildings such as those of the Indian architect Charles Correa.

Music, dance and film

Music

Indian music can trace its origins to the metrical hymns and chants of the Vedas, in which the production of sound according to strict rules was thought to be vital to the continuing order of the Universe. Through more than 3000 years of development, India's musical tradition has been handed on almost entirely by ear. The chants of the **Rig Veda** developed into songs in the **Sama Veda** and music found expression in every sphere of life, reflecting the cycle of seasons and the rhythm of work.

Over the centuries the original three notes, which were sung strictly in descending order, were extended to five and then seven and developed to allow freedom to move up and down the scale. The scale increased to 12 with the addition of flats and sharps and finally to 22 with the further subdivision of semitones. Books of musical rules go back at least as far as the third century AD. Classical music was totally intertwined with dance and drama, an interweaving reflected in the term *sangita*.

At some point after the Muslim influence made itself felt in the north, North and South Indian styles diverged, to become Carnatic (Karnatak) music in the south and Hindustani music in the north. However, they still share important common features: *svara* (pitch), *raga* (the melodic structure) and *tala* or *talam* (metre).

Hindustani music probably originated in the Delhi Sultanate during the 13th century, when the most widely known of North Indian musical instruments, the *sitar*, was believed to have been invented. **Amir Khusrau** is also believed to have invented the small drums, the *tabla*. Hindustani music is held to have reached its peak under *Tansen*, a court musician of Akbar. The other important northern instruments are the stringed *sarod*, the reed instrument *shahnai* and the wooden flute. Most Hindustani compositions have devotional texts, though they encompass a great emotional and thematic range. A common classical form of vocal performance is the *dhrupad*, a four-part composition.

The essential structure of a melody is known as a **raga** which usually has five to seven notes and can have as many as nine (or even 12 in mixed ragas). The music is improvised by the performer within certain rules and although theoretically thousands of ragas are possible, only around a 100 are commonly performed. Ragas have become associated with particular moods and specific times of the day. Music festivals often include all night sessions to allow performers a wider choice of repertoire.

Dance

The rules for classical dance were laid down in the Natya shastra in the second century BC, which is still one of the bases for modern dance forms. The most common sources for Indian dance are the epics, but there are three essential aspects of the dance itself, Nritta (pure dance), Nrittya (emotional expression) and Natya (drama). The religious influence in dance was exemplified by the tradition of temple dancers, *devadasis*, girls and women who were dedicated to the deity in major temples. In South and East India there were thousands of *devadasis* associated with temple worship, though the practice fell into widespread disrepute and was banned in independent India. Various dance forms (for example Odissi, Manipuri, Bharat Natyam, Kathakali, Mohinyattam) developed in different parts of the country. India is also rich in folk dance traditions which are widely performed during festivals.

Film

Film goers around the world are taking greater note of Indian cinema, both home-grown and that produced and directed by Indians abroad. Not all fall into the category of a Bollywood '*masala* movie' or 'curry western' churned out by the Mumbai (Bombay) film industry but many offer an insight into what draws millions to watch diverse versions of Indian life on the silver screen. A few titles, both all time favourites as well as new releases include: *The Apu Trilogy, Mother India; Titash Ekti Nadir Naam; Sholay; Bombay; Kuch Kuch Hota Hai; Lagaan; Kabhie Khushi Kabhie Cham; Monsoon Wedding; The Guru; The Warrior; Choker Bali; Nayagan (The Leader); Junoon.*

Religion

It is impossible to write briefly about religion in India without greatly oversimplifying. Over 80% of Indians are Hindu, but there are significant minorities. Muslims number about 125 million and there are over 23 million Christians, 19 million Sikhs, six million Buddhists and a number of other religious groups. One of the most persistent features of Indian religious and social life is the caste system. This has undergone substantial changes since Independence, especially in towns and cities, but most people in India are still clearly identified as a member of a particular caste group. The government has introduced measures to help the backward, or 'scheduled' castes, though in recent years this has produced a major political backlash.

Hinduism

It has always been easier to define Hinduism by what it is not than by what it is. Indeed, the name 'Hindu' was given by foreigners to the peoples of the subcontinent who did not profess the other major faiths, such as Muslims or Christians. While some aspects of modern Hinduism can be traced back more than 4000 years before that, other features are recent.

Key ideas

According to the great Indian philosopher and former president of India, S Radhakrishnan, religion for the Hindu "is not an idea but a power, not an intellectual proposition but a life conviction. Religion is consciousness of ultimate reality, not a theory about God". There is no Hindu organization, such as a church, with the authority to define belief or establish official practice. Not all Hindu groups believe in a single supreme God. In view of these characteristics, many authorities argue that it is misleading to think of Hinduism as a religion at all. Be that as it may, the evidence of the living importance of Hinduism is visible across India. Hindu philosophy and practice has also touched many of those who belong to other religious traditions, particularly in terms of social institutions such as caste, and in post-Independence India religious identity has become an increasingly politicized feature of national life.

Darshan One of Hinduism's recurring themes is 'vision', 'sight' or 'view' – **darshan**. Applied to the different philosophical systems themselves, such as *yoga* or *vedanta*, 'darshan' is also used to describe the sight of the deity that worshippers hope to gain when they visit a temple or shrine hoping for the sight of a 'guru' (teacher). Equally it may apply to the religious insight gained through meditation or prayer.

The four human goals Many Hindus also accept that there are four major human goals; material prosperity (*artha*), the satisfaction of desires (*kama*) and performing the duties laid down according to your position in life (*dharma*). Beyond those is the goal of achieving liberation from the endless cycle of rebirths into which everyone is locked (*moksha*). It is to the search for liberation that the major schools of Indian philosophy have devoted most attention. Together with dharma, it is basic to Hindu thought.

The *Mahabharata* lists 10 embodiments of **dharma**: good name, truth, self-control, cleanness of mind and body, simplicity, endurance, resoluteness of character, giving and sharing, austerities and continence. In *dharmic* thinking these are inseparable from five patterns of behaviour: non-violence, an attitude of equality, peace and tranquillity, lack of aggression and cruelty and absence of envy. Dharma, an essentially secular concept, represents the order inherent in human life.

Karma The idea of *karma*, 'the effect of former actions', is central to achieving liberation. As C Rajagopalachari put it: "Every act has its appointed effect, whether the act be thought, word or deed. The cause holds the effect, so to say, in its womb. If we reflect deeply and objectively, the entire world will be found to obey unalterable laws. That is the doctrine of karma." See also box, page 339.

Rebirth The belief in the transmigration of souls (*samsara*) in a neverending cycle of rebirth has been Hinduism's most distinctive and important contribution to Indian culture. The earliest reference is in one of the *Upanishads*, around the seventh century BC, at about the same time as the doctrine of *karma* made its first appearance.

Ahimsa AL Basham pointed out that belief in transmigration must have encouraged a further distinctive doctrine, that of non-violence or non-injury – *ahimsa*. The belief in rebirth meant that all living things and creatures of the spirit – people, devils, gods, animals, even worms – possessed the same essential soul. One inscription threatens that anyone who interferes with the rights of Brahmins to land given to them by the king will 'suffer rebirth for 80,000 years as a worm in dung'. Belief in the cycle of rebirth was essential to give such a threat any weight!

Schools of philosophy
It is common now to talk of six major schools of Hindu philosophy. *Nyaya, Vaisheshika, Sankhya, Yoga, Purvamimansa* and *Vedanta*.

Yoga Yoga can be traced back to at least the third century AD. It seeks a synthesis of the spirit, the soul and the flesh and is concerned with systems of meditation and self denial that lead to the realization of the Divine within oneself and can ultimately release one from the cycle of rebirth.

Vedanta These are literally the final parts of the Vedic literature, the *Upanishads*. The basic texts also include the Brahmasutra of Badrayana, written about the first century AD and the most important of all, the *Bhagavad-Gita*, which is a part of the epic the *Mahabharata*. There are many interpretations of these basic texts. Three are given here.

Advaita Vedanta holds that there is no division between the cosmic force or principle, *Brahman* and the individual Self, *atman* (also referred to as 'soul'). The fact that we appear to see different and separate individuals is simply a result of ignorance. This is termed *maya* (illusion), but Vedanta philosophy does not suggest that the world in which we live is an illusion. *Jnana* (knowledge) is held as the key to understanding the full and real unity of Self and Brahman. **Shankaracharya**, born at Kalady in modern Kerala, in the seventh century AD, is the best known Advaitin Hindu philosopher. He argued that there was no individual Self or soul separate from the creative force of the universe, or Brahman and that it was impossible to achieve liberation (*moksha*) through meditation and devotional worship, which he saw as signs of remaining on a lower level and of being unprepared for true liberation.

The 11-12th-century philosopher, **Ramanuja**, repudiated ideas of **Vishishtad-vaita**. He transformed the idea of God from an impersonal force to a personal God and viewed both the Self and the World as real but only as part of the whole. In contrast to Shankaracharya's view, Ramanuja saw *bhakti* (devotion) as of central importance to achieving liberation and service to the Lord as the highest goal of life.

Dvaita Vedanta was developed by the 14th-century philosopher, Madhva. He believed that Brahman, the Self and the World are completely distinct. Worship of God is a key means of achieving liberation.

Worship

Puja For most Hindus today, worship ('performing puja') is an integral part of their faith. The great majority of Hindu homes will have a shrine to one of the gods of the Hindu pantheon. Individuals and families will often visit shrines or temples and on special occasions will travel long distances to particularly holy places such as Benaras or Puri. Such sites may have temples dedicated to a major deity but may also have numerous other shrines in the vicinity dedicated to other favourite gods.

Acts of devotion are often aimed at the granting of favours and the meeting of urgent needs for this life – good health, finding a suitable wife or husband, the birth of a son, prosperity and good fortune. Puja involves making an offering to God and *darshan* (having a view of the deity). Hindu worship is generally, though not always, an act performed by individuals. Thus Hindu temples may be little more than a shrine on a river bank or in the middle of the street, tended by a priest and visited at special times when a darshan of the resident God can be obtained. When it has been consecrated, the image, if exactly made, becomes the channel for the godhead to work.

Holy places Certain rivers and towns are particularly sacred to Hindus. Thus there are seven holy rivers – the Ganga, Yamuna, Indus and mythical Sarasvati in the north and the Narmada, Godavari and Kaveri in the Peninsula. There are also seven holy places – Haridwar, Mathura, Ayodhya and Varanasi, again in the north, Ujjain, Dwarka and Kanchipuram to the south. In addition to these seven holy places there are four holy abodes: Badrinath, Puri and Ramesvaram, with Dwarka in modern Gujarat having the unique distinction of being both a holy abode and a holy place.

The four stages of life

Popular Hindu belief holds that an ideal life has four stages: the student, the householder, the forest dweller and the wandering dependent/beggar (sannyasi). These stages represent the phases through which an individual learns of life's goals and of the means of achieving them.

One of the most striking sights today is that of the saffron-clad sannyasi (sadhu) seeking gifts of food and money to support himself in the final stage of his life. There may have been sadhus even before the Aryans arrived. Today, most of these have given up material possessions, carrying only a strip of cloth, a danda (staff), a crutch to support the chin during achal (meditation), prayer beads, a fan to ward off evil spirits, a water pot, a drinking vessel, which may be a human skull and a begging bowl.

Rituals and festivals The temple rituals often follow through the cycle of day and night, as well as yearly lifecycles. The priests may wake the deity from sleep, bathe, clothe and feed it. Worshippers will be invited to share in this process by bringing offerings of clothes and food. Gifts of money will usually be made and in some temples there is a charge levied for taking up positions in front of the deity in order to obtain a darshan at the appropriate times.

Every temple has its special festivals. At festival times you can see villagers walking in small groups, brightly dressed and often high spirited, sometimes as far as 80-100 km.

Hindu deities

Today three Gods are widely seen as all-powerful: Brahma, Vishnu and Siva. While Brahma is regarded as the ultimate source of creation, Siva also has a creative role alongside his function as destroyer. Vishnu in contrast is seen as the preserver or protector of the universe. Vishnu and Siva are widely represented and have come to be seen as the most powerful and important. Their followers are referred to as Vaishnavite and Shaivites respectively and numerically they form the two largest sects in India.

Brahma Popularly Brahma is interpreted as the Creator in a trinity, alongside Vishnu as Preserver and Siva as Destroyer. In the literal sense the name Brahma is the masculine and personalized form of the neuter word Brahman.

In the early Vedic writing, Brahman represented the universal and impersonal principle which governed the Universe. Gradually, as Vedic philosophy moved towards a monotheistic interpretation of the universe and its origins, this impersonal power was increasingly personalized. In the Upanishads, Brahman was seen as a universal and elemental creative spirit. Brahma, described in early myths as having been born from a golden egg and then to have created the Earth, assumed the identity of the earlier Vedic deity Prajapati and became identified as the creator.

By the fourth and fifth centuries AD, the height of the classical period of Hinduism, Brahma was seen as one of the trinity of Gods – Trimurti – in which Vishnu, Siva and Brahma represented three forms of the unmanifested supreme being. It is from Brahma that Hindu cosmology takes its structure. The basic cycle through which the whole cosmos passes is described as one day in the life of Brahma – the kalpa. It equals 4320 million years, with an equally long night. One year of Brahma's life – a cosmic year – lasts 360 days and nights. The universe is expected to last for 100 years of Brahma's life, who is currently believed to be 51 years old.

By the sixth century AD Brahma worship had effectively ceased (before the great period of temple building), which accounts for the fact that there are remarkably few temples dedicated to Brahma. Nonetheless images of Brahma are found in most temples. Characteristically he is shown with four faces, a fifth having been destroyed by the fire from Siva's third eye. In his four arms he usually holds a copy of the Vedas, a sceptre and a water jug or a bow. He is accompanied by the goose, symbolizing knowledge.

Sarasvati Seen by some Hindus as the 'active power' of Brahma, popularly thought of as his consort, Sarasvati has survived into the modern Hindu world as a far more important figure than Brahma himself. In popular worship Sarasvati represents the goddess of education and learning, worshipped in schools and colleges with gifts of fruit, flowers and incense. She represents 'the word' itself, which began to be deified as part of the process of the writing of the Vedas, which ascribed magical power to words. The development of her identity represented the rebirth of the concept of a mother goddess, which had been strong in the Indus Valley Civilization over 1000 years before and may have been continued in popular ideas through the worship of female spirits.

In addition to her role as Brahma's wife, Sarasvati is also variously seen as the wife of Vishnu and Manu or as Daksha's daughter, among other interpretations. Normally white coloured, riding on a swan and carrying a book, she is often shown playing a vina. She may have many arms and heads, representing her role as patron of all the sciences and arts.

Vishnu Vishnu is seen as the God with the human face. From the second century a new and passionate devotional worship of Vishnu's incarnation as Krishna developed in the South. By AD 1000 Vaishnavism had spread across South India and it became closely associated with the devotional form of Hinduism preached by **Ramanuja**, whose followers spread the worship of Vishnu and his 10 successive incarnations in animal and human form. For Vaishnavites, God took these different forms in order to save the world from impending disaster. AL Basham has summarized the 10 incarnations.

Rama and Krishna By far the most influential incarnations of Vishnu are those in which he was believed to take recognizable human form, especially as Rama (twice) and Krishna. As the Prince of Ayodhya, history and myth blend, for Rama was probably a chief who lived in the eighth or seventh century BC. Although Rama is now seen as an earlier incarnation of Vishnu than Krishna, he came to be regarded as divine very late, probably after the Muslim invasions of the 12th century AD. Rama (or Ram, pronounced to rhyme with *calm*) is a powerful figure in contemporary India. His supposed birthplace at Ayodhya became the focus of fierce disputes between Hindus and Muslims in the early 1990s which continue today. Krishna is worshipped extremely widely as perhaps the most human of the gods. His advice on the battlefield of the *Mahabharata* is one of the major sources of guidance for the rules of daily living for many Hindus today.

Lakshmi Commonly represented as Vishnu's wife, Lakshmi is widely worshipped as the goddess of wealth. Earlier representations of Vishnu's consorts portrayed her as Sridevi, often shown in statues on Vishnu's right, while Bhudevi, also known as Prithvi, who represented the earth, was on his left. Lakshmi is popularly shown in her own right as standing on a lotus flower, although eight forms of Lakshmi are recognized.

Karma – an eye to the future

According to the doctrine of karma, every person, animal or god has a being or 'self' which has existed without beginning. Every action, except those that are done without any consideration of the results, leaves an indelible mark on that Self, carried forward into the next life.

The overall character of the imprint on each person's Self determines three features of the next life: the nature of his next birth (animal, human or god), the kind of family he will be born into if human and the length of the next life. Finally, it controls the good or bad experiences that the self will experience. However, it does not imply a fatalistic belief that the nature of action in this life is unimportant. Rather, it suggests that the path followed by the individual in the present life is vital to the nature of its next life and ultimately to the chance of gaining release from this world.

Hanuman The *Ramayana* tells how Hanuman, Rama's faithful servant, went across India and finally into the demon Ravana's forest home of Lanka at the head of his monkey army in search of the abducted Sita. He used his powers to jump the sea channel separating India from Sri Lanka and managed after a series of heroic and magical feats to find and rescue his master's wife. Whatever form he is shown in, he remains almost instantly recognizable.

Siva Professor Wendy Doniger O'Flaherty argues that the key to the myths through which Siva's character is understood, lies in the explicit ambiguity of Siva as the great ascetic and at the same time as the erotic force of the universe.

Siva is interpreted as both creator and destroyer, the power through whom the universe evolves. He lives on Mount Kailasa with his wife **Parvati** (also known as **Uma**, **Sati**, **Kali** and **Durga**) and two sons, the elephant-headed Ganesh and the six-headed Karttikeya, known in South India as Subrahmanya. In sculptural representations Siva is normally accompanied by his 'vehicle', the bull (*Nandi* or *Nandin*).

Siva is also represented in Shaivite temples throughout India by the *linga*, literally meaning 'sign' or 'mark', but referring in this context to the sign of gender or phallus and *yoni*. On the one hand a symbol of energy, fertility and potency, as Siva's symbol it also represents the yogic power of sexual abstinence and penance. The *linga* is now the most important symbol of the cult of Siva. O'Flaherty suggests that the worship of the *linga* of Siva can be traced back to the pre-Vedic societies of the Indus Valley civilization (circa 2000 BC), but that it first appears in Hindu iconography in the second century BC. From that time a wide variety of myths appeared to explain the origin of *linga* worship. The myths surrounding the 12 **jyotirlinga** (*linga* of light) found at centres such as Ujjain go back to the second century BC and were developed to explain and justify *linga* worship.

Siva's alternative names Although Siva is not seen as having a series of rebirths, like Vishnu, he none the less appears in very many forms representing different aspects of his varied powers. Some of the more common are:

Chandrasekhara – the moon (*chandra*) symbolizes the powers of creation and destruction.

Mahadeva – the representation of Siva as the god of supreme power, which came relatively late into Hindu thought, shown as the *linga* in combination with the *yoni*, or female genitalia.

Hindu deities

Deity	Association	Relationship
Brahma	Creator	One of Trinity
Sarasvati	Education and culture, "the word"	Wife of Brahma
Siva	Creator/destroyer	One of Trinity
Bhairava	Fierce aspect of Siva	
Parvati (Uma)	Benevolent aspect of female divine power	Consort of Siva, mother of Ganesh
Kali	The energy that destroys evil	Consort of Siva
Durga	In fighting attitude	Consort of Siva
Ganesh/ Ganapati	God of good beginnings, clearer of obstacles	Son of Siva
Skanda	God of War/bringer of disease (Karttikkeya, Murugan, Subrahmanya)	Son of Siva and Ganga
Vishnu	Preserver	One of Trinity
Prithvi/ Bhudevi	Goddess of Earth	Wife of Vishnu
Lakshmi	Goddess of Wealth	Wife of Vishnu
Agni	God of Fire	
Indra	Rain, lightning and thunder	
Ravana	King of the demons	

Nataraja – the Lord of the Cosmic Dance. The story is based on a legend in which Siva and Vishnu went to the forest to overcome 10,000 heretics. In their anger the heretics attacked Siva first by sending a tiger, then a snake and thirdly a fierce black dwarf with a club. Siva killed the tiger, tamed the snake and wore it like a garland and then put his foot on the dwarf and performed a dance of such power that the dwarf and the heretics acknowledged Siva as the Lord.

Rudra – Siva's early prototype, who may date back to the Indus Valley Civilization.

Virabhadra – Siva created Virabhadra to avenge himself on his wife Sati's father, Daksha, who had insulted Siva by not inviting him to a special sacrifice. Sati attended the ceremony against Siva's wishes and when she heard her father grossly abusing Siva she committed suicide by jumping into the sacrificial fire. This act gave rise to the term *sati* (*suttee*, a word which simply means a good or virtuous woman). Recorded in the *Vedas*, the self immolation of a woman on her husband's funeral pyre probably did not become accepted practice until the early centuries BC. Even then it was mainly restricted to those of the Kshatriya caste.

Nandi – Siva's vehicle, the bull, is one of the most widespread of sacred symbols of the ancient world and may represent a link with Rudra, who was sometimes represented as a bull in pre-Hindu India. Strength and virility are key attributes and pilgrims to Siva temples will often touch the Nandi's testicles on their way into the shrine.

Attributes	Vehicle
4 heads, 4 arms, upper left holds water pot and rosary or sacrificial spoon, sacred thread across left shoulder	Hamsa – (goose/swan)
Two or more arms, vina, lotus, plam leaves, rosary	Hamsa
Linga; Rudra, matted hair, 3 eyes, drum, fire, deer, trident; Nataraja, Lord of the Dance	Nandi – bull
Trident, sword, noose, naked, snakes, garland of skulls, dishevelled hair, carrying destructive weapons	Dog
2 arms when shown with Siva, 4 when on her own, blue lily in right hand, left hand hangs down	Lion
Trident, noose, human skulls, sword, shield, black colour	Lion
4 arms, conch, disc, bow, arrow, bell, sword, shield	Lion or tiger
Goad, noose, broken tusk, fruits	Rat/ mouse/ shrew
6 heads, 12 arms, spear, arrow, sword, discus, noose cock, bow, shield, conch and plough	Peacock
4 arms, high crown, discus and conch in upper arms, club and sword (or lotus) in lower	Garuda – mythical eagle
Right hand in abhaya gesture, left holds pomegranate, left leg on treasure pot	
Seated/standing on red lotus, 4 hands, lotuses, vessel, fruit	Lotus
Sacred thread, axe, wood, bellows, torch, sacrificial spoon	2-headed ram
Bow, thunderbolt, lances	
10 heads, 20 arms, bow and arrow	

Ganesh One of Hinduism's most popular gods, Ganesh is seen as the great clearer of obstacles. Shown at gateways and on door lintels with his elephant head and pot belly, his image is revered across India. Meetings, functions and special family gatherings will often start with prayers to Ganesh and any new venture, from the opening of a building to inaugurating a company, will not be deemed complete without a Ganesh *puja*.

Shakti, The Mother Goddess Shakti is a female divinity often worshipped in the form of Siva's wife Durga or Kali. As Durga she agreed to do battle with Mahish, an *asura* (demon) who threatened to dethrone the gods. Many sculptures and paintings illustrate the story in which, during the terrifying struggle which ensued, the demon changed into a buffalo, an elephant and a giant with 1000 arms. Durga, clutching weapons in each of her 10 hands, eventually emerges victorious. As Kali ('black') the mother goddess takes on her most fearsome form and character. Fighting with the chief of the demons, she was forced to use every weapon in her armoury, but every drop of blood that she drew became 1000 new giants just as strong as he. The only way she could win was by drinking the blood of all her enemies. Having succeeded she was so elated that her dance of triumph threatened the earth. Ignoring the pleas of the gods to stop, she even threw her husband Siva to the ground and trampled over him, until she realized to her shame what she had done. She is always shown with a sword in one hand, the severed head of the giant in another, two corpses for earrings and a necklace of human skulls. She is often shown standing with one foot on the body and the other on the leg of Siva.

The worship of female goddesses developed into the widely practised form of devotional worship called Tantrism. Goddesses such as Kali became the focus of worship which often involved practices that flew in the face of wider Hindu moral and legal codes. Animal and even human sacrifices and ritual sexual intercourse were part of Tantric belief and practice, the evidence for which may still be seen in the art and sculpture of some major temples. Tantric practice affected both Hinduism and Buddhism from the eighth century AD; its influence is shown vividly in the sculptures of Khajuraho and Konark and in the distinctive Hindu and Buddhist practices of the Kathmandu Valley in Nepal.

Skanda The God of War, Skanda (known as Murugan in Tamil Nadu and by other regional names) became known as the son of Siva and Parvati. One legend suggests that he was conceived by the Goddess Ganga from Siva's seed.

Gods of the warrior caste Modern Hinduism has brought into its pantheon over many generations gods who were worshipped by the earlier pre-Hindu Aryan civilizations. The most important is **Indra**, often shown as the god of rain, thunder and lightning. To the early Aryans, Indra destroyed demons in battle, the most important being his victory over Vritra, 'the Obstructor'. By this victory Indra released waters from the clouds, allowing the earth to become fertile. To the early Vedic writers the clouds of the southwest monsoon were seen as hostile, determined to keep their precious treasure of water to themselves and only releasing it when forced to by a greater power. Indra, carrying a bow in one hand, a thunderbolt in another and lances in the others and riding on his vehicle Airavata, the elephant, is thus the Lord of Heaven. His wife is the relatively insignificant **Indrani**.

Mitra and **Varuna** have the power both of gods and demons. Their role is to sustain order, Mitra taking responsibility for friendship and Varuna for oaths and as they have to keep watch for 24 hours a day Mitra has become the god of the day or the sun, Varuna the god of the moon.

Agni, the god of fire, is a god whose origins lie with the priestly caste rather than with the Kshatriyas, or warriors. He was seen in the Vedas as being born from the rubbing together of two pieces of dead wood and as Masson-Oursel writes "the poets marvel at the sight of a being so alive leaping from dry dead wood. His very growth is miraculous". Riding on a ram, wearing a sacred thread, he is often shown with flames leaping from his mouth and he carries an axe, wood, bellows or a fan, a torch and a sacrificial spoon, for he is the god of ritual fire.

The juice of the soma plant, the nectar of the gods guaranteeing eternal life, **Soma** is also a deity taking many forms. Born from the churning of the ocean of milk in later stories Soma was identified with the moon. The golden haired and golden skinned god **Savitri** is an intermediary with the great power to forgive sin and as king of heaven he gives the gods their immortality. **Surya**, the god of the sun, fittingly of overpowering splendour is often described as being dark red, sitting on a red lotus or riding a chariot pulled by the seven horses of the dawn (representing the days of the week). **Usha**, sometimes referred to as Surya's wife, is the goddess of the dawn, daughter of Heaven and sister of the night. She rides in a chariot drawn by cows or horses.

Devas and Asuras In Hindu popular mythology the world is also populated by innumerable gods and demons, with a somewhat uncertain dividing line between them. Both have great power and moral character and there are frequent conflicts and battles between them.

The **Rakshasas** form another category of semi-divine beings devoted to performing magic. Although they are not themselves evil, they are destined to cause havoc and evil in the real world.

The multiple-hooded cobra head often seen in sculptures represents the fabulous snake gods the **Nagas**, though they may often be shown in other forms, even human. In South India it is particularly common to find statues of divine Nagas being worshipped. They are usually placed on uncultivated ground under trees in the hope and belief, as Masson-Oursel puts it, that "if the snakes have their own domain left to them they are more likely to spare human beings". The Nagas and their wives, the **Naginis**, are often the agents of death in mythical stories.

Hindu society

Dharma Dharma is seen as the most important of the objectives of individual and social life. But what were the obligations imposed by dharma? Hindu law givers, such as those who compiled the code of Manu (AD 100-300), laid down rules of family conduct and social obligations related to the institutions of caste and jati which were beginning to take shape at the same time.

Caste Although the word caste was given by the Portuguese in the 15th century AD, the main feature of the system emerged at the end of the Vedic period. Two terms – varna and jati – are used in India itself and have come to be used interchangeably and confusingly with the word caste.

Varna, which literally means colour, had a fourfold division. By 600 BC this had become a standard means of classifying the population. The fair-skinned Aryans distinguished themselves from the darker skinned earlier inhabitants. The priestly varna, the Brahmins, were seen as coming from the mouth of Brahma; the Kshatriyas were warriors, coming from Brahma's arms; the Vaishyas, a trading community, came from Brahma's thighs and the Sudras, classified as agriculturalists, from his feet. Relegated beyond the pale of civilized Hindu society were the untouchables or outcastes, who were left with the jobs which were regarded as impure, usually associated with dealing with the dead (human or animal) or with excrement.

Many Brahmins and Rajputs are conscious of their varna status, but the great majority of Indians do not put themselves into one of the four varna categories, but into a **jati** group. There are thousands of different jatis across the country. None of the groups regard themselves as equal in status to any other, but all are part of local or regional hierarchies. These are not organized in any institutional sense and traditionally there was no formal record of caste status. While individuals found it impossible to change caste or to move up the social scale, groups would sometimes try to gain recognition as higher caste by adopting practices of the Brahmins such as becoming vegetarians. Many used to be identified with particular activities and occupations used to be hereditary. Caste membership is decided by birth. Although you can be evicted from your caste by your fellow members, usually for disobedience to caste rules such as over marriage, you cannot join another caste and technically you become an outcaste.

Right up until Independence in 1947 such punishment was a drastic penalty for disobeying one's dharmic duty. In many areas all avenues into normal life could be blocked, families would disregard outcaste members and it could even be impossible for the outcaste to continue to work within the locality.

Gandhi spearheaded his campaign for independence from British colonial rule with a powerful campaign to abolish the disabilities imposed by the caste system. Coining the term *Harijan* (meaning 'person of God'), which he gave to all former outcastes, Gandhi demanded that discrimination on the grounds of caste be outlawed. Lists – or 'schedules' – of backward castes were drawn up during the early part of this century in order to provide positive help to such groups. The term itself has now been widely rejected by many former outcastes as paternalistic and as implying an adherence to Hindu beliefs (Hari being a Hindu deity) which some explicitly reject and today the use of the secular term '**dalits**' – the 'oppressed' has been adopted in its place. There are several websites devoted to dalit issues, including www.dalits.org.

Marriage, which is still generally arranged by members of all religious communities, continues to be dictated almost entirely by caste and clan rules. Even in cities, where traditional means of arranging marriages have often broken down and where many people resort to advertising for marriage partners in the columns of the Sunday newspapers, caste is frequently stated as a requirement. Marriage is mainly seen as an alliance between two families. Great efforts are made to match caste, social status and economic position, although rules governing eligibility vary from region to region. In some groups marriage between first cousins is common, while among others marriage between any branch of the same clan is strictly prohibited.

Hindu reform movements

In the 19th-century English education and European literature and modern scientific thought, alongside the religious ideas of Christian missionaries, all became powerful influences on the newly emerging Western-educated Hindu opinion. That opinion was challenged to re-examine inherited Hindu beliefs and practice.

Some reform movements have had regional importance. Two of these originated, like the **Brahmo Samaj**, in Bengal. The **Ramakrishna Mission** was named after a temple priest in the Kali temple in Calcutta, Ramakrishna (1834-1886), who was a great mystic, preaching the basic doctrine that 'all religions are true'. He believed that the best religion for any individual was that into which he or she was born. One of his followers, **Vivekananda**, became the founder of the Ramakrishna Mission, which has been an important vehicle of social and religious reform, notably in Bengal, see page 73.

Aurobindo Ghose (1872-1950) links the great reformers from the 19th century with the post-Independence period. Educated in English – and for 14 years in England itself – he developed the idea of India as 'the Mother', a concept linked with the pre-Hindu idea of Shakti, or the Mother Goddess. For him 'nationalism was religion'. After imprisonment in 1908 he retired to Pondicherry, where his ashram became a focus of an Indian and international movement.

The Hindu calendar While for its secular life India follows the Gregorian calendar, for Hindus, much of religious and personal life follows the Hindu calendar. This is based on the lunar cycle of 29 days, but the clever bit comes in the way it is synchronized with the 365 day Gregorian solar calendar of the west by the addition of an 'extra month' (*adhik maas*), every 2½-3 years.

Hindus follow two distinct eras. The *Vikrama Samvat*, which began in 57 BC (and is followed in Goa), and the *Salivahan Saka* which dates from AD 78 and has been the official

Auspicious signs

Some of Hinduism's sacred symbols are thought to have originated in the Aryan religion of the Vedic period.

Om The Primordial sound of the universe, 'Om' (or more correctly the three-in-one 'Aum') is the Supreme syllable. It is the opening, and sometimes closing, chant for Hindu prayers. Some attribute the three constituents to the Hindu triad of Brahma, Vishnu and Siva. It is believed to be the cosmic sound of Creation which encompasses all states from wakefulness to deep sleep and though it is the essence of all sound, it is outside our hearing.

Svastika Representing the Sun and its energy, the svastika usually appears on doors or walls of temples, in red, the colour associated with good fortune and luck. The term, derived from the Sanskrit 'svasti', is repeated in Hindu chants. The arms of the symbol point in the cardinal directions which may reflect the ancient practice of lighting fire sticks in the four directions. When the svastika appears to rotate clockwise it symbolizes the positive creative energy of the sun; the anti-clockwise svastika, symbolizing the autumn/winter sun, is considered to be unlucky.

Six-pointed star The intersecting triangles in the 'Star of David' symbol represents Spirit and Matter held in balance. A central dot signifies a particle of Divinity. The star is incorporated as a decorative element in some Muslim buildings such as Humayun's Tomb in Delhi.

Lotus The 'padma' or 'kamal' flower with its many petals appears not only in art and architecture but also in association with gods and godesses. Some deities are seen holding one, others are portrayed seated or standing on the flower, or as with Padmanabha it appears from Vishnu's navel. The lotus represents purity, peace and beauty, a symbol also shared by Buddhists and Jains and as in nature stands away and above the impure, murky water from which it emerges. In architecture, the lotus motif occurs frequently.

Om

Svastika

Six-pointed star

Lotus

Indian calendar since 1957. The *Saka* new year starts on 22 March and has the same length as the Gregorian calendar. In most of South India (except Tamil Nadu) the New Year is celebrated in the first month, *Chaitra* (corresponding to March-April). In North India (and Tamil Nadu) it is celebrated in the second month of *Vaisakh*.

The year itself is divided into two, the first six solar months being when the sun 'moves' north, known as the *Makar Sankranti* (which is marked by special festivals), and the second half when it moves south, the *Karka Sankranti*. The first begins in January and the second in June. The 29 day lunar month with its 'dark' (*Krishna*) and 'bright' (*Shukla*) halves, based on the new (*Amavasya*) and full moons (*Purnima*), are named after the 12 constellations, and total a 354 day year. The day itself is divided into eight *praharas* of three hours each and the year into six seasons: *Vasant* (spring), *Grishha* (summer), *Varsha* (rains), *Sharat* (early autumn), *Hemanta* (late autumn), *Shishir* (winter).

Islam

Even after partition in 1947 over 40 million Muslims remained in India and today there are around 120 million. Islamic contact with India was first made around AD 636 and then by the navies of the Arab Mohammad al Qasim in AD 710-712. These conquerors of Sindh made very few converts, although they did have to develop a legal recognition for the status of non-Muslims in a Muslim-ruled state. From the creation of the Delhi Sultanate in 1206, by Turkish rather than Arab power, Islam became a permanent living religion in India.

The victory of the Turkish ruler of Ghazni over the Rajputs in AD 1192 established a 500-year period of Muslim power in India. By AD 1200 the Turkish sultans had annexed Bihar in the east, in the process wiping out the last traces of Buddhism with the massacre of a Buddhist monastic order, sacked Varanasi and captured Gwalior. Within 30 years Bengal had been added to the Turkish empire and by AD 1311 a new Turkish dynasty, the Khaljis, had extended the power of the Delhi Sultanate to the doors of Madurai.

The early Muslim rulers looked to the Turkish ruling class and to the Arab caliphs for their legitimacy and to the Turkish elite for their cultural authority. From the middle of the 13th century, when the Mongols crushed the Arab caliphate, the Delhi sultans were left on their own to exercise Islamic authority in India. From then onwards the main external influences were from Persia. Small numbers of migrants, mainly the skilled and the educated, continued to flow into the Indian courts. Periodically their numbers were augmented by refugees from Mongol repression in the regions to India's northwest as the Delhi Sultanate provided a refuge for craftsmen and artists from the territories the Mongols had conquered from Lahore westwards.

Muslim populations Muslims only became a majority of the South Asian population in the plains of the Indus and west Punjab and in parts of Bengal. Elsewhere they formed important minorities, notably in the towns of the central heartland such as Lucknow. The concentration at the east and west ends of the Ganga valley reflected the policies pursued by successive Muslim rulers of colonizing forested and previously uncultivated land. In the central plains there was already a densely populated, Hindu region, where little attempt was made to achieve converts.

The Mughals wanted to expand their territory and their economic base. To pursue this they made enormous grants of land to those who had served the empire and particularly in Bengal, new land was brought into cultivation. At the same time, shrines were established to Sufi saints who attracted peasant farmers. The mosques built in East Bengal were the centres of devotional worship where saints were venerated. By the 18th century many Muslims had joined the **Sunni** sect of Islam. The characteristics of Islamic practice in both these regions continues to reflect this background.

In some areas Muslim society shared many of the characteristic features of the Hindu society from which the majority of them came. Many of the Muslim migrants from Iran or Turkey, the elite **Ashraf** communities, continued to identify with the Islamic elites from which they traced their descent. They held high military and civil posts in imperial service. In sharp contrast, many of the non-Ashraf Muslim communities in the towns and cities were organized in social groups very much like the *jatis* of their neighbouring Hindu communities. While the elites followed Islamic practices close to those based on the Qur'an as interpreted by scholars, the poorer, less literate communities followed devotional and pietistic forms of Islam.

The five pillars of Islam

In addition to the belief that there is one God and that Mohammed is his prophet, there are four requirements imposed on Muslims. Daily prayers are prescribed at daybreak, noon, afternoon, sunset and nightfall. Muslims must give alms to the poor. They must observe a strict fast during Ramadan (no eating or drinking from sunrise to sunset). Lastly, they should attempt the pilgrimage to the Ka'aba in Mecca, known as the Hajj. Those who have done so are entitled to the prefix Hajji before their name.

Islamic rules differ from Hindu practice in several other aspects of daily life. Muslims are strictly forbidden to drink alcohol (though some suggest that this prohibition is restricted to the use of fermented grape juice, that is wine, it is commonly accepted to apply to all alcohol). Eating pork, or any meat from an animal not killed by draining its blood while alive, is also prohibited. Meat prepared in the appropriate way is called *halal*. Finally, usury (charging interest on loans) and games of chance are forbidden.

Muslim beliefs The beliefs of Islam (which means 'submission to God') could apparently scarcely be more different from those of Hinduism. Islam, often described as having "five pillars" of faith (see box above), has a fundamental creed; 'There is no God but God; and Mohammad is the Prophet of God' (*La Illaha illa 'llah Mohammad Rasulu 'llah*). One book, the Qur'an, is the supreme authority on Islamic teaching and faith. Islam preaches the belief in bodily resurrection after death and in the reality of heaven and hell.

The idea of heaven as paradise is pre-Islamic. Alexander the Great is believed to have brought the word into Greek from Persia, where he used it to describe the walled Persian gardens that were found even three centuries before the birth of Christ. For Muslims, Paradise is believed to be filled with sensuous delights and pleasures, while hell is a place of eternal terror and torture, which is the certain fate of all who deny the unity of God.

Islam has no priesthood. The authority of Imams derives from social custom and from their authority to interpret the scriptures, rather than from a defined status within the Islamic community. Islam also prohibits any distinction on the basis of race or colour and most Muslims believe it is wrong to represent the human figure. It is often thought, inaccurately, that this ban stems from the Qur'an itself. In fact it probably has its origins in the belief of Mohammad that images were likely to be turned into idols.

Muslim sects During the first century after Mohammad's death Islam split in to two sects which were divided on political and religious grounds, the Shi'is and Sunni's. The religious basis for the division lay in the interpretation of verses in the Qur'an and of traditional sayings of Mohammad, the Hadis. Both sects venerate the Qur'an but have different *Hadis*. They also have different views as to Mohammad's successor.

The **Sunnis** – always the majority in South Asia – believe that Mohammad did not appoint a successor and that Abu Bak'r, Omar and Othman were the first three caliphs (or vice-regents) after Mohammad's death. Ali, whom the Sunni's count as the fourth caliph, is regarded as the first legitimate caliph by the Shi'is, who consider Abu Bak'r and Omar to be usurpers. While the Sunni's believe in the principle of election of caliphs, Shi'is believe that although Mohammad is the last prophet there is a continuing need for intermediaries between God and man. Such intermediaries are termed Imams and they base both their law and religious practice on the teaching of the Imams.

Akbar, the most eclectic of Mughal emperors, went as far as banning activities such as cow slaughter which were offensive to Hindus and celebrated Hindu festivals in court. In contrast, the later Mughal Emperor, Aurangzeb, pursued a far more hostile approach to Hindus and Hinduism, trying to point up the distinctiveness of Islam and denying the validity of Hindu religious beliefs. That attitude generally became stronger in the 20th century, related to the growing sense of the Muslim's minority position within South Asia and the fear of being subjected to Hindu rule.

The Islamic calendar The calendar begins on 16 July 622 AD, the date of the Prophet's migration from Mecca to Medina, the Hijra, hence AH (Anno Hejirae). *Murray's Handbook for travellers in India* gave a wonderfully precise method of calculating the current date in the Christian year from the AH date: "To correlate the Hijra year with the Christian year, express the former in years and decimals of a year, multiply by .970225, add 621.54 and the total will correspond exactly with the Christian year."

The Muslim year is divided into 12 lunar months, totalling 354 or 355 days, hence Islamic festivals usually move 11 days earlier each year according to the solar (Gregorian) calendar. The first month of the year is *Moharram*, followed by *Safar, Rabi-ul-Awwal, Rabi-ul-Sani, Jumada-ul-Awwal, Jumada-ul-Sani, Rajab, Shaban, Ramadan, Shawwal, Ziquad* and *Zilhaj*.

Buddhism

India was the home of Buddhism, which had its roots in the early Hinduism, or Brahmanism, of its time. Today it is practised only on the margins of the subcontinent, from Ladakh, Nepal and Bhutan in the north to Sri Lanka in the south, where it is the religion of the majority Sinhalese community. Most are very recent converts, the last adherents of the early schools of Buddhism having been killed or converted by the Muslim invaders of the 13th century. However, India's Buddhist significance is now mainly as the home for the extraordinarily beautiful artistic and architectural remnants of what was for several centuries the region's dominant religion.

India has sites of great significance for Buddhists around the world. Some say that the Buddha himself spoke of the four places his followers should visit. **Lumbini**, the Buddha's birthplace, is in the Nepali foothills, near the present border with India. **Bodh Gaya**, where he attained what Buddhists term his 'supreme enlightenment', is about 80 km south of the modern Indian city of Patna; the deer park at **Sarnath**, where he preached his first sermon and set in motion the Wheel of the Law, is just outside Varanasi; and **Kushinagara**, where he died at the age of 80, is 50 km east of Gorakhpur. There were four other sacred places of pilgrimage – **Rajgir**, where he tamed a wild elephant; **Vaishali**, where a monkey offered him honey; **Sravasti**, associated with his great miracle; and **Sankasya**, where he descended from heaven. The eight significant events associated with the holy places are repeatedly represented in Buddhist art.

In addition there are remarkable monuments, sculptures and works of art, from Gandhara in modern Pakistan to Sanchi and Ajanta in central India, where it is still possible to see the vivid evidence of the flowering of Buddhist culture in South Asia. In Sri Lanka, Bhutan and Nepal the traditions remain alive.

The Buddha's Life Siddharta Gautama, who came to be given the title of the Buddha – the Enlightened One – was born a prince into the warrior caste in about 563 BC. He was married at the age of 16 and his wife had a son. When he reached the age of 29 he left home and wandered as a beggar and ascetic. After about six years he spent some time in Bodh Gaya. Sitting under the Bo tree, meditating, he was tempted by the demon Mara, with all the desires of the world. Resisting these temptations, he received enlightenment. These scenes are common motifs of Buddhist art.

The next landmark was the preaching of his first sermon on 'The Foundation of Righteousness' in the deer park near Benaras. By the time he died the Buddha had established a small band of monks and nuns known as the *Sangha* and had followers across North India. His body was cremated and the ashes, regarded as precious relics, were divided among the peoples to whom he had preached. Some have been discovered as far west as Peshawar, in Pakistan and at Piprawa, close to his birthplace.

After the Buddha's death From the Buddha's death, or *parinirvana*, to the destruction of Nalanda (the last Buddhist stronghold in India) in AD 1197, Buddhism in India went through three phases. These are often referred to as Hinayana, Mahayana and Vajrayana, though they were not mutually exclusive, being followed simultaneously in different regions.

Hinayana The Hinayana or Lesser Way insists on a monastic way of life as the only path to the personal goal of *nirvana*, see box page 350, achieved through an austere life. Divided into many schools, the only surviving Hinayana tradition is the **Theravada Buddhism**, which was taken to Sri Lanka by the Emperor Asoka's son Mahinda, where it became the state religion, and spread to southeast Asia as practised in Thailand, Myanmar, Cambodia and Laos today. Suffering, sorrow and dissatisfaction are the nature of ordinary life and can only be eliminated by giving up desire. In turn, desire is a result of the misplaced belief in the reality of individual existence. Theravada Buddhism taught that there is no soul and ultimately no God. *Nirvana* is a state of rest beyond the universe, once found never lost.

Mahayana In contrast to the Hinayana schools, the followers of the Mahayana school (the Great Way) believed in the possibility of salvation for all. They practised a far more devotional form of meditation and new figures came to play a prominent part in their beliefs and their worship – the **Bodhisattvas**, saints who were predestined to reach the state of enlightenment through thousands of rebirths. They aspired to Buddhahood, however, not for their own sake but for the sake of all living things. The Buddha is believed to have passed through numerous existences in preparation for his final mission. Mahayana Buddhism became dominant over most of South Asia and its influence is evidenced in Buddhist art from Gandhara in north Pakistan to Ajanta in Central India and Sigiriya in Sri Lanka.

Vajrayana A new branch of Buddhism, Vajrayana, or the Vehicle of the Thunderbold, appeared which began to lay stress on secret magical rituals and cults of female divinities. This new 'Diamond Way' adopted the practice of magic, yoga and meditation. It became associated with secret ceremonies, chanting of mystical 'mantras' and taking part in orgiastic rituals in the cause of spiritual gain in order to help others. The ideal of Vajrayana Buddhists is to be 'so fully in harmony with the cosmos as to be able to manipulate the cosmic forces within and outside himself'. It had developed in the north of India by the seventh century AD, matching the parallel growth of Hindu Tantrism. The magical power associated with Vajrayana requires instruction from a teacher or Lama, hence the Tibetan form is sometimes referred to as 'Lamaistic'.

The Buddha's Four Noble Truths

The Buddha preached Four Noble Truths: that life is painful; that suffering is caused by ignorance and desire; that beyond the suffering of life there is a state which cannot be described but which he termed nirvana; and that nirvana can be reached by following an eightfold path.

The concept of nirvana is often understood in the West in an entirely negative sense – that of 'non-being'. The word has the rough meaning of 'blow out', meaning to blow out the fires of greed, lust and desire. In a more positive sense it has been described by one Buddhist scholar as "the state of absolute illumination, supreme bliss, infinite love and compassion, unshakeable serenity and unrestricted spiritual freedom". The essential elements of the eightfold path are the perfection of wisdom, morality and meditation.

Buddhist beliefs Buddhism is based on the Buddha's own preaching. However, when he died none of those teachings had been written down. He developed his beliefs in reaction to the Brahmanism of his time, rejecting several of the doctrines of Vedic religion which were widely held in his lifetime: the Vedic gods, scriptures and priesthood and all social distinctions based on caste. However, he did accept the belief in the cyclical nature of life and that the nature of an individual's existence is determined by a natural process of reward and punishment for deeds in previous lives – the Hindu doctrine of karma, see page 335. In the Buddha's view, though, there is no eternal soul. He denied the identification of the Self with the everchanging Mind-Body (here, some see parallels in the Advaita Vedanta philosophy of Self-*Brahman* in Hinduism). In Buddhism, *Anatta* (no-Self) overcame the egoistical Self, given to attachment and selfishness.

Following the Buddha's death a succession of councils was called to try and reach agreement on doctrine. The first three were held within 140 years of the Buddha's death, the fourth being held at Pataliputra (modern Patna) during the reign of the Emperor Asoka (272-232 BC), who had recently been converted to Buddhism. Under his reign Buddhism spread throughout South Asia and opened the routes through Northwest India for Buddhism to travel into China, where it had become a force by the first century AD.

Buddhism's decline The decline of Buddhism in India probably stemmed as much from the growing similarity in the practice of Hinduism and Buddhism as from direct attacks. Mahayana Buddhism, with its reverence for Bodhisattvas and its devotional character, was increasingly difficult to distinguish from the revivalist Hinduism characteristic of several parts of North India from the seventh to the 12th centuries AD. The Muslim conquest dealt the final death blow, as it was also accompanied by the large-scale slaughter of monks as well as the destruction of monasteries. Without their institutional support Buddhism faded away.

Jainism

Like Buddhism, Jainism started as a reform movement of the Brahmanic religious beliefs of the sixth century BC. Its founder was a widely revered saint and ascetic, Vardhamma, who became known as **Mahavir** – 'great hero'. Mahavir was born in the same border region of India and Nepal as the Buddha, just 50 km north of modern Patna, probably in 599 BC. His family, also royal, were followers of an ascetic saint, Parsvanatha, who according to Jain tradition had lived 200 years previously.

Mahavir's life story is embellished with legends, but there is no doubt that he left his royal home for a life of the strict ascetic. He is believed to have received enlightenment after 12 years of rigorous hardship, penance and meditation. Afterwards he travelled and preached for 30 years, stopping only in the rainy season. He died aged 72 in 527 BC. His death was commemorated by a special lamp festival in the region of Bihar, which Jains claim is the basis of the now-common Hindu festival of lights, Diwali.

Unlike Buddhism, Jainism never spread beyond India, but it has survived continuously into modern India, with four million adherents. In part this may be because Jain beliefs have much in common with puritanical forms of Hinduism and are greatly respected and admired. Some Jain ideas, such as vegetarianism and reverence for all life, are widely recognized by Hindus as highly commendable. The value Jains place on non-violence has contributed to their importance in business, as they regard nearly all occupations except banking and commerce as violent.

Jain beliefs Jains (from the word Jina, literally meaning 'descendants of conquerors') believe that there are two fundamental principles, the living (*jiva*) and the non-living (*ajiva*). The essence of Jain belief is that all life is sacred and that every living entity, even the smallest insect, has within it an indestructible and immortal soul. Jains developed the view of ahimsa – often translated as 'non-violence', but better perhaps as 'non-harming'. Ahimsa was the basis for the entire scheme of Jain values and ethics and alternative codes of practice were defined for householders and for ascetics.

The five vows may be taken both by monks and by lay people: not to harm any living beings (Jains must practise strict vegetarianism – and even some vegetables, such as potatoes and onions, are believed to have microscopic souls); to speak the truth; not to steal; to give up sexual relations and practice complete chastity; to give up all possessions – for the *Digambara* sect that includes clothes.

Celibacy is necessary to combat physical desire. Jains also regard the manner of dying as extremely important. Although suicide is deeply opposed, vows of fasting to death voluntarily may be regarded as earning merit in the proper context. Mahavir himself is believed to have died of self-starvation. The essence of all the rules is to avoid intentional injury, which is the worst of all sins. Like Hindus, the Jains believe in *karma*.

Jains have two main **sects**, whose origins can be traced back to the fourth century BC. The more numerous **Svetambaras** – the 'white clad' – concentrated more in eastern and western India, separated from the **Digambaras** – or 'sky-clad'– who often go naked. The Digambaras may well have been forced to move south by drought and famine in the northern region of the Deccan and they are now concentrated in the south of India.

Unlike Buddhists, Jains accept the idea of God, but not as a creator of the universe. They see him in the lives of the 24 **Tirthankaras** (prophets, or literally 'makers of fords' – a reference to their role in building crossing points for the spiritual journey over the river of life), or leaders of Jainism, whose lives are recounted in the Kalpsutra – the third century BC book of ritual for the Svetambaras. Mahavir is regarded as the last of these great spiritual leaders. Much Jain art details stories from these accounts and the Tirthankaras play a similar role for Jains as the Bodhisattvas do for Mahayana Buddhists. The first and most revered of the Tirthankaras, Adinatha, also known as Rishabnath, is widely represented in Jain temples.

Sikhism

Guru Nanak, the founder of the religion, was born just west of Lahore and grew up in what is now the Pakistani town of Sultanpur. His followers, the Sikhs (derived from the Sanskrit word for 'disciples'), form perhaps one of India's most recognizable groups. Beards and turbans give them a very distinctive presence and although they represent less than 2% of the population they are both politically and economically significant.

Sikh beliefs The first Guru, accepted the ideas of *samsara* – the cycle of rebirths – and *karma*, see page 335, from Hinduism. However, Sikhism is unequivocal in its belief in the oneness of God, rejecting idolatry and any worship of objects or images. Guru Nanak believed that God is One, formless, eternal and beyond description.

Guru Nanak also fiercely opposed discrimination on the grounds of caste. He saw God as present everywhere, visible to anyone who cared to look and as essentially full of grace and compassion. Some of Guru Nanak's teachings are close to the ideas of the Benaras mystic **Kabir**, who, in common with the Muslim mystic sufis, believed in mystical union with God. Kabir's belief in the nature of God was matched by his view that man was deliberately blind and unwilling to recognize God's nature. He transformed the Hindu concept of *maya* into the belief that the values commonly held by the world were an illusion.

Guru Nanak preached that salvation depended on accepting the nature of God. If people recognized the true harmony of the divine order (*hookam*) they would be saved. Rejecting the prevailing Hindu belief that such harmony could be achieved by ascetic practices, he emphasized three actions: meditating on and repeating God's name (*naam*), 'giving' or charity (*daan*), and bathing (*isnaan*).

Many of the features now associated with Sikhism can be attributed to **Guru Gobind Singh**, who on 15 April 1699, started the new brotherhood called the *Khalsa* (meaning 'the pure', from the Persian word *khales*), an inner core of the faithful, accepted by baptism (*amrit*). The 'five ks' date from this period: *kesh* (uncut hair), the most important, followed by *kangha* (comb, usually of wood), *kirpan* (dagger or short sword), *kara* (steel bangle), and *kachh* (similar to 'boxer' shorts). The dagger and the shorts reflect military influence.

In addition to the compulsory 'five ks', the new code prohibited smoking, eating *halal* meat and sexual intercourse with Muslim women. These date from the 18th century, when the Sikhs were often in conflict with the Muslims. Other strict prohibitions include: idolatry, caste discrimination, hypocrisy and pilgrimage to Hindu sacred places. The Khalsa also explicitly forbade the seclusion of women, one of the common practices of Islam. It was only under the warrior king Ranjit Singh (1799-1838) that the idea of the Guru's presence in meetings of the Sikh community (the *Panth*) gave way to the now universally held belief in the total authority of the **Guru Granth**, the recorded words of the Guru in the scripture.

Sikh worship The meditative worship Guru Nanak commended is a part of the life of every devout Sikh today, who starts each day with private meditation and a recitation of the verses of Guru Nanak himself, the *Japji*. However, from the time of the third Guru, Sikhs have also worshipped as congregations in Gurudwaras ('gateways to the Guru'). The Golden Temple in Amritsar, built at the end of the 16th century, is the holiest site of Sikhism.

Hill tribes

The hill tribes of the 635 'scheduled' tribes listed in the Indian Constitution, 213 have their traditional homelands in the remote hill states of Northeast India. Bordered by Bhutan and China to the north, Myanmar to the east and Bangladesh to the west, the people are of Mongoloid origin, speaking a variety of Sino-Tibetan languages. Tribal culture and religion is firmly rooted in the flora and fauna of the forests that once covered this humid tropical region; traditional dress comprises woven shawls, often in black, red and yellow, sometimes accompanied by extravagant headgear decorated with the beaks and feathers of the indigenous hornbill. Early anthropologists declared the various tribal religions to be animistic, but many scholars argue that the core tribal belief is in a single 'High God' – a fact that may have expedited the widespread conversion to Christianity, now the dominant religion in the region. Until the arrival of the British in the 1820s, the hill tribes had remained beyond the reach of colonizing Indian empires, but since the creation of Assam, a strategic move in the 19th century 'Great Game' designed to forestall Chinese expansion in India, and especially since the creation of Bangladesh after Partition in 1947, the hill regions have been flooded with immigrants from the Ganges delta. Despite the government granting ethnically based territories to some of the major tribal groups – the states of Nagland, Mizoram and Manipur – displacement by Bengali migrants has rendered tribes a minority elsewhere in the northeast. Rapid economic development in the region has caused much of the region's cultural heritage to disappear, while separatist groups in Nagaland, Manipur and Assam have begun to adopt political violence as a means to win independence from India.

The present institutions of Sikhism owe their origins to 19th-century reform movements. Under the Sikh Gurudwaras Act of 1925 all temples were restored to the management of a Central Gurudwara Management Committee, thereby removing them from the administrative control of the Hindus under which many had come. This body has acted as the religion's controlling body ever since.

Christianity

There are about 23 million Christians in India. Christianity ranks third in terms of religious affiliation after Hinduism and Islam and there are Christian congregations in all the major towns of India.

The great majority of the Protestant Christians in India are now members of the Church of South India, formed from the major Protestant denominations in 1947, or the Church of North India, which followed suit in 1970. Together they account for approximately half the total number of Christians. Roman Catholics make up the majority of the rest. Many of the church congregations, both in towns and villages, are active centres of Christian worship.

Origins Some of the churches owe their origin either to the modern missionary movement of the late 18th century onwards, or to the colonial presence of the European powers. However, Christians probably arrived in India during the first century after the birth of Christ. There is evidence that one of Christ's Apostles, **Thomas**, reached India in

AD 52, only 20 years after Christ was crucified. He settled in Malabar and then expanded his missionary work to China. It is widely believed that he was martyred in Tamil Nadu on his return to India in AD 72 and is buried in Mylapore, in the suburbs of modern Chennai. St Thomas' Mount, a small rocky hill just north of Chennai airport, takes its name from him. Today there is still a church of Thomas Christians in Kerala.

Northern missions Protestant missions in Bengal from the end of the 18th century had a profound influence on cultural and religious development. In November 1793 the Baptist missionary **William Carey** reached the Hugli River. Although he went to India to preach, he was also interested in languages and education and the work of 19th-century missions rapidly widened to cover educational and medical work as well.

Converts were made most readily among the backward castes and in the tribal areas. The Christian populations of the tribal hill areas of Nagaland and Assam stem from such late 19th-century and 20th-century movements. But the influence of Christian missions in education and medical work was greater than as a proselytizing force. Education in Christian schools stimulated reformist movements in Hinduism itself and mission hospitals supplemented government-run hospitals, particularly in remote areas. Some of these Christian-run hospitals, such as that at Vellore, continue to provide high class medical care.

Christian beliefs Christian theology had its roots in Judaism, with its belief in one God, the eternal Creator of the universe. Judaism saw the Jewish people as the vehicle for God's salvation, the 'chosen people of God' and pointed to a time when God would send his Saviour, or Messiah. Jesus, whom Christians believe was 'the Christ' or Messiah, was born in the village of Bethlehem, some 20 km south of Jerusalem. Very little is known of his early life except that he was brought up in a devout Jewish family. At the age of 29 or 30 he gathered a small group of followers and began to preach in the region between the Dead Sea and the Sea of Galilee. Two years later he was crucified in Jerusalem by the authorities on the charge of blasphemy – that he claimed to be the son of God.

Christians believe that all people live in a state of sin, in the sense that they are separated from God and fail to do his will. They believe that God is personal, 'like a father'. As God's son, Jesus accepted the cost of that separation and sinfulness himself through his death on the cross. Christians believe that Jesus was raised from the dead on the third day after he was crucified and that he appeared to his closest followers. They believe that his spirit continues to live today and that he makes it possible for people to come back to God.

The New Testament of the Bible, which, alongside the Old Testament, is the text to which Christians refer as the ultimate scriptural authority, consists of four 'Gospels' (meaning 'good news') and a series of letters by several early Christians referring to the nature of the Christian life.

Christian worship Although Christians are encouraged to worship individually as well as together, most forms of Christian worship centre on the gathering of the church congregation for praise, prayer and the preaching of God's word, which usually takes verses from the Bible as its starting point. Different denominations place varying emphases on the main elements of worship, but in most church services today the congregation will take part in singing hymns (songs of praise), prayers will be led by the minister, priest or a member of the congregation, readings from the Bible will be given and a sermon preached. For many Christians the most important service is the act of Holy Communion (Protestant) or Mass (Catholic) which celebrates the death and resurrection of Jesus in sharing bread and wine, which are held to represent Christ's body and blood given to save people from their sin.

Zoroastrianism

The first Zoroastrians arrived on the west coast of India in the mid-eighth century AD, forced out from their native Iran by persecution of the invading Islamic Arabs. Until 1477 they lost all contact with Iran and then for nearly 300 years maintained contact with Persian Zoroastrians through a continuous exchange of letters. They became known by their now much more familiar name, the **Parsis** (or Persians).

Although they are a tiny minority (approximately 100,000), even in the cities where they are concentrated, they have been a prominent economic and social influence, especially in West India. Parsis adopted Westernized customs and dress and took to the new economic opportunities that came with colonial industrialization. Families in West India such as the Tatas continue to be among India's leading industrialists, just part of a community that in recent generations has spread to Europe and north America.

Origins Zoroastrians trace their beliefs to the prophet Zarathustra, who lived in Northeast Iran around the seventh or sixth century BC. His place and even date of birth are uncertain, but he almost certainly enjoyed the patronage of the father of Darius the Great. The passage of Alexander the Great through Iran severely weakened support for Zoroastrianism, but between the sixth century BC and the seventh century AD it was the major religion of peoples living from North India to central Turkey. The spread of Islam reduced the number of Zoroastrians dramatically and forced those who did not retreat to the desert to emigrate.

Parsi beliefs The early development of Zoroastrianism marked a movement towards belief in a single God. **Ahura Mazda**, the Good Religion of God, was shown in rejecting evil and in purifying thought, word and action. Fire plays a central and symbolic part in Zoroastrian worship, representing the presence of God. There are eight Atash Bahram – major fire temples – in India; four are in Mumbai, two in Surat and one each in Navsari and Udwada. There are many more minor temples, where the rituals are far less complex – perhaps 40 in Mumbai alone.

Earth, fire and air are all regarded as sacred, while death is the result of evil. Dead matter pollutes all it touches. Where there is a suitable space therefore, dead bodies are simply placed in the open to be consumed by vultures, as at the Towers of Silence in Mumbai. However, burial and cremation are also common.

Land and environment

Geography

The origins of India's landscapes

Only 100 million years ago the Indian Peninsula was still attached to the great land mass called 'Pangaea' alongside South Africa, Australia and Antarctica. Then as the great plates on which the earth's southern continents stood broke up, the Indian Plate started its dramatic shift northwards, eventually colliding with the Asian plate. As the Indian Plate continues to get pushed under the Tibetan Plateau so the Himalaya continue to rise. Northeast India falls into two major geological regions. The north is enclosed by the great arc of the Himalaya, while along their southern flank lie the alluvial plains of the Ganga.

The Himalaya The Himilaya dominate the northern borders of India, stretching 2500 km from northwest to southeast. Of the 94 mountains in Asia above 7300 m, all but two are in the Himalaya. Nowhere else in the world are there mountains as high. The Himalaya proper, stretching from the Pamirs in Pakistan to the easternmost bend of the Brahmaputra in Assam, can be divided into three broad zones. On the southern flank are the Shiwaliks, or Outer Ranges. To their immediate north run the parallel Middle Ranges of Pir Panjal and Dhauladhar and to the north again is the third zone, the Inner Himalaya, which has the highest peaks, many of them in Nepal. The central core of the Himalayan ranges did not begin to rise until about 35 million years ago. The latest mountain building period, responsible for the Shiwaliks, began less than five million years ago and is still continuing, raising some of the high peaks by as much as 5 mm a year. Such movement comes at a price and the boundary between the plains and the Himalayan ranges is a zone of continuing violent earthquakes and massive erosion.

The Gangetic Plains As the Himalaya began their dramatic uplift, the trough which formed to the south of the newly emerging mountains was steadily filled with the debris washed down from the hills, creating the Indo-Gangetic plains. Today the alluvium reaches depths of over 3000 m in places (and over 22 km at the mouth of the Ganga in Bangladesh), and contains some of the largest reserves of underground water in the world. These have made possible extensive well irrigation, especially in Northwest India, contributing to the rapid agricultural changes which have taken place.

The Indo-Gangetic plains are still being extended and modified. The southern part of Bengal only emerged from the sea during the last 5000 years. The Ganga and the Indus have each been estimated to carry over one million tonnes of silt every year – considerably more than the Mississippi. The silts washed down from the Himalaya have made it possible for intensive rice cultivation to be practised continuously for hundreds of years, though they cause problems for modern irrigation development. Dams in the Himalayan region are being rapidly filled by silt, over 33 million tonnes being deposited behind the Bhakra Dam on the Sutlej River alone.

Vegetation

India's tropical location and its position astride the wet monsoonal winds ensured that 16 different forest types were represented in India. The most widespread was tropical dry deciduous forest. Areas with more than 1700 mm of rainfall had tropical moist deciduous, semi-evergreen or wet evergreen forest, while much of the remainder had types ranging from tropical dry deciduous woodland to dry alpine scrub, found at high altitudes. However, today forest cover has been reduced to about 13% of the surface area, mainly the result of the great demand for wood as a fuel.

Deciduous forest Two types of deciduous tree remain particularly important, **Sal** (*Shorea robusta*), now found mainly in eastern India, and **Teak** (*Tectona grandis*). Most teak today has been planted. Both are resistant to burning, which helped to protect them where people used fire as a means of clearing the forest.

Mountain forests and grassland At between 1000-2000 m in the eastern hill ranges of India and in Bhutan, for example, wet hill forest includes evergreen oaks and chestnuts. Further west in the foothills of the Himalaya are belts of subtropical pine at roughly the same altitudes. Deodars (*Cedrus deodarus*) form large stands and moist temperate forest, with pines, cedars, firs and spruce, is dominant, giving many of the valleys a beautifully fresh, alpine feel. Between 3000-4000 m alpine forest predominates. Rhododendron are often mixed with other forest types. Birch, juniper, poplars and pine are widespread.

There are several varieties of coarse grassland found along the southern edge of the Terai and alpine grasses are important for grazing above altitudes of 2000 m. A totally distinctive grassland is the bamboo (*Dendo calamus*) region, which is found in the eastern Himalaya.

Trees

Flowering trees Many Indian trees are planted along roadsides to provide shade and they often also produce beautiful flowers. The **silk cotton tree** (*Bombax ceiba*), up to 25 m in height, is one of the most dramatic. The pale greyish bark of this buttressed tree usually bears conical spines. It has wide spreading branches and keeps its leaves for most of the year. The flowers, which appear when the tree is leafless, are cup-shaped, with curling, rather fleshy red petals up to 12 cm long while the fruit produce the fine, silky cotton which gives it its name.

Other common trees with red or orange flowers include the Dhak (also called 'flame of the forest' or *Palas*), the gulmohur, the Indian coral tree and the tulip tree. The smallish (6 m) deciduous **dhak** (*Butea monosperma*) has light grey bark and a gnarled, twisted trunk and thick, leathery leaves. The large, bright orange and sweet pea-shaped flowers appear on leafless branches. The 8-9-m-high umbrella-shaped **gulmohur** (*Delonix regia*), a native of Madagascar, is grown as a shade tree in towns. The fiery coloured flowers make a magnificent display after the tree has shed its feathery leaves. The scarlet flowers of the **Indian coral tree** (*Erythrina indica*) appear when its branches with thorny bark are leafless. The tall **tulip tree** (*Spathodea campanulata*) (not to be confused with the North American one) has a straight, darkish brown, slender trunk. It is usually evergreen except in the drier parts of India. The scarlet bell-shaped, tulip-like flowers grow in profusion at the ends of the branches from November to March.

Often seen along roadsides the **jacaranda** (*Jacaranda mimosaefolia*) has attractive feathery foliage and purple-blue thimble-shaped flowers up to 40 mm long. When not in flower it resembles a gulmohur, but differs in its general shape. The valuable **tamarind** (*Tamarindus indica*), with a short straight trunk and a spreading crown, often grows along the roadside. An evergreen with feathery leaves, it bears small clusters of yellow and red flowers. The noticeable fruit pods are long, curved and swollen at intervals. In parts of India, the rights to the fruit are auctioned off annually for up to Rs 4000 (US$100) per tree.

Of these trees the silk cotton, the dhak and the Indian coral are native to India. Others were introduced mostly during the last century: the tulip tree from East Africa, the jacaranda from Brazil and the tamarind, possibly from Africa.

Fruit trees   The familiar apple, plum, apricot and cherry grow in the cool upland areas of India. In the warmer plains tropical fruits flourish. The large, spreading **mango** (*Mangifera indica*) bears the delicious, distinctively shaped fruit that comes in hundreds of varieties. The evergreen **jackfruit** (*Artocarpus heterophyllus*) has dark green leathery leaves. The huge fruit (up to 90 cm long and 40 cm thick), growing from a short stem directly off the trunk and branches, has a rough, almost prickly skin and is almost sickly sweet. The **banana** plant (*Musa*), actually a gigantic herb (up to 5 m high) arising from an underground stem, has very large leaves which grow directly off the trunk. Each large purplish flower produces bunches of up to 100 bananas. The **papaya** (*Carica papaya*) grows to about 4 m with the large hand-shaped leaves clustered near the top. Only the female tree bears the fruit, which hang down close to the trunk just below the leaves.

Palm trees   **Coconut palms** (*Cocos nucifera*) are extremely common all round the coast of India. It has tall (15-25 m), slender, unbranched trunks, feathery leaves and large green or golden fruit with soft white flesh filled with milky water, so different from the brown fibre-covered inner nut which makes its way to Europe. The 10-15-m-high **palmyra palms** (*Borassus flabellifer*), indigenous to South and East India, have very distinctive fan-like leaves, as much as 150 cm across. The fruit, which is smaller than a coconut, is round, almost black and very shiny. The **betel nut palm** (*Areca catechu*) resembles the coconut palm, its slender trunk bearing ring marks left by fallen leaf stems. The smooth, round nuts, only about 3 cm across, grow in large hanging bunches. **Wild date palms** (*Phoenix sylvestris*), originally came from North Africa. About 20-25 m tall, the trunks are also marked with the ring bases of the leaves which drop off. The distinctive leaflets which stick out from the central vein give the leaf a spiky appearance. Bunches of dates are only borne by the female tree.

All these palm trees are of considerable **commercial importance**. From the fruit alone the coconut palm produces coir from the outer husk, copra from the fleshy kernel from which coconut oil or coconut butter is extracted, in addition to the desiccated coconut and coconut milk. The sap is fermented to a drink called toddy. A similar drink is produced from the sap of the wild date and the palmyra palms which are also important for sugar production. The fruit of the betel nut palm is wrapped in a special leaf and chewed. The trunks and leaves of all the palms are widely used in building and thatching.

Other trees   Of all Indian trees the **banyan** (*Ficus benghalensis*) is probably the best known. It is planted by temples, in villages and along roads. The seeds often germinate in the cracks of old walls, the growing roots splitting the wall apart. If it grows in the bark of another tree, it sends down roots towards the ground. As it grows, more roots appear from the branches, until the original host tree is surrounded by a 'cage' which eventually strangles it. The famous one in Kolkata's Botanical Gardens is more than 400 m in circumference.

Related to the banyan, the **pipal** or peepul (*Ficus religiosa*) also cracks open walls and strangles other trees with its roots. With a smooth grey bark, it too is commonly found near temples and shrines. You can distinguish it from the banyan by the absence of aerial roots and its large, heart-shaped leaf with a point tapering into a pronounced 'tail'. It bears abundant 'figs' of a purplish tinge which are about 1 cm across.

The **ashok** or **mast** (*Polyalthia longifolia*) is a tall evergreen which can reach 15 m or more in height. One variety, often seen in avenues, is trimmed and tapers towards the top. The leaves are long, slender and shiny and narrow to a long point.

Acacia trees with their feathery leaves are fairly common in the drier parts of India. The best known is the **babul** (*Acacia arabica*) with a rough, dark bark. The leaves have long silvery white thorns at the base and consist of many leaflets while the flowers grow in golden balls about 1 cm across.

The **eucalyptus** or **gum tree** (*Eucalyptus grandis*), introduced from Australia in the 19th century, is now widespread and is planted near villages to provide both shade and firewood. There are various forms but all may be readily recognized by their height, their characteristic long, thin leaves which have a pleasant fresh smell and the colourful peeling bark.

The wispy **casuarina** (*Casuarina*) grows in poor sandy soil, especially on the coast and on village waste land. It has the typical leaves of a pine tree and the cones are small and prickly to walk on. It is said to attract lightning during a thunder storm.

Bamboo (*Bambusa*) strictly speaking is a grass which can vary in size from small ornamental clumps to the enormous wild plant whose stems are so strong and thick that they are used for construction and for scaffolding and as pipes in rural irrigation schemes.

Flowering plants

Common in the Himalaya is the beautiful flowering shrub or tree, which can be as tall as 12 m, the **rhododendron** which is indigenous to this region. In the wild the commonest colour of the flowers is crimson, but other colours, such as pale purple occur too. From March to May the flowers are very noticeable on the hill sides. Another common wild flowering shrub is **lantana**. This is a fairly small untidy looking bush with rough, toothed oval leaves, which grow in pairs on the square and prickly stem. The flowers grow together in a flattened head, the ones near the middle being usually yellowish, while those at the rim are pink, pale purple or orange. The fruit is a shiny black berry.

Many other flowering plants are cultivated in parks, gardens and roadside verges. The attractive **frangipani** (*Plumeria acutifolia*) has a rather crooked trunk and stubby branches, which if broken give out a white milky juice which can be irritating to the skin. The big, leathery leaves taper to a point at each end and have noticeable parallel veins. The sweetly scented waxy flowers are white, pale yellow or pink. The **bougainvillea** grows as a dense bush or climber with small oval leaves and rather long thorns. The brightly coloured part (which can be pinkish-purple, crimson, orange, yellow, etc) which appears like a flower is not formed of petals, which are quite small and undistinguished, but by large papery bracts.

The unusual shape of the **hibiscus**. The trumpet shaped flower, as much as 7 or 8 cm across, has a very long 'tongue' growing out from the centre and varies in colour from scarlet to yellow or white. The leaves are somewhat oval or heart-shaped with jagged edges. In municipal flowerbeds the commonest planted flower is probably the **canna lily**. It has large leaves which are either green or bronzed and lots of large bright red or yellow flowers. The plant can be more than 1 m high.

On many ponds and tanks the floating plants of the **lotus** (*Nelumbo nucifera*) and the **water hyacinth** (*Eichornia crassipes*) are seen. Lotus flowers which rise on stalks above the water can be white, pink or a deep red and up to 25 cm across. The very large leaves either float on the surface or rise above the water. Many dwarf varieties are cultivated. The rather fleshy leaves and lilac flowers of the water hyacinth float to form a dense carpet, often clogging the waterways.

Crops

Of India's enormous variety, the single most widespread crop is **rice** (commonly *Orysa indica*). This forms the most important staple in South and East India, though other cereals and some root crops are also important elsewhere. The rice plant grows in flooded fields called *paddies* and virtually all planting or harvesting is done by hand. Millets are favoured in drier areas inland, while wheat is the most important crop in the northwest.

There are many different sorts of millet, but the ones most often seen are finger millet, pearl millet (bajra) and sorghum (jowar). **Finger millet**, commonly known as ragi (*Eleusine corocana*), is so-called because the ear has several spikes which radiate out, a bit like the fingers of a hand. Usually less than 1 m high, it is grown extensively in the south. Both **pearl millet** (*Pennisetum typhoideum*, known as *bajra* in the north and *cumbu* in Tamil Nadu) and **sorghum** (*Sorghum vulgare*, known as *jowar* in the north and *cholam* in the south) look superficially similar to the more familiar maize though each can be easily distinguished when the seed heads appear. Pearl millet, mainly grown in the north, has a tall single spike which gives it its other name of bulrush millet. Sorghum bears an open ear at the top of the plant.

Tea (*Camellia sinensis*) is grown on a commercial scale in tea gardens in areas of high rainfall, often in highland regions. Over 90% comes from Assam and West Bengal in the Northeast and Tamil Nadu and Kerala in the South. Left to itself tea grows into a tree 10 m tall. In the tea gardens it is pruned to waist height for the convenience of the tea pluckers and forms flat topped bushes, with shiny bright green oval leaves.

Coffee (*Coffea*) is not as widely grown as tea, but high quality arabica is an important crop in parts of South India. Coffee is also a bush, with fairly long, shiny dark green leaves. The white, sweet smelling flowers, which yield the coffee berry, grow in groups along the stems. The coffee berries start off green and turn red when ripe.

Sugar cane (*Saccharum*) is another important crop. It looks like a large grass, standing up to 3 m tall. The crude brown sugar is sold as jaggery and tastes like molasses.

Of the many spices grown in India, the two climbers pepper and vanilla and the grass-like cardamom are the ones most often seen. The **pepper** vine (*Piper Nigrum*) is indigenous to India where it grows in the warm moist regions. As it is a vine it needs support such as a trellis or a tree. It is frequently planted up against the betel nut palm and appears as a leafy vine with almost heart-shaped leaves. The peppercorns cluster along hanging spikes and are red when ripe. Both black and white pepper is produced from the same plant, the difference being in the processing.

Vanilla (*Vanilla planifolium*), which belongs to the orchid family, also grows up trees for support and attaches itself to the bark by small roots. It is native to South America, but grows well in India in areas of high rainfall. It is a rather fleshy looking plant, with white flowers and long slender pods.

Cardamom (*Elettaria cardomomum*) is native to India and is planted under shade. It grows well in highland areas such as Sikkim and the Western Ghats. It is a herbaceous plant looking like a big clump of grass, with long leafy shoots springing out of the ground up to 2-3 m. The white flowers grow on shoots which can be upright, but usually sprawl on the ground. It is from these flowers that the seed bearing capsules grow.

The **cashew nut** tree (*Anacardium occidentale*) was introduced into India, but now grows wild as well as being cultivated. It is a medium sized tree with bright green, shiny, rounded leaves. The nut grows on a fleshy fruit called a cashew apple and hangs down below this. **Cotton** (*Gossypium*) is important in parts of the west and south. The cotton bush is a small knee-high bush and the cotton boll appears after the flower has withered. This splits when ripe to show the white cotton lint inside.

The **castor oil** plant (*Ricinus Communis*) is cultivated as a cash crop and is planted in small holdings among other crops and along roads and paths. It is a handsome plant up to about 2 m in height, with very large leaves which are divided into some 12 'fingers'. The young stems are reddish and shiny. The well known castor oil is extracted from the bean which is a mottled brown in colour.

Wildlife

India has an extremely rich and varied wildlife, though many species only survive in very restricted environments. Alarmed by the rapid loss of wildlife habitat the Indian government established the first conservation measures in 1972, followed by the setting up of national parks and reserves. Some 25,000 sq km were set aside in 1973 for Project Tiger. Tigers are reported to be increasing steadily in several game reserves but threats to their survival continue, mainly due to poaching. The same is true of other less well-known species. Their natural habitat has been destroyed both by people and by domesticated animals. There are now nearly 70 national parks and 330 sanctuaries, as well as programmes of afforestation and coastline preservation. Most sanctuaries and parks are open October-March; in the northeast they are closed April-September.

The animals

The big cats Of the three Indian big cats the Asiatic lion is virtually confined to a single reserve. The other two, the tiger and leopard, occasionally occur outside. The **tiger** (*Panthera tigris*), which prefers to live in fairly dense cover, is most likely to be glimpsed as it lies in long grass or in dappled shadow or in the mangroves of the Sunderbans. The **Asiatic lion** (*Panthera leo*) is now found only in the Gir National Park. Less sleek than the African lion, it has a more shaggy coat and a smaller, often black mane. The **leopard**, or **panther** as it is often called in India (*Panthera pardus*), is far more numerous than the tiger, but is even more elusive. The all-black form is not uncommon in areas of higher rainfall in Northeast India, though the typical form is seen more often.

Elephant and rhino The **Indian elephant** (*Elephas maximus*) has been domesticated for centuries and today it is still used as a beast of burden. In the wild it inhabits hilly country with forest and bamboo, where it lives in herds which can number as many as 50 or more individuals. They are adaptable animals and can live in all sorts of forest, except in dry areas. Wild elephants are mainly confined to reserves, but occasionally move out into cultivation, where they cause great damage. The **great Indian one-horned rhinoceros** (*Rhinoceros unicornis*) has folds of skin which look like rivet covered armour plating. It stands at up to 170 cm at the shoulder.

Deer, antelope, oxen and their relatives Once widespread, these animals are now largely confined to the reserves. The male deer (stags) carry antlers which are branched, each 'spike' on the antler being called a tine. Antelopes and oxen, on the other hand, have horns which are not branched. There are several deer species in India, mainly confined to very restricted ranges. Three species are quite common. The largest and one of the most widespread is the magnificent **sambar** (*Cervus unicolor*) which can be up to 150 cm. It has a noticeably shaggy coat, which varies in colour from brown with a yellow or grey tinge through to dark, almost black, in the older stags. The sambar is often found on wooded hillsides and lives in groups of up to 10, though solitary individuals are also seen. The

Elephants – a future in the wild?

The Indian elephant (*Elephas maximas*), smaller than the African, is the world's second largest land mammal. Unlike the African elephant, the male rarely reaches a height of over 3 m; it also has smaller ears. Other distinguishing features include the high domed forehead, the rounded shape of the back and the smooth trunk with a single 'finger' at the end. Also the female is often tuskless or bears small ones called tushes and even the male is sometimes tuskless (*makhnas*). The Indian elephant has five nails on its front feet and four on the back (compared to the African's four and three respectively). There are approximately 6500 elephants living in the wild in northern West Bengal, Assam and Bhutan.

The loss of habitat has made wild elephants an increasing danger to humans and about 300 people are killed every year by wild elephants, mainly in the northeast. The tribal people have developed skilled techniques for capturing and training wild elephants, which have been domesticated in India for about 5000 years. They need a lot of feeding – about 18 hours a day. Working elephants are fed on a special diet, by hand straight at the mouth and they eat between 100 and 300 kg per day.

barasingha or **swamp deer** (*Cervus duvauceli*), standing about 130 cm at the shoulder, is also quite common. The females are usually lighter and some are spotted, as are the young. The antlers are much more complex than those of the sambar, having as many as 20 tines, but 12 is more usual. Barasingha prefer swampy habitat, but are also seen in grassy areas, often in large herds. The small **chital** or **spotted deer** (*Axis axis*), only about 90 cm tall, are seen in herds of 20 or so, in grassy areas. The bright rufous coat spotted with white is unmistakable; the stags carry antlers with three tines.

These animals live in open grasslands, never too far from water. The beautiful **blackbuck** or **Indian antelope** (*Antilope cervicapra*), up to 80 cm at the shoulder, occurs in large herds. The distinctive colouring and the long spiral horns make the stag easy to identify. The coat is chocolate brown above, sharply demarcated from the white of the underparts. The females do not usually bear horns and like the young, have yellowish brown coats. The larger, heavier **nilgai** or **blue bull** (*Boselaphus tragocamelus*) is about 140 cm at the shoulder and has a horse-like sloping back. The male has a dark grey coat; the female is sandy coloured. Both sexes have two white marks on the cheek, white throats and a white ring above each hoof. The male carries short, forward-curving horns and has a tuft of long black hairs on the front of the neck.

The very graceful **chinkara** or **Indian gazelle** (*Gazella gazella*) is only 65 cm at the shoulder. The light russet colour of the body has a distinct line along the side where the paler underparts start. Both sexes carry slightly S-shaped horns. Chinkara live in small groups in rather broken hilly countryside.

The commonest member of the oxen group is the **Asiatic wild buffalo** or water buffalo (*Bubalus bubalis*). About 170 cm at the shoulder, the wild buffalo, which can be aggressive, occurs in herds on grassy plains and swamps near rivers and lakes. The black coat and wide-spreading curved horns, carried by both sexes, are distinctive.

In the high Himalaya, the **yak** (*Bos grunniens*) is domesticated. The wild yak, found on bleak Himalayan hillsides, has a shaggy, blackish brown coat and large horns; the domesticated animals are often piebald and the horns much smaller.

The **Indian bison** or **gaur** (*Bos gaurus*) can be up to 200 cm at the shoulder with a heavy muscular ridge across it. Both sexes carry curved horns. The young gaur is a light sandy colour, which darkens with age, the old bulls being nearly black with pale sandy coloured 'socks' and a pale forehead. Basically hill animals, they live in forests and bamboo clumps and emerge from the trees to graze.

The rare **asiatic wild ass** (*Equus hemionus*) is confined to the deserts of the Little Rann of Kachchh. The fawn body has a distinctive dark stripe along the back. The dark mane is short and erect. The **wild boar** (*Sus scrofa*) has a mainly black body and a pig-like head; the hairs thicken down the spine to form a sort of mane. A mature male stands 90 cm at the shoulder and, unlike the female, bears tusks. The young are striped. Quite widespread, they can often cause great destruction among crops.

One of the most important scavengers of the open countryside, the **striped hyena** (*Hyena hyena*) usually comes out at night. It is about 90 cm at the shoulder with a large head with a noticeable crest of hairs along its sloping back.

The **common giant flying squirrel** (*Petaurista petaurista*) is common in the larger forests of India, except in the northeast. The body can be 45 cm long and the tail another 50 cm. They glide from tree to tree using a membrane stretching from front leg to back leg which acts like a parachute.

In towns and villages The **common langur** (*Presbytis entellus*), 75 cm, is a long-tailed monkey with a distinctive black face, hands and feet. Usually a forest dweller, it is found almost throughout India. The **rhesus macaque** (*Macaca mulatta*), 60 cm, is more solid looking with shorter limbs and a shorter tail. It can be distinguished by the orange-red fur on its rump and flanks.

Palm squirrels are very common. The **five-striped** (*Funambulus pennanti*) and the **three-striped palm squirrel** (*Funambulus palmarum*) are both about the same size (30 cm long, about half of which is tail). The five-striped is usually seen in towns.

The two bats most commonly seen in towns differ enormously in size. The larger so-called **flying fox** (*Pteropus giganteus*) has a wing span of 120 cm. These fruit eating bats, found throughout, except in the driest areas, roost in large noisy colonies where they look like folded umbrellas hanging from the trees. In the evening they can be seen leaving the roost with slow measured wing beats. The much smaller **Indian pipistrelle** (*Pipistrellus coromandra*), with a wing span of about 15 cm, is an insect eater. It comes into houses at dusk, roosting under eaves and has a fast, erratic flight.

The **jackal** (*Canis aureus*), a lone scavenger in towns and villages, looks like a cross between a dog and a fox and varies from brown to black. The bushy tail has a dark tip.

The **common mongoose** (*Herpestes edwardsi*) lives in scrub and open jungle. It kills snakes, but will also take rats, mice and chicken. Tawny coloured with a grey grizzled tinge, it is about 90 cm in length, of which half is pale-tipped tail.

The **sloth bear** (*Melursus ursinus*), about 75 cm at the shoulder, lives in broken forest, but may be seen on a lead accompanying a street entertainer who makes it 'dance' to music as part of an act. They have a long snout, a pendulous lower lip and a shaggy black coat with a yellowish V-shaped mark on the chest.

If you take a boat trip on the Ganga or the Brahmaputra rivers, look out for the fresh water **gangetic dolphin** (*Platanista gangetica*) as it comes to the surface to breathe.

Birds

Town and village birds Some birds perform a useful function scavenging and clearing refuse. One of the most widespread is the brown **pariah kite** (*Milvus migrans*, 65 cm). The more handsome chestnut and white **brahminy kite** (*Haliastur indus*, 48 cm) is largely confined to the waterside. The common brown **white-backed vulture** (*Gyps bengalensis*, 90 cm) looks ungainly and has a bare and scrawny head and neck. The smaller **scavenger vulture** (*Neophron percnopterus*, 65 cm) is mainly white, but often has dirty looking plumage and the bare head and neck of all vultures. In flight its wedge-shaped tail and black and white colouring are characteristic.

The **house crow** (*Corvus splendens*, 45 cm) on the other hand is a very smart looking bird with a grey body and black tail, wings, face and throat. It occurs in almost every town and village in India. The **jungle crow** (*Corvus macrorhynchos*, 50 cm) originally a bird of the countryside has started to move into populated areas and in the hill stations tends to replace the house crow. Unlike the house crow it is a glossy black all over and has a much deeper, hoarser caw.

The **feral pigeon**, or **blue rock dove** (*Columba livia*, 32 cm), found throughout the world, is generally a slatey grey in colour. It invariably has two dark bars on the wing and a white rump. The **little brown dove** (*Streptopelia senegalensis*, 25 cm) is bluey grey and brown above, with a pink head and underparts and a speckled pattern on the neck. The **collared dove** (*Streptopelia decaocto*, 30 cm), with a distinct half collar on the back of its neck, is common, especially in the drier parts of India.

Bulbuls are common in gardens and parks. The **red-vented bulbul** (*Pycnonotus cafer*, 20 cm), a mainly brown bird, can be identified by the slight crest and a bright red patch under the tail. The **house sparrow** (*Passer domesticus*, 15 cm) can be seen in towns. The ubiquitous **common myna** (*Acridotheres tristis*, 22 cm) feeds on lawns, especially after rain or watering. Look for the white under the tail and the bare yellow skin around the eye, yellow bill and legs and in flight the large white wing patch.

A less common but more striking bird also seen feeding in open spaces is the **hoopoe** (*Upupa epops*, 30 cm), easily identified by its sandy plumage with black and white stripes and long thin curved bill. The marvellous fan-shaped crest is sometimes raised. Finally there is a member of the cuckoo family which is heard more often than seen. The **koel** (*Eudynamys scolopacea*, 42 cm) is commonly heard during the hot weather: kuoo-kuoo-kuoo, the double note starts off low and flute-like, rises in pitch and intensity, then suddenly stops, only to start all over again. The male is all black with a greenish bill and a red eye; the female streaked and barred.

Water and waterside birds The *jheels* (marshes or swamps) of India form one of the richest bird habitats in the world. Cormorants abound; the commonest, the **little cormorant** (*Phalacrocorax niger*, 50 cm) is found on most inland waters. An almost entirely black bird with just a little white on the throat, it has a long tail and a hooked bill. The **coot** (*Fulica atra*, 40 cm), another common black bird, seen especially in winter has a noticeable white shield on the forehead.

The magnificent **sarus crane** (*Grus antigone*, 150 cm) is one of India's tallest birds. It is widespread year round across northern India, usually in pairs. The bare red head and long red legs combined with its height and grey plumage make it easy to identify. The commonest migrant crane is the **common crane** (*Grus grus*, 120 cm), present only in winter, often in flocks. It has grey plumage with a black head and neck. There is a white streak running down the side of the neck and above the eye is a tuft of red feathers.

The **openbill stork** (*Anastomus oscitans*, 80 cm) and the **painted stork** (*Ibis leucocephalus*, 100 cm) are common too and breed in large colonies. The former is white with black wing feathers and a curiously shaped bill. The latter, mainly white, has a pinkish tinge on the back and dark marks on the wings and a broken black band on the lower chest. The bare yellow face and yellow down-curved bill are conspicuous.

By almost every swamp, ditch or rice paddy up to about 1200 m you will see the **paddy bird** (*Ardeola grayii*, 45 cm). An inconspicuous, buff-coloured bird, it is easily overlooked as it stands hunched up by the waterside. As soon as it takes off, its white wings and rump make it very noticeable. The **bronze-winged jacana** (*Metopidius indicus*, 27 cm) has very long toes which enable it to walk on the floating leaves of water-lilies and there is a noticeable white streak over and above the eye. Village ponds often have their resident bird.

The commonest and most widespread of the Indian kingfishers is the jewel-like **common kingfisher** (*Alcedo atthis*, 18 cm). With its brilliant blue upperparts and orange breast it is usually seen perched on a twig or a reed beside the water.

Open grassland, light woodland and cultivated land   The **cattle egret** (*Bubulcus ibis*, 50 cm), a small white heron, is usually seen near herds of cattle, frequently perched on the backs of the animals. Equal in height to the sarus crane is the impressive, but ugly **adjutant stork** (*Leptopilos dubius*, 150 cm). This often dishevelled bird is a scavenger and is thus seen near rubbish dumps and carcasses. It has a naked red head and neck, a huge bill and a large fleshy pouch which hangs down the front of the neck.

The **rose-ringed parakeet** (*Psittacula krameri*, 40 cm) is found throughout India up to about 1500 m while the **pied myna** (*Sturnus contra*, 23 cm) is restricted to northern and central India. The rose-ringed parakeet often forms huge flocks, an impressive sight coming in to roost. The long tail is noticeable both in flight and when the bird is perched. They can be very destructive to crops, but are attractive birds which are frequently kept as pets. The pied myna, with its smart black and white plumage, is conspicuous, usually in small flocks in grazing land or cultivation. It feeds on the ground and on village rubbish dumps. The all black **drongo** (*Dicrurus adsimilis*, 30 cm) is invariably seen perched on telegraph wires or bare branches. Its distinctively forked tail makes it easy to identify.

Weaver birds are a family of mainly yellow birds, all remarkable for the intricate nests they build. The most widespread is the **baya weaver** (*Ploceus philippinus*, 15cm) which nest in large colonies, often near villages. The male in the breeding season combines a black face and throat with a contrasting yellow top of the head and the yellow breast band. In the non-breeding season both sexes are brownish sparrow-like birds.

Hill birds   Land above 1500 m supports different species, although some, such as the ubiquitous **common myna**, are found in the highlands as well as in lower lying terrain.

The highland equivalent of the red-vented bulbul is the **white-cheeked bulbul** (*Pycnonotus leucogenys*, 20 cm) which is found in gardens and woodland in the Himalaya up to about 2500 m. It has white underparts with a yellow patch under the tail and a black head. The crest varies in length and is most prominent in birds found in Kashmir, where it is very common in gardens. The **red-whiskered bulbul** (*Pycnonotus jocosus*, 20 cm) is widespread in the Himalaya and the hills of South India up to about 2500 m. Its pronounced pointed crest, which is sometimes so long that it flops forward towards the bill, white underparts and red and white 'whiskers' serve to distinguish it. It has a red patch under the tail.

In the summer the delightful **verditer flycatcher** (*Muscicapa thalassina*, 15 cm) is a common breeding bird in the Himalaya up to about 3000 m. It is tame and confiding, often builds its nest on verandas and is seen perching on telegraph wires. In winter it is more widely distributed throughout the country. It is an active little bird which flicks its tail up and down in a characteristic manner. The male is all bright blue green with darker wings and a black patch in front of the eyes. The female is similar, but duller.

Another species associated with man is the **white wagtail** (*Motacilla alba*, 21 cm), very common in the Himalayan summer up to about 3000 m. It is found near water, by streams and lakes, on floating vegetation and among the house boats in Kashmir. Its black and white plumage and constantly wagging tail make it easy to identify.

Yet another species common in Kashmir and in other Himalayan hill stations is the **red-billed blue magpie** (*Urocissa erythrorhyncha*, 65 cm). With a long tail and pale blue plumage, contrasting with its black head, it is usually seen in small flocks as it flies from tree to tree. Its habitats of choice are tea gardens, open woodland and cultivation.

The highlands of India, especially the Himalaya, are the home of the ancestors of **domestic hens** and also of numerous beautiful **pheasants**. These are mainly forest dwellers and are not easy to see as they tend to be shy and wary of man.

Last but not least is India's national bird, the magnificent **Peafowl** (*Pavo cristatus*, male 210 cm, female 100 cm), which is more commonly known as the peacock. Semi-domesticated birds are commonly seen and heard around towns and villages, especially in the northwest of India. In the wild it favours hilly jungles and dense scrub.

Reptiles and amphibians

India is famous for its reptiles, especially its snakes, which feature in many stories and legends. One of the most common is the **Indian rock python** (*Python molurus*), a 'constrictor' which kills its prey by suffocation. Usually about 4 m in length, they can be much longer. Their docile nature make them favourites of snake handlers.

The other large snakes favoured by street entertainers are cobras. The various species all have a hood which is spread when the snake draws itself up to strike. They are all highly venomous and the snake charmers prudently de-fang them to render them harmless. The best known is probably the **spectacled cobra** (*Naja naja*), which has a mark like a pair of spectacles on the back of its hood. The largest venomous snake in the world is the **king cobra** (*Ophiophagus hannah*) which is 5 m in length. It is usually brown, but can vary from cream to black and lacks the spectacle marks of the other. In their natural state cobras are generally inhabitants of forest regions.

In houses everywhere you cannot fail to see the **gecko** (*Hemidactylus*). This small harmless lizard is active after dark. It lives in houses behind pictures and curtain rails and at night emerges to run across the walls and ceilings to hunt insects. It is not usually more than about 14 cm long, with a transparent, pale yellowish brown body.

At the other end of the scale is the **monitor lizard** (*Varanus*), which can grow to 2 m in length. They can vary from a colourful black and yellow, to plain or speckled brown. They live in different habitats from cultivation and scrub to waterside places and desert.

The most widespread crocodile is the freshwater **mugger** or Marsh crocodile (*Crocodilus palustris*) which grows to 3-4 m in length. The only similar fresh water species is the **gharial** (*Gavialis gangeticus*) which lives in large, fast flowing rivers. Twice the length of the mugger, it is a fish-eating crocodile with a long thin snout and, in the case of the male, an extraordinary bulbous growth on the end of the snout.

The huge, aggressive **estuarine** or **saltwater crocodile** (*Crocodilus porosus*) is restricted to the brackish waters of the Sundarbans, on the east coast and in the Andaman and Nicobar Islands. It grows to 7 m in length and is sleeker than the mugger.

Books

The literature on India is as huge and varied as the subcontinent itself. India is a good place to buy English language books as foreign books are often much cheaper than the published price. There are also cheap Indian editions and occasionally reprints of out-of-print books. There are excellent bookshops in all the major Indian cities. Below are a few suggestions.

Art and architecture

Burton, TR *Hindu Art*, British Museum P. Well illustrated; broad view of art and religion.
Cooper, I and Dawson, B *Traditional Buildings of India*, Thames & Hudson.
Michell, G *The Hindu Temple*, Univ of Chicago Press, 1988. An authoritative account of Hindu architectural development.
Sterlin, H *Hindu India*. Köln, Taschen, 1998. Traces the development from early rock-cut shrines, detailing famous examples; clearly written, well illustrated.

Cities, sites and places

Kolkata
Humphrey, K *Walking Calcutta*, Grosvenor House, 2009. One of the best ways to discover the city and its inhabitants, off the tourist trail.
Moorhouse, G *Calcutta*, 1971. It has dated somewhat, but is still a classic appraisal of the city. Written during Calcutta's bleaker moments.
Winchester, S *Lonely Planet*, 2004. Engaging essays by father and son, utilizing many worthy sources of travel literature.

Varanasi
Gol *A Pilgrimage to Kashi*, Indica, 1999. Rs 275. An accessible cartoon strip; the city's history and culture as seen by modern-day visitors.
Parry, JP *Death in Banaras*, Cambridge UP, 1994.

Current affairs and politics

French, P *Liberty or Death*, Harper Collins, 1997. Well researched, serious, but very readable.
Granta 57 *India: the Golden Jubilee*. Superb edition devoted to India's 50th anniversary of Independence, 22 international writers give brilliant snapshot accounts of India today.
Khilnani, S *The idea of India*, Penguin, 1997. Excellent introduction to contemporary India.
Silver, RB and Epstein, B *India: a mosaic*. New York, NYRB, 2000. Distinguished essays on history, politics and literature. Amartya Sen on Tagore, Pankaj Mishra on nuclear India.
Tharur, S *India: from midnight to the millennium*. Viking, 1997.
Tully, M *No full stops in India*, Viking, 1991. An often superbly observed but controversially interpreted view of contemporary India.

History: medieval and modern

Beames, J *Memoirs of a Bengal Civilian*. A readable insight into the British Raj in the post-Mutiny period, London, Eland, 1991.
Edwardes, M *The Myth of the Mahatma*. Presents Gandhi in a whole new light.
Gandhi, R *The Good Boatman*, Viking/Penguin 1995. An excellent biography by one of Gandhi's noted grandson's.
Gascoigne, B *The Great Moghuls*, London, Cape, 1987.
Keay, J *India: a History*, Harper Collins, 2000. A major new popular history of the subcontinent.
Nehru, J *The discovery of India*, New Delhi, ICCR, 1976.
Robinson, F (ed) *Cambridge Encyclopaedia of India*, Cambridge, 1989. An introduction to many aspects of South Asian society.
Spear, P and Thapar, R *A history of India*, 2 vols, Penguin, 1978.
Wolpert, S *A new history of India*, OUP 1990.

History: pre- and early history

Allchin, B and R *Origins of a civilisation*, Viking, Penguin Books, 1997. The most authoritative up-to-date survey of the origins of Indian civilizations.

Basham, AL *The Wonder that was India*, London, Sidgwick & Jackson, 1985. One of the most comprehensive and readable accounts of the development of India's culture.

Language

Snell, R and Weightman, S *Teach Yourself Hindi*. An excellent, accessible teaching guides with cassette tapes.

Yule, H and Burnell, AC (eds) *Hobson-Jobson*, 1886. New paperback edition, 1986. A delightful insight into Anglo-Indian words and phrases.

Literature

Anand, Mulk Raj *Untouchable*. Penguin Classics, 1935. A day in the life of a casteless toilet-sweeper.

Chatterjee, U *English August*. London, Faber, 1988. A wry modern account of an Indian civil servant's year in a rural posting.

Chaudhuri, N Vivid, witty and often sharply critical accounts of India across the 20th century. *The autobiography of an unknown Indian*, Macmillan, London; *Thy Hand, Great Anarch!*, London, Chatto & Windus, 1987.

Desai, Kiran *The Inheritance of Loss*, Hamish Hamilton 2006. Set in Kalimpong in the 1980s during the Gorkha uprising. Winner of the Man Booker Prize.

Farrell, JG *The Siege of Krishnapur*, 1973. Comic, horrific and gripping fiction about the 1857 mutiny.

Lapierre, Dominique *City of Joy*, 1985. Every volunteer in Kolkata will find themselves reading this story of a rickshaw-wallah and a priest. It's no great work of literature,

unfortunately. There's also a film version, starring the late Patrick Swayze.

Mistry, R *A fine balance*. Faber, 1995. A tale of the struggle to survive in the modern Indian city.

Naipaul, VS *A million mutinies now*, Penguin, 1992. 'Revisionist' account of India turns away from the despondency of his earlier books (*An Area of darkness* and *India: a wounded civilisation*).

Ramanuja, AK *The collected essays*. Ed by V Dhawadker. New Delhi, OUP, 1999. Brilliant essays on Indian culture and literature.

Rushdie, S *Midnight's children*, London, Picador, 1981. India since Independence, with funny and sharp critiques of South Asian life in the 1980s. *The Moor's Last Sigh*, Viking, 1996, is of particular interest to those travelling to Kochi and Mumbai.

Scott, P *The Raj Quartet*, Panther, London, 1973; *Staying on*, Longmans, 1985. Outstandingly perceptive novels of the end of the Raj.

Scott, P *Staying On*. Heinemann, 1977. Very funny, very poignant evocation of life in a hill station. Won the Booker Prize.

Seth, V *A Suitable Boy*, Phoenix House London, 1993. Prize-winning novel of modern Indian life.

Weightman, S (ed) *Travellers Literary Companion: the Indian Sub-continent*. Invaluable introduction to the diversity of Indian writing.

Music and cinema

Menon, RR *Penguin Dictionary of Indian Classical Music*, Penguin, New Delhi, 1995.

Mohan, L *Bollywood, Popular Indian Cinema*, Joshi (Dakini).

People

Bumiller, E *May you be the mother of one hundred sons*, Penguin, 1991. An American woman journalist's account of coming to understand the issues that face India's women.

Holmstrom, L *The Inner Courtyard*. A series of short stories by Indian women, translated into English, Rupa, 1992.
Lewis, N *A Goddess in the Stones*. An insight into tribal life in Orissa and Bihar.
Varma, PK *Being Indian*. Penguin, 2004.
Bijapurkar, R *We are like that only*, Penguin 2007. To understand consumer India.
Lloyd, S *An Indian Attachment*, London, Eland, 1992. A very personal and engaging account of time spent in an Indian village.

Religion

Doniger O'Flaherty, W *Hindu Myths*, London, Penguin, 1974. A sourcebook translated from the Sanskrit.
Jain, JP *Religion and Culture of the Jains,* 3rd ed, New Delhi, Bharatiya Jnanapith, 1981.
Qureshi, IH *The Muslim Community of the Indo-Pakistan Sub-Continent 610-1947*, OUP, Karachi, 1977.
Rahula, W *What the Buddha Taught.*
Singh, H *The heritage of the Sikhs*, 2nd ed, New Delhi, 1983.
Waterstone, R *India, the cultural companion*, Duncan Baird, Winchester, 2002. India's spiritual traditions brought up to date, well illustrated.
Zaehner, RC *Hinduism*, OUP.

Travel

Dalrymple, W *White Moghuls*, Harper-Collins 2002. The early days of the East India Company, classic Dalrymple, readable history.
Fishlock, T *Cobra Road*, London, John Murray, 1991. Impressions of a news journalist.
Frater, A *Chasing the monsoon*, London, Viking, 1990. Prize-winning account of the human impact of the monsoon's sweep across India.
Hatt, J *The tropical traveller: the essential guide to travel in hot countries*, Penguin, 3rd ed, 1992. Wide ranging and clearly written, based on extensive experience and research.

Keay, J *Into India*, London, John Murray, 1999. Seasoned traveller's introduction to understanding and enjoying India.
Parkes, Fanny *Begums, Thugs and White Moghuls*. Eland, 2001. The jounals of this intrepid lady, who immersed herself in Indian culture during the early years of the Raj, are honest, illuminating and immensely readable.

Trekking

Bonnington, C *Annapurna South Face*, London, Cassell, 1971; *Everest the hard way*, London, Hodder & Stoughton, 1979.
Hillary, E *High Adventure*, New York, Dutton, 1955. Classic account of Himalayan climbs.
Salkeld, A *The History of Great Climbs*, 1995, The Royal Geographical Society. A magnificently illustrated and written account of historic climbs.

More practical publications include:
Iozawa, T *Trekking in the Himalayas*, Delhi, Allied Publishers, 1980. *Nest & Wings*, Post Box 4531, New Delhi 110016, T011-644 2245: 'Trekking', 'Holiday & Trekking' and 'Trekking Map' titles (Rs 40-140) cover most trekking destinations in the Indian Himalaya; trekking itineraries are listed in brief but some booklets give additional insight into the history and culture of the area.

Also useful are:
Himalayan Club's *Himalayan Journal* (annual) from PO Box 1905, Mumbai 400001.

Wildlife and vegetation

Ali, S *Indian hill birds*, OUP.
Ali, Sand Dillon Ripley, S *Handbook of the birds of India & Pakistan* (compact ed).
Cowen, DV *Flowering Trees and Shrubs in India.*
Grimmet, R, and Inskipp, C and T *Pocket guide to Birds of the Indian Sub-Continent*, 1999.
Ives, R *Of tigers and men*, Doubleday, 1995.

Kazmierczak, K and Singh, R *A birdwatcher's guide to India*. Prion, 1998, Sandy, Beds, UK. Well researched and carrying lots of practical information for all birders.
Nair, SM *Endangered animals of India*, New Delhi, NBT, 1992.

Polunin, O and Stainton, A *Flowers of the Himalaya*, OUP, 1984.
Prater, SH *The Book of Indian Animals*.
Sippy, S and Kapoor, S *The Ultimate Ranthambhore Guide*, 2001. Informative, practical guide stressing conservation.

Contents

Footnotes

Basic Hindi words and phrases

Pronunciation: 'a' as in *ah*; 'i' as in *bee*; 'o' as in *oh*; 'u' as *oo* in *book*
Hello *namaste/nomoshkar*
Thank you/no thank you *dhanyavad or shukriya/nahin shukriya*
Yes/no *ji han/ji nahin*
What is your name? *apka nam kya hai?*
My name is... *mera nam... hai*
How are you? *kya hal hai?*
I am well, thanks, and you? *main thik hun, aur ap?*
How much? *kitna?*
That is very expensive! *bahut mahanga hai!*

Food and drink glossary

Meat and fish

gosht, mas	meat, usually mutton (sheep)
jhinga	prawns
macchli	fish
murgh	chicken

Vegetables (sabzi)

aloo	potato	**khumbhi**	mushroom
baingan	aubergine	**matar**	peas
band gobi	cabbage	**piaz**	onion
bhindi	okra, ladies' fingers	**phool gobi**	cauliflower
gajar	carrots	**sag**	spinach

Styles of cooking

Many items on restaurant menus are named according to methods of preparation, roughly equivalent to terms such as 'Provençal' or 'sauté'.

bhoona in a thick, fairly spicy sauce

chops minced meat, fish or vegetables, covered with mashed potato, crumbed and fried

cutlet minced meat, fish, vegetables formed into flat rounds or ovals, crumbed and fried (eg prawn cutlet, flattened king prawn)

do piaza with onions (added twice during cooking)

dum pukht steam baked

jhal frazi spicy, hot sauce with tomatoes and chillies

jhol thin gravy (Bengali)

Kashmiri cooked with mild spices, ground almonds and yoghurt, often with fruit

kebab skewered (or minced and shaped) meat or fish; a dry spicy dish cooked on a fire

kima minced meat (usually 'mutton')

kofta minced meat or vegetable balls

korma in fairly mild rich sauce using cream/yoghurt

masala marinated in spices (fairly hot)

Madras hot

makhani in butter rich sauce

moli South Indian dishes cooked in coconut milk and green chilli sauce

Mughlai rich North Indian style

Nargisi dish using boiled eggs

navratan curry ('9 jewels') colourful mixed vegetables and fruit in mild sauce

Peshwari rich with dried fruit and nuts (Northwest Indian)

tandoori baked in a tandoor (special clay oven) or one imitating it

tikka marinated meat pieces, baked quite dry

vindaloo hot and sour Goan meat dish using vinegar

Typical dishes

aloo gosht potato and mutton stew

aloo gobi dry potato and cauliflower with cumin

aloo, matar, kumbhi potato, peas, mushrooms in a dryish mildly spicy sauce

bhindi bhaji lady's fingers fried with onions and mild spices

boti kebab marinated pieces of meat, skewered and cooked over a fire

dhal makhani lentils cooked with butter

dum aloo potato curry with a spicy yoghurt, tomato and onion sauce

matar panir curd cheese cubes with peas and spices (and often tomatoes)

murgh massallam chicken in creamy marinade of yoghurt, spices and herbs with nuts

nargisi kofta boiled eggs covered in minced lamb, cooked in a thick sauce

rogan josh rich, mutton/beef pieces in creamy, red sauce

sag panir drained curd (panir) sautéed with chopped spinach in mild spices

sarson-ke-sag and **makkai-ki-roti** mustard leaf cooked dry with spices served with maize four roti from Punjab

shabdeg a special Mughlai mutton dish with vegetables

yakhni lamb stew

Rice

bhat/sada chawal plain boiled rice

biriyani partially cooked rice layered over meat and baked with saffron

khichari rice and lentils cooked with turmeric and other spices

pulao/pilau fried rice cooked with spices (cloves, cardamom, cinnamon) with dried fruit, nuts or vegetables. Sometimes cooked with meat, like a biriyani

Roti – breads

chapati (roti) thin, plain, wholemeal unleavened bread cooked on a tawa (griddle), usually made from ata (wheat flour). Makkaikiroti is with maize flour.

nan oven baked (traditionally in a tandoor) white flour leavened bread often large and triangular; sometimes stuffed with almonds and dried fruit

paratha fried bread layered with ghi (sometimes cooked with egg or with potatoes)

poori thin deepfried, puffed rounds of flour

Sweets

These are often made with reduced/thickened milk, drained curd cheese or powdered lentils and nuts. They are sometimes covered with a decorative, edible silver leaf.

barfi fudgelike rectangles/diamonds

gulab jamun dark fried spongy balls, soaked in syrup

halwa rich sweet made from cereal, fruit, vegetable, nuts and sugar

khir, payasam, paesh thickened milk rice/vermicelli pudding

kulfi cone-shaped Indian ice cream with pistachios/almonds, uneven in texture

jalebi spirals of fried batter soaked in syrup

laddoo lentil based batter 'grains' shaped into rounds

rasgulla (roshgulla) balls of curd in clear syrup

sandesh dry sweet made of curd cheese

Snacks

bhaji, pakora vegetable fritters (onions, potatoes, cauliflower etc) deep-fried in batter

chat sweet and sour fruit and vegetables flavoured with tamarind paste and chillis

chana choor, chioora ('Bombay mix') lentil and flattened rice snacks mixed with nuts and dried fruit

dosai South Indian pancake made with rice and lentil flour; served with a mild potato and onion filling (masala dosai) or without (ravai or plain dosai)

iddli steamed South Indian rice cakes, a bland breakfast given flavour by spiced accompaniments

kachori fried pastry rounds stuffed with spiced lentil/peas/potato filling

momos Tibetan stuffed pastas

samosa cooked vegetable or meat wrapped in pastry triangles and deep fried

utthappam thick South Indian rice and lentil flour pancake cooked with spices/onions/tomatoes

vadai deep-fried, small savoury lentil 'doughnut' rings. **Dahi vada** are similar rounds in yoghurt

Glossary

Words in *italics* are common elements of words, often making up part of a place name

A

aarti (arati) Hindu worship with lamps

abad peopled

acharya religious teacher

Adi Granth Guru Granth Sahib, holy book of the Sikhs

Adinatha first of the 24 Tirthankaras, distinguished by his bull mount

agarbathi incense

Agni Vedic fire divinity, intermediary between gods and men; guardian of the Southeast

ahimsa non-harming, non-violence

amrita ambrosia; drink of immortality

ananda joy

Ananda the Buddha's chief disciple

Ananta a huge snake on whose coils Vishnu rests

anna (ana) 1/16 of a rupee

Annapurna Goddess of abundance; one aspect of Devi

apsara celestial nymph

Ardhanarisvara Siva represented as half-male and half-female

Arjuna hero of the *Mahabharata*, to whom Krishna delivered the *Bhagavad Gita*

arrack alcoholic spirit fermented from potatoes or grain

asana a seat or throne (Buddha's) pose

ashram hermitage or retreat

Ashta Matrikas The eight mother goddesses who attended on Siva or Skanda

astanah threshold

atman philosophical concept of universal soul or spirit

aus summer rice crop (Apr-Aug) Bengal

Avalokiteshwara Lord who looks down; Bodhisattva, the Compassionate

avatara 'descent'; incarnation of a divinity

ayah nursemaid

B

babu clerk

bagh garden

bahadur title, meaning 'the brave'

baksheesh tip 'bribe'

Balabhadra Balarama, elder brother of Krishna

bandh a strike

Bangla (Bangaldar) curved roof, based on thatched roofs in Bengal

bania merchant caste

basti Jain temple

bazar market

begum Muslim princess/woman's courtesy title

Bhagavad-Gita Song of the Lord; section of the *Mahabharata*

Bhagiratha the king who prayed to Ganga to descend to earth

bhai brother

Bhairava Siva, the Fearful

bhakti adoration of a deity

bhang Indian hemp

Bharata half-brother of Rama

bhavan building or house

bhikku Buddhist monk

Bhima Pandava hero of the *Mahabharata*, famous for his strength

Bhimsen Deity worshipped for his strength and courage

bidi (beedi) Indian cigarette, tobacco wrapped in tendu leaves

bo-tree (or Bodhi) *Ficus religiosa*, pipal tree associated with the Buddha

Bodhisattva Enlightened One, destined to become Buddha

bodi tuft of hair on back of the shaven head (also *tikki*)

Brahma Universal self-existing power; Creator in the Hindu Triad

Brahmachari religious student, accepting rigorous discipline (eg chastity)

Brahman (Brahmin) highest Hindu (and Jain) caste of priests

Brahmanism ancient Indian religion, precursor of modern Hinduism

bundh (literally closed) a strike

burqa (burkha) over-dress worn by Muslim women observing purdah

bustee slum

C

cantonment planned military or civil area in town

chaam Himalayan Buddhist masked dance

chadar sheet worn as clothing

chai tea

chakra sacred Buddhist wheel of the law; also Vishnu's discus

chala Bengali curved roof

Chamunda terrifying form of the goddess Durga

Chandra Moon; a planetary deity

char bagh formal Mughal garden, divided into quarters

char bangla (char-chala) 'four temples' in Bengal, built like huts

charpai 'four legs' – wooden frame string bed

chatt(r)a ceremonial umbrella on stupa (Buddhist)

chaukidar (chowkidar) night-watchman; guard

chhang strong mountain beer of fermented barley maize rye or millet or rice

chhatri umbrella shaped dome or pavilion

chhetri (kshatriya) Hindu warrior caste

chikan shadow embroidery on fine cotton

chogyal heavenly king (Sikkim)

choli blouse

chorten Himalayan Buddhist relic shrine or a memorial stupa

chowk (chauk) a block; open place in a city where the market is held

coir fibre from coconut husk

crore 10 million

D

dacoit bandit

dada (dadu) grandfather; elder brother

dahi yoghurt

dak post

dakini sorceress

Dakshineshvara Lord of the South; name of Siva

dan gift

dandi wooden 'seat' carried by bearers

darbar (durbar) a royal gathering

darshan (darshana) viewing of a deity or spiritual leader

darwaza gateway, door

deodar Himalayan cedar; from *deva-daru*, the 'wood of the gods'

dervish member of Muslim brotherhood, committed to poverty

deul in Bengal and Orissa, generic name for temple; the sanctuary

devala temple or shrine (Buddhist or Hindu)

Devi Goddess; later, the Supreme Goddess

dhaba roadside restaurant

dharamshala (dharamsala) pilgrims' rest house

dharma moral and religious duty

dharmachakra wheel of 'moral' law (Buddhist)

dhobi washerman

dhol drums

dhooli (dhooli) swinging chair on a pole, carried by bearers

dhoti loose loincloth worn by Indian men

dhyana meditation

digambara literally 'sky-clad' Jain sect in which the monks go naked

dighi village pond (Bengal)

dikshitar person who makes oblations or offerings

divan (diwan) smoking-room; also a chief minister

Diwali festival of lights (Oct-Nov)

diwan chief financial minister

diwan-i-am hall of public audience

diwan-i-khas hall of private audience

Draupadi wife-in-common of the five Pandava brothers in the *Mahabharata*

duar (dwar) door, gateway

dun valley

dupatta long scarf worn by Punjabi women

Durga principal goddess of the Shakti cult

durrie (dhurrie) thick handloom rug

E

ek the number 1, a symbol of unity

ekka one horse carriage

F

firman edict or grant issued by a sovereign

G

gaddi throne

gadi/gari car, cart, train

gali (galli) lane; an alley

gana child figures in art

Ganesh (Ganapati) elephant-headed son of Siva and Parvati

Ganga goddess personifying the Ganges

ganj market

ganja Indian hemp

gaon village

garbhagriha literally 'womb- chamber'; a temple sanctuary

garh fort

Garuda Mythical eagle, half-human Vishnu's vehicle

Gauri 'Fair One'; Parvati, consort of Shiva

Gaurishankara Siva with Parvati

ghagra (ghongra) long flared skirt

ghanta bell

ghat hill range, hill road; landing place; steps on the river bank

ghazal Urdu lyric poetry/love songs, often erotic

ghee clarified butter for cooking

gherao industrial action, surrounding home or office of politician or industrial manager

giri hill

godown warehouse

gola conical-shaped storehouse

gompa Tibetan Buddhist monastery

Gopala (Govinda) cowherd; a name of Krishna

Gopis cowherd girls; milk maids who played with Krishna

Gorakhnath historically, an 11th-century yogi who founded a Saivite cult; an incarnation of Siva

gosain monk or devotee (Hindi)

gram chick pea, pulse

gram village; gramadan, gift of village

gumbaz (gumbad) dome

gur gur salted butter tea (Ladakh)

gurudwara (literally 'entrance to the house of God'); Sikh religious complex

---

H

Haj (Hajj) annual Muslim pilgrimage to Mecca

hakim judge; a physician (usually Muslim)

halwa a special sweetmeat

Hanuman Monkey devotee of Rama; bringer of success to armies

Hara (Hara Siddhi) Siva

Hari Vishnu Harihara, Vishnu-Siva as a single divinity

hartal general strike

hat (haat) market

hathi (hati) elephant

hathi pol elephant gate

hauz tank or reservoir

haveli a merchant's house usually in Rajasthan

havildar army sergeant

hindola swing

hiti a water channel; a bath or tank with water spouts

Holi spring festival (Feb-Mar)

hookah 'hubble bubble' or smoking vase

howdah seat on elephant's back, sometimes canopied

hundi temple offering

huzra a Muslim tomb chamber

I

Iat pillar, column

Id principal Muslim festivals

Idgah open space for Id prayers

ikat 'resist-dyed' woven fabric

imam Muslim religious leader

imambara tomb of a Shiite Muslim holy man; focus of Muharram procession

Indra King of the gods; God of rain; guardian of the East

Ishana Guardian of the North East

Ishvara Lord; Siva

iwan main arch in mosque

J

jadu magic

jaga mohan audience hall or ante-chamber of an Orissan temple

Jagadambi literally Mother of the World; Parvati

Jagannath literally Lord of the World; particularly, Krishna worshipped at Puri

jagati railed parapet

jaggery brown sugar, made from palm sap

jahaz ship: building in form of ship

Jambudvipa Continent of the Rose-Apple Tree; the earth

Jami masjid (Jama, Jumma) Friday mosque, for congregational worship

Jamuna Hindu goddess who rides a tortoise; river

Janaka Father of Sita

jangha broad band of sculpture on the outside of the temple wall

jarokha balcony

jataka stories accounts of the previous lives of the Buddha

jatra Bengali folk theatre

jawab literally 'answer,' a building which duplicates another to provide symmetry

jawan army recruit, soldier

jheel (jhil) lake; a marsh; a swamp

jhilmil projecting canopy over a window or door opening

-ji (jee) honorific suffix added to names out of reverence and/or politeness; also abbreviated 'yes' (Hindi/Urdu)

Jina literally 'victor'; spiritual conqueror or Tirthankara, after whom Jainism is named

Jogini mystical goddess

jorbangla double hut-like temple in Bengal

Jyotirlinga luminous energy of Siva manifested at 12 holy places, miraculously formed lingams

K

kabigan folk debate in verse

kacheri (kutchery) a court; an office for public business

Kailasa mountain home of Siva

Kali literally 'black'; terrifying form of the goddess Durga, wearing a necklace of skulls/heads

Kalki future incarnation of Vishnu on horseback

kalyanamandapa marriage hall

kameez women's shirt

kanga comb (one of five Sikh symbols)

kantha Bengali quilting

kapok the silk cotton tree

karma impurity resulting from past misdeeds

Kartikkeya (Kartik) Son of Siva, God of war

kati-roll Muslim snack of meat rolled in a 'paratha' bread

khadi cotton cloth made from home-spun cotton (or silk) yarn

khal creek; a canal

khana food or meal, also suffix for room/office/place

khanqah Muslim (Sufi) hospice

khet field

khola river or stream in Nepal

khondalite crudely grained basalt

khukri traditional curved Gurkha weapon

kirti-stambha 'pillar of fame', free standing pillar in front of temple

kos minars Mughal 'mile' stones

kot (kota/kottai/kotte) fort

kothi house

kotla citadel

Kubera chief yaksha; keeper of the treasures of the earth, Guardian of the North

kumar a young man

Kumari virgin; Durga

Kumbhayog auspicious time for bathing to wash away sins

kumhar (kumar) potter

kund lake, well or pool

kurta Punjabi shirt

kurti-kanchali small blouse

kutcha (cutcha/kacha) raw; crude; unpaved; built with sun-dried bricks

kwabgah bedroom; literally 'palace of dreams'

L

la Himalayan mountain pass

lakh 100,000

Lakshmana younger brother of Rama

Lakshmi Goddess of wealth and good fortune, consort of Vishnu

lama Buddhist priest in Tibet

lassi iced yoghurt drink

lathi bamboo stick with metal bindings, used by police

lena cave, usually a rock-cut sanctuary

lingam (linga) Siva as the phallic emblem

Lingaraja Siva worshipped at Bhubaneswar

Lokeshwar 'Lord of the World', Avalokiteshwara to Buddhists and form of Siva to Hindus

lungi wrapped-around loin cloth, normally checked

M

madrassa Islamic theological school or college

maha great

Mahabharata Sanskrit epic about the battle between the Pandavas and Kauravas

Mahabodhi Great Enlightenment of Buddha

Mahadeva 'Great Lord'; Siva

mahal palace, grand building

mahalla (mohulla) division of a town; a quarter; a ward

mahant head of a monastery

maharaja great king

maharani great queen

maharishi (Maharshi) literally 'great teacher'

Mahavira literally 'Great Hero'; last of the 24 Tirthankaras, founder of Jainism

Mahayana The Greater Vehicle; form of Buddhism practised in East Asia, Tibet and Nepal

Mahesha (Maheshvara) Great Lord; Siva

mahout elephant driver/keeper

mahseer large freshwater fish found especially in Himalayan rivers

maidan large open grassy area in a town

Maitreya the future Buddha
makara crocodile-shaped mythical creature symbolizing the river Ganga
makhan butter
mali gardener
Manasa Snake goddess; Sakti
mandala geometric diagram symbolizing the structure of the Universe
mandi market
mandir temple
mani stones with sacred inscriptions at Buddhist sites
Mara Tempter, who sent his daughters (and soldiers) to disturb the Buddha's meditation
marg wide roadway
masjid literally 'place of prostration'; mosque
mata mother
math Hindu or Jain monastery
maulana scholar (Muslim)
maulvi religious teacher (Muslim)
maund measure of weight about 20 kg
maya illusion
meena enamel work
mela festival or fair, usually Hindu
memsahib married European woman, term used mainly before Independence
Meru mountain supporting the heavens
mihrab niche in the western wall of a mosque
mimbar pulpit in mosque
Minakshi literally 'fish-eyed'; Parvati
minar (minaret) slender tower of a mosque
mitthai Indian sweets
mithuna couple in sexual embrace
mofussil the country as distinct from the town
moksha salvation, enlightenment; literally 'release'
mudra symbolic hand gesture
muezzin mosque official who calls the faithful to prayer
Muharram period of mourning in remembrance of Hasan and Hussain, murdered sons of Ali
mullah religious teacher (Muslim)
musalla prayer mat
muthi measure equal to 'a handful'

N

nadi river
Naga (nagi/nagini) Snake deity; associated with fertility and protection
nagara city, sometimes capital
nallah (nullah) ditch, channel
namaaz Muslim prayers, worship
namaste Hindu greeting (with joined palms) translated as: 'I salute all divine qualities in you'
namda rug
Nandi a bull, Siva's vehicle and a symbol of fertility
Narayana Vishnu as the creator of life
Nataraja Siva, Lord of the cosmic dance
nath literally 'place' eg Amarnath
natya the art of dance
nautch display by dancing girls
navagraha nine planets, represented usually on the lintel or architrave of the front door of a temple
navaranga central hall of temple
navaratri literally '9 nights'; name of the Dasara festival
nawab prince, wealthy Muslim, sometimes used as a title
niwas small palace
nritya pure dance

P

pada foot or base
padam dance which tells a story
padma lotus flower, Padmasana, lotus seat; posture of meditating figures
paga projecting pilaster-like surface of an Orissan temple
pahar hill
paisa (poisa) one hundredth of a rupee
palanquin covered litter for one, carried on poles
pali language of Buddhist scriptures
palli village
pan leaf of the betel vine; sliced areca nut, lime and other ingredients wrapped in leaf for chewing
panchayat a 'council of five'; a government system of elected councils

pandal marquee made of bamboo and cloth

pandas temple priests

pandit teacher or wise man; a Sanskrit scholar

pankah (punkha) fan, formerly pulled by a cord

Parinirvana the Buddha's state prior to nirvana, shown usually as a reclining figure

parishads political division of group of villages

Parsi (Parsee) Zoroastrians who fled from Iran to West India in the 8th century to avoid persecution

Parvati daughter of the Mountain; Siva's consort

Pashupati literally Lord of the Beasts; Siva

pata painted hanging scroll

patan town or city (Sanskrit)

patel village headman

pattachitra specially painted cloth (especially Orissan)

pau measure for vegetables and fruit equal to 250 g

peon servant, messenger (from Portuguese *peao*)

pida (pitha) basement

pida deul hall with a pyramidal roof in an Orissan temple

pinjrapol animal hospital (Jain)

pipal Ficus religiosa, the Bodhi tree

pir Muslim holy man

pithasthana place of pilgrimage

pralaya the end of the world

prasadam consecrated temple food

prayag confluence considered sacred by Hindus

puja ritual offerings to the gods; worship (Hindu)

pujari worshipper; one who performs puja (Hindu)

pukka literally 'ripe' or 'finished'; reliable; solidly built

punya merit earned through actions and religious devotion (Buddhist)

Puranas literally 'the old' Sanskrit sacred poems

purdah seclusion of Muslim women from public view (literally curtains)

pushkarani sacred pool or tank

Q

qabr Muslim grave

qibla direction for Muslim prayer

qila fort

qutb axis or pivot

R

rabi winter/spring season crop

Radha Krishna's favourite consort

raj rule or government

raja king, ruler (variations include rao, rawal)

rajbari palaces of a small kingdom

Rajput dynasties of western and central India

Rakshakas Earth spirits

Rama Seventh incarnation of Vishnu

Ramayana Sanskrit epic – the story of Rama

Ramazan (Ramadan) Muslim month of fasting

rana warrior (Nepal)

rani queen

rath chariot or temple car

Ravana Demon king of Lanka; kidnapper of Sita

rawal head priest

Rig (Rg) Veda oldest and most sacred of the Vedas

Rimpoche blessed incarnation; abbot of a Tibetan Buddhist monastery (gompa)

rishi 'seer'; inspired poet, philosopher

ryot (rayat/raiyat) a subject; a cultivator; a farmer

S

sabha columned hall (sabha mandapa, assembly hall)

sabzi vegetables, vegetable curry

sadar (sadr/saddar) chief, main especially Sikh

sadhu ascetic; religious mendicant, holy man

sagar lake; reservoir

sahib title of address, like 'sir'

Saiva (Shaiva) the cult of Siva

sal a hall

sal hardwood tree of the lower slopes of the Himalayan foothills

salaam literally 'peace'; greeting (Muslim)

salwar (shalwar) loose trousers (Punjab)

samadh(i) literally concentrated thought, meditation; a funerary memorial

samsara transmigration of the soul

samudra large tank or inland sea

sangam junction of rivers

sangarama monastery

sangha ascetic order founded by Buddha

sankha (shankha) the conch shell (symbolically held by Vishnu); the shell bangle worn by Bengali women

sanyasi wandering ascetic; final stage in the ideal life of a man

sarai caravansarai, halting place

saranghi small four-stringed viola shaped from a single piece of wood

Saraswati wife of Brahma and goddess of knowledge

sarkar the government; the state; a writer; an accountant

sarod Indian stringed musical instrument

sarvodaya uplift, improvement of all

sati (suttee) a virtuous woman; act of self-immolation on a husband's funeral pyre

Sati wife of Siva who destroyed herself by fire

satyagraha 'truth force'; passive resistance

seer (ser) weight (about 1 kg)

sepoy (sepai) Indian soldier, private

serow a wild Himalayan antelope

seth merchant, businessman

seva voluntary service

shahtush very fine wool from the Tibetan antelope

Shakti Energy; female divinity often associated with Siva

Shankara Siva

sharia corpus of Muslim theological law

shastras ancient texts defining temple architecture

shastri religious title (Hindu)

sheesh mahal palace apartment with mirror work

sherwani knee-length coat for men

Shesha (Sesha) serpent who supports Vishnu

shikar hunting

shloka (sloka) Sanskrit sacred verse

sindur vermilion powder used in temple ritual; married women mark their hair parting with it (East India)

singh (sinha) lion; Rajput caste name adopted by Sikhs

Sita Rama's wife, heroine of the *Ramayana* epic

sitar classical stringed musical instrument with a gourd for soundbox

Siva (Shiva) The Destroyer in the Hindu triad of Gods

Sivaratri literally 'Siva's night'; a festival (Feb-Mar)

soma sacred drink mentioned in the *Vedas*

sri (shri) honorific title, often used for 'Mr'; a sign of great respect

stupa hemispheric Buddhist funerary mound

subahdar (subedar) the governor of a province; viceroy under the Mughals

sudra lowest of the Hindu castes

sufi Muslim mystic; sufism, Muslim mystic worship

Surya Sun; Sun God

svami (swami) holy man; a suffix for temple deities

svastika (swastika) auspicious Hindu/Buddhist cross-like sign

swadeshi home-made goods

swaraj home rule

swatantra freedom

T

tabla a pair of drums

tahr wild goat

takht throne

talao (*tal*, talar) water tank

taluk administrative subdivision of a district

tamasha spectacle; festive celebration

tandava (dance) of Siva

tapas (tapasya) ascetic meditative self-denial

Tara literally 'star'; a goddess

tarkashi Orissan silver filigree

Teej Hindu festival

tehsil subdivision of a district (North India)
tempo three-wheeler vehicle
terai narrow strip of land along Himalayan foothills
thakur high Hindu caste; deity (Bengal)
thakur bari temple sanctuary (Bengal)
thana a police jurisdiction; police station
thangka (thankha) cloth (often silk) painted with a Tibetan Mahayana deity
tiffin snack, light meal
tika (tilak) vermilion powder, auspicious mark on the forehead; often decorative
tirtha ford, bathing place, holy spot (Sanskrit)
Tirthankara literally 'ford-maker'; title given to 24 religious 'teachers', worshipped by Jains
Tollywood the Bengali film industry
tonga two-wheeled horse carriage
Trimurti the Hindu Triad, Brahma, Vishnu and Siva
trisul the trident chief symbol of the god Siva
triveni triple-braided
tsampa ground, roasted barley, eaten dry or mixed with milk, tea or water (Himalayan)
tulsi sacred basil plant

U

Uma Siva's consort in one of her many forms
untouchable 'outcastes', with whom contact of any kind was believed by high caste Hindus to be defiling
Upanishads ancient Sanskrit philosophical texts, part of the Vedas
ustad master
uttarayana northwards

V

vahana 'vehicle' of the deity
vaisya the 'middle-class' caste of merchants and farmers
Valmiki sage, author of the *Ramayana* epic
Vamana dwarf incarnation of Vishnu

vana grove, forest
Varaha boar incarnation of Vishnu
varna 'colour'; social division of Hindus into Brahmin, Kshatriya, Vaishya and Sudra
Varuna Guardian of the West, accompanied by Makara
Veda (Vedic) oldest known Hindu religious texts
vedi (bedi) altar, also a wall or screen
vihara Buddhist or Jain monastery with cells around a courtyard
Vishnu a principal Hindu deity; the Preserver (and Creator)

W

-wallah suffix often used with a occupational name, eg rickshaw-wallah
wazir chief minister of a raja (from Turkish 'vizier')

Y

yagya (yajna) major ceremonial sacrifice
Yaksha (Yakshi) a demi-god, associated with nature
Yama God of death, judge of the living
yantra magical diagram used in meditation; instrument
yatra pilgrimage
Yellow Hat Gelugpa Sect of Tibetan Buddhism – monks wear yellow headdress
yoni a hole symbolizing female sexuality; vagina

Z

zamindar a landlord granted income under the Mughals
zari silver and gold thread for weaving or embroidery
zarih cenotaph in a Muslim tomb
zenana segregated women's apartments
ziarat holy Muslim tomb
zilla (zillah) district

Index → *Entries in bold refer to maps.*

Acknowledgements

Firstly, grateful thanks to Robert and Roma Bradnock for the enormous amount of work they put in to compiling the core of the India handbooks, which builds on 15 years of research. Many thanks are also due to David Stott for all his input and work on the first edition of the *Northeast India Handbook*, as well as for his comradeship and good advice. Particular thanks also go out to Wil Lee-Wright for his research and help on the Bodh Gaya and Bishnupur sections. And great thanks for your time, help and company to: Asit Biswas, Sanjoy Biswas, Bibhuti Borah, Katharine Bowerman, Lorraine Close, Dudu, Charlotte Good, Adil Khan, Niamh Moran, Sandip Samaddar and Eran Shaham. And, of course, thank you to Nicola Gibbs, Felicity Laughton and Alan Murphy at Footprint.

Credits

Footprint credits
Project Editor: Felicity Laughton
Layout and production: Emma Bryers
Maps: Kevin Feeney
Colour section: Robert Lunn, Kevin Feeney
Series design: Mytton Williams
Proofreader: Stephanie Rebello
Cover design: Robert Lunn

Managing Director: Andy Riddle
Commercial Director: Patrick Dawson
Publisher: Alan Murphy
Publishing Managers: Felicity Laughton,
Jo Williams, Jenny Haddington
Digital Editor: Alice Little
Marketing: Liz Harper
Sales: Jeremy Parr
Advertising: Renu Sibal
Finance and administration: Elizabeth Taylor

Photography credits
Front cover: Thomas David Pinzer/Alamy
Back cover: Imagestate Media Partners Ltd -
Impact Photos/Alamy
Opener: age fotostock/Superstock
Introduction: Sandeep Subba/istock
Montage pic 1: Hemis/Superstock; pic 2: Amit
Pasricha/Photolibrary; pic 3: age fotostock/
Superstock; pic 4: Dinodia Images/Alamy;
pic 5: Richard Durnan/SuperStock;
pic 6: Jeremy Richards/Shutterstock;
pics 7, 9 and 10: Vanessa Betts;
pic 8: Hidekazu Nishibata/SuperStock

Manufactured in India by Nutech
Pulp from sustainable forests

Footprint feedback
We try as hard as we can to make each
Footprint guide as up to date as possible
but, of course, things always change. If you
want to let us know about your experiences –
good, bad or ugly – then don't delay, go to
footprinttravelguides.com and send in
your comments.

Publishing information
Footprint Northeast India
2nd edition
© Footprint Handbooks Ltd
November 2010

ISBN: 9781907263187
CIP DATA: A catalogue record for this book
is available from the British Library

® Footprint Handbooks and the Footprint
mark are a registered trademark of Footprint
Handbooks Ltd

Published by Footprint
6 Riverside Court
Lower Bristol Road
Bath BA2 3DZ, UK
T +44 (0)1225 469141
F +44 (0)1225 469461
footprinttravelguides.com

Distributed in the USA by Globe Pequot Press,
Guilford, Connecticut